Handbook of Parenting

Volume 2
Biology and Ecology of Parenting

Handbook of Parenting

Second Edition

Volume 2
Biology and Ecology of Parenting

Edited by

Marc H. Bornstein

National Institute of Child Health and Human Development

 LAWRENCE ERLBAUM ASSOCIATES, PUBLISHERS
2002   Mahwah, New Jersey   London

KH

Editor:	Bill Webber
Editorial Assistant:	Erica Kica
Cover Design:	Kathryn Houghtaling Lacey
Textbook Production Manager:	Paul Smolenski
Full-Service Compositor:	TechBooks
Text and Cover Printer:	Hamilton Printing Company

This book was typeset in 10/11.5 pt. Times, Italic, Bold, Bold Italic.
The heads were typeset in Helvetica, Italic, Bold, Bold Italic.

Lawrence Erlbaum Associates, Inc., Publishers
10 Industrial Avenue
Mahwah, New Jersey 07430

Library of Congress Cataloging-in-Publication Data

Handbook of parenting / edited by Marc H. Bornstein.—2nd ed.
    p. cm.
    Includes bibliographical references and indexes.
    Contents: v. 1. Children and parenting—v. 2. Biology and ecology of parenting—v. 3. Being
and becoming a parent—v. 4. Social conditions and applied parenting—v. 5. practical issues
in parenting.
    ISBN 0-8058-3778-7 (hc : v. 1 : alk. paper)—ISBN 0-8058-3779-5 (hc : v. 2 : alk. paper)—
ISBN 0-8058-3780-9 (hc : v. 3 : alk. paper)—ISBN 0-8058-3781-7 (hc : v. 4 : alk. paper)—
ISBN 0-8058-3782-5 (hc : v. 5 : alk. paper)
    1. Parenting.   2. Parents.   I. Bornstein, Marc H.

HQ755.8.H357   2002
649'.1—dc21   2001058458

Books published by Lawrence Erlbaum Associates are printed on
acid-free paper, and their bindings are chosen for strength and
durability.

Printed in the United States of America
10 9 8 7 6 5 4 3 2 1

10/19/06

For *Marian* and *Harold Sackrowitz*

Contents of Volume 2:
Biology and Ecology of Parenting

PART I: BIOLOGY OF PARENTING

Preface

This new edition of the *Handbook of Parenting* appears at a time that is momentous in the history of parenting. The family generally, and parenting specifically, are today in a greater state of flux, question, and redefinition than perhaps ever before. We are witnessing the emergence of striking permutations on the theme of parenting: blended families, lesbian and gay parents, teen versus fifties first-time moms and dads. One cannot but be awed on the biological front by technology that now renders postmenopausal women capable of childbearing and with the possibility of designing babies. Similarly, on the sociological front, single parenthood is a modern-day fact of life, adult–child dependency is on the rise, and parents are ever less certain of their roles, even in the face of rising environmental and institutional demands that they take increasing responsibility for their offspring. The *Handbook of Parenting* is concerned with all facets of parenting.

Despite the fact that most people become parents and everyone who has ever lived has had parents, parenting remains a most mystifying subject. Who is ultimately responsible for parenting? Does parenting come naturally, or must we learn how to parent? How do parents conceive of parenting? Of childhood? What does it mean to parent a preterm baby, twins, or a child with a disability? To be a younger or an older parent, or one who is divorced, disabled, or drug abusing? What do theories in psychology (psychoanalysis, personality theory, and behavior genetics, for example) contribute to our understanding of parenting? What are the goals parents have for themselves? For their children? What are the functions of parents' beliefs? Of parents' behaviors? What accounts for parents' believing or behaving in similar ways? What accounts for all the attitudes and actions of parents that differ? How do children influence their parents? How do personality, knowledge, and world view affect parenting? How do social status, culture, and history shape parenthood? How can parents effectively relate to schools, daycare, their children's pediatricians?

These are some of the questions addressed in this second edition of the *Handbook of Parenting* . . . for this is a book on *how to parent* as much as it is one on *what being a parent is all about*.

Put succinctly, parents create people. It is the entrusted and abiding task of parents to prepare their offspring for the physical, psychosocial, and economic conditions in which they will eventually fare and, it is hoped, flourish. Amidst the many influences on child development, parents are the "final common pathway" to children's development and stature, adjustment and success. Human social inquiry—at least since Athenian interest in Spartan childrearing practices—has always, as a matter of course, included reports of parenting. Yet Freud opined that childrearing is one of three "impossible professions"—the other two being governing nations and psychoanalysis. And one encounters as many views as the number of people one asks about the relative merits of being an at-home or a working mother, about whether daycare, family care, or parent care is best for a child, about whether good parenting reflects intuition or experience.

The *Handbook of Parenting* concerns itself with different types of parents—mothers and fathers, single, adolescent, and adoptive parents; with basic characteristics of parenting—behaviors, knowledge, beliefs, and expectations about parenting; with forces that shape parenting—employment, social status, culture, environment, and history; with problems faced by parents—handicaps, marital difficulties, drug addiction; and with practical concerns of parenting—how to promote children's health, foster social adjustment and cognitive competence, and interact with school, legal, and public officials. Contributors to the *Handbook of Parenting* have worked in different ways toward understanding all these diverse aspects of parenting, and all look to the most recent research and thinking in the field to shed light on many topics every parent wonders about.

Parenthood is a job whose primary object of attention and action is the child. But parenting also has consequences for parents. Parenthood is giving and responsibility, but parenting has its own intrinsic pleasures, privileges, and profits as well as frustrations, fears, and failures. Parenthood can enhance psychological development, self-confidence, and sense of well-being, and parenthood also affords opportunities to confront new challenges and to test and display diverse competencies. Parents can derive considerable and continuing pleasure in their relationships and activities with their children. But parenting is also fraught with small and large stresses and disappointments. The transition to parenting is formidable; the onrush of new stages of parenthood is relentless. In the final analysis, however, parents receive a great deal "in kind" for the hard work of parenting—they are often recipients of unconditional love, they gain skills, and they even pretend to immortality. This edition of the *Handbook of Parenting* presents the many positives that accompany parenting and offers solutions for the many challenges.

The *Handbook of Parenting* encompasses the broad themes of who are parents, whom parents parent, the scope of parenting and its many effects, the determinants of parenting, and the nature, structure, and meaning of parenthood for parents. This second edition of the *Handbook of Parenting* is divided into five volumes, each with two parts:

Volume 1 concerns CHILDREN AND PARENTING. Parenthood is, perhaps first and foremost, a functional status in the life cycle: Parents issue as well as protect, care for, and represent their progeny. But human development is too subtle, dynamic, and intricate to admit that parental caregiving alone determines the developmental course and outcome of ontogeny. Volume 1 of the *Handbook of Parenting* begins with chapters concerned with how children influence parenting. The origins of parenting are, of course, complex, but certain factors are of obvious importance. First, children affect parenting: Notable are their more obvious characteristics, like age or developmental stage; but more subtle ones, like gender, physical state, temperament, mental ability, and other individual-differences factors, are also instrumental. The chapters in Part I, on Parenting Children and Older People, discuss the unique rewards and special demands of parenting children of different ages—infants, toddlers, youngsters in middle childhood, and adolescents—as well as the modern notion of parent–child relationships in adulthood and later years. The chapters in Part II, on Parenting Children of Varying Status, discuss the common matters of parenting siblings and girls versus boys as well as more unique situations of parenting twins, adopted and foster children, and children with special needs, such as those born preterm, with mental retardation, or aggressive and withdrawn disorders.

Volume 2 concerns the BIOLOGY AND ECOLOGY OF PARENTING. For parenting to be understood as a whole, psychophysiological and sociological determinants of parenting need to be brought into the picture. Volume 2 of the *Handbook* relates parenting to its biological roots and sets parenting within its ecological framework. Some aspects of parenting are influenced by the biological makeup of human beings, and the chapters in Part I, on the Biology of Parenting, examine the evolution of parenting, hormonal and psychobiological determinants of parenting in nonhumans and in human beings, parenting in primates, and intuitive universals in human parenting. A deep understanding of what it means to parent also depends on the ecologies in which parenting takes place. Beyond the nuclear family, parents are embedded in, influence, and are themselves affected by larger social systems. The chapters in Part II, on the Social Ecology of Parenting, examine employment status and parenting, the socioeconomic, cultural, environmental, and historical contexts of parenting, and provide an overarching developmental contextual perspective on parenting.

Volume 3 concerns BEING AND BECOMING A PARENT. A large cast of characters is responsible for parenting, each has her or his own customs and agenda, and the psychological makeups and social interests of those individuals are revealing of what parenting is. Chapters in Part I, on The Parent, show how rich and multifaceted is the constellation of children's caregivers. Considered successively are mothers, fathers, coparenting, single parenthood, grandparenthood, adolescent parenthood, nonparental caregiving, sibling caregivers, parenting in divorced and remarried families, lesbian and gay parents, and the role of contemporary reproductive technologies in parenting. Parenting also draws on transient and enduring physical, personality, and intellectual characteristics of the individual. The chapters in Part II, on Becoming and Being a Parent, consider the transition to parenting, stages of parental development, personality and parenting, parents' knowledge of, beliefs in, cognitions about, attributions for, and attitudes toward childrearing, as well as relations between psychoanalysis and parenthood. Such parental cognitions serve many functions: They generate and shape parental behaviors, mediate the effectiveness of parenting, and help to organize parenting.

Volume 4 concerns SOCIAL CONDITIONS AND APPLIED PARENTING. Parenting is not uniform in all communities, groups, or cultures; rather, parenting is subject to wide variation. Volume 4 of the *Handbook* describes socially defined groups of parents and social conditions that promote variation in parenting. The chapters in Part I, on Social Conditions of Parenting, include ethnic and minority parenting in general and parenting among Latino, African American, and Asian populations, in particular, as well as parents in poverty and parenting and social networks. Parents are ordinarily the most consistent and caring people in the lives of children. In everyday life, however, parenting does not always go right or well. Information, education, and support programs can remedy these ills. The chapters in Part II, on Applied Issues in Parenting, explore parenting competence, maternal deprivation, marital relationships and conflict, parenting with a sensory or physical disability, parental psychopathology, substance-abusing parents, parental child maltreatment, and parent education.

Volume 5 concerns PRACTICAL ISSUES IN PARENTING. Parents meet the biological, physical, and health requirements of children. Parents interact with children socially. Parents stimulate children to engage and understand the environment and to enter the world of learning. Parents provision, organize, and arrange children's home and local environments and the media to which children are exposed. Parents also manage child development vis-à-vis childcare, school, the worlds of medicine and law, as well as other social institutions through their active citizenship. Volume 5 of the *Handbook* describes the nuts and bolts of parenting as well as the promotion of positive parenting practices. The chapters in Part I, on Practical Parenting, review the ethics of parenting, parenting and attachment, child compliance, the development of children's self-regulation, children's prosocial and moral development, socialization and children's values, maximizing children's cognitive abilities, parenting talented children, play in parent–child interactions, everyday stresses and parenting, parents and children's peer relationships, and health promotion. Such caregiving principles and practices have direct effects on children. Parents indirectly influence children as well, for example, through their relationships with each other and their local or larger community. The chapters in Part II, on Parents and Social Institutions, explore parents and their children's childcare, schools, media, and doctors and delve into relations between parenthood and the law and public policy.

Each chapter in the second edition of the *Handbook of Parenting* addresses a different but central topic in parenting; each is rooted in current thinking and theory as well as in classical and modern research in that topic; each has been written to be read and absorbed in a single sitting. Each chapter in this new *Handbook* follows a standard organization, including an introduction to the chapter as a whole, followed by historical considerations of the topic, a discussion of central issues and theory, a review of classical and modern research, forecasts of future directions of theory and research, and a set of conclusions. Of course, each chapter considers the contributors' own convictions and research, but contributions to this new edition of the *Handbook of Parenting* present all major points of view and central lines of inquiry and interpret them broadly. The *Handbook of Parenting* is intended to be both comprehensive and state of the art. To assert that parenting is complex is to understate the obvious. As the expanded scope of this second edition of the *Handbook of Parenting* amply shows, parenting is naturally and closely allied with many other fields.

The *Handbook of Parenting* is concerned with child outcomes of parenting but also with the nature and dimensions of variations in parenting per se. Beyond an impressive range of information, readers will find *passim* critical discussions of typologies of parenting (e.g., authoritarian–autocratic, indulgent–permissive, indifferent–uninvolved, authoritative–reciprocal), theories of parenting (e.g., ecological, psychoanalytic, behavior genetic, ethological, behavioral, sociobiological), conditions of parenting (e.g., mother versus father, cross cultural, situation-by-age-by-style), recurrent themes in parenting studies (e.g., attachment, transaction, systems), and even aphorisms (e.g., "A child should have strict discipline in order to develop a fine, strong character," "The child is father to the man").

In the course of editing this new edition of the *Handbook*, I set about to extract central messages and critical perspectives expressed in each chapter, fully intending to construct a comprehensive Introduction to these volumes. In the end, I took away two significant impressions from my own efforts and the texts of my many collaborators in this work. First, my notes cumulated to a monograph on parenting . . . clearly inappropriate for an Introduction. Second, when all was written and done, I found the chorus of contributors to this new edition of the *Handbook* more eloquent and compelling than one lone voice could ever be. Each chapter in the *Handbook of Parenting* begins with an articulate and persuasive Introduction that lays out, in a clarity, expressiveness, and force (I frankly envy), the meanings and implications of that contribution and that perspective to parenting. In lieu of one Introduction, readers are urged to browse the many Introductions that will lead their way into the *Handbook of Parenting*.

Once upon a time, parenting was a seemingly simple thing: Mothers mothered; Fathers fathered. Today, parenting has many motives, many meanings, and many manifestations. Contemporary parenting is viewed as immensely time consuming and effortful. The perfect mother or father or family is a figment of past imagination. Modern society recognizes "subdivisions" of the call: genetic mother, gestational mother, biological mother, birth mother, social mother. For some, the individual sacrifices that mark parenting arise for the sole and selfish purpose of passing one's genes on to succeeding generations. For others, a second child is conceived to save the life of a first child. A multitude of factors influence the unrelenting advance of events and decisions that surround parenting—biopsychological, dyadic, contextual, historical. Recognizing this complexity is important to informing people's thinking about parenting, especially information-hungry parents themselves. This second edition of the *Handbook of Parenting* explores all these motives, meanings, and manifestations of parenting.

Each day more than three fourths of a million adults around the world experience the rewards and the challenges as well as the joys and the heartaches of becoming parents. The human race succeeds because of parenting. From the start, parenting is a "24/7" job. Parenting formally begins during or before pregnancy and can continue throughout the lifespan: Practically speaking for most, *once a parent, always a parent*. But parenting is a subject about which people hold strong opinions and about which too little solid information or considered reflection exists. Parenting has never come with a *Handbook* . . . until now.

ACKNOWLEDGMENTS

I would like to express my sincere gratitude to the staffs at Lawrence Erlbaum Associates, Publishers, and TechBooks who perfectly parented production of the *Handbook of Parenting*: Victoria Danahy, Susan Detwiler, Sheila Johnston, Arthur M. Lizza, Paul Smolenski, and Christopher Thornton.

—Marc H. Bornstein

Contents of Volume 1:
Children and Parenting

Contents of Volume 3:
Being and Becoming a Parent

Contents of Volume 4:
Social Conditions and Applied Parenting

PART II: APPLIED ISSUES IN PARENTING

Contents of Volume 5:
Practical Issues in Parenting

PART I: PRACTICAL PARENTING

About the Authors in Volume 2

KIM A. BARD is a Senior Lecturer in the Department of Psychology, University of Portsmouth, U.K. She was educated at Wheaton College (B.A.) and Georgia State University (M.A. and Ph.D.). Bard previously held positions at Emory University as a Research Scientist at the Yerkes Regional Primate Research Center and at the Clinical Developmental and Applied Research Program of the Human Genetics Laboratory and as a Research Fellow in the Department of Psychology. Bard is an Associate Fellow of the British Psychological Society, sits on the Council of the Primate Society of Great Britain, and is a member of the International Society for Infant Studies, American Psychological Society, International Society for Developmental Psychobiology, American Society of Primatologists, Society for Research in Child Development, and International Primatological Society. She is on the editorial boards of *Infancy* and *Primates*. Bard studies the early development of emotional expressions, self-recognition, imitation, and laterality in chimpanzees and the influence of rearing practices on the development of emotions, cognition, and social skills in chimpanzees, orangutans, and sometimes human infants. Bard is the author of *Responsive Care: Behavioral Intervention for Nursery-Reared Chimpanzees* and a coeditor of *Reaching into Thought: The Minds of the Great Apes*.

* * *

KAY BATHURST is a Professor of Psychology at California State University, Fullerton. Her Ph.D. is from the University of California, Los Angeles. Bathurst's areas of interest include psychological assessment and test-taking behavior, family functioning and divorce, and intelligence and cerebral asymmetry. Bathurst has received awards for outstanding research and teaching at CSUF and for being an outstanding alumna at CSUF. She is coauthor of *Gifted IQ: Early Developmental Aspects*.

* * *

DAVID F. BJORKLUND is a Professor of Psychology at Florida Atlantic University. He received his Ph.D. from the University of North Carolina at Chapel Hill. He has served as Associate Editor of *Child Development*, on the editorial boards of the *Journal of Experimental Child Psychology*, *Developmental Psychology*, *Cognitive Development*, *Developmental Review*, *Journal of Cognition and Development*, and *School Psychology Quarterly*, and as a contributing editor to *Parents Magazine*. His current research interests include children's memory and strategy development, cognitive developmental primatology, and evolutionary developmental psychology. He is the author of several books, including *Children's Thinking: Developmental Function and Individual Differences*, and he is coauthor of *Evolution and Development: The Origins of Human Nature*.

* * *

SHIREEN BOULOS is pursuing her Ph.D. in Applied Child Development at the Eliot-Pearson Department of Child Development at Tufts University. She received her M.A. from Teachers College, Columbia University, and her B.A. from Harvard University. Her research interests focus on social policy for children and families, with a particular emphasis on adolescent parenting, homelessness, and childcare.

* * *

ROBERT H. BRADLEY is Professor at the Center for Applied Studies in Education at the University of Arkansas at Little Rock and Adjunct Professor of Pediatrics at the University of Arkansas for Medical Sciences. Bradley received his Ph.D. from the University of North Carolina. He was formerly Director of the Center for Research on Teaching & Learning and Director of the University of Arkansas University Affiliated Program in Developmental Disabilities. Bradley has served on the Board of Editors for *Child Development* and currently serves on the Board of Editors for *Parenting*. He also serves as President of the Southwestern Society for Research in Human Development. His primary research interests include the family environment and its relation to children's health and development, particularly children living in poverty and children with disabilities or serious health problems, daycare, fathering, and early intervention. He is the coauthor, along with Bettye Caldwell, of the *Home Observation for Measurement of the Environment* (HOME Inventory).

* * *

DOMINI R. CASTELLINO is a Research Scholar at the Center for Child and Family Policy at Duke University. Castellino received her B.A. from the Pennsylvania State University and her Ph.D. from Michigan State University. She was a NICHD postdoctoral fellow at the Center for Developmental Science at the University of North Carolina–Chapel Hill. Castellino's research focuses on parenting, children's achievement, and the application of developmental theory to policies and programs related to children, youth, and families.

* * *

CARL M. CORTER is Professor in the Department of Human Development and Applied Psychology and Associate Dean at the Ontario Institute for Studies in Education of the University of Toronto. He received his B.A. from Davidson College and his Ph.D. from the University of North Carolina, Chapel Hill. His research interests include parenting and early childhood education.

* * *

ALISON S. FLEMING is a Professor in the Department of Psychology at the University of Toronto–Mississauga. She received her B.Sc. from Columbia University and her M.A. and Ph.D. from the Institute of Animal Behavior, Rutgers University, Newark, New Jersey. She is Secretary of the Society for Behavioral Neuroendocrinology, a member of the Society for Neurosciences, and on the Editorial Board of *Hormones and Behavior*. Her research interests include the study of sensory, experiential, neural, and neurochemical mechanisms underlying the regulation of maternal behavior in the rat. She also studies the sensory, experiential, and endocrine correlates of parental behavior in humans and marmoset monkeys.

* * *

VALERIE FRENCH is Associate Professor of History at The American University, Washington, D.C. She has been active in professional organizations on women's and minorities' issues. She has published extensively on ancient childhood, women in antiquity, Alexander the Great, and Greek historiography. French is coauthor of *Historians and the Living Past: The Theory and Practice of Historical Study*.

* * *

ADELE ESKELES GOTTFRIED is Professor, Department of Educational Psychology and Counseling, California State University, Northridge. She was awarded the Ph.D. from the Graduate School of the City University of New York. She is a Fellow of the American Psychological Association, recipient of the Mensa Award for Excellence in Research, and she has served as Action Editor for *Child Development* and currently serves on the Editorial Boards of *Parenting: Science and Practice* and the *Journal of Educational Psychology.* Her major research programs are in the areas of maternal- and dual-earner employment and children's development, home environment and children's development, and the development of children's academic intrinsic motivation. Gottfried's books include *Maternal Employment and Children's Development: Longitudinal Research*, *Redefining Families: Implications for Children's Development, Gifted IQ: Developmental Aspects*, and she is the author of the *Children's Academic Intrinsic Motivation Inventory.*

* * *

ALLEN W. GOTTFRIED is Professor of Psychology, California State University, Fullerton, Clinical Professor of Pediatrics at the University of Southern California School of Medicine, and Director of the Fullerton Longitudinal Study. His Ph.D. is from the New School for Social Research. Gottfried is a Fellow of the American Psychological Association, the American Psychological Society, and the Western Psychological Association. His areas of interest include infancy, home/family environment development relations, intelligence, and longitudinal research. His books include *Home Environment and Early Cognitive Development: Longitudinal Research, Maternal Employment and Children's Development: Longitudinal Research, Infant Stress under Intensive Care, Play Interactions: Role of Play Materials and Parental Involvement to Children's Development, Redefining Families: Implications for Children's Development, Gifted IQ: Early Developmental Aspects,* and *Temperament: Infancy Through Adolescence–The Fullerton Longitudinal Study.*

* * *

SARA HARKNESS is Professor in the School of Family Studies and Director of the Center for the Study of Culture, Health and Human Development at the University of Connecticut, Storrs. She received her Ph.D. at Harvard University, where she also earned a M.P.H. She has taught at Pennsylvania State University, the University of Leiden (The Netherlands), Harvard, and the University of Rhode Island. She has done research on parents and children in Kenya, Guatemala, The Netherlands, and the United States. She is currently directing the Parenting-21 Study, a seven-nation collaborative study of parents, children, and schools. She is editor of *Ethos* and coeditor of *Parents' Cultural Belief Systems: Their Origins, Expressions and Consequences* and *Variability in the Social Construction of the Child.*

* * *

ERIKA HOFF is Professor of Psychology at Florida Atlantic University. She holds a Ph.D. from the University of Michigan. Hoff conducts research on the role of input in early language development, including studies of the relation of family socioeconomic status to mother–child interaction and to children's language development. She is the author of *Language Development.*

* * *

BRETT LAURSEN is Professor of Psychology at Florida Atlantic University. He is an Institute of Child Development, University of Minnesota, Ph.D. Laursen is on the Editorial Boards of *Child Development, Journal of Research on Adolescence*, and *Merrill-Palmer Quarterly*. His current research addresses adolescent relationships with parents and friends and their influence on social adjustment and academic achievement. He is the editor of *Close Friendships in Adolescence* and coeditor of *Relationships as Developmental Contexts.*

* * *

RICHARD M. LERNER is the Bergstrom Chair in Applied Developmental Science at Tufts University. Lerner received a Ph.D. from the City University of New York. He has been a Fellow at the Center for Advanced Study in the Behavioral Sciences and is a Fellow of the American Association for the Advancement of Science, the American Psychological Association, and the American Psychological Society. He was on the faculty and held administrative posts at Michigan State University, Pennsylvania State University, and Boston College, where he was the Anita L. Brennan Professor of Education and the Director of the Center for Child, Family, and Community Partnerships. Lerner has held the Tyner Eminent Scholar Chair in the Human Sciences at Florida State University. Lerner is the author or editor of 45 books and more than 300 scholarly articles and chapters. He edited Volume 1, on "Theoretical Models of Human Development," for the fifth edition of the *Handbook of Child Psychology*. He is the founding editor of the *Journal of Research on Adolescence* and *Applied Developmental Science*.

*   *   *

MING LI is a Ph.D. candidate at the University of Toronto. He received his B.Sc. and M.Sc. from Beijing University, China. His research interests include the study of neuroanatomical and neurochemical bases of motivated behaviors, especially maternal behavior.

*   *   *

HANUŠ PAPOUŠEK was Professor of Developmental Psychobiology at the Max-Planck Institute for Psychiatry and the Pediatric Department of the University of Munich. He earned his medical degree at Purkinje (formerly Masaryk) University in Brno, Czechoslovakia, and he received the Doctor of Sciences degree at Charles University in Prague. After postdoctoral training in pediatrics, he led a research lying-in unit for interdisciplinary research on behavioral development and immunological resistance at the Research Institute for Mother and Child Care in Prague. Papoušek was Visiting Professor of Developmental Psychology at the University of Denver and Developmental Psychobiology at Harvard University, Professor of Developmental Psychobiology at the Ludwig-Maximilian University of Munich, Visiting Senior Scientist in the Laboratory of Comparative Ethology of the National Institute of Child Health and Human Development, Special Professor of Developmental Psychology at the Free University of Amsterdam, The Netherlands, and Visiting Professor of Charles University, Prague and Pilsen, CFR. His scientific awards include Prochaska's Prize, Hoffmann's Medal, the Arnold-Lucius-Gesell Prize, and the Society for Research in Child Development Award for Distinguished Scientific Contributions to Child Development. He was elected President of the International Society for Infancy Studies. Papoušek's research focused on early development of learning and cognitive abilities, early social and communicative development, early musical abilities and play, and on intuitive forms of parental support to these abilities. Papoušek edited *Nonverbal Vocal Communication*.

*   *   *

MECHTHILD PAPOUŠEK is Associate Professor of Developmental Psychobiology in the Institute for Social Pediatrics and Youth Medicine, University of Munich, where she directs The Research and Intervention Unit for Early Development and Parenting. She received her medical education at the University of Tübingen. She collaborated with her husband, Hanuš Papoušek, at the Research Unit of Developmental Psychobiology, Max-Planck Institute for Psychiatry in Munich, with particular interests in preverbal communication between infants and caregivers, vocal development, infant-directed speech, and intuitive parenting. She carried out cross-cultural comparisons of preverbal communication in the Laboratory of Comparative Ethology, National Institute of Child Health and Human Development, NIH, as a Fellow of the Hughes Foundation. Her program of research integrates clinical and scientific approaches to the study of infants with excessive crying, feeding, and sleeping problems in the context of preverbal communication and early parent-infant relationships. Papoušek was president of the German-Speaking Association for Infant Mental Health. She is author of *Vom ersten Schrei zum ersten Wort* (*On Preverbal Origins of Language Acquisition*).

*   *   *

ANTHONY D. PELLEGRINI is a Professor of Educational Psychology at the University of Minnesota, Twin Cities Campus. He received his Ph.D. from the Ohio State University and has served on the faculties of the Universities of Rhode Island and Georgia, as well as having visiting posts at Cardiff University, Leiden University, and Sheffield University. Pellegrini is a Fellow of the American Psychological Association as well as a Visiting Fellow of the British Psychological Society and an Honourary Professor at Cardiff University. His research interests currently relate to evolution and human development. He published *Evolution and Development: The Origins of Human Nature* and *Observing Children in Their Natural Worlds: A Methodological Primer*.

* * *

JAY S. ROSENBLATT is Daniel S. Lehrman Professor of Psychobiology of the Psychology Department of Rutgers University and the Rutgers/UMDNJ Integrative Neuroscience Program located in Newark, New Jersey. He received his B.A. and Ph.D. from New York University. He is a Fellow of the American Psychological Association and the Animal Behavior Society, past President of the International Society of Developmental Psychobiology, and a member of the Society for Behavioral Neuroendocrinology. He has received Honorary Degrees in Philosophy from the University of Gøteborg and the National University for Education at a Distance, Madrid. His research interests include the study of maternal behavior in the rat and rabbit and behavioral development is these species. He is former editor and current associate editor of *Advances in the Study of Behavior* and coeditor of the series *Parental Behavior*.

* * *

FRED ROTHBAUM is a Professor in the Eliot-Pearson Department of Child Development at Tufts University. He received his Ph.D. from Yale University and was a faculty member at Bryn Mawr College. Rothbaum's research is on parent–child relationships, children's problem behavior and perceived control, and cultural differences. Rothbaum serves on the Office of Policy and Communications at the Society of Research in Child Development and is developing the Child & Family WebGuide–a service for parents and students that reviews and evaluates web sites that provide information about child development.

* * *

CHARLES M. SUPER is Professor and Dean in the School of Family Studies at the University of Connecticut. He received his education at Yale (B.A.) and Harvard (Ph.D.) and received training in child clinical psychology at the Judge Baker Children's Center in Boston. He has held academic positions at Harvard, Clark, and Pennsylvania State Universities and the University of Leiden (The Netherlands). In clinical practice, Super specialized in therapy and developmental counseling for children and families, and frequently served as an expert witness in court. He has carried out research on children and families in Kenya, Colombia, Guatemala, Bangladesh, the Netherlands, and the United States, and served as consultant in Haiti, India, and Bangladesh for agencies of the United Nations. Super is particularly interested in the evolution and promotion of interdisciplinary understanding and collaboration. His published volumes include *Parents' Cultural Belief Systems: Their Origins, Expressions, and Consequences*, *Life Roles, Values, and Careers: International Findings of the Work Importance Study*, and *The Role of Culture in Developmental Dysfunction*.

* * *

TWILA ZOE TARDIF is Associate Professor of Psychology at the Chinese University of Hong Kong. She is a Ph.D.from Yale University. Tardif is Editor of the *Journal of Psychology in Chinese Societies*. She has published on Chinese children's early language learning, and she has conducted research on socioeconomic status and parenting in several cultures including rural and urban China, Hong Kong, Japan, and the United States.

* * *

JENNIFER L. YUNGER is a graduate student at Florida Atlantic University. She is a member of the American Psychological Association, the American Psychological Society, the Human Behavior and Evolution Society, and the Society for Research in Child Development. Her research interests include the study of aggression, evolutionary psychology, gender identity, parenting, and peer victimization.

*   *   *

Handbook of Parenting

Volume 2
Biology and Ecology of Parenting

PART I

BIOLOGY OF PARENTING

1

The Evolution of Parenting and Evolutionary Approaches to Childrearing

David F. Bjorklund
Jennifer L. Yunger
Florida Atlantic University
Anthony D. Pellegrini
University of Minnesota

INTRODUCTION

Child and developmental psychologists, sociologists, educators, and policymakers have long viewed parenting and the family as the most significant influences on the developing child. As such, parenting has traditionally been viewed as an important source of "environmental" variability in the long-debated (and still controversial) nature–nurture dichotomy. At one level, of course, this is correct. An infant's very survival depends on parents. There is nothing in the external world so critical to a child's success in life as her or his parents. Yet parenting also straddles the nature side of the traditional continuum. Parenting is important not only to humans, but it is central to the survival of many species of animals, including all mammals and many birds (Rosenblatt, in Vol. 2 of this *Handbook*). Evolutionary biologists have long recognized this fact, arguing that, in order for individuals to get their genes into the next generation, they must make investments in mating and, following conception, parenting (Hamilton, 1964; Trivers, 1972). How much is invested in mating versus parenting will vary among species and between females and males within a species, depending on characteristics of the developing offspring and ecological conditions. But parenting—the care and nurturing of offspring between conception and independence—is universal among mammals and, depending on the species-typical pattern of such investment, influences how offspring are reared and relationships among the sexes.

Homo sapiens, however, have taken parenting to new heights, not simply because of our use of language, advanced cognition, cultural transmission of knowledge, or societal institutions, but primarily because of the extended period of immaturity of our young. As for all mammals, human children are conceived within their mothers' bodies, fed after birth with mother-produced milk, and are eventually mature enough to be able to fend for themselves. However, the period of immaturity and dependency is extended in humans relative to that of other primates. This prolonged period of youth is seemingly necessitated by the intellectual demands of human society; children cannot learn enough in a decade of life to function effectively in any human group. This intellectual immaturity is accompanied by physical immaturity that puts extraordinary demands on human parents, surpassing those of any other land mammal. Such pressures have shaped how parents around the world treat children, the structure of the human family, and relationships between women and men.

In this chapter, we provide an evolutionary view of human parenting. In the next section, we review briefly the basic tenets of evolution by natural selection and some of the major ideas of the emerging field of evolutionary psychology, particularly evolutionary *developmental* psychology. We then review a more specific evolutionary theory, Trivers's (1972) *parental investment theory*, which accounts for the amount of investment females and males put into parenting (all actions related to rearing an offspring to reproductive age) versus mating (including the seeking, attaining, and maintaining of a mate). We next examine the phylogenetic history of *H. sapiens*, the selection pressures that produced our species, and how those pressures led to patterns of parenting and the structure of the family that characterize our species today. We next take a closer look at some of the factors influencing the decisions parents and other people make for investing in children. The final major section of this chapter examines how an evolutionary perspective can provide a better understanding of some aspects of modern parenting. In all, we argue that an evolutionary perspective tells us not only from where patterns of childrearing came, but where they may head in the future as ecological conditions change and how many problems of contemporary parenting can be understood and perhaps solved.

PRINCIPLES OF EVOLUTION AND EVOLUTIONARY DEVELOPMENTAL PSYCHOLOGY

Evolution by Natural Selection

The basic ideas behind Charles Darwin's (1859) great theory of "descent with modification" are surprisingly simple yet frequently misunderstood, particularly when applied to human behavior. The core of evolutionary theory is the concept of *natural selection*, which, simply stated, refers to the fact that individuals who are well suited to their environment leave more progeny than do less well-suited (or less fit) individuals. Natural selection works because there is *variation* among members of a generation; that is, there are different combinations of physical and behavioral traits among individuals within a species. Critically, these traits, as well as individual differences in these traits, are heritable. Characteristics that result in an individual's surviving and reproducing are passed down from one generation to the next, whereas characteristics that are associated with early death or low levels of reproduction decrease in frequency in the population. Note that characteristics of the individual interact with features of the local ecology, and it is this interaction that is responsible for increases and decreases in characteristics over time. This is the process of *selection*, and through this process, adaptive changes in individuals, and eventually species, are brought about.

Natural selection is a highly interactive process, involving an active organism's response to a sometimes changing environment. Evolutionary theorists often use phrases such as "the trait was selected by the environment" as a shorthand to refer to this complex interaction among an organism, heritable traits of that organism, and the environment. It is worth remembering, however, that the term selection does not imply some deliberate or foresighted process (e.g., selecting for more "advanced" individuals). Natural selection and thus evolution are blind to the future; individuals who fit well within a current environment survive, and althose who fit less well die. Nevertheless, the process, although blind, is an active one, reflecting the bidirectional relation between an organism with heritable traits and the environment.

Although debate on the level at which natural selection works continues, contemporary theory assumes that natural selection operates on *individuals and their genes* and not on groups or on the species as a whole (but see Wilson, 1997). In other words, natural selection does not necessarily produce what is "best for the group." However, although the individual may be the target for natural selection, evolution occurs not in individuals per se, but within *populations* of individuals. Thus a mutation that results in some benefit to an individual must spread through a local population of similar individuals if a change at the species level is to occur (Tattersall, 1998).

Darwin used the term *reproductive fitness* to refer to the likelihood that an individual will become a parent and a grandparent. Contemporary evolutionary theorists, taking advantage of the scientific advances in genetics that have occurred since Darwin's time, use the concept of *inclusive fitness* (Hamilton, 1964) to take into consideration the influence that an individual may have in getting additional copies of her or his genes into subsequent generations. For example, a child possesses 50% of a parent's genes. Thus it is in the parent's best genetic interest to see that an offspring survives so that copies of the parent's genes are passed on to grandchildren (each of whom will possess 25% of a grandparent's genes). A person can further benefit the transmission of her or his genes by helping relatives, who share a smaller percentage of genes. For example, by helping to rear a sister's four children, each of whom shares, on average, 25% of her genes, a woman can further increase her genetic contribution to the next generation, thereby increasing her inclusive fitness. Of course, none of this happens intentionally or consciously. After all, people do not walk around calculating exactly how related they are to one another before deciding to act altruistically. Rather, the underlying mechanisms are in terms of unconscious "strategies," influenced by genes. Moreover, such patterns are observed in nonhuman mammals, birds, and social insects, indicating that self-awareness is not ordinarily involved.

Principles of Evolutionary Developmental Psychology

Although the principles of evolution should be the same for physical, behavioral, or cognitive characteristics, psychologists investigating the evolution of behavior or cognition, particularly *human* behavior or cognition, have made explicit some of these principles. Moreover, *developmentalists* have added to or modified slightly some of these principles in order to achieve a better understanding of the role of evolution in contemporary human behavior (Bjorklund and Pellegrini, 2000, 2002; Geary and Bjorklund, 2000), and we list these principles briefly here.

First, an evolutionary account of a behavioral or a cognitive characteristic does not imply genetic determinism. Certainly evolutionary change implies change in the frequency of genes within a population; but evolutionary psychologists argue that behavioral change occurs as a result of a transactional relation between an organism and its environment and that the eventual behavioral phenotype of an organism is not predetermined by its genes. From this perspective, development involves the expression of evolved, epigenetic programs, from conception through old age, as described by the *developmental systems approach* (e.g., Gottlieb, 1991, 2000; Gottlieb, Wahlsten, and Lickliter, 1998; Oyama, 2000). Development occurs as a result of the bidirectional relationship between all levels of biological and experiential factors, from the genetic through the cultural. *Experience*, from this perspective, involves not only exogenous events but also self-produced activity, as reflected by the firing of a nerve cell in response to solely endogenous factors. Functioning at one level (e.g., the genetic) influences functioning at adjacent levels (e.g., neuronal) with constant feedback between levels. Evolved psychological mechanisms can be thought of as genetically coded "messages" that, following epigenetic rules, interact with the environment over time to produce behavior.

Because the experiences of each individual are unique, there should be substantial plasticity in development. Yet there is much that is universal about humans (or any species), and this seeming discrepancy is resolved when we recognize that infants of a species, beginning at conception, inherit not only a species-typical genome but also a species-typical environment. To the extent that individuals grow up in environments similar to those of their ancestors, development should follow a species-typical pattern. From the developmental systems perspective, there are no simple cases of either genetic or environmental determinism. Infants are not born as blank slates; evolution has prepared them to "expect" certain types of environments and to process some types of information more readily than others. Yet it is the constant and bidirectional interaction between various levels of organization, which changes over the course of development, that produces behavior. For example, differences in the quality and the quantity of parental investment affect children's development and influence their subsequent reproductive and childcare strategies (e.g., Belsky, Steinberg, and Draper, 1991; Surbey, 1998a; see subsequent discussion).

Second, there is a need for an extended childhood so that children can learn the complexities of human communities. *H. sapiens* spend a disproportionate amount of time as prereproductives. From an evolutionary perspective, the benefits associated with an extended period of immaturity must have outweighted the costs. We believe that the most important and difficult things children need to learn are related to the social complexity of human groups (e.g., Alexander, 1989; Bjorklund and Pellegrini, 2002; Humphrey, 1976), although the time to master tool use and food-acquisition techniques (e.g., Kaplan, Hill, Lancaster, and Hurtado, 2000) would also require an extended juvenile period.

Third, many aspects of childhood serve as preparations for adulthood and were selected over the course of evolution. Many gender differences in social and cognitive abilities are good examples (see Geary, 1998). Evolutionary psychologists have often focused on gender differences, proposing that women and men have different self-interests and thus have evolved different psychologies. This is reflected especially in gender differences with regard to mating, childrearing, and intra-sex competition. However, these behaviors, dispositions, and cognitions do not appear with the first blast of pubertal hormones or on hearing the cries of one's newborn infant, but have developmental histories, with children adapting their gender-specific behavior to local norms, based on evolved predispositions. Such gender differences should not be viewed as a form of biological determinism, destining women and men to narrow and unchanging roles. Rather, girls and boys are biased toward different environments and experiences through evolved epigenetic rules, and, to the extent that their environment supports those biases, children will develop in a species-typical fashion. However, although these epigenetic rules may be necessary, they are not sufficient to produce a particular developmental pattern (Wachs, 2000). Human behavior is highly flexible, and although some outcomes are more likely than others, all require environmental support to be realized.

Fourth, there have been different selection pressures on organisms at different times in ontogeny. Although some aspects of infancy and childhood can be seen as preparations for later life, other features have been selected in evolution to serve an adaptive function at that time in development only and not to prepare the child for later life (Bjorklund, 1997). For example, some aspects of infancy may serve to foster the attachment between an infant and mother *to increase the chances of survival at that time in ontogeny*, and not only to prepare the child for later adult relationships. Evolution, we propose, has endowed children (and the juveniles of other species) with many characteristics that adapt them well to their immediate environments and not solely prepare them for a future one.

Fifth, many, but not all, evolved psychological mechanisms are domain specific in nature, selected to deal with relatively specific types of problems that our ancestors would have faced in the ancient environments in which they lived and in which most current adaptive psychological mechanisms likely evolved, also referred to as the environment of evolutionary adaptedness (see the following discussion). Rather than seeing the human mind as consisting of a general-purpose processing mechanism that can be applied to a wide range of problems, evolutionary psychologists typically see the mind as consisting of a set of modules, each specialized to deal with a certain type of problem (Buss, 1995; Tooby and Cosmides, 1992). Within social psychology, domain-specific abilities have been hypothesized for attachment, hierarchical power, coalition groups, reciprocity, and mating, among others (Bugental, 2000; Geary, 2001), several of which are relevant for our subsequent discussion on the evolution of parenting.

Sixth, simply because some social, behavioral, or cognitive tendency was adaptive for our ancestors, it does not mean that it continues to be adaptive for modern humans. Similarly, just because some tendencies (such as violence among young adult males) are "natural," based on evolutionary examination, does not mean that they are morally "good," excusable, or inevitable. For example, humans' penchant for sweet and fatty foods can be seen as a formerly adaptive disposition that, in modern environments with grocery stores and Ben and Jerry's Rocky Road Ice Cream, produces increased risk of strokes and heart attacks. Similarly, formal schooling represents a situation in which many of children's evolved tendencies do not fit well with the demands of modern society. From the perspective of evolutionary psychology, much of what we teach children in school is "unnatural" in that teaching involves tasks never encountered by our ancestors (e.g., Pellegrini and Bjorklund, 1997). Many other aspects of social and childrearing behavior, perhaps adaptive for small groups of hunters and gatherers living on the brink of survival, may not be adaptive for modern people living in nation–state societies.

PARENTAL INVESTMENT THEORY

Human parents, particularly mothers, devote substantial time, resources, and energy to rearing their children. Given humans' extended period of youth, there is likely no other species that devotes as much time and energy to their offspring from conception to adulthood as *H. sapiens*. To try to make sense of exactly why parents are so involved in a child's life, it is important to understand the evolutionary reasons why selection would act to produce parents who invest so much in their children. First, children are a parent's most direct route to genetic immortality. Although a person can serve her or his inclusive fitness by helping rear nieces, nephews, and younger siblings, reproductive fitness is most directly served by a person's having children who grow up to become reproductive members of the community. From this perspective, evolution should operate to select parents who provide the means by which their offspring attain maturity and later carry on their parents' reproductive lineage. This includes not only the physical means necessary for survival (e.g., food, shelter), but also the means by which a child develops competencies in the social groups in which humans live.

If at first glance it may seem as if both females and males should be equally likely to invest in their children, this is not the case. For most species, including humans, females invest more heavily in their offspring than males do. This observation and the theory developed around it known as parental investment theory was first postulated by Trivers (1972). Trivers based his ideas on Darwin's (1871) theory of *sexual selection*. Darwin believed that sexual selection would occur for two reasons: First, there would be competition within one sex for access to the other and, second, there would be differential choice of mate selection by members of one sex for members of the other. Generally, sexual selection takes the form of males competing with one another for access to females, whereas females choose among males, often based upon signs of a male's genetic fitness, successful domination over competing males, and the likelihood of his providing resources to her and her offspring.

But why is this pattern, with males competing and females choosing, found so clearly, both cross culturally and across species? The answer, Trivers theorized, lies in the amount of parental investment each parent has contributed, and will contribute, to an offspring. Differential amounts of parental investment actually occur before the child is even conceived. For mammals, this is because females produce a finite number of eggs that are large and immobile. Males, in contrast, produce an unlimited number of small, mobile sperm throughout their lifetimes. This difference in sex-cell size causes females' eggs to be more costly metabolically and thus a limited resource relative to sperm. Furthermore, the fact that her eggs are immobile means that conception will happen inside the female's body, and she will then carry the child through the gestational period and usually be primarily responsible for the lactation and the care of the infant after birth. Male investment can theoretically end following copulation. As such, males have higher potential reproductive rates, in that, following insemination of a female, they can seek additional mating opportunities; in contrast, once conception has occurred, females' mating opportunities end (at least temporarily) and their parenting efforts begin. The end result is that mammal males typically invest more in mating than in parenting, whereas the reverse pattern is found for females. This greater initial investment by females, Trivers argued, is what sets in motion two differing strategies as to how to go about finding and maintaining a mate and rearing subsequent offspring.

Depending on the requirements of the young, there are substantial species differences in the amount of postcopulatory investment males provide to their offspring. Males of some species contribute literally no support to their progeny or mother, whereas others may spend considerable time and energy garnering resources for their offspring, and even spend time in childcare. However, in greater than 95% of mammals, males provide little or no postnatal investment to their offspring (Clutton-Brock, 1991).

Human males are an exception to the typical mammalian pattern. However, despite the well-known role of fathers as providers ("bringing home the bacon") and to a lesser extent as caregivers, women in all cultures provide more support and engage their children more frequently than men do (Barnard and Solchany, in Vol. 3 of this *Handbook*; Parke, in Vol. 3 of this *Handbook*). This pattern is observed in traditional cultures (Eibl-Eibesfeldt, 1989) and in industrialized societies (Whiting and Whiting, 1975) and persists in modern societies in which women work outside the home (Hetherington, Henderson, and Reiss, 1999). There have been changes in Western cultures over the twentieth century, with many fathers spending significant time with their children, sometimes approaching the time investment made by mothers. However, in these same societies, the number of children living in homes headed by females has increased fourfold since 1960 (see Cabrera, Tamis-LeMonda, Bradley, Hofferth, and Lamb, 2000). Thus social forces in today's world influence the degree of paternal investment, but the overall pattern is still that of women devoting more of their time to child care than men do, even in the most enlightened families.

The consequences of such differential investment in offspring have important implications for gender differences in behavior (see Bjorklund and Shackelford, 1999; Buss and Schmidt, 1993; Keller, 2000 for reviews of parental investment theory applied specifically to humans). For women, sexual intercourse brings with it possible conception and pregnancy. Until recently, infants required breast milk to survive, and this could be provided only by the mother or other lactating females. Fathers in generations past could not take the 3 a.m. feeding; the responsibility for feeding infants fell solely to the mothers, making postnatal parental investment for women obligatory (as it is for females of other mammalian species). Men's minimum required investment is today, and surely was in the ancient past, substantially less.

As a direct result of this differential minimum investment between women and men, women tend to be more cautious in assenting to sex than men are (Oliver and Hyde, 1993). Women must not only evaluate the physical qualities of a potential mate (is he healthy, strong, fertile, and so forth), but they also must evaluate his access to resources (is he wealthy, of high status, or otherwise capable of supporting a family) and the likelihood of his sharing them with her and her offspring. In contrast, men are less concerned with the resources of a future mate or her likelihood of sharing. His greater interest lies with her genetic fitness (is she healthy) and her ability to conceive, give birth, and care for a child. These are not necessarily conscious concerns of either sex, for they are reflected in the behavior of nonhuman animals as well (Clutton-Brock, 1991; Trivers, 1972, 1985).

As noted earlier, members of the less investing sex compete with one another for access to the more investing sex. In many mammals, the result of such competition is a physically larger male. Increased size and strength afford males a competitive edge with other males and are associated, in many species, with higher social status and greater access to females (see Geary, 1998, 2000). (High status or otherwise successful males do not simply "take" females as mates; rather, by being successful in competition with other males, they possess traits that females, over evolutionary time, have come to prefer.) Females, of course, also compete with one another over males (Smuts, 1995), but female–female competition is rarely as physically fierce as that between males and is much less apt to result in injury or death. Moreover, most females will eventually find a mate, even if an undesirable one; in contrast, some males will be have no access to females, "shut out" of the Darwinian game altogether.

Finally, whereas maternity is always certain, paternity never is. It is within the women's body that the child is conceived and carried to term, making maternity a sure thing. Males, in contrast, have no such assurance. A man could spend time, energy, and other resources investing in another man's biological child, which would not be adaptive from an evolutionary (reproductive fitness) perspective. As a result, men are apt to question the paternity of their children and may be less likely to invest in a child when that child's paternity is in question. In general, males may be more likely to invest minimally in their offspring because they know that females will continue to invest in their child, even if the male invests little, or even deserts her completely.

In sum, evolutionary theory predicts that mothers will be more likely than fathers to invest heavily in their offspring. This phenomenon is seen both cross culturally and in other species of mammals (as well as in most sexually reproducing species). When fathers do invest, they are most likely to do so when they are sure that the child is genetically their own, and they are sure that the child is healthy enough to reach reproductive age. This pattern is prevalent in humans today, but it is widely assumed that it is an old one that has evolved in our species over the past 5 million years.

BECOMING HUMAN

We can never know with certainty the precise phylogeny of our species and how our ancient ancestors lived. However, evidence from the fossil record, genetic analyses of humans and related species, archeological records (particularly of tool use), examination of the lifestyles of traditional peoples, and the cognitive and social skills of extant great apes provide a picture of what our ancestors might have looked like, their intellectual abilities, and their social organization. This information can also provide us with an idea of how females and males interacted and their respective roles in childrearing. In this section, we first describe briefly the natural history of *H. sapiens* and the environmental conditions under which our species evolved. We then examine some of the factors that may have been responsible for human evolution, particularly as they relate to the formation of the human family and parenting.

The Natural History of *Homo sapiens*

Depending on how we define modern humans, animals identifiable as *H. sapiens* appear in the fossil record as long ago as 300,000 years before the present in the form of *Archaic H. sapiens*, or as late as 35,000 years ago, when the first unambiguous evidence of artistic expression is seen. Anatomically modern humans are found in the fossil records dating back approximately 100,000 years (see Johanson and Edgar, 1996; Tattersall, 1998). However, humanlike creatures, collectively termed hominids to refer to bipedal (upward-walking) apes including humans and our ancient ancestors, date back 4.5 to 5 million years ago (mya). Hominids include members of the *Homo* genus, but also members of the *Australopithecus* and the *Ardipithecus* genera. Although determining with certainty the species to which any fossil belongs is difficult, it is nonetheless certain that many physically and presumably behaviorally different species of hominids have existed over the past 5 million years, with several different species of hominids living at the same time. *H. sapiens* are the only living members of this group; all others have become extinct.

Although there are not other hominids around, humans do have some close relatives. Chimpanzees (*Pan troglodytes*) and bonobos, sometimes referred to as pygmy chimpanzees (*Pan paniscus*), each share approximately 98% of their genetic material with modern people (Sibley and Ahlquist, 1984), making these species more genetically similar to humans than horses are to zebras, for example. Humans share slightly less genetic information with the other great apes, gorillas (*Gorilla gorilla*) and orangutans (*Pongo pygmaeus*). From both the fossil record and genetic analysis, it is estimated that modern humans and modern chimpanzees last shared a common ancestor between 5 and 7 mya.

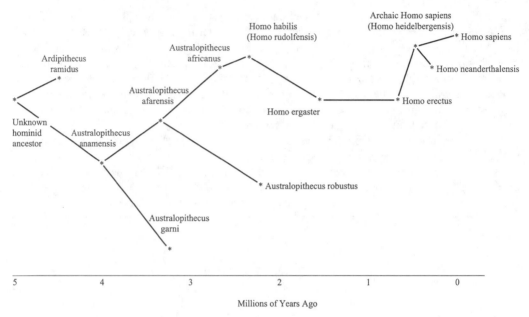

FIGURE 1.1. One possible phylogenetic tree of human evolution.

Since that time, chimpanzees have displayed relatively little physical change from the common ancestor (they are an evolutionary conservative species), and it is likely that the common ancestor of both humans and chimps was substantially chimplike. Hominids, in contrast, displayed substantial change over this relatively brief (in geological time) period, evolving a bipedal stance, expanding the brain and thus cognitive ability, and creating, to an extent not found elsewhere in the animal kingdom, the use of tools and a sophisticated communication system in the form of language. Other species do use tools (most importantly chimpanzees), and many species have complicated communication systems; but these abilities, along with the complexity and diversity of social systems, are qualitatively different in *H. sapiens* than in other species.

Figure 1.1 presents one possible (and greatly simplified) phylogenetic tree of hominid evolution, dating back to the first known hominid, *Ardipithecus ramidus*. Little is know about these animals, that date back approximately 4.5 mya, and only a little more is known about the next oldest species in the human line, *Australopithecus anamensis*. This species, however, is believed to be a direct ancestor to the oldest species in the human line for which there is good fossil evidence, *Australopithecus afarensis* (of which famous Lucy was a member; Johanson and Edgar, 1996). *A. afarensis* were small animals, with females being approximately 3.5 ft tall. They walked upright, much as modern humans do, but had skulls (and thus presumably brains) not much larger than those of modern chimpanzees (~400 cc). *A. afarensis* apparently spawned several sister species, some, such as *Australopithecus garhi*, may have used tools (Asfaw, White, Lovejoy, Latimer, Simpson, and Suwa, 1999), whereas others evolved sturdy bones and jaws, but retained a small (relative to body size) skull (*Australopithecus robustus*). One line led to what paleoanthropologists call the *Homo* (true humans) genus beginning approximately 2.5 mya.

The first member of the *Homo* genus was *Homo habilis* (or perhaps *Homo rudolfensis*, a related species living at approximately the same time), who had a larger brain (~650 cc) than that of the australopithecines and used primitive stone tools. (It is, of course, possible that australopithecines could have used tools made of wood or bone, but because these materials do not preserve well, evidence for tool use other than those made from stone must remain speculative.) *H. habilis*, as were the australopithecines, were confined to Africa and gave rise to *Homo ergaster* approximately 1.8 mya, near the beginning of the geological age referred to as the Pleistocene. Although there are several related scenarios about *Homo* phylogeny from this point, one likely alternative is that *H. ergaster* gave rise to *Homo erectus*, who had larger brains (~900 cc), created more complex tools than its ancestors, and may have used fire. *H. erectus* (or perhaps *H. ergaster*) was the first species to leave Africa, emigrating to what today is the Middle East, Europe, and Asia between 1.7 and 2 mya (Gabunia et al., 2000). *H. erectus* became extinct approximately 250,000 years ago. The ancestral *H. ergaster* species that remained in Africa was replaced by *Archaic H. sapiens* (classified by some as *Homo heidelbergensis*) approximately 300,000 years ago. These individuals had characteristics of both *H. ergaster* and modern *H. sapiens*. Modern humans with large brains (~1,300 cc) apparently evolved in Africa within the past 100,000 years (possibly as early as 52,000 years ago; see Ingman, Kaessmann, Pääbo, and Gyllensten, 2000). They migrated out of Africa and replaced, according to most paleoanthropologists, the aboriginal *Homo* species they encountered (for example, *Neanderthals* in Europe), either by killing or by outcompeting them (Eccles, 1989; Johanson and Edgar, 1996; Wood, 1994).

H. sapiens is a relatively young species that has not changed much over the past 100,000 years, at least physically, and certainly little at all over the past 35,000 years or so. But humans' physical conservatism belies a behavioral and cognitive flexibility that has resulted in a radical change in how we live as a species. The advent of agriculture and a sedentary lifestyle beginning approximately 12,000 years ago changed drastically how most human beings lived. For most of the history of *H. sapiens* and its immediate forbears, individuals lived in small nomadic, groups, living off the land, gathering fruits and vegetables (mainly the work of women), scavenging from the kills made by other animals, and hunting (mainly the work of men). In one form or another, it was in such hunting–gathering–scavenging environments in which the modern human mind evolved. Although life has changed substantially for most members of our species since the advent of agriculture and sedentary lifestyles, there has not been sufficient time for our brains, and the evolved psychological mechanisms within them, to evolve. Basically, modern humans possess brains and minds adapted for life in a very different environment than that in which they find themselves living today. This ancient environment is often referred to as the environment of evolutionary adaptedness. What was this like, how did our ancestors behave, and what pressures were there that resulted in the modern human mind, and, importantly for this chapter, how did these pressures lead to the human way of rearing children?

The Environment of Evolutionary Adaptedness

It is impossible to specify exactly what the environment of evolutionary adaptedness was like, in part because it is impossible to define precisely what time period this term represents. On the one hand, humans share an evolutionary history with all extant primates and mammals. Thus historical environments in which these ancestral mammals and, later primates, evolved are also relevant to modern humans. If we take as our starting point, however, the period in which the genetic line that would eventually lead to *H. sapiens* separated from the line that would lead to modern chimpanzees, we find a period of approximately 5 to 7 million years, beginning in the forests and the savannas of Africa. Because of the dearth of fossil and archeological evidence for periods much before 2 mya, it is difficult to say anything with confidence about the lifestyles of the various species of australopithecines. However, based on what fossil evidence we do have and on the way in which chimpanzees live today, it is highly likely that hominids were always a social species. Based again on limited fossil evidence, the organization of chimpanzee and bonobo troops, and the lifestyles of contemporary hunter–gatherers, it is likely that the size of most social groups during the Pleistocene age was relatively small (probably between 30 and 60 people), consisting of both closely related and unrelated individuals who interacted on a regular basis. Like modern female chimpanzees, female humans were more likely to leave their natal group to find a mate than were males. This is a phenomenon seen in many (but not all) traditional cultures today and is supported by patterns of genetic diversity. Across the globe, the variation in human mitochondrial DNA, which is passed to offspring only from their mothers, is similar to the variation found for genes on autosomal (nonsex) chromosomes, such that between 81% and 85% of mitochondrial and autosomal DNA is found in all cultures. This is in contrast to variation in DNA found on the male Y chromosome. Most human populations share only $\sim$36% of the possible genetic variation on the Y chromosome, with 53% of variation being attributed to the continent on which men reside (Owens and King, 1999; Seielstad, Minch, and Cavalli-Sforza, 1998). This pattern suggests that ancient women migrated more than men, leaving their birthplaces to live with their mates. Most female migration would not have involved long distances, but over hundreds of generations, the genetic effects would accumulate.

As in all societies today and for the vast majority of mammals, mothers were the primary caregivers to their children. Fathers likely provided protection to their mates and offspring and support in the form of food and other tangible resources (Kaplan et al., 2000), but likely spent relatively little time in direct childcare. Some males surely had several mates, meaning that some females shared the resources and attention of a single male and that some males had no access to reproductive females. Females probably reached puberty relatively late (late teens, early 20s), and gave birth every 3 to 5 years, with pregnancy often following the cessation of nursing a previous child (Kaplan et al., 2000). Infant mortality was surely high, and, even for those who did survive to adulthood, life was relatively brief by contemporary standards, with few people living past 40 years of age (Austad, 1997). However, if contemporary hunter–gatherer societies are any indication, it is likely that there were always some "old" people (i.e., beyond 60 or 70 years of age) in every group (Hill and Hurtado, 1991; Kaplan et al., 2000).

Although hominid groups were usually small, social relationships, especially among large-brained members of the *Homo* genus, were surely complex. Humans in all societies around the world cooperate and compete with one another and with people from outside groups. Trade among different social groups is universal to humans, as is warfare. We are aware of no other mammal that engages in trade, and only the chimpanzee displays anything similar to war parties, attacking and killing members of another group of their own species (Goodall, 1986).

It is worth pointing out that the picture of a consistent and stable Pleistocene environment is likely more fiction than fact. There were substantial climatic changes over the past 2 million years, and individuals who could deal with unpredictable changes in climate and habitat were the ones who reproduced to become our ancestors (Potts, 1998, 2000). This implies that behavioral flexibility characterized ancient *Homo* populations, which is further bolstered by the fact that *H. erectus* and, later, *H. sapiens* emigrated out of Africa and populated much of the Old World, and, in the process, surely encountered a wide range of ecological conditions. Despite this ecological instability, some characteristics of hominid lifestyle, such as its social complexity, division of labor, and tool use, have likely always characterized our ancestors, and these may have served as the foundation for domain-specific and species-universal psychological mechanisms that underlie the modern human mind.

WHAT WERE THE SELECTION PRESSURES THAT LED TO THE MODERN HUMAN MIND AND THE HUMAN FAMILY?

There have been many hypotheses about the "causes" of human evolution. Selection pressures related to hunting, tool use, navigating large environments, coping with variable environments, diet, and dealing with conspecifics have all been suggested (among others) as the principal cause of human evolution. There is, of course, no single cause for the evolution of any species, including humans. Rather, evolution surely proceeded as the result of a confluence of interacting factors, with no single one identified as a simple cause or consequence of another. This does not mean, however, that some hypotheses of human evolution are not better than others, and the one we prefer, which we believe accounts well for humans' unique cognitive abilities and style of childrearing, focuses on three interrelated factors: an enlarged brain and the accompanying cognitive abilities, increased social organization and the need to better cooperate and compete with conspecifics, and an extended juvenile period (Bjorklund and Pellegrini, 2002). Each of these factors in concert with the others contributed to changes in what it took for infants to survive and to grow up to become reproductive members of their group. We describe briefly here the role of social intelligence and "big brains" in the human evolution story and focus on how these factors may have contributed to a prolonged juvenile period, necessitating increased parental investment.

The Significance of Social Intelligence

We (e.g., Bjorklund and Harnishfeger, 1995; Bjorklund and Pellegrini, 2002, in press) and many others (e.g., Alexander, 1989; Byrne and Whiten, 1988; Humphrey, 1976; Jolly, 1966, 1999) have argued that the single most important selection pressure in the evolution of human intelligence was dealing with other members of the species. As hominid groups became more complex, a greater social intelligence was required for maneuvering the often stormy waters within small groups of long-lived conspecifics. Individuals who could reflect on their own knowledge, intentions, and desires, and, importantly, the knowledge, intentions, and desires of others (theory of mind) would have been at an advantage in cooperating and competing with others both within and without their immediate group.

As social cohesion became more important in primate and hominid groups, the need to control sexual and aggressive responses also increased in importance. This may have been particularly true for early humans, attributed, in part, to changes in females' receptivity to sex. In many primates, there is considerable competition between males for access to estrous females. The receptivity of females to sexual advances varies across species, with female chimpanzees, bonobos, and some monkeys being receptive for an extended period of time beyond the period of estrus, resulting in extended competition among males. In contrast to other great ape females, human females do not show any outward signs of ovulation, and, unlike other mammals, they present permanently swollen mammaries, whether nursing or not, that have become constant sexual signals for males, despite their unreliability in predicting sexual receptivity or ovulation. Thus sexual receptivity, in both human females and males, cannot be determined by physical body signs, such as swollen genitals in apes. Moreover, both females and males are, in theory, continually receptive sexually, with their willingness to copulate being primarily under the control of social and not hormonal factors. The opportunity for continuous mating would result in continuous conflict among males if some mechanisms for inhibiting sexual responses had not evolved. Several theorists have proposed that, in response to these pressures, the inhibitory control of sexual and aggressive behavior became increasingly under cortical control (Bjorklund and Harnishfeger, 1995; Chance, 1962).

These changes in female sexual behavior (potentially receptive even when not ovulating) and appearances (no outward sign of sexual receptivity or ovulation) may have contributed significantly, along with other factors, to human pair bonding. For a male hominid, whose investment is required if his long-dependent offspring are to survive, it is critical that he be confident that his resources are going to his genetic progeny and not to the offspring of another male. However, this can be problematic in a species in which ovulation, and thus fertility, cannot be known by the male and when females, as well as males, are potentially sexually receptive at all times. To counteract this dilemma, males may resort to some form of mate guarding, in which they hover near their mates during her fertile time, preventing her access to other males; but males cannot guard their mates all of the time. Also, although it may seem to be to the female's advantage to have as many options in terms of potential mates as she can, mating with a large number of males would do her little good if none of them contributed significantly to the support of her offspring, which seems to have been, if not necessary, at least highly desirable in hominids (see Geary, 1998). One solution to these problems may have been the "invention" of neurochemical systems (opioids and oxytocin) that fostered strong emotional bonds between a female and male, producing marginally (and temporary) monogamous behavior in the pair, long enough so that their children could reach an age so that they could care for themselves (Fisher, 1992).

As we have suggested, one condition necessary for substantial paternal investment to evolve would be a high degree of paternity certainty. This seems to have been achieved in contemporary humans. Studies from a broad range of countries have estimated the degree of paternity discrepancy (in which the domestic father is not the genetic father) to be between 7% and 15% (see Bellis and Baker, 1990; Lerner and von Eye, 1992). Thus, although women clearly engage in extramate copulations (surely enough for men to have evolved mechanisms to guard against cuckoldry), they apparently do not frequently make cuckolds of their mates. The result is a male who can be relatively confident of the paternity of his offspring, a female who obtains resources for herself and her offspring from her mate, and an offspring who survives past infancy.

Inhibitory abilities necessary for increasing the control of sexual and aggressive behaviors would require increased neural capacity, and they may have been part of the selective pressures that led to enhanced brain size, particularly of the neocortex, in the hominid line. Alternatively, other factors may have been primarily responsible for the increase in brain size seen in hominids over the past 4 million years, with greater inhibitory abilities being a by-product of this increase, co-opting neural circuits that had been selected for other purposes. Nonetheless, once inhibitory abilities did increase, the behaviors they produced were subject to natural selection. And whether they were primarily a cause or a consequence of increased brain power, what is undeniable is that brain size did increase, and, for better or worse, *H. sapiens*' large brain and resulting cognitive processes define us, more than any other feature, as a species.

Large Brains

Humans have disproportionately large brains relative to their body size (Deacon, 1997; Jerison, 1973). Brains are very expensive in terms of the calories they consume, so that having "more brain" than needed to control the body must have substantial benefits for survival. *H. sapiens*' large cranium did not materialize out of thin air, however. Primates in general have larger brains than expected by their body size (represented by the encephalization quotient [EQ] that reflects brain size relative to the expected brain size for an animal of a specified body size, Jerison, 1973); humans merely reflect an extension of a pattern already observed in primates. Figure 1.2 shows the EQ for chimpanzees and for several hominid species. (An EQ of 1.0 is the "expected" value, with EQs greater than 1.0 reflecting "more brain" than that predicted for an animal of a specified size.) As can be seen, the EQ for *A. afarensis* was only slightly greater than that of modern chimpanzees. From this point on in evolution, brain weight relative to body weight increased at a rapid rate. As we stated earlier, one set of factors responsible for this change was related to the increased social complexity of hominid groups, although changes in diet, technology, and responses to modifications in climate all likely played interacting and contributory roles (e.g., Kaplan et al., 2000; Potts, 1998). But regardless of the reasons (i.e., selective pressures) for increased brain size, there must be some mechanisms within the organism for achieving this change. One important mechanism, we believe, can be found in alterations of patterns of development that, in turn, would provide additional changes that must pass through the sieve of natural selection.

The Consequences of Delaying Development

Although humans' brains are bigger than those of their ancestors, somewhat ironically, one mechanism by which brains increased in size was the process of delayed development. Some evolutionary changes can be brought about by a change in patterns of development. Genetic-based differences in developmental rate have been referred to as heterochrony (de Beer, 1958; Gould, 1977; McKinney, 1998; Shea, 1989). For simplicity's sake, we talk about only two general forms of heterochrony,

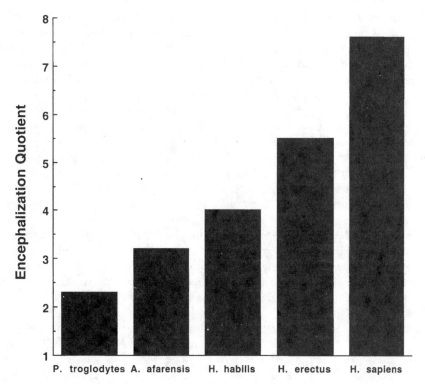

FIGURE 1.2. EQs for chimpanzees (*P. troglodytes*) and four hominid species (data for chimpanzees from Jerison, 1973; data for hominids from Tobias, 1987).

acceleration, in which the rate of development (ontogeny) in an individual is accelerated or extended relative to one's ancestors, and *retardation*, in which development is slowed down or delayed in comparison with ancestral patterns. In one sense, big brains are a good example of accelerated development. The development of the brain of *H. sapiens* is clearly extended beyond that of its progenitors. Yet, achieving that extension required the delaying of a pattern of growth rate typical of the prenatal period to postnatal life.

The primate brain develops rapidly in comparison with the growth rate of the overall size of the body (see Bonner, 1988). For chimpanzees, macaque monkeys, and other primates, brain growth slows quickly after birth; this is much less so for humans. Rather, the rate of prenatal brain growth for humans continues over the first 2 years of life (see Gould, 1977). By 2 years of age, the human brain has attained 50% of its eventual adult weight; in contrast, total body weight is only ~20% of what it will eventually be (Tanner, 1978). Increasing the time the brain grows increases the number of neurons that are produced (Finlay and Darlington, 1995; Finlay, Darlington, and Nicastro, 2001) and also results in the extension of dendritic and synaptic growth, so that the human brain has more neurons and more interconnections among neurons than the brains of other primates (Finlay et al., 2001; Gibson, 1991). Although most parts of the brain have undergone enlargement in human evolution, the effects are most pronounced on the neocortex, the so-called thinking portion of the brain (Deacon, 1997; Eccles, 1989).

The extension of embryonic growth rates for the brain into the second year of life was necessitated by some physical limitations of human females. Big brains require big skulls, and if a human newborn's skull were as large as "expected," given the eventual adult size (and given the standard primate rate of prenatal and postnatal brain development), the infant's head would be too large to fit through the birth canal. The size of a woman's hips (which determine the size of the birth canal) is limited by the need for bipedality. A woman with hips large enough for giving birth to an infant who has a cranium the size of that of a contemporary 2-year-old child would not be able to walk. Thus evolutionary pressures that resulted in an enlarged brain required that pregnancy be extended only to the point at which the infant skull would fit through the birth canal. The result is a physically immature infant, motorically and perceptually far behind the sophistication of other primate infants (see Antinucci, 1989; Gibson, 1991). However, human brain and cognitive development soon became accelerated relative to their primate cousins (because, in large part, of the retention of fetal brain-growth rate) (Langer, 1998; McKinney, 1998; Parker and McKinney, 1999).

Rate of brain development is not the only aspect of ontogeny that is delayed. As a species, humans spend a disproportionate amount of time as prereproductives. Worldwide today, the average age of menarche is between 12.5 and 13.5 years. However, for both girls and boys, there is typically a period of low fertility, extending the nonreproductive years even further (Bogin, 1999; Tanner, 1978). Based on historical data and data from traditional cultures (Hill and Hurtado, 1996; Kaplan et al., 2000), it is likely that our ancient ancestors were closer to 18 to 20 years of age before being fully reproductive. This is all the more impressive when we consider that the likely life expectancy of our hominid forebears was substantially less than ours today, meaning that many children would die before reaching reproductive age and that many others would have only a limited number of reproductive years. Many women, for example, surely died in childbirth. When looked on in hindsight, our delayed maturation had substantial risks. Given these risks, the selective pressures for this delayed maturation must have been derived from strong compensatory advantages of the immature state, most notably increased flexibility of learning.

Human development is different from that of other primates not only in quantitative terms (i.e., being slow and extended), but also in qualitative terms. For example, Bogin (1997, 1999) proposed five stages of development for *H. sapiens*: infancy, childhood, juvenility, adolescence, and adulthood, two of which, childhood and adolescence, are not observed in any other species. Infancy ends with the cessation of nursing and is followed in other mammals by the juvenile period, in which the young animal is no longer dependent on its parents but is not yet sexually mature. In contrast, weaning in humans occurs between 2 and 5 years of age, but it is another several years before children can eat an adult diet and otherwise fend for themselves. The juvenile period in humans is followed by adolescence, with its characteristic growth spurt, and continues until sexual maturity, typically in the late teen years. No other species displays this rapid growth spurt before adulthood, although chimpanzees and bonobos also apparently have a postmenarche period of infertility (see Bogin, 1999).

From fossil evidence, Bogin (1997, 1999) has estimated that the life stages of our australopithecine ancestors were similar to those of chimpanzees (*P. troglodytes*), consisting of a period of infancy last-ing 5 or 6 years, followed by a juvenile period, with adulthood beginning at approximately 12 years of age. According to Bogin, it is only with the beginning of the *Homo* line that a period of child-hood is seen, and only in modern *H. sapiens* is there evidence for a period of adolescence. In addition to the emergence of childhood and adolescence, the length of juvenility and adulthood is longer in humans than in other primates and is almost certainly longer than for our hominid an-cestors. There is also evidence from fossil dental and cranial development that brain development in Neanderthals was much faster than in modern humans (e.g., Akazawa, Muhesen, Dodo, Kondo, and Mizouguchi, 1995; Dean, Stringer, and Bromage, 1986; Zollikofer, Ponce de León, Martin, and Stucki, 1995). Mithen (1996) has used this evidence to suggest that the modern human mind, with the ability to communicate between different cognitive modules, required an extended juvenile period.

There are many possible reasons for the extension of developmental periods in humans (see Bogin, 1999), but the very fact of this developmental extension indicates that ancient members of the *Homo* line were able to keep children alive long enough to reach an age at which they could reproduce themselves. Note also that the extended developmental period is associated with an enlarged brain. As argued previously in this chapter, we, and others (Bogin, 1999; Dunbar, 1992, 1995), believe that the extended period of youth and an enlarged brain were necessary to master the increasing complexity of the social environment. In fact, research showing the relation among large brains, an extended immaturity, and social complexity has been reported by Joffe (1997), who compared aspects of brain size with length of the prereproductive period and aspects of social complexity for 27 primates, including humans. Joffe reported that the proportion of the lifespan spent as a juvenile was positively correlated with group size *and* the relative size of the nonvisual neocortex. This is the part of the primate brain that is associated with complex problem solving, including memory. Joffe argued that social complexity exerted selection pressures for increased nonvisual neocortex in primates and an extension of the juvenile period.

Extended childhoods would also be useful for mastering other important skills in addition to social intelligence. For example, Kaplan et al. (2000) proposed that it was ancient humans' shift to a higher-quality diet that necessitated greater cognitive skills and thus an extended childhood for learning. Chimpanzees, for example, rely primarily on a diet of easily extracted fruit and plants with low-nutrition density. Such foods, when available, can be obtained relatively easily even by juveniles. Chimpanzees obtain only a small portion of their diet by hunting, which provides foods of high-nutrition density. Hunting, however, is engaged in mainly by adults (usually males) and takes considerable time to learn. Kaplan et al. (2000) examined food-gathering procedures in contemporary hunter–gatherer societies and noted that, similar to chimpanzees, children often forage for low-density easily accessible foods, such as ripe fruit, at young ages and become relatively adept at the task. Extracting foods of higher nutrition density, such as roots and tubers or vertebrate meat through hunting, is performed effectively only by older individuals and requires many years to master.

INVESTING IN CHILDREN

What does all this have to do with the formation of the human family and patterns of parenting? First, as we mentioned, the enlargement of the *Homo* brain required that much of the brain growth be done postnatally, because of restrictions of the female anatomy. This meant that human children would be physically dependent on their parents for a longer period of time. This was coupled with an extended childhood that was due to the need to learn the complexity of one's social environment (or possibly, in addition, to learn the mechanisms for processing high-quality food), which further extended the time children spent as prereproductives.

If children are to grow to become sexually mature and economically productive members of their community, they require substantial support from their parents, particularly their mothers. Parents allocate effort and resources to their offspring that could otherwise be devoted to mating effort or spent on their own physical development and acquisition of resources. Yet allocating resources to an infant not only limits one's own ontogeny and mating efforts, but also compromises opportunities to invest in other offspring, both those born and unborn (Keller, 2000). Although it may seem obvious that parents, particularly mothers, will do anything to enhance the survival of their children, there are factors, in both contemporary and ancient environments, that affect how much mothers are willing to invest. These include the health of a child, the conditions of the local economy/ecology, the presence of additional children, the age and reproductive status of the parents (particularly the mother), and the amount of social support available to help rear a child, among other factors.

We focus here on the issue of social support. Human mothers likely have never reared a child "alone." Because of the extended dependency of their offspring, human mothers must spend more time caring for their offspring than do mothers of other mammals, leaving less time for activities that would be important for their own growth and that of their other offspring. This has made it necessary for a mother to receive assistance from others; this includes resources and some childcare from the father, but also support from members in the community. In this section, we discuss briefly the two most likely sources of support for a mother and her offspring: fathers and grandparents.

The Importance of Paternal Investment

The long period of offspring dependency meant that a male's genetic success could not be measured just by how many children he sired. His inclusive fitness would depend on how many of his offspring reached sexual maturity, ensuring his becoming a grandfather. To increase the odds of this happening, his help in rearing his children would be needed. Human males devote more time to "parenting" than the vast majority of mammals do (Clutton-Brock, 1991) and, in most contemporary hunter–gatherer societies, they provide the majority of calories consumed by both their offspring and their mates (see Kaplan et al., 2000). Increased paternal investment permitted human females to rear multiple dependent offspring and to cut the childhood mortality rate in half in comparison with that of other primates and group-hunting carnivores (Lancaster and Lancaster, 1987).

The significance to survival and success of paternal investment are not just speculative, but are supported by evidence from modern societies, contemporary hunter–gatherers, and historical records (see Geary, 1998, 2000, for reviews). For all types of data sets, children's mortality rates are higher and their social status is lower when fathers are absent. Moreover, in contemporary America, the quality of a father's active and supportive involvement in his children's lives is positively associated with emotional regulation, academic achievement, and social competence (see Cabrera et al., 2000; Lamb, 1997).

Grandparental Support

Although fathers may be the most important source of support to a mother and her children, in all societies, support also comes from related kin, most often from grandparents. The conditions under which grandparents are apt to provide support are similar to the conditions under which fathers are likely to make investments: when genetic relatedness is high. Maternal grandparents, like the mothers themselves, can be quite confident that the baby is related to them, whereas paternal grandparents, as fathers, can never be 100% certain of paternity. As such, evolutionary theory predicts that, on average, maternal grandparents will invest more in their grandchildren than will paternal grandparents, and the research literature has consistently confirmed this relation (Smith and Drew, in Vol. 3 of this *Handbook*). Studies from a variety of countries have shown that maternal grandparents have more contact with and show greater solicitude toward their grandchildren than do paternal grandparents, even after researchers control for distances the grandparents live from their grandchildren (Smith and Drew, in Vol. 3 of this *Handbook*). Moreover, maternal grandfathers are viewed as devoting more care to their grandchildren than are paternal grandmothers, despite the greater childcare role that women play in all cultures (e.g., Eisenberg, 1988; Euler and Weitzel, 1996; Hoffman, 1978/1979; Rossi and Rossi, 1990; Salmon, 1999). A similar pattern of investment has been found for aunts and uncles, with maternal agnates being seen by college participants as expressing more concern for them than paternal agnates do (Gaulin, McBurney, and Brakeman-Wartell, 1997).

The only published exception to this phenomenon that we are aware of is from a study in which German and Greek adults evaluated how much each of their grandparents had cared for them (Pashos, 2000). Patterns were as predicted for the Germans and for the Greek participants from urban areas (i.e., greater care from maternal than from paternal grandparents). However, participants from rural areas of Greece stated that their *paternal* grandparents provided more care for them than their maternal grandparents. This pattern was due, in part, to the custom in rural Greece in which paternal grandparents have the social obligation of caring for their grandchildren; moreover, children usually live closer to their paternal grandparents, often in the same house. The increased physical closeness of the paternal family may result in greater paternity certainty than is the case in urban settings. When the movements of women (daughters-in-law) are known and controlled in part by the husband's family, there is little uncertainty about paternity. As a result, paternal grandparents can invest in their grandchildren with relative certainty. In contrast, in urban areas, in which social customs serve to reduce paternity certainty, paternal grandparental investment is reduced.

Grandparents who contribute to the success of their adult offspring and their grandoffspring can serve to decrease infant mortality and morbidity rates, which increases their inclusive fitness. Some have even speculated that such grandparental investment has contributed significantly to

H. sapiens' longevity (e.g., Gaulin, 1980; Hamilton, 1966; Hawkes, O'Connell, and Blurton Jones, 1997; O'Connell, Hawkes, and Blurton Jones, 1999). Characteristics associated with longevity can be selected for if older people continue to reproduce; that is, long-lived individuals can pass these characteristics directly to their offspring. However, most human females in traditional societies have their last children 20 or 30 years before they die. Thus both women who live long lives and those who live shorter lives are likely to have reproduced before natural selection will have had an effect on the genes associated with longevity. However, genes for longevity can be selected for if long-lived (but nonreproducing) individuals foster their grandchildren's survival.

There is evidence from a variety of species for the "grandmother hypothesis" (because it is primarily grandmothers and not grandfathers who provide support to their grandchildren). Vervet monkeys, baboons, lions, and humans in traditional societies all benefit from the presence of a grandmother (Hawkes et al., 1997; Packer, Tatar, and Collins, 1998). For example, research with the Hadza, a small group of foragers living in Africa's Rift Valley, found that older women's foraging was particularly important for the nutrition of young children who had been weaned but who were not yet prepared to eat adult food (Hawkes et al., 1997; O'Connell et al., 1999). Hawkes et al. (1997) reported that, in families in which mothers were nursing, the nutritional status of weaned children was related to the foraging efforts of their *grandmothers* rather than those of their mothers. If this pattern reflects ancestral populations, the result would have been to increase fertility by permitting mothers to wean a child earlier and become pregnant again sooner. Without grandmother support for weaned children, nursing would likely continue for several more years, reducing the total number of children a female could expect to have.

EVOLUTIONARY PERSPECTIVES ON MODERN PARENTING

Evolutionary theory can provide some insights into how patterns of human parenting came to be, but does an evolutionary approach to parenting provide anything more than an interesting historical perspective? We argue that it does, that looking at parenting through the lens of evolutionary theory can be useful for understanding important aspects of childrearing relevant to people in contemporary societies (Belsky, 1997, 2000; Bjorklund and Pellegrini, 2000, 2002, in press; Geary and Bjorklund, 2000; Keller, 2000; Surbey, 1998b). Perhaps the most empirical research related to parenting from an evolutionary perspective concerns attachment and the consequences that styles of attachment have for subsequent development. This is because, in part, Bowlby (1969), the founder of modern attachment theory, saw attachment from an ethological (as well as psychoanalytic) perspective, believing that attachment served an adaptive function to infants in the environment of evolutionary adaptedness. More recently, Belsky et al. (1991) suggested that different styles of childrearing can result in different patterns of attachment and have consequences on subsequent mating behaviors, consistent with evolutionary theory. Other theorists taking an evolutionary perspective, however, have questioned the degree to which individual differences in parenting style (including, but not restricted to, attachment) affect personality and intellectual development (Harris, 1995; Scarr, 1992), and we examine briefly this issue later. Before examining these important topics, however, we first look at how evolutionary explanations can be helpful in understanding the possible psychological mechanisms in play when parenting "goes wrong," resulting in the neglect, abuse, or even the death of children at the hands of their parents.

Evolved Mechanisms Underlying Neglect, Abuse, and Infanticide

It seems a given that all parents want the best for their children—that children are parents' route to immortality. From a Darwinian perspective, reproduction is the *sine qua non* of success, making situations in which parents do not act in the best interests of their children paradoxical. These situations become a bit easier to understand, however, when we consider that any given child is only one of potentially many offspring, some of whom may be better candidates for continuing a parent's genetic heritage than others.

Differential parental investment. Parents often choose to invest differentially in their off-spring, investing the most in those who have the greatest chance of reaching reproductive age and thus carrying on the parents' genes. Parents must balance costs associated with care of a specific child against resources that can be used for other children, both those born and those unborn, and for the parents themselves. Differential investment in offspring is most apparent in the behaviors of mothers. In ages past, it seems likely that mothers who were skilled at identifying cues to a child's future reproductive success could invest more time, energy, and resources in those children, influencing substantially the likely survival of their various offspring. Mothers who were less proficient at making these discriminations or were less reluctant to act on perceived differences were likely to squander scarce resources on a child who may not make it to adulthood, no matter the degree of investment made. From this perspective, evolution has selected mothers who are skillful at identifying which children, as well as which circumstances, are best suited to rearing a child to reproductive years.

Reduced maternal investment can take many forms. Children may be neglected, receiving less attention, medical care, and food than they might need; they may be abused, wet-nursed, fostered out with relatives or even strangers, or left in the custody of a religious institution. Infants and children in some cultures have been sold into slavery, or at the extreme, put to death (Hrdy, 1999).

Under what conditions would parents, particularly mothers, decide to reduce investment in children? One set of salient cues comes directly from infants themselves. Sickly babies may be a bad investment, particularly if caring for a sickly child means devoting fewer resources to healthier children or postponing becoming pregnant again with the chance of having a healthy baby who is more likely to survive and thrive. Although our society places a high value on the life of even the most sickly infants, this is not universal. For example, anthropological data indicate that the killing of a deformed or seriously ill infant was sanctioned in approximately one third of the traditional cultures studied (Daly and Wilson, 1984). In our own society, children with mental retardation or those who have other congenital defects such as Down's syndrome, spina bifida, cystic fibrosis, or cleft palate are abused at rates 2 to 10 times higher than those of unaffected children (see Daly and Wilson, 1981 for review); and when these children are institutionalized parental interest rapidly decreases, and many are not visited ever (Daly and Wilson, 1988).

Differential investment in sickly infants is often less severe, as indicated by research by Mann (1992), who examined the interaction between mothers and their premature and extremely low-birth-weight twins. Although there were few differences in the interaction patterns between mothers and each of their twins at 4 months of age, when the twins were 8 months old, all mothers in the study showed more positive behavior toward the healthier of the two twins; that is, maternal preferences were clearly linked to the baby's health, mediated, quite surely, by the differential behavior and appearance of the two siblings (Sameroff and Suomi, 1996).

Other factors that influence maternal investment include the child's age, such that older children (who, by living as long as they have, demonstrate viability) often receive more investment than younger children, particularly in times of high stress and low resources (see Daly and Wilson, 1988); mother's reproductive status, with younger mothers being more likely to neglect, abuse, or kill their infants than older mothers (see Daly and Wilson, 1988; Lee and George, 1999; Overpeck, Brenner, Trumble, Trifiletti, and Berendes, 1998), presumably because younger mothers have greater opportunity for having more children than older mothers; and social support, with mothers who have little social support being more likely to abandon an infant than mothers with greater social support (see Daly and Wilson, 1988; Lancaster, 1989).

We have provided evidence of neglect, abuse, and infanticide to illustrate the extremes that parents (particularly mothers) sometimes go in making decisions about parental investment. From a broader perspective, human parents are generally supportive of their children, with abuse and infanticide being relatively rare phenomena. However, the circumstances under which humans abandon their infants are similar to those seen for many other species (Hrdy, 1999). Hrdy (1999) suggests that mothers may kill their own infants when other means of birth control are unavailable and they were unwilling or unable to commit themselves to further care of the infant. However, with notable exceptions, mothers rarely plan to kill their babies. To quote Hrdy (1999, p. 297):

> Rather, abandonment is at one extreme of a continuum that ranges between termination of investment and the total commitment of a mother carrying her baby everywhere and nursing on demand. Abandonment is, you might say, the default mode for a mother terminating investment. Infanticide occurs when circumstances (including fear of discovery) prevent a mother from abandoning it. Although legally and morally there is a difference, biologically the two phenomena are inseparable.

Stepparent investment. Incidences of neglect, abuse, and even death, although still rare, are more likely to occur at the hands of stepparents rather than biological parents. From a strictly inclusive fitness perspective, any resource a stepparent provides to stepchildren will not benefit that parent's fitness. The stepchild possesses none of the stepparent's genes, and presumably the adult's resources could be better spent supporting her or his own genetic offspring. Yet stepparenting is widespread throughout the world and through recorded history, and despite the myths and realities of the fate of children at the hands of stepparents, the vast majority of stepparents love and care for their children (Hetherington and Stanley-Hagan, in Vol. 3 of this *Handbook*). Perhaps the first question we should ask is, "Why should a stepparent provide *any* resources to a stepchild?"

Most evolutionary psychologists have suggested that parental investment from a stepparent is actually investment in mating, not investment in parenting (e.g., Anderson, Kaplan, and Lancaster, 1999b; Hawkes, Rogers, and Charnov, 1995; Rowher, Herron, and Daly, 1999; van Schaik and Paul, 1996). For example, a stepfather provides support to his wife's children from a previous mating to maintain sexual access to her and for the children he will father with her. Women with children from a previous male select men who will not only provide support for themselves and their future offspring, but also for their children from previous matings.

However, stepparents rarely provide the same level of support to their stepchildren as they do to their natural children. Research from a wide range of cultures indicates that the amount of financial resources parents provide and the amount of time spent interacting with stepchildren is significantly less than for natural children (e.g., Anderson, Kaplan, Lam, and Lancaster, 1999a, Anderson et al., 1999b; Flinn, 1988; Flinn, Leone, and Quinlan, 1999; Marlowe, 1999; Zvoch, 1999). For example, Anderson et al. (1999b) found that the amount of financial resources children in the United States are likely to receive for their college education was considerably less for families that consisted of a stepfather and a biological mother than for families consisting of two biological parents. In an observational study of the Hazda, biological fathers communicated, played with, and nurtured (held, fed, pacified, cleaned) their natural children more than they did their stepchildren (Marlowe, 1999), despite adults' claims of equal feelings and care for natural children and stepchildren.

Not providing as much money for college for a stepchild as for a biological child or playing more with a natural child than with a stepchild reflects pancultural differences in the amount of parental investment made to biological versus nonbiological offspring, consistent with the tenets of parental investment theory. However, having a smaller college fund for a stepchild than for a biological offspring is far from stepchild abuse. Yet all cultures appear to have their own versions of Cinderella. Such folklore, unfortunately, has a basis in reality.

Child abuse and homicide are both more likely when a child lives with a stepparent than with two biological parents (Daly and Wilson, 1988, 1996). In an extensive Canadian study, Daly and Wilson (1985) reported that children were 40 times more likely to be abused if they lived with a stepparent than with two natural parents. Differences remained substantial even after potentially confounding factors such as poverty, mother's age, and family size were statistically controlled. Perhaps even more disturbing are findings for child homicide, a crime that, unlike child abuse, is almost always reported to authorities. Daly and Wilson (1988) examined the results of several surveys of crime data from around the world and reported a similar pattern independent of country: Children were more likely to be killed by a stepparent than by a genetic parent, with this difference being particularly large for children under 2 years of age. Rates of child homicide were sometimes more than 100 times larger for stepchildren than for biological children.

Murder of one's stepchildren, of course, is not sanctioned by modern societies. (Although in some contemporary hunter–gatherer societies, when a man marries a woman with children, it is acceptable for her young children be put to death; see Daly and Wilson, 1988.) Men who kill their stepchildren are inevitably convicted and incarcerated, so there is no adaptive value to the killing of a stepchild. Yet the fact that abuse and murder are enormously greater for stepchildren than for natural children suggests that the restraints against acting violently toward nonrelated children are much less than the restraints involved with one's genetic children. The love and affection that parents "naturally" feel toward their biological children must be nurtured, often with substantial effort, to be felt for stepchildren. We are not suggesting that the killing of stepchildren, or unrelated children in general, was once adaptive in our evolutionary past and that the higher rates of abuse and homicide observed for stepchildren than for natural children represent the activation of these atavistic mechanisms. Rather, we argue that in high-stress situations in which violence is apt to occur, the evolved tendencies that inhibit aggression against one's biological children are not as easily activated for one's stepchildren.

How Important Are Parents for Healthy Psychological Development?

From what we have presented to this point, as well as from a commonsense perspective, there should be no debate that parents play a key role in their children's development. However, although parental investment may be necessary for a child's survival, how critical is it in determining psychological characteristics such as personality and intelligence, traits that are of greater interest to academic psychologists and educators than "mere" survival? Taking what many consider to be an extreme view, Scarr (1992, 1993) proposed that "ordinary differences between families have little effect on children's development, unless the family is outside of a normal, developmental range. Good enough, ordinary parents probably have the same effects on their children's development as culturally defined super-parents" (Scarr, 1992, p. 15). In other words, "superparenting" is not required for rearing a successful adult; rather, children adapt to variations in childrearing, which, claimed Scarr, is a product of natural selection. A species such as *H. sapiens*, which lives in varied environments and under a broad array of cultural traditions, must be flexible to the vagaries of "ordinary" parenting if it is to continue.

Scarr's claim is based on the strength of what she has termed active genotype → environment effects (Scarr and McCartney, 1983), in which genetically based dispositions cause children to seek environments consistent with their genotypes. These effects increase with age as children become less dependent on their parents for providing environments in which they behave. Experiences in these environments shape children's intellects and personalities; but it is the genes that drive experience and thus that eventually are responsible for the adult phenotype.

Understandably, Scarr's approach has been severely criticized (Baumrind, 1993; Jackson, 1993). As we see in the next subsection, children in a wide range of environments will grow up to be reproductive members of their species, but their particular mating strategies (among other behaviors) are influenced by a history of parental interaction (Belsky et al., 1991). Moreover, granting the significance of active genotype → environment effects in influencing children's selection of environments, children must have the opportunities to seek their niche. If children's opportunities are restricted (for example, a child with a disposition toward high literacy reared in an environment without books and that does not reward academic achievement), they will not be able to "reach their full potential."

Scarr (1993) acknowledges that in some environments "good enough" parents may not be good enough. Children lacking opportunities and experiences of the dominant culture will be at a disadvantage relative to children in the majority culture, although these effects can often be ameliorated by education. The difference between Scarr and her critics seems primarily to be one of focus: Scarr is looking at how individual children become functioning members of their species; her critics are focusing instead on individual differences among children within a culture.

Scarr is right, we believe, in stating that human children have evolved the ability to tolerate a wide range of parental behaviors and still grow up to be functioning adults. This does not mean, however, that all adults function equally well, especially when adaptation to modern ecological environments, and not just procreation, is the litmus test. It is at this level of individual differences that patterns of parenting contribute importantly to psychological development. Moreover, children's psychological development is influenced by factors beyond their family as well (Collins, Maccoby, Steinberg, Hetherington, and Bornstein, 2000; Harris, 1995), so that predicting adult adjustment solely as a function of parenting style is difficult, if not impossible. Parents can neither take all the credit nor need they take all the blame for their children's lot in life.

Infant–Mother Attachment from an Evolutionary Perspective

Infant–mother attachment is common throughout the animal world, particularly in mammals and birds. Bowlby (1969) saw an analogy between the "instinctive" behaviors of proximity seeking in precocial birds and behaviors that kept human infants in close contact with their mothers. Both were adaptive for keeping the infant alive. But human attachment, Bowlby believed, was more complicated, in that, although all but the most deprived of infants become attached to their mothers or mother figures, there are measurable differences in the *quality* of attachment, with some forms of attachment (notably secure) being associated with better psychological outcomes than others (notably insecure). Moreover, it was behaviors of mothers that served to establish and maintain style of attachment. Research by Ainsworth and colleagues (e.g., Ainsworth, Blehar, Waters, and Wall, 1978; Ainsworth and Wittig, 1969) over the past 30 years has generally supported Bowlby's contention. For example, securely attached infants are likely to have mothers (or other caregivers) who respond to them contingently and who are responsive to their signals of physical and social need (e.g., Isabella and Belsky, 1991; Egeland and Farber, 1984); and longitudinal research has demonstrated that children and adolescents who were classified as securely attached as infants and toddlers display better social and cognitive functioning than did those who had been classified as insecurely attached (e.g., Jacobsen, Edelstein, and Hofmann, 1994; Lewis, Feiring, McGuffog, and Jaskir, 1984; Pipp, Easterbrooks, and Harmon, 1992). These relatively robust patterns led many to the conclusion, consistent with Bowlby's original proclamation, that secure attachment represents the most adaptive style, with aspects of insecure attachment being predictive of poor adjustment and psychopathology (Karen, 1990).

In addition to serving to promote the survival of infants, attachment systems evolved to adapt individuals to subsequent environments (e.g., Belsky, 1997, 2000; Chisholm, 1996; Hinde, 1980; Wiley and Carlin, 1999). From this perspective, different patterns of attachment should develop as a function of the ecological conditions of a child's local environment (including amount of parental investment). Moreover, attachment classifications should reflect adjustments to contemporary environments and should not necessarily be stable over time when ecological conditions vary (Lewis, Feiring, and Rosenthal, 2000).

The evolutionary-based theory that has generated the most research and controversy in this area is that of Belsky et al. (1991). They proposed that aspects of children's environments affect their attachment style and also important aspects of later reproductive strategies. According to Belsky et al. (1991, p. 650),

> a principal evolutionary function of early experience—the first 5 to 7 years—is to induce in the child an understanding of the availability and predictability of resources (broadly defined) in the environment, of the trustworthiness of others, and of the enduringness of close interpersonal relationships, all of which will affect how the developing person apportions reproductive effort.

Rather than viewing secure attachment as being the "best strategy" for a child to follow, they proposed that humans have evolved mechanisms that are sensitive to features of the early childhood environment that induce rate of pubertal maturation and influence reproductive strategies. Specifically, they suggested that children from homes characterized by high stress, insecure attachment, and father absence attain physical maturity early, are sexually promiscuous, and form unstable pair bonds. This is in contrast to children from low-stress, secure attachment, and father-present homes, who reach puberty later, delay sexual activity, and form more stable pair bonds. The former strategy may be adaptive for children growing up in unpredictable environments with little expectation of social support. In such cases, both females and males invest relatively more in mating than in parenting, taking a "quantity over quality" perspective. In the latter case, in which children receive social support in a low-stress, adequately resourced environment, they invest relatively more in parenting than in mating, taking a "quality over quantity" perspective. In other words, Belsky and his colleagues proposed that children follow alternative reproductive strategies, depending on the availability of resources in their rearing environment, which results in differential investment in the next generation.

Although it is beyond our scope in this chapter to review the literature that has accumulated on this issue, the hypothesis has generally been supported by the research literature (see Belsky, 2000; Bjorklund and Pellegrini, 2002). Girls from high-stress father-absent homes reach puberty earlier than do girls living with their biological fathers (e.g., Ellis, McFadyen-Ketchum, Dodge, Pettit, and Bates 1999; Garber, Brooks-Gunn, and Warren, 1995; Surbey, 1990; Wierson, Long, and Forehand, 1993). Effects are smaller or nonexistent for boys (Kim, Smith, and Palermiti, 1997), although boys from high-stress father-absent homes tend to be noncompliant and aggressive (Draper and Harpending, 1987). This sex difference of enhanced effects for girls makes sense, given the differential investment in offspring by females and males. Because females' investment in any conception is greater than males', females should be more sensitive to environmental factors that may affect the rearing of offspring (such as malnutrition, stress, lack of resources) than males are (Surbey, 1998a). Part of this effect may be related to genetics, in that early maturing girls have mothers who themselves matured quickly (Surbey, 1990). However, researchers still find effects of stress and father absence after controlling for the age at which mothers reached puberty (Ellis and Garber, 2000; Chasiotis, Scheffer, Restmeier, and Keller, 1998), indicating that it is likely that not only genetic factors are contributing to the "rate-of-maturation" effect.

One way in which genetic differences may contribute to the rate-of-maturation effect is to produce differences in children's receptivity to variations in rearing environments. Belsky (2000) has reviewed research consistent with this idea. Some children, Belsky proposes, are more sensitive to individual differences in parenting. This greater plasticity is advantageous when environments are unpredictable, permitting children to adjust as well as possible to a wide range of conditions (e.g., father absence, insecure attachment). Other children, however, do best in an environment that provides high levels of support and secure attachment. This is presumably the more "typical" environment, and it makes sense that some children (perhaps most children) will adapt to this species-typical environment. As with any set of traits, variability provides the stuff on which natural selection works, and parents can hedge their bets by producing some children who are receptive to change and others who will thrive in the "expected" environment.

One provocative study has indicated that the presence of a stepfather or mother's boyfriend was a mitigating factor in influencing girls' maturation rates. Ellis and Garber (2000) reported that there was a significant relation between pubertal maturation and age of the daughter when a stepfather or mother's boyfriend came into her life ($r = -.37$), such that the younger the girl was when the unrelated father figure arrived, the earlier she attained puberty. In contrast, the relation between pubertal timing and the age at which the biological father left was not significant ($r = -.13$). Thus, Ellis and Garber proposed, it is not father absence, per se, that is responsible for accelerated pubertal timing, but the presence of an unrelated adult male (see also Surbey, 1990). Although speculative, they suggested that this effect is mediated by pheromones from unrelated males that accelerate pubertal timing, consistent with both animal (e.g., Drickamer, 1988; see Sanders and Reinisch, 1990) and human (e.g., Cutler, Krieger, Huggins, Garcia, and Lawley, 1986) research. In nonhuman animals, the presence of unrelated adult males hastens the onset of puberty in females, affording greater reproductive opportunity between the older males and the younger females (Sanders and Reinisch, 1990). Because of the complex social relations between mates that have evolved in humans, probably in both contemporary and in ancient human groups, sexual activity between a stepdaughter and stepfather would likely be a source of stress, not something that would be adaptive to the family structure nor to (most, if any) individuals in the family.

This new line of attachment research has produced some unexpected results and reveals how evolutionary theory can be applied in a novel way to well-studied topics. Since Bowlby, attachment has been seen as being a species' way of ensuring that its young receive the support they need to survive and that behaviors surrounding infant–mother attachment were selected for this survival value over the course of evolution. But this more recent theorizing demonstrates how *individual differences* in attachment relations and the associated parenting styles can lead to different adaptive routes. Evolutionary theory is not just for describing species' universals anymore; with its emphasis on the expression of epigenetic programs in interaction with the environment over the course of development, evolutionary theory can provide new insights into how variations in parenting can yield different adaptive responses, producing different phenotypes.

CONCLUSIONS

Ever since Darwin, there has been the recognition of continuity in cognitive and social functioning among different species. *H. sapiens* share a heritage with other primates and mammals, and evolutionary theory provides the means of assessing that heritage. In many ways, when it comes to parenting, humans are just another mammal. They invest substantially in their offspring, with females investing disproportionately more than males; they consider the availability of resource and the likelihood of a "payoff" when devoting resources to their children; males' and grandparents' investments are based on a degree of genetic certainty; and the sex differential in parental investment dictates, to a substantial degree, the ways females and males relate to one another. Yet, in other ways, human parenting is different from that of other mammals, and this also is predicted from evolutionary theory. Because of the confluence of a number of factors, including a big brain and the cognitive ability that accompanies it, increased social complexity, and, most critically we believe, an extended period of youth, human children require greater investment for reaching maturity than do the young of other primates. This means that fathers must contribute more to their offspring if their offspring are to be successful than is the case for the vast majority of males from other mammalian species. This has led directly to the formation of the human family, which, although taking many specific forms, is universal in our species. Evolutionary theory provides the "big picture" for how the human family and our particular way of parenting have come about. It is a fascinating story, we believe, but it is more than just history; it also provides a perspective that helps us understand important issues of parenting in contemporary societies.

Many people unfamiliar with evolutionary theory assume that it is concerned only with species universals—traits that characterize all normal members of the species (or all members of one sex). Individual differences, the argument goes, are ignored or handled poorly by evolutionary theory. As the examples provided above of the application of parental investment theory to the phenomenon of child abuse and to quality of attachment indicate, this depiction of evolutionary theory is inaccurate. Evolutionary psychological approaches consider how evolved mechanisms become expressed over development as a function of local ecological conditions. Although evolutionary psychology certainly proposes that there are universal mechanisms characterizing members of a species, this is not equivalent to proposing hardwired "instincts," impervious to environmental variations. Just as an individual inherits a species-typical genome, that individual also inherits a species-typical environment. Both genome and environment are constrained, in that there can be only so much variation to still produce a viable organism. However, that variation can be substantial, and evolutionary theory can be useful in predicting and explaining individual differences in important social, emotional, and cognitive realms, and possibly in suggesting means to deal with persistent societal problems.

REFERENCES

Ainsworth, M. D. S., Blehar, M. C., Waters, E., and Wall, S. (1978). *Patterns of attachment: A psychological study of the Strange Situation*. Hillsdale, NJ: Lawrence Erlbaum Associates.

Ainsworth, M. D. S., and Wittig, D. S. (1969). Attachment and exploratory behavior of one-year-olds in a strange situation. In B. M. Foss (Ed.), *Determinants of infant behavior* (Vol. 4, pp. 113–136). London: Methuen.

Akazawa, T., Muhesen, S., Dodo, Y., Kondo, O., and Mizouguchi, Y. (1995). Neanderthal infant burial. *Nature (Paris), 377*, 585–586.

Alexander, R. D. (1989). Evolution of the human psyche. In P. Mellers and C. Stringer (Eds.), *The human revolution: Behavioural and biological perspectives on the origins of modern humans* (pp. 455–513). Princeton, NJ: Princeton University Press.

Anderson, K. G., Kaplan, H., Lam, D., and Lancaster, J. (1999a). Paternal care by genetic fathers and stepfathers II: Reports by Xhosa high school students. *Evolution and Human Behavior, 20*, 433–451.

Anderson, K. G., Kaplan, H., and Lancaster, J. (1999b). Paternal care by genetic fathers and stepfathers I: Reports from Albuquerque men. *Evolution and Human Behavior, 20*, 405–431.

Antinucci, F. (Ed.). (1989). *Cognitive structure and development in nonhuman primates*. Hillsdale, NJ: Lawrence Erlbaum Associates.

Asfaw, B., White, T., Lovejoy, O., Latimer, B., Simpson, S., and Suwa, G. (1999). *Australopithecus garhi*: A new species of early hominid from Ethiopia. *Science, 284*, 629–635.

Austad, S. N. (1997). *Why we age: What science is discovering about the body's journey through life*. New York: Wiley.

Baumrind, D. (1993). The average expectable environment is not good enough: A response to Scarr. *Child Development, 64*, 1299–1317.

Bellis, M. A., and Baker, R. R. (1990). Do females promote sperm competition? Data for humans. *Animal Behaviour, 40*, 997–999.

Belsky, J. (1997). Attachment, mating, and parenting: An evolutionary interpretation. *Human Nature, 8*, 361–381.

Belsky, J. (2000). Conditional and alternative reproductive strategies: Individual differences in susceptibility to rearing experience. In J. Rodgers and D. Rowe (Eds.), *Genetic influences on fertility and sexuality* (pp. 127–146). Boston, MA: Kluwer Academic.

Belsky, J., Steinberg, L., and Draper, P. (1991). Childhood experience, interpersonal development, and reproductive strategy: An evolutionary theory of socialization. *Child Development, 62*, 647–670.

Bjorklund, D. F. (1997). The role of immaturity in human development. *Psychological Bulletin, 122*, 153–169.

Bjorklund, D. F., and Harnishfeger, K. K. (1995). The role of inhibition mechanisms in the evolution of human cognition and behavior. In F. N. Dempster and C. J. Brainerd (Eds.), *New perspectives on interference and inhibition in cognition* (pp. 141–173). New York: Academic.

Bjorklund, D. F., and Pellegrini, A. D. (2000). Child development and evolutionary psychology. *Child Development, 71*, 1687–1798.

Bjorklund, D. F., and Pellegrini, A. D. (2002). *The origins of human nature: Evolutionary developmental psychology*. Washington, DC: American Psychological Association.

Bjorklund, D. F., and Pellegrini, A. D. (in press). Evolutionary perspectives on social development. In P. K. Smith and C. Hart, *Handbook of social development*. London: Blackwell.

Bjorklund, D. F., and Shackelford, T. K. (1999). Differences in parental investment contribute to important differences between women and men. *Current Directions in Psychological Science, 8*, 86–89.

Bogin, B. (1997). Evolutionary hypotheses for human childhood. *Yearbook of Physical Anthropology, 40*, 63–89.

Bogin, B. (1999). *Patterns of human growth* (2nd ed.). Cambridge, England: Cambridge University Press.

Bonner, J. T. (1988). *The evolution of complexity by means of natural selection*. Princeton, NJ: Princeton University Press.

Bowlby, J. (1969). *Attachment and loss: Vol. 1: Attachment*. London: Hogarth.

Bugental, D. B. (2000). Acquisition of the algorithms of social life: A domain-based approach. *Psychological Bulletin, 126*, 187–219.

Buss, D. M. (1995). Evolutionary psychology. *Psychological Inquiry, 6*, 1–30.

Buss, D. M., and Schmidt, D. P. (1993). Sexual strategies theory: An evolutionary perspective on human mating. *Psychological Review, 100*, 204–232.

Byrne, R., and Whiten, A. (Eds.). (1988). *Machiavellian intelligence: Social expertise and the evolution of intellect in monkeys, apes, and humans*. Oxford, England: Clarendon.

Cabrera, N. J., Tamis-LeMonda, C. S., Bradley, R. H., Hofferth, S., and Lamb, M. E. (2000). Fatherhood in the twenty-first century. *Child Development, 71*, 127–136.

Chance, M. R. A. (1962). Social behaviour and primate evolution. In M. F. A. Montagu (Ed.), *Culture and the evolution of man*. New York: Oxford University Press.

Chasiotis, A., Scheffer, D., Restmeier, R., and Keller, H. (1998). Intergenerational context discontinuity affects the onset of puberty: A comparison of parent–child dyads in West and East Germany. *Human Nature, 9*, 321–339.

Chisholm J. S. (1996). The evolutionary ecology of attachment organization. *Human Nature, 7*, 1–37.

Clutton-Brock, T. H. (1991). *The evolution of parental care*. Princeton, NJ: Princeton University Press.

Collins, W. A., Maccoby, E. E., Steinberg, L., Hetherington, E. M., and Bornstein, M. H. (2000). Contemporary research on parenting: The case for nature *and* nurture. *American Psychologist, 55*, 218–232.

Cutler, W. B., Krieger, A., Huggins, G. R., Garcia, C. R., and Lawley, H. J. (1986). Human axillary secretions influence women's menstrual cycles: The role of donor extracts from men. *Hormones and Behavior, 20*, 463–473.

Daly, M., and Wilson, M. (1981). Abuse and neglect of children in evolutionary perspective. In R. D. Alexander and D. W. Tinkle (Eds.), *Natural selection and social behavior* (pp. 405–416). New York: Chiron.

Daly, M., and Wilson, M. (1984). A sociobiological analysis of human infanticide. In G. Hausfater and S. B. Hrdy (Eds.), *Infanticide: Comparative and Evolutionary Perspectives* (pp. 487–502). New York: Aldine de Gruyter.

Daly, M., and Wilson, M. (1985). Child abuse and other risks of not living with both parents. *Ethology and Sociobiology, 6*, 197–210.

Daly, M., and Wilson, M. (1988). *Homicide*. New York: Aldine de Gruyter.

Daly, M., and Wilson, M. (1996). Violence against children. *Current Directions in Psychological Science, 5*, 77–81.

Darwin, C. (1859). *The origin of species*. New York: Modern Library.

Darwin, C. (1871). *The descent of man, and selection in relation to sex*. London: Murray.

Deacon, T. W. (1997). *The symbolic species: The co-evolution of language and the brain*. New York: Norton.

de Beer, G. (1958). *Embryos and ancestors* (3rd ed.). Oxford, England: Clarendon.

Dean, M. C., Stringer, C. B., and Bromage, T. G. (1986). Age at death of the Neanderthal child from Devil's Tower, Gibraltar and the implications for studies of general growth and development in Neanderthals. *American Journal of Anthropology, 70*, 301–309.

Draper, P., and Harpending, H. (1987). A sociobiological perspective on human reproductive strategies. In K. B. MacDonald (Ed.). *Sociobioloigcal perspectives on human development* (pp. 340–372). New York: Springer-Verlag.

Drickamer, L. C. (1988). Preweaning stimulation with urinary chemosignals and age of puberty in female mice. *Developmental Psychobiology, 21*, 77–87.

Dunbar, R. I. M. (1992). Neocortex size as a constraint on group size in primates. *Journal of Human Evolution, 20*, 469–493.

Dunbar, R. I. M. (1995). Neocortex size and group size in primates: A test of the hypothesis. *Journal of Human Evolution, 28*, 287–296.

Eccles, J. C. (1989). *Evolution of the brain: Creation of the self*. New York: Routledge.

Egeland, B., and Farber, E. A. (1984). Infant–mother attachment: Factors related to its development and changes over time. *Child Development, 55*, 753–771.

Eibl-Eibesfeldt, I. (1989). *Human ethology*. New York: Aldine de Gruyter.

Eisenberg, A. R. (1988). Grandchildren's perspectives on relationships with grandparents: The influence of gender across generations. *Sex Roles, 19*, 295–217.

Ellis, B. J., and Garber, J. (2000). Psychosocial antecedents of variation in girls' pubertal timing: Maternal depression, stepfather presence, and marital and family stress. *Child Development, 71*, 485–501.

Ellis, B. J., McFadyen-Ketchum, S., Dodge, K. A., Pettit, G. S., and Bates, J. E. (1999). Quality of early family relationships and individual differences in the timing of pubertal maturation in girls: A longitudinal test of an evolutionary model. *Journal of Personality and Social Psychology, 77*, 387–401.

Euler, H. A., and Weitzel, B. (1996). Discriminative grandparental solicitude as reproductive strategy. *Human Nature, 7*, 39–59.

Finlay, B. L., and Darlington, R. D. (1995). Linked regularities in the development and evolution of mammalian brains. *Science, 268*, 1579–1584.

Finlay, B. L., Darlington, R. B., and Nicastro, N. (2001). Developmental structure in brain evolution. *Behavioral and Brain Sciences, 24*, 263–308.

Fisher, H. E. (1992). *Anatomy of love: The natural history of monogamy, adultery, and divorce*. New York: Norton.

Flinn, M. V. (1988). Step and genetic parent/offspring relationships in a Caribbean village. *Ethology and Sociobiology, 9*, 335–369.

Flinn, M. V., Leone, D. V., and Quinlan, R. J. (1999). Growth and fluctuating asymmetry of stepchildren. *Evolution and Human Behavior, 20*, 465–479.

Gabunia, L., Vekua, A., Lordkipanidze, D., Swisher, III, C. C., Ferring, R., Justus, A., Nioradze, M., Tvalchrelidze, M., Antón, S. C., Bosinski, G., Jöris, O., de Lumley, M.-A., Majsuradze, G., and Mouskhelishvili, A. (2000). Earliest Pleistocene hominid cranial remains from Dmanisi, Republic of Georgia: Taxonomy, setting, and age. *Science, 288,* 1019–1025.

Garber, J. A., Brooks-Gunn, J., and Warren, M. P. (1995). The antecedents of menarcheal age: Heredity, family environment and stressful life events. *Child Development, 66,* 346–359.

Gaulin, S. J. (1980). Sexual dimorphism in the human post-reproductive lifespan: Possible causes. *Human Evolution, 9,* 227–232.

Gaulin, S. J. C., McBurney, D. H., and Brakeman-Wartell, S. L. (1997). Matrilateral biases in the investment of aunts and uncles: A consequence and measure of paternity certainty. *Human Nature, 8,* 139–151.

Geary, D. C. (1998). *Male, female: The evolution of human sex differences.* Washington, DC: American Psychological Association.

Geary, D. C. (2000). Evolution and proximate expression of human paternal investment. *Psychological Bulletin, 126,* 55–77.

Geary, D. C. (2001). Sexual selection and sex differences in social cognition. In A. V. McGillicuddy-DeLisi and R. DeLisi (Eds.), *Biology, society, and behavior: The development of sex differences in cognition* (pp. 23–53). Greenwich, CT: Ablex.

Geary, D. C., and Bjorklund, D. F. (2000). Evolutionary developmental psychology. *Child Development, 71,* 57–65.

Gibson, K. R. (1991). Myelination and behavioral development: A comparative perspective on questions of neoteny, altriciality and intelligence. In K. R. Gibson and A. C. Petersen (Eds.), *Brain maturation and cognitive development: Comparative and cross-cultural perspectives* (pp. 29–63). New York: Aldine de Gruyter.

Goodall, J. (1986). *The chimpanzees of Gombe.* Cambridge, MA: Belknap.

Gottlieb, G. (1991). Experiential canalization of behavioral development: Theory. *Developmental Psychology, 27,* 4–13.

Gottlieb, G. (2000). Environmental and behavioral influences on gene activity. *Current Directions in Psychological Science, 9,* 93–102.

Gottlieb, G., Wahlsten, D., and Lickliter, R. (1998). The significance of biology for human development: A developmental psychobiological systems view. In R. M. Lerner (Vol. Ed.), *Theoretical models of human development* (Vol. 1, pp. 233–273), in W. Damon (Gen. Ed.), *Handbook of child psychology.* New York: Wiley.

Gould, S. J. (1977). *Ontogeny and phylogeny.* Cambridge, MA: Harvard University Press.

Hamilton, W. D. (1964). The genetical theory of social behavior. *Journal of Theoretical Biology, 7,* 1–52.

Hamilton, W. D. (1966). The moulding of senescence by natural selection. *Journal of Theoretical Biology, 12,* 12–45.

Harris, J. R. (1995). Where is the child's environment? A group socialization theory of development. *Psychological Review, 102,* 458–489.

Hawkes, K., O'Connell, J. F., and Blurton Jones, N. G. (1997). Hadza women's time allocation, offspring provisioning, and the evolution of post-menopausal lifespans. *Current Anthropology, 38,* 551–578.

Hawkes, K., Rogers, A. R., and Charnov, E. L. (1995). The male's dilemma: Increased offspring production is more paternity to steal. *Evolutionary Ecology, 9,* 662–677.

Hetherington, E. M., Henderson, S. H., and Reiss, D. (1999). Adolescent siblings in stepfamilies: Family functioning and adolescent adjustment. *Monographs of the Society for Research in Child Development, 64* (No. 259).

Hill, K., and Hurtado, A. M. (1991). The evolution of premature reproductive senescence and menopause in human females: An evaluation of the "grandmother hypothesis." *Human Nature, 2,* 313–350.

Hill, K., and Hurtado, A. M. (1996). *Ache life history: The ecology and demography of a foraging people.* New York: Aldine de Gruyter.

Hinde, R. A. (1980). *Ethology.* London: Fontana.

Hoffman, E. (1978/1979). Young adults' relations with their grandparents: An exploratory study. *International Journal of Aging and Human Development, 10,* 299–310.

Hrdy, S. B. (1999). *Mother nature: A history of mothers, infants, and natural selection.* New York: Pantheon Books.

Humphrey, N. K. (1976). The social function of intellect. In P. P. G. Bateson and R. A. Hinde (Eds.), *Growing points in ethology* (pp. 303–317). Cambridge, England: Cambridge University Press.

Ingman, M., Kaessmann, H., Pääbo, S., and Gyllensten, U. (2000). Mitochondrial genome variation and the origin of modern humans. *Nature (London), 408,* 708–713.

Isabella, R. A., and Belsky, J. (1991). Interactional synchrony and the origins of infant–mother attachment. *Child Development, 62,* 373–384.

Jackson, J. F. (1993). Human behavioral genetics: Scarr's theory, and her views on intervention: A critical review and commentary on their implications for African American children. *Child Development, 64,* 1318–1332.

Jacobsen, T., Edelstein, W., and Hofmann, V. (1994). A longitudinal study of the relation between representations of attachment in childhood and cognitive functioning in childhood and adolescence. *Developmental Psychology, 30,* 112–124.

Jerison, H. J. (1973). *Evolution of the brain and intelligence.* New York: Academic.

Joffe, T. H. (1997). Social pressures have selected for an extended juvenile period in primates. *Journal of Human Evolution, 32,* 593–605.

Johanson, D., and Edgar, B. (1996). *From Lucy to language.* New York: Simon and Schuster.

Jolly, A. (1966). Lemur social behavior and primate intelligence. *Science, 153,* 501–506.

Jolly, A. (1999). *Lucy's legacy: Sex and intelligence in human evolution.* Cambridge, MA: Harvard University Press.

Kaplan, H., Hill, K., Lancaster, J., and Hurtado, A. M. (2000). A theory of human life history evolution: Diet, intelligence, and longevity. *Evolutionary Anthropology, 9,* 156–185.

Karen, R. (1990, February). Becoming attached. *Atlantic Monthly,* 35–70.

Keller, H. (2000). Human parent–child relationships from an evolutionary perspective. *American Behavioral Scientist, 43,* 957–969.

Kim, K., Smith, P. K., and Palermiti, A. (1997). Conflict in childhood and reproductive development. *Evolution and Human Development, 18,* 109–142.

Lamb, M. E. (Ed.). (1997). *The role of the father in child development* (3rd ed.). New York: Wiley.

Lancaster, J. B. (1989). Evolutionary and cross-cultural perspectives on single-parenthood. In R. W. Bell and N. J. Bell (Eds.), *Sociobiology and the social sciences* (pp. 63–72). Austin, Texas: Texas University Press.

Lancaster, J. B., and Lancaster, C. S. (1987). The watershed: Change in parental-investment and family-formation strategies in the course of human evolution. In J. B. Lancaster, J. Altmann, A. S. Rossi, and L. R. Sherrod (Eds.), *Parenting across the life span: Biosocial dimensions* (pp. 187–205). New York: Aldine de Gruyter.

Langer, J. (1998). Phylogenetic and ontogenetic origins of cognition: Classification. In J. Langer and M. Killen (Eds.), *Piaget, evolution, and development* (pp. 33–54). Mahwah, NJ: Lawrence Erlbaum Associates.

Lee, B. J., and George, R. M. (1999). Poverty, early childbearing and child maltreatment: A multinomial analysis. *Children and Youth Services Review, 21,* 755–780.

Lerner, R. M., and von Eye, A. (1992). Sociobiology and human development: Arguments and evidence. *Human Development, 35,* 12–33.

Lewis, M., Feiring, C., McGuffog, C., and Jaskir, J. (1984). Predicting psychopathology in six-year-olds from early social relations. *Child Development, 55,* 123–136.

Lewis, M., Feiring, C., and Rosenthal, S. (2000). Attachment over time. *Child Development, 71,* 707–720.

Mann, J. (1992). Nurture or negligence: Maternal psychology and behavioral preference among preterm twins. In J. Barkow, L. Cosmides, and J. Tooby (Eds.), *The adapted mind: Evolutionary psychology and the generation of culture* (pp. 367–390). New York: Oxford University Press.

Marlowe, F. (1999). Showoffs or providers? The parenting effort of Hazda men. *Evolution and Human Behavior, 20,* 391–404.

McKinney, M. L. (1998). Cognitive evolution by extending brain development: On recapitulation, progress, and other heresies. In J. Langer and M. Killen (Eds.), *Piaget, evolution, and development* (pp. 9–31). Mahwah, NJ: Lawrence Erlbaum Associates.

Mithen, S. (1996). *The prehistory of the mind: The cognitive origins of art, religion and science.* London: Thames and Hudson.

O'Connell, J. F., Hawkes, K., and Blurton Jones, N. G. (1999). Grandmothering and the evolution of *Homo erectus. Journal of Human Evolution, 36,* 461–485.

Oliver, M. B., and Hyde, J. S. (1993). Gender differences in sexuality: A meta-analysis. *Psychological Bulletin, 114,* 29–36.

Overpeck, M. D., Brenner, R. A., Trumble, A. C., Trifiletti, L. B., and Berendes, H. W. (1998). Risk factors for infant homicide in the United States. *New England Journal of Medicine, 339,* 1211–1216.

Owens, K., and King, M.-C. (1999). Genomic views of human history. *Science, 286,* 451–453.

Oyama, S. (2000). *The ontogeny of information: Developmental systems and evolution* (2nd ed.). Durham, NC: Duke University Press.

Packer, C., Tatar, M., and Collins, A. (1998). Reproductive cessation in female mammals. *Nature (London), 392,* 807–811.

Parker, S. T., and McKinney, M. L. (1999). *Origins of intelligence: The evolution of cognitive development in monkeys, apes, and humans.* Baltimore: Johns Hopkins University Press.

Pashos, A. (2000). Does paternal uncertainty explain discriminative grandparental solicitude? A cross-cultural study in Greece and Germany. *Evolution and Human Behavior, 21,* 97–109.

Pellegrini, A. D., and Bjorklund, D. F. (1997). The role of recess in children's cognitive performance. *Educational Psychologist, 32,* 35–40.

Pipp, S., Easterbrooks, M. A., and Harmon, R. J. (1992). The relation between attachment and knowledge of self and mother in one- to three-year-old infants. *Child Development, 63,* 738–750.

Potts, R. (1998). Variability selection in hominid evolution. *Evolutionary Anthropology, 7,* 81–96.

Potts, R. (2000, June). *The adaptive crunch: Habitat instability as the context of early human behavioral evolution.* Paper presented at meeting of Human Evolution and Behavior Society, Amherst, MA.

Rossi, A. S., and Rossi, P. H. (1990). *Of human bonding: Parent–child relations across the life course.* Hawthorne, NY: Aldine de Gruyter.

Rowher, S., Herron, J. C., and Daly, M. (1999). Stepparental behavior as mating effort in birds and other animals. *Evolution and Human Behavior, 20,* 367–390.

Salmon, C. A. (1999). On the impact of sex and birth order on contact with kin. *Human Nature, 10,* 183–197.

Sameroff, A. J., and Suomi, S. J. (1996). Primates and persons: A comparative developmental understanding of social organization. In R. B. Cairns, G. H. Elder, Jr., and E. J. Costello (Eds.), *Developmental Science* (pp. 97–120). New York: Cambridge University Press.

Sanders, S. A., and Reinisch, J. M. (1990). Biological and social influences on the endocrinology of puberty: Some additional considerations. In J. Bancroft and J. M. Reinisch (Eds.), *Adolescence and puberty* (pp. 50–62). New York: Oxford University Press.

Scarr, S. (1992). Developmental theories for the 1990s: Development and individual differences. *Child Development, 63,* 1–19.

Scarr, S. (1993). Biological and cultural diversity: The legacy of Darwin for development. *Child Development, 64,* 1333–1353.

Scarr, S., and McCartney, K. (1983). How people make their own environments: A theory of genotype → environment effects. *Child Development, 54,* 424–435.

Seielstad, M. T., Minch, E., and Cavalli-Sforza, L. L. (1998). Genetic evidence for a higher female migration rate in humans. *Nature Genetics, 20,* 278–280.

Shea, B. T. (1989). Heterochrony in human evolution: The case for neoteny revisited. *Yearbook of Physical Anthropology, 32,* 69–101.

Sibley, C. G., and Ahlquist, J. E. (1984). The phylogeny of hominid primates, as indicated by DNA–DNA hybridization. *Journal of Molecular Evolution, 20,* 2–15.

Smuts, B. B. (1995). The evolutionary origins of patriarchy. *Human Nature, 6,* 1–32.

Surbey, M. K. (1990). Family composition, stress, and the timing of human menarche. In T. E. Ziegler and F. B. Bercovitvch (Eds.), *Socioendocrinology of primate reproduction* (pp. 11–32). New York: Wiley-Liss.

Surbey, M. K. (1998a). Parent and offspring strategies in the transition at adolescence. *Human Nature, 9,* 67–94.

Surbey, M. K. (1998b). Developmental psychology and modern Darwinism. In C. B. Crawford and D. Krebs (Eds.), *Handbook of evolutionary psychology: Ideas, issues, and applications* (pp. 369–404). Mahwah, NJ: Lawrence Erlbaum Associates.

Tanner, J. M. (1978). *Fetus into man: Physical growth from conception to maturity.* Cambridge, MA: Harvard University Press.

Tattersall, I. (1998). *Becoming human: Evolution and human intelligence.* San Diego, CA: Harcourt Brace Jovanovitch.

Tobias, P. V. (1987). The brain of *Homo habilis*: A new level of organization in cerebral evolution. *Journal of Human Evolution, 16,* 741–761.

Tooby, J., and Cosmides, L. (1992). The psychological foundations of culture. In J. H. Barkow, L. Cosmides, and J. Tooby (Eds.), *The adapted mind: Evolutionary psychology and the generation of culture* (pp. 19–139). New York: Oxford University Press.

Trivers, R. (1972). Parental investment and sexual selection. In B. Campbell (Ed.), *Sexual selection and the descent of man* (pp. 136–179). New York: Aldine de Gruyter.

Trivers, R. L. (1985). *Social evolution.* Menlo Park, CA: Benjamin/Cummings.

van Schaik, C. P., and Paul, A. (1996). Male care in primates: Does it ever reflect paternity? *Evolutionary Anthropology, 5,* 152–156.

Wachs, T. D. (2000). *Necessary but not sufficient: The respective roles of single and multiple influences on individual development.* Washington, DC: American Psychological Association.

Whiting, B. B., and Whiting, J. W. (1975). *Children of six cultures: A psycho-cultural analysis.* Cambridge, MA: Harvard University Press.

Wierson, M., Long, P. J., and Forehand, R. L. (1993). Toward a new understanding of early menarche: The role of environmental stress in pubertal timing. *Adolescence, 23,* 913–924.

Wiley, A. S., and Carlin, L. C. (1999). Demographic contexts and the adaptive role of mother–infant attachment: A hypothesis. *Human Nature, 10,* 135–161.

Wilson, D. S. (1997). Incorporating group selection into the adaptationist program: A case study involving human decision making. In J. A. Simpson and D. T. Kenrick (Eds.), *Evolutionary social psychology* (pp. 345–386). Mahwah, NJ: Lawrence Erlbaum Associates.

Wood, B. A. (1994). The oldest hominid yet. *Nature (London), 317,* 280–281.

Zollikofer, C. P. E., Ponce de León, M. S., Martin, R. D., and Stucki, P. (1995). Neanderthal computer skulls. *Nature (London), 375,* 283–285.

Zvoch, K. (1999). Family type and investment in education: A comparison of genetic and stepparent families. *Evolution and Human Behavior, 20,* 453–464.

2

Hormonal Bases of Parenting in Mammals

Jay S. Rosenblatt

Rutgers University–Newark Campus

INTRODUCTION

Parental behavior is inherently interesting to all of us, but for specialists in behavioral biology it is perhaps the most compelling and important behavior we can study. In evolution, an individual female's own survival is the measure of her individual fitness or successful adaptation to her environment; it is only the first step that enables her to take the next important step, that is, to become a parent. Producing children and rearing them until they themselves reproduce is the ultimate measure of successful adaptation among all organisms. It is the measure of their inclusive fitness because in this way parents pass on their genes to generations of descendents. In the performance of parental behavior therefore females (and males in many species) mobilize their physiological and behavioral capacities most fully to ensure the survival and the growth of their offspring.

Parental behavior consists of behavior that is either directed at the offspring (nursing, carrying, cleaning, warming, grouping the offspring) or at establishing a nesting and feeding site (nest building), and it includes aggressive behavior directed at threatening species mates or predators that might harm the offspring (parental aggression). Often the parents and the offspring (family) are not part of a larger social group, but more often the family is a member of a social group consisting of many families (herds, colonies, troops, communities). Families are better protected from predators by living in larger social groups. Also, they can forage for food more effectively, and the children can find agemate companions to develop their social skills and later for reproduction.

Types of Parental Behavior

There are three types of parental behavior that have evolved among the mammals. They are based on the maturity or immaturity of the offspring at birth and the extent and nature of the care that the mother and the father must provide them.

Nesting.   Among species that bear helpless, immature infants (i.e., altricial newborns), which includes most rodents and carnivores, the mother builds a nest before or during parturition and deposits her offspring there. The offspring remain huddled together in the nest for warmth when she leaves them to forage for food in the vicinity of the nest. She returns periodically to nurse them and to warm and clean them (anogenital licking), and she carries them back to the nest (retrieving) if they have strayed from it. The mother also protects her offspring by exhibiting parental aggression: She attacks and bites species mates as well as interspecific predators that threaten her offspring.

Mothers may hide their infants, to avoid predators, by camouflaging their nests or by constructing nests underground. Nursing the infants may be frequent, at least once per hour, as among rats, hamsters, cats and dogs, or infrequent, only once per day, as among rabbits and hares. Some mothers may not nurse their infants for several days (tree shrew) or for a week (seals). Offspring develop at different rates in different species and weaning, therefore, occurs at very different ages. Small mammals such as rats, mice, and hamsters are weaned at between 3 and 4 weeks of age, but it may be several years before lions are fully weaned. Most unusual is the hooded seal, which is weaned after only 4 days of nursing and parental care (Perry and Stenson, 1992)!

In more primitive mammals, monotreme (e.g., platypus and spiny anteater) mothers lay eggs, even though they are mammals, which they deposit in nests they have previously built underground in tunnels they have excavated. They incubate the eggs, and when the eggs hatch the mother begins to take care of her infants as in nesting species of mammals.

Leading–following.   Many ungulate species (sheep, goats, cows, horses) bear infants that are relatively mature at birth (precocial newborn). They are able to stand and walk, to respond to visual and auditory stimulation, to vocalize, and to engage in suckling by standing up and walking to the mother within minutes of being born. In sheep and goats parental behavior consists of nudging the young with the nose, licking them, emitting low bleats, and accepting them at the udder. When the infants are removed the mother issues distress vocalizations. These are herd animals in most instances; therefore the mother and her offspring must be able to rejoin the herd within a few days after she gives birth. Parental behavior is adapted to this mode of life. The mother leads the offspring that follow her as she moves with the foraging herd or, in solitary species, as she forages individually.

There may be a brief postpartum period during which the newborns remain in the clearing away from the herd, where they were born. There they are hidden from predators while they are still too weak to escape them even with the help of the mother.

An important and special characteristic of parental behavior in these subprimate species is that the mother recognizes her own offspring by an odor, which it partially receives from the mother, and she will allow only her own infants to suckle, rejecting the attempts of alien offspring.

Clinging–carrying pattern.   All primates bear infants that can see and hear at birth but that are limited in their motor abilities and are unable to feed independently (semialtricial). They cling to the mother or are carried by her at birth and for some time afterward (Bard, in Vol. 2 of this *Handbook*). Nursing is a prominent part of this pattern of parental care, which also includes grooming the infant, remaining in close contact with it, and protecting it from threatening conspecifics and predators. Mothers become attached to their own infants and infants to their mothers, individually.

There is another form of carrying newborns that is quite different from that seen among the primates. Marsupial mothers also carry their infants, but they carry their infants in their pouches or their infants cling to the mothers' nipples and are "carried" in this way as the mothers travel. Marsupial newborns are the least developed among the mammals at birth; in most species they are little more than tiny undeveloped fetuses with large mouths for clinging to the nipple and well-developed forelimbs for crawling into the mother's pouch. They attach to nipples in the pouch and remain there for many months, or they attach to the mother's teats and hang from them as she moves about.

Aims and Methods of Research on the Hormonal Bases of Parental Behavior

Because it has long been acknowledged that the onset of parental behavior in female mammals is stimulated by hormones, the aims of research have been to identify which hormones are involved and the sources of these hormones, how their secretion is regulated, and, most important, to determine how they effectively stimulate parental behavior. Hormones elicit parental behavior from females by stimulating neural sites in the central nervous sytem. This enables them to respond to stimulation from their offspring (odors, vocalizations, visual characteristics and newborn behavior, and contact and thermal stimuli) and to perform specific patterns of behavior that parents use in the care of their offspring. Parental aggression is also stimulated by hormones that stimulate the onset of parental behavior.

Pregnancy and Parturition

Parental behavior in mammals arises out of the endocrine processes of pregnancy and parturition. There are three reproductive events of crucial importance for the mother and her offspring that are closely synchronized with one another. They are, first, parturition, which terminates pregnancy, second, the initiation of lactation, and third, the onset of parental behavior. As a consequence of these events, the newborns that are delivered at parturition are provided with milk and the mother is prepared to take care of them. Moreover, during the course of the mother's interaction with her infants at parturition, she develops a behavioral relationship with them, and over the next few weeks this relationship plays an important role in maintaining her parental behavior. Fathers normally are not present during parturition in subhuman animals and, of course, they lack the hormones of pregnancy. However, in several species, fathers or at least male consorts may be present shortly after parturition, and they may assist the female in care of the infants. For example, in the California mouse males perform parental care, except for lactation and nursing, from birth onward, and in the common marmoset, a subhuman primate, the male carries the twin infants from the end of the first week on (Dixson and George, 1982; Gubernick and Nelson, 1989). Males therefore receive stimulation from the infants as do females, and this results in parental care by males of several species of rodents, carnivores, and primates.

In this chapter, the focus is on the hormonal bases of parental behavior among the mammals. This has been studied for only a small number of species. They are principally nesting species of rodents (rats, mice, hamsters), lagomorphs (rabbits), and also ungulates (sheep and goats) that exhibit the leading–following type of parental behavior. Few clinging–carrying primates have been studied in this respect, but the number is increasing, and the evidence that is available is reviewed. The first section reviews which hormones stimulate the onset of the diverse patterns of parental behavior in different mammals and how hormones act in the brain to produce their effects on parental behavior. In the second section, the nature of these effects on behavior is discussed.

HORMONAL BASES OF PARENTAL BEHAVIOR AMONG THE MAMMALS

Evolutionary Background of Mammalian Parental Behavior

Among the vertebrates, of which the mammals are one important class, parental behavior directed at offspring appeared late in evolution (Bjorklund, Yunger, and Pelligrini, in Vol. 2 of this *Handbook*). Early in vertebrate evolution, large numbers of eggs that had been fertilized externally were scattered broadly; then later in evolution they were deposited more carefully in selected or prepared nest sites without the eggs or hatchlings being guarded. These modes of reproduction are common among fish and are the principal reproductive modes in amphibians. Among the reptiles, internally fertilized eggs may be buried on various beaches and left to hatch by themselves without parental guarding (Rosenblatt, 1992).

These wasteful parental modes of reproduction, which sacrificed most of the eggs to predation, were superseded in evolution by new modes of reproduction that reduced predation and reduced the energetic cost of egg production. Fewer eggs were laid, but they were guarded by the parent(s) or carried on the body surface in specially evolved structures or in the mouth or various internal structures temporarily modifed for the purpose. External fertilization of the eggs during mating allowed either parent to guard or carry the eggs when the other left. Parental care of the developing eggs or the offspring therefore was performed as readily by males as by females. Except for a few species of fish and frogs, however, guarding or carrying the eggs during embryonic development was no guarantee that the hatchlings would receive parental care. In most species parental interest in offspring waned as soon as the eggs hatched.

Not until internal fertilization arose, in which the male inseminates the female internally and then leaves and the female carries the fertilized egg or developing embryo, did gender-differentiated patterns of parental behavior arise in evolution. The significance of this evolutionary innovation cannot be overestimated. As a consequnce of internal fertilization, only the female is present to take care of the offspring when they are released at various stages of embryonic development. Internal fertilization arose in only a few fish; it is rare among amphibians, but is universal among reptiles. Gender-differentiated patterns of parental behavior performed by females were firmly established in birds and mammals as a consequence of this evolutionary innovation.

Parental care has been elaborated most extensively in two classes of vertebrates, the birds and mammals, although it is also present in several species of reptiles. Birds and mammals differ reproductively mainly in the fact that birds incubate their eggs externally whereas mammals incubate their eggs internally. Also, most birds feed their young by foraging and carrying food back to the nest; mammals feed their young by lactating and nursing them.

There are two phases of parental care in birds: In the first phase, birds construct a nest in which they lay their eggs and incubate them (guarding them also). When the eggs hatch, females exhibit parental behavior toward their offspring during the second phase. Egg incubation and parental behavior are stimulated by ovarian and pituitary hormones, and in selected species these hormones are also involved in enabling parents to feed their infants with milk produced by their crop glands. However, parental feeding of offspring in this manner is rare among birds. Feeding offspring by delivering food to them for which the parent(s) has foraged and may have partially digested is more common.

Among the mammals, internal incubation of fertilized ova was made possible by the evolution of neuroendocrine mechanisms for extending the sexual cycle following successful mating, from its normal length to a multiple of the sexual cycle (e.g., in rats, five times the length of the estrous cycle, and in humans, nine times the length of the menstrual cycle). Gestation or pregnancy in mammals is considered a behaviorally quiescent period because there are no marked changes in the female's behavior that are indicative of her forthcoming parental behavior (exceptions to this are given in the next subsection). In mammals therefore the onset of parental behavior at parturition is not preceded by a prolonged period of behavioral interaction with the eggs, as among birds, and there is no provision for a smooth transition from care of eggs to care of hatchlings. Parental behavior in mammals has an abrupt onset; in the rat, it arises ~$3\frac{1}{2}$ hr before parturition, as shown when prepartum females are tested with foster newborns before they deliver their own (Mayer and Rosenblatt, 1984). In subhuman primates, the female may show no sign of parental behavior until the fetus has already begun to emerge from the vaginal opening (Rosenblatt, 1990).

Just as the establishment of pregnancy required the evolution of special neuroendocrine mechanisms to extend the sexual cycle, the termination of pregnancy also required the evolution of special mechanisms, but these mechanisms have added complexities. The termination of pregnancy must be coordinated with the status of the developing fetus, and this is done through a hormonal signal that is transmitted from the fetus to the mother (Nathanielsz, 1998; Smith, 1999). Mainly, however, parturition must synchronized with the onset of parental behavior and with the beginning of lactation. Synchrony among these three events is crucial for the survival of the newborn among all mammals. Synchrony is based on the fact that the hormonal changes that terminate pregnancy also initiate parturition, and, in the course of these changes, through endocrine, neuroendocrine, and sensory stimulation (e.g., fetuses passing through the birth canal; Komisaruk et al., 2000), parental behavior is initiated and lactation is started (this is described in the next subsection).

In several species fathers or at least male consorts may be present shortly after parturition, and they may assist the female in care of the young (next subsection).

Hormonal Secretions During Pregnancy

Hormones from endocrine glands are released directly into the circulatory system and act widely throughout the body to coordinate and regulate basic cellular physiological processes. Hormones are also synthesized in the brain and released there, where they may act to stimulate behavior. Hormones from the endocrine glands can enter the brain by crossing the blood–brain barrier and are taken up at various brain sites by cells that contain specific hormone receptors. Once a hormone has been taken up by a cell, its effects are determined by the nature of the cell.

The principal hormones that have been studied in connection with the onset of maternal behavior are the steroid hormones estradiol-17β (E2) and progesterone (P), which are secreted by the ovaries and placentas of pregnant females, the anterior pituitary gland hormones, prolactin (PROL) and the growth hormone (GH), and oxytocin (OT), a hormone that is synthesized in the brain and transported to various sites in the brain. It is also released from storage in the posterior pituitary gland in response to sensory stimulation during parturition and nursing. Additional hormones secreted by the fetal placenta, the placental lactogens, and chorionic gonadotropin may also be involved in parental behavior. Regulation of the secretion of hormones differs greatly in the different species. As one example of how hormonal secretions are regulated during pregnancy, we examine the rat.

Regulation of pregnancy in the rat. Following mating, pregnancy is established in the rat by E2 and P acting on the uterus to prepare the endometrium over the next 6 days for implantation of the fertilized ova (attachment of ova that have formed multicellular blastocysts to the wall of the uterus). The pituitary gland regulates this process, initially through the mating-induced release of the luteinizing hormone (LH) that establishes the corpora lutea (CL) of pregnancy and later through the secretion of PROL. Early in pregnancy, E2 synthesized in the ovary stimulates P synthesis and maintains growth and survival of the CL. PROL at this time increases the effectiveness of E2 actions in the CL (Gibori, Richards, and Keyes, 1979). Androgen, initially from the ovary and later from the placenta, also plays a role in maintaining CL progesterone secretion by its conversion to E2 in the ovary. The fetal placenta forms soon after implantation and begins to secrete placental lactogen at approximately the end of the first week. This marks the beginning of the transition from pituitary gland to placental regulation of the ovarian secretion of E2 and P and maintenance of pregnancy (Gibori et al., 1988; Terkel, 1988). The pituitary gland can be removed at this time (i.e., hypophysectomy), and pregnancy will continue to term. At the end of pregnancy, the pituitary gland once again controls ovarian secretion of E2 and P and regulates the timing of parturition.

Most notable among the hormones in the rat during pregnancy that are concerned with parental behavior is P, which increases in circulation early in pregnancy, remains high through the middle period, and declines during late pregnancy. E2 levels are initially high but then decline and remain low until late pregnancy, when they rise sharply. PROL levels are low throughout pregnancy but also rise sharply at the end just before parturition. The rise in PROL is due to E2, which stimulates the synthesis of this hormone by the pituitary gland and also causes its release.

At the end of pregnancy the female is prepared for delivery by a reversal in the ratio of E2 and P in circulation, the release of OT, which stimulates vigorous uterine contractions, and by relaxin, which

Removal of the ovaries or pituitary in pregnancy and its effect on the maintenance of gestation in various species

	Approximate stage of pregnancy when operation performed			
Animal and length of gestation (days)	Ovariectomy First half	Ovariectomy Second half	Hypophysectomy First half	Hypophysectomy Second half
Woman (267)	+	+	+	+
Rhesus monkey (165)	+	+	+	+
Tammar wallaby (29)*	+	+	+	+
Quokka (27)*	+	+		
Guinea pig (68)	±	+	+	+
Sheep (148)	−	+	−	+
Horse (350)	−	+		
Brush-tailed possum (17)	−	+		
Rat (22)	−	±	−	+
Cat (63)	−	±		±
Ferret (42)	−	±	−	±
Cow (282)	−	±		
Dog (61)	−		−	±
Rabbit (28)	−	−	−	−
Mouse (19)	−	−	±	+
Hamster (16)	−	−	−	+
Goat (150)	−	−	−	−
Pig (113)	−	−	−	−
Virginia opossum (13)	−	−		
Armadillo (150)	Implantation may occur	−		

+, Fetuses survive; ±, some fetuses survive; −, fetuses aborted or resorbed.
* From ovulation to birth, excluding the period of diapause.

FIGURE 2.1. Hormonal secretions from the ovaries, pituitary gland, and placentas that are required in different species for maintaining pregnancy. Ovariectomy removes the ovarian source of estrogen and P, and hypophysectomy removes the pituitary source of PROL. Species that maintain pregnancy after ovariectomy depend on placental secretion of these hormones; those that maintain their pregnancies after hypophysectomy depend on placental lactogen and chorionic gonadotopin. (Reproduced with the permission of Cambridge University Press from Heap and Flint, 1986.)

prepares the uterus to respond to E2 and also relaxes the pubic symphysis to enable it to expand to enable the fetus to be delivered (Landgraf, Neumann, Russell, and Pittman, 1990).

Regulation of pregnancy in other mammals. Mammals differ in the regulation of pregnancy by secretions from the pituitary gland, the ovaries, and the placenta (Heap and Flint, 1986). In Figure 2.1, for example, in the rabbit, ovaries and pituitary glands are needed throughout pregnancy, whereas in humans, from 1 month onward, only the placenta is needed to maintain pregnancy. In all species, E2 and P are required, but in different species these hormones may be secreted by the ovaries under the control of the pituitary gland or the placenta or they may be secreted directly by the placenta. The trend in evolution has been for the fetus, through its placenta, increasingly to regulate the pregnancy by means of the regulation of the mother's reproductive physiology (Davis and Ryan, 1972).

A similar trend in evolution is the increasing control by the fetus of termination of the mother's pregnancy. In the rat, the fetus signals its developmental status in the womb by secreting the adrenocortical hormone, cortisol, which enters the mother's circulation and initiates the gradual process of decline in P secretion by the corpus luteum of the ovary. In sheep, the fetal signal for the release of cortisol arises in its paraventricular nucleus (PVN), which secretes the corticotropin-releasing hormone. Lesions of this nucleus during late pregnancy prevent the initiation of parturition in this species (Gluckman, Mallard, and Boshier, 1991; McDonald and Nathanielsz, 1991; Nathanielisz, 1998; Smith, 1999). Among primates, P secretion during pregnancy is maintained by the fetal placenta rather than by the maternal adrenal gland. Maternal OT and fetal prostaglandins combine to condition the uterus to initiate contractions that expel the fetus.

Mammary gland development in the rat.   Mammary gland development in the rat and other species is under the control of E2 and P, adrenal corticoids, somatotropin, PROL, placental lactogen, insulin, and thyroid hormones; milk synthesis or lactogenesis is stimulated by PROL and adrenal glucocorticoids.

Behavior during pregnancy also plays a role in preparing the pregnant rat for lactation. As pregnancy advances, the female increasingly licks her nipple region and genital area (Roth and Rosenblatt, 1967). In females that are prevented from licking their nipples and the genital area, mammary glands are only half the size of normal glands, containing little milk (Roth and Rosenblatt, 1968). Self-licking of the nipples and the genital region by pregnant females plays an important role in mammary gland growth and differentiation and in lactation. The underlying mechanism for the effectiveness of licking is not known, but it is very likely a neuroendocrine response to tactile stimulation.

HORMONAL STIMULATION OF PARENTAL BEHAVIOR

Rat

Steroid hormones.   Injecting a schedule of steroid hormones and PROL derived from the spectrum of hormones that maintains pregnancy and promotes mammary gland development and lactation produced the first effective hormone treatment for stimulating parental behavior in female rats (Moltz, Lubin, Leon, and Numan, 1970; Zarrow, Gandelman, and Denenberg, 1971). The ovaries were removed to eliminate endogenous ovarian steroids; females were injected under the skin with the steroids for either 11 or 20 days (Figure 2.2); then they were given PROL and tested with pups until they initiated parental behavior. Latencies for parental behavior were quite short, 35 to 40 hr of pup exposure in one experiment (Moltz et al., 1970) and almost immediately in the other (Zarrow et al., 1971).

As shown in Figure 2.2, each hormone treatment consisted of a period in which the same doses of E2 and P were given daily for either 11 days or 20 days. This is similar to what happens during most of pregnancy when E2 and P are secreted at the same levels daily. In the experiments, the P treatment was terminated at the end of either 11 days or 20 days and E2 treatment was continued. Again this resembles what happens at the end of pregnancy when P secretion declines and E2 secretion increases. The ratio of E2 to P in circulation favors P during most of pregnancy but this is reversed at the end of pregnancy when it favors E2. This reversal, on the background of the previous E2 plus P stimulation, proved to be the trigger for parental behavior; in the uterus it triggers parturition and in the mammary gland lactogenesis because the removal of P from circulation allows PROL, stimulated by E2, to initiate milk production.

We obtained similar results of a rapid initiation of parental behavior when pregnant females were hysterectomized (i.e., the surgical removal of the uteruses, fetuses, and placentas) during late pregnancy (16th day), which terminated their pregnancies (Rosenblatt and Siegel, 1975; Siegel and Rosenblatt, 1975a). Following hysterectomy there was a decline in P secretion and an increase in E2 secretion. By 48 hr later most females exhibited parental behavior shortly after they were given pups.

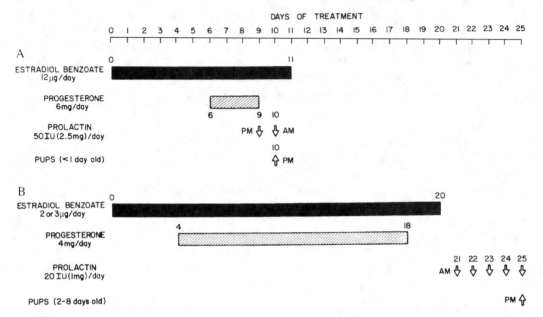

FIGURE 2.2. Hormone treatments that stimulate parental behavior in nonpregnant, ovariectomized female rats. Both treatments consisted of estradiol benzoate, P, and PROL. Note the termination of the P treatment shortly before the termination of the estradiol benzoate treatment and the treatment with PROL after the end of the P treatment. A, from Moltz, Lubin, Leon, and Numan (1970); B, from Zarrow, Gandelman, and Denenberg (1971).

When the females were ovariectomized in addition to being hysterectomized, the decline in P occurred but the rise in E2 was prevented. This resulted in longer latencies for parental behavior, indicating that it was the previous rise in E2 that stimulated parental behavior; short latencies for parental behavior were restored in the ovariectomized females by giving them an injection of E2 at the time of surgery (Siegel and Rosenblatt, 1975a). Nonpregnant ovariectomized–hysterectomized females could also be stimulated to show parental behavior by an injection of estrogen (Siegel and Rosenblatt, 1975b).

Another method for stimulating parental behavior in female rats does not depend on hormones and can be done with nonpregnant females. When females are exposed continuously to pups, which are exchanged daily for freshly nursed pups, they begin to show parental behavior after 4 to 7 days (Fleming and Rosenblatt, 1974a; Rosenblatt, 1967). Their behavior closely resembles the parental behavior of lactating females (these females do not lactate) and they even "wean" pups at the normal age (Reisbick, Rosenblatt, and Mayer, 1975). This procedure is called sensitization, and the females that exhibit parental behavior are referred to as sensitized. Sensitization does not require stimulation by hormones: Females can be ovariectomized or hypophysectomized and still can be sensitized. Males also, whether intact or castrated, can be sensitized. The latency of sensitized females (number of days of exposure to pups to show parental behavior) is the baseline against which the effectiveness of all other treatments is measured. To be shown to be effective in stimulating parental behavior, these treatments must produce shorter latencies than the sensitization latencies of untreated females.

Although estrogen is directly responsible for the hormonal stimulation of parental behavior, P plays a most important role, which justifies its name as the hormone that promotes gestation. In fact, it plays two roles: first by maintaining pregnancy and suppressing the display of growing parental responsiveness during pregnancy (Bridges, Feder, and Rosenblatt, 1977; Bridges, Rosenblatt, and

Feder, 1978; Numan, 1978); and second, through its decline at the end of pregnancy, it facilitates the action of estrogen and other hormones involved in the onset of parental behavior.

In studies of pregnant females therefore it was found that they would not display parental behavior while they remained pregnant even when they were given foster pups for testing Only by terminating their pregnancies and ovariectomizing them (to remove any further action of E2 and P) during the second half of pregnancy (11th to 19th day) could it be shown that female latencies have become shorter, and by day 19 nearly all females were immediately responsive to pups when tested on day 21 (Rosenblatt, Olufowobi, and Siegel, 1998).

Because P normally declines on day 20, ~30 hr before parturition and E2 rises 1 day before parturition, females are ready to respond to pups before they actually give birth (Rosenblatt and Siegel, 1975; Slotnick, Carpenter, and Fusco, 1973). The timing of the onset of maternal behavior is fine tuned by feedback from uterine contractions 3 to 4 hr before parturition and by uterine–cervical–vaginal stimulation by the fetuses passing through the birth canal (Komisaruk et al., 2000; Mayer and Rosenblatt, 1984; Yeo and Keverne, 1986).

Underlying the effects of these hormones on parental behavior is their action on the brain at sites that mediate maternal behavior. E2 acts on the medial preoptic area (MPOA) of the forebrain (and other brain sites related to maternal behavior) (Cohn and Gerall, 1989; Fahrbach and Pfaff, 1986; Numan, 1974, 1978; Numan, Rosenblatt, and Komisaruk, 1977). Cells within this brain area contain protein receptors that bind the hormone and transport it to the nucleus where many cofactors are involved in its action on estrogen-responsive sites of the genome. Neurons stimulated by E2 transmit the effects of this stimulation by producing neuroactive substances (neurotransmitters, neuropeptides) that are released at synapses stimulating parental behavior.

Although pregnancy is "behaviorally silent," nevertheless, there is an increase in parental responsiveness. This is correlated with evidence that neurons in the MPOA are responding to E2 by increasing the binding of E2 to nuclear estrogen receptors in these cells. A sharp increase in binding of E2 to these receptors over a period of 48 hr plays an important role in stimulating parental behavior in hormonally primed females (Giordano, Ahdieh, Mayer, Siegel, and Rosenblatt, 1990; Giordano, Siegel, and Rosenblatt, 1989). How increased binding of E2 in cells of the MPOA results in parental behavior is not yet known.

Less is known about the inhibition by progesterone of E2 stimulation of parental behavior. It has been shown that the inhibition is mediated by a P receptor mechanism. When RU 486, an intracellular P receptor agonist, was used, P inhibition of E2 was blocked (Numan et al., 1999). The inhibition probably occurs in the Medial Preoptic Nucleus (MPN) which has a high concentration of mRNA for the progesterone receptor (Shughrue, Lane, and Merchenthaler, 1997). Another possible inhibitory mechanism is the high affinity P binding sites found in the membranes of cells of the MPOA and the anterior hypothalmus (Caldwell et al., 1995).

Additional sites of inhibition of parental behavior, in this instance by E2 and P, are the ventromedial and dorsal/anterior hypothalamic areas, which have efferent neural connections with the MPOA (Bridges, Mann, and Coppeta, 1999). Lesions of these areas release the inhibition and accelerate the onset of maternal behavior of females treated with E2 and P. Through the use of c-fos immunochemistry to detect brain regions that are active during the inhibition of parental behavior in nonpregant females, a number of regions have been found, which include the MPOA, the bed nucleus of the stria terminalis (BNST), the anterior commissure nucleus (ACN), several amygdala nuclei, and the PVN, among others (Sheehan, Cirrito, Numan, and Numan, 2000). Hormonally primed females that were undergoing inhibition of parental behavior showed increased c-fos activity in the above brain regions, reported by Bridges et al. (1999), and additional nuclei in the amygdala known to inhibit parental behavior.

Prolactin. PROL is a polypeptide protein hormone synthesized mainly in the pituitary gland and released during lactation to stimulate the production of milk by the mammary glands. Because of its intimate connection with lactation and nursing, early investigators of parental behavior in mammals, and in birds as well, proposed that PROL was the "maternal hormone" (Riddle, Lahr, and Bates, 1942). Later studies were unable to confirm this (Numan et al., 1977; Rodriguez-Sierra and Rosenblatt, 1977), but more recent studies have led to reevaluation of the role of PROL in parental behavior in the rat, and it is now recognized that it is important for the initiation of parental behavior.

The role of PROL in parental behavior was shown in studies in which females were hypophysectomized (thereby removing the pituitary gland source of prolactin) before they were treated with E2. This delayed the onset of parental behavior (Bridges, 1990). When the hypophysectomized females were injected with PROL or were implanted with a pituitary gland in the kidney capsule, where it secretes large amounts of PROL, short-latency parental behavior was restored in females that had been primed with E2 (Bridges and Millard, 1988).

Most convincing is a study in which PROL was placed directly in the MPOA where it stimulated short-latency parental behavior in E2 primed females (Bridges, Numan, Ronsheim, Mann and Lupini 1990). Recent studies have extended this finding: First, both PROL and rat placental lactogen I (rPl-I), implanted in the MPOA, were found to be equally effective in stimulating parental behavior, and, second, the most effective steroid hormone treatment for priming these effects was exposure to P by subcutaneous implants for 11 days followed by removal of the P implants and insertion of an E2 implant. This treatment was more effective than either P or E2 alone, which were ineffective (Bridges et al., 1997).

The increase in circulating prolactin at the end of pregnancy and the distribution of PROL receptor mRNA support the behavioral evidence of the role of PROL in parental behavior. The source of the PROL that stimulates parental behavior is believed to be both the pituitary gland and the brain itself. PROL released by the pituitary gland into the circulatory system reaches the brain by transport across the blood–brain barrier (Walsh, Slaby, and Posner, 1987). PROL is also synthesized and released in the region of the lateral hypothalamus (DeVito, 1989; DeVito, Connors and Hedge, 1987; Emanuele et al., 1992).

There are two forms of PROL receptor mRNA that are distributed in various brain nuclei, including the MPOA (Pi and Grattan, 1998). Of particular interest is the long form of PROL and the receptor mRNA for the long form because this increases during pregnancy and may, therefore, be more closely related than the short form to PROL stimulation of parental behavior (Bakowska and Morrell, 1997; Sugiyama, Minoura, Kawabe, Tanaka, and Nakashima, 1994).

It is not clear what role rPL-I plays in parental behavior because it is secreted by fetal placentas at approximately midpregnancy (beginning on day 12) and does not stimulate parental behavior at that time. It may play a role in the priming of parental behavior in the rat, a role that had been assigned to PROL (see preceding discussion), in addition to its role in promoting embryo growth (Seyoum, Robertson, Persaud, Paterson, and Shiu, 1999). The role of PROL may be to trigger the onset of parental behavior in females that have been exposed over pregnancy to E2 and P and to rPL-I during the latter half of pregnancy.

Oxytocin. OT, a neuropeptide, is synthesized in several brain nuclei (the supraoptic nucleus [SON], the PVN, and the ACN). It is stored in the posterior pituitary gland and released during parturition, producing vigorous and coordinated uterine contractions in response to cervical stimulation (Ferguson reflex) and during nursing, causing milk "let-down" in response to sucking stimulaton. Recently, studies have shown that OT is also transmitted from the PVN chiefly to other regions of the brain, in which it has been shown to be involved in parental behavior in the rat and several other species.

In the initial studies, ovariectomized female rats were treated with E2, and 48 hr later OT was injected directly into the lateral ventricles (intracerebroventricularly, [icv]). Their response was rapid, within 2 hr nearly all of the females had displayed all of the components of parental behavior (Pedersen and Prange, 1979). This effect was duplicated by Fahrbach, Morrell, and Pfaff (1984, 1985), but other investigators were not able to confirm these findings with different strains of rats (Bolwerk and Swanson, 1984; Rubin, Menniti, and Bridges,1983). In one strain that failed to respond to OT given icv, the descrepancy between the different studies was resolved when Wamboldt and Insel (1987) showed that OT was effective only when combined with anosmia (unresponsiveness to olfactory stimuli). Because pup odors are initially aversive to females (see subsequent discussion), anosmia reduced the aversive response of these females to the pups and only then was OT able to stimulate positive, parental responses.

Using OT antagonists consisting either of OT antiserum to OT an antioxytocin is another method for showing that OT is involved in the stimulation of parental behavior. Pregnancy-terminated females that are ovariectomized and given estradiol benzoate (EB) normally show parental behavior immediately at 48 hr but when they were injected icv with either antiserum to OT or an antioxytocin they were delayed by 24 hr (Caldwell, Greer, Johnson, Prange, and Pedersen, 1987; Pedersen, Caldwell, Johnson, Fort, and Prange, 1985; Fahrbach et al., 1985). Moreover, if the antioxytocin is given to females that have begun to give birth, there is a delay of several hours in their initial retrieving and grouping of pups (van Leengoed, Kerker, and Swanson, 1987). Lesions of the PVN that destroy cells that produce OT also cause deficits in specific aspects of parental behavior (Insel and Harbaugh, 1989; Olazabal and Ferreira, 1997).

Estrogen at the end of pregnancy plays an important role in OT stimulation of parental behavior. It is found in the cytoplasm of oxytocinergic cells (Jirikowska, Caldwell, Pilgrim, Stumpf, and Pedersen, 1990), where it regulates the synthesis of OT in magnocellular cells of the PVN, the SON, and neighboring regions. The increase in E2 at the end of pregnancy also enables OT to be behaviorally effective because it stimulates the increase at parturition in mRNA for OT (OT-mRNA) in the nuclei of magnocellular OT-secreting cells (Douglas et al., 1998).

Localization of OT–receptor–mRNA (OT-R-mRNA) in various brain regions provides the initial basis for determining where OT, secreted by the preceding nuclei, is likely to act in stimulating parental behavior (Yoshimura et al., 1993).There are high concentrations of OT-R-mRNA in diencephalic nuclei (MPOA, PVN, Ventromedial nucleus of the hypothalmus [VMH]), amygdala nuclei, and the anterior olfactory nucleus of the olfactory bulb, and low concentrations in other cell layers of the olfactory bulb (periglomerular, mitral, and granular), all of which may be relevant for parental behavior.

During pregnancy on days 13 to15 there are increases in OT-R-mRNA in the MPOA but not on the morning of parturition (Young, Muns, Wang, and Insel, 1997), and smaller increases are also found in additional brain regions involved in parental behavior, including the BNST, PVN, SON, and suprachiasmatic nucleus (SCN). These increases are regulated by estrogen, which also regulates the increase in binding affinity of the OT receptor in the MPOA and the anterior hypothalmus (AH) (Caldwell, Walker, Pedersen, Barakat, and Mason,1994; Young et al., 1997).

In summary, during pregnancy E2 and P, acting by means of their receptors in the MPOA and other nuclei in the neural circuit of maternal behavior, and perhaps rat placental hormone-I, stimulate an increase in parental responsiveness that becomes apparent when P levels decline at the end of pregnancy. At this time PROL and OT, primed by E2, combine with E2 to trigger the onset of maternal behavior. Fine tuning of the onset of parental behavior is based on the MPOA response to vigorous and regular uterine contractions and to fetal stimulaton of the birth canal during parturition.

Males. Male rats possess the neural circuitry and responsiveness to E2 and P stimulation of parental behavior similar to those of females (Lubin, Leon, Moltz, and Numan, 1972), and they can be sensitized (see subsection on steroid hormones). Gonadectomized (removal of testes) males treated with E2 and P for 16 days respond to an injection of E2 (at a higher dose than that required by females) with the rapid onset of parental behavior. E2 implanted in the MPOA of males is as effective in stimulating parental behavior as it is in females, and lesions of the MPOA produce the same deficits in the onset or the maintenance of male parental behavior (Rosenblatt and Ceus, 1998; Rosenblatt, Hazelwood, and Poole, 1996; Sturgis and Bridges, 1997). In evolution therefore neuroendocrine circuits for maternal behavior have been retained in males despite the fact that male rats rarely engage in parental behavior. What is lacking in the male rat, normally, are the hormones of pregnancy to stimulate these neural circuits. This allows for the possibility that males of other mammalian species in which parental behavior is more typical and functional may be hormonally stimulated to perform parental behavior.

Mouse

Parental behavior in the mouse is similar to that of the rat and other small mammals, and includes nursing, retrieving pups, anogenital licking, nest building, and nest defense. In some strains parental behavior is elicited by pups almost immediately in nonpregrant females and in males also. In others, however, females must undergo pregnancy, and parental behavior is stimulated by hormones at parturition or earlier.

Steroid hormones. In the mouse, nest building arises early in pregnancy (rather than just before parturition as in most nest-building mammals), when circulating E2 levels are declining and P levels are rising. It is stimulated by the synergy (i.e., successive, joint action) of these hormones in the proper dosage levels and timing (Lisk, 1971). Parental responsiveness also arises during pregnancy, as shown by parental responses of females that are given pups during pregnancy or when they are tested in a lever-pressing apparatus from which they receive a single pup each time they press the lever. It develops gradually, in stages: Licking pups alone appears earliest, at approximately days 3 and 4 of pregnancy, then in combination with retrieving or nest building between days 3 and 10. On days 11 to 19 (day of parturition), females presented with pups are likely to exhibit licking with retrieving, nest building, with adopting a nursing position following soon after (Saito and Takahashi, 1980).

Parental responsiveness has also been shown to increase during pregnancy in the mouse that uses the operant response of lever pressing. Females are willing to perform a greater number of lever presses (which deliver pups to the female) after pregnancy termination by hysterectomy on day 18 of pregnancy than earlier in pregnancy on day 8 (Hauser and Gandelman, 1985). The increase is therefore based on E2; ovariectomy reduces it and only E2 restores it. Response to E2 increases with experience: Koch and Ehret (1989) implanted ovariectomized females subcutaneously (sc) with silastic capsules of E2, and the females retrieved pups in 40% of the cases if they were inexperienced and in nearly 100% of cases when they had previous parental experience. Later, Ehret and Buckenmaier (1994) found that previous experience increased estrogen receptor concentrations of brain areas associated with olfaction in females that exhibit high levels of maternal behavior.

In several strains of mice, females (and males) can be stimulated to exhibit parental behavior almost immediately when they are presented with young pups (Beniest-Noirot, 1958; LeBlond, 1938). All components of parental behavior are performed in a manner that is not distinguishable from that of postpartum females except, of course, that these females do not lactate. It has been proposed that in all strains, once parental behavior is established by hormones, it no longer depends on them but is responsive to pup stimulation (Köller, 1955; LeBlond, 1938).

Prolactin and oxytocin. PROL also plays a role in parental nest building in mice. Virgins exposed to pups can also be stimulated to nest build, but hypophysectomy, which removes the source of PROL, prevents this (Saito, Takahashi, and Imamichi, 1983). High levels of P alone do not stimulate nest building if PROL is absent. In an early study, PROL administered to virgin mice enhanced nursing behavior, gathering of pups in the nest, and attending them by virgin mice (Voci and Carlson, 1973).

Although PROL does not play a role in gathering of pups in the nest and warming them by virgin wild mice, it has been reported that OT does (McCarthy, 1990; McCarthy, Bare, and vom Saal, 1986; but see the following discussion). E2, which stimulates retrieving in house mice, also causes the release of PROL; nevertheless, Koch and Ehret (1989) found that retrieving was not affected by postpartum depletion of PROL in the blood.

New molecular biological methods for manipulating genes that regulate the synthesis of protein receptors for PROL have shown that PROL is essential for maternal behavior in mice (Lucas, Ormandy, Binart, Bridges, and Kelly, 1998; Ormandy et al., 1997). Females that are heterozygous for the germ line null mutation of the prolactin receptor are prevented from synthesizing the receptor. Nevertheless, they are able to give birth (homozygous females are sterile), but only 20% of the females had surviving pups and only 15% of the pups survived. These females exhibited deficits in all aspects of maternal behavior and these deficits were not based on deficits in learning, memory, or in olfaction.

Mice with a null mutation resulting in the absence of OT were able to show normal maternal behavior, but they lost all of their offspring because of failure of milk ejection. When the mothers were injected with OT, the offspring were rescued (Nishimori et al., 1996). These studies indicate that PROL, but not OT, is an essential component of the hormonal basis of maternal behavior among mice.

Males. Male mice of several strains readily show parental behavior on their first contact with pups. The behavior resembles that of females, and, in fact, males housed with pregnant females become increasingly parental toward pups as the female's pregnancy advances (Beniest-Noirot, 1958).

Although voles are of a different rodent family than that of mice, their parental behavior is very similar, with the important difference that in several species males are as parental as females (prairie voles) whereas in others males are completley nonparental (montane voles). This behavioral difference has enabled investigators to relate two neuropeptides, arginine vasopressin (AVP) and OT to differences in parental behavior of males. There are differences in the distribution of these neuropeptides in the brain and in the distribution of receptor mRNA for them (DeVries and Villaba, 1997; Wang, Young, De Vries, and Insel, 1998). The parental males among prairie voles have a wide distribution of AVP receptors in various brain regions (olfactory bulb, BNST, amygdala, and thalamus) that is absent in the nonparental montane voles. Vasopressin gene expression following parturition also increased in male prairie voles but not in male montane voles. Females of these species do not differ from one another in the distribution of AVP fibers and AVP receptor mRNA but differ from the males of the two species. OT receptor distributions in females of the two species also differ. OT receptor binding in postpartum females of both species increased in the VMH of both species; however, it is not yet clear to what extent OT is involved in the parental behavior of either female or male voles (Wang, Liu, Young, and Insel, 2000). There have been no studies on the role of gonadal hormones, E2 and P, on parental behavior of either males or females.

Hamsters

Several unique features mark the parental behavior of the Syrian hamster. In addition to having the shortest gestation period of any placental mammal (16 days after the day of mating), unlike those of all other mammals, E2 levels in circulation in hamsters do not rise at the end of pregnancy, but like P they decline and there is no reversal of the E2 and P ratio at the end of pregnancy. Hamsters have evolved a reproductive strategy that depends on a short gestation period, no postpartum estrus and mating, and rapid development and weaning of the young. There is an early postpartum period of infanticidal behavior during which females reduce the size of their litters to that which they can successfully raise given the availability of adequate food supplies early in reproduction and environmental conditions at the time of lactation (Day and Galef, 1977; Schneider and Wade, 1991).

Steroid hormones. In other respects the parental behavior of the hamster is similar to that of other small mammals in the performance of nest building, nursing, retrieving, licking of the young, and nest defense or parental aggression. Nest building arises during pregnancy in hamsters placed in a seminatural environment and reaches a peak before delivery: It begins as digging behavior during the last 4 days of pregnancy, then shifts to nest building (Daly, 1972). Implants of E2 and P in ovariectomized females, over a period corresponding to the length of pregnancy, stimulates nest building similar to that which occurs in pregnant females (Richards, 1969). During pregnancy there is also a gradual increase in parental responsiveness, which is measured by the decreasing amount of daily exposure needed to initiate retrieving: By day 15 of pregnancy a single exposure is sufficient (Buntin, Jaffe, and Lisk, 1984; Siegel, Clark, and Rosenblatt, 1983). Parental behavior arises spontaneously several hours before parturition, but studies of the steroid hormone basis of this behavior have not provided conclusive answers to how these hormones are involved in the onset of parental behavior in the hamster. Neither E2 nor P, given either separately or in combination 24 hr prepartum, alters the prepartum onset of parental behavior nor does 10 days of treatment with these hormones alter latencies for parental behavior in ovariectomized females. Pregnancy termination by hysterectomy, which is effective in stimulating the onset of maternal behavior in mice and rats, has no effect on parental behavior in hamsters (Siegel, 1985; Siegel and Rosenblatt, 1979).

Like the rat and the mouse, virgin hamsters can be induced to show parental behavior if they are simply exposed to pups (Buntin, Jaffe, and Lisk, 1979; Siegel and Rosenblatt, 1978; Swanson and Campbell, 1979). Latencies range from 18 hr, when the pups presented to them are 6 to 12 days of age, to 43 hr, when pups are 1 to 2 days of age and exposure is for a short period twice daily (Siegel and Rosenblatt, 1978). Considering that virgin females have a tendency to exhibit infanticidal behavior toward pups of less than 6 days of age, eliciting parental behavior was unexpected but shows that the substrate for parental behavior can be activated by sensory stimuli even in the absence of ovarian steroids (Siegel, 1985).

Prolactin.   In the Syrian hamster, PROL plays a crucial role in parental behavior. When PROL release is blocked in new mothers, they abruptly stop performing parental behavior, no longer exhibit nest defense, and frequently kill their pups (Wise and Pryor, 1977). Hamster PROL, partially restores parental behavior and nest defense in these animals (McCarthy, Curran, and Siegel, 1994).

Males.   A unique and remarkable instance of male parental behavior has been reported in the Djungarian hamster in which males actively participate in the birth of the young (Jones and Wynne-Edwards, 2000). They lick amniotic fluid before birth, assist the delivery, initiate respiration in the newborn by clearing their nostrils of fluid, lick and sniff pups as they are born, clean birth membranes, and eat the placentas. Males undergo a series of hormonal changes before the birth of their first litter that may "prime" them to exhibit paternal behavior. Males of a closely related species, the Siberian hamster, do not provide paternal care: In this species inexperienced males attack pups and experienced males are only slightly less aggressive toward pups (Gibber, Piontkewitz, and Terkel, 1984).

Rabbits

Rabbits, which bear altrical newborn, have a most unusual pattern of parental behavior. Shortly before parturition rabbit mothers build nests of straw in burrows they have dug underground, and then they line them with loosened fur that they pluck from the ventrum. During parturition they deposit their young in the nest and return only once a day to nurse them for approximately 3 min (González-Mariscal, Melo, Jiménez-Estrada, Beyer, and Rosenblatt, 1994; Zarrow, Denenberg, and Anderson, 1965). Although contact with their pups is brief at parturition and during nursing, it is essential if parental care is to be maintained (González-Mariscal, Melo, Chirino et al., (1998). Separating mothers from their pups at parturition or during succeeding days results in severe deficits in parental care (González-Mariscal and Rosenblatt, 1996).

Hares that bear precocial young, rather than altrical young, make shallow depressions where they deposit their young at parturition and nurse them once each day for several days (Broekhuizen and

Maaskamp, 1975). The young then disperse and remain hidden in nearby bushes and return to the parturition site when the mother appears once each day at dusk to nurse them.

These unique parental care patterns are adaptations to avoid predation of the young. They are designed to hide the young and not reveal their location except, of necessity, when the mother nurses them once a day. Other small mammals are able to defend their young by becoming aggressive and fighting off intruders, but rabbits resort to a less energetic method for doing so.

Despite the abbreviated pattern of parental behavior, there are no differences, compared with that of other mammals, in the pattern of hormonal secretions of E2, P, and PROL during pregnancy and at parturition in the rabbit. To a greater extent than in other mammals, however, in the rabbit these hormones stimulate an elaborate pattern of nest-building behavior that results in a fur-lined underground straw nest. In view of the minimal postpartum parental care that the female provides for her young, leaving them for long periods, the elaborate nest that she builds before parturition is necessary.

The female first exhibits digging behavior starting at approximately 2 weeks before parturition, and this declines during the last week as straw carrying to the nest site increases (González-Mariscal, Díaz-Sanchez, Melo, Beyer, and Rosenblatt, 1994; González-Mariscal, Melo, Jiménez-Estrada, Beyer, and Rosenblatt, 1996). Hair pulling from her ventrum arises abruptly the day before parturition and continues for the next 4 days; the female lines the nest with the hair, and this provides insulation and also absorbs moisture from the pups after they urinate (González-Mariscal, Cuamatzi, and Rosenblatt, 1998).

Steroid Hormones. The early studies by Zarrow, Gandelman, and Denenberg (1971) used various regimens of EB and P, which were modeled after circulating levels of these hormones during pregnancy, to stimulate nest building. These were the first studies to establish the role of gonadal hormones in parental behavior in the rabbit. Most effective were treatments in which EB was administered for 18 days, and P from day 2 to day 15; nearly all females started to nest build shortly after this treatment. The hormonal basis of parental behavior was not studied directly (Zarrow, Sawin, Ross, and Denenberg, 1962).

More detailed studies of steroid horomone control of the various phases of nest building were done by González-Mariscal and Rosenblatt (1996). Digging, the preliminary to nest building, was stimulated by the combination of low levels of E2 and high levels of P, characteristic of pregnant females at approximately day 20. The decline of P after day 20 and an increase in E2 levels stimulated straw carrying to construct the nest in the excavated underground burrow. Hair loosening of the ventrum and flanks and lining the straw nest with the hair obtained occurred at the end of pregnancy and for a few days postpartum. Testosterone, which is also secreted in large amounts during pregnancy, was also able to stimulate digging and hair loosening but not straw carrying, and it was not necessarily through conversion to estrogen (González-Mariscal, Melo, Jiménez, Beyer, and Rosenblatt, 1996).

Study of E2 stimulation of maternal nest building has been extended to the brain to determine the sites of behavioral response to E2. Implants of E2 were made specifically in the MPOA together with systemic injections of P, and they elicited digging and straw carrying (after withdrawal of P). Hair pulling was not elicited by the implants. The effectiveness of E2 implants was due to high concentrations of immunoreactive estrogen receptors in the MPOA (also found in the BNST and the amygdala, which are also involved in E2 stimulation of maternal behavior in the rat; Caba, Beyer, González-Mariscal, and Morrell, 2001).

Prolactin. The hormonal control of nursing after parturition has not previously been studied in rabbits, although nursing itself has been described during the lactation period (González-Mariscal et al., 1996; Zarrow et al., 1965). Suckling by the young is facilitated by a nipple pheromone (stimulated by E2 and P) that guides their nipple-searching behavior and elicits nipple grasping (Hudson and Distel, 1983).

Early studies of the role of PROL in maternal nest building, in which a PROL release inhibitor (ergocornine) was used, revealed deficits in nest building and in maternal behavior (Anderson, Zarrow, Fuller, and Denenberg, 1971; Zarrow et al., 1971). Recent studies have confirmed these findings and have established PROL as the principal hormone in the onset of maternal behavior (González-Mariscal et al., 1996; González-Mariscal, Melo, Parlow, Beyer, and Rosenblatt, 2000). PROL release was prevented (by bromocryptine) either prepartum, postpartum, or during both periods, and females were either suckled or their mammary glands were removed (thelectomy) to prevent suckling stimulation. PROL levels were low or absent in females that were administered bromocryptine, and they were tested in their responses to pups placed in the nest.

Straw carrying and hair pulling were abolished when the release of PROL was prevented. In addition, there were severe deficits in parental behavior when PROL release was prevented during the last 5 days of pregnancy and even greater deficits when it was prevented for an additional 5 days after parturition. Specifically, crouching over the young as in nursing was prevented in females that entered the nest in response to the pups. The absence of suckling in the thelectomized females did not prevent females from performing maternal behavior.

PROL receptors in the rabbit brain, which provide the basis for the behavioral effects of PROL, have also been measured in pregnant and postpartum females. PROL receptor immunoreactivity was not found in brain sites usually associated with parental behavior, the MPOA, amygdala, BNST, or VMH, but was present in the medial habenula, mesencephalic central gray, and several thalamic nuclei (González-Mariscal, Melo, and Beyer, 1998).

OT has not been studied with respect to parental behavior in the rabbit.

Sheep and Goats

Sheep and goats present more complex patterns of parental behavior (i.e., leading–following) toward their precocial offspring than do nesting species with altricial newborn. The onset of parental behavior occurs at parturition and consists of licking the lamb or kid to clean it, low-pitch bleating, and allowing the newborn to suckle. Shortly after parturition, as a result of contact with her own offspring, the mother responds parentally to only her own newborn and within a short period (i.e., 2 hr in sheep and several minutes in goats); the mother no longer allows alien offspring to approach and suckle from her (Poindron and Le Neindre, 1980).

Normally the mothers' responses to their own offspring are based on its individually specific odor, and making mothers anosmic (unable to smell) prevents them from developing this exclusive bond with their own offspring. Parental responsiveness itself does not depend on developing this exclusive bond as shown by the fact that anosmic mothers are parental toward infants but not just toward their own offspring. In sheep and other ungulates, we can distinguish parental responsiveness from selective response to the mother's own offspring, which grows out of parental responsiveness and is based on learning. Recently it has been shown that anosmic mothers eventually do develop an exclusive bond with their own offspring based on the specific vocalizations and individual appearance of the young (Terrazas et al., 1999).

Steroid hormones. The role of steroid hormones in parental behavior has been studied only in sheep. Early studies showed an increase in responsiveness to lambs by females during estrus when E2 levels are high and at prepartum when E2 levels also were high. When E2 or P was injected in multiparous ovariectomized ewes over a 7-day period or on 1 day only, parental behavior was stimulated in more than 75% of the females by E2, which proved to be more effective than P (Poindron and Le Neindre, 1980). Normally, females initiate parental behavior and establish recognition of their lamb just after they have received strong vaginal–cervical stimulation by passage of the fetus through the birth canal during delivery. The effect of experimentally applied vaginal–cervical stimulation on parental behavior has been studied, and stimulation with E2 and P combined with vaginal–cervical stimulation has been found to be more effective in stimulating parental care than either of the treatments alone were, especially in experienced ewes (Kendrick and Keverne, 1991). In inexperienced females, E2 alone was ineffective in stimulating parental behavior, but when combined with vaginal–cervical stimulation, the effects of E2 were strengthened and aggression and negative behavior toward lambs were reduced. In experienced ewes this combined treatment elicited positive parental responses of licking, sniffing, approaching the lamb, and emitting low-pitched bleats. As we see in the next two subsections, vaginal–cervical stimulation causes the release of OT in the brain, which plays an important role in the parental behavior of ewes. Ewes depend on continued stimulation from their lambs during the first 24 hr for maintaining parental behavior. If lambs are removed at parturition, only 25% of females retain their parental behavior 12 hr later, but if E2 is maintained at a high level during this period, more that 60% of females remain parental (Poindron and Le Neindre, 1980). This in another indication that E2 is important in parental behavior in ewes.

Prolactin. Among sheep only one study has tested the possibility that PROL plays a role in parental care shortly after parturition. When dexamethasone was used to induce labor at term, PROL levels were high for at least 24 hr postpartum. Nevertheless, this did not prevent the decline in parental responsiveness following removal of the lambs at parturition during the first 24 hr (Poindron and LeNeindre, 1980). Although PROL may not maintain parental behavior, as shown in this study, it may play a role in its onset.

Oxytocin. The strongest evidence of a role for OT in stimulating parental behavior in mammals has been found in sheep. The first evidence that OT might be involved in parental behavior was obtained in studies in which vaginal–cervical stimulation was shown to synergize with E2 and P to induce parental behavior in ewes (Keverne, Lévy, Poindron, and Lindsay, 1983). Vaginal–cervical stimulation causes the release of OT from the pituitary gland into the general circulation during parturition, and these findings suggest that there may also be a release of OT directly in the brain. This was shown to be the case when dialysis of cerebrospinal fluid (selective removal of chemical components of cerebrospinal fluid through a tube inserted into the ventricles of the brain) taken from ewes during labor and parturition was found to contain high concentrations of OT (Kendrick, Keverne, Baldwin, and Sharman, 1986; Kendrick, Keverne, Chapman, and Baldwin, 1988a, 1988b).

The link between OT and parental behavior was established more definitively when OT, infused directly into the cerebrospinal fluid of EB-primed females, elicited parental behavior (low-pitched bleats, accepting suckling, approaching and following lambs, and sniffing and licking them; Kendrick, Keverne and Baldwin, 1987). The behavior was short lived but led to studies in which females were subjected to spinal anesthesia during parturition to prevent the spinal nerves that innervate the birth canal from stimulating the release of OT by means of feedback during parturition (Krehbiel, Poindron, Lévy, and Prud'Homme, 1987). Parental behavior was blocked in these females but not in females that were also subjected to the blocking effects of spinal anesthesia after parturition was nearly completed. As a final proof of the role of OT, the effects of spinal anesthesia on parental behavior could be prevented if females were injected icv with OT; this treatment restored the behavior in a large proportion of the females (Lévy, Kendrick, Keverne, Piketty, and Poindron, 1992).

OT exerts additional effects related to parental behavior in sheep. After the critical period for accepting alien lambs for nursing has passed (2 hr after parturition), vaginal–cervical stimulation will reopen it for a short period and females will again accept these newborn young (Keverne et al., 1983). This abrupt change in the female's behavior is based on the release of OT by the vaginal–cervical stimulation. It enables females that have given birth to one lamb and become attached to it to accept a second lamb when it is born because of the birth canal stimulation during the second delivery.

In developing their parental responsiveness, ewes must first overcome their aversion to the amniotic fluid that will cover the newborn when it emerges from the birth canal. They show this aversion experimentally by refusing to eat food that has been mixed with amniotic fluid (Lévy, Poindron, and Le Neindre, 1983). Shortly before parturition, however, this aversion disappears: Ewes develop a preference for amniotic fluid that lasts for several hours postpartum. This preference is lost in females subjected to spinal anesthesia but is restored if OT is injected icv, into the females 1 hr after delivery. It can also be extended beyond its normal duration if vaginal–cervical stimulation is applied to postpartum females as the effect is waning (Lévy, Keverne, Piketty, and Poindron, 1990; Lévy et al., 1992).

Primates

Except for several species among the more primitive primates (prosimians), in which parental care resembles that of nesting species of mammals (lemurs), parental behavior among the primates falls within the broad category of clinging and carrying (Bard, in Vol. 2 of this *Handbook*; Jolly, 1966). However, beyond this characterization, parental care among the primates involves a wide range of behaviors that are not easily categorized as in the lower mammalian species that have been described (Bornstein, in Vol. 1 of this *Handbook*). Clinging and carrying characterize one aspect of the relationship between mother and young, which also includes nursing, cleaning, protecting, and in general attending the physical and the psychosocial needs of the young. The obvious psychological relationship between the mother and her offspring has obscured the underlying hormonal basis of the female's parental behavior, and few studies until recently (Pryce, 1996) were carried out on this aspect of parental care among the primates.

Steroid hormones. Among primates, including humans, only recently have studies been reported on the role of hormones, including steroidal hormones, in the onset of parental behavior (Capitanio, Weissberg, and Reite, 1985; Pryce, Abbott, Hodges, and Martin, 1988; Pryce, Döbeli, and Martin, 1993). In one study, red-bellied tamarin mothers were rated as "good" or "poor" depending on their behavior during the first 2 hr postpartum. Good mothers carried their infants, nursed them, and licked and groomed them for longer periods than poor mothers did, and their infants spent more time on them and less often were pushed off the mother. Good mothering was correlated with high levels of urinary E2 during the last 3 weeks of pregnancy in experienced mothers and the last week in females without such experience. Poor mothers showed a decline in urinary E2 levels during this terminal period of pregnancy, whereas in good mothers urinary E2 remained level or increased. This was the first indication that in primates, as in rodents and ungulates, E2 played an important role in parental behavior.

This led to further studies by Pryce et al. (1993) in which common marmoset females were trained to press a lever to illuminate a model of an infant and, at the same time, terminate infant distress calls that are disturbing to mothers. During the first 10 days postpartum, high frequencies of lever pressing were correlated in individual mothers with observations of the duration of carrying infants (almost invariably twins) and also with short latencies to respond to crying infants and long latencies to exhibit aggression toward their infants. Lever pressing was shown therefore to be a good measure of female parental responsiveness to infants and could be used to measure changes in responsiveness during pregnancy and in response to hormone treatments.

Lever pressing increased in the marmoset females during the last 35 days of pregnancy (which lasts approximately 142 days). The increase was correlated with an initial rise in plasma levels of E2 and P 70 to 30 days before parturition and a sharp decline in P starting at approximately 25 days and a further increase in plasma E2 levels.

In the next study, noncycling females were treated with a combination of E2 and P at dose levels that mimicked the relative concentrations of these hormones at the end of pregnancy. In response to lengthy treatment with these hormones, lever pressing increased to levels approximating those during the natural prepartum rise. This study, the first in which hormones were used to stimulate parental responsiveness in a primate, gave results that are very similar to those found in other subprimate species with respect to the role of steroid hormones in parental responsiveness.

Among group-living pigtailed monkeys, pregnant females increase their rate of handling infants of other mothers of the group at approximately week 18 of their 24-week pregnancy (Maestripieri and Zehr, 1998). The increase is correlated with a decrease in plasma P after week 12 and an increase in the plasma concentration of E2 during week 22. When females were ovariectomized and given E2, handling of infants increased over the level of ovariectomized untreated females. Interestingly, as in the rat, exposure to infants alone, without hormones, stimulates handling in intact, nonpregnant females.

Social relationships with other group members were not, however, disrupted to any great extent in the group-living pregnant females (Maestripieri, 1999). There was reduced grooming in the first month of pregnancy, reduced aggressiveness in the last month, and a general decline in social behavior during the last week. Through pregnancy there was decrease in sexual behavior with males of the group.

Prolactin. PROL is involved in the parental behavior of male primates of several species. In the marmoset, a New World monkey, females always have twin infants. The male exhibits parental care of the twins after the first week when they become too heavy for the female to carry them, handing them over to the females for nursing. There is an increase in plasma PROL levels in males, but only when the male has been carrying the infant shortly before the blood sample is taken (Dixson and George, 1982). Mota and Sousa (2000) found a basal level of PROL in paternal males of the common marmoset, and this was elevated following carrying behavior; nonparental male helpers that carried the infants also had elevated PROL levels.

Among cotton-top tamarins, the males' care of infants begins at parturition and consists of carrying the infants at least as often as females and also food sharing with the young during weaning (Ziegler, Wegner, and Snowdon, 1996). Closely correlated with infant carrying is a rise in the fathers' plasma PROL levels during the first 2 weeks postpartum; experienced fathers had higher prolactin levels than inexperienced fathers did.

Most interesting was the finding that for 2 weeks preceding parturition, inexperienced male partners showed an increase in PROL levels and this increase was also greater in experienced males. The larger the number of births fathers had participated in, the greater was the correlation between plasma PROL levels and fathering during the first 2 weeks.

Among females the relation between PROL and parental behavior has not been studied despite the close temporal relation between the rise in circulating levels of PROL at the end of pregnancy and the onset of parental behavior.

Abrupt Onset of Parental Behavior in Subhuman Primates

In addition to the direct evidence of the role of steroid hormones in the onset of parental behavior among the primates, there is circumstantial evidence. This consists of the appearance of parental responsiveness during pregnancy and the initial responses of females to their young during parturition and immediately afterward (Rosenblatt, 1990). In general, among subhuman primates there are no striking behavioral changes during pregnancy that reveal any change in the female's parental responsiveness toward infants. Rhesus monkeys, pregnant for the first time, exhibit no regular, increased parental responsiveness to infants up to 2 weeks of age (Gibber, 1986), and these was only a slight tendency in experienced females (Gibber and Goy, 1985). Contrary to these studies, shortly before parturition, rhesus monkeys licked amniotic fluid and ate the placenta of another female giving birth (Tinklepaugh and Hartman, 1930), and late pregnant squirrel monkeys approached and explored infants, even making contact with them and retrieving them, which they would not do earlier in pregnancy (Rosenblum, 1972).

The literature on subhuman primate parental behavior during pregnancy (as evidence of hormonal stimulation), with the exception of the few studies described in the preceding paragraph, which were done on animals living in captivity, leads to the conclusion that the sudden appearance of parental behavior during parturition provides the best evidence of the effects of hormonal stimulation (Rosenblatt, 1990). The lack of marked behavioral changes in pregnant females observed in nature can be understood as an adaptation to the nomadic life of primate troops, which does not permit females to be handicapped by any behavioral changes during pregnancy that would force them to lose contact with their troop because of the ever-present danger of predation (Altmann, 1987).

Pregnancy hormones might be responsible, however, for shifts in sociability of subhuman primate females. Goodall (1960) reported that the late pregnant (155 to 230 days) chimpanzee in the wild separates herself from some members of her troop and from heterosexual foraging groups, and Coe (1990) described increased social responsiveness in late pregnant chimpanzees to female conspecifics and decreased responsiveness to infants and juveniles in the troop and, in general, to males.

One would expect that the most reliable indication of hormonal effects on parental behavior in primates is the behavior of the female toward the infant during parturition when the hormonal changes that initate parental behavior in subprimate mammals have occurred. Yet in primates, without experimental evidence, it is difficult to distinguish during parturition between hormonal effects on the female and the effects of the physiological aspects of delivery. Uterine contractions, birth fluids, and emerging fetus present a combination of strong stimuli that direct the female's attention and behavior to the newborn infant, making it difficult to define the specific role of hormones in the parental behavior observed. The experience of parturition is evidently quite important in two species of *Macaca* (*Macaca mulatta* and *Macaca fascicularis*). Among 211 females that were delivered by Caesarean-section at term, only 7 accepted infants after the delivery (Lundblad and Hogden, 1980). Only when Caesarean-section-delivered infants were smeared with the vaginal secretions of near-term mothers were they accepted by their mothers; infants that were not smeared with those secretions were not accepted by their mothers.

Behavioral Effects of Hormones on Parental Behavior

After identifying the hormones that stimulate parental behavior, we are left with the following question: What are the behavioral effects of these hormones? Although we may not be able to identify all of the neurohormonal processes that underlie parental behavior, we can identify their behavioral contributions to parental care.

The basic components of parental care in the rat (and presumably other mammals) already exist in the central nervous system before hormones act to stimulate them, and they are undoubtedly under genetic control. In fact, they are present in both prepubertal female and male rats as early as the third week of life while the young are still suckling from their mother and have not yet been stimulated by the hormones of puberty (Bridges, Zarrow, Goldman, and Denenberg, 1974; Brunelli and Hofer, 1990; Mayer and Rosenblatt, 1979).

The ability to stimulate parental behavior in prepubertal rats by exposing them to pups contin-uously for several days testifies to the nonhormonally based neural processes underlying parental behavior. Even as adults females and males can be stimulated nonhormonally to initiate parental behavior by continuous exposure to pups (Cosnier, 1963; Rosenblatt, 1967; Wiesner and Sheard, 1933). However, it requires nearly a week of exposure to pups to stimulate parental behavior in adult rats without hormones, whereas females that give birth perform parental behavior under hormonal stimulation almost immediately. Hormones therefore shorten the period of pup stimulation required for activating parental behavior from several days to several minutes.

Insight into why pup stimulation alone requires such a lengthy period of exposure was obtained in studies in which adult virgin females were made anosmic before being exposed to pups for the first time, thereby removing pup odors as a source of stimulation. The effect was surprising: The anosmic females initiated parental behavior more rapidly, rather than less rapidly, as might have been expected when such an important source of stimulation is removed (Fleming and Rosenblatt, 1974b, 1974c; Mayer and Rosenblatt, 1975). The results of these studies implied that the odors of the pups initially prevent females (and males) from exhibiting parental behavior. It had been noted earlier that virgin females initially sniffed pups and then avoided them for several days (Terkel and Rosenblatt, 1971). Also, Cosnier (1963) has shown that virgins exposed to pups initially display infanticidal behavior and avoidance, and only gradually over several days did their negative responses decline and their positive, parental responses increase.

Previously, the general view held by many investigators (e.g., Beach, 1948) was that hormonal stimulation combined with sensory stimuli from the pups to stimulate regions of the brain that mediate parental behavior. When the combined stimulation reached a threshold value this triggered the performance of parental behavior (Rosenblatt and Mayer, 1995). This has been labeled the threshold theory of parental behavior. According to this theory an additional effect of hormones is to lower neural–sensory thresholds for eliciting parental behavior.

It is difficult to maintain such a theory, however, if the removal of a principal sensory stimulus, olfaction, actually shortens virgin female latencies for initiating parental behavior. Moreover, removal of the ability to smell pup odors also eliminates female avoidance of pups after initial contact with them. This had led to the concept that pups initially elicit both approach and withdrawal (or avoidance) responses from nonpregant females (and males) and that these may conflict with one another to inhibit parental behavior (Fleming and Li, in Vol. 2 of this *Handbook*; Rosenblatt and Mayer, 1995). Other investigators have proposed a similar concept with respect to rats (Fleming, 1986; Sheehan et al., 2000) and also subhuman primates (Pryce, 1992, 1996).

Approach–withdrawal is a broad theory (Schneirla, 1965) that includes the concept of neural thresholds for parental behavior but goes much further. It proposes that two opposing systems determine whether females will show either parental behavior when exposed to pups or avoid them and perhaps attack them. In Figure 2.3 these two systems are labeled approach and withdrawal with their associated behavioral, motivational, and emotional responses. As the figure shows, sensory stimuli do not simply summate as proposed by threshold theory but, as shown at the input side of this figure, they are sorted out by a perceptual mechanism that differentiates between those stimuli that elicit approach and those that elicit withdrawal. Each of these separately activates either the approach

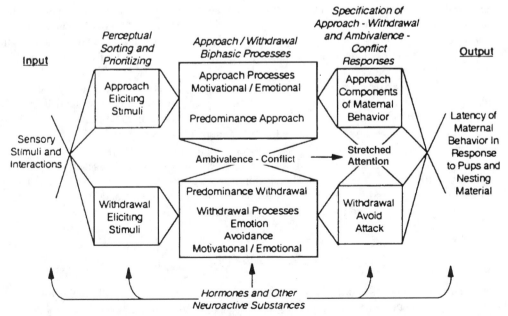

FIGURE 2.3. The mechanisms underlying stimulation of parental behavior according to the approach–withdrawal processes concept (see text for explanation; Rosenblatt and Mayer, 1995).

or the withdrawal systems, and it is the balance between these two systems that determines whether a female will approach the pups and exhibit parental behavior or avoid and perhaps attack them.

Ordinarily during pup exposure, virgins start by avoiding pups after sniffing them, then gradually over several days they adapt to the pups' odors, which enables them to respond to the positive (somatosensory, auditory, and gustatory) stimuli presented by the pups. This may take several days, but the first sign that they have begun to adapt is when they lick the pups (Fleming and Rosenblatt, 1974a; Stern, 1983).

Figure 2.3 also shows that a conflict between approach and withdrawal systems may occur, resulting in behavior that expresses the conflict (e.g., "stretched attention"). The actual parental behaviors performed by the female (or male), including their patterning, frequency, and duration, are determined by the behavior of the pups and the ongoing behavioral state of the female.

Hormones play a role in this conception of the organization of parental behavior at many points (Rosenblatt and Mayer, 1995). Hormones may amplify the effect of pup stimulation by acting on skin receptive fields (i.e., smaller or larger areas on the skin sensory surface represented by single neurons in the cortex) of snout and breast tactile sensory receptors (Stern, 1996), and they may change the nature of the response to olfactory stimulation from negative or indifferent to positive (Kinsley and Bridges, 1990). For example, one effect of OT in female rats is to bind to OT receptors in the olfactory bulb, which results in reducing responsiveness of the olfactory system to pup odors, thereby facilitating approach responses to pups and the onset of maternal behavior (Yu, Kaba, Okutani, Takahashi, and Higuchi, 1996; Yu, Kaba, Okutani, Takahashi, Higuchi, and Seto, 1996). OT may also facilitate learning and retention of pups' odors as positive stimuli, once parental behavior has been established (Nelson and Panksepp, 1996). Females may also become selectively more sensitive to certain pup stimuli, and they may respond positively to specific pup vocalizations more than to others (Ehret and Haack, 1982).

Motivational and emotional responses are also subject to the influence of hormones. It has been shown that parental females, under the influence of hormones, are better able to resolve conflicts between approach and avoidance responses, for example, in a feeding situation that requires the female to receive a shock in order to reach food (Ferreira, Hansen, Nielsen, Archer, and Minor, 1989). During parental care female rats are less responsive to stressful stimuli (i.e., measured by adrenal cortical hormone release). Thermoregulation emerges as an important aspect of their behavior. They produce excessive heat and therefore seek lower environmental temperatures. Thermoregulation also governs their behavior during pregnancy, and during postpartum lactation it plays an important role in nursing and nest-building behavior (Wilson and Stricker, 1979; Woodside and Jans, 1988; Woodside, Pelchat, and Leon, 1980).

On the performance side, hormones give rise to behavior patterns not seen at other times when females are not exhibiting parental behavior. Retrieving, nest building, and anogenital licking of pups are rare in females that are not stimulated by hormones to exhibit parental behavior. Aggression toward intruders at the nest site is exhibited only by mothers that are guarding pups, otherwise females rarely show aggression (Erskine, Barfield, and Goldman, 1978).

Approach–withdrawal theory enables us to bring together a large number of experimental findings to explain how they play a role in parental behavior. It integrates observations of parental behavior with underlying neural and hormonal processes and enables us to understand how each of these levels of analysis contributes to our understanding of parental behavior.

CONCLUSIONS

Several generalizations arise from this review of the hormonal basis of parenting behavior among the mammals. The hormones that are emerging as principal in stimulating the onset of parental behavior in females are estrogen, P, and PROL. The former two, which are present during most of pregnancy, appear to prime females to respond to terminal hormonal changes, which include a decline in P and increases in estrogen, PROL, and, in several species, OT. These hormones trigger the onset of parental behavior in conjunction with birth canal stimulation before and during parturition. P plays a dual role in stimulating latent parental responsiveness and in inhibiting its expression during pregnancy. Moreover, its decline at the end of pregnancy allows estrogen and other hormones to act. OT is important in the parental behavior of rats, but is of even greater importance in sheep, in which it plays an important role in the selective parental responsiveness of ewes to their lambs, which is established through olfactory stimulation at parturition when OT levels are high.

The neural substrate of parental responsiveness has been only briefly reviewed insofar as it enables us to understand how hormones act to produce their behavioral effects. Hormones are effective in stimulating parental behavior because the brain regions in which this behavior is organized become selectively responsive to the different hormones and to interactions among the hormones during pregnancy and at parturition.

In addition to the uniformity of hormonal effects on parental behavior, there is the diversity of effects because hormones are only one component among the multiple determinants of parental behavior. Rabbits use steroidal hormones and PROL to produce elaborate nests but little parental behavior, whereas ungulates build no nests under the influence of these hormones during pregnancy but instead these hormones prime their response to OT and its effects on individual recognition and parental behavior toward lambs. Ecological and social factors play an important role in how hormones are involved in parental behavior among the mammals.

There is a growing consensus that the behavioral effects of hormones on parental behavior are mediated by changes in the relation between underlying approach–withdrawal processes rather than simply by changes in thresholds for eliciting individual parental responses. Females of many species initially avoid newborns (olfactory aversive responses and timidity). Hormones act by changing the female's responses to newborns. These hormones produce their behavioral effects by reducing fear and timidity, increasing positive responsiveness to stimuli from the newborn, mobilizing early experiences with offspring, and altering basic motivational processes. Males in several species that have been studied are fully capable of performing parental behaviors (Parke, in Vol. 3 of this *Handbook*). Even in species in which males do not ordinarily take care of infants, they are capable of doing so if they are either treated with pregnancy hormones or exposed to infants for a period. In these species it has been shown that they possess the neural substrate of parental behavior, but normally they lack the necessary hormonal stimulation. In those species in which male parental behavior has been elaborated as an essential part of infant care—species of voles, hamsters, and several primates—hormonal stimulation of male parental care does occur.

ACKNOWLEDGMENT

The research from my laboratory reported here is the work of a large number of students but particularly of my former research associate, Anne D. Mayer.

REFERENCES

Altmann, J. (1987). Life span aspects of reproduction and parental care in anthropoid primates. In J. B. Lancaster, J. Altmann, A. S. Rossi, and L. R. Sherrod (Eds.), *Parenting across the life span* (pp. 15–29). New York: Aldine de Gruyter.

Anderson, C. O., Zarrow, M. X., Fuller, G. B., and Denenberg, V. H. (1971). Pituitary involvement in maternal nest-building in the rabbit. *Hormones and Behavior, 2,* 183–189.

Bakowska J. C., and Morrell, J. I. (1997). Atlas of the neurons that express mRNA for the long form of the prolactin receptor in the forebrain of the female rat. *Journal of Comparative Neurology, 386,* 161–177.

Bard, K. A. (1995). Parenting in primates. In M. H. Bornstein (Ed.), *Handbook of parenting: Vol. 2. Biology and Ecology of Parenting* (pp. 27–58). Mahwah, NJ: Lawrence Erlbaum Associates.

Beach, F. A. (1948). *Hormones and behavior*. New York: Hoeber.

Beniest-Noirot, E. (1958). Analyse du comportement dit 'maternel' chez la souris [Analysis of 'maternal' behavior in mice]. *Monograph Français Psychologie, 1*. Paris: Centre National de la Recherches Scientifique.

Bolwerk, E. L. M., and Swanson, H. H. (1984). Does oxytocin play a role in the onset of maternal behaviour in the rat? *Journal of Endocrinology, 101*, 353–357.

Bridges, R. S. (1990). Endocrine regulation of parental behavior in rodents. In N. A. Krasnegor, and R. S. Bridges (Eds.), *Mammalian parenting* (pp. 93–132). New York: Oxford University Press.

Bridges, R. S., Feder, H. F., and Rosenblatt, J. S. (1977). Induction of maternal behaviors in primigravid rats by ovariectomy, or ovariectomy plus hysterectomy: Effect of length of gestation. *Hormones and Behavior, 9*, 156–169.

Bridges, R. S., Mann, P. E., and Coppeta, J. S. (1999). Hypothalamic involvement in the regulation of maternal behaviour in the rat: Inhibitory roles for the ventromedial hypothalamus and the dorsal/anterior hypothalamic areas. *Journal of Neuroendocrinolgy, 11*, 259–266.

Bridges, R. S., and Millard, W. J. (1988). Growth hormone is secreted by ectopic pituitary grafts and stimulates maternal behavior in rats. *Hormones and Behavior, 22*, 194–206.

Bridges, R. S., Numan, M., Ronsheim, P. M., Mann, P. E., and Lupini, C. E. (1990). Central prolactin infusions stimulate maternal behavior in steroid- treated, nulliparous female rats. *Proceedings of the National Academy of Sciences, U.S.A., 87*, 8003–8007.

Bridges, R. S., Robertson, M. C., Shiu, R. P., Sturgis, J. D., Henriquez, B. M., and Mann, P. E. (1997). Central lactogenic regulation of maternal behavior in rats: steroid dependence, hormone specificity, and behavioral potencies of rat placental lactogen I. *Endocrinology, 138*, 756–763.

Bridges, R. S., Rosenblatt, J. S., and Feder, H. H. (1978). Serum progesterone concentrations and maternal behavior in rats after pregnancy termination: Behavioral stimulation following progesterone withdrawal and inhibition by progesterone maintenance. *Endocrinology, 102*, 258–267.

Bridges, R. S., Zarrow, M. X., Goldman, B. D., and Denenberg, V. H. (1974). A developmental study of maternal responsiveness in the rat. *Physiology and Behavior, 12*, 149–151.

Broekhuizen, S., and Maaskamp, F. (1975). Behaviour and maternal relations of young European hares (*Lepus europaeus Pallas*) during the nursing period. *Congré Gibier, Lisbon* (R.I.N. communication nr. 123), 24.

Brunelli, S. A., and Hofer, M. A. (1990). Parental behavior in juvenile rats: Environmental and biological determinants. In N. A. Krasnegor and R. S. Bridges (Eds.), *Mammalian parenting* (pp. 372–399). New York: Oxford University Press.

Buntin, J. D., Jaffe, S., and Lisk, R. D. (1979, June). Physiological and experiential influences on pup-induced maternal behavior in female hamsters. Paper presented at the Eastern Conference on Reproductive Behavior, New Orleans, LA.

Buntin, J. D., Jaffe, S., and Lisk, R. D. (1984). Changes in responsiveness to newborn pups in pregnant, nulliparous golden hamsters. *Physiology and Behavior, 32*, 437–439.

Caba, M., Beyer, C., González-Mariscal, G., and Morrell, J. I. (2001). Atlas of neurons that express alpha-estrogen receptor in the forebrain of female rabbits. *Journal of Comparative Neurology*. (In Press).

Caldwell, J. D., Greer, E. R., Johnson, M. F., Prange, Jr., A. J., and Pedersen, C. A. (1987). Oxytocin and vasopressin immunoreactivity in hypothalamic and extrahypothalamic sites in late pregnant and post-partum rats. *Neuroendocrinology, 46*, 39–47.

Caldwell, J. D., Walker, C. H., Faggin, B. M., Carr, R. B. Pedersen, C. A., and Mason, G. A. (1995). Characterization of progesterone-3-[125I-BSA] binding sites in the medial preoptic area and anterior hypothalamus. *Brain Research, 693*, 225–232.

Caldwell, J. D., Walker, C. H., Pedersen, C. A., Barakat, A. S., and Mason, G. A. (1994). Estrogen increases affinity of oxytocin receptors in the medial preoptic-anterior hypothalamus. *Peptides, 15*, 1079–1084.

Capitanio, J. P., Weissberg, M., and Reite, M. (1985). Biology of maternal behavior: recent findings and implications, In M. Reite and T. Field (Eds.), *The psychobiology of attachment and separation* (pp. 51–91). New York: Academic.

Coe, C. L. (1990). Psychobiology of maternal behavior in nonhuman primates, In N. A. Krasnegor and R. W. Bridges (Eds.), *Mammalian parenting* (pp. 157–183). New York: Oxford University Press.

Cohn, J., and Gerall, A. A. (1989). Pre- and postpubertal medial preoptic area lesions and maternal behavior in the rat. *Physiology and Behavior, 46*, 333–336.

Cosnier, J. (1963). Quelques problemes posés par le comportement maternel provoqué chéz la ratte [Some problems posed by maternal behavior stimulated in the rat]. *Psychophysiologie Compte Rendu Société Biologie, 157*, 1611–1613.

Daly, M. (1972). The maternal behaviour cycle in golden hamsters. *Zeitschrift für Tierpsychologie, 31*, 289–299.

Davis, I. J., and Ryan, K. J. (1972). Comparative endocrinology of gestation. *Vitamins and Hormones, 30*, 223–279.

Day, C. S. D., and Galef, B. D. (1977). Pup cannibalism: One aspect of maternal behavior in golden hamsters. *Journal of Comparative and Physiological Psychology, 91*, 1179–1189.

DeVito, W. J. (1989). Immunoreactive prolactin in the hypothalamus and cerebrospinal fluid of male and female rats. *Neuroendocrinology, 50*, 182–186.

DeVito, W. J., Connors, J. M., and Hedge, G. A. (1987). Immunoreactive prolactin in the rat hypothalamus: In vitro release and subcellar localization. *Neuroendocrinology, 46,* 155–161.

De Vries, G. J., and Villaba C. (1997). Brain sexual dimorphism and sex differences in parental and other social behaviors. *Annals of the New York Academy of Sciences, 807,* 273–286.

Dixson, A. F., and George, L. (1982). Prolactin and parental behavior in a male New World monkey. *Nature (London), 299,* 551–553.

Douglas, A. J., Meeren, H. K., Jonstone, L. E., Pfaff, D. W., Russell, J. A., and Brooks, P. J. (1998). Stimulation of expression of the oxytocin gene in rat supraoptic neurons at parturition. *Brain Research, 782,* 167–174.

Ehret, G., and Buckenmaier, J. (1994). Estrogen-receptor occurrence in the female mouse—brain-effects of maternal experience, ovariectomy, estrogen and anosmia. *Journal of Physiology Paris, 88,* 315–329.

Ehret, G., and Haack, B. (1982). Ultrasound recognition in house mice: Key stimulus configuration and recognition mechanism. *Journal of Comparative and Physiological Psychology, 148,* 245–251.

Emanuele, N. V., Jurgens, J. K., Halloran, M. M., Tentler, J. J., Lawrence, A. M., and Kelley, M. R. (1992). The rat prolactin gene is expressed in brain tissue: Detection of normal and alternately spliced prolactin messenger RNA. *Molecular Endocrinology, 6,* 35–42.

Erskine, M. S., Barfield, R. J., and Goldman, B. D. (1978). Intraspecific fighting during late pregnancy and lactation in rats and effects of litter removal. *Behavioral Biology, 23,* 206–218.

Fahrbach, S. E., Morrell, J. I., and Pfaff, D. W. (1984). Oxytocin induction of short-latency maternal behavior in nulliparous, estrogen- primed female rats. *Hormones and Behavior, 18,* 267–286.

Fahrbach, S. E., Morrell, J. I., and Pfaff, D. W. (1985). Possible role for endogenous oxytocin in estrogen-facilitated maternal behavior in rats. *Neuroendocrinology, 40,* 526–532.

Fahrbach, S. E., and Pfaff, D. W. (1986). Effects of preoptic region implants of dilute estradiol on the maternal behavior of ovariectomized, nulliparous rats. *Hormones and Behavior, 20,* 354–363.

Ferreira, A., Hansen, S., Nielsen, M., Archer, T., and Minor, B. G. (1989). Behavior of mother rats in conflict tests sensitive to antianxiety agents. *Behavioral Neuroscience, 103,* 193–201.

Fleming, A. S. (1986). Psychobiology of rat maternal behavior: How and where hormones act to promote maternal behavior at parturition. In B. R. Komisaruk, H. I. Siegel, M-F. Cheng, and H. H. Feder (Eds.), *Reproduction: A Behavioral and Neuroendocrine Perspective* (pp. 234–251). New York: New York Academy of Science.

Fleming, A. S., and Corter, C. M. (1995). Psychobiology of maternal behavior in nonhuman mammals. In M. H. Bornstein (Ed.), *Handbook of parenting: Vol. 2. Biology and Ecology of Parenting* (pp. 59–85). Mahwah, NJ: Lawrence Erlbaum Associates, Publishers.

Fleming, A. S., and Rosenblatt, J. S. (1974a). Maternal behavior in the virgin and lactating rat. *Journal of Comparative and Physiological Psychology, 86,* 957–972.

Fleming, A. S., and Rosenblatt, J. S. (1974b). Olfactory regulation of maternal behavior in rats: I. Effects of olfactory bulb removal in experienced and inexperienced lactating and cycling females. *Journal of Comparative and Physiological Psychology, 86,* 221–232.

Fleming, A. S., and Rosenblatt, J. S. (1974c). Olfactory regulation of maternal behavior in rats: II. Effects of peripherally induced anosmia and lesions of the lateral olfactory tract in pup-induced virgins. *Journal of Comparative and Physiological Psychology, 86,* 233–246.

Gibber, J. R. (1986). Infant-directed behavior of rhesus monkeys during their first pregnancy and parturition. *Folia Primatologica, 46,* 118–124.

Gibber, J. R., and Goy, R. W. (1985). Infant-directed behavior in young rhesus monkeys: Sex differences and effects of prenatal androgens. *American Journal of Primatology, 8,* 225–237.

Gibber, J. R., Piontkewitz, Y., and Terkel, J. (1984). Response of male and female Siberian hamsters towards pups. *Behavioral and Neural Biology, 42,* 177–182.

Gibori, G., Khan, I., Warshaw, M. L., McLean, M. P., Puryear, T. K., Nelson, S., Durkee, T. J., Azhar, S., Steinschneider, A., and Rao, M. C. (1988). Placental-derived regulators and the complex control of luteal cell function. *Recent Progress in Hormone Research, 44,* 377–429.

Gibori, G., Richards, J. S., and Keyes, P. L. (1979). Synergistic effects of prolactin and estradiol in the luteotropic process in the pregnant rat: Regulation of estradiol receptor by prolactin. *Biology of Reproduction, 21,* 419–423.

Giordano, A. L., Ahdieh, H. B., Mayer, A. D., Siegel, H. I., and Rosenblatt, J. S. (1990). Cytosol and nuclear estrogen receptor binding in the preoptic area and hypothalamus of female rats during pregnancy and ovariectomized rats after steroid priming correlation with maternal behavior. *Hormones and Behavior, 24,* 231–255.

Giordano, A. L., Siegel, H. I., and Rosenblatt, J. S. (1989). Nuclear estrogen receptor binding in the preoptic area and hypothalamus of pregnancy-terminated rats: Correlation with the onset of maternal behavior. *Neuroendocrinology, 50,* 248–258.

Gluckman, P. D., Mallard, C., and Boshier, D. P. (1991). The effect of hypothalamic lesions on the length of gestation in fetal sheep. *American Journal of Obstetrics and Gynecology, 165,* 1464–1468.

González-Mariscal, G., Cuamatzi, E., and Rosenblatt, J. S. (1998). Hormones and external factors: Are they "on/off" signals for maternal nestbuilding in rabbits? *Hormones and Behavior, 33,* 1–8.

González-Mariscal, G., Díaz-Sánchez, V., Melo, A. I., Jiménez-Estrada, Beyer, C., and Rosenblatt, J. S. (1994). Maternal behavior in New Zealand white rabbits: Quantification of somatic events, motor patterns, and steroid plasma levels. *Physiology and Behavior, 55*, 1081–1089.

González-Mariscal, G., Melo, A. I., and Beyer, C. (1998). Prolactin receptor-immunoreactivity in female rabbit brain: Variations across the reproductive cycle. *Society of Neuroscience Abstracts, 53*, 6.

González-Mariscal, G., Melo, A. I., Chirino, R., Jiménez, P., Beyer, C., and Rosenblatt, J. S. (1998). Importance of mother/young contact at parturition and across lactation for the expression of maternal behavior in rabbits. *Developmental Psychobiology, 32*, 101–11.

González-Mariscal, G., Melo, A. I., Jiménez, P., Beyer, C., and Rosenblatt, J. S. (1996). Estradiol, progesterone, and prolactin regulate maternal nestbuilding in rabbits. *Journal of Neuroendocrinology, 8*, 901–907.

González-Mariscal, G., Melo, A. I., Jiménez-Estrada, Beyer, C., and Rosenblatt, J. S. (1994). Maternal behavior in rabbits: Description and assessment of the role of steroid hormones. *Physiology and Behavior, 55*, 1081–1089.

González-Mariscal, G., Melo, A. I., Parlow, A. F., Beyer, C., and Rosenblatt, J. S. (2000). Pharmacological evidence that prolactin acts from late gestation to promote maternal behavior in rabbits. *Journal of Neuroendocrinology. 12*, 1–12.

González-Mariscal, G., and Rosenblatt, J. S. (1996). Maternal behavior in rabbits: A historical and multidisciplinary perspective. *Advances in the Study of Behavior, 25*, 333–360.

Goodall, J. (1986). *The chimpanzees of Gombe*. Cambridge, MA: Belknap.

Gubernick, D. J., and Nelson, R. J. (1989). Prolactin and paternal behavior in the biparental California mouse, *Peromyscus californicus. Hormones and Behavior, 23*, 203–210.

Hauser, H., and Gandelman, R. (1985). Lever pressing for pups: Evidence for hormonal influence upon maternal behavior of mice. *Hormones and Behavior, 19*, 454–468.

Heap, R. B., and Flint, A. P. F. (1986). Pregnancy. In C. R. Austin and R. V. Short (Eds.), *Hormonal control of reproduction* (2nd ed., pp. 153–194). Cambridge, MA: Cambridge University Press.

Hudson, R., and Distel, H. (1983). Nipple location by newborn rabbits: Evidence for pheromonal guidance. *Behaviour, 81*, 260–275.

Insel, T. R., and Harbaugh, C. R. (1989). Lesions of the hypothalamic paraventrcular nucleus disrupt the initiation of maternal behavior. *Physiology and Behavior, 45*, 1033–1041.

Jirikowski, G. F., Caldwell, J. D., Pilgrim, C., Stumpf, W. E., and Pedersen, C. A. (1990). Changes in immunostaining for oxytocin in the forebrain of the female rat during late pregnancy, parturition and early lactation. *Cell Tissue Res.* 1989; *256*(2):411–417.

Jirikowski, G. F., Caldwell, J. S., Pilgrim, C., Stumpf, W. E., and Pedersen, C. A. (1989). Changes in immunostaining for oxytocin in the forebrain of the female rat during late pregnancy, parturition and early lactation. *Cell Tissue Research, 256*, 411–417.

Jolly, A. (1966). *Lemur behavior. A Madagascar field study*. Chicago: University of Chicago Press.

Jones, J. S., and Wynne-Edwards, K. E. (2000). Paternal hamsters mechanically assist the delivery, consume amniotic fluid and placenta, remove fetal membranes, and provide parental care during the birth process. *Hormones and Behavior, 37*, 116–125.

Kendrick, K. M., and Keverne, E. B. (1991). Importance of progesterone and estrogen priming for the induction of maternal behavior by vaginal stimulation in sheep: Effects of maternal experience. *Physiolology and Behavior, 49*, 745–750.

Kendrick, K. M., Keverne, E. B., and Baldwin, B. A. (1987). Intracerebroventricular oxytocin stimulates maternal behaviour in the sheep. *Neuroendocrinology, 46*, 56–61.

Kendrick, K. M., Keverne, E. B., Baldwin, B. A., and Sharman, D. F. (1986). Cerebrospinal fluid levels of acetylcholinesterase, monoamines and oxytocin during labour, parturition, vaginocervical stimulation, lamb separation and suckling in sheep. *Brain Research, 439*, 1–10.

Kendrick, K. M., Keverne, E. B., Chapman, C., and Baldwin, B. A. (1988a). Microdialysis measurement of oxytocin, aspartate, amma-aminobutyric acid and glutamate release from the olfactory bulb of the sheep during vaginocervical stimulation. *Brain Research, 442*, 171–174.

Kendrick, K. M., Keverne, E. B., Chapman, C., and Baldwin, B. A. (1988b). Intracranial dialysis measurement of oxytocin, monoamine uric acid release from the olfactory bulb and substantia nigra of sheep during parturition, suckling, separation from lambs and eating. *Brain Research, 439*, 1–10.

Keverne, E. B., Lévy, F., Poindron, P., and Lindsay, D. (1983). Vaginal stimulation: An important determinant of maternal bonding in sheep. *Science, 219*, 81–83.

Kinsley, C. H., and Bridges, R. S. (1990). Morphine treatment and reproductive condition alter olfactory preferences for pup and adult male odors. *Developmental Psychobiology, 23*, 331–347.

Koch, M., and Ehret, G. (1989). Estradiol and parental experience but not prolactin is necessary for ultrasound recognition and pup-retrieving in the mouse. *Physiology and Behavior, 45*, 771–776.

Köller, G. (1955). Hormonale und psychische Steuerung beim Nestbau weiser Mäuse [Hormonal and psychic controls of nest building in the white mouse], *Zoolischer Anzieger (Supplemental volume) 19*, 123–132.

Komisaruk, B. R., Rosenblatt, J. S., Barona, M. L., Chinapen, S., Nissanov, J., O'Bannon III, R. T., Johnson, B. M., and Del Cerro, M. C. (2000). Combined c-*fos* and C-2-deoxyglucose method to differentiate site-specific excitation from disinhibition: analysis of maternal behavior in the rat. *Brain Research, 859*, 262–272.

Krehbiel, D., Poindron, P., Lévy, F., and Prud'Homme, M. J. (1987). Peridural anesthesia disturbs maternal behavior in primiparous and multiparous parturient ewes. *Physiology and Behavior, 40*, 463–472.

Landgraf, R., Neumann, I., Russell, J. A., and Pittman, Q. J. (1990). Push–pull perfusion and microdialysis studies of central oxytocin and vasopressin release in freely moving rats during pregnancy, parturition, and lactation. In C. A. Pedersen, J. D. Caldwell, G. F. Jirikowki, and T. R. Insel (Eds.), *Oxytocin and maternal, sexual, and social behaviors. Annals of the New York Academy of Sciences, 652*, 326–339.

LeBlond, C. P. (1938). Extra-hormonal factors in maternal behavior. *Proceedings of the Society for Experimental Biology, 38*, 66–70.

Lévy, F., Kendrick, K. M., Keverne, E. B., Piketty, V., and Poindron, P. (1992). Intracerebral oxytocin is important for the onset of maternal behavior in inexperienced ewes delivered under peridural anesthesia. *Behavioral Neuroscience, 106*, 427–432.

Lévy, F., Keverne, E. B., Piketty, V., and Poindron, P. (1990). Physiological determinism of olfactory attraction for amniotic fluids in sheep. In D. W. MacDonald, D. Muller-Swarze, and S. E. Natinczuk (Eds.), *Chemical signals in vertebrates*, (Vol. 5, pp. 162–165) Oxford, England: Oxford University Press.

Lévy, F., Poindron, P., and Le Neindre, P. (1983). Attraction and repulsion by amniotic fluids and their olfactory control in the ewe around parturition. *Physiology and Behavior, 31*, 687–692.

Lisk, R. D. (1971). Oestrogen and progesterone synergism and elicitation of maternal nestbuilding in the mouse (*Mus musculus*). *Animal Behaviour, 19*, 606–610.

Lubin, M., Leon, M., Moltz, H., and Numan, M. (1972). Hormones and maternal behavior in the male rat. *Hormones and Behavior, 3*, 369–374.

Lucas, B. K., Ormandy, C. J., Binart, N., Bridges, R. S., and Kelly, P. A. (1998). Null mutation of the prolactin receptor gene produces a defect in maternal behavior. *Endocrinology, 139*, 4102–4107.

Lundblad, E. G., and Hodgen, G. D. (1980). Induction of maternal–infant bonding in rhesus and cynomologous monkeys after Caesarean delivery. *Laboratory Animal Science, 30*, 913.

Maestripieri, D. (1999). Changes in social behavior and their hormonal correlates during pregnancy in pig-tailed macaques. *International Journal of Primatology, 20*, 707–718.

Maestripieri, D., and Zehr, J. L. (1998). Maternal responsiveness increases during pregnancy and after estrogen treatment in macaques. *Hormones and Behavior, 34*, 223–230.

Mayer, A. D., and Rosenblatt, J. S. (1975). Olfactory basis for the delayed onset of maternal behavior in virgin female rats: Experiential basis. *Journal of Comparative and Physiological Psychology, 89*, 701–710.

Mayer, A. D. and Rosenblatt, J. S. (1979). Ontogeny of maternal behavior in the laboratory rat: Early origins in 18–27-day old young. *Developmental Psychobiology, 12*, 407–424.

Mayer, A. D., and Rosenblatt, J. S. (1984). Prepartum changes in maternal responsiveness and nest defense in *Rattus norvegicus*. *Journal of Comparative Psychology, 98*, 177–188.

McCarthy, M. M. (1990). Oxytocin inhibits infanticide in female house mice (*Mus domesticus*). *Hormones and Behavior, 24*, 365–375.

McCarthy, M. M., Bare, J. E., and vom Saal, F. S. (1986). Infanticide and parental behavior in wild female house mice: Effects of ovariectomy, adrenalectomy, and administration of oxytocin and prostaglandin F2 alpha. *Physiology and Behavior, 36*, 17–23.

McCarthy, M. M., Curran, G. H., and Siegel, H. I. (1994). Evidence for the involvement of prolactin in the maternal behavior of the hamster. *Physiology and Behavior, 55*, 181–184.

McDonald, T. J., and Nathanielsz, P. W. (1991). Bilateral destruction of the fetal paraventricular nuclei prolongs gestation in sheep. *American Journal of Obstetrics and Gynecology, 165*, 764–770.

Moltz, H., Lubin, M., Leon, M., and Numan, M. (1970). Hormonal induction of maternal behavior in the ovariectomized nulliparous rat. *Physiology and Behavior, 5*, 1373–1377.

Mota, M. T., and Sousa, M. B. (2000). Prolactin levels in fathers and helpers related to alloparental care in common marmosets, *callithrix jacchus*. *Folia Primatology (Basel), 71*, 22–26.

Nathanielsz , P. W. (1998). Comparative studies on the initiation of labor. *European Journal of Obstetrics, Gynecology, and Reproductive Biology, 78*, 127–132.

Nelson, E., and Panksepp, J. (1996). Oxytocin mediates acquisition of maternally associated odor preferences in preweanling rat pups. *Behavioral Neuroscience, 110*, 583–592.

Nishimori, K., Young, L. J., Guo, Q., Wang, Z., Insel, T. R., and Matzuk, M. M. (1996). Oxytocin is required for nursing but is not essential for parturition or reproductive behavior. *Proceedings of the National Academy of Sciences, U.S.A., 93*, 699–704.

Numan, M. (1974). Medial preoptic area and maternal behavior in the female rat. *Jounal of Comparative and Physiological Psychology, 87*, 746–759.

Numan, M. (1978). Progesterone inhibition of maternal behavior in the rat. *Hormones and Behavior, 11*, 209–231.

Numan, M., Roach, J. K., del Cerro, M. C. R., Guillamón, A., Segovia, S., Sheehan, T. P., and Numan, M. J. (1999). Expression of intracellular progesterone receptors in rat brain during different reproducive states, and involvement in maternal behavior. *Brain Research, 830,* 358–371.

Numan, M., Rosenblatt, J. S., and Komisaruk, B. R. (1977). Medial preoptic area and onset of maternal behavior in the rat. *Journal of Comparative and Physiological Psychology, 91,* 146–164.

Olazabal, D. E., and Ferreira, A. (1997). Maternal behavior in rats with kainic acid-induced lesions of the hypothalamic paraventricular nucleus. *Physiology and Behavior, 61,* 779–784.

Ormandy, C. J., Camus, A., Barra, J., Damotte, D., Lucas, B., Buteau, H., Edery, M., Brousse, N., Babinet, C., Binart, N., and Kelly, P. A. (1997). Null mutation of the prolactin receptor produces multiple defects in the mouse. *Genes and Development, 11,* 167–178.

Pedersen, C. A., Caldwell, J. D., Johnson, M. F., Fort, S. A., and Prange, A. J., Jr. (1985). Oxytocin antiserum delays onset of ovarian steroid-induced maternal behavior. *Neuropeptides, 6,* 175–182.

Pedersen, C. A., and Prange, A. J., Jr. (1979). Induction of maternal behavior in virgin rats after intracerebroventricular administration of oxytocin. *Proceedings of the National Academy of Sciences, U.S.A., 76,* 6661–6665.

Perry, E. A., and Stenson, G. B. (1992). Observations on nursing behaviour of hooded seals, *Cystophora cristata. Behaviour, 122,* 1–10.

Pi, X. J., and Grattan, D. R. (1998). Differential expression of the two forms of prolactin receptor mRNA within microdissected hypothalamic nuclei of the rat. *Brain Reseach Molecular Brain Reseach, 15,* 1–12.

Poindron, P., and P., Le Neindre (1980). Endocrine and sensory regulation of maternal behaviour in the ewe. *Advances in the Study of Behavior, 11,* 75–119.

Pryce, C. R. (1992). A comparative systems model of the regulation of maternal motivation in mammals. *Animal Behavior, 43,* 417–444.

Pryce, C. R. (1996). Socialization, hormones, and the regulation of maternal behavior in nonhuman simian primates. *Advances in the Study of Behavior, 25,* 423–473.

Pryce, C. R., Abbott, D. H., Hodges, J. K., and Martin, R. D. (1988). Maternal behavior is related to prepartum urinary estradiol levels in red-bellied tamarin monkeys. *Physiology and Behavior, 44,* 717–726.

Pryce, C. R., Döbeli, M., and Martin, R. D. (1993). Effects of sex steroids on maternal motivation in the common marmoset (*Callithrix jacchus*): Development and application of an operant system with maternal reinforcement. *Journal of Comparative Psychology, 107,* 99–115.

Reisbick, S., Rosenblatt, J. S., and Mayer, A. D. (1975). Decline in maternal behavior in the virgin and lactating rat. *Journal of Comparative and Physiological Psychology, 89,* 722–732.

Richards, M. P. M. (1969). Effects of estrogen and progesterone on nestbuilding in the golden hamster. *Animal Behavior, 17,* 356–361.

Riddle, O., Lahr, E. L., and Bates, R. W. (1942). The role of hormones in the initiation of maternal behavior in rats. *American Journal of Physiology, 137,* 299–317.

Rodriguez-Sierra, J. F., and Rosenblatt, J. S. (1977). Does prolactin play a role in estrogen-induced maternal behavior in rats: Apomorphine reduction of prolactin release. *Hormones and Behavior, 9,* 1–7.

Rosenblatt, J. S. (1967). Nonhormonal basis of maternal behavior in the rat. *Science, 156,* 1512–1514.

Rosenblatt, J. S. (1990). A psychobiological approach to maternal behaviour among the primates. In P. Bateson (Ed.), *The development and integration of behaviour* (pp. 191–222). Cambridge, England: Cambridge, University Press.

Rosenblatt, J. S. (1992). Hormone-behavior relationships in the regulation of parental behavior. In J. Becker, D. Crews, and S. M. Breedlove (Eds.), *Behavioral endocrinology* (pp. 219–259). Cambridge, MA: MIT Press.

Rosenblattt, J. S., and Ceus, K. (1998). Estrogen implants in the medial preoptic area stimulate maternal behavior in male rats. *Hormones and Behavior, 33,* 23–30.

Rosenblatt, J. S., Hazelwood, S., and Poole, J. (1996). Maternal behavior in male rats: Effects of medial preoptic area lesions and presence of maternal aggression. *Hormones and Behavior, 30,* 201–215.

Rosenblatt, J. S., and Mayer, A. D. (1995). An analysis of approach/withdrawal processes in the initiation of maternal behavior in the laboratory rat. In K. E. Hood (Ed.), *Behavioral development in comparative perspective: The approach/withdrawal theory of T. C. Schneirla* (pp. 177–230). New York: Garland.

Rosenblatt, J. S., Olufowobi, A., and Siegel, H. I. (1998). Effects of pregnancy hormones on maternal responsiveness to estrogen stimulation. *Hormones and Behavior, 33,* 104–114.

Rosenblatt, J. S., and Siegel, H. I. (1975). Hysterectomy-induced maternal behavior during pregnancy in the rat, *Journal of Comparative and Physiological Psychology, 89,* 685–700.

Rosenblum, L. A. (1972). Sex and age differences in response to infant squirrel monkeys. *Brain, Behavior, and Evolution, 5,* 30–40.

Roth, L. L., and Rosenblatt, J. S. (1967). Changes in self-licking during pregnancy in the rat. *Journal of Comparative and Physiological Psychology, 63,* 397–400.

Roth, L. L., and Rosenblatt, J. S. (1968). Self-licking and mammary development during pregnancy in the rat. *Journal of Endocrinology, 42,* 363–378.

Rubin, B. S., Menniti, F. S., and Bridges, R. S. (1983). Intracerebroventricular administration of oxytocin and maternal behavior in rats after prolonged and acute steroid pretreatment. *Hormones and Behavior, 17*, 45–53.

Saito, T. R., Takahashi, K. W., and Imamichi, T. (1983). Role of progesterone and prolactin in the maternal nestbuilding of mice. *Zoological Magazine, 92*, 342–355.

Saito,T. R., and Takahashi, K. W. (1980). Studies on maternal behavior in the mouse. III. The maternal behavior of pregnant mice. *Japanese Journal of Animal Reproduction, 26*, 43–45.

Schneider, J. E., and Wade, G. N. (1991). Effects of ambient temperature and body fat content on maternal litter reduction in Syrian hamsters. *Physiology and Behavior, 49*, 135–139.

Schneirla, T. C. (1965). Aspects of stimulation and organization in approach/withdrawal processes underlying vertebrate behavioral development. *Advances in the Study of Behavior, 1*, 1–74.

Seyoum, G., Robertson, M. C., Persaud, T. V., Paterson, J. A., and Shiu R. P. (1999). Influence of rat placental lactogen-I on the development of whole rat embryos in culture. *Journal of Endocrinology, 160*, 231–237.

Sheehan, T. P., Cirrito, J., Numan, M. J., and Numan, M. (2000). Using c-Fos immunochemistry to identify forebrain regions that may inhibit maternal behavior in rats. *Behavioral Neuroscience, 114*, 337–352.

Shughrue, P. J., Lane, M. V., and Merchenthaler, I. (1997). Regulation of progesterone receptor messenger ribonucleic acid in the rat medial preoptic nucleus by estrogenic and antiestrogenic compounds: An in situ hybridization study. *Endocrinology, 138*, 5476–5484.

Siegel, H. I. (1985). Parental behavior. In H. I. Siegel (Ed.), *The hamster. Reproduction and behavior* (pp. 207–228). New York: Plenum.

Siegel, H. I., Clark, M. C., and Rosenblatt, J. S. (1983). Maternal responsiveness during pregnancy in the hamster (*Mesocricetus auratus*). *Animal Behavior, 31*, 497–502.

Siegel, H. I., and Rosenblatt, J. S. (1975a). Hormonal basis of hysterectomy-induced maternal behavior during pregnancy in the rat. *Hormones and Behavior, 62*, 211–222.

Siegel, H. I., and Rosenblatt, J. S. (1975b). Estrogen-induced maternal behavior in hysterectomized-ovariectomized virgin rats. *Physiology and Behavior, 14*, 465–471.

Siegel, H. I., and Rosenblatt, J. S. (1978, June). Short-latency induction of maternal behavior in nulliparous hamsters. Paper presented at the Eastern Conference on Reproductive Behavior, Madison, WI.

Siegel, H. I., and Rosenblatt, J. S. (1979). Hormonal and behavioral aspects of maternal care in the hamster: A review. *Neuroscience Biobehavioral Reviews, 4*, 17–26.

Slotnick, B. M., Carpenter, M. L., and Fusco, R. (1973). Initiation of maternal behavior in pregnant nulliparous rats. *Hormones and Behavior, 4*, 53–59.

Smith, P. E. (1954). Continuation of pregnancy in rhesus monkeys (*Macaca mulatta*) following hypophysectomy. *Endocrinology, 55*, 655–664.

Smith, R. (1999). The timing of birth. *Scientific American, 279*, 68–75.

Stern, J. M. (1983). Maternal behavior priming in virgin and Caesarean-delivered Long-Evans rats: Effects of brief contact or continuous exteroceptive pup stimulation. *Physiology and Behavior, 31*, 757–763.

Stern, J. M. (1996). Somatosensation and maternal care in Norway rats. *Advances in the Study of Behavior, 25*, 243–294.

Sturgis, J. D., and Bridges, R. S. (1997) *N*-methyl-DL-aspartic acid lesions of the medial preoptic area disrupt ongoing parental behavior in male rats. *Physiology and Behavior, 62*, 305–310.

Sugiyama, T., Minoura, H., Kawabe, N., Tanaka, M., and Nakashima, K. (1994). Preferential expression of long form prolactin receptor mRNA in the rat brain during the oestrous cycle, pregnancy and lactation: Hormones involved in gene expression. *Journal of Endocrinology, 141*, 325–333.

Swanson, L. J., and Campbell, C. S. (1979). Induction of maternal behavior in nulliparous golden hamsters (*Mesocricetus auratus*). *Behavioral and Neural Biology, 26*, 364–371.

Terkel, J. (1988). Neuroendocrine processes in the establishment of pregnancy and pseudopregnancy. *Psychoneuroendocrinology, 13*, 5–28.

Terkel, J., and Rosenblatt, J. S. (1971). Aspects of nonhormonal maternal behavior in the rat. *Hormones and Behavior, 2*, 161–171.

Terrazas, A., Ferreira, G., Lévy, F., Nowak, R., Serafin, R., Orgeur, P., Soto, R., and Poindron, P. (1999). Do ewes recognize their lambs within the first day postpartum without the help of olfactory cues? *Behavioural Processes, 47*, 19–29.

Tinklepaugh, O. L., and Hartman, K. G. (1930). Behavioral aspects of parturition in the monkey (*Macaca rhesus*). *Comparative Psychology, 11*, 63–98.

van Leengoed, E., Kerker, E., and Swanson, H. H. (1987). Inhibition of post-partum maternal behaviour in the rat by injecting an oxytocin antagonist into the cerebral ventricles. *Journal of Endocrinology, 112*, 275–282.

Voci, V. E., and Carlson, N. R. (1973). Enhancement of maternal behavior and nest building following systemic and diencephalic administration of prolactin and progesterone in the mouse. *Journal of Comparative and Physiological Psycholology, 83*, 388–393.

Walsh, R. J., Slaby, F. J., and Posner, B. I. (1987). A receptor-mediated mechanism for the transport of prolactin from blood to cerebrospinal fluid. *Endocrinology, 120*, 1846–1850.

Wamboldt, M. Z., and Insel, R. T. (1987). The ability of oxytocin to induce short latency maternal behavior is dependent on peripheral anosmia. *Behavioral Neuroscience, 101*, 439–441.

Wang, Z. X., Liu, Y., Young, L. J., and Insel, T. R. (2000). Hypothalamic vasopressin gene expression increases in both males and females postpartum in a biparental parent. *Journal of Neuroendocrinology, 12*, 111–120.

Wang, Z., Young, L. J., De Vries, G. J., and Insel, T. R. (1998). Voles and vasopressin: A review of molecular, cellular, and behavioral studies of pair bonding and paternal behaviors. *Progress in Brain Research, 119*, 483–499.

Wiesner, B. P., and Sheard, N. M. (1933). *Maternal behaviour in the rat.* London: Oliver and Boyd.

Wilson, N. E., and Stricker, E. M. (1979). Thermal homeostasis in pregnant rats during heat stress. *Journal of Comparative and Physiological Psychology, 93*, 585–594.

Wise, D. A., and Pryor T. L. (1977). Effects of ergocornine and prolactin on aggression in the postpartum golden hamster. *Hormones and Behavior, 8*, 30–39.

Woodside, B., and Jans, J. E. (1988). Neuroendocrine basis of thermally regulated maternal responses to young in the rat. *Psychoneuroendocrinology, 13*, 79–98.

Woodside, B., Pelchat, R., and Leon, M. (1980). Acute elevation of the heat load of mother rats curtails maternal nest bouts. *Endocrinology, 9*, 61–68.

Yeo, J. A. G., and Keverne, E. G. (1986). The importance of vaginal–cervical stimulation for maternal behaviour in the rat. *Physiology and Behavior, 37*, 23–26.

Yoshimura, R., Kiyama, H., Kimura, T. Araki, T., Maeno, H., Tanizawa, O., and Tohyama, M. (1993). Localization of oxytocin receptor message ribonucleic acid in the rat brain. *Endocrinology, 133*, 1239–1246.

Young, L. J., Muns, S. Wang, Z., and Insel, T. R. (1997). Changes in oxytocin mRNA in rat brain during pregnancy and the effect of estrogen and interleukin-6. *Journal of Neuroendocrinology, 9*, 859–865.

Yu, G.-Z., Kaba, H., Okutani, F., Takahashi, S., and Higuchi, T. (1996). The olfactory bulb: A critical site of action for oxytocin in the induction of maternal behaviour in the rat. *Neuroscience, 72*, 1083–1088.

Yu, G.-Z., Kaba, H., Okutani, F., Takahashi, S., Higuchi, T., and Seto, K. (1996). The action of oxytocin originating in the hypothalamic paraventricular nucleus on mitral and granule cells in the rat main olfactory bulb. *Neuroscience, 72*, 1073–1082.

Zarrow, M. X., Denenberg, V. H., and Anderson, C. O. (1965). Rabbit: Frequency of suckling in the pup. *Science, 150*, 1835–1836.

Zarrow, M. X., Gandelman, R. T., and Denenberg, V. H. (1971). Prolactin: Is it an essential hormone for maternal behavior in mammals? *Hormones and Behavior, 2*: 343–354.

Zarrow, M. X., Sawin, P. B., Ross S., and Denenberg, V. H. (1962). Maternal behavior and its endocrine basis in the rabbit. In E. L. Bliss (Ed.), *Roots of behavior* (pp. 187–197). New York: Harper.

Ziegler, T. E., Wegner, F. S., and Snowdon, C. T. (1996). Hormonal responses to parental and nonparental conditions in male cotton–top tamarins, *Saguinus oedipus*, a New World primate. *Hormones and Behavior, 30*, 287–297.

3

Psychobiology of Maternal Behavior and Its Early Determinants in Nonhuman Mammals

Alison S. Fleming

Ming Li

University of Toronto

INTRODUCTION

Mammalian mothers of different species may differ in the extent to which physiological or psychological factors contribute to the postpartum expression of their nurturant behavior. In all species that have been studied, however, the physiological determinants are realized only in individuals who have had certain developmental histories and who are psychologically "prepared" by their physical and psychological environments (Rosenblatt and Snowdon, 1996). In many mammalian species, the hormonal changes associated with late pregnancy and parturition predispose the newly parturient female to be nurturant with her offspring, to nurse, clean, and protect them (see Rosenblatt, in Vol. 2 of this *Handbook*). However, whether these nurturant behaviors in fact occur at the appropriate time and in the appropriate way depends on a host of psychological factors. Enhanced morbidity or mortality of young or reduced responsiveness by mammalian mothers occurs if mothers are stressed during pregnancy or parturition, severely food deprived, or are placed in low-resource environments (Lyons, Kim, Schatzberg, and Levine, 1998), if ambient temperature precipitously rises, if pups are sickly, or if the nesting area is inadequate (Herskin, Jensen, and Thodberg, 1998; Kinsley, 1990; Leon, Coopersmith, Beasley, and Sullivan, 1990). However, mothers are also quite robust; to eliminate maternal behavior entirely, environmental restrictions or debilitations experienced by mothers have to be quite extreme (Aubert, Goodall, Dantzer, and Gheusi, 1997; McQuire, Pachon, Butler, and Rasmussen, 1995). In sheep, the specific odor characteristics of the young, as well as the mother sheep's earliest postpartum experiences, also determine whether hormone-induced responsiveness is expressed in nurturance and maternal behavior or in rejection (Lévy, Kendrick, Keverne, Proter, and Romeyer, 1996; Poindron and Lévy, 1990). In primates, examples of the importance of interactive influences of early experiences and hormones on mothering are still more pronounced. Harlow's "motherless" monkeys, raised in social isolation and on wire mothers or monkeys who were young and inexperienced, neglected or battered their own (usually first) offspring, despite having apparently normal pregnancies and childbirths (Coe, 1990; Harlow, 1963; Ruppenthal, Arling, Harlow, Sackett, and Suomi, 1976). In human beings, a host of background and psychological factors increase risk of mothering disorders, including poverty, low education, social isolation, lack of supports, immaturity, and being themselves victims of abuse (Moore and Brooks-Gunn, in Vol. 3 of this *Handbook*; Cochran and Niego, in Vol. 4 of this *Handbook*; Daly, 1990; Eisenberg, 1990; Magnuson and Duncan, in Vol. 4 of this *Handbook*).

These examples indicate that, even in "lower" species and situations in which hormones exert clear and powerful influences on maternal behavior, the behaviors will not occur or will be masked by competing responses, given dysfunctional past or present experiences. Conversely, in primates and human beings, in particular, the clear importance of these background and situational factors may seem to mask the role of biological factors in early mothering; however, a variety of approaches detailed by Corter and Fleming (in Vol. 2 of this *Handbook*) help to unmask contributions of these biological influences.

In this chapter we focus on the interaction between psychological and physiological influences in the expression of maternal behavior and in its development in nonhuman mammalian mothers. We discuss experiential, sensory, neural, and early experience factors that regulate maternal behavior in nonprimate mammals (rats primarily). This chapter follows quite directly from discussions of hormonal mechanisms regulating the onset of responsiveness (see Rosenblatt, in Vol. 2 of this *Handbook*). The specific approach adapted here assumes that maternal behavior is not regulated in a unitary fashion, but depends for its expression on activation of a variety of behavioral systems, mediated by multiple neurochemical and neuranatomical substrates. It assumes further that hormones do not automatically trigger behavior, but instead that they act on substrates whose activation is influenced by the animal's social–psychological and physical environments, both present and past. We argue that the development of the capacity to both express and modify maternal behavior patterns in adulthood depends on mechanisms that were themselves activated and later tuned by early experience. The interaction between newborn and mother alters the basic mechanism of behavioral expression in both. How the mother responds determines, in part, how the neurobiological and the behavioral changes in the infant proceeds. Changes in an infant may eventually play out as to how the individual will respond to his or her offspring as an adult, and so on. In this chapter, the maternal behavior of rodents receives considerably more attention than maternal behavior in other nonprimate mammals. This orientation is based on a number of considerations. First, comparisons among rat and other nonprimate mammals (for which appropriate data exist) show many similarities in physiological regulation of parenting. In addition, most research on mechanisms of maternal behavior focuses on *Rattus norvegicus* mothers, and, as a result, understanding of this species is more complete. Finally, despite large differences in cognitive organization between the two, the rat has proved to be a productive model for the analysis of human maternal behavior and has provided insights into possible mechanisms at work in human beings (Corter and Fleming, 1990; Fleming, Ruble, Krieger, and Wong, 1997; Fleming, Steiner, and Corter, 1997). However, because of the extent of research on rodent maternal behavior, this review does not attempt to be complete and exhaustive (see too Krasnegor and Bridges, 1990; Numan, 1994; Rosenblatt and Snowdon, 1996; Stern, 1989).

This chapter is divided into a number of sections. The first part describes the basic techniques used in the study of maternal behavior. The second part discusses the effects of the maternal hormones on maternal behavior and on other behaviors that undergo change when a female gives birth. This part also describes the transition that occurs in the regulation of maternal behavior after the initial period of hormonal priming and emphasizes factors regulating the long-term maintenance of maternal behavior. In this section the roles of learning, memory, and reinforcement are considered. The third part of the chapter considers the role of sensory factors in the onset and maintenance of maternal behavior, with particular attention given to olfactory and somatosensory input during mother–litter interactions. The fourth and the fifth parts of the chapter describe in considerable detail what we know about the neurochemistry and the neuroanatomy of maternal behavior and of other behaviors that co-occur with maternal behavior in the postpartum animal. The sixth section describes recent work on the ontogeny of maternal behavior and its underlying neurobiology, with a short subsection devoted to gene effects. The final part of the chapter summarizes some of the main themes raised in the chapter and issues yet to be explored.

METHODOLOGICAL ISSUES

The popularity of the rat as the animal of choice in the analysis of the physiology of parenting is based on both practical and scientific considerations. The laboratory rat is an easy animal to breed, care for, and test. Its use permits the application of experimental manipulations, providing greater control over physiological or psychobiological variables than is possible with nonlaboratory animals, primate models, or human beings. For instance, to understand the role of hormones in the regulation of parenting, we can analyze the behavior before and after the removal of the gland that produces the suspected hormone or before and after the administration (by injection or capsule) of the suspected hormone. Using a similar "extirpation and replacement" paradigm, we can evaluate the involvement of different sensory systems or different neural circuits in behavioral regulation by observing behavior before and after the destruction of specific neuronal cell groups within the brain by a variety of lesioning techniques or by use of antagonist drugs that block the functioning of specific neurotransmitters in the brain. Conversely, we can attempt to augment or facilitate the expression of the behavior in initially nonmaternal animals by the application of electrical, hormonal, or agonist neurochemical stimulation that mimics the action of naturally occurring neurotransmitters. In some cases, in which a longitudinal design is impractical, different groups sustaining different experimental and control conditions are compared in their responses. Thus, for instance, we might test the behavior of a group of animals that have been injected with a particular hormone or chemical that we suspect is normally released when animals become maternal at parturition and compare their maternal behavior with the behavior shown by a control group of animals which have received injections containing a related but biologically inert substance.

Convergent with these invasive experimental approaches, we can also undertake correlational, rather than experimental, analyses and relate changes in physiology to changes in ongoing behavior; thus we can explore electrical events or hormonal or neurochemical changes that occur when an animal expresses maternal behavior. For instance, recent innovations in technology permit the measurement, by a technique called microdialysis, of neurotransmitters that are released during ongoing behavior. Alternatively, by means of immunocytochemical staining techniques, we can determine whether particular proteins, neuropeptides, or other brain chemicals are produced in the mother's brain in response to interactions with offspring. The role of early experiences in the development of the behavior can be studied by a comparison of adult behavior and neurobiology of animals that have been raised under different early environmental conditions, with or without a mother or siblings or with and without certain nest-related cues. Effects of adverse early experiences prenatally as well as postnatally can be assessed by evaluation of the adult behavior of offspring of mothers who are stressed, malnourished, or who are administered agents or toxins, like cocaine or alcohol. The effects of genotype and these maternal effects can then be parceled out by a comparison of animals that have been raised by their own mothers and those raised by foster mothers. Finally, least well formulated are the technologies associated with establishing which genes or gene complexes regulate adult maternal behavior. Strategies that have been used to study heredity and genetic factors in the regulation of maternal behavior include a comparison of different strains, cross fostering within and between strains, the analysis of transgenic mice mutants that lack specific genes (so-called knockout mice) that underlie the production of specific proteins and receptors in brain that are involved in the expression of maternal behavior (Crusio and Gerlai, 1999) and use of molecular techniques that assess activation of particular genes during ongoing behavior (Lytton with Gallagher, in Vol. 1 of this *Handbook*). In the discussion that follows many of these techniques, strategies, or approaches previously described have been adapted to augment our understanding of the physiology of parenting. To facilitate navigation through the somewhat more technical portions of this chapter we provide a brief description of the relevant terminology and techniques at the beginning of some of the more technical sections.

DESCRIPTION OF MATERNAL BEHAVIOR AT PARTURITION

Although the study of maternal behavior in rodents has generated a smaller literature than has the study of many of the other species-typical behaviors, it is by no means a new area of interest. In fact, some of the most detailed and informative descriptions of the rat mother–litter interactions were provided by Wiesner and Sheard in their seminal book titled *Maternal Behaviour in the Rat*, published in 1933.

From this long history of research, we have a relatively complete picture of the phenomenology of rat maternal behavior. The new mother rat is maternally responsive to newborn pups as soon as they emerge from the birth canal (Hudson, Cruz, Lucio, Ninomiya, and Martinez-Gomez, 1999; Rosenblatt and Lehrman, 1963). At the parturition, she pulls off the amniotic sac, eats the placentas, and cleans off the pups (Hudson et al., 1999; Kristal, Thompson, Heller, and Komisaruk, 1986). Within the first 30 min after parturition, she gathers all the pups together, retrieves them to a nest site, mouths and licks them, and adopts a nursing posture over them; she does all this without prior experience of interacting with pups (Fleming and Rosenblatt, 1974a). Moreover, the high motivational state of the new mother is illustrated by observations that, if new mothers are prevented from actively exhibiting these proactive maternal behaviors (by application of a muzzle over their snouts), they nevertheless spend considerable time nudging and pushing at the pups and manipulating them with their forepaws (Stern and Keer, 1999). The virgin animal, by contrast, is not maternally responsive when first presented with newborn foster pups (Rosenblatt, 1967; Wiesner and Sheard, 1933). In fact, initially she moves away from them and actively avoids them (Fleming and Luebke, 1981; Terkel and Rosenblatt, 1971). However, within 1 to 2 days of continuous pup stimulation, the virgin becomes habituated to pups and is willing to lie down in close proximity to them (Fleming and Luebke, 1981; Fleming and Rosenblatt, 1974a; Terkel and Rosenblatt, 1971); after 5 to 10 days of continuous contact with foster pups, the virgin eventually begins to respond maternally (Rosenblatt, 1967), showing a pattern of behavior that resembles that of the new mother, but also showing some differences (Lonstein and De Vries, 1999). This procedure has come to be known as pup induction or pup sensitization.

HORMONAL EFFECTS ON THE ONSET OF MATERNAL BEHAVIOR

Although early endocrine studies (Beach and Wilson, 1963; Lott and Fuchs, 1962; Riddle, Lahr, and Bates, 1935) did not provide conclusive evidence for endocrine involvement in the regulation of maternal behavior, the studies provided an approach to the analysis of the hormonal control of behavior by use of extirpation and replacement strategies. As described by Rosenblatt (in Vol. 2 of this *Handbook*), there is now substantial evidence that the hormones associated with late pregnancy and the parturitional period acting on brain receptors (Numan, 1994) account for the rapid activation of maternal responsiveness seen at parturition (see Terkel and Rosenblatt, 1972); these include the steroid hormones, estradiol and progesterone, which are synthesized by the ovaries and released into the circulatory system, as well as the protein hormones, prolactin and oxytocin, which are released within the brain and from cells or nerve terminals within the "master" endocrine organ, the pituitary gland (see Bridges, 1990; Insel, 1990; Numan, 1994; Rosenblatt, in Vol. 2 of this *Handbook*, Rosenblatt, 1990; Rosenblatt and Snowdon, 1996). Associated with parturition, there also occurs a release of the hypothalamic neurohormones, oxytocin, norepinephrine, and gamma-aminobutyric acid (GABA), and a decline in preoptic β-endorphins (Bridges, 1990; Caldwell, Greer, Johnson, Prange, and Pedersen, 1987; Insel, 1990; Keverne and Kendrick, 1990; Rosenberg, Leidahl, Halaris, and Moltz, 1976; Stafisso-Sandoz, Polley, Holt, Lambert, and Kinsley, 1998; Young, Muns, Wang, and Insel, 1997). These neurohormones are synthesized by brain cells and are released by their nerve terminals. They act either as neurotransmitters across the junctions between two nerve cells, altering the neural activity of the receiving neurons, or they exert modulatory effects, changing the probability that nerve cells will become activated by other stimuli or hormones.

These hormones and neurochemicals serve multiple functions. They prepare the prospective mother physiologically by acting on mammary tissue before the initiation of lactation (Tucker, 1988) and by acting on the uteri, first, to maintain the integrity of the implanted conceptus and then to promote uterine contractions and parturition as well as analgesia during the birth process (Challis and Olson, 1988; Hodgen and Itskovitz, 1988; Kristal et al., 1986). As documented by Rosenblatt (in Vol. 2 of this *Handbook*), these hormones also contribute to elevated maternal responsiveness shown by the newly parturient mother (Bridges, 1990; Insel, 1990; Rosenblatt, 1990). When a regimen of hormones designed to simulate these pregnancy and parturitional changes is administered to maternally inexperienced virgins through injection or by silastic capsules or into the brain directly, it acts on the brain to induce a very rapid onset of retrieval, crouching, and licking in response to foster pups (Bridges, 1990; Insel, 1990; Rosenblatt, 1990).

Although the parturitional hormones might seem to activate maternal behavior in a unitary fashion, in fact the different hormones and neurochemicals probably exert somewhat different behavioral effects, and any one hormone or neurochemical probably exerts multiple effects. Moreover, their varied effects probably result from their action on a variety of different neural pathways. For instance, the hormones progesterone and estradiol might facilitate the expression of maternal behavior by altering a number of behavioral propensities, and these alterations provide the behavioral environment in which maternal responses can be most easily expressed (Fleming, 1987; Fleming and Corter, 1988). Specifically, as shown schematically in Fig. 3.1, these hormones promote changes in the female's attraction to the odors of pups, reduce her fearfulness in their presence, and facilitate the ease with which she learns about their characteristics, possibly by augmenting the pups' reinforcing value. Together, these hormonal effects are seen to augment maternal responsiveness indirectly during the periparturitional period by reducing the competing effects of alternative nonmaternal behaviors and by ensuring that dams will continue to respond to pups when the period of hormonal priming ends.

Thus, as discussed in the next two subsections, postpartum animals differ from virgins on a number of psychological dimensions because of the action of hormones.

Emotional Changes in the New Mother

Naturally parturient females are less avoidant when presented with pups than are virgin animals. More generally, they are less neophobic, being more willing to approach an unfamiliar intruder and to enter and explore a novel environment (Fleming and Luebke, 1981). Among mice, Ghiraldi and Svare (in Svare, 1990) reported a postpartum "docility" that permits females to remate with males during a postpartum estrus. These emotionality differences appear to be hormonally mediated; the regimen of progesterone and estradiol that facilitates maternal behavior in the virgin rat also reduces pup avoidance and measures of timidity in an open-field apparatus (Fleming, Cheung, Myhal, and Kessler, 1989). Moreover, there is now a substantial literature that shows marked hyporesponsiveness of the stress system in lactating animals and differences between virgin and lactating females in their hypothalamic–pituitary–adrenal (HPA) responses to stressors, in which virgins show an enhanced stressor-induced release of corticosterone, adrenocorticotropic hormone (ACTH), and an enhanced baseline corticotropin-releasing factor (CRF) in the paraventricular nucleus region of the hypothalamus (Neumann et al., 1998; Windle et al., 1997). Moreover, these HPA differences are associated with differences in a variety of emotionality tasks (Neumann et al., 1998; Silva, Bernardi, Nasello,

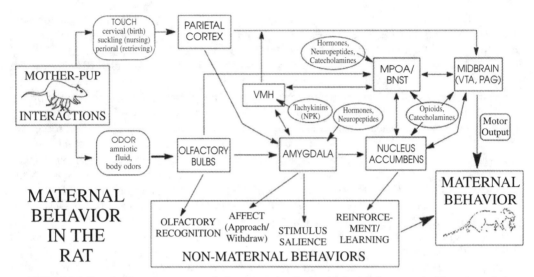

FIGURE 3.1. Functional neuroanatomy mediating maternal and related behaviors in mammals. Neuroanatomical structures include olfactory bulbs, amygdala, nucleus accumbens, bed nucleus of the stria terminalis (BNST), medial preoptic area (MPOA), ventromedial hypothalamus (VMH), midbrain, and parietal cortex. Relevant neurochemistry includes the catecholamines, NE, and dopamine, the neuropeptides, and the opioids (adapted from Fleming, O'Day, and Kraemer, 1999).

and Felicio, 1997). Finally, the assumption that reduced timidity contributes to elevated maternal responsiveness is supported by findings that drugs or manipulations that reduce the animals' timidity or anxiety, like benzodiazepines (Hansen, Ferreira, and Selart, 1985) or early handling (Mayer, 1983), also facilitate maternal responding. As well, Panesar and Fleming (2000) found that high concentrations of glucocorticoids injected into an adrenalectomized virgin animal inhibits the expression of many components of pup-induced maternal behavior, whereas the same high concentration facilitates maternal behavior in the postpartum animal.

Sensory Changes in the New Mother

In addition to their effects on the dam's affective state, parturitional hormones also alter her responsiveness to pup-related cues. In the following discussion we first describe hormonal effects on olfactory-mediated responses and then on their somatosensory processing.

Odor cues. The study of the sensory control of maternal behavior was begun by Beach and Jaynes in 1956; it involved observing maternal behavior in experienced mother rats after the systematic removal of the different sensory systems, either singly or in combination (Beach and Jaynes, 1956a, 1956b). This early study suggested that no single sensory system is essential for the expression of the behavior but that their combined removal produces additive deficits, leading Beach and Jaynes to conclude that maternal behavior is under multisensory control. Although these results seem to apply quite well to animals who have had maternal experience, we now know that single denervations of a number of sensory systems can have quite profound effects on the expression of maternal behavior in the maternally inexperienced animal (Fleming and Rosenblatt, 1974a; Stern, 1989) and that specific sensory cues from the pups play an important role both in motivating responsiveness and in guiding ongoing behavior.

Compared with virgins, new mothers without direct experience with pups prefer nest material taken from the nest of a new mother and her pups to material taken from a virgin's nest or clean material. Virgins show no such preference (Bauer, 1983; Fleming et al., 1989). Moreover, virgins treated with a regimen of hormones designed to mimic the parturitional changes in progesterone and estradiol also exhibit a preference for pup-related odors (Fleming et al., 1989); the additional observation that injections of morphine can induce an aversion to pup odors (Bridges, 1990; Kinsley and Bridges, 1988; Kinsley, Morse, Zoumas, Corl, and Billack, 1995) suggests that, at the time of parturition, low concentrations of this neurochemical in relevant parts of the brain permits heightened attraction to pup-related odors. Experience with these odors can facilitate maternal responses; adult virgin rats show more rapid maternal inductions if they have been preexposed to pup odors and vocalizations during their early development (Gray and Chesley, 1984; Moretto, Paclik, and Fleming, 1986). Although difficult to demonstrate, it seems that preexposure to pup cues at a distance (primarily odors and vocalizations) in adulthood also facilitates maternal responses, at least among females whose responsiveness is high to begin with. Thus a higher proportion of animals exhibits immediate maternal behavior during maternal tests if they have been preexposed to pup odors than if they have not been (Orpen and Fleming, 1987). Finally, if virgins are rendered unable to smell pups by olfactory bulb removal, which mediates the sense of smell, they are not avoidant with pups, but instead exhibit a very rapid onset of maternal behavior, as though the pups' odors in the context of other pup cues are aversive (Fleming and Rosenblatt, 1974b, 1974c; Fleming, Vaccarino, Tambosso, and Chee, 1979).

In rats, we have no idea which specific pups or pup-related odors influence the dam's attraction to pups, although recent evidence suggests that pup anogenital licking by the mother is facilitated by secretions from the pup preputial glands (glands around the anal region) (Brouette-Lahlou, Vernet-Maury, and Chanel, 1991). Moreover, the relevent component in the secretion seems to be a pheromonelike compound called dodecyl propionate (Brouette-Lahlou, Amouroux et al., 1991). It appears likely that, because rats do not become attached to individual offspring or even to individual litters, the odor of individual pups or litters is less relevant than is the odor that characterizes the developmental age of the pups and/or the mother's postpartum stage; these odors could derive from many sources in addition to preputial glands, including uterine fluids, mother's milk, maternal diet, and maternal excretory products. In mice, for instance, Doane and Porter (1978) found that dams could discriminate among pups being nursed by females fed the same diet as themselves from those nursed by mothers fed a different diet. The existence of nest-specific odors is also suggested by the works of Bauer (1983), Kinsley (1990), Kinsley and Bridges (1988), and Leon (1978).

In sheep, on the other hand, there is considerable evidence that at parturition the ewe develops an attraction to amniotic fluids, to which she had been aversive before giving birth, and this attraction begins to fade by 2 hr postpartum (Lévy, Poindron, and Le Neindre, 1983; Poindron and Lévy, 1990). This attraction is apparently induced by the synergistic action of prepartum estrogen, genital stimulation, and oxytocin release associated with the parturition (Poindron and Lévy, 1990) and functions to enhance the ewe's maternal licking, grooming, and willingness to accept the neonatal lamb (Lévy and Poindron, 1984, 1987). Finally, olfactory input clearly constitutes the initial basis of the ewe's selective bond with her lamb. Ewes that are unable to smell their lambs exhibit enhanced maternal behavior to all lambs and do not develop a selective bond with any one lamb.

Touch cues. As previously indicated, hormones exert their effects on multiple sensory systems. We now discuss effects on somatosensory function. Rat mothering involves physical interactions with pups that activate the mothers' somatosensory systems. When mothers mouth, lick, and retrieve pups they receive tactile input to the very sensitive mouth (perioral) region. Work by Kenyon, Cronin, and Keeble (1983) and by Stern and colleagues (Stern, 1990; Stern and Johnson, 1989; Stern and Kolunie, 1989) indicates that this stimulation of the mouth region is essential to the complete expression of maternal behavior during the early postpartum period. Stern and her colleagues (Stern and Johnson, 1989; Stern and Kolunie, 1989) found that if the mouth region is desensitized through use of a muzzle, anesthesia injected into the cheek region, or transection of the nerves in this region, mother rats will not exhibit normal crouching behavior. If anesthetized and transected, they also do not retrieve or lick pups. In fact, tactile stimulation of the mouth area seems to be necessary for activation of the pronounced nursing posture (ventroflexion) necessary for successful suckling by young (Stern, 1990; Stern, 1996). Given the clear importance of tactile sensation of the mouth and the cheek regions, it is interesting that estradiol also enlarges the area of responsiveness of this facial area (Bereiter and Barker, 1975, 1980; Bereiter, Stanford, and Barker, 1980), presumably heightening maternal sensitivity to pup-generated touch cues.

The ventral trunk region with its teats is obviously another important contributor to somatostimulation. When dams crouch over and nurse pups, they receive tactile input through touch receptors in the ventral skin surface and teat stimulation by suckling pups. The importance of suckling stimulation for the release of prolactin, glucocorticoids, and oxytocin (the hormones of lactation) and activation of the milk ejection or "let-down" reflex is well known (Wakerly, Clarke, and Sumerlee, 1988). However, the fact that thelectomized females (with teats removed) or females whose individual teats have been anesthetized engage in motivated maternal behavior suggests that teat stimulation by suckling young is not necessary for the retrieval, licking, or hovering over pups, although teat stimulation is clearly necessary for the occurrence of the high crouch involved in nursing behavior (Stern, Dix, Bellomo, and Thramann, 1992; Stern, Dix, Pointek, and Thramann, 1990). Similarly, insufficient ventral stimulation that is due to the presence of too few pups, chilled pups, or pups prevented from suckling fails to elicit the high-arch crouch in dams (Stern and Johnson, 1989). Although teat stimulation may not be necessary for the expression of most maternal behaviors, the ventral surface surrounding the nipples may be. If a dam is given a local anesthetic that desensitizes the ventrum (Stern and Johnson, 1989) or wears a specially devised spandex jacket covering the ventrum (Morgan, Fleming, and Stern, 1992), pups do not gather under the mother's ventrum and attach to the teats but instead gravitate to her exposed neck region, where the fur presumably has the right tactile, temperature, and odor characteristics (Magnusson and Fleming, 1995; Morgan et al., 1992). Under these conditions, licking and a variety of other maternal behaviors are considerably distorted.

Other sensory cues.   Although somatosensory (touch), thermal (temperature), and olfactory (odor) cues are probably most important for the regulation of maternal behavior, other cues may also contribute to the proximal control of behavior and may be influenced by hormones. For instance, ultrasonic calls, above the range of human hearing, emitted by pups when they are in distress, cold, or out of the nest, result in the mother's locating them from a distance and retrieving them back into the nest (Allin and Banks, 1972; Brewster and Leon, 1980); such directional orientation to pup ultrasounds is facilitated by associated pup-odor cues (Smotherman, Bell, Starzec, Elias, and Zachman, 1974). In fact, Brouette-Lahlou, Vernet-Maury, and Vigouroux (1992) reported that pup ultrasounds stimulate the initiation of maternal anogenital licking of pups, which is then facilitated or patterned by pup preputial secretions acting on the maternal vomeronasal system (Brouette-Lahlou, Vernet-Maury, Godinot, and Chanel, 1992; Brouette-Lahlou, Godinot, and Vernet-Maury, 1999). That ultrasonic calls may acquire motivational properties is suggested by the observation that virgin animals do not awaken in response to these calls, whereas postpartum mothers do. Visual cues may also contribute to maternal responsiveness, although their role must be restricted to proximal interactions and distances over which the dam can see (newborn pups are more effective at eliciting retrieval in the newly parturient dam than are older pups; Peters and Kristal, 1983; see also Stern, 1985). That said, there is evidence that neither sight nor hearing is necessary for the expression of maternal behavior. In the absence of both, maternally experienced dams show normal interactions with pups (Beach and Jaynes, 1956a, 1956b; Herrenkohl and Rosenberg, 1972).

Taken together, these data suggest that the effects of hormones in reducing pup avoidance, in augmenting the dam's attraction to pup-related odorants, and in sensitizing the mother to tactile cues promote a rapid onset of maternal behavior at parturition.

EXPERIENTIAL EFFECTS ON THE MAINTENANCE
AND THE RETENTION OF MATERNAL BEHAVIOR

Processes regulating the long-term maintenance of maternal behavior are quite different from those involved in its onset. The female first undergoes a transition period during which hormones interact with environmental and experiential processes in the regulation of behavior. However, once this transition period is over, by the end of the first postpartum week, behavior is maintained primarily by sensory influences and processes of learning and reinforcement. Hormonal effects on maternal behavior at this time are minimal.

Behavioral Changes from Birth to Weaning

Mothers respond to their offspring for a considerable period after parturition, although the quality of responsiveness changes as the young grow and mature. In general, young are weaned at approximately 20 to 25 days of age, and although mothers continue nursing young over this period, nursing bouts become shorter, interbout intervals become longer, and dams spend increasing amounts of time away from their young (Leon, Croskerry, and Smith, 1978). In fact, once the young are mobile, by 12 to 15 days of age, the mother increasingly distances herself from the pups; she rarely retrieves them, her nest becomes matted, and she terminates nursing bouts before the infants have had their fill (Fleming and Blass, 1994). By 15 to 20 days of age, pups begin to supplement their diet with solid food, which they first encounter in the mother's milk, then as particles of food in the mother's saliva or on the mothers body (mouth, head, and fur), and then when they follow their mother to the food source (Alberts and Cramer, 1988; Galef, 1989; Galef and Beck, 1990).

At a more proximal level, after the first few postpartum days, mothers and litter develop a rhythm of interaction in which the dam alternates between being in the nest and nursing the young and leaving the nest, out of litter contact. Leon et al. (1990) showed that the duration of the long nursing nest bouts is regulated by an interaction of hormonal factors and the thermal characteristics of the nest, the huddle of pups, and the mother. Dams experience a rise in body temperature when nursing and get off the pups when they experience acute hyperthermia (Leon et al., 1978). Compared with nonlactating animals, dams have a chronically elevated core temperature, making them more vulnerable to hyperthermia (Jans and Leon, 1983a, 1983b). Moreover, endocrine changes associated with suckling and lactation contribute to the elevated core body temperature. The developing pups induce their mothers to release both prolactin and ACTH, which provoke the release of progesterone and corticosterone, respectively. Progesterone then elevates the maternal thermal set point, and corticosterone increases maternal heat production and possibly heat retention. The resulting chronic increase in maternal heat load makes the mothers vulnerable to a further acute increase in their heat load, eventually driving up maternal brain temperature and forcing the interruption of pup contact (Leon et al. 1990, p. 404).

Although many hormones are associated with lactation, the primary ones are the peptides, prolactin, adrenocortical hormone, oxytocin, and adrenal steroids, not the "parturitional" hormones known to be associated with the onset of responsiveness. Although both prolactin and oxytocin have been implicated in the onset of maternal responsiveness (Bridges, 1990; Insel, 1990), there is no evidence that these lactational hormones contribute directly to the dam's motivation to continue to respond nurturantly during the lactational period.

Effects of Postpartum Experiences

As noted in the preceding subsection, the continued expression of maternal behavior after 4 to 5 days postparturition seems no longer to be based on hormones but is, instead, based both on experiences acquired by the mother when she interacts with pups under the influence of hormones and on experiences acquired during the lactational period (Fleming, Morgan, and Walsh, 1996). Thus processes of learning and memory sustain the behavior beyond the period of hormonal priming and into the next parity.

If pups are removed from newly parturient (or Cesarean-delivered) females before dams have had the opportunity to interact with the pups, maternal responsiveness declines over the next 3 to 5 days and reaches low virgin levels by day 10, by which time animals have usually reinitiated their estrous cycles (Orpen, Furman, Wong, and Fleming, 1987). However, if females give birth (or are C-sectioned) and within 24 to 36 hr are permitted to interact with pups for as little as 1/2 hr before separation, dams continue to be quite maternal in tests undertaken 10 days later (Orpen and Fleming, 1987). Not surprisingly, a longer interactive exposure period results in a longer retention of responsiveness (Bridges, 1975, 1977; Cohen and Bridges, 1981; Fleming and Sarker, 1990). This long-term change in behavior as a result of experience in interacting with pups has come to be known as the maternal experience effect and has now been demonstrated in other species (e.g., rabbit; Gonzalez-Mariscal et al., 1998).

That these experience effects are not due to hormonal stimulation is indicated by the fact that, whether or not animals have received postpartum exposure to pups, on day 10 most animals have resumed their estrous cycles and preparturitional hormonal state. However, the parturitional hormones influence the robustness of maternal learning. Animals that acquire maternal experience under the influence of the parturitional hormones (whether postpartum animals or virgins treated with hormones) exhibit better retention of maternal behavior 30 days later than do animals who are not being stimulated with hormones at the time of the maternal experience (virgins or nonparous but experienced animals). Moreover, the optimal condition for the expression of maternal behavior occurs when both the initial experience and the test occur during a period of hormonal priming (Fleming and Sarker, 1990). There is considerable evidence that multiparous animals (which have experienced a previous pregnancy, parturition, and period of pup rearing) are less disturbed than primiparous mothers are by a variety of experimental manipulations including C-section (Moltz, Robbins, and Parks, 1966), endocrine manipulations (Moltz and Wiener, 1966; Moltz, Levin, and Leon, 1969), morphine administration (Bridges, 1990; Kinsley and Bridges, 1988), and brain lesions (Fleming and Rosenblatt, 1974b; Franz, Leo, Steuer, and Kristal, 1986; Numan, 1994; Schlein, Zarrow, Cohen, Denenberg, and Johnson, 1972) that could disrupt maternal behavior. In addition, pup cues that are initially ineffective in eliciting maternal behavior in first-time mothers, come to be effective in multiparous animals (Noirot, 1972). Finally, among ewes, exogenous hormones are most effective in enhancing responsiveness in experienced animals (Poindron and Le Neindre, 1980).

Although most work in this area has focused on mother's learning about her offspring, this enhanced learning ability seems not to be specific to the maternal context; in comparison with virgins or nonmothers, new mothers during the postpartum period also show enhanced learning in other contexts, involving other forms of social learning (Fleming, Kuchera, Lee, and Winocur, 1994) as well as spatial learning (Kinsley et al., 1999).

Taken together, these studies indicate that experiences acquired under hormones are also more easily activated by a combination of hormones and exposure to relevant pup stimuli in the absence of hormones. There are a number of ways hormones could act to promote these robust experience effects. They could increase the salience of associative cues, most likely unconditioned pup cues (e.g., proximal tactile or olfactory) during the learning phase; they could act to facilitate or strengthen the association between the conditioned and the unconditioned pup-associated cues; finally, they could produce internal cues that themselves act as conditioned stimuli, a mechanism that could explain the apparent state dependency of the maternal–hormone interactions previously described. Research has not yet identified which of these hormone mechanisms is important.

Sensory Mechanisms Involved in Maternal Experience

Although it is clear that interactive experience is important for the long-term retention of behavior, which aspect of the experience is important is not known. In this subsection, we consider the different sensory experiences the animal acquires while interacting with pups. As becomes apparent, both somatosensory and chemosensory inputs are important.

When a female interacts with her litter after the birth, she engages in many proximal interactions. After the nest has been constructed and the pups have been retrieved into it, the dam spends a considerable proportion of her time mouthing and licking the pups, especially their anogenital regions

(Moore, 1990), a behavior that functions to promote urination and elimination by the offspring and to maintain the dam's fluid balance (Friedman, Bruno, and Alberts, 1981). The dam also gathers the young underneath her ventrum, permitting pups to gain access to her teats and suckle (Stern, 1989). Once the pups begin to suckle, the dam usually adopts a high-arch crouch posture over them and becomes immobile for a period (Stern, 1989, 1990; Stern et al., 1992). During early interactions with pups, the dam is multiply stimulated by distal visual and auditory cues and by more proximal tactual, chemosensory, and, possibly, thermal cues, and these may well be important aspects of the maternal experience (Stern, 1989).

The importance of somatosensory and chemosensory stimulation for the maintenance of maternal responding is well established; if the mother is prevented from crouching over her young during the postpartum period but receives other distal inputs, her responsiveness declines more rapidly with earlier weaning (Jakubowski and Terkel, 1986; Stern, 1983). Moreover, Orpen and Fleming (1987) found that if mothers were separated from their litters by a wire mesh floor during the 1-hr postpartum exposure phase, so that they could see, hear, and distally smell pups but receive no tactile or proximal chemosensory input, on tests 10 days later they showed no long-term benefit of maternal experience, but instead responded to pups as virgins do. These data indicate that ventral stimulation is probably an essential feature of the maternal experience. The additional findings that dams need to receive somatosensory perioral input from the mouth region to exhibit normal maternal licking and crouching (Stern and Johnson, 1989; Stern and Kolunie, 1989) and that licking during exposure is correlated with responsiveness during test (Morgan et al., 1992) point also to the importance of chemosensory and perioral stimulation for the maternal experience effect.

Effects of somatosensory input.   To determine the relative contributions of perioral and ventral stimulation to the maternal experience effect, Morgan et al. (1992) tested different groups of C-sectioned dams; one group was rendered insensitive to touch stimulation of the mouth region (by injection of a local anesthetic into the mystacial pads), one group experienced reduced stimulation of the teat ventral trunk region by means of application of a spandex jacket that precluded teat attachment, one group received both forms of desensitization, and the control groups received sham manipulations. Results showed that, although desensitization of either perioral or ventral regions alone did not substantially block the maternal experience effect, desensitization of both together did, indicating that somatosensory stimulation of either the trunk or the perioral region provides a sufficient experience to the dam to produce long-term changes. However, when both sources of stimulation are precluded, the remaining modalities are not sufficient.

Effects of olfactory–chemosensory input.   During interactions with pups, dams learn about specific olfactory and chemosensory features of the pups. If pups are scented with an artificial odorant during the exposure phase, in tests 10 days later dams respond more rapidly to pups labeled with the same scent than to those labeled with a discrepant scent. That this effect depends on the association of the odors with the pups is shown by the additional observation that preexposure to the odor on its own (in the absence of pups) does not result in the same facilitation of responsiveness to similarly scented pups (Malenfant, Barry, and Fleming, 1991). Moreover, how dams respond to pup-associated scents depends on the quality of their interactions with pups during the initial pup-odor pairings. If mothers interact proximally with pups during the pairing and spend time sniffing and licking them, the mothers develop a strong long-term preference for that scent over a novel scent; however, if during the pairing mothers do not respond maternally and remain at a distance from pups, then the dams do not develop a preference for the paired scent. Although pup-associated scents can be learned, olfactory input is apparently not necessary for a maternal experience. Transections of the vomeronasal nerve of the main olfactory bulbs or application of zinc sulfate before an experience do not block the long-term influence of pup-associated odors (Fleming, Gavarth, and Sarker, 1992; Mayer and Rosenblatt, 1977).

Stimulus Salience of Pups

As previously indicated, postpartum and virgin animals differ in the number of respects. As we have seen, one difference is in the effects of a maternal experience. In the next subsection, we consider the generalizability of these learning differences and ask whether they occur in contexts not related to pups.

Parity differences in learning capacity. That the dam shows a more robust experience effect than does the virgin is, apparently, due both to differences in the dams' learning capacities (Fleming, Kuchera et al., 1994) and to differences in the reinforcing value of rat pups (Fleming, Korsmit, and Deller, 1994). Fleming, Kuchera et al. (1994) compared postpartum and virgin female rats in their acquisition of two social olfactory learning tasks, one involving olfactory recognition of a food experienced in the context of interactions with a conspecific and the other involving the recognition of a juvenile animal to whom adult rats had been preexposed. In both situations, the postpartum animals exhibited a more robust recognition, although both groups of animals were very adept at recognizing preexposed stimuli with quite long exposure-test intervals. These effects are not restricted to social tasks. In fact, Kinsley et al. (1999) reported enhancement of spatial learning in maternal animals over nonmaternal animals. Although the postpartum hormones may facilitate this effect, the experience of being maternal is sufficient, as enhancement in a radial-arm maze occurs in maternal virgins as well.

Parity differences in pup reinforcement. Despite these parity differences in general olfactory learning, the primary reason the postpartum animal expresses such a robust maternal experience is because rat pups acquire highly reinforcing properties for the maternal animal (Fleming, Korsmit, and Deller, 1994). In a series of studies addressing this issue, Fleming and colleagues (Fleming, Kuchera et al., 1994; Lee, Clancy, and Fleming, 2000) compared postpartum and virgin animals under a variety of different temporal, hormonal, experiential, deprivation, and stimulus conditions on a conditioned place preference (CPP) paradigm or in an operant box by using either rat pups or food as the reinforcing stimulus. In the CPP tests, animals were examined for their preference for one of two white boxes, one with vertical black stripes and the other with horizontal black stripes, after a preexposure regimen in which rat pups (or food) were paired repeatedly with one of the striped environments but not with the other. Pups are more reinforcing to postpartum animals than to virgins, whereas the reverse is true for food stimuli. However, when virgins are induced to become maternal as a result of extensive experience with pups, pups take on heightened reinforcing properties in the absence of the parturitional hormones. The fact that pups are more reinforcing to the maternal postpartum animal than to the maternal virgin suggests, however, that hormones augment the salience of the pup stimulus (Fleming, Korsmit, and Deller, 1994). Consistent with this interpretation, in the virgin the parturitional hormones enhance the reinforcing effects of pups, but only if the hormones also activate the expression of maternal behavior in virgins. Hormones have no effect on the reinforcing properties of food stimuli. In a second test of pup reinforcement, Lee et al. (2000) found that, during pregnancy, females will not bar press for pups although they will bar press for food, but that after the birth of the litter, bar-pressing for pups increases tenfold. Again hormones augment this effect but are not necessary for it, because animals commence bar pressing outside the postpartum period, as soon as they begin showing maternal responses in the home cage. That pups are the relevant reinforcing stimulus, the maintenance of bar pressing responses is indicated by the observations that, if pups are removed, the bar press response extinguishes almost immediately.

These studies indicate that, for animals to respond maternally to pups during the initial encounters, pups do not have to be strongly reinforcing. Presumably the attraction to pups induced by hormones is adequate to ensure that the mother will respond nurturantly. However, for maternal responsiveness to be sustained in the absence of hormones, females must gain experience in interacting with pups, which in general occurs in the presence of hormones; as a result of this experience, pups acquire strongly reinforcing properties.

Reinforcing characteristics of the mother–litter interaction. To determine precisely what aspects or features of the pups are reinforcing to the maternal animal, Magnusson and Fleming (1995) tested the relative contributions of chemosensory and somatosensory stimulation during maternal interactions on the development of a CPP. They found that pups do not acquire reinforcing properties as readily if dams are exposed to pups placed in a Plexiglas cube, permitting visual, auditory, and olfactory stimulation but preventing the proximal somatosensory and chemosensory inputs normally associated with mouthing, licking, retrieving, and crouching. Thus for pups to be reinforcing they must provide proximal stimulation to the dam. These conclusions were reinforced by subsequent studies that showed that, if dams are prevented from receiving full somatosensory input by being locally anesthetized with a topical anesthetic [EMLA (eutectic mixture of lidocaine and prilocaine) cream] in either the perioral region, the ventrum, or both regions, pups no longer sustain their reinforcing properties. Finally, the reinforcing properties of pups also depend on their odor characteristics. Pups will not sustain a CPP if dams are rendered anosmic by peripheral infusion of zinc sulphate, a drug that destroys the nasal epithelial cells. Thus, by reducing either tactile or olfactory pup input, dams no longer find pups as reinforcing.

Taken together, these studies show that maternal learning is a robust phenomenon that is based on activation of both chemosensory and somatosensory systems during mother–litter interactions. Although the new mother seems primed to respond to certain cues over others by the action of hormones, the primary effect of the maternal hormones is to activate maternal behavior. Once maternal behavior has been exhibited, general mechanisms of learning and memory are utilized to further consolidate experiences acquired during mother–litter interactions. These experiences include the activation in the mother of both chemosensory and somatosensory systems.

NEUROANATOMY AND NEUROCHEMISTRY OF MATERNAL BEHAVIOR

Although there is substantial evidence that some of the parturitional hormones exert their effects on maternal responsiveness by acting on neural substrates in the brain, which hormones exert central effects and what brain systems are implicated, and by what specific behavioral mechanisms, are not totally understood. Of interest also is whether the systems that mediate the onset of maternal behavior and the maternal experience effect are the same, different, or overlapping.

As can be seen in Fig. 3.1, the neural systems that are most important include the the olfactory systems, the limbic system, and the hypothalamus (Numan, 1994, Numan and Sheehan, 1997). The olfactory system mediates the sense of smell and comprises two parts: The main olfactory system detects odor molecules in the air that activate the olfactory receptors in the nose when an animal sniffs an object, and the accessory olfactory system detects molecules in a liquid medium that activate receptors in the vomeronasal organ, also situated in the nose, when an animal touches an object with its snout. The limbic system involves groups of neurons and their axons that have been implicated in the regulation of emotional behavior and memory processes and species-characteristic behaviors. Included in this circuit are the neural structures, the amygdala, the nucleus accumbens, and the hippocampus. The hypothalamus sits at the base of the brain above the pituitary gland and consists of different groups of cells involved in the control of a variety of reproductive behaviors and the release of hormones from the pituitary gland. Two important nuclear groups within this region are the medial preoptic area (MPOA), which is situated somewhat anterior to the hypothalamus, and the ventral part of the bed nucleus of the stria terminalis (vBNST), which sits adjacent and dorsal to the MPOA. Also within the hypothalamus are the ventromedial hypothalamic nucleus (VMH) and the paraventricular nucleus, which are positioned close to the midline but posterior to the MPOA, closer to the pituitary. All four hypothalamic structures respond to environmental stimuli and to circulating hormones. These different brain areas are interconnected by a series of neural pathways. For instance, the two olfactory systems have direct connections with the limbic system (especially the amygdala) and the hypothalamus by means of the lateral olfactory tract. The amygdala, in turn, is interconnected with the nucleus accumbens, and both are connected with the hypothalamus.

Before the work of Numan (1974), little was known about the neuroanatomy of maternal behavior. The early work by Beach (1937) focused on neocortical structures and suggested that no one area of the cortex is crucial to the expression of maternal behavior. However, the greater the cortical mass removed, the greater the deficits in behavior. Subsequent to these early studies on neocortex, other studies focused on the midline cortex and associated limbic structures, the hippocampus and septum (Fleischer and Slotnick, 1978; Slotnick, 1967; Stamm, 1955; Terlecki and Sainsbury, 1978; Wilsoncroft, 1963). Although small lesions of these regions disrupt maternal behavior, the deficits were primarily related to motor sequencing and patterning, not to maternal motivation. Thus animals with these forebrain lesions continued to respond to pups but in a disorganized fashion (Slotnick, 1967; Stamm, 1955).

The Expression of Maternal Behavior

The neural bases involved in the regulation of the expression of maternal behavior at the time of parturition are in many ways well understood. There are at least two antagonistic neural systems that govern the expression of maternal behavior (Numan and Sheehan, 1997). One is the excitatory neural system that deals with the activation of maternal responses towards pups; the other is an inhibitory neural system that may regulate avoidance and aversive responses to pups or pup-related stimuli. The balance between these two systems determines whether maternal behavior will be expressed at the time of parturition. The combination of sensory cues, parturitional hormones, and experiential factors exerts its effects on the excitatory system to bring animals close to pups by increasing the attractive quality of pups or pup-related stimuli and to initiate and maintain maternal care; these factors exert effects on the inhibitory system to inhibit animals' naturally fearful responses toward novel pups (Rosenblatt, 1990; Schneirla, 1959).

The excitatory system. The excitatory system is controlled primarily by neurons in the MPOA and the vBNST and their efferent projections to the brain stem (Numan, 1988, 1994; Numan and Sheehan, 1997). Lesions of MPOA/vBNST cell bodies or knife cuts transecting their lateral projections completely abolish maternal behavior in the new mother or maternal virgin (Numan, Corodimas, Numan, Factor, and Piers, 1988; Numan, McSparren, and Numan, 1990; Numan and Numan, 1996), whereas "kindlinglike" electrical stimulation of this site facilitates maternal response (Morgan, Watchus, Milgram, and Fleming, 1999). Hormones that activate maternal behavior act on the MPOA: implants into MPOA of either estradiol, prolactin, or oxytocin (albeit under somewhat different conditions) facilitate maternal responding (Bridges, Numan, Ronsheim, Mann, and Lupini, 1990; Insel, 1990; Numan, Rosenblatt, and Komisaruk, 1977), whereas the infusion of oxytocin antagonists, morphine, or β-endorphin into the MPOA impair maternal behavior (Mann and Bridges, 1992; Pedersen, Caldwell, Walker, Ayers, and Mason, 1994; Rubin and Bridges, 1984). Implants of antiestrogen in the MPOA also delay the onset of maternal behavior (Ahdieh, Mayer, and Rosenblatt, 1987).

Another line of evidence supporting the importance of MPOA/vBNST neurons in the control of maternal expression comes from studies with c-fos immunohistochemistry. The proto-oncogene c-fos is one of a class of genes (known as immediate early genes) that are expressed in response to a variety of stimulus conditions (Sagar, Sharp, and Curran, 1988) by producing a protein, called the Fos protein. Fos expression is often used as a marker for detection of neuronal activation. Several studies have demonstrated that there exists a population of neurons in the MPOA/vBNST, which regulates maternal responsiveness independent of sensory input. For example, Fleming, Suh, Korsmit, and Rusak (1994) found that postpartum rats exposed to pups had higher numbers of cells showing Fos within the MPOA nuclei than did those exposed to adult conspecifics or left alone. Numan and Numan (1994) also found that postpartum rats exposed to pups had more Fos-labeled neurons in the MPOA and the vBNST than did the postpartum control females exposed to candy. These effects require that the animal be actively maternal and crouch over pups; however, they do not depend on activation by many of the pup-associated sensory inputs. Heightened MPOA c-fos expression persists in maternally active animals even after animals are rendered anosmic (unable to smell), anaptic (unable to feel touch sensations around the muzzle), or after temporary anesthetization of the ventral nipple area (Numan and Numan, 1995; Walsh, Fleming, Lee, and Magnusson, 1996).

To understand the function of the MPOA/vBNST in maternal behavior, Numan and his colleagues have investigated the MPOA/vBNST projections implicated in maternal response (see review, Numan and Sheehan, 1997). By combining the c-fos immunohistochemistry technique with the neural tract-tracing technique, Numan and Numan (1997) found that "maternal" neurons (visualized by Fos labeling) in the MPOA mainly project to the lateral septum (LS), the VMH, and the periaqueductal gray (PAG) whereas the "maternal" neurons in the vBNST project to the retrorubral field, the PAG, and the ventral tegmental area (VTA). The importance of these projections in the control of maternal behavior is consistent with the involvement of these regions in maternal behavior. For instance, the LS has been implicated in the control of the sequential organization of the maternal pattern (Fleischer and Slotnick, 1978); the VTA has been linked to the motivational aspect of maternal behavior (Hansen, Harthon, Wallin, Löfberg, and Svensson, 1991b; see the next subsection for details); the VMH is involved in the control of aversive reactions toward pups (Bridges, Mann, and Coppeta, 1999; Sheehan and Numan, 1997); and the PAG is found to be specifically important for the regulation of the upright nursing posture (Lonstein, Simmons, and Stern, 1998; Lonstein and Stern, 1997). It is interesting to speculate that these projections may contribute to different aspects of maternal behavior control. As stated by Numan and Sheehan (1997, p. 105), "the hormonally primed preoptic area projects to some regions to facilitate the appetitive aspects of maternal behavior, projects to other regions to potentiate consummatory components, and projects to still other neuronal groups to depress aversive reactions to pup stimuli."

The inhibitory system. The MPOA/vBNST not only projects to the midbrain and the motor system involved in the expression of maternal behavior, these nuclear groups also receive input from other parts of the brain, in particular, from the olfactory and limbic systems (Fleming, 1987; Numan, 1988; see Fig. 3.1) that exert inhibitory influences on the functions of the MPOA/vBNST. For instance, a major input to the MPOA comes from the amygdala, which in turn receives input from the main and the accessory olfactory bulbs (Fleming, 1987). Thus removal of main or accessory olfactory inputs facilitates the expression of the maternal behavior in nonresponsive virgin animals, while at the same time reducing certain olfactory-mediated components (like licking) in both virgins and postpartum animals who are maximally responsive. These data are consistent with the observation that pup odors within the context of other pup cues are aversive in virgin animals but attractive in the postpartum dams (Fleming et al., 1989; Fleming et al., 1974; Fleming and Rosenblatt, 1974b, 1974c). The findings that infusions of oxytocin into the olfactory bulb facilitate the appearance of maternal behavior whereas infusions of an oxytocin antagonist markedly delay all components of maternal behavior suggest that the olfactory bulb is one such site where parturitional hormones act to antagonize the inhibitory control on maternal behavior (Yu, Kaba, Okutani, Takahashi, and Higuchi, 1996). Behavioral inhibition is also exerted by sites that receive chemosensory projections and that project to the MPOA, such as the medial and cortical nuclei of the amygdala and the VMH. The amygdala receives inputs from both olfactory systems and the VMH and projects directly to the MPOA and the VMH. Activation of the olfactory systems increases medial amygdala neuronal activity, whereas electrical stimulation of the medial amygdala predominantly inhibits MPOA neurons as well as the onset of maternal behavior (Gardner and Phillips, 1977; Morgan, Watchus, Milgram, and Fleming, 1999). Lesions of the medial amygdala, the stria terminalis (the major efferent pathway from the medial amygdala), the BNST, or the VMH all result in the disinhibition of maternal retrieving and crouching in virgin animals exposed to foster pups (Bridges et al., 1999; Fleming, 1987; Fleming et al., 1979; Fleming et al., 1992; Fleming, Vaccarino, and Luebke, 1980; Numan, Numan, and English, 1993). Importantly, the facilitation of maternal behavior produced by amygdala lesions is abolished by lesions of the MPOA, confirming that the input from amygdala acts through the MPOA to exert its inhibitory role in maternal behavior (Fleming, Miceli, and Moretto, 1983). On the other hand, applications of various doses of neuropeptide K into the VMH were also found to inhibit maternal behavior (Sheehan and Numan, 1997).

Komisaruk et al. (2000) provided support for the notion of an active inhibitory system in the regulation of maternal behavior. They combined the ^{14}C-2-deoxyglucose (2-DG) autoradiographic method with c-fos immunocytochemistry to make visible the neural activities in specific brain regions under different maternal conditions. The 2-DG method provides information about the metabolic activity of neuronal input. On the other hand, c-fos immunocytochemistry detects postsynaptic neuronal activity; therefore it indicates the metabolic activity level of neuronal output. Information from the combined methods can reveal the input–output relations in certain brain areas. They found that in parturient and hormonally primed maternal animals, there were elevated 2-DG and c-fos activities in the MPOA and in sites that receive accessory olfactory bulb input (e.g., medial amygdala) indicating an increase in the input and the output activities of these areas. In contrast, maternal virgin animals showed a decrease of 2-DG activity but an increase of c-fos activity in the medial amygdala indicating a decrease in the input but an increase in output activity. These results suggest that for the virgin animals to become maternal through pup induction, the input activity in the vomeronasal nuclei must be decreased, which in turn, disinhibits the output neurons in stimulating the neurons in the MPOA and, in so doing, activates the whole excitatory system.

The amygdala mediates fear.   The evidence previously cited suggests that the amygdala, especially the medial part, has an inhibitory influence on the onset of maternal behavior. The inhibitory circuits consist of olfactory systems-to-amygdala-to-MPOA/vBNST and olfactory systems-to-amygdala-to-VMH-to-MPOA/vBNST (Numan and Sheehan, 1997). Because it has been demonstrated that virgins that sustain amygdala lesions differ from controls in not withdrawing from pups and in maintaining closer proximity to them and that they are less fearful in a series of emotionality tests (Fleming et al., 1980), it is proposed that these circuits "depresses maternal behavior by activating a central aversion system" (Numan and Sheehan, 1997, p. 123). These effects of amygdala lesions on the animal's affect are consistent with an extensive literature relating the amygdala to emotional behavior within other contexts (Davis, 1992; Everitt and Robbins, 1992; LeDoux, 1992). One interesting feature of these olfactory limbic structures is that a number of these sites contain receptors for estradiol (Pfaff and Keiner, 1973), progesterone (Numan et al., 1999), oxytocin (Brinton, Wamsley, Gee, Wann, and Yamamura, 1984), and the opiates (Bridges, 1990; Hammer, 1984) and therefore constitute likely sites for the hormonal and the neurochemical alteration of maternal affect. However, no studies to date have been published that show that the maternal hormones or neurotransmitters act on these limbic sites to influence maternal affect in general or maternal behavior specifically.

Taken together, maternal behavior is under the joint control by two antagonistic neural systems: the excitatory system, which mainly consists of the efferents from MPOA/vBNST neurons to various brain areas, and the inhibitory system, which mainly refers to the projections from the medial amygdala to the MPOA/vBNST and the VMH. These systems may coordinately regulate neuroendocrine, sensory, and autonomic components necessary for the elaboration of maternal behavior.

The preceding neural circuitry analysis does not incorporate all the known brain structures involved in maternal behavior, one of which is the lateral habenula (LH) (Corodimas, Rosenblatt, Canfield, and Morrell, 1993; Corodimas, Rosenblatt, and Morrell, 1992; Felton, Linton, Rosenblatt, and Morrell, 1998; Matthews-Felton, Corodimas, Rosenblatt, and Morrell, 1995). Lesion studies clearly implicate the involvement of LH in maternal behavior, but the mechanism is still unclear (Matthews-Felton, Linton, Rosenblatt, and Morrell, 1999).

Maternal Motivation and Pups as Reinforcing Stimuli

Maternal animals are willing to cross an electric grid to touch pups (Nissen, 1930), bar press for the delivery of pups (Lee et al., 2000; Wilsoncroft, 1969), prefer a place associated with pups before (Fleming, Korsmit, and Deller, 1994), and retrieve pups from a T-shaped maze (Stern and MacKinnon, 1976). Maternal behavior is very robust, goal-directed, motivated behavior, and pups are reinforcing stimuli for the maternal animal. Most studies on maternal motivation have focused on pup-retrieval, because it is the most dramatic behavior and is very easy to quantify. By looking at the pup-retrieval latency and the number of pups retrieved during certain test period, one can assess an animal's interest in pups and the intensity of her "motivation" to be in proximity to them. Probably the most important system in the regulation of maternal motivation is the mesolimbic dopamine (DA) system, which originates in the midbrain and releases the neurotransmitter, DA, in the nucleus accumbens. The current hypothesis is that the normal dopaminergic transmission is key for the normal expression of maternal motivation. According to this theory, DA disturbance leads to disrupted motivational performance by means of its interconnections with the maternal circuit, especially the MPOA/vBNST. For instance, the systemic injection of certain DA receptor antagonists, such as haloperidol or raclopride, suppresses pup retrieval and nest building but not nursing behavior (Giordano, Johnson, and Rosenblatt, 1990; Hansen et al., 1991b; Stern and Taylor, 1991). In all these studies, the drug-treated animals generally have longer latencies to retrieve pups or retrieve fewer pups than vehicle-treated animals do, although at lower drug doses they show only minimal motor deficits. That these effects reflect motivational deficits is reflected in similar effects of DA antagonists on many types of "approach" behaviors. For instance, if new mother rats are fitted with a muzzle so they cannot retrieve pups, they will push pups with their snouts and paws. DA antagonists also block this response at concentrations that are too low to affect actual pup retrieval (Stern and Keer, 1999).

That the DA function within the nucleus accumbens is important for these effects is suggested by additional studies that show that if DA-containing cells within the nucleus accumbens or the midbrain (the VTA) are destroyed with a neurotoxin (6-hydroxydopamine) or if DA antagonists are infused into the nucleus accumbens, new mother rats retrieve pups more slowly, although other maternal behaviors, such as nursing, nest building, and maternal aggression are not affected (Hansen et al., 1991a, 1991b; Keer and Stern, 1999). Recent studies indicate that the limbic shell, rather than the core region of the nucleus accumbens, is important for this effect (Keer and Stern, 1999). That motivation rather than consummatory behavior is affected by the DA antagonists is further supported by results showing that DA antagonists, administered to new mother rats, also block the formation of a CPP for an environment that was previously paired with rat pups (Fleming, Korsmit, and Deller, 1994). The fact that these maternal deficits occur only if mothers have recently interacted with pups but not if they have experienced a period of separation from them, suggests that blocking brain DA primarily affects motivation to retrieve and not the motor mechanisms of retrieval (Hansen, 1994). Finally, pups, as strong reinforcers, were found to be able to increase the DA activity in the accumbens area (Hansen, Bergvall, and Nyiredi, 1993). What happens behaviorally when an animal experiences a deficit in the DA function is an open question. Many behavioral mechanisms can be invoked. Disruption of the DA function might (1) produce a general ahedonia, in which pups are no longer experienced as pleasurable stimuli (Wise's hedonia hypothesis; Wise, 1985; Wise, Spindler, deWit, and Gerberg, 1978), or (2) dampen an animal's incentive motivation to approach pups (Bindra, 1978; Bolles 1972), or (3) inhibit the flexible approach responses toward pups by impairing the behavioral invigoration process induced by pups (Ikemoto and Panksepp, 1999).

These data strongly support the conclusion that the mesolimbic system controls maternal motivation, and the integrity of this system is required for animals to exhibit normal motivated behavior.

This conclusion is consistent with a large body of evidence that has implicated the mesolimbic DA system in other motivated behaviors, including feeding (Bassareo and Di Chiara, 1999; Wilson, Nomikos, Collu, and Fibiger, 1995), food foraging (Whishaw and Kornelsen, 1993), drinking (Miyazaki, Mogi, Araki, and Matsumoto, 1998), drug seeking (Di Chiara, 1998; Wise, 1998), and sexual behavior (Everitt, 1990; Mitchell and Gratton, 1994).

We hypothesize that the mesolimbic DA system exerts its influence on maternal motivation by interacting with the MPOA and vBNST. The nucleus accumbens has reciprocal neural connections with MPOA and vBNST (Chiba and Murata, 1985; Numan and Numan, 1996, 1997). Also, the nucleus accumbens has long been regarded as the limbic–motor interface and is responsible for converting information from the limbic systems (hippocampus, amygdalal and prefrontal cortex, and so forth) into motor actions (Willner and Scheel-Kruger, 1991). It is interesting to speculate that the function of the MPOA/vBNST in the control of maternal motivation is to provide specific maternal information and pass it to the mesolimbic DA system, which in turn, activates the motivation and the motor control systems (extrapyramidal motor system) to execute the motor outputs. The mesolimbic DA system may also feed back to the MPOA/vBNST to regulate the appetitive component of maternal behavior.

Maternal Learning and Experience Effects

In this subsection, we discuss the neural and the chemical controls of the maternal experience effect. As we already know, maternal behavior beyond 1 week after parturition is maintained primarily by sensory influences and the processes of learning and reinforcement. It suggests that the neuroanatomical and the neurochemical substrates of maternal experience effect may not be the same as those underlying the expression of maternal behavior. Brain sites, which are involved in the control of sensory processing and learning and memory processes, may be involved.

Neurochemical bases of maternal experience.   Because the maternal experiences at parturiton result in a long-term facilitation of behavior, similar to other forms of learning, there must occur mediating structural (i.e., synaptic) or functional (i.e., neurotransmitter, receptor) changes within the brain. One approach to understanding neuromolecular changes associated with maternal experience was adapted by Fleming, Cheung, and Barry (1990), who asked whether maternal memory requires the synthesis of proteins in the brain in the same way as do other more traditional forms of memory (Davis and Squire, 1984). In their investigations of the maternal experience effect, Fleming et al. (1990) and Malenfant, Barry, and Fleming (1991) found that, if a drug that inhibits protein synthesis was injected into dams immediately after a 1-hr exposure, the long-term retention of maternal behavior was blocked and at test animals behaved like inexperienced virgin animals. Moreover, the consolidation of a specifically olfactory experience acquired during the exposure phase was also blocked by drugs that inhibit protein synthesis (Malenfant, Barry, and Fleming, 1991).

It is unclear how these synthesis-blocking drugs interfere with the retention of the maternal experience. One interesting possibility is the noradrenergic system. Moffat, Suh, and Fleming (1993) injected noradrenergic antagonists or agonists into dams immediately after a brief maternal experience and tested the dams 10 days later for the retention of maternal behavior. Animals receiving the adrenergic blocker exhibited reduced responsiveness, whereas those receiving the agonist exhibited elevated responsiveness during subsequent induction tests. Although these data indicate that the noradrenergic system may indeed be involved in the consolidation of the maternal experience effect, the fact that latencies among animals injected with antagonists were not as long as those found for virgin or inexperienced animals suggests that more than one neurochemical system is probably involved. Possible candidates include the cholinergic system (Ferreira, Gervais, Durkin, and Lévy, 1999) and the neuromodulators, oxytocin (Amico, Thomas, and Hollinghead, 1997; Broad et al., 1999; Pederson et al., 1995), and the endorphins (Byrnes and Bridges, 2000). These peptides are present at parturition, influence maternal behavior, and have been shown in other contexts to influence learning and/or memory formation (Martinez and Kesner, 1991). In fact, work by Hatton's group demonstrated that maternal rats, either real mothers or virgins induced to be maternal by continuous exposure of pups, have profound morphological and physiological changes in their oxytocinergic neurons in the supraoptic nucleus, one of the major sites responsible for oxytocin synthesis and release. These changes include increases in multiple synapses and electrical synapses and decreases in astrocytic processes (Hatton and Tweedle, 1982; Hatton, Yang, and Cobbett, 1987; Perlmutter, Tweedle, and Hatton, 1984; Theodosis and Poulain, 1984; Yang and Hatton, 1988). On the other hand, other work shows that, with the increase of maternal experiences, opiate receptor densities in the MPOA were also elevated (Bridges and Hammer, 1992) and treatment with opioid antagonists before parturition interefered with the formation of a maternal memory (Byrnes and Bridges, 2000; Mann and Bridges, 1992). From these results it is clear that changes in multiple systems are probably involved in the experience-based elevations in behavioral responsiveness.

Neuroanatomical bases of maternal experience.   Which specific brain sites are involved in the formation of a maternal memory has been the focus of a number of recent immunocytochemical and lesion studies. These show that a number of structures within the maternal circuit are implicated in the the formation of a long-term maternal experience, including the MPOA, the amygdala, and the nucleus accumbens.

Neural and glial activation with experience: Immunocytochemistry.   Using immunocyto-chemical techniques to elucidate experience-based changes in neuronal and glial functions, Fleming and her colleagues assessed the distribution in the brain of neurons and astroglial cells that expressed the Fos protein and/or the glial fibrillary acidic protein (GFAP) in maternally experienced and inex-perienced postpartum females (Featherstone, Fleming, and Ivy, 2000; Fleming and Korsmit, 1996). In one study (Fleming and Korsmit, 1996), four groups of postpartum female rats were assessed. Two groups received a 2-hr interactive experience with pups on the day after parturition; during the same period, the other two groups were left alone in their home cages. All groups were then separated from pups for a number of days and then reexposed to pups or to pup-associated cues. At the end of the 2-hr reexposure period, rats were sacrificed in preparation for Fos immunohisto-chemistry. The results revealed that experienced mothers had a significantly higher level of Fos-like immunoreactivities in the MPOA, the basolateral amygdala (BLA), and the parietal cortex compared with that of the inexperienced mothers when they were exposed to the pups. Subsequent experi-ments indicate that this experience-based enhancement of neuronal activation in the MPOA and the BLA is independent of the animals' hormonal state or the time interval between exposure and test phrases. Moreover, the same effect was found when animals were tested with pup-associated distal cues (e.g., pup odors, visual characteristics, and so forth) or even in response to other cues that had become associated with pups (Fleming and Korsmit, 1996). The changes in amygdala and parietal cortex are quite consistent with other learning research that shows the experience-based plasticities in the amygdala and somatosensory cortex in other learning contexts (Izquierdo et al., 1998; Rogan, Staubli, and LeDoux, 1997; Rosen, Fanselow, Young, Sitcoske, and Maren, 1998). In addition to experience effects on neuronal activity, Featherstone et al. (2000) demonstrated that glial astrocytes in the MPOA and the amygdala also undergo long-term changes with experience. These investigators found significantly higher numbers of GFAP positive cells in the MPOA 4 days after the experience in multiparous rats when compared with those of the pup-exposed primiparous rats. The opposite effect was found for the medial amygdala, in which reduced levels were associated with experience. These results are interesting because astrocytes are known to contribute to the growth and the repair of nerve cells and to have an impact on the metabolism of synaptic transmitters. The increase of astrocytes in the MPOA and the decrease in the medial amydala are consistent with their respective roles in the excitation and the inhibition of maternal behavior.

Effects of lesions on experience.   In addition to examining the distribution in brain of molecular changes associated with a long-term maternal experience, in a series of lesion studies Fleming and colleagues investigated experimentally which brain sites are implicated in the formation of the experience (Lee, Li, Watchus, and Fleming, 1999). We were interested to know whether lesions in neural sites that had been implicated either in the actual expression of maternal behavior or in the formation of memories within other behavioral contexts would disrupt the long-term experience-based retention of maternal behavior. Of all the sites lesioned, only lesions to the nucleus accumbens prevented the formation of a long-term maternal experience effect. Animals receiving nucleus accumbens lesions either before or immediately after, but not 24 h after, a maternal experience did not show the facilitatory effects of the experience when tested 10 days later. Instead they responded to pups in much the same way as did the totally inexperienced animals, with long maternal onset latencies. These and other data suggest that the nucleus accumbens are involved in the consolidation of maternal memory rather than in its acquisition or long-term storage.

The involvement of the nucleus accumbens in the maternal memory is consistent with its role in the consolidation of other forms of memory (Setlow and McGaugh, 1998; Setlow, Roozendaal, and McGaugh, 2000; Winnicka, 1999). The nucleus accumbers has long been implicated in the mediation of reward-related processes (Ikemoto and Panksepp, 1999) and is reciprocally connected with both the MPOA and amygdala (Everitt et al., 1999; Holland and Soedjono, 1981), it is possible that the nucleus accumbens in combination with these structures mediates the formation of maternal memory through its role in both reinforcement and associative processes.

EFFECTS OF MOTHERING AND ITS ABSENCE ON THE DEVELOPMENT OF MATERNAL BEHAVIOR

Many factors influence a new mother's responses to her offspring. Some are situational; others are physiological. These factors exert effects by acting on an organism that has a genotype and a developmental history. The adult characteristics and sensitivities do not emerge *de novo*, but come about as a result of a host of earlier influences acting in relation to a genetic background. These include influences exerted during the earliest stages of development, during the prenatal period; influences exerted in the nest during the neonatal period; and influences during development through the juvenile and the adolescent periods. These influences also take many forms; they include various forms of physical stimulation (associated with variations in temperature, nutritional factors, endocrine factors, and so forth); they also include social influences experienced in the nest with mother and littermates and with littermates and conspecifics during later periods of development.

There is now good evidence from a number of species that earlier experiences during preweaning life can exert profound effects on the quality and the intensity of mothering the new mother provides to her offspring postpartum (Fairbanks, 1996; see Fleming, O'Day, and Kraemer, 1999). Moreover, from rat and monkey work, it seems that these earlier experiences exert their effects throughout development by means of multiple routes to alter the neurobiology of the juvenile animal and of the adult animal and the mechanisms that mediate maternal behavior at these two time points (see Fig. 3.2) (Francis, Diorio, Liu, and Meaney, 1999; Francis, Caldji, Champagne, Plotsky, and Meaney, 1999; Gonzalez, Lovic, Ward, Wainwright, and Fleming, 2000; Fleming et al., 1999; Kraemer, 1992; Suomi and Ripp, 1983).

The Genetics of Maternal Behavior—In Its Infancy

The role of genetic factors in the expression of maternal behavior is poorly understood. Although the analysis of behavior in transgenic and knockout mice is being done with exponential frequency, as more and more knockouts are being produced, we still have a very poor understanding of the meaning

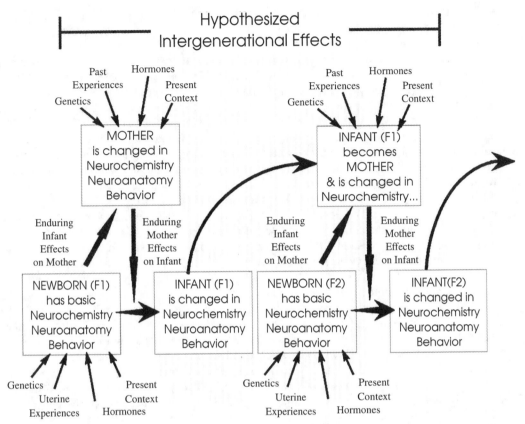

FIGURE 3.2. Schematic showing factors that affect the newborn infant's response to the mother and the mother's response to infants. In this "intergenerational" model, we describe the hypothesized transmission of experiences received by the infant (F1 generation) in the nest and in relation to their own mothers on the quality of mothering the offspring show toward their offspring (F2 generation) when they grow up. The assumption is that the transmission of experience effects persists across generations, from generations F1 to F2 to F3, and so forth. Influences experienced by the developing offspring are determined in part by their genetic makeup, by uterine experiences, by hormones (both prenatally and postnatally), and by present context in the nest and with other siblings. Experiences alter the psychobiology of the offspring, changing their subsequent neuroanatomy, chemistry, endocrinology, and, hence, behavior. These offspring then grow up and gain experiences throughout their lives that, together with their earlier experiences, will determine how they respond to their offspring (From Fleming, O'Day, and Kraemer, 1999).

of the behavioral deficits. Although deficits in maternal behavior have been reported for mice that are deficient in a whole variety of different genes, why the deficit occurs has received less attention; hence deficits have been reported for mice deficient in the Peg3 gene (Li et al., 1999; Li, Szeto, Cattanach, Ishino, and Surani, 2000), the Peg 1 (Mest) gene (Lefebvre et al., 1998), and the Fos-B gene (Brown et al., 1996), the 5HT1B receptor gene (Brunner, Buhot, Hen, and Hofer, 1999), and the PRLR receptor gene (Lucas, Ormandy, Binart, Bridges, and Kelly, 1998), to name a few. In some cases the knockout involves a gene that regulates the synthesis of one of the maternally relevant hormones or its receptors. When this is the case, the expected deficits in maternal behavior often occur, as with the PRLR receptor knockout (Lucas et al., 1998); however, sometimes the expected deficits do not occur, as with the oxytocin knockouts, which continue to show robust maternal behavior (Young, Winslow et al., 1997). In this case only the synthesis of the hormone was eliminated, not the oxytocin receptors that could be activated by other ligands. Other deficits in maternal behavior seen in the knockouts may be due to the absence of genes that regulate activity and inhibition or ability to learn (e.g., Brunner et al., 1999). To illustrate the problems in interpretation that use of knockouts can produce, we studied maternal behavior in the c-fos knockout (Honrado and Fleming, unpublished observation). The rationale behind this effect was that with the expression of maternal behavior, the c-fos gene is expressed in the maternal circuit (see Fleming et al., 1996). To determine whether the c-fos gene is essential for the expression of the behavior, rather than simply a side effect of some other process, we investigated maternal behavior in the c-fos knockout mouse. We found that, in this mutant mouse, pup retrieval and crouching were indeed disrupted. However, closer inspection indicated that these animals also had skeleton and bone problems and had no teeth and hence did not retrieve pups into a single nest site. However, if pups were placed into one site, then the mother would crouch over them and lick them intensively. To conclude that the c-fos gene is essential to maternal behavior—based on these data—would be true in only its most trivial sense. However, this interpretation does not apply to the clear deficits in maternal retrieving seen in the Fos-B knock-out (Brown et al., 1996). Why these animals show deficits requires further analysis.

In short, caution should be taken in the interpretation of results from the knockout mice. To understand precisely what the knocked-out genes are doing in the expression of the behavior, it is important to evaluate the animal on multiple behavioral and perceptual tasks, and also, because the knocked-out gene in question is absent from inception and was never present, to evaluate how the systems underlying behavior develop may be altered and what different developmental routes may be taken. To determine the role of particular genes in adulthood, it is therefore necessary to use convergent techniques and look for comparable outcomes. Hence if a knockout shows the same kinds of deficits in adult behavior as those produced by the intracerebral application in the adult organism of antisense to production of that gene's proteins, then the role of that gene and of associated gene complexes in behavior is more likely. Finally, and perhaps most importantly, genes do not develop in a vacuum; they develop within the context on an environment. Hence a single gene and gene complex could lead to multiple adult phenotypes and one phenotype could be produced by a variety of gene–environment interactions. Genes and environment interact to produce the adult behavior. To understand the role of genes, then, it is important to systematically covary the genetics and the environmental influences present during development. We now turn to a review of early environmental influences that affect adult mothering.

Early Environmental Influences in the Nest on Adult Maternal Behavior

The mother and the maternal nest provide a host of stimuli that the young can learn about and that can form the basis of their later behavior. The newborn pups preferentially approach and learn to recognize the mother and the nest site based on their unique odors (Polan and Hofer, 1998). Their first attachments to the teats are guided and activated by the odor and taste of amniotic fluid first experienced by the young *in utero* (Pedersen and Blass, 1981; see also Goursaud and Nowak, 1999) as well as by compression of labor, the decline in ambient temperature with the birth, and licking stimulation provided by the mother (Abel, Ronca, and Alberts, 1998). The subsequent attraction to mother's odors, which helps the infant orient to the mother (Leon, 1978) and, in some spcies, locate a nipple position (Rosenblatt, 1971), as well as providing a basis for later food preferences (Galef, 1990), comes about as a result of the pairing of mother's odors with licking stimulation provided by the mother before a nursing bout (Wilson and Sullivan, 1994). In fact, the neurobiology of this early conditioning is now well worked out and involves neural and neurochemical systems that are also involved in later learning (see Wilson and Sullivan, 1994). The long-term effects of this learned attraction to mother's odors are now clear. If female young are exposed to mothers scented with an artificial odorant during the preweaning period, when they grow up and give birth, they are more responsive to pups (licking them more) scented with that same odorant over unscented control pups (Shah, Oxley, Lovic, and Fleming, submitted). Interestingly, among male young the early nest odors influence their mating in adulthood; if the partner is scented with the same artificial odorant as the male offspring was exposed to on the mother, mating proceeds more efficiently (Fillion and Blass, 1986). Among ungulates a similar situation obtains, but preference in this case is based on visual experiences; in experiments in cross fostering sheep and goats, Kendrick, Hinton, Atkins, Haupt, and Skinner (1998) found that in adulthood male offspring showed a preference for the facial characteristics of female partners that resembled the species by whom they were raised.

The early experiences of being mothered also have long-term effects on the quality of mothering that offspring that will show toward their own offspring when they grow up. In this case, the experience of receiving more somatosensory stimulation and more varied nest experiences may directly affect the animals' physiology and maturational processes; active associative processes may not be involved. Meaney and colleagues demonstrated that young that receive more licking from their mothers grow up to show higher levels of licking toward their own offspring compared with those who received low licking (Francis, Diorio et al., 1999). This effect was also found if the young from high- and low-licking mothers were cross fostered to mothers showing the opposite pattern of licking than that of their biological mothers. Hence if offspring from high-licking mothers are cross fostered to low-licking mothers they show a low-licking pattern when they grow up. This cross-generational effect of licking provides a nongenomic mechanism for the transmission of behavioral phenotypes (see also Gonzalez et al., 2000).

One can also actively manipulate the early environment experienced by the offspring and make marked changes in their adult maternal behavior. Gonzalez et al. (2000) raised rat pups artificially from day 3 to day 18 of life in cups floating in a warm bath. Pups were fed a nutritionally balanced (for rat pups) diet at 1-hr intervals and received either a high level of simulated licking daily (six times daily with a paintbrush) or low levels of licking (two times daily). Sham operated and intact, sibling pups remained with their mothers. On day 18 all animals were raised in pairs until adulthood and then mated. When compared with their mother-raised siblings in the quality of their maternal behavior after birth of their own litters, the artificially raised mothers showed clear deficits in maternal licking and crouching, but no deficits in retrieval responses. Interestingly, the artificially raised offspring that received additional lickinglike stimulation (six daily bouts of stroking) while in the cups showed levels of maternal licking and crouching more similar to those of their mother-raised siblings. A full 24-hr period of maternal deprivation is not necessary to produce these behavioral deficits in adulthood; 3 or 5 hr of deprivation from the mother and the littermates daily during the preweaning period produces maternal behavior deficits in adulthood that are almost as severe (Lovic, Gonzalez, and Fleming, submitted; Rees and Fleming, in press). Moreover, the effects of early mothering deprivation experienced by one generation are also experienced by subsequent generations that did not experience the maternal deprivation regime. Hence the female offspring of artificially raised mothers who received reduced licking themselves licked their offspring less when they grew up (Gonzalez et al., 2000). These early experience effects can therefore be transmitted from one generation to the next and very likely depend on somatosensory experiences associated with licking stimulation.

In addition to affecting the quality of mothering, early experiences being mothered also affect the development of fear and emotionality (Francis, Diorio et al., 1999; Gonzalez et al., 2000) and fear conditioning (Antoniadis, Gonzalez, Lovic, Mcdonald, and Fleming, in preparation). Females who are raised artificially (Gonzalez et al., 2000) or who receive reduced licking from their mothers show reduced exploration in the open-field test of emotionality and reduced emission of ultrasonic calls in a novel environment (Francis, Diorio et al., 1999; Antoniadis, Gonzalez, and Fleming, in preparation). Fear conditioning is also disrupted, although only when ultrasound is used as the dependent measure (Antoniadis et al., in preparation). The mechanisms through which this early experience affects the animal's later maternal behavior is not known. Mechanisms through which these same experiences affect the fear system is better understood; their interdependence has yet to be demonstrated. However, there are a number of potential mechanisms. Maternally deprived animals do not receive the same olfactory and somatosensory stimulations that are necessary for normal development of responses to social cues later on. Pups who are exposed to the species-characteristic odor of the mother (or, indeed, any artificial odor) while she is licking them become classically conditioned to that odor; in adulthood that odor continues to have a positive valence, and males will more readily copulate with females with that odor and females will more readily lick pups with that odor (Fillion and Blass, 1986; Shah et al., submitted).

These early experiences of olfactory–somatosensory associations are encoded by the brain and produce long-lasting changes in brain. Formation of the association between licking and maternal odor produces changes in the olfactory bulbs, altering their neurochemical and structural properties (Najbauer and Leon, 1995, Wilson and Sullivan, 1994); and depends on the activation of the noradrenergic system that originates in the midbrain locus coereleus and terminates in the olfactory bulbs (Wilson and Sullivan, 1994). In fact, infusions of norepinephrine agonists into the olfactory bulbs of neonates during odor exposure mimic the reinforcing effects of stroking stimulation and induce olfactory conditioning (R. M. Sullivan, Stackenwalt, Nasr, Lemon, and Wilson, 2000). There are substantial data that additional environmental manipulations, in addition to olfactory mechanisms, during the preweaning period (including somatosensory stimulation) produce changes in cortex, hippocampus, and other limbic areas (Cramer, 1988; Pascual and Figueroa, 1996; Post et al., 1998; Rosenzweig and Bennett, 1996). Given the importance of pup odors in the regulation of normal pup identification and licking by maternal animals (Brouette-Lahlou, Godinot, and Vernet-Maury, 1999; Fleming and Rosenblatt, 1974a, 1974b, 1974c; Moore, 1995), tactile stimulation from the pups for normal mouthing, retrieving, and high-arched crouching (Stern, 1996; Stern and Johnson, 1989; Stern and Kolunie, 1991), and infant ultrasounds in the regulation of search and retrieval (Brunelli, Shair, and Hofer, 1994), it remains to be seen whether or not the behavioral deficits seen in maternally deprived animals are due to the absence of normal early learning and hence disruptions in brain systems that mediate these experience effects. Also not known at this point is the extent to which early maternal stimulation or its deprivation alters adult maternal responsiveness to offspring by altering the maternal neural circuit directly (Numan, 1994) or possibly by altering its plasticity, which underlies postpartum experience effects acquired in adulthood (Fleming et al., 1996; Fleming and Korsmit, 1996; Fleming, Korsmit, and Deller, 1994; Numan and Numan, 1994; Walsh et al., 1996). It is possible that early deprivation from the mother alters the development of the MPOA or its afferent (amygdala, BNST) or efferent (midbrain tegmentum) connections (Numan, 1994). In fact, we have recent evidence that indicates that animals that do not receive adequate mothering, compared with those that do, show reduced c-fos activation in the MPOA, the BLA, and the parietal cortex (all parts of the maternal circuit) in response to pups when they are tested during the juvenile period (Gonzalez and Fleming, in preparation). Alternatively, it is possible that early maternal deprivation alters the development of receptor systems normally activated by the parturitional hormones that reside in this maternal circuit (see subsequent discussion).

In light of these findings, it would be interesting to know whether manipulations of maternal odors, vocalizations, and/or thermal cues in conjunction with stroking stimulation, in the pup-in-the-cup paradigm, would affect animals' subsequent responses to their pups and their cues and whether there occurs an associated change in olfactory, limbic, and hypothalamic mechanisms.

Deprivation of maternal behavior is known to induce a variety of other physiological, behavioral, metabolic, and neurochemical changes that are differentially regulated by environmental and social stimuli (Hall, 1998) and that could influence a mother's response to her offspring. There is a large body of research that demonstrates the negative effects of maternal deprivation on the HPA axis. Maternal deprivation produces pups that have enhanced corticosterone response to various stressors, increased adrenal sensitivity to the pituitary hormone, ACTH, and changes in glucocorticoid receptor systems in the brain (Kuhn and Schanberg, 1998; Liu et al., 1997; Suchecki, Nelson, van Oers, and Levine, 1995; Suchecki, Rosenfeld, and Levine, 1993; van Oers, de Kloet, Whelan, and Levine, 1998; Vazquez, van Oers, Levine, and Akil, 1996). Stroking has also been found to suppress the elevated ACTH stress response that is characteristic of deprived rats and to normalize corticosterone receptor mRNA levels (van Oers et al., 1998), and growth hormone secretion and ornithine decarboxylase activity (Suchecki et al., 1993; Evoniuk, Kuhn, and Schanberg, 1979). Hence, if the critical components of the dams' nurturing behavior are reinstated, some of the negative physiological responses that are due to maternal deprivation can be reversed.

Alterations seen in HPA activity occur not only as a function of maternal deprivation and stroking stimulation; they have also been found with normal variations in maternal care (Caldji et al., 1998; Francis, Caldji et al., 1999; Francis, Diorio et al., 1999; Francis and Meaney, 1999; Liu et al., 1997). Variations in maternal licking and grooming of rat pups produce differences in the regulation of HPA activity in the pups. Offspring from mothers who received high amounts of licking in the nest show decreased plasma ACTH and corticosterone response to stress, increased hippocampal glucocorticoid receptor expression, decreased levels of hypothalamic expression of the CRF, increases in the density of receptor binding of the central benzodiazepine receptor and $\alpha 2$ adrenoreceptor and corticotropin-releasing hormone binding in the amygdala and the locus coreleus (Caldji et al., 1998; Liu et al., 1997). Taken together, these studies show plasticity of various systems that mediate stress and fearfulness in the adult rat that is affected by early maternal care. Although, to date, a direct link between HPA activity and maternal behavior has not been established, a study comparing virgin and postpartum animals in their responses to exogenous cortiosterone (Panesar and Fleming, 2000) found that elevated concentrations of the glucocorticoid inhibited maternal licking in the virgin, but facilitated it in the postpartum animal. The implications of these findings for the early experience effects reported here have yet to be established. However, it is quite likely that this effect is mediated by a corticoid effect on emotional responsivity. It is possible that maternal deprivation produces in the pups an HPA system that causes animals to be more reactive to even mildly stressful stimuli in the environment. All maternally deprived animals exhibit maternal behavior after the birth of their litters, for example retrieving of pups to the nest, but they are easily distracted by outside noise and activity and engage in a host of unusual behaviors. It may well be that their reduced licking and crouching are reflections of this distractibility.

There are multiple other mechanisms altered by early maternal deprivation that could underlie these deficits in adult maternal behavior. For instance, there are changes in the oxytocin system (Boccia and Pedersen, 1999; Noonan et al., 1994), important for affiliation and postpartum maternal behavior (Insel, 1997; Noonan et al., 1994; Panksepp, Nelson, and Siviy, 1994); there are also changes in the DA system (Hall et al., 1998; Kehoe, Shoemaker, Arons, Triano, and Suresh, 1998; Kehoe, Shoemaker, Triano, Callahan, and Rappolt, 1998), also known to be important for maternal behavior (Hansen, 1994; Hansen et al., 1993; Keer and Stern, 1999; Stern and Keer, 1999) as well as for processes of reinforcement, stimulus salience, and learning in a biologically relevant context (Matthews, Wilkinson, and Robbins, 1996; Fleming, Korsmit, and Deller, 1994).

CONCLUSIONS

Despite the extent of our knowledge of the control of maternal behavior in nonhuman rodents, there is much still to learn. We know a great deal about the role of hormones in the onset of maternal behavior, but very little about their role in its long-term maintenance. We know that the parturitional hormones exert multiple effects on behavior, but we have very little understanding of where they act in the brain to effect their behavioral changes; hormone-binding sites outside the MPOA must surely be involved. We know that the MPOA/vBNST is a critical part of the neural circuitry, but we do not really understand its precise function; it seems not to function as a sensory integrator or a motivational "center"; it may simply function as part of the effector mechanism. Despite the popularity of the neuropeptides and the neurotransmitters in the behavioral neurosciences, we have limited information on which of these neurochemical systems is activated in the maternal animal or their mode of action. Our understanding of the sensory regulation of maternal behavior is somewhat more complete, but even in this area there is some debate regarding the extent to which single versus multiple modalities are involved in the onset and in the maintenance of maternal behavior. We know that even very brief experiences acquired when the mother interacts with the young can have robust long-term effects, profoundly altering the dam's response to subsequent external stimulation and to hormones. However, our understanding of where these long-term effects are encoded in the brain and by what mechanism(s) is still not complete. Finally, our knowledge of the genetics of maternal behavior and of the interactive effects of genes and the developmental environment in which the young grow on adult maternal behavior is in its infancy. Work on the effects of the early environment in the nest and the effects of being mothered on the development of maternal behavior is striking and provocative. However, how these experiences influence the developmental neurobiology of the organism and the neurochemistry and the neuroanatomy that underlie maternal and associated behaviors are poorly understood. An additional set of issues, not touched on in this review but that would be extremely fruitful to pursue, is a consideration of the natural history and the social factors in the regulation of both maternal behavior and its physiological underpinnings. Many of the animals discussed, and rodents in particular, live in social groups in a natural environment characterized by seasonal variations in temperature, food sources, and photoperiod. All these factors could substantially constrain the maternal system.

Although maternal behavior in the rat has a specific, quite stereotyped, species-characteristic pattern, its expression depends on the activation of general processes that are activated in a variety of diverse contexts. The onset of maternal behavior involves a hormonally mediated change in the dam's affective state and in the salience of pup-related olfactory and somatosensory cues. These changes increase the likelihood that the dam will approach and maintain proximal contact with pups, thereby creating the possibility for pup stimuli to elicit the specific maternal responses. Once the maternal behavior is expressed, other processes become activated to ensure that the behavior will be sustained beyond the period of hormonal priming. Once again, these other processes are not specific to the maternal system, but occur within other functional contexts, as well. For instance, when the mother interacts with the young, pups acquire heightened reinforcing properties and, through perceptual learning and/or other associative processes, the mother sustains responsiveness to them until weaning commences. All these processes occur in the adult animal that has had numerous experiences earlier in its life—experiences being mothered and experiences interacting with peers—and these influence the quality of maternal behavior expressed in adulthood. This expression in turns affects the subsequent development of offspring and how they, in turn, will respond to their own offspring.

Moreover, the general nature of many of the behavioral processes activated in the maternal animal is accomplished through the mediation of physiological mechanisms that are recruited in a variety of functional and stimulus contexts and that have had a particular developmental history. Thus olfactory, limbic, and hypothalamic systems and their associated neurotransmitters, known to influence the expression and maintenance of maternal behavior, are also activated during the acquisition and/or consolidation of learned behaviors within aversive, feeding, and sexual contexts.

Finally, it appears that many of these general processes also play a role in the regulation of maternal behavior in other mammalian species (Pryce, 1992), including human beings (see Corter and Fleming, in Vol. 2 of this *Handbook*). As a result, our understanding of the control of different species-characteristic patterns may be enhanced by an understanding of some of these more general processes, with the rat model providing a useful heuristic for their analysis.

ACKNOWLEDGMENTS

Many thanks to all the lab technicians, animal care workers, and undergraduate and graduate students who made many of the studies reported herein possible. They know who they are. Thanks also to our families who have patiently withstood the absences necessitated by work reflected in this chapter. Work reported in this chapter was supported by National Sciences Engineering Research and Medical Research Councils of Canada.

REFERENCES

Abel, R. A., Ronca, A. E., and Alberts, J. R. (1998). Perinatal stimulation facilitates suckling onset in newborn rats. *Developmental Psychobiology, 32,* 91–99.

Ahdieh, H. B., Mayer, A. D., and Rosenblatt, J. S. (1987). Effects of brain antiestrogen implants on maternal behavior and on postpartum estrus in pregnant rats. *Neuroendocrinology, 46,* 522–531.

Alberts, J. R., and Cramer, C. P. (1988). Ecology and experience: Sources of means and meaning of developmental change. In E. M. Blass (Ed.), *Handbook of behavioral neurobiology* (Vol. 9, pp. 1–39). New York: Plenum.

Allin, J. R., and Banks, E. M. (1972). Functional aspects of ultrasound production by infant albino rats. *Animal Behaviour, 20,* 175–185.

Amico, J. A., Thomas, A., and Hollinghead, D. J. (1997). The duration of estradiol and progesterone exposure prior to progesterone withdrawal regulates oxytocin mRNA levels in the paraventricular nucleus of the rat. *Endocrine Research, 23,* 141–156.

Antoniadis, E., Gonzalez, A., and Fleming, A. S. (in preparation). Effects of artificial rearing on emotionality and fear-conditioning in the rat.

Aubert, A., Goodall, G., Dantzer, R., and Gheusi, G. (1997). Differential effects of lipopolysaccharide on pup retrieving and nest building in lactating mice. *Brain, Behavior, and Immunity, 11,* 107–118.

Bassareo, V., and Di Chiara, G. (1999). Modulation of feeding-induced activation of mesolimbic dopamine transmission by appetitive stimuli and its relation to motivational state. *European Journal of Neuroscience, 11,* 4389–4397.

Bauer, J. H. (1983). Effects of maternal state on the responsiveness to nest odors of hooded rats. *Physiology and Behavior, 30,* 229–232.

Beach, F. A. (1937). The neural basis of innate behavior. I. Effects of cortical lesions upon the maternal behavior pattern in the rat. *Journal of Comparative Psychology, 24,* 393–436.

Beach, F. A., and Jaynes, J. (1956a). Studies of maternal retrieving in rats. I. Recognition of young. *Journal of Mammology, 37,* 177–180.

Beach, F. A., and Jaynes, J. (1956b). Studies of maternal retrieving in rats. III. Sensory cues involved in lactating female's response to her young. *Behavior, 10,* 104–125.

Beach, F. A., and Wilson, J. R. (1963). Effects of prolactin, progesterone and estrogen on reactions of nonpregnant rats to foster young. *Psychological Reports, 13,* 231–239.

Bereiter, D. A., and Barker, D. J. (1975). Facial receptive fields of trigeminal neurons: Increased size following estrogen treatment in female rats. *Neuroendocrinology, 18,* 115–124.

Bereiter, D. A., and Barker, D. J. (1980). Hormone-induced enlargement of receptive fields in trigeminal mechanoreceptive neurons. I. Time course, hormone, sex and modality specificity. *Brain Research, 184,* 395–410.

Bereiter, D. A, Stanford, I. R., and Barker, D. J. (1980). Hormone-induced enlargement of receptive fields in trigeminal mechanoreceptive neurons. II. Possible mechanisms, *Brain Research, 184,* 411–423.

Bindra, D. (1978). How adaptive behavior is produced: A perceptual-motivational alternative to response-reinforcement. *Behavioural Brain Research, 1,* 41–91.

Boccia, M. L., and Pedersen, C. A. (1999). Early maternal seperation alters postpartum pup-licking and grooming, lactation-associated changes in aggression and anxiety, and central oxytocin binding in female offspring. *Society for Neuroscience, 25,* 872.

Bolles, R. C. (1972). Reinforcement, expectancy, and learning. *Psychological Review, 79,* 394–409.

Brewster, J. A., and Leon, M. (1980). Relocation of the site of mother-young contact: Maternal transport behavior in Norway rats. *Journal of Comparative and Physiological Psychology, 94,* 69–79.

Bridges, R. S. (1975). Long-term effects of pregnancy and parturition upon maternal responsiveness in the rat. *Physiology and Behavior, 14,* 245–249.

Bridges, R. S. (1977). Parturition: Its role in the long-term retention of maternal behavior in the rat. *Physiology and Behavior, 18,* 487–490.

Bridges, R. S. (1990). Endocrine regulation of parental behavior in rodents. In N. A. Krasnegor and R. S. Bridges (Eds.), *Mammalian parenting: Biochemical, neurobiological, and behavioral determinants* (pp. 93–117). New York: Oxford University Press.

Bridges, R. S., and Hammer, R. P., Jr. (1992). Parity-associated alterations of medial preoptic opiate receptors in female rats. *Brain Research, 578,* 269–274.

Bridges, R. S., Mann, P. E., and Coppeta, J. S. (1999). Hypothalamic involvement in the regulation of maternal behavior in the rat: Inhibitory roles for the ventromedial hypothalamus and the dorsal/anterior hypothalamic areas. *Journal of Neuroendocrinology, 11,* 259–266.

Bridges, R. S., Numan, M., Ronsheim, P. M., Mann, P. E., and Lupini, C. E. (1990). Central prolactin infusions stimulate maternal behavior in steroid-treated, nulliparous female rats. *Proceedings of the National Academy of Sciences U.S.A., 87,* 8003–8007.

Brinton, R. E., Wamsley, J. K., Gee, K. W., Wan, Y. P., and Yamamura, H. I. (1984). H-oxytocin binding-sites demonstrated in the rat brain by quantitative light microscopic autoradiography. *European Journal of Pharmocology, 102*, 365–367.

Broad, K. D., Lévy, F., Evans, G., Kimura, T., Keverne, E. B., and Kendrick, K. M. (1999). Previous maternal experience potentiates the effect of parturition on oxytocin receptor mRNA expression in the paraventricular nucleus. *European Journal of Neuroscience, 11*, 3725–3737.

Brouette-Lahlou, I., Amouroux, R., Chastrett, I., Cosnier, J., Stoffelsma, J., and Vernet-Maury, E. (1991). Dodecyl propionate, the attractant from rat pups' preputial gland, characterization and identification. *Journal of Chemical Ecology, 17*, 1343–1354.

Brouette-Lahlou, I., Godinot, F., and Vernet-Maury, E. (1999). The mother rat's vomeronasal organ is involved in detection of dodecyl propionate, the pup's preputial gland pheromone. *Physiology and Behavior, 66*, 427–436.

Brouette-Lahlou, I., Vernet-Maury, E., and Chanel, J. (1991). Is rat dam licking behavior regulated by pups' preputial gland secretion? *Animal Learning and Behavior, 19*, 177–184.

Brouette-Lahlou, I., Vernet-Maury, E., Godinot, F., and Chanel, J. (1992). Vomeronasal organ sustains pups' anogenital licking in primiparous rats. In R. L. Doty and D. Müoler-Schwarze (Eds.), *Chemical signals in vertebrates* (Vol. 6, pp. 551–555). New York: Plenum.

Brown et al., 1996. A defect in nurturing in mice lacking the immediate early gene fos B. *Cell, 86*, 297–309.

Brunelli, S. A., Shair, H. N., and Hofer, M. A. (1994). Hypothermic vocalizations of rat pups (Rattus norvegicus) elicit and direct maternal search behavior. *Journal of Comparative Psychology, 108*, 298–303.

Brunner, D., Buhot, M. C., Hen, R., and Hofer, M. (1999). Anxiety, motor activation, and maternal-infant interactions in 5HT1B knockout mice. *Behavioral Neuroscience, 113*, 587–601.

Byrnes, E. M., and Bridges, R. S. (2000). Endogenous opioid facilitation of maternal memory in rats. *Behavioral Neuroscience, 114*, 797–804.

Caldji, C., Tannenbaum, B., Sharma, S., Francis, D., Plotsky, P. M., and Meaney, M. J. (1998). Maternal care during infancy regulates the development of neural systems mediating the expression of fearfulness in the rat. *Proceedings of the National Academy of Sciences U.S.A., 95*, 5335–5340.

Caldwell, J. D., Greer, E. R., Johnson, M. F., Prange, A. J., Jr., and Pedersen, C. A. (1987). Oxytocin and vasopressin immunoreactivity in hypothalamic and extrahypothalamic sites in late pregnant and postpartum rats. *Neuroendocrinology, 46*, 39–47.

Challis, J. R. G., and Olsen, D. M. (1988). Parturition. In E. Knobil, J. D. Neill, L. L. Ewing, C. L. Market, G. S. Greenwald, and D. W. Pfaff (Eds.), *Physiology of Reproduction* (pp. 2177–2216). New York: Raven.

Chiba, T., and Murata, Y. (1985). Afferent and efferent connections of the medial preoptic area in the rat: a WGA-HRP study. *Brain Research Bulletin, 14*, 261–272.

Coe, C. L. (1990). Psychobiology of maternal behavior in nonhuman primates. In N. A. Krasnegor and R. S. Bridges (Eds.), *Mammalian parenting: Biochemical, neurobiological, and behavioral determinants* (pp. 157–183). New York: Oxford University Press.

Cohen, J., and Bridges, R. S. (1981). Retention of maternal behavior in nulliparous and primiparous rats: Effects of duration of previous maternal experience. *Journal of Comparative and Physiological Psychology, 95*, 450–459.

Corodimas, K. P., Rosenblatt, J. S., Canfield, M. E., and Morrell, J. I. (1993). Neurons in the lateral subdivision of the habenular complex mediate the hormonal onset of maternal behavior in rats. *Behavioral Neuroscience, 107*, 827–843.

Corodimas, K. P., Rosenblatt, J. S., and Morrell, J. I. (1992). The habenular complex mediates hormonal stimulation of maternal behavior in rats. *Behavioral Neuroscience, 106*, 853–865.

Corter, C., and Fleming, A. S. (1990). Maternal responsiveness in humans: Emotional, cognitive, and biological factors. *Advances in the study of behavior, 19*, 83–136.

Cramer, C. P. (1988). Experience during suckling increases weight and volume of rat hippocampus. *Brain Research, 470*, 151–155.

Crusio, W. E., and Gerlai, R. T. (Eds.). (1999). *Handbook of molecular–genetic techniques for brain and behavior research* (Vol. 13). New York: Elsevier Science.

Daly, M. (1990). Evolutinary theory and parental motives. In N. A. Krasnegor and R. S. Bridges (Eds.), *Mammalian parenting: Biochemical, neurobiological, and behavioral determinants* (pp. 25–39). New York: Oxford University Press.

Davis, H. P., and Squire, L. R. (1984). Protein synthesis and memory: A review. *Psychological Bulletin, 96*, 518–559.

Davis, M. (1992). The role of the amygdala in conditioned fear. In J. Aggleton (Ed.), *The amygdala: Neurobiological aspects of emotion, memory, and mental dysfunction* (pp. 255–306). New York: Wiley-Liss.

Di Chiara, G. (1998). A motivational learning hypothesis of the role of mesolimbic dopamine in compulsive drug use. *Journal of Psychopharmacology, 12*, 54–67.

Doane, H., and Porter, R. H. (1978). The role of diet in mother–infant reciprocity in the spiny mouse. *Developmental Psychobiology, 11*, 271–277.

Eisenberg, L. (1990). The biosocial context of parenting in human families. In N. A. Krasnegor and R. S. Bridges (Eds.), *Mammalian parenting: Biochemical, neurobiological, and behavioral determinants* (pp. 9–24). New York: Oxford University Press.

Everitt, B. J. (1990). Sexual motivation: a neural and behavioural analysis of the mechanisms underlying appetitive and copulatory responses of male rats. *Neuroscience and Biobehavioral Reviews, 14*, 217–232.

Everitt, B. J., Parkinson, J. A., Olmstead, M. C., Arroyo, M., Robledo, P., and Robbins, T. W. (1999). Associative processes in addiction and reward. The role of amygdala–ventral striatal subsystems. *Annals of the New York Academy of Sciences, 877*, 412–438.

Everitt, B. J., and Robbins, T. W. (1992). Amygdala–ventral striatal interactions and reward-related processes. In J. Aggleton (Ed.), *The amygdala: Neurobiological aspects of emotion, memory, and mental dysfunction* (pp. 401–429). New York: Wiley-Liss.

Evoniuk, G. E., Kuhn, C. M., and Schanberg, S. M. (1979). The effect of tactile stimulation on serum growth hormone and tissue ornithine decarboxylase activity during maternal deprivation in rat pups. *Communications in Psychopharmacology, 3*, 363–370.

Fairbanks, L. A. (1996). Individual differences in maternal style: causes and consequences for mothers and offspring. *Advances in the study of behavior, 25*, 579–611.

Featherstone, R. E., Fleming, A. S., and Ivy, G. O. (2000). Plasticity in the maternal circuit: effects of experience and partum condition on brain astrocyte number in female rats. *Behavioral Neuroscience, 114*, 158–172.

Felton, T. M., Linton, L., Rosenblatt, J. S., and Morrell, J. I. (1998). Intact neurons of the lateral habenular nucleus are necessary for the nonhormonal, pup-mediated display of maternal behavior in sensitized virgin female rats. *Behavioral Neuroscience, 112*, 1458–1465.

Ferreira, G., Gervais, R., Durkin, T. P., and Lévy, F. (1999). Postacquisition scopolamine treatments reveal the time course for the formation of lamb odor recognition memory in parturient ewes. *Behavioral Neuroscience, 113*, 136–142.

Fillion, T. J., and Blass, E. M. (1986). Infantile experience with suckling odors determines adult sexual behavior in male rats. *Science, 231*, 729–731.

Fleischer, S., and Slotnick, B. M. (1978). Disruption of maternal behavior in rats with lesions of the septal area. *Physiology and Behavior, 21*, 189–200.

Fleming, A. S. (1987). Psychobiology of rat maternal behavior: How and where hormones act to promote maternal behavior at parturition. In B. R. Komisaruk, H. I. Siegel, M.-F. Cheng, and H. H. Feder (Eds.), *Reproduction: A behavioral and neuroendocrine perspective* (Vol. 474, pp. 234–251). New York: New York Academy of Sciences.

Fleming, A. S., and Blass, E. M. (1994). Psychobiology of the early mother-young relationship. In J. A. Hogan, J. J. Bolhuis, J. P. Kruijt (Eds.), *Causal mechanisms of behavioural development* (pp. 212–241). Cambridge, England: Cambridge University Press.

Fleming, A. S., Cheung, U., Myhal, N., and Kessler, Z. (1989). Effects of maternal hormones on 'timidity' and attraction to pup-related odors in female rats. *Physiology and Behavior, 46*, 449–453.

Fleming, A. S., Cheung, U. S., and Barry, M. (1990). Cycloheximide blocks the retention of maternal experience in postpartum rats. *Behavioral and Neural Biology, 53*, 64–73.

Fleming, A. S., and Corter, C. (1988). Factors influencing maternal responsiveness in humans: usefulness of an animal model. *Psychoneuroendocrinology, 13*, 189–212.

Fleming, A. S., Gavarth, K., and Sarker, J. (1992). Effects of transections to the vomeronasal nerves or to the main olfactory bulbs on the initiation and long-term retention of maternal behavior in primiparous rats. *Behavioral and Neural Biology, 57*, 177–188.

Fleming, A. S., and Korsmit, M. (1996). Plasticity in the maternal circuit: Effects of maternal experience on Fos-lir in hypothalamic, limbic, and cortical structures in the postpartum rat. *Behavioral Neuroscience, 110*, 567–582.

Fleming, A. S., Korsmit, M., and Deller, M. (1994). Rat pups are potent reinforcers to the maternal animal: Effects of experience, parity, hormones and dopamine function. *Psychobiology, 22*, 44–53.

Fleming, A. S., Kuchera, C., Lee, A., and Winocur, G. (1994). Olfactory-based social learning varies as a function of parity in female rats. *Psychobiology, 22*, 37–43.

Fleming, A. S., and Luebke, C. (1981). Timidity prevents the virgin female rat from being a good mother: Emotionality differences between nulliparous and parturient females. *Physiology and Behavior, 27*, 863–868.

Fleming, A. S., Miceli, M., and Moretto, D. (1983). Lesions of the medial preoptic area prevent the facilitation of maternal behavior produced by amygdala lesions. *Physiology and Behavior, 31*, 503–510.

Fleming, A. S., Morgan, H. D., and Walsh, C. (1996). Experiential factors in postpartum regulation of maternal care. *Advances in the study of behavior, 25*, 295–332.

Fleming, A. S., O'Day, D. H., and Kraemer, G. W. (1999). Neurobiology of mother–infant interactions: Experience and central nervous system plasticity across development and generations. *Neuroscience and Biobehavioral Reviews, 23*, 673–685.

Fleming, A. S., and Rosenblatt, J. S. (1974a). Maternal behavior in the virgin and lactating rat. *Journal of Comparative and Physiological Psychology, 86*, 957–972.

Fleming, A. S., and Rosenblatt, J. S. (1974b). Olfactory regulation of maternal behavior in rats. I. Effects of olfactory bulb removal in experienced and inexperienced lactating and cycling females. *Journal of Comparative and Physiological Psychology, 86*, 221–232.

Fleming, A. S., and Rosenblatt, J. S. (1974c). Olfactory regulation of maternal behavior in rats. II. Effects of peripherally induced anosmia and lesions of the lateral olfactory tract in pup-induced virgins. *Journal of Comparative and Physiological Psychology, 86*, 233–246.

Fleming, A. S., Ruble, D., Krieger, H., and Wong, P. Y. (1997). Hormonal and experiential correlates of maternal responsiveness during pregnancy and the puerperium in human mothers. *Hormones and Behavior, 31*, 145–158.

Fleming, A. S., and Sarker, J. (1990). Experience–hormone interactions and maternal behavior in rats. *Physiology and Behavior, 47*, 1165–1173.

Fleming, A. S., Steiner, M., and Corter, C. (1997). Cortisol, hedonics, and maternal responsiveness in human mothers. *Hormones and Behavior, 32*, 85–98.

Fleming, A. S., Suh, E. J., Korsmit, M., and Rusak, B. (1994). Activation of Fos-like immunoreactivity in the medial preoptic area and limbic structures by maternal and social interactions in rats. *Behavioral Neuroscience, 108*, 724–734.

Fleming, A. S., Vaccarino, F., and Luebke, C. (1980). Amygdaloid inhibition of maternal behavior in the nulliparous female rat. *Physiology and Behavior, 25*, 731–743.

Fleming, A., Vaccarino, F., Tambosso, L., and Chee, P. (1979). Vomeronasal and olfactory system modulation of maternal behavior in the rat. *Science, 203*, 372–374.

Francis, D., Diorio, J., Liu, D., and Meaney, M. J. (1999). Nongenomic transmission across generations of maternal behavior and stress responses in the rat. *Science, 286*, 1155–1158.

Francis, D. D., Caldji, C., Champagne, F., Plotsky, P. M., and Meaney, M. J. (1999). The role of corticotropin-releasing factor—norepinephrine systems in mediating the effects of early experience on the development of behavioral and endocrine responses to stress. *Biological Psychiatry, 46*, 1153–1166.

Francis, D. D., and Meaney, M. J. (1999). Maternal care and the development of stress responses. *Current Opinion In Neurobiology, 9*, 128–134.

Franz, J. R., Leo, R. J., Steuer, M. A., and Kristal, M. B. (1986). Effects of hypothalamic knife cuts and experience on maternal behavior in the rat. *Physiology and Behavior, 38*, 629–640.

Friedman, M. I., Bruno, J. P., and Alberts, J. R. (1981). Physiological and behavioral consequences in rats of water recycling during lactation. *Journal of Comparative and Physiological Psychology, 95*, 26–35.

Galef, B. G. J. (1989). Socially-mediated attenuation of taste-aversion learning in Norway rats: Preventing development of food phobias. *Animal Learning and Behavior, 17*, 468–474.

Galef, B. G. J. (1990). An adaptationist perspective on social learning, social feeding, and social foraging in Norway rats. In D. A. Dewsbury (Ed.), *Contemporary issues in comparative psychology* (pp. 55–79). Suderland, MA: Sinauer.

Galef, B. G. J., and Beck, M. (1990). Diet selection and poison avoidance by mammals individually and in social groups. In E. M. Stricker (Ed.), *Handbook of behavior and neurobiology: Neurobiology and food intake* (Vol. 10, pp. 329–352). New York: Plenum.

Gardner, C. R., and Phillips, S. W. (1977). The influence of the amygdala on the basal septum and preoptic area of the rat. *Experimental Brain Research, 29*, 249–263.

Giordano, A. L., Johnson, A. E., and Rosenblatt, J. S. (1990). Haloperidol-induced disruption of retrieval behavior and reversal with apomorphine in lactating rats. *Physiology and Behavior, 48*, 211–214.

Gonzalez, A., and Fleming, A. S. (in preparation). Artificial rearing alters c-fos expression in juvenile rats.

Gonzalez, A., Lovic, V., Ward, G. R., Wainwright, P. E., and Fleming, A. (2000). Intergenerational effects of complete maternal deprivation and replacement stimulation on maternal behavior and emotionality in female rats. *Developmental Psychobiology, 38*, 11–32.

González-Mariscal, G., Melo, A. I., Chirino, R., Jiménez, P., Beyer, C., and Rosenblatt, J. S. (1998). Importance of mother/young contact at parturition and across lactation for the expression of maternal behavior in rabbits. *Developmental Psychobiology, 32*, 101–111.

Goursaud, A. P., and Nowak, R. (1999). Colostrum mediates the development of mother preference by newborn lambs. *Physiology and Behavior, 67*, 49–56.

Gray, P., and Chesley, S. (1984). Development of maternal behavior in nulliparous rats (*Rattus Norvegicus*): Effects of sex and early maternal experience. *Journal of Comparative Psychology, 98*, 91–99.

Hall, F. S. (1998). Social deprivation of neonatal, adolescent, and adult rats has distinct neurochemical and behavioral consequences. *Critical Reviews in Neurobiology, 12*, 129–162.

Hall, F. S., Wilkinson, L. S., Humby, T., Inglis, W., Kendall, D. A., Marsden, C. A., and Robbins, T. W. (1998). Isolation rearing in rats: Pre- and postsynaptic changes in striatal dopaminergic systems. *Pharmacology Biochemistry and Behavior, 59*, 859–872.

Hammer, R. P., Jr. (1984). The sexually dimorphic region of the preoptic area in rats contains denser opiate receptor binding sites in females. *Brain Research, 308*, 172–176.

Hansen, S. (1994). Maternal behavior of female rats with 6-OHDA lesions in the ventral striatum: Characterization of the pup retrieval deficit. *Physiology and Behavior, 55*, 615–620.

Hansen, S., Bergvall, A. H., and Nyiredi, S. (1993). Interaction with pups enhances dopamine release in the ventral striatum of maternal rats: a microdialysis study. *Pharmacology Biochemistry and Behavior, 45*, 673–676.

Hansen, S., Ferreira, A., and Selart, M. E. (1985). Behavioural similarities between mother rats and benzodiazepine-treated non-maternal animals. *Psychopharmacology*, *86*, 344–347.

Hansen, S., Harthon, C., Wallin, E., Löfberg, L., and Svensson, K. (1991a). The effects of 6-OHDA-induced dopamine depletions in the ventral or dorsal striatum on maternal and sexual behavior in the female rat. *Pharmacology Biochemistry and Behavior*, *39*, 71–77.

Hansen, S., Harthon, C., Wallin, E., Löfberg, L., and Svensson, K. (1991b). Mesotelencephalic dopamine system and reproductive behavior in the female rat: Effects of ventral tegmental 6-hydroxydopamine lesions on maternal and sexual responsiveness. *Behavioral Neuroscience*, *105*, 588–598.

Harlow, H. F. (1963). The manteral affectional system of rhesus monkeys. In H. L. Rheingold (Ed.), *Maternal behavior in mammals* (pp. 254–281). New York: Wiley.

Hatton, G. I., and Tweedle, C. D. (1982). Magnocellular neuropeptidergic neurons in hypothalamus: increases in membrane apposition and number of specialized synapses from pregnancy to lactation. *Brain Research Bulletin*, *8*, 197–204.

Hatton, G. I., Yang, Q. Z., and Cobbett, P. (1987). Dye coupling among immunocytochemically identified neurons in the supraoptic nucleus: increased incidence in lactating rats. *Neuroscience*, *21*, 923–930.

Herrenkohl, L. R., and Rosenberg, P. A. (1972). Exteroceptive stimulation of maternal behavior in the naive rat. *Physiology and Behavior*, *8*, 595–598.

Herskin, M. S., Jensen, K. H., and Thodberg, K. (1998). Influence of environmental stimuli on maternal behavior related to bonding, reactivity and crushing in domestic sows. *Applied Animal Behaviour Science*, *58*, 241–254.

Hodgen, G. D., and Itskovitz, J. (1988). Recognition and maintenance of pregnancy. In E. Knobil, J. D. Neill, L. L. Ewing, C. L., Market, G. S. Greenwald, and D. W. Pfaff (Eds.), *Physiology of reproduction* (pp. 1995–2022). New York: Raven.

Holland, R. C., and Soedjono, A. (1981). Electrophysiological studies of the nucleus accumbens. In R. B. Chronister and J. F. DeFrance (Eds.), *The Neurobiology of the nucleus accumbens* (pp. 253–258). Brunswick, Me: Haer Institute of Electrophysiological Research.

Honrado, G., and Fleming, A. S. (unpublished observation). Maternal behavior in the c-fos "knockout" mouse.

Hudson, R., Cruz, Y., Lucio, R. A., Ninomiya, J., and Martinez-Gomez, M. (1999). Temporal and behavioral patterning of parturition in rabbits and rats. *Physiology and Behavior*, *66*, 599–604.

Ikemoto, S., and Panksepp, J. (1999). The role of nucleus accumbens dopamine in motivated behavior: A unifying interpretation with special reference to reward-seeking. *Brain Research Reviews*, *31*, 6–41.

Insel, T. (1990). Oxytocin and maternal behavior. In N. A. Krasnegor and R. S. Bridges (Eds.), *Mammalian parenting: Biochemical, neurobiological, and behavioral determinants* (pp. 260–280). New York: Oxford University Press.

Insel, T. R. (1997). A neurobiological basis of social attachment. *American Journal of Psychiatry*, *154*, 726–735.

Izquierdo, I., Izquierdo, L. A., Barros, D. M., Mello è Souza, T., de Souza, M. M., Quevedo, J., Rodrigues, C., Sant'Anna, M. K., Madruga, M., and Medina, J. H. (1998). Differential involvement of cortical receptor mechanisms in working, short-term and long-term memory. *Behavioral Pharmacology*, *9*, 421–427.

Jakubowski, M., and Terkel, J. (1986). Establishment and maintenance of maternal responsiveness in postpartum Wistar rats. *Animal Behaviour*, *34*, 256–262.

Jans, J. E., and Leon, M. (1983a). Determinants of mother–young contact in Norway rats. *Physiology and Behavior*, *30*, 919–935.

Jans, J. E., and Leon, M. (1983b). The effects of lactation and ambient temperature on the body temperature of female Norway rats. *Physiology and Behavior*, *30*, 959–961.

Keer, S. E., and Stern, J. M. (1999). Dopamine receptor blockade in the nucleus accumbens inhibits maternal retrieval and licking, but enhances nursing behavior in lactating rats. *Physiology and Behavior*, *67*, 659–669.

Kehoe, P., Shoemaker, W. J., Arons, C., Triano, L., and Suresh, G. (1998). Repeated isolation stress in the neonatal rat: Relation to brain dopamine systems in the 10-day-old rat. *Behavioral Neuroscience*, *112*, 1466–1474.

Kehoe, P., Shoemaker, W. J., Triano, L., Callahan, M., and Rappolt, G. (1998). Adult rats stressed as neonates show exaggerated behavioral responses to both pharmacological and environmental challenges. *Behavioral Neuroscience*, *112*, 116–125.

Kendrick, K. M., Hinton, M. R., Atkins, K., Haupt, M. A., and Skinner, J. D. (1998). Mothers determine sexual preferences [letter]. *Nature (London)*, *395*, 229–230.

Kenyon, P., Cronin, P., and Keeble, S. (1983). Role of the infraorbital nerve in retrieving behavior in lactating rats. *Behavioral Neuroscience*, *97*, 255–269.

Keverne, E. B., and Kendrick, K. M. (1990). Neurochemical changes accompanying parturition and their significance for maternal behavior. In N. A. Krasnegor and R. S. Bridges (Eds.), *Mammalian parenting: Biochemical, neurobiological, and behavioral determinants* (pp. 281–304). New York: Oxford University Press.

Kinsley, C. H. (1990). Prenatal and postnatal influences on parental behavioral in rodents. In N. A. Krasnegor and R. S. Bridges (Eds.), *Mammalian parenting: Biochemical, neurobiological, and behavioral determinants* (pp. 347–371). New York: Oxford University Press.

Kinsley, C. H., and Bridges, R. S. (1988). Prolactin modulation of the maternal-like behavior displayed by juvenile rats. *Hormones and Behavior*, *22*, 49–65.

Kinsley, C. H., Madonia, L., Gifford, G. W., Tureski, K., Griffin, G. R., Lowry, C., Williams, J., Collins, J., McLearie, H., and Lambert, K. G. (1999). Motherhood improves learning and memory. *Nature (London)*, *402*, 137–138.

Kinsley, C. H., Morse, A. C., Zoumas, C., Corl, S., and Billack, B. (1995). Intracerebroventricular infusions of morphine, and blockade with naloxone, modify the olfactory preferences for pup odors in lactating rats. *Brain Research Bulletin*, *37*, 103–107.

Komisaruk, B. R., Rosenblatt, J. S., Barona, M. L., Chinapen, S., Nissanov, J., O'Bannon, R. T., Johnson, B. M., and Del Cerro, M. C. (2000). Combined c-fos and 14C-2-deoxyglucose method to differentiate site-specific excitation from disinhibition: analysis of maternal behavior in the rat. *Brain Research*, *859*, 262–272.

Kraemer, G. W. (1992). A psychobiological theory of attachment. *Behavioral and Brain Sciences*, *15*, 493–541.

Krasnegor, N. A., and Bridges, R. S. (1990). *Mammalian parenting: Biochemical, neurobiological, and behavioral determinants*. New York: Oxford University Press.

Kristal, M. B., Thompson, A. C., Heller, S. B., and Komisaruk, B. R. (1986). Placenta ingestion enhances analgesia produced by vaginal/cervical stimulation in rats. *Physiology and Behavior*, *36*, 1017–1020.

Kuhn, C. M., and Schanberg, S. M. (1998). Responses to maternal separation: Mechanisms and mediators. *International Journal of Developmental Neuroscience*, *16*, 261–270.

LeDoux, J. E. (1992). Emotion and the amygdala. In J. Aggleton (Ed.), *The amygdala: Neurobiological aspects of emotion, memory, and mental dysfunction* (pp. 339–351). New York: Wiley-Liss.

Lee, A., Clancy, S., and Fleming, A. S. (2000). Mother rats bar-press for pups: Effects of lesions of the mpoa and limbic sites on maternal behavior and operant responding for pup-reinforcement [corrected and republished article originally printed in *Behavioural Brain Research* 1999, *100*, 15–31]. *Behavioural Brain Research*, *108*, 215–231.

Lee, A., Li, M., Watchus, J., and Fleming, A. S. (1999). Neuroanatomical basis of maternal memory in postpartum rats: Selective role for the nucleus accumbens. *Behavioral Neuroscience*, *113*, 523–538.

Lefebvre, L., Viville, S., Barton, S. C., Ishino, F., Keverne, E. B., and Surani, M. A. (1998). Abnormal maternal behaviour and growth retardation associated with loss of the imprinted gene Mest. *Nature Genetics*, *20*, 163–169.

Leon, M. (1978). Filial responsiveness to olfactory cues in the laboratory rat. In D. S. Lehrman, R. A. Hinde, and E. Shaw (Eds.), *Advances in the study of behavior* (pp. 117–153). New York: Academic Press.

Leon, M., Coopersmith, R., Beasley, L., and Sullivan, R. M. (1990). Thermal aspects of parenting. In N. A. Krasnegor and R. S. Bridges (Eds.), *Mammalian parenting: Biochemical, neurobiological, and behavioral determinants* (pp. 400–415). New York: Oxford University Press.

Leon, M., Croskerry, P. G., and Smith, G. K. (1978). Thermal control of mother–young contact in rats. *Physiology and Behavior*, *21*, 790–811.

Lévy, F., Kendrick, K. M., Keverne, E. B., Proter, R. H., and Romeyer, A. (1996). Physiological, sensory, and experiential factors of prenatal care in sheep. In J. S. Rosenblatt and C. T. Snowdon (Eds.), *Advances in the study of behavior* (Vol. 25, pp. 385–416). San Diego: Academic.

Lévy, F., and Poindron, P. (1984). Influence du liquide amniotique sur la manifestation du comportement maternel chez la brebis parturiente [The influence of amniotic fluid on maternal behavior in parturient sheep]. *Biology and Behavior*, *9*, 65–88.

Lévy, F., and Poindron, P. (1987). The importance of amniotic fluids for the establishment of maternal behavior in experienced and non-experienced ewes. *Animal Behaviour*, *35*, 1188–1192.

Lévy, F., Poindron, P., and Le Neindre, P. (1983). Attraction and repulsion by amniotic fluids and their olfactory control in the ewe around parturition. *Physiology and Behavior*, *31*, 687–692.

Li, L., Keverne, E. B., Aparicio, S. A., Ishino, F., Barton, S. C., and Surani, M. A. (1999). Regulation of maternal behavior and offspring growth by paternally expressed Peg3. *Science*, *284*, 330–333.

Li, L. L., Szeto, I. Y., Cattanach, B. M., Ishino, F., and Surani, M. A. (2000). Organization and parent-of-origin-specific methylation of imprinted Peg3 gene on mouse proximal chromosome 7. *Genomics*, *63*, 333–340.

Liu, D., Diorio, J., Tannenbaum, B., Caldji, C., Francis, D., Freedman, A., Sharma, S., Pearson, D., Plotsky, P. M., and Meaney, M. J. (1997). Maternal care, hippocampal glucocorticoid receptors, and hypothalamic–pituitary–adrenal responses to stress [see comments]. *Science*, *277*, 1659–1662.

Lonstein, J. S., and De Vries, G. J. (1999). Sex differences in the parental behaviour of adult virgin prairie voles: Independence from gonadal hormones and vasopressin. *Journal of Neuroendocrinology*, *11*, 441–449.

Lonstein, J. S., Simmons, D. A., and Stern, J. M. (1998). Functions of the caudal periaqueductal gray in lactating rats: Kyphosis, lordosis, maternal aggression, and fearfulness. *Behavioral Neuroscience*, *112*, 1502–1518.

Lonstein, J. S., and Stern, J. M. (1997). Role of the midbrain periaqueductal gray in maternal nurturance and aggression: c-fos and electrolytic lesion studies in lactating rats. *Journal of Neuroscience*, *17*, 3364–3378.

Lott, D. L., and Fuchs, S. S. (1962). Failure to induce retrieving by sensitization or the injection of prolactin. *Journal of Comparative and Physiological Psychology*, *65*, 111–113.

Lovic, V., Gonzalez, A., and Fleming, A. (2001). Maternally separated rats show deficits in maternal care in adulthood. *Developmental Psychobiology*, *39*, 19–33.

Lucas, B. K., Ormandy, C. J., Binart, N., Bridges, R. S., and Kelly, P. A. (1998). Null mutation of the prolactin receptor gene produces a defect in maternal behavior. *Endocrinology*, *139*, 4102–4107.

Lyons, D. M., Kim, S., Schatzberg, A. F., and Levine, S. (1998). Postnatal foraging demands alter adrenocortical activity and psychosocial development. *Developmental Psychobiology, 32*, 285–291.

Magnusson, J. E., and Fleming, A. S. (1995). Rat pups are reinforcing to the maternal rat: Role of sensory cues. *Psychobiology, 23*, 69–75.

Malenfant, S. A., Barry, M., and Fleming, A. S. (1991). Effects of cycloheximide on the retention of olfactory learning and maternal experience effects in postpartum rats. *Physiology and Behavior, 49*, 289–294.

Mann, P. E., and Bridges, R. S. (1992). Neural and endocrine sensitivities to opioids decline as a function of multiparity in the rat. *Brain Research, 580*, 241–248.

Martinez, J. L. J., and Kesner, R. P. (1991). Pharmacology and biochemistry: Memory: drugs and hormones. In J. L. J. Martinez and R. P. Kesner (Eds.), *Learning and memory: A biological view* (pp. 127–163). Orlando, FL: Academic.

Matthews-Felton, T., Corodimas, M. C., Rosenblatt, J. S., and Morrell J. I. (1995). Lateral habenula neurons are necessary for the hormonal onset of maternal behavior and for the display of postpartum estrus in naturally parturient female rats. *Behavioral Neuroscience, 109*, 1172–88.

Matthews-Felton, T., Linton, L. N., Rosenblatt, J. S., and Morrell, J. I. (1999). Estrogen implants in the lateral habenular nucleus do not stimulate the onset of maternal behavior in female rats. *Hormones and Behavior, 35*, 71–80.

Matthews, K., Wilkinson, L. S., and Robbins, T. W. (1996). Repeated maternal separation of preweanling rats attenuates behavioral responses to primary and conditioned incentives in adulthood. *Physiology and Behavior, 59*, 99–107.

Mayer, A. D. (1983). The ontogeny of maternal behavior in rodents. In R. W. Elwood (Ed.), *Parental behavior of rodents* (pp. 1–20). Chichester, England: Wiley.

Mayer, A. D., and Rosenblatt, J. S. (1977). Effects of intranasal zinc sulfate on open field and maternal behavior in female rats. *Physiology and Behavior, 18*, 101–109.

McQuire, M. K., Pachon, H., Butler, W. R., and Rasmussen, K. M. (1995). Food restriction, gonadotropins, and behavior in the lactating rat. *Physiology and Behavior, 58*, 1243–1249.

Mitchell, J. B., and Gratton, A. (1994). Involvement of mesolimbic dopamine neurons in sexual behaviors: Implications for the neurobiology of motivation. *Review of Neuroscience, 5*, 317–329.

Miyazaki, K., Mogi, E., Araki, N., and Matsumoto, G. (1998). Reward-quality dependent anticipation in rat nucleus accumbens. *Neuroreport, 9*, 3943–3948.

Moffat, S. D., Suh, E. J., and Fleming, A. S. (1993). Noradrenergic involvement in the consolidation of maternal experience in postpartum rats. *Physiology and Behavior, 53*, 805–811.

Moltz, H., Levin, R., and Leon, M. (1969). Differential effects of progesterone on the maternal behavior of primiparous and multiparous rats. *Journal of Comparative and Physiological Psychology, 67*, 36–40.

Moltz, H., Robbins, D., and Parks, M. (1966). Caesarean delivery and maternal behavior of primiparous and multiparous rats. *Journal of Comparative and Physiological Psychology, 61*, 455–460.

Moltz, H., and Wiener, E. (1966). Effects of ovariectomy on maternal behavior of primiparous and multiparous rats. *Journal of Comparative and Physiological Psychology, 61*, 455–460.

Moore, C. (1995). Maternal contributions to mammalian reproductive development and the divergence of males and females. In P. J. B. Slater, J. S. Rosenblatt, C. T. Snowdon, and M. Milinski (Eds.), *Advances in the study of behavior* (Vol. 24, pp. 47–118). San Diego: Academic.

Moore, C. L. (1990). Comparative development of vertebrate sexual behavior: Levels, cascades, and webs. In D. A. Dewsbury (Ed.), *Contemporary issues in comparative psychology* (pp. 278–299). Suderland, MA: Sinauer.

Moretto, D., Paclik, L., and Fleming, A. (1986). The effects of early rearing environments on maternal behavior in adult female rats. *Developmental Psychobiology, 19*, 581–591.

Morgan, H. D., Fleming, A. S., and Stern, J. M. (1992). Somatosensory control of the onset and retention of maternal responsiveness in primiparous Sprague-Dawley rats. *Physiology and Behavior, 51*, 549–555.

Morgan, H. D., Watchus, J. A., Milgram, N. W., and Fleming, A. S. (1999). The long lasting effects of electrical simulation of the medial preoptic area and medial amygdala on maternal behavior in female rats. *Behavioural Brain Research, 99*, 61–73.

Najbauer, J., and Leon, M. (1995). Olfactory experience modulated apoptosis in the developing olfactory bulb. *Brain Research, 674*, 245–251.

Neumann, I. D., Johnstone, H. A., Hatzinger, M., Liebsch, G., Shipston, M., Russell, J. A., Landgraf, R., and Douglas, A. J. (1998). Attenuated neuroendocrine responses to emotional aqnd physical stressors in pregnant rats involve adeno-hypophyseal changes. *Journal of Physiology, 508*, 289–300.

Nissen, H. (1930). A study of maternal behavior in the white rat by means of the obstruction method. *Journal of Genetic Psychology, 87*, 377–393.

Noirot, E. (1972). The onset of maternal behavior in rats, hamsters, and mice. In D. S. Lehrman, R. A. Hinde, and E. Shaw (Eds.), *Advances in the study of behavior* (Vol. 4, pp. 107–140). New York: Academic.

Noonan, L. R., Caldwell, J. D., Li, L., Walker, C. H., Pedersen, C. A., and Mason, G. A. (1994). Neonatal stress transiently alters the development of hippocampal oxytocin receptors. *Developmental Brain Research, 80*, 115–120.

Numan, M. (1974). Medial preoptic area and maternal behavior in the female rat. *Journal of Comparative and Physiological Psychology, 87*, 746–759.

Numan, M. (1988). Neural basis of maternal behavior in the rat. *Psychoneuroendocrinology, 13*, 47–62.

Numan, M. (1994). Maternal behavior. In E. Knobil and J. D. Neill (Eds.), *The physiology of reproduction* (2nd ed., pp. 221–302). New York: Raven.

Numan, M., Corodimas, K. P., Numan, M. J., Factor, E. M., and Piers, W. D. (1988). Axon-sparing lesions of the preoptic region and substantia innominata disrupt maternal behavior in rats. *Behavioral Neuroscience, 102*, 381–396.

Numan, M., McSparren, J., and Numan, M. J. (1990). Dorsolateral connections of the medial preoptic area and maternal behavior in rats. *Behavioral Neuroscience, 104*, 964–979.

Numan, M., and Numan, M. (1996). A lesion and neuroanatomical tract-tracing analysis of the role of the bed nucleus of the stria terminalis in retrieval behavior and other aspects of maternal responsiveness in rats. *Developmental Psychobiology, 29*, 23–51.

Numan, M., and Numan, M. J. (1994). Expression of Fos-like immunoreactivity in the preoptic area of maternally behaving virgin and postpartum rats. *Behavioral Neuroscience, 108*, 379–394.

Numan, M., and Numan, M. J. (1995). Importance of pup-related sensory inputs and maternal performance for the expression of Fos-like immunoreactivity in the preoptic area and ventral bed nucleus of the stria terminalis of postpartum rats. *Behavioral Neuroscience, 109*, 135–149.

Numan, M., and Numan, M. J. (1997). Projection sites of medial preoptic area and ventral bed nucleus of the stria terminalis neurons that express Fos during maternal behavior in female rats. *Journal of Neuroendocrinology, 9*, 369–384.

Numan, M., Numan, M. J., and English, J. B. (1993). Excitotoxic amino acid injections into the medial amygdala facilitate maternal behavior in virgin female rats. *Hormones and Behavior, 27*, 56–81.

Numan, M., Roach, J. K., del Cerro, M. C., Guillamon, A., Segovia, S., Sheehan, T. P., and Numan, M. J. (1999). Expression of intracellular progesterone receptors in rat brain during different reproductive states, and involvement in. maternal behavior. *Brain Research, 830*, 358–371.

Numan, M., Rosenblatt, J., and Komisaruk, B. R. (1977). Medial preoptic area and onset of maternal behavior in the rat. *Journal of Comparative and Physiological Psychology, 91*, 146–164.

Numan, M., and Sheehan, T. P. (1997). Neuroanatomical circuitry for mammalian maternal behavior. *Annals of the New York Academy of Sciences, 807*, 101–125.

Orpen, B. G., and Fleming, A. S. (1987). Experience with pups sustains maternal responding in postpartum rats. *Physiology and Behavior, 40*, 47–54.

Orpen, B. G., Furman, N., Wong, P. Y., and Fleming, A. S. (1987). Hormonal influences on the duration of postpartum maternal responsiveness in the rat. *Physiology and Behavior, 40*, 307–315.

Panesar, S., and Fleming, A. (Nov. 2000). *Effects of adrenalectomy and corticosterone replacement on maternal behavior in virgin and postpartum rats.* Paper presented at the meeting of the Society for Neuroscience, New Orleans, LA.

Panksepp, J., Nelson, E., and Siviy, S. (1994). Brain opioids and mother-infant social motivation. *Acta Paediatric Supplement, 397*, 40–46.

Pascual, R., and Figueroa, H. (1996). Effects of preweaning sensorimotor stimulation on behavioral and neuronal development in motor and visual cortex of the rat. *Biology of the Neonate, 69*, 399–404.

Pedersen, C. A., Caldwell, J. D., Walker, C., Ayers, G., and Mason, G. A. (1994). Oxytocin activates the postpartum onset of rat maternal behavior in the ventral tegmental and medial preoptic areas. *Behavioral Neuroscience, 108*, 1163–1171.

Pedersen, C. A., Johns, J. M., Musiol, I., Perez-Delgado, M., Ayers, G., Faggin, B., and Caldwell, J. D. (1995). Interfering with somatosensory stimulation from pups sensitizes experienced, postpartum rat mothers to oxytocin antagonist inhibition of maternal behavior. *Behavioral Neuroscience, 109*, 980–990.

Pederson, C., and Blass, E. (1981). Olfactory control over suckling in albino rats. In R. N. Aslin, J. R. Alberts, and M. R. Petersen (Eds.), *Development of perception: Psychobiological perspectives* (pp. 359–381). New York: Academic.

Perlmutter, L. S., Tweedle, C. D., and Hatton, G. I. (1984). Neuronal/glial plasticity in the supraoptic dendritic zone: dendritic bundling and double synapse formation at parturition. *Neuroscience, 13*, 769–779.

Peters, L. C., and Kristal, M. B. (1983). Suppression of infanticide in mother rats. *Journal of Comparative Psychology, 97*, 167–177.

Pfaff, D., and Keiner, M. (1973). Atlas of estradiol-concentrating cells in the central nervous system of the female rat. *Journal of Comparative Neurology, 151*, 121–158.

Poindron, P., and Le Neindre, P. (1980). Endocrine and sensory regulation of maternal behavior in the ewe. In J. S. Rosenblatt, R. A. Hinde, and C. Beer (Eds.), *Advances in the study of behavior* (Vol. 11, pp. 75–119). New York: Academic.

Poindron, P., and Lévy, F. (1990). Physiological, sensory and experiential determinants of maternal behavior in sheep. In N. A. Krasnegor and R. S. Bridges (Eds.), *Mammalian parenting: Biochemical, neurobiological, and behavioral determinants* (pp. 133–157). New York: Oxford University Press.

Polan, H. J., and Hofer, M. A. (1998). Olfactory preference for mother over home nest havings by newborn rats. *Developmental Psychobiology, 33*, 5–20.

Post, R. M., Weiss, S. R., Li, H., Smith, M. A., Zhang, L. X., Xing, G., Osuch, E. A., and McCann, U. D. (1998). Neural plasticity and emotional memory. *Developmental Psychopathology, 10*, 829–855.

Pryce, C. R. (1992). A comparative systems model of the regulation of maternal motivation in mammals. *Animal Behaviour*, *43*, 417–441.

Rees, S. L., and Fleming, A. S. (in press). How early maternal seperation and juvenile experience with pups affect maternal behavior and emotionality in adult postpartum rats. *Animal Learning and Behavior*, *29*(3).

Riddle, O., Lahr, E. L., and Bates, R. W. (1935). Maternal behavior induced in virgin rats by prolactin. *Proceedings of the Society for Experimental Biology and Medicine*, *32*, 730–734.

Rogan, M. T., Staubli, U. V., and LeDoux, J. E. (1997). Fear conditioning induces associative long-term potentiation in the amygdala [see comments] [published erratum appears in *Nature (London)*, 1998, *391*, 818]. *Nature (London)*, *390*, 604–607.

Rosen, J. B., Fanselow, M. S.,Young, S. L., Sitcoske, M., and Maren, S. (1998). Immediate-early gene expression in the amygdala following footshock stress and contextual fear conditioning. *Brain Research*, *796*, 132–142.

Rosenberg, P., Leidahl, L., Halaris, A., and Moltz, H. (1976). Changes in the metabolism of hypothalamic norepinephrine associated with the onset of maternal behavior in the nulliparous rat. *Pharmacology Biochemistry and Behavior*, *4*, 647–649.

Rosenblatt, J. S. (1967). Nonhormonal basis of maternal behavior in the rat. *Science*, *156*, 1512–1514.

Rosenblatt, J. S. (1971). Suckling and home orientation in the kitten: A comparative developmental study. In E. Tobach, L. Aronson, and E. Shaw (Eds.), *The biopsychology of development* (pp. 345–410). New York: Academic.

Rosenblatt, J. S. (1990). Landmarks in the physiological study of maternal behavior with special reference to the rat. In N. A. Krasnegor and R. S. Bridges (Eds.), *Mammalian parenting: Biochemical, neurobiological, and behavioral determinants* (pp. 40–60). New York: Oxford University Press.

Rosenblatt, J. S., and Lehrman, D. S. (1963). Maternal behavior in the laboratory rat. In H. L. Rheingold (Ed.), *Maternal behavior in mammals* (pp. 8–57). New York: Wiley.

Rosenblatt, J. S., and Snowdon, C. T. (Eds.). (1996). *Advances in the study of behavior*. San Diego: Academic.

Rosenzweig, M. R., and Bennett, E. L. (1996). Psychobiology of plasticity: Effects of training and experience on brain and behavior. *Behavioural Brain Research*, *78*, 57–65.

Rubin, B. S., and Bridges, R. S. (1984). Disruption of ongoing maternal responsiveness in rats by central administration of morphine sulfate. *Brain Research*, *307*, 91–97.

Ruppenthal, G. C., Arling, G. L., Harlow, H. F., Sackett, G. P., and Suomi, S. J. (1976). A 10-year perspective of motherless-mother monkey behavior. *Journal of Abnormal Psychololgy*, *85*, 341–349.

Sagar, S. M., Sharp, F. R., and Curran, T. (1988). Expression of c-fos protein in brain: Metabolic mapping at the cellular level. *Science*, *240*, 1328–1331.

Schlein, P. A., Zarrow, M. X., Cohen, H. A., Denenberg, V. H., and Johnson, N. P. (1972). The differential effect of anosmia on maternal behaviour in the virgin and primiparous rat. *Journal of Reproductive Fertility*, *30*, 139–142.

Schneirla, T. C. (1959). An evolutionaary and developmental theory of biphasic process underlying approach and withdrawal. In M. R. Jones (Ed.), *Nebraska symposium on motivation* (Vol. 7, pp. 1–42). Lincoln, NE: University of Nebraska Press.

Setlow, B., and McGaugh, J. L. (1998). Sulpiride infused into the nucleus accumbens posttraining impairs memory of spatial water maze training. *Behavioral Neuroscience*, *112*, 603–610.

Setlow, B., Roozendaal, B., and McGaugh, J. L. (2000). Involvement of a basolateral amygdala complex-nucleus accumbens pathway in glucocorticoid-induced modulation of memory consolidation. *European Journal of Neuroscience*, *12*, 367–375.

Shah, A., Oxley, G., Lovic, V., and Fleming, A. S. (submitted). Effects of early olfactory experience in nest on maternal behavior in the adult offspring. *Developmental Psychobiology*.

Sheehan, T. P., and Numan, M. (1997). Microinjection of the tachykinin neuropeptide K into the ventromedial hypothalamus disrupts the hormonal onset of maternal behavior in female rats. *Journal of Neuroendocrinology*, *9*, 677–687.

Silva, M. R., Bernardi, M. M., Nasello, A. G., and Felicio, L. F. (1997). Influence of lactation on motor activity and elevated plus maze behavior. *Brazil Journal of Medical and Biological Research*, *30*, 241–244.

Slotnick, B. M. (1967). Disturbances of maternal behavior in the rat following lesions of the cingulate cortex. *Behaviour*, *29*, 204–236.

Smotherman, W. P., Bell, R. W., Starzec, J., Elias, J., and Zachman, T. A. (1974). Maternal responses to infant vocalizations and olfactory cues in rats and mice. *Behavioral Biology*, *12*, 55–66.

Stafisso-Sandoz, G., Polley, D., Holt, E., Lambert, K. G., and Kinsley, C. H. (1998). Opiate disruption of maternal behavior: Morphine reduces, and naloxone restores, c-fos activity in the medial preoptic area of lactating rats. *Brain Research Bulletin*, *45*, 307–313.

Stamm, J. S. (1955). The function of the median cerebral cortex in maternal behavior in rats. *Journal of Comparative and Physiological Psychology*, *48*, 347–356.

Stern, J. M. (1983). Maternal behavior priming in virgin and Caesarean-delivered Long-Evans rats: Effects of brief contact or continuous exteroceptive pup stimulation. *Physiology and Behavior*, *31*, 757–763.

Stern, J. M. (1985). Parturition influences initial pup preferences at later onset of maternal behavior in primiparous rats. *Physiology and Behavior*, *35*, 25–31.

Stern, J. M. (1989). Maternal behavior: Sensory, hormonal, and neural determinants. In F. R. Brush and S. Levine (Eds.), *Psychoendocrinology* (pp. 105–226). New York: Academic.

Stern, J. M. (1990). Multisensory regulation of maternal behavior and masculine sexual behavior: A revised view. *Neuroscience and Biobehavioral Reviews, 14*, 183–200.

Stern, J. M. (1996). Trigeminal lesions and maternal behavior in Norway rats: II. Disruption of parturition. *Physiology and Behavior, 60*, 187–190.

Stern, J. M., Dix, L., Bellomo, C., and Thramann, C. (1992). Ventral trunk somatosensory determinants of nursing behavior in Norway rats: Role of nipple and surrounding sensations. *Psychobiology, 20*, 71–80.

Stern, J. M., Dix, L., Pointek, C., and Thramann, C. (1990). Ventral somatosensory determinants of nursing behavior in rats: Effects of nipple loss or anesthesia. *Society for Neuroscience, 16*, 600.

Stern, J. M., and Johnson, S. K. (1989). Perioral somatosensory determinants of nursing behavior in Norway rats (*Rattus norvegicus*). *Journal of Comparative Psychology, 103*, 269–280.

Stern, J. M., and Keer, S. E. (1999). Maternal motivation of lactating rats is disrupted by low dosages of haloperidol. *Behavioural Brain Research, 99*, 231–239.

Stern, J. M., and Kolunie, J. M. (1989). Perioral anesthesia disrupts maternal behavior during early lactation in Long-Evans rats. *Behavioral and Neural Biology, 52*, 20–38.

Stern, J. M., and Kolunie, J. M. (1991). Trigeminal lesions and maternal behavior in Norway rats: I. Effects of cutaneous rostral snout denervation on maintenance of nurturance and maternal aggression. *Behavioral Neuroscience, 105*, 984–997.

Stern, J. M., and MacKinnon, D. A. (1976). Postpartum, hormonal, and nonhormonal induction of maternal behavior in rats: Effects on T-maze retrieval of pups. *Hormones and Behavior, 7*, 305–316.

Stern, J. M., and Taylor, L. A. (1991). Haloperidol inhibits maternal retrieval and licking, but facilitates nursing behavior and milk ejection in lactating rats. *Journal of Neuroendocrinology, 3*, 591–596.

Suchecki, D., Nelson, D. Y., van Oers, H., and Levine, S. (1995). Activation and inhibition of the hypothalamic-pituitary-adrenal axis of the neonatal rat: Effects of maternal deprivation. *Psychoneuroendocrinology, 20*, 169–182.

Suchecki, D., Rosenfeld, P., and Levine, S. (1993). Maternal regulation of the hypothalamic–pituitary–adrenal axis in the infant rat: The roles of feeding and stroking. *Developmental Brain Research, 75*, 185–192.

Sullivan, R. M., Stackenwalt, G., Nasr, F., Lemon, C., and Wilson, D. A. (2000). Association of an odor with activation of olfactory bulb noradrenergic beta-receptors or locus coeruleus stimulation is sufficient to produce learned approach responses to that odor in neonatal rats. *Behavioral Neuroscience, 114*, 957–62.

Suomi, S. J., and Ripp, C. (1983). A history of motherless mothering at the University of Wisconsin Primate Laboratory. In M. Reite and N. Caine (Eds.), *Child abuse: The non-human primate data* (pp. 49–78). New York: Liss.

Svare, B. (1990). Maternal aggression: Hormonal, genetic, and developmental determinants. In N. A. Krasnegor and R. S. Bridges (Eds.), *Mammalian parenting: Biochemical, neurobiological, and behavioral determinants* (pp. 118–132). New York: Oxford University Press.

Terkel, J., and Rosenblatt, J. S. (1971). Aspects of nonhormonal maternal behavior in the rat. *Hormones and Behavior, 2*, 167–171.

Terkel, J., and Rosenblatt, J. S. (1972). Humoral factors underlying maternal behavior at parturition: Corss transfusion between freely moving rats. *Journal of Comparative and Physiological Psychology, 80*, 365–371.

Terlecki, L. J., and Sainsbury, R. S. (1978). Effects of fimbria lesions on maternal behavior in the rat. *Physiology and Behavior, 21*, 89–97.

Theodosis, D. T., and Poulain, D. A. (1984). Evidence for structural plasticity in the supraoptic nucleus of the rat hypothalamus in relation to gestation and lactation. *Neuroscience, 11*, 183–193.

Tucker, H. A. (1988). Lactation and its hormonal control. In E. Knobil, J. D. Neill, L. L. Ewing, C. L. Market, G. S. Greenwald, and D. W. Pfaff (Eds.), *Physiology of reproduction* (pp. 2235–2264). New York: Raven.

van Oers, H. J., de Kloet, E. R., Whelan, T., and Levine, S. (1998). Maternal deprivation effect on the infant's neural stress markers is reversed by tactile stimulation and feeding but not by suppressing corticosterone. *Journal of Neuroscience, 18*, 10171–10179.

Vazquez, D. M., van Oers, H., Levine, S., and Akil, H. (1996). Regulation of glucocorticoid and mineralocorticoid receptor mRNAs in the hippocampus of the maternally deprived infant rat. *Brain Research, 731*, 79–90.

Wakerly, J. B., Clarke, G., and Sumerlee, A. J. (1988). Milk ejection and its control. In E. Knobil, J. D. Neill, L. L. Ewing, C. L. Market, G. S. Greenwald, and D. W. Pfaff (Eds.), *Physiology of reproduction* (pp. 2283–2321). New York: Raven.

Walsh, C. J., Fleming, A. S., Lee, A., and Magnusson, J. E. (1996). The effects of olfactory and somatosensory desensitization on Fos-like immunoreactivity in the brains of pup-exposed postpartum rats. *Behavioral Neuroscience, 110*, 134–153.

Whishaw, I. Q., and Kornelsen, R. A. (1993). Two types of motivation revealed by ibotenic acid nucleus accumbens lesions: Dissociation of food carrying and hoarding and the role of primary and incentive motivation. *Behavioural Brain Research, 55*, 283–295.

Wiesner, B. P., and Sheard, N. M. (1933). *Maternal behaviour in the rat*. Edinburgh: Oliver.

Willner, P., and Scheel-Kruger, J. (Eds.). (1991). *The mesolimbic dopamine system: From motivation to action*. New York: Wiley.

Wilson, C., Nomikos, G. G., Collu, M., and Fibiger, H. C. (1995). Dopaminergic correlates of motivated behavior: Importance of drive. *Journal of Neuroscience, 15,* 5169–5178.

Wilson, D. A., and Sullivan, R. M. (1994). Neurobiology of associative learning in the neonate: Early olfactory learning. *Behavioral and Neural Biology, 61,* 1–18.

Wilsoncroft, V. (1969). Babies by bar-press: Maternal behaviour in the rat. *Behavior Research Methods and Instrumentation, 1,* 229–230.

Wilsoncroft, W. E. (1963). Effects of median cortex lesions on the maternal behavior of the rat. *Psychological Reports, 13,* 835–838.

Windle, R. J., Wood, S., Shanks, N., Perks, P., Conde, G. L., da Costa, A. P., Ingram, C. D., and Lightman, S. L. (1997). Endocrine and behavioural responses to noise stress: Comparison of virgin and lactating female rats during non-disrupted maternal activity. *Journal of Neuroendocrinology, 9,* 407–414.

Winnicka, M. M. (1999). Dopaminergic projection to the nucleus accumbens mediates the memory-enhancing effect of angiotensins in rats. *Pharmacology Biochemistry and Behavior, 62,* 625–630.

Wise, R. A. (1985). The anhedonia hypothesis: Mark III. *Behavioral and Brain Sciences, 8,* 178–186.

Wise, R. A. (1998). Drug-activation of brain reward pathways. *Drug and Alcohol Dependence, 51,* 13–22.

Wise, R. A., Spindler, J., deWit, H., and Gerberg, G. J. (1978). Neuroleptic-induced "anhedonia" in rats: Pimozide blocks reward quality of food. *Science, 201,* 262–264.

Yang, Q. Z., and Hatton, G. I. (1988). Direct evidence for electrical coupling among rat supraoptic nucleus neurons. *Brain Research, 463,* 47–56.

Young, L. J., Muns, S., Wang, Z., and Insel, T. R. (1997). Changes in oxytocin receptor mRNA in rat brain during pregnancy and the effects of estrogen and interleukin-6. *Journal of Neuroendocrinology, 9,* 859–865.

Young, L. J., Winslow, J. T., Wang, Z., Gingrich, B., Guo, Q., Matzuk, M. M., and Insel, T. R. (1997). Gene targeting approaches to neuroendocrinology: Oxytocin, maternal behavior, and affiliation. *Hormones and Behavior, 31,* 221–231.

Yu, G. Z., Kaba, H., Okutani, F., Takahashi, S., and Higuchi, T. (1996). The olfactory bulb: A critical site of action for oxytocin in the induction of maternal behaviour in the rat. *Neuroscience, 72,* 1083–1088.

4

Primate Parenting

Kim A. Bard
University of Portsmouth

INTRODUCTION

The conceptual and the practical issues associated with parenting in nonhuman primates in general and with maternal competence in chimpanzees specifically are addressed in this chapter. What does it take to be a good parent if you are a primate? How can we characterize the ontogeny of maternal and paternal skills? Are there biological bases in primate parenting? What are the learning mechanisms involved in parenting in primates? It seems evident that there are specific behaviors that must be learned in order to be a competent parent; however, the learning mechanisms remain unknown. It is unclear whether behavior patterns must be learned through actual practice or whether other mechanisms, such as observational learning, are equally effective. In addition, the influence of early experience on maternal capability remains an unknown factor. These central questions of parenting in primates have been asked for the past 30 years and still have not been satisfactorily answered (e.g., Rogers and Davenport, 1970).

Primates were studied in their natural habitat in the 1920s, 1930s, and 1940s in order to document the variety of primate species and to specify the habitat, group demographics, and gross aspects of behavior in each species (e.g., Bingham, 1932; Carpenter, 1964; Nissen, 1931; Zuckerman, 1932). In 1938, a monkey colony was established at Cayo Santiago with rhesus imported from India, and the long-term study of Japanese macaques was begun (Dolhinow, 1972). Studies of the finer details of behavior during this time were conducted in the laboratory (e.g., Harlow, 1958; Kluver, 1933; Kohler, 1925; Yerkes and Yerkes, 1929) or in the home as a laboratory (e.g., Jacobsen, Jacobsen, and Yoshioka, 1932; Kellogg and Kellogg, 1933; Kohts, 1935).

In the 1950s, there was a burst of long-term field studies and an equivalent burst of laboratory studies, but few species were studied in depth. Basics about mother–infant relations and social systems were described in some species of macaques, especially Japanese macaques (Itani, 1959), rhesus (Altmann, 1962), baboons (DeVore, 1963; Hall, 1962; Rowell, 1966), and langurs (Jay, 1962).

In the 1950s and 1960s, Harlow and colleagues experimentally manipulated aspects of the mother–infant relation (Harlow, 1958; Kaufman and Rosenblum, 1969; Seay, Hansen, and Harlow, 1962), and Hinde and colleagues studied mother–infant relations in group-living captive rhesus (e.g., Hinde, 1969; Hinde and Spencer-Booth, 1967; Rowell, Hinde, and Spencer-Booth, 1964). These research efforts in connection with Ainsworth's (1967; Ainsworth and Bell, 1970) study of human mother–infant relations greatly affected Bowlby's (1969; 1973) theoretical works on attachment.

The 1960s was the beginning of long-term field work of great apes (Nishida, 1968; Reynolds, 1965; Schaller, 1963; van Lawick-Goodall, 1968), prosimians (Jolly, 1966), and baboons (Kummer, 1967) and could be considered the beginning of the explosion of psychological, biological, anthropological, and evolutionary studies of primates that took place in the laboratory (e.g., Schrier, Harlow, and Stollnitz, 1965), seminatural settings (e.g., Altmann, 1962), and the natural habitat (Altmann, 1967; DeVore, 1965; Dolhinow, 1972; Jay, 1968; Morris, 1967). In addition, primate research centers were established at Kyoto University (The Japan Monkey Center), the University of Wisconsin, and Emory University (Yerkes Regional Primate Research Center; Parker, 1990).

The foundation of basic knowledge provided by these studies allowed specific issues to be addressed, such as the following: (1) What are the genetic and the evolutionary bases of parental care (e.g., Trivers, 1974)? (2) What functions are served by nonparents providing infant care (e.g., Hrdy, 1976; Lancaster, 1971; McKenna, 1979; Quiatt, 1979; Rowell, Hinde, and Spencer-Booth, 1964)? (3) Why does infanticide occur (e.g., Hausfater and Hrdy, 1984; Hrdy, 1976; Nicolson, 1987; Quiatt, 1979)? (4) How do disruptions or dysfunctions in parental care influence infants, e.g., child abuse (Nadler, 1980; Reite and Caine, 1983)? (5) What is the evolution of male–infant relations (Deag and Crook, 1971; Strum, 1984; Whitten, 1987)? and (6) How do social systems influence patterns of parental care (e.g., Hinde and Spencer-Booth, 1967; Maestripieri, 1994)?

These central issues have been further investigated, raising more specific questions. For instance, what are the major factors that influence the evolution of cooperative care? It was thought that males would provide care when paternity was certain, so monogamy was considered to be the best predictor of cooperative care. When types of care were compared across monogamous primates, some did have cooperative care but others did not (Wright, 1990). The ratio of infant(s) weight to mother's weight was also considered to be a predictor of cooperative care, but it was also found to be a poor candidate (Gursky, 2000). Cooperative care of infants is associated with increased vigilance and defense against predators (Caine, 1993; Snowdon, 1996). A constant issue is how primate parenting relates to human parenting (Goodall, 1967; Higley and Suomi, 1986; Hinde, 1969; Hinde and Stevenson-Hinde, 1990; Nicolson, 1991; Rheingold, 1963), and this is considered in more detail in the final section of the chapter.

This chapter is concerned with describing parenting behavior in primates. Chimpanzees are used as the basis for comparison with other primate species. Chimpanzees are our closest evolutionary relatives, sharing over 90% similarity in genetic material (King and Wilson, 1975), and provide important information relevant to human behavior. In addition, parental prerequisites are proposed. As a result of research with chimpanzees, a proposal is made that there are optimal or sensitive periods during which different aspects of parental behavior are readily learned (e.g., Bornstein, 1989). Intervention strategies to maximize parental competence in chimpanzees are presented; optimal learning periods and ways to facilitate learning a full range of necessary behaviors are discussed.

The majority of research on primate parenting has been conducted in a relatively limited number of primate species. This chapter, as a product of our limited knowledge, focuses on the well-studied species listed in Table 4.1. Parenting behaviors in chimpanzees are described in detail, and explicit comparisons are made in parenting behavior among chimpanzees and other primates. Social dynamics may also influence parenting styles (for example, see Maestripieri, 1994), and these are listed in Table 4.2, but because of lack of space are not discussed in detail here (see Smuts, Cheney, Seyfarth, Wrangham, and Shruhsaker, 1987). In addition, issues pertaining to the development and the ontogeny of adequate parental behaviors are highlighted. This perspective provides insights on

TABLE 4.1
Primate Taxonomy (with Familiar Species Listed)

Prosimians

Suborder: Strepsirhini	**Superfamily**: Lemuroidea (Malagasy
Lemur catta, ring-tailed lemurs	lemurs)
	Superfamily: Lorisoidea

Loris tardigradus, slender loris; *Galago senagalensis*, lesser bushbaby

Suborder: Haplorhini	**Superfamily**: Tarsioidea

Tarsius bancanus, Borneo tarsier; *Tarsius spectrum*, spectral tarsier

New World Monkeys	**Superfamily**: Ceboidea
Family: Callitrichidae (tamarins	
and marmosets)	

Callithrix jacchus, common marmoset; *Saguinus oedipus*, cotton-top tamarin

Family: Cebidae (Cebid monkeys)

Cebus apella, tufted capuchin; *Callicebus moloch*, Titi monkey; *Saimiri sciureus*, squirrel monkey; *Alouatta palliata*, mantled howler monkey; *Ateles paniscus*, black spider monkey

Old World Monkeys	**Superfamily**: Cercopithecoidea
Subfamily: Cercopithecinae	

Macaca mulatta, rhesus macaque; *Cercocebus torquatus*, sooty mangabey; *Papio hamadryas*, hamadryas baboon; *Erythrocebus patas*, patas monkey

Subfamily: Colobinae

Presbytius entellus, hanuman langur; *Nasalis larvatus*, proboscis monkey; *Cercopithecus aethiops*, vervet monkey; *Colobus badius*, red colobus monkey

Apes and Humans	
	Superfamily: Hominoidea

Hylobates lar, gibbon; *Pongo pygmaeus*, orangutan; *Pan troglodytes*, chimpanzee; *Pan paniscus*, bonobo or pygmy chimpanzee; *Gorilla gorilla*, gorilla; *Homo sapiens*, human

---

Abstracted from Jolly (1985); Napier and Napier (1967).

primate parenting because the focus is on different parenting behaviors that are required for offspring of different ages.

This chapter also presents data and specific hypotheses on parenting prerequisites in chimpanzees. The description that follows illustrates events that were instrumental in the formation of some of the ideas and research described in this chapter. Barbara, a 14-year-old chimpanzee was pregnant for the second time. Would she be a competent mother and raise her infant in a species-typical manner? Barbara was born at the Yerkes Research Center of Emory University, and had been raised by her mother, Sonia, who was born in Africa. Sonia, a gentle and extremely competent adult female, had been a good mother to Barbara (Miller and Nadler, 1981). In 1987, when Barbara gave birth to her first infant, everyone's expectation was that she would be a "good" mother because after all Barbara was mother reared, housed with other adult chimpanzees (an indication that she had good social skills), and exhibited sufficiently sophisticated sexual behavior to become pregnant through natural means. When her first baby, Winston, was born, however, Barbara did not pick him up. Barbara gave every indication of the best intentions toward Winston: She was disturbed by his crying and made herself available to him, she attentively leaned over him, stayed in close proximity to him, and leaned more solicitously whenever he cried. Barbara, however, had no maternal behaviors; she did not pick him up and did not cradle him. After a few hours, Winston was placed in the nursery because he could not have survived without Barbara picking him up. Because Barbara was so solicitous but lacking in behavior, it was concluded that she did not know what to do with a baby.

TABLE 4.2
Social Dynamics and Parenting in Primates

Primate	Group Structure	Breeding	Migration	Raising of Young
Prosimians				
Ring-tailed lemur	Matrilineal Multimale			Mother
Slender loris	Solitary			Mother
Bushbaby	Matrilineal	Polygynous	Male	Twins: nested carried in mouth by mothers
Tarsier	Solitary	Pairs: polygynous		
New World Monkeys				
Marmoset	Monogamous family	Pairs	Male and female	Twins: mother and father and older siblings
Tamarin	Monogamous family	Pairs	Male and female	Mothers, fathers, siblings + helpers
Tufted capuchin	Multifemale Multimale	One male	Male	Mothers (allomothers)
Squirrel monkey	Multimale Multifemale	Polygynous	Male	Mothers (+ allomothers)
Howler monkey	Multimale	Polygynous	Female	Mother
Spider monkey	Multimale Multifemale	Polygynous		Mother
Old World Monkey				
Barbary macaque	Multimale	Polygynous		Mothers (fathers play, etc.)
Rhesus macaque	Matrilineal		Male	Mothers
Hamadryas baboon	Harem	One male	Female	Mothers
Hanuman langur	Matrilineal	Multimale	Male	Mothers + allomothers
Vervet monkey	Multimale		Male	Mothers + allomothers
Red colobus	Multifemale Patrilineal	Multimales One male	Female	Mothers
Apes				
Gibbon/Siamang	Monogamous, family	Pairs	Male and female	Mother, father
Orangutan	Solitary matrilineal	One male	Male	Mother
Gorilla	Harem	One male	Female	Mother (father plays)
Chimpanzee	Multimale Multifemale	Polygamous	Female	Mother

Note. Polygynous: one female + many males; polygamous: either sex multiple mates.

A plan developed to provide a remedial intervention for Barbara. Conan, a 1-year-old chimpanzee infant, had been temporarily moved to the great ape nursery at this time in order for his mother to resume her menstrual cycle. The veterinary staff at the Yerkes Center decided to put Conan and Barbara together, hoping that both would benefit. Barbara was as solicitous as she had been toward Winston, her biological offspring, but Conan, a more capable 1-year-old infant, was quite different. Initially he avoided Barbara because she was a stranger. Finally, after 2 to 3 days, Conan rushed into Barbara's arms, accepting her as a substitute for his absent mother. In the next 3 to 5 months, Barbara was observed developing maternal behaviors; she was seen cradling Conan, allowing him to nurse, and gathering him up before she moved. Conan was allowed to remain with Barbara, his adopted mother, rather than disrupt him again with a return to his biological mother. Three years later, Barbara gave birth to her second baby, Kevin. No one was surprised that now Barbara exhibited the full range of appropriate species-typical maternal behaviors; she picked up Kevin and cradled him immediately. The experience involved in interacting with a motorically competent 1-year-old infant seemed to give Barbara the opportunity to learn how to pick up and cradle infants. It was clear that, in this case, Barbara's motivation to provide care was equal for Winston and for Conan. The difference in her maternal competence, however, before and after her hands-on experiences with Conan was striking and led to the specification of maternal competence in chimpanzees and necessary precursors (Bard, 1994a, 1995a).

This chapter contains two main parts, descriptions of species-typical parental behaviors and theoretical discussions of prerequisites for the expression of parental behavior. The section describing species-typical parental behavior is further divided by taxonomic divisions and by offspring age, beginning with parental behaviors directed toward newborn chimpanzees and ending with parental behaviors directed toward adolescent prosimians. Two small subsections contain information on intuitive parenting and teaching in nonhuman primates. In the section on ontogeny of maternal behavior, the influence of different precursors of parental behavior is evaluated. The variables considered include early experience and observational learning. Discussions of the influence of these variables on general behavior have a long history (Whiten and Ham, 1992), as do discussions of their influence on parental behavior, in particular. A brief subsection describes a prospective study in chimpanzees to manipulate the amount of "hands-on" experience with infants and to evaluate the subsequent effect on parental behaviors. The final section describes some of the ways in which primate parenting relates to human parenting.

PARENTING BEHAVIORS IN NONHUMAN PRIMATES

Different skills are required for parental care of infants of different ages (e.g., Tardif, Harrison, and Simek, 1993). The ages of individuals within each period differ among the species on account of different rates of development. Therefore parenting behaviors are discussed for newborns, infants, juveniles, and adolescents. The *newborn* period is defined as the initial period after birth during which the infant is unable to survive without parental support. *Infancy* is the period during which the offspring is physically dependent on the mother's milk. The *juvenile* period is distinguished by longer times spent further away from the parent(s) and sometimes accompanying changes in coat color. Weaning marks the end of the juvenile period. The *adolescent* period begins at puberty and ends at the time when effective reproduction occurs (Walters, 1987). The skills necessary for parenting offspring at each of the developmental periods may have different developmental histories. Therefore both the skills and their ontogeny are discussed within each age period separately. Parenting behaviors are additionally presented within sections by order (see Table 4.1). There are major differences between species in the skills required for maternal competence. For many species of monkey, the infants are motorically capable soon after birth. Maternal competence in many monkeys therefore involves only acceptance of the infant, i.e., allowing the infant to cling. For example, rhesus infants at birth are able to cling, climb on the mother's body, and suckle. In other words, rhesus infants can survive as a result of their own behavior, as long as the mother does not actively reject them (i.e., pull them off her body and prevent them from clinging). In contrast, for chimpanzees, as in humans, maternal competence requires active cradling and nurturing. Newborn chimpanzees are as helpless to survive without maternal support as are human newborns. Winston, Barbara's baby, could not move into her arms; Barbara needed to take the active role and to pick him up—but this was one of the behavioral skills that she lacked. Maternal competence in chimpanzees therefore requires the mother to take positive action, including picking up the helpless newborn. Competence in all species is defined broadly as the ability to raise offspring to adulthood.

This section of the chapter concentrates on parenting during infancy for a number of reasons. Primarily, parenting responsibilities are greatest during this period when offspring are least capable of coping on their own. The second reason is that there are already good reviews on juveniles (i.e., Pereira and Fairbanks, 1993) and adolescents (Bernstein, Ruehlmann, Judge, Lindquist, and Weed, 1991; Caine, 1986), although little is known about parenting juveniles and adolescents.

Adolescence is typically the time when emigration occurs, and offspring may permanently leave the family group. In most primate species, it is the sons who leave and the daughters who stay in close proximity to their mothers. Although parental status within the group may be crucial to the long-term outcome for an adolescent, the observable parent–offspring interactions are minimal.

Parenting Newborn Chimpanzees and Apes

The newborn period is defined as the initial period after birth during which the infant is unable to survive without parental support. For some species there is really no clearly definable neonatal period subsequent to the minutes after birth; for others the period lasts through the first 30 days, as is true for human newborns (e.g., Brazelton, 1984). In this section those special parental skills applied to newborns are discussed, distinct from parental behaviors to infants. The term infants refer to nonhuman primate infants: Human infants are distinguished explicitly.

Existing field studies of free-living chimpanzees do not richly describe newborn chimpanzee behavior because the very small neonate is difficult to detect on the body of the mother who must be observed amid the trees and grasses of the chimpanzee's African habitats (Plooij, 1984). The chimpanzee newborn and mother are in constant ventral–ventral contact during the first 30 days of life (van Lawick-Goodall, 1968). Newborn chimpanzees are as helpless to survive without maternal support as are human newborns. Newborn chimpanzees and humans have a strong grasping reflex (Bard, Hopkins, and Fort, 1990) but it is insufficient to support the infant for more than a few seconds at a time. Unlike most primates, chimpanzees are unable to support their own weight independently for at least the first 2 months of life (Bard, Platzman, Lester, and Suomi, 1992; van Lawick-Goodall, 1968; Plooij, 1984; Rijt-Plooij and Plooij, 1987). Mothers provide the majority of physical support during this time, although they seldom help the neonates to suckle. Feedings are short in duration and irregularly spaced (Brown and Pieper, 1973; Dienske and Vreeswijk, 1987; Plooij, 1984).

Detailed observations of newborn chimpanzees with their mothers are possible in the laboratory setting, such as at the Yerkes Research Center of Emory University. These observations reveal that sleep is the predominant infant state throughout the first 30 days of life, ~50% of observation time (Bard, Platzman, and Coffman, 1989). The newborn is alert and quiet for considerable periods, especially on the first day of life and increasingly through the first month, an average of 25% of the time. Active alert states are apparent but account for less than 10% of observation time during the chimpanzee's first month of life. Newborn chimpanzees do cry and fuss but it is rare and for short periods of time (Bard, 2000). Nuzzling, rooting, and nursing account for approximately 20% of the infant's time during the first month. In addition, electroencephalogram sleep patterns are evident in newborn chimpanzee and are similar to those of human newborns (Balsamo, Bradley, Bradley, Pegram, and Rhodes, 1972).

The vast majority of maternal behavior is simply cradling newborn infants, providing the support they need to remain in physical contact (over 80% of the time; Bard, 1994a; Fig. 4.1). Other activities, in addition to cradling, occur on an average of 10 min/hr. These additional activities include grooming the infant (6%), playing with the infant and eliciting some smiles (3%), examining the infant (2.5%), assessing the behavioral and physical state of the newborn (2%), and encouraging the infant's motor development with physical exercises (1%).

Gaze is an important aspect of primate behavior. On average, chimpanzee mothers spend 12 min/hr looking at their newborn infants (Bard, 1994a). Half of that time is spent looking at the infants' face during activities of assessing, examining, playing, and grooming. Newborn infants also gaze at the face of their mother (Goodall, 1986, p. 86). Numerous instances of mutual gaze occur between mother and infant, 10 times in an hour on the average (Bard, 1994a). Although not explicitly investigated, it seems that chimpanzee mothers encourage brief mutual glances, in striking contrast to the extended mutual gaze encouraged by human mothers (e.g., Trevarthen, 1979; Tronick, Als, and Adamson, 1979). Preliminary data from another chimpanzee colony suggest that there may be cultural differences in mutual eye gaze (Bard, Myowa-Yamakoshi, and Tomonaga, 2001).

FIGURE 4.1. Mother chimpanzees, such as Vivienne, provide cradling support to their newborns. Keith, at 20 days of age, is quiet and alert and able to focus on the photographer, K. A. Bard, who is 10 ft away.

The social structures of orangutans and gorillas differ from that of chimpanzees, and one might expect differences in parenting. Orangutans are the most solitary of the great apes, and gorilla groups consist of a dominant male silverback and 5 to 7 unrelated females (i.e., harem). Newborn orangutans and gorillas appear more capable motorically compared with chimpanzees (Fig. 4.2). Orangutan mothers do not travel far or quickly, and they rest frequently with newborns (Galdikas, 1982). Maternal support of the infant may be minimal, even on the infant's first day of life, and the placenta may or may not be eaten (Fossey, 1979; Galdikas, 1982). Gorilla mothers with newborns are given preferential proximity to the father, the silverback male. Newborn gorillas can cling unsupported by mother for up to 3 min (Fossey, 1979). The social group is important for the maintenance of maternal competence in gorilla, perhaps heightening protective responses (Nadler, 1983). New gorilla mothers isolated from the group typically exhibit abusive behavior (Joines, 1977; Nadler, 1983).

The lesser apes, gibbons and siamangs, are monogamous and territorial. In fact, as expected, the males engage in paternal care, but mothers provide exclusive care to newborn lesser apes. A gibbon mother provides cradling support to her newborn and repositions the infant to a safer spot on her body before leaping between trees (Carpenter, 1964).

Parenting Infant Chimpanzees and Apes

Infancy is the period in which the offspring is physically dependent on the mother's milk, and infancy could be differentiated into an early time, during which no independent locomotion occurs, and a time during which there is some independent locomotion but the infant remains close to the parent(s) during the day and the night. Great apes (chimpanzees, orangutans, bonobos, and gorillas) remain in an infancy period for 4 to 6 years. Goodall classifies infancy in chimpanzees as the period from birth to the time of weaning (and cessation of travel on the mother's body), which occurs

FIGURE 4.2. Orangutan newborns, in contrast to chimpanzees, are capable of clinging without maternal support, at least for minutes at a time. Photograph by K. A. Bard.

at approximately 5 years of age (e.g., Clark, 1977; van Lawick-Goodall, 1968). The early infancy period is characterized by almost constant physical contact. The first break in contact is typically initiated by the 3- or 4-month-old laboratory infant (Miller and Nadler, 1981; van Lawick-Goodall, 1968). By the time an infants is 3 months of age, the amount of maternal restraint of infant movement has increased fivefold (Bard, 1994a), indicating both how active the infant is and that the mother is responsible for maintaining the proximity to the infant.

In the first three months of their infants' lives, chimpanzee mothers (with good maternal competence) engage their infants in a variety of interactions (Bard, 1994a; van Lawick-Goodall, 1968; Plooij, 1984). There are many instances of encouragement or exercising of skills in infants during this time. Motor development is stimulated through maternal maneuvers such as mothers standing their infants while holding their hands. Mothers repeatedly and alternatively stimulate their infants to hold their weight with legs and then with arms. Encouraging of early crawling is accomplished in a similar way. Because mother–infant contact is rarely broken in these early months, these stimulating exercises are typically performed on mother's body. "Sooner or later every mother encourages and variously aids her baby to learn to creep, stand erect, climb, and finally to walk and run" (Yerkes and Tomilin, 1935, p. 333).

Early mother–infant communication in chimpanzees is often accomplished with touch (Plooij, 1979) and accompanied by vision and audition. Mothers monitor their infants' behavioral state by stretching and moving their infants' toes, fingers, arms, and legs and sometimes just by looking at them. During play, infant smiles are sometimes "marked" as critical features by the mother with an emphasized touch (e.g., Adamson and Bakeman, 1984). When the infant smiles in response to a tickle in the neck or groin, a mother may place her index finger on the infant's lower gums and exaggerate the smile by pushing gently on the lower gums.

Mothers appear to be sensitive to infants' eye gaze and, in same captive populations will shift their own gaze away whenever mutual eye gaze is attained (Bard, 1994a). Chimpanzee mothers spend considerable amounts of their time gazing at their young infants and gazing at the infant's face. There are numerous instances of mutual gaze every hour within the infant's first months of life. The role played by maternal eye gaze and mutual eye gaze in chimpanzees is still uncertain and may be different from that of human mother–infant pairs in which mutual eye gaze is the foundation for interpersonal communication (Tronick et al., 1979) and interaction (Trevarthen, 1979). In Old World monkeys, mutual eye gaze is exceedingly rare and prolonged gaze by an individual monkey constitutes a threat. In chimpanzees, mothers are very attentive to infants, even to the extent of monitoring behavioral states as subtle as sleep and cessation of nursing. Chimpanzee infants gaze at their mothers' faces. Very young infant chimpanzees appear to have a greater visual acuity at 30 cm than at 15 cm, but see quite comparably with human infants at 15 cm (Bard, Street, McCrary, and Booth, 1995; Fig. 4.1). Moreover, neonatal chimpanzees reared with human adults engage in extended eye-to-eye contact (Bard, 1998b; Bard et al., 1992). Previous reports indicate very limited episodes of mutual gaze in mother–infant great apes (e.g., Papoušek, Papoušek, Suomi, and Rahn, 1991; Plooij, 1979; Rijt-Plooij and Plooij, 1987). Early social environments seem to influence the expression of behavior as early as 30 days of life (Bard, 1994b; Bard et al., 1992). It appears that chimpanzee mothers in the Yerkes colony regulate the duration of mutual gazes by looking away within seconds of achieving mutual eye contact. In contrast, chimpanzee mothers at the Primate Research Institute, Kyoto University, actively encourage mutual gaze by turning their infants' head toward their face while gazing at their infants (Bard, Myowa-Yamakoshi, and Tomonaga, 2001). Thus it may be that one of the early behaviors that is "culturally" regulated in chimpanzees is eye gaze (e.g., Bard and Gardner, 1996; Fig. 4.3).

From 5 to 7 months of age, the infant begins to ride on the mother's back. Typically it is not until 1½ years of age that infant chimpanzees reliably respond to the mother's communicative signals to "climb aboard" (van Lawick-Goodall, 1968). However, one mother was explicitly observed to teach her young infant to climb on her back when she displayed a hunched posture while looking over

FIGURE 4.3. Mother–newborn chimpanzees engage in mutual gaze, 10 times an hour on the average. This picture illustrates the typical situation when the infant is 3 months of age. The mother tickles the infant while *en face*, but the infant keeps her eyes tightly closed. Photograph by J. A. Schneider.

the shoulder, which constitutes the communicative signal (Rijt-Plooij and Plooij, 1987). When the infant is 5 or 6 months of age, the mother places the infant on her back or repositions the infant from ventral to dorsal position. Independent quadrupedal steps and climbing appear when the infant is as young as 4 months of age (Rijt-Plooij and Plooij, 1987). Some researchers argue that mothers act aggressively toward their infants in order to attain dorsal riding and breaks in contact, but careful reading suggests that typical maternal behavior is determined rather than aggressive (Rijt-Plooij and Plooij, 1987). Chimpanzee mothers provide both physical support and encouragement for these motor developments (Bard, 1994a; Goodall, 1967; Yerkes and Tomilin, 1935).

From 8 months of age, infants and their mothers are comfortable out of physical contact and within arm's reach, but infants whimper when their mothers move too far away (Rijt-Plooij and Plooij, 1987). It is perhaps no different from increased attachment and separation anxiety that surrounds the period during 7 to 9 months of age when developing cognitive processing allows both human and chimpanzee infants to distinguish novel from familiar (Ainsworth and Bell, 1970; Bard and Gardner, 1996; Bowlby, 1969, 1973; Fritz and Fritz, 1985; Plooij, 1984; Rijt-Plooij and Plooij, 1987). A reasonable conclusion from the descriptive data of Rijt-Plooij and Plooij is that between 8 and 11 months of age the infant becomes responsible for maintaining contact and proximity with the mother in contrast to the earlier time when the mother is primarily responsible. When the infant is approximately 11 months of age, there appears to be an infantile regression and ventral contact is again predominant. However, from 12 to 18 months of age, infants return to being comfortable within mothers' arm's reach, and as they get older they spend increasing amounts of time more distant from the mother.

Social skills such as greeting social partners and using communicative signals to initiate play or grooming develop first in infants' interactions with their mothers and then are used in interaction with older siblings and peers. In the second month of life, infant chimpanzees respond to mothers' tickles with smiles and very quiet laughter (Bard, 1998b; Plooij, 1979). In the third month, infants reach, with a smile, to initiate tickle games with the mother and sometimes with older siblings (van Lawick-Goodall, 1968; Plooij, 1979). In the second half-year of life, infants initiate social interactions with others by approaching them with vocal greetings. Mothers monitor infants' interactions with others and immediately rush to pick them up at the first signs that their infants are becoming distressed.

Infants learn a great deal of social communicative signals in the first 2 years of life. Communicative signals constitute all the ways that social partners negotiate social interactions. Some might label these communicative signals the natural "language" of chimpanzees. The sharing of food is a negotiated event that involves communicative signals (Fig. 4.4). It can serve as one example of this type of social skill development. Food sharing is a phenomenon that occurs in chimpanzees (Goodall, 1986) and orangutans (Bard, 1992). Mothers typically allow young infants of approximately 4 or 5 months of age to take some food from her mouth. Chimpanzee infants use communicative gestures to request food when they are between 9 and 12 months of age (Plooij, 1984). These food-begging communicative gestures also allow individuals, when they are older, to obtain some meat from adult males. It appears that chimpanzee mothers selectively share only the more difficult to process or difficult to obtain foods as the infant matures (Silk, 1978, 1979).

From 2 to 5 years of age, chimpanzee youth have much to learn about food, food processing, traveling, and hunting. Chimpanzee mothers monitor what infants eat and prevent them from manipulating or eating undesirable objects. Mothers serve as models for older infants to learn termite fishing (Goodall, 1986), tool manufacture (Wright, 1972), plant foraging (McGrew, 1974, 1977), food processing (Lefebvre, 1985), and locomotory behaviors (Bard, 1993, 1995b). There is an increasing amount of evidence that great ape mothers actively instruct their infants under some circumstances. Boesch (1991) argues convincingly that chimpanzee mothers "take an active part in the apprenticeship of their female offspring" (Boesch and Boesch, 1981, p. 592) to crack nuts with a hammer tool. Chimpanzee mothers facilitate arboreal locomotory behavior by "bridging" gaps between trees, allowing the young infants to cross the gap on her body and allowing older infants to cross the gap on branches that she holds close together (Bard, 1995b; Goodall, 1986). It is likely that adult male chimpanzees play a teaching role in the apprenticeship of male offspring in cooperative hunting (Boesch and Boesch, 1989; Boesch and Boesch-Achermann, 2000).

FIGURE 4.4. Juvenile chimpanzees practice social skills. In this photograph, food is exchanged between juvenile and infant chimpanzees when appropriate communicative signals are used. Photograph by J. A. Schneider.

The subtle communication between mothers and infants is documented in "meshing." Rijt-Plooij and Plooij (1987) discuss meshing in only the locomotor context and define it as maternal anticipation of and coordination with the infant's contact behavior. Meshing occurs when the infants are between 8 to 24 months of age, but monthly levels rise and fall in correspondence with the infants' responsibility for contact maintenance. "It is the mother's role to (force) teach the infant how to use newly emerged abilities it might not, or not fully, have used otherwise" (Rijt-Plooij and Plooij, 1987, p. 72).

Clark (1977, p. 235) describes the 2-year gradual weaning process in 2- to 4-year-old chimpanzees as a period when infants may "display many elements of depression." It begins with mothers who prevent access to the breast by holding their infants away, pushing their infants away, or physically blocking access with an arm or knee pressed firmly against their own chests. Mothers often distract their infants with play or grooming when they attempt to suckle, and mothers may move away from the infant as the infant approaches to suckle. It is extremely rare for any mother to exhibit aggressive behavior in relation to weaning her infant. In response to these tactics, infants whimper and become physically more intrusive in their attempt to gain access to the nipple. As the infant grows older and weaning is more strictly enforced, temper tantrums ensue. However, as weaning progresses, elements of depressive response are seen in the infant, including decrease in play, loss of appetite, huddled posture and resumption of infantile behavior with the mother, including ventral riding and increased contact (Yoshida, Norikoshi, and Kitahara, 1991).

All 4- to 5-year-old infants exhibit distress when their mothers' milk is no longer available and within months make no further attempts to suckle. Clark (1977) notes that all mothers appear "remarkably tolerant and gentle with the infants during the weaning period" (p. 252) and increase their attentiveness to the infant through grooming and waiting for them in traveling. Infants, however, appear depressed through the period of the birth of the younger siblings. Their depression is exhibited in lethargic movements, lack of positive emotions, and sometimes decreased appetite and moderate weight loss.

Orangutan infants of less than 2 years of age are less frequently out of contact with the mother compared with chimpanzee infants (Bard, 1993, 1995b). Mothers may tolerate relatively close proximity with other mothers in order to allow their infants to play. Fewer peers are available for socialization in orangutans compared with chimpanzees during the entire infancy period up to 5 years of age (Bard, personal observation). Orangutan infants are weaned between 4 and 8 years of age (Bard, 1993; Galdikas, 1979).

The gorilla infant in early infancy is motorically more advanced than chimpanzees, chewing food items in the first 2 months of life, clinging to the mother's hair without support by 2 months and reaching for objects earlier. Mothers spend time grooming the infant and begin to rebuff suckling attempts before their infants' first birthday. Gorilla mothers encourage the development of infant locomotor skills in a manner similar to that of chimpanzees (Whiten, 1999). By 2 years of age, infants travel primarily independently but they retain the white tail tuft that indicates an infant through part of the third year (Fossey, 1979).

Infancy in the lesser apes lasts from 2 to 2½ years (Leighton, 1987). When the gibbon mother rests, her 6-week-old infant begins to move a little distance from her. Infant gibbons in the first weeks of life may eat some solid food and engage in locomotor play (Carpenter, 1964). One of the most striking behaviors exhibited by gibbon parents is their vocal duet; songs are given morning and evening. "Infants often squeal during a mother's great call" (Leighton, 1987, p. 140). As older infants travel independently, they sometimes are unable to cross gaps between trees, and they "cry" until the mother retrieves them (Carpenter, 1964). In the second year of their infants' lives, fathers carry gibbon and siamang infants and groom them. Paternal care can be as high as 78% of the day (Whitten, 1987); the infant returns to the mother to nurse and to sleep at night (Alberts, 1987).

Gorilla infants and their fathers play frequently in notably contrast to chimpanzees (Fig. 4.5). In addition, gorilla fathers carry some young infants (Tilford and Nadler, 1978). Some gorilla infants spend more time near or interacting with their fathers than with their mothers (Fossey, 1979, 1983; Harcourt, 1979). "Gorilla males often groom, cuddle, and nest with their 3- and 4-year old offspring" (Whitten, 1987, p. 346). The fathers also monitor play between infants and stops it before it becomes too rough (Fossey, 1979). Gorilla fathers appear through these early interactions to form a particularly close relationship with at least one male infant who will remain in the father's group (Harcourt and Stewart, 1981; Tilford and Nadler, 1978). Chimpanzee males are remarkably tolerant when infants attempt to interfere with mating, and males may reassure uneasy infants with a touch. The tolerance of infancy appears to continue as long as the infant retains the tail tuft, long white hairs at the base of the spine (Goodall, 1986). Chimpanzee males in captivity do engage in play with infants, showing that there is a capability (Bingham, 1927; Taub and Redican, 1984). The difference between gorilla and chimpanzee fathers may be that paternity in chimpanzees is usually not known either by observers or apparently by the chimpanzees (Gagneux, Woodruff, and Boesch, 1997; Goodall, 1986), but in gorilla harems, paternity is certain. Male orangutans rarely engage in interactions with infants.

Parenting Juvenile Chimpanzees and Apes

The juvenile period is distinguished by the infants' spending longer times farther away from the parents and sometimes by accompanying changes in coat color. In chimpanzees the end of infancy is indicated by disappearance of the white tail tuft. Attention turns from mothers to peers in the juvenile period (e.g., Horvat and Kraemer, 1981). Maternal responsibilities in terms of providing milk and transportation diminish while responsibilities for increasing offspring independence increase. It is

FIGURE 4.5. Among the great apes, gorilla fathers are unique in the amount of time they spend interacting with infants. This silverback, with a big smile, allows the youngster to pull on his hair and bite his hand. Photograph by F. Kiernan.

when offspring reach this period of semi-independence that mothers facilitate learning of travel techniques (Goodall, 1986), of food processing (McGrew, 1977), including tool use (Boesch, 1991), and of socialization. Puberty marks the end of the juvenile period.

Juvenile chimpanzees are weaned but remain in close association with their mothers (Hiraiwa-Hasegawa, 1990). Mothers groom juvenile daughters and sons, but daughters more often groom family members than sons do (Preuschoft, Chivers, Brockelman, and Creel, 1984). Juvenile sons and daughters play, groom, and carry young infants who may or may not be siblings (Nishida, 1983). All juveniles exhibit submissive behaviors to adult males, for example, presenting their hindquarters and pant grunting. Occasionally juveniles display and attack adolescent females, but this occurs only when the mother joins to support her son or daughter (Pusey, 1990).

Juvenile lesser apes (2 to 4 years of age) begin to receive aggressive behaviors from their parents: Typically, mothers harass daughters and fathers harass sons (Preuschoft et al., 1984). Fights ensue most often over access to food (Leighton, 1987). Juvenile lesser apes may join in singing the duet with their parents. The song tends to be gender appropriate but imperfect (Leighton, 1987).

Parenting Adolescent Chimpanzees and Apes

The beginning of adolescence, signaled in females with small sexual swellings, occurs at approximately 9 years of age in wild chimpanzees (Nishida, 1988) and orangutans (Galdikas, 1979) and 5 1/2 years in the laboratory (S. Phythyon, personal communication, 1993). Menarche and full sexual swellings occur when a chimpanzee is 11 to 12 years of age in the wild and 8 to 10 years of age in the laboratory. The adolescent period includes the time when offspring travel independently throughout days and nights, sometimes engaging in sexual activity and reproductive behavior, but the individual is neither socially nor physically fully adult. Adolescence lasts from the age of 9 to 14 years in wild female chimpanzees (Nishida, 1988), until 15 years in male chimpanzees (Nishida, 1988) and until 21 years in male orangutans (Galdikas, 1979). The adolescent period begins at puberty and ends at the time when effective reproduction occurs (Walters, 1987). Some physical changes that characterize the adult status include coat color (e.g., silver-colored hair on the backs in the dominant male gorilla), secondary sexual characteristics (e.g., cheek flanges in male orangutans), and full growth (e.g., canines, testes, and general body size).

At adolescence, there are striking differences between chimpanzee daughters' and sons' behavior in whom they groom and with whom they spend their time. Sons are more often in the company of adult males than daughters are. Mothers provide support to their daughters in agonistic encounters whereas sons solicit and receive support from older brothers. The behavior of adolescent males is molded by adult males who touch to quiet adolescent males during boundary patrols (Pusey, 1990) and guide adolescent males in assuming complimentary and cooperative roles while hunting colobus monkeys (Boesch and Boesch, 1989; Boesch and Boesch-Achermann, 2000). It is during midadolescence, when females exhibit adult-sized sexual swellings, that daughters leave their mother, join a new group, and are solicited and protected by adult males (Pusey, 1990).

During adolescence in lesser apes, fighting occurs over breeding access and adolescents are eventually evicted from the family. Male adolescent gibbons appear to be inhibited from singing with their parents, but females emit great calls simultaneously with their mother. Fathers and adolescent sons form a coalition in territorial defense against intruders. Fathers may facilitate the process of their sons establishing their own territory, either by joining the sons to usurp neighbors' territory or by expanding the home territory and then leaving the son in the new area (Leighton, 1987). Young adult male gibbons sing solo, apparently to attract unmated females, but unmated females rarely sing alone (Leighton, 1987).

Parenting Newborn Old World Monkeys

Macaques (e.g., rhesus, cynomologus, pigtails, and bonnets) have a strong crawling and grasping reflex that may actually aid in the birth process (Rosenblum, 1971; Tinklepaugh and Hartman, 1932). Their "strong righting reflexes and negative geotropism $\cdots$ function to produce the proper orientation" (Rosenblum, 1971, p. 324). Mothers must provide a supportive base during the expelling of the newborn, especially important when the mother is in an arboreal environment or else the infant may not initially get a grasp of the mother's hair (Rosenblum, 1971; Timmermans and Vossen, 1996).

Little attention is paid to the newborn. The placenta is eaten during the initial birthing period. This period is followed by a period of intense grooming of the infant. Mothers may gaze at their newborn infants and infants may gaze at their mother's face (Higley and Suomi, 1986). Newborn macaques, through reflexive behaviors, suckle without maternal aid. Nipple contact is maintained over 80% of the time during the first month of the infant's life (Higley and Suomi, 1986), in striking contrast to the 20% nipple contact of chimpanzees.

Paternal behaviors toward newborns vary by species but generally range within the indifferent category. Mothers with newborns may stay in close proximity to adult males in baboons (*Papio anubis*; Hrdy, 1976). One-week-old Barbary macaques are carried by adult males as well as by juvenile and subadult males (Deag and Crook, 1971), and there is a report of the dominant male holding an infant four times on the day it was born (Burton, 1972, cited in Hrdy, 1976).

Parenting Old World Monkey Infants

Most macaques remain in infancy for only 1 to 1½ years. Baboon infants have black hair and pink skin in contrast to the light hair and the black skin of adults and have a new sibling when 1½ to 2 years of age, so are weaned at 1 to 1½ years of age (Altmann, 1980; Strum, 1987). Macaque infants mature quickly and begin to crawl/walk in the first days after birth. Mothers monitor the infants and remain ready to retrieve and protect the infants. Some mothers of some species, however, encourage infant locomotion (in pigtails; Bolwig, 1980; Hinde and Simpson, 1975; Ransom and Rowell, 1972; see section on teaching). Macaque infants typically engage in independent excursions in their third and fourth weeks of life. Mothers provide a "secure base" from which their infants travel (Harlow and Harlow, 1965). "Mothers now become psychologically more than physically important for their infants" (Higley and Suomi, 1986, p. 160). However, during this time mothers are providing kinesthetic and vestibular stimulation through grooming and physical contact while traveling and contingent responsive stimulation in their social interactions. Mothers respond to infant cries and seem to respond selectively or at least differentially in positive, negative, or neutral manner to all infant social communicative signals (e.g., Maestripieri and Call, 1996). It is this type of selective and contingent social responsiveness that mothers in particular provide to infants that peers do not. However, it is rare that macaque mothers engage in extended play with their infants (e.g., Suomi, 1979). Play in macaques is primarily a peer activity.

Parental behavior in Old World monkeys varies considerably among species (Taub, 1984a). Mothers stay close to adult males in baboon species, and male langurs may respond to infants in distress with protection and rescue (Hrdy, 1976). Young mangabeys spend most of their time with an adult male rather than with their mothers. Intensive caretaking by males is found in one species of Old World Monkeys, the Barbary macaque. Adult males "groom, nuzzle, and mouth infants, lick and smell them, manipulate their genitalia, and teeth chatter at them" (Whitten, 1987; p. 345), engaging in interactions analogous to those of mothers (Taub, 1984b). Males may temporarily foster an infant or permanently adopt an orphaned infant anubis baboon (DeVore, 1963), Japanese macaque (Itani, 1959), or hamadryas baboon (Kummer, 1967). In fact, Kummer reports that motherless infant hamadryas are invariably adopted by young adult males. However, males in each of these species, and in langurs and vervets, also use infants as an "agonistic buffer," which puts the infant at risk for injury or death. Males carry an infant to or near another male: The presence of the infant inhibits aggression and the males interact in a less tense environment. Cases of infanticide in langurs and rhesus by adult males typically involve nonfathers and appear to be cases whereby the adult male is maximizing his inclusive fitness (Trivers, 1974), whereas cases of infant care, play, and other affiliative interactions are by dominant males who are likely fathers (Hrdy, 1976). Infants are used by adult males as agonistic buffers regardless of genetic relatedness (Whitten, 1987).

Maternal style is the term used to differentiate both species differences and individual differences in maternal behaviors toward older infants that reflect the balance between permissive and restrictive rearing (e.g., Hinde and Simpson, 1975). Maternal style in early infancy is reflected by how contact and proximity are regulated and how much contact the infant is allowed with others. In rhesus and pig-tail macaques and in baboon species, none may touch the newborn infant for many weeks. In contrast, colobus and langur mothers may allow others to carry away their newborns (Bennett, 1988; Fimbel, 1992). Bonnet macaque mothers allow their infants to interact in a limited fashion with others in the social group but not immediately after birth. It is common, however, for these mothers to allow older siblings limited access to infants. Mothers exhibit consistent rejection rates with each of their offspring and across the development of each offspring. Moreover, there is consistency in maternal style across generations. Therefore it appears conclusive that maternal style is a characteristic of the mother and not of the mother–infant bond in rhesus (Berman, 1990) and vervet monkeys (Fairbanks, 1989).

Maternal style is also apparent at weaning. Frequency of rejection and punishment has been documented to be a stable maternal characteristic in rhesus monkeys (Berman, 1990). Rejection and punishment as a weaning style clearly differentiate species; rhesus have high rejection rates compared with bonnets, for instance (Rosenblum, 1971). By the end of the infants' first year of life, weaning is complete in Old World monkeys. Baboon mothers hit, push, grab, and bite at infants. Individual differences between mothers occur, but by the time that infants are 5 months of age they have experienced maternal aggression at least once (Altmann, 1980). Weaning occurs when the infant is between 4 and 6 months of age. Weaning begins somewhat later in hanuman langurs and different responses are noted from male and female offspring, but all mothers are harsh, punitive, or indifferent (Rajpurohit and Mohnot, 1991).

Baboon mothers encourage independent locomotor behavior when infants are 7 months of age. The mother may descend from the sleeping trees without carrying the infant. Infants "protest" with whimpers. Sometimes mothers return halfway up the tree, still requiring that the infant descend part of the way independently. Mothers always monitor the tree, even if they do not facilitate any of the travel, until the infant travels down. Typically, the infant immediately runs to the mother and nurses. By the end of 1 month of these "lessons," the 8- or 9-month-old infants descend from the sleeping tree independently.

Competing theories have suggested either that punishment–rejection facilitates, if not causes, independence (e.g., Hansen, 1966; Hinde and Spencer-Booth, 1967) or that high levels of punishment–rejection cause increased dependence and delays in the attainment of independence (Kaufman and Rosenblum, 1969; Rosenblum and Harlow, 1963). In experiments on cross-fostered rhesus monkeys, Suomi (1987) evaluated the independent contributions of inherited reactivity, foster caregiver reactivity, and foster caregiver style on infant reactivity. Foster caregiving style is a better index of infants' behavioral reactivity than inherited temperament or caregiver temperament under stable environmental conditions. However, when presented with environmental challenges, such as a brief separation from the caregiver, infant reactivity was best predicted by inherited reactivity. When the infants were initially returned to the foster mother, then the caregiver reactivity best predicted the infants' behavior (Suomi, 1987).

Parenting Juvenile Old World Monkeys

In rhesus macaques, baboons, and Japanese macaques, the age of menarche is $5\frac{1}{2}$ years of age on the average but can be influenced by hierarchical dominance status (Pereira and Fairbanks, 1993). Male testes descend when baboons are approximately $5\frac{1}{2}$ years of age (Altmann, Altmann, Hausfater, and McCuskey, 1977). Infant and juvenile baboons are given the preferential center location during group travel.

Mother macaques allow juvenile daughters to handle infant siblings and juvenile sons to play with infant siblings. Mothers also allow unrelated juvenile females access to infants. Sometimes mothers are intimidated by juveniles of high-ranking matrilines and their infants are kidnapped (Hrdy, 1976; Maestripieri, 1993). In agonistic encounters, the entire matriline will support their kin. Juveniles begin to acquire ranks similar to those of their mothers and exercise dominance toward all females that are subordinate to their mothers.

In hamadryas baboons, adult males form "special relationships" with juvenile females. These begin as friendships but grow to be consortships. Juvenile males may have strong affiliative bonds with an adult male or with male peers, which develop into coalitions later in life (Kummer, 1967; Walters, 1987).

Parenting Adolescent Old World Monkeys

There is a great deal of variance in the age of adolescence in Old World Monkeys. In baboons, full adult size is reached by females at approximately 7 years of age, and full secondary sexual characteristics are developed by 10 years of age in males (Altmann et al., 1977). In vervets, breeding is seen when they are 3 years of age, but females are not adult in size until 4 years of age and males not before 5 years of age (Fairbanks, 1990). Rhesus monkeys are in early adolescence between the ages of $2\frac{1}{2}$ and $4\frac{1}{2}$ years (Bernstein, Judge, and Ruehlmann, 1993) but may remain in adolescence for 4 or more years (Bernstein et al., 1991).

In rhesus monkeys, the males leave the birth group during adolescence. Few specifics on parenting are known to account for the large differences between male and female behavior. Female rhesus spend significantly more time grooming and males spend more time with male peers. The result of these differences in behavior is a loosening of the sons' bonds with mother and sisters and a strengthening of the daughters' bonds with mother and sisters. The role played by the mother during the process is unspecified. "Male macaques and vervets frequently emigrate in the company of brothers or natal group peers" (Walters, 1987, p. 365). In hamadryas baboons, the alpha male acts aggressively toward subadult males, eventually evicting them from the natal group (Caine, 1986). It is the daughters in red colobus groups, however, that migrate as adolescents (Caine, 1986).

Parenting Newborn New World Monkeys

New World monkeys are arboreal and forest dwelling. Care of infants is different for the species who are pair bonded (e.g., marmosets, tamarins, titi monkeys) and for the species who live in large social groups (e.g., squirrel monkeys, howler monkeys, and capuchins).

Newborn squirrel monkeys and capuchins can move independently from the ventral position used in nursing to the dorsal position used in travel. Early field studies of newborn howlers documented that mothers regularly restrained and pulled the infants as they continually climbed up the mother's ventrum (Carpenter, 1964). Although newborn New World monkeys can support their weight with their tails, it appears that newborns are uncoordinated with their tails (Carpenter, 1964: Fragaszy and Bard, 1997). From the day of birth, squirrel monkey infants respond visually and vocally to the communication of others. Adult females and juveniles are allowed to touch newborn squirrel monkeys, but many mothers avoid adult males or prevent them from touching the newborns (Hopf, 1981). Adults vocalize "caregiver calls" to newborns, and newborns vocalize responsively (Biben, 1994). These vocal exchanges occur when infants and adults are engaged in mutual gaze. It is noteworthy that these communicative exchanges are not between infant and mother but rather between infant and other adult members of the group.

Marmosets, tamarins, and titi monkeys are monogamous species. Marmoset and tamarins typically give birth to twins (80%); triplets are as common as single births. The amount of maternal care relative to paternal care varies among the species as does the amount of care by nonparents; however, in all these species there are substantial amounts of infant care by individuals other than the mother (Goldizen, 1987). Systematic research indicates that helpers of specific age, gender, and experience levels participate with care of infants of different ages (e.g., Price, 1992). Mothers typically provide infant care exclusively in the neonatal period. Infants ride on the mother's back. In titi monkeys, the mother and father work as a team from birth. From the first week of life, however, the father carries the infant more than 70 percent of the time (Mason and Mendoza, 1998). For marmosets and tamarins, multiple births are the norm. Specialized behavior has developed to cope with twin births (fraternal twinning is typical; Tardif, Carson, and Gangaware, 1992), specifically, "helpers" to carry the infants, which includes fathers. Helpers become an important factor during infancy but after the newborn period. Behavior to newborns, however, appears to be similar to that in Old World monkeys. Mothers are primarily responsible for carrying and totally responsible for feeding the newborns (e.g., Box, 1977; Rothe, Darms, Koenig, Radespiel, and Juenemann, 1993; Wamboldt, Gelhard, and Insel, 1988).

Infants can be actively rejected by mothers who have insufficient prior experience (see, e.g., Johnson, Petto, and Sehgal, 1991; Tardif, Richter, and Carson, 1984), and these mothers show some fear and avoidance of the newborn presumably because of the lack of prior experience (Pryce, Abbott, Hodges, and Martin, 1988). Although deaths of newborns occur because of lack of sustenance, most early deaths appear to be due to falls (i.e., skull fractures found in autopsies of newborn squirrel monkeys; Hopf, 1981). Tamarin, marmoset, squirrel monkey, and capuchin mothers actively reject an infant by rubbing the infant off their body. It appears for these species that maternal cradling of newborns does not occur. In fact, New World monkey infants, even at birth, have sufficient strength and motor maturity to support their own weight and to maneuver to the nipple. However, the survival rate of infants born to first-time tamarin mothers is quite low (i.e., 10 percent, Snowdon, 1996). This appears to be due to the first-time tamarin mother's doing most of the carrying of her twins:

Experienced mothers typically carry their infants only 50% of the time during their infants' first week of life.

Parenting Infant New World Monkeys

The infancy period in New World monkeys is relatively short (approximately 5 months). Squirrel monkeys are weaned within the first 3 months of life (Biben, 1994), as are capuchins (Wamboldt et al., 1988). Marmoset and tamarins, however, appear to be weaned at approximately 6 months of age. Both adult and adolescent squirrel monkey females carry and play with infants (Robinson and Janson, 1987). Mothers groom their infants regularly. Cebus infants, 2 months old or older, are occasionally left with the dominant male who either huddles with them or is tolerant of their play (Robinson and Janson, 1987). Food is shared with infants through an exchange of infant vocalization and tolerated taking.

Many view the commonalities in infantcare patterns within the cooperatively breeding species of New World monkeys but "variation and flexibility emerged as major themes" when parenting in cooperatively breeding species such as tamarins, marmosets, and titi monkeys was considered (Snowdon, 1996, p. 682). In some monogamous species, mothers have primary responsibility for infantcare at birth. The infant is able to crawl ventrally to nurse, and otherwise the infant rides on the mother's back. In some monogamous species, fathers have primary responsibility for the infant from shortly after birth. In titi and night monkeys, fathers carry the infant up to 90% of the time, and the infant forms a strong attachment to the father (Wright, 1990). In these species, mothers hold the infants only for nursing. Mothers rarely groom their infants. Infants transfer to other carriers for the majority of their time. Initially, the infant's transfer is facilitated by the helper adopting a different posture, "including extension of the arms toward the infant and direction of the infant's crawling motions" (Tardif et al., 1992, p. 156). Both male and female nonparents act as helpers with equal frequency in cotton-top tamarins, but which gender helps may be constrained by age. Females carry more than males as subadults, but as adults, males carry more than female nonparents. Very young infants are more often carried by adults than by subadults, but subadults carry more than juveniles do (Yamomato, Box, Albuquerque, and Arruda, 1996). There is evidence that in some species (red-bellied tamarins) younger, less experienced helpers are not allowed access to very young infants (Pryce et al., 1988). Weaning is accomplished by the eighth month of life, when mothers were observed to act aggressively to infants who attempted to nurse (Snowdon, 1996).

The squirrel monkey pattern of mutual gaze and responsive vocalizing that occurs between newborns and reproductively active females becomes a characteristic pattern between the squirrel monkey infant and mother when the infant begins to leave mother in independent forays in the third or fourth week of life (Biben, 1994). Infant position, riding on the mother's back, influences the infant's ability to engage in eye contact with the mother. Constant physical contact in the early days of life also makes it unlikely that contact-resuming vocalizations will be directed at the mother. Perhaps these vocal exchanges or dialogues serve socialization purposes, acquainting infants with the sounds of group members (Biben, 1994).

A noticeable aspect of paternal care in tamarins, *Cebus apella* and *Ateles*, is food sharing, which is tolerated taking by infants. Some males, in some species, are reported to initiate food taking with specific vocalizations (Brown and Mack, 1978) but primarily it is the infant who begs. Older siblings also participate in sharing food with infants. As is the case for chimpanzees, the types of shared foods are those that the infants find difficult to process or difficult to obtain (Whitten, 1987).

Fathers will defend infants against intruders and rescue them, at some risk to their own welfare. Typically parental caretaking of this sort is given only to very young infants, i.e., until infants can locomote independently (Whitten, 1987). Titi and night monkey fathers, however, are reported to guard their infants for their first full year of the infants' lives (Wright, 1990). Adult male howler monkeys may carry and play with infants for short periods of time (Vogt, 1984).

Parenting Juvenile New World Monkeys

In tamarins, marmosets, and squirrel monkeys, the juvenile period begins at approximately 5 months of age and ends at puberty, at approximately 14 months of age (Tardif et al., 1992). In some calli-trichids, the presence of the mothers inhibit their daughters' sexual development (Walters, 1987). In cotton-top tamarins, juveniles, $6^1/_2$ to 15 months of age, react with stress to the birth of new infants. Parents and juveniles are seen to be more often in conflict. Initially, it was thought that this conflict was due to competition for parental resources (that is, conflict between the juveniles and the infants). However, when the parents were not carrying the new infants there was no conflict, so it was clear that the conflict was due to competition for the infants. When juveniles were allowed to carry the infants, approximately 4 to 6 weeks after the infants were born, then all conflicts ceased.

Parenting Adolescent New World Monkeys

Adolescents play less than juveniles do, and when the newest set of twins is born then adolescent behaviors becomes more adultlike (Caine, 1986). Adolescent sons and daughters help with infantcare by grooming and caring for younger siblings. For marmosets and tamarins, adolescence appears to end at approximately 3 years of age (Santos, French, and Otta, 1997). Before achieving adult stature, however, both males and females leave the family. In New World monkeys, squirrel monkeys for example, primiparous females give birth at approximately 3 years of age (Hopf, 1981), but males are not fully mature before the age of 5 years (Biben, 1992). Adolescent squirrel monkeys continue to play, but play takes on sexual elements (Caine, 1986). It appears that adult females actively reject adolescent males who are forced to the periphery of the group (Caine, 1986).

Parenting Newborn Prosimians

Some prosimian newborns cling and are carried ventrally (without support) by mothers. In some species, transport of infants is by mouth and infants are left unattended in nests or left "parked," meaning that they are grasping on tree branches (Higley and Suomi, 1986; Klopfer and Boskoff, 1979). In these prosimian species, mothers may leave their infants unattended for up to 12 hr. Mothers may scent mark the infants for identification, an indicator that mothers do not visually identify their infants as individuals (Niemitz, 1979). Prosimians are the most quickly maturing of primate species and reach sexual maturity by 1 year of age.

Parenting Infant Prosimians

Infant prosimians ride dorsally on the mother. Infant accomplish this by 2 weeks of age in *Lemur catta* and by 4 weeks of age in *Lemur fulvus*. In *Varecia variegata*, however, infants engage in independent excursions away from the mother by 3 weeks of age (Klopfer and Boskoff, 1979). Mothers groom their infants frequently. In contrast to monkeys, but like chimpanzees, prosimian mothers may play for extended periods of time with their infants (Charles-Dominique, 1977; Niemitz, 1979). Prosimians, which are the most evolutionarily distant from humans, are weaned by the age of 2, 3, or 4 months, depending on the species (Jolly, 1985; Klopfer and Boskoff, 1979).

Prosimian fathers tend not to participate at all in infant care (Vogt, 1984). Male *L. catta* involvement tends to be limited to occasional grooming or sniffing of the infant, but if the mother is removed from the group the amount of time that the infant spends in contact with the male increases (Vogt, 1984).

Parenting Juvenile and Adolescent Prosimians

Very little is known about parental influence on older prosimian offspring. Dispersal by sons appears to be voluntary. Immature male bushbabies may leave by following an adult male when he travels through the mother's home range. Daughters remain close to their mothers; even as adults, daughters sleep close to mother at night (Charles-Dominique, 1977).

INTUITIVE PARENTING IN PRIMATES

The concept of intuitive parenting is considered in order to summarize the behaviors involved in parenting across primate species. Intuitive parenting consists of a psychobiological preadaptedness to stimulate infants' integrative development (Papoušek and Papoušek, 1987). The behaviors are neither reflexive nor based on rational thought, but they appear to require prior experience with infants.

Chimpanzee mothers act responsively, contingently, and nurture development in their infants. Of special significance are the intuitive parenting behaviors utilized to support development in motor behaviors and in communicative behaviors (Bard, 1994a, 1996; Rijt-Plooij and Plooij, 1987). Those behaviors that support motor development have been called exercising (Yerkes and Tomilin, 1935) and occur for up to 20% of the time while the mother is engaged with her young infant (Bard, 1994a). Similar observations have been made in a gorilla mother (Whiten, 1999). Orangutan mothers appear to "scaffold," crossing gaps between trees by staying in the gap longer than usual. When the infant is very young, the mother waits for the infant to move from clinging to her body to crossing the gap, and, as the infant gets older, the mother waits for infant to cross on the branches that she holds (Bard, 1995b).

The lesser apes, gibbons, and siamangs also facilitate infants' motor development by providing scaffolding to travel between trees. Fathers, in particular, are frequently noted as helping their older offspring become well socialized and helping sons establish new independent home territories (Leighton, 1987).

Among Old World monkeys there are scattered reports of facilitation in motor development consisting basically of the encouragement of early walking. Some rhesus mothers and pigtail mothers engage in elaborate "games" (Hinde and Simpson, 1975), when the mother leaves a short distance, turns back to look at the infant, and gives a retrieval signal (either a facial expression, vocalization expression, or whole body posture that indicates that the infant should approach the mother). The mother may move away again before the infant fully approaches, as long as the infant does not show signs of distress, in which case the mother immediately returns. There is strong evidence that such intuitive parenting serves to enhance the locomotor development of the infant (significantly, but only by 4 days; Maestripieri, 1995). There are striking individual differences, even among Old World monkey mothers, in sensitivity to infants' needs. When infants are sick, for example, mothers increase contact time and carry them more frequently (Nicolson, 1991). Comparisons of maternal parenting style across Old World monkey species and across different environments illustrate the influence of foraging demands (in terms of predictability and availability of food; Rosenblum and Paully, 1984), of social rank (low-ranking mothers tend to be more restrictive of infants than high-ranking mothers, and species with strict dominance hierarchies tend to be more restrictive than species with looser or little dominance; Nicolson, 1991), and maternal temperament (reactive versus laid back; Suomi, 1987). Evolutionary benefits are said to be the basis of intuitive parenting of locomotor skills in monkeys, including early cessation of infant carrying, early weaning, and thus an increase in the likelihood of a shorter interval to the next birth (Maestripieri, 1995).

New World monkeys exhibit components of intuitive parenting consisting of vocal exchanges accompanies by eye gaze (Biben, 1994) and the sharing of food, also accompanied by vocalizations and eye gaze (Starin, 1978). It is important to note that group members of a family are frequent exhibitors of intuitive parenting in New World monkeys. Typically there is no indication that mothers facilitate their infants' motor development. In special circumstances, however, when infants are artificially handicapped (e.g., temporary taping of infants' arms), mothers compensate for the infants' inability to hold on (Rumbaugh, 1965).

Prosimian mothers (nonlemur) spend relatively little time with their young infants as they are solitary foragers and leave their infants in a nest of tree branch except for feedings. Lemurs, however, are group living, and adult females in addition to mothers provide care to infants.

TEACHING IN NONHUMAN PRIMATES

Teaching has reemerged as a controversial topic and is considered here as distinct from intuitive parenting. As much of infant learning was once labeled "imitation," much of parental behavior was once labeled "teaching." Therefore it is not surprising to find that there are major debates about the definition: What constitutes teaching in nonhuman primate parents? At one extreme are those who argue that teaching should be reserved for those instances in which the instructor (usually the mother) "intends" that the other learn, as is the case with some human instruction (e.g., Tomasello and Call, 1997). However, because much of the teaching even in human parents occurs without full conscious awareness (in teaching early socialization of eye gaze patterns, for instance), this definition seems unnecessarily limiting. Another view is that teaching should be used to reflect those instances in which performance is enhanced by the purposeful (in the sense of being goal directed) efforts of an instructor (Caro and Hauser, 1992). More specifically, teaching is evident whenever the instructor modifies the learner's behavior in a manner that is sensitive and responsive to the performance of the learner. In this latter sense, scaffolding (a term used to mean maternal support of infant development; Wood, Bruner and Ross, 1976) can be evidence of teaching. That is, teaching occurs when the instructor helps to structure the environment, structure the activity, or otherwise acts to help the infant, in a way that allows them together to accomplish a task that the infant could not perform alone.

Boesch and Boesch-Achermann (2000) distinguish three different types of pedagogy with reference to the acquisition of nut-cracking skills: stimulation, facilitation, and teaching. Stimulation appears to be an aspect of scaffolding that involves setting the environment conditions for the infants to practice the behavior on their own. Facilitation involves more active intervention by the mother, such as giving the offspring her own good-quality tool while she uses the poor-quality tool that her offspring had tried unsuccessfully to use. The mother must work harder to crack nuts with the poorer tool but the offspring is more successful. Because facilitation is often a teaching strategy used with older, 4- to 5-year-old, offspring, and stimulation was the strategy most often used for younger, 3-year-old, offspring, there seems to be clear evidence that the mother adjusts her strategy to the competence of her offspring. Boesch (1991) argues that active teaching of specific actions is seen when the offspring experience "technical problems" and mothers adjust their pupils' grip on the tool or adjusts the position of a nut on the anvil in a slow, exaggerated, and deliberate way to emphasize the technical solution.

A similar sort of developmental analysis could be applied to orangutan mothers, who teach their offspring to bridge the gap between two trees (Bard, 1993, 1995b). Two types of stimulation occur. Initially, the mother pauses in the middle of crossing a gap and waits for the infant to stop clinging and to walk across to the next tree. When the infant is walking independently, the mother crosses a gap ahead of the infant but waits in the middle so that the infant can cross on her body or on the branches that she holds. Orangutan mothers facilitate learning when they cross ahead but wait to release the tree branches until the offspring are in position to catch the tree on the backswing. Active teaching of this arboreal behavior was difficult to identify with certainty in orangutans (Bard, 1995b).

THE ONTOGENY OF MATERNAL COMPETENCE

In chimpanzees, maternal competence includes providing supportive care (i.e., cradling, grooming), enjoying interactions (i.e., playing), being responsive (i.e., soothing, assessing, inspecting), and nurturing development (i.e., exercising; Bard, 1994a; Rogers and Davenport, 1970; Yerkes, 1943).

Chimpanzee mothers with marginal skills exhibit some of these behaviors, but there appears to be some mismatching of emotional signals between infants and marginal mothers (Bard, 1994a). The mismatch may include insensitivity to infant crying, treating newborns as if they were much older infants, and either a lack of enjoyment or a lack of gentleness. The overall impression given by chimpanzees with marginal maternal competence is that they are out of tune with their infants. Infant cues of discomfort tend to be disregarded by mothers with marginal skills. Caregiving is applied with the mother's personal agendum, rather than that of the infant.

A review of the literature on great apes makes clear that there is probably not a single factor responsible for all cases of inadequate parenting in primates. In addition, parenting behaviors that are important for the care of newborns are very different from those that are important for care of juveniles. The following subsections delineate prerequisite variables in understanding primate parenting and reviews remedial interventions. This section on ontogeny of maternal competence focuses on the learning mechanisms by which individual chimpanzees acquire behaviors that accompany maternal competence. Early experience, observational learning, and direct learning are discussed in turn.

Primate Parental Prerequisites

There is a great interest in providing remediation of some sort for cases of inadequate parenting in primates. Initially a lack of knowledge of natural conditions and later various constraints of captive conditions resulted in adult primates with insufficient or inadequate parenting behaviors. For example, initial efforts at captive breeding of tamarins and marmosets consisted of removing fathers and older siblings from the cage when mothers gave birth to twins. Without the presence of helpers, many infants died. Older siblings, denied opportunities to interact with infants, were subsequently less efficient in parental behaviors as adults.

Maternal competence in chimpanzees is not instinctual. Although hormones may influence some aspects of maternal behavior, hormones do not determine maternal competence (Coe, 1990; Maestripieri, 1999). Early experience (i.e., whether an individual was raised with the biological mother) is not sufficient in itself to promote maternal competence. Some individual chimpanzees raised with their mothers show maternal competence and some do not; therefore there must be additional factors involved. Observational learning (i.e., watching another individual provide adequate care for offspring) may provide familiarization with infants, but again is not a sufficient condition in itself to promote maternal competence in chimpanzees. The crucial factor may be individual learning through direct hands-on interaction with an infant, a younger individual. A behavioral intervention was designed to maximize maternal competence, in which natural learning conditions were approximated, giving juvenile chimpanzees monitored and limited exposure to younger infants (Bard, 1996). This discussion is focused on the evolutionary and comparative foundations of maternal behavior and maternal competence.

Early Experience

This subsection presents support for the conclusion that early experience is not sufficient in itself to promote maternal competence in chimpanzees. Although early experience may influence a number of variables, such as maternal attitudes in humans (Fleming, 1990), familiarity with infants in rhesus monkeys (Dienske, van Vreeswijk, and Kongis, 1980), coping style in chimpanzees (Fritz and Fritz, 1985), security of attachment in chimpanzees and humans (Goodall, 1986), or other variables that relate to temperamental responsiveness (Fairbanks, 1996; Rijt-Plooij and Plooij, 1987), including cognitive style in problem solving (Capitanio and Mason, 2000), early experience (i.e., being mother reared) in itself does not result in maternal competence.

It has been thought that adult competence in chimpanzees was practically ensured as long as infants were raised with their mother. In fact, when mother rearing includes social groups of mixed ages and genders with family membership approximating that found in the wild, then adult competence appears to be the rule (van Lawick-Goodall, 1968, 1986). "A female who has had a prolonged and positive relationship in infancy with her own mother, contact with peers, and an opportunity to handle or observe infants is very likely to become a good mother herself" (Nicolson, 1991, p. 41). When mother rearing does not include the addition of social groups, such as in conditions with limited space or limited social relations (e.g., when mothers and infants may remain together for 1 or 2 years or when the only other social companions are adults), then maternal competence is not a likely result (Fritz, 1989; Goosen, Schrama, Brinkhof, Schonk, and van Hoek, 1988; Seal and Flesness, 1986). From this information alone, we can conclude that maternal competencies in chimpanzees are not instinctual (Rogers and Davenport, 1970).

The most basic primate parental behavior necessary but not in itself sufficient for survival of the newborn is physical contact. Physical contact, either in the form of allowing the infant to cling (as in rhesus monkeys) or in the form of maternal active cradling (as in chimpanzees), is required for nursing, protection from predators, and thermoregulation. Harlow's (1958) studies demonstrated the preference of monkeys for surrogate mothers who provide "contact comfort" rather than those who provided food as a secure base. Additional information from rhesus monkeys illuminated the requirement that newborns be something familiar. This is necessary in order for isolation-reared mothers to acquire maternal behaviors. Experience with infants before becoming a mother is essential in order for female macaques to find neonates attractive (Sackett and Ruppenthal, 1974). Isolation-reared Japanese macaques are frightened of newborns. When the infant is born, they move away and threaten the neonate (Negayana, Negayana, and Kondo, 1986). Dienske et al. (1980) demonstrated that one of the most important initial responses of rhesus monkeys to new infants is tolerating physical contact. If new mothers had never before seen a newborn infant, they forcibly removed the clinging infant; hence the origin of the term rejection. If provided with opportunities to observe adequate mothers, even from a distance and through Plexiglass barriers, then new rhesus mothers were less likely physically to reject the newborn. Additionally, if infants spent at least 2 days with the mother then the mother's behavior was significantly improved for the second infant (Ruppenthal, Arling, Harlow, Sackett, and Suomi, 1976). Note that in Java macaques, however, only extensive peer contact is required for adequate maternal behavior (Kemps, Timmermans, and Vossen, 1989); however, differences were found in maternal behavior of rhesus monkeys as a function of early rearing (Champoux, Byrne, DeLizio, and Suomi, 1992).

The picture is more complicated in chimpanzees even with respect to newborn behavior. Chimpanzee newborns cannot cling independently at birth. If chimpanzee mothers are frightened of their newborns, they simply do not pick them up. In fact, chimpanzee mothers must engage in active nurturing behaviors: New mothers must pick up the infant and then must provide cradling support for 2 to 3 months, a much longer period of time than is the case with monkey infants. Baboon mothers provide support to their newborns for the first day or two of life (Altmann, 1980; Strum, 1987), but rhesus infants can survive if the mother does not actively reject them. In contrast, chimpanzee infants cannot survive if the mother does not actively accept them.

For any primate infant to survive past the first days of life, sustenance must be provided. This is another area in which mothers must have competent behavior. In almost all primate species (prosimians, New World monkeys, Old World monkeys, and great apes) infants have sufficient reflexive behavior to suckle provided that the mother does not actively interfere. Mothers can interfere with infants' attempts to suckle by preventing them from attaining proximity to the nipple and by actively disengaging them from the nipple. Although these behaviors are species-typical maternal patterns, they are used appropriately at the time that the infant is weaned (e.g., Nicolson, 1987) and they are not adaptive when they occur at birth.

Tactile experience with an infant may also be required for learning the normal holding or carrying postures. This is true for rhesus (Dienske et al., 1980) and callitrichids (especially for male and sibling helpers; Tardif et al., 1992). In callitrichids, holding is less important than appropriate behaviors to facilitate the transfer of the infant from the mother's body to that of the helper. Previous knowledge of both body postures and handling by the individual who will carry the infant aids the transfer process.

When extensive observations indicate that an adult female chimpanzee does not provide adequate care to her offspring, then that infant must be reared under alternative conditions to ensure the survival of the infant. At the Yerkes Research Center of Emory University in the 1970s, nursery-reared chimpanzees began to be raised in same-age peer groups as an alternative to either isolation rearing or rearing with exclusive human contact. Initial social groups began as early as when an infant was 30 days of age and were rarely delayed beyond 4 months of age. Nursery-reared chimpanzees were *not* isolation reared, and each individual was given extensive contact both with conspecifics and human caregivers. Chimpanzees left the nursery when they were approximately 4 to 6 years old and most were placed in mixed-age and mixed-gender social groups in the Great Ape Wing. This policy provided chimpanzees with social experiences that lead in adulthood to most chimpanzees' displaying relatively normal behavioral repertoires. Most chimpanzees raised under these conditions interact appropriately in social situations, including reproduction. Male and female nursery-reared chimpanzees exhibit appropriate mating behavior and the females become pregnant. Despite concerted efforts of researchers and veterinarians, however, many chimpanzee mothers did not exhibit sufficient maternal behavior to raise their own offspring through the first year of life.

An analysis was conducted on the historical records at the Yerkes Center to assess whether there was a relation between an individual herself experiencing adequate maternal care and her subsequent maternal competence. The rearing history of each female at the Yerkes Main Center who had given birth to an infant from January 1, 1987, through January 1, 1992, was collated. The historical records of 30 female chimpanzees allowed them to be classified into one of two early experience categories: mother reared (which included those females who were probably wild born) and nursery reared. The maternal competence of each female was then classified as either "poor" (i.e., their infants were nursery reared) or "good" (i.e., mother reared). Poor is defined as not cradling the infant; good is defined as cradling and providing sufficient care for the infant to remain with the mother. A third classification, "marginal," was required for the mothers who picked up and cradled their infants and allowed them initially to nurse but did not provide sufficient care for the infant to remain with her for 3 months. Only one infant was counted for each mother so as not to bias the count: mothers whose infants were reared in the nursery gave birth to more infants than mothers who had good maternal competence. Some mothers gave birth to more than one infant during this period. Typically, each of the infants could be classified in the same category. For those mothers whose maternal competence status changed, the better rating was used for analysis.

The results revealed that there was no relation between the early experience (i.e., rearing history) of an individual and her subsequent maternal competence ($\chi^2 = 1.43$, *ns*). Of the mothers, 14 were themselves mother reared and 16 were nursery reared. Of the infants, 15 stayed with their mother immediately after birth and 15 were placed in the nursery, but almost twice as many infants were in the nursery at 3 months of age than were with their mothers (18 versus 12). Mothers with marginal maternal competence account for this difference. They picked up their infants, carried them, and allowed them to nurse but did not provide adequate care for longer than several weeks. There were no differences in the results of the statistical analysis if marginal mothers were counted as good or as poor mothers. For marginal mothers, it appeared that additional factors contributed to inadequate care of their offspring, such as low rank within the group or a lack of adult grooming partners. If conditions could be optimized for these mothers, perhaps they could all provide adequate care.

Thus the mother's rearing history, her early experience, does not predict the rearing status of her infant. There was an equal distribution of maternal competence in individuals who were nursery reared and mother reared, although approximately half of the mothers exhibited some maternal behaviors. An individual will not necessarily exhibit maternal competence just because that individual was mother reared. Therefore one must look elsewhere for those variables that are sufficient for the expression of maternal competence. Among the candidate variables, discussed in the following subsections, are observational learning of maternal behaviors and, most importantly, direct hands-on experience with a younger infant.

Observational Learning and Imitation

It is widely believed that chimpanzees can learn behavior patterns through the observation of others and furthermore can imitate the observed behaviors of others. The extent to which observational learning accounts for the development of new skills continues to be a highly debated issue (e.g., Bard and Russell, 1999; Custance and Bard, 1994; Russon and Galdikas, 1993; Tomasello, Davis-Dasilva, Camak, and Bard, 1987; Visalberghi and Fragaszy, 1990; Whiten and Ham, 1992). Experiments indicate that 4-year-old nursery-reared chimpanzees can imitate arbitrary actions (Custance, Whiten, and Bard, 1995), can imitate actions on a foraging task (Whiten, Custance, Gomez, Teixidor, and Bard, 1996) and a 3-year-old chimpanzee's performance on a tool task was enhanced by the presence of a model (Bard, Fragaszy, and Visalberghi, 1995). Yet there remains surprisingly little published evidence of imitative copying of actions on objects by any great ape (Tomasello and Call, 1997).

The historical records of chimpanzees and available social companions do not provide sufficiently clear information to evaluate the singular role of observation (i.e., in the absence of direct learning opportunities) in the development of maternal competence. Research with rhesus monkeys suggests that observation of competent mothers by juveniles facilitates maternal competence (Dienske et al., 1980). Familiarization with neonates is undoubtedly an important prerequisite for the expression of maternal competence and may be obtained through observation without direct contact (Rogers and Davenport, 1970). The fact that some multiparous chimpanzees continue to exhibit poor maternal behavior and some chimpanzee mothers show a decrement in performance with subsequent infants (Struthers, Bloomsmith, and Alford, 1990) are strong arguments against the singular variable of familiarity through observation. The conclusion therefore is that observation of maternal competence by another individual is not a sufficient condition for the expression of maternal competence in chimpanzees.

Direct Hands-on Learning

Although observation may indeed facilitate the learning process, the hypothesis of this subsection is that the crucial variable in acquiring appropriate maternal skills is direct hands-on interaction with an infant. It is suggested that each individual must learn maternal behaviors individually through her own interactions with infants. One of the most fundamental skills that is lacking in chimpanzee mothers with poor maternal competence is picking up the baby. Although some new mothers are actively avoidant and fearful of the newborn, even the most interested of chimpanzee mothers cannot successfully rear her infant if she does not pick up and cradle the infant for the first months of the infant's life.

At the most fundamental level, a chimpanzee mother must pick up her newborn and support the infant against her until the infant is strong enough to accomplish this independently, usually at 2 to 3 months of age (Miller and Nadler, 1981). In addition, basic maternal competence includes allowing the infant to suckle. In the captive setting, these behaviors will ensure infant survival, barring illness or injury. Responsive caregiving and contingent responding are additional characteristics of chimpanzee mothers with good maternal competence (Rogers and Davenport, 1970; Yerkes, 1943).

In wild chimpanzee groups, juvenile and adolescent females show keen interest in their younger siblings (Goodall, 1986; van Lawick-Goodall, 1968). Unrelated subadult females, as well as older female siblings, acquire access to infants by enticement, invitation, or grooming the mother before taking the infant from her arms (Nishida, 1983). When the infant cries or screams, then the mother always retrieves it. Therefore, when the juvenile or adolescent wants to handle the infant for extended periods, she must learn to handle the infant in a manner that does not create infant distress. Such interactions with infants by juveniles, adolescent, or nulliparous females has been called allomothering (Nishida, 1983), play mothering (Lancaster, 1971), and aunting (Rowell et al., 1964), and have been given privileged status as a strategy used by mothers to reduce parental investment (e.g., Bales, Dietz, Baker, Miller, and Tardif, 2000; Fairbanks, 1990; Hrdy, 1976; Sánchez, Peláez, Gil-Bürmann, and Kaumanns, 1999; Trivers, 1974).

Long-term naturalistic observations of both monkeys and apes provide strong documentation that allomothering serves as direct hands-on practice of maternal behaviors. This is the learning-to-mother hypothesis of allomothering. Specifically, the learning-to-mother thesis is supported by fieldwork with chimpanzees (Nishida, 1983), by studies of both captive (Fairbanks, 1990) and free-ranging (Lancaster, 1971) vervet monkeys and patas monkeys (e.g., Chism, 1986), and by more theoretical considerations. One study compared species characteristics and found those species with higher firstborn mortality are those with limited direct opportunities to handle young infants (Nicolson, 1991). Further research with human beings indicates that the infants of adolescent rather than adult mothers are at greater risk for neglect and abuse (Field, Widmayer, Stringer, and Ignatoff, 1980).

The learning-to-mother hypothesis does not explain all allocarer interactions with infants. For instance, female–female competition is suggested to be at the root of the harassment of macaque infants by others (Maestripieri, 1994). In bonnet macaques, there was no difference in infant handling between young and old females, and allocarers who handled infants more often did not have enhanced reproductive success compared with those who handled infants less (Silk, 1999). In wild capuchins, infant handling appears to be a mechanism by which allocarers assess their current relationship with mothers: If the mother is willing to allow the allocarer to handle the infant then the relationship between the allocarer and the mother is good (Manson, 1999). It is important to assess separately the costs and benefits to each member of the infant–mother–allocarer triad: There are likely to be different functions served for each member, and these are likely to vary across primates (Paul, 1999; Ross and MacLarnon, 2000).

Young female chimpanzees do appear to learn mothering behaviors through interactions with younger individuals. Evidence from the field indicates that, of all age and gender classes, subadult female chimpanzees engage in the most hugging and transport of young infants. Mothers differentially allow access of infants to their own daughters, but even touching of infants less than 2 months old is rarely tolerated (Nishida, 1983). Multigenerational observations of vervet monkeys demonstrate that juveniles who spend more time carrying infants have increased survivorship of first offspring compared with juveniles who spend less time engaged in allomothering (Fairbanks, 1990).

Direct learning by each individual is suggested to be a necessary variable for the expression of maternal competence in chimpanzees. Experimental support of this proposition is limited to interventions involving resocialization experiences (Nankivell, Fritz, Nash, and Fritz, 1988) and specific interventions designed to maximize the likelihood of direct interaction with younger individuals (e.g., Hannah and Brotman, 1990). These studies and a prospective longitudinal study (Bard, 1996) are discussed in the following section.

INTERVENTION STRATEGIES TO IMPROVE PARENTAL COMPETENCE

Often it is the case that remedial interventions by humans are required for facilitating species-typical behavior of individuals, such as a chimpanzee who has had insufficient social experiences (e.g., Fritz, 1986, 1989), or opportunities exist to design programs to provide remedial intervention (e.g., Keiter, Reichard, and Simmons, 1983; Mehren and Rapley, 1979). There are many examples of remedial training (e.g., Fritz, 1986) but the emphasis of this section is on preventive intervention, i.e., intervention provided before an individual reaches adulthood, and intervention strategies that relate to improving maternal competence. Interventions should be designed to provide many avenues for the development of species-typical skills.

Resocialization

Remedial procedures have been successfully implemented to maximize the likelihood of maternal competence in adult females through resocialization with conspecifics of individuals before adulthood. One of the reports of successful intervention with a hand-reared chimpanzee involved 6 years of extensive resocialization involving contact with at least six infants; the result was a chimpanzee female with good maternal competence (Nankivell et al., 1988). Many other successful projects have provided remedial experiences to some or many adult chimpanzees, usually those already pregnant or already with a newborn to maximize maternal skills.

It is time intensive and potentially very dangerous for humans to provide experiences to maximize maternal skills to an adult chimpanzee (but see Fouts, Hirsch, and Fouts, 1982; Fritz, 1986). Often the success of the project depends on the adult female's having a particular temperamental style (e.g., very responsive to human interactions). One extremely successful project (Hannah and Brotman, 1990) provided first-time pregnant chimpanzee females with opportunities to interact with infants. Although all females were pregnant, all were still quite young (i.e., most were less than 10 years old) and would be considered subadult (Goodall, 1986; Davis, Fouts, and Hannum, 1981). Of the females, 9 out of 10 who were given exposure to infants successfully reared their infants whereas none of the 8 females without exposure to infants was successful. The results appear to support conclusively the importance of previous handling of infants for the expression of good maternal competence in chimpanzees.

There is much evidence that under "normal" circumstances (i.e., chimpanzees raised in family groups with older and younger siblings and offspring of other individuals), the learning of basic maternal skills, such as picking up, holding, and providing support to infants, occurs when individuals are juveniles or adolescents (Goodall, 1986; see previous section; Nishida, 1983). In nature, the offspring may be 5 to 8 years old when this occurs. In the laboratory setting, in which maturation is more rapid and females routinely give birth at 8 to 10 years of age, it seems appropriate to give exposure when individuals are 3 to 5 years old.

Foster Care

Two fostering projects at the Yerkes Center were conducted, one with a group of 1-year-old nursery-reared chimpanzees, the other with a group of 2-year-old nursery-reared chimpanzees. With a gradual introduction process, the individuals of the groups, now young adults, successfully interact with adult males and with adult females, some of who have offspring of similar age as the nursery-reared individuals. It is not the case, however, that any adult female has "adopted" any nursery-reared subject. In the future, this project may provide prospective evidence of whether observational learning and exposure to adults is sufficient to promote maternal competence. It is possible that these nursery-reared infants will develop to be more socially competent adults than will nonfostered nursery-reared chimpanzees because of exposure to older individuals. It is possible that the fostered individuals will not exhibit enhanced maternal competence because of a lack of exposure to individuals younger than themselves. An alternative possibility is that, because of the long-term nature of the fostering situation, the infants eventually will develop affiliative bonds with the adult females and with their subsequent infants. As the fostered infants grow, it is hoped that the affiliative bonds will grow and that the fostered individuals will be allowed to allomother and obtain direct hands-on experience with individuals younger than themselves.

Another fostering alternative is to give a nursery infant to a lactating female who is without an infant. Potential foster mothers at the Yerkes Center, however, are exceedingly rare. If a female is a good mother then she generally is caring for her own biological offspring. If she does not have good maternal competence, then she would not be a good candidate to be a foster mother for a newborn. Occasionally, opportunities arise and successful fostering is accomplished (e.g., Blersch and Schmidt, 1992; van Wulfften Pathe and van Hooff, 1975). In the wild, juveniles have been adopted by adolescent and adult males as well as by females (Thierry and Anderson, 1986).

Intervention Designed to Enhance Maternal Competence in Chimpanzees

Behavioral and developmental research on both nursery-reared chimpanzees and mother-reared chimpanzees has been conducted at the Yerkes Center (for example, Bard, 1991, 1994a, 1994b, 1998a, 1998b, 2000; Bard and Gardner, 1996; Bard et al., 1992; Hopkins and Bard, 1993, 2000; Lin, Bard, and Anderson, 1992; Russell, Bard and Adamson, 1997). Major goals of the National Chimpanzee Breeding and Research Program were to produce behaviorally normal chimpanzees and to produce a self-sustaining population of chimpanzees (Seal and Flesness, 1986). With the rapidly increasing population of laboratory chimpanzees, management policies that foster the expression of the full range of adult competencies, including social, reproductive, and especially maternal competence, are vital. If self-sustaining populations of laboratory chimpanzees are desired, the urgency for using corrective interventions remains great.

A direct hands-on protocol was designed for use in the Great Ape Nursery of the Yerkes Center. This behavioral intervention was designed to enhance maternal competence by providing a juvenile chimpanzee with hands-on experience with a younger infant. The first nursery-reared female that participated in this study was Katrina. Previous to this experience, the juvenile had only direct experience with peers (individuals of the same age as herself), visual exposure to younger infants, and experience with many adult human caregivers and researchers. Two adult human females were available to mediate and protect each individual. We introduced Katrina when she was 3 years old into a large outdoor area in which Duff, a 1-year-old infant, was already comfortable. On introduction, although very excited, the 3-year-old female gently hugged the 1-year-old infant and lay on her back to gently pull the infant higher on her chest. Although this juvenile might have been one of those individuals who are nursery reared but exhibit good maternal competence, we are confident that now, with the direct hands-on experience, she will exhibit good maternal competence. As we continue this project in the years ahead and give every juvenile nursery-reared chimpanzee experience with younger infants, we maximize the likelihood that every adult female will prove competent with her own offspring (Bard, 1996). The potential explication of the proximate causes of behavioral inadequacies in maternal, reproductive, and social competence makes long-term research such as this extremely valuable.

HOW DOES PRIMATE PARENTING RELATE TO HUMAN PARENTING?

One explicit rationale for the study of parenting in primates is to learn more about the evolutionary basis of parenting in the human primate. Primate mother–infant studies have been especially useful in the development of attachment theory, for example, in which the "parental caregiving system is seen as reciprocal to an infant's attachment system" (Hinde and Stevenson-Hinde, 1990, p. 62). This brief section presents primate models of human parenting and primate models of dysfunctions in parenting. The aim is to better understand both what "works" in primate parenting, things that might be adapted to improve human parenting (Goodall, 1967; Higley and Suomi, 1986; Hinde, 1969; Hinde and Stevenson-Hinde, 1990; Nicolson, 1991; Rheingold, 1963; Yogman, 1990), and models of primate parenting that might provide insight to resolving problematic issues in human parenting.

Primate Models of Human Parenting

A biosocial model of motherhood, incorporating primate and nonprimate research, incorporates many variables thought to be important in determining good parenting, including genetically based temperament, attachment (quality of attachment in infancy through to working models of attachment in adulthood), environmental responsiveness (e.g., to stress), neurobiological responsiveness, and extent of social support (Pryce, 1995). The model has been criticized, however, because it is not useful for predicting maternal competence, does not differentiate maternal neglect from maternal abuse (Maestripieri, 1999), and is based on research with nonprimate species. Nonhuman primates serve as a better model: "The rich behavioral and emotional repertoires and cognitive capabilities of monkeys and apes provide opportunities for modeling aspects of human stress response patterns that are simply not feasible with rodents." (Suomi and Levine, 1998, p. 627).

There is a danger in drawing explicit comparisons between a particular primate species and a particular human society. Perhaps every facet of human parenting can be found to occur in some other primate species, yet clearly no one other primate species exhibits a complete repertoire of human parenting. It is perhaps more helpful to abstract principles from primate studies of parenting and to utilize these principles to better understand human parenting (Hinde, 1987). One principle might be the importance of physical contact in the developing mother–infant relationship (e.g., Harlow's work providing the evidence that contact comfort is an important primary need). Another principle is that attachment with the mother provides protection from danger. The evolutionary basis of attachment can account for some of young children's fears, for example of being alone at night (Hinde, 1987). Another principle, derived from Hrdy's (1976) research in support of Trivers' (1974) theory, is that the optimal mothering style for the mother may not equate to the optimal mothering style for the infant. There are selective pressures that support infanticide, infant neglect, and nonmaternal care given certain social, environmental, and individual conditions. There may not be a single optimal maternal style.

One of the principles of parenting that can be derived from the studies of abuse and separation is that early stress can have long-lasting consequences. Stress experienced early in life may induce changes in emotional reactions to stress, and these changed responses may last a lifetime (Suomi and Levine, 1998). Emotional behavior, mediated by the limbic system, results in emotional reactions that are easily transferred to other individuals and to the next generation (e.g., phobic reactions; Mineka, Davidson, Cooke, and Keir, 1984). It is important to note that the magnitude of disturbance in adults is clearly related to the magnitude of the stress response in infancy. Therefore one could argue that it is not the experience itself, be it abuse or separation-induced stress, but the individual's *experience of the event* that significantly predicts the degree of effect later in life.

As we develop new primate models of human parenting, it will be important to integrate findings about the emotional components of parenting. There is substantial information about the role of the limbic system in emotional behavior but little work utilizing our sophistication in localizing brain activity (e.g., functional magnetic resonance imaging and positron emission tomography) to better understand its role in maternal behavior (Coe, 1990; Suomi and Levine, 1998). Krasnegor and Bridges (1990) advocate that we look more closely at how the brain changes in response to parenting behavior, how parenting, once established, is maintained, and how reproductive and parenting experiences might cause long-term changes in both the neurochemical and the neuroanatomical substrates of parenting. Emotional attitudes toward infants could be considered a theme to explain some causes of abuse and some causes of neglect (for example, emotions are definitely involved in phobic reactions to newborns).

Evolution may have acted, in part, on the reinforcing aspect of bonding with infants. The opioid system is an underexplored aspect of parenting. For example, sucrose appears to act by means of an opioid pathway to produce sustained calming in newborn human infants. By the time the infant is 4 weeks of age, however, sucrose must be paired with eye contact in order to continue to be effective in calming crying babies (Zeifman, Delaney, and Blass, 1996). There has been a great deal of research on the effects of stress and fear, but we have not spent equivalent energy in investigating the effects of positive emotions and attachments (Panksepp, 1986). Providing positive emotional responsiveness to infant chimpanzees, for as little as 4 hr/day, had dramatic effects on cooperation, social responsiveness, and on emotional expressiveness (increasing positive affect). In contrast, early stress had equally dramatic effects but on different systems—early stress caused deficits in attention span, goal-directed efforts, and on emotional expressiveness (increasing fearful responses; Bard and Gardner, 1996). Beta-endorphins are important in primate social relationships and may be implicated in both the initiation and maintenance of maternal behavior (e.g., Keverne, 1992). Coe (1990, p. 179) challenges us to "develop holistic psychobiological models" of parenting.

Modeling Dysfunctional Human Parenting

Major disruptions in the environment can cause maternal dysfunction. Lack of species-typical social support, for example, has an impact on maternal competence. In rhesus, mothers with good competence when raising infants within the social group will abuse their infants when forced to raise them in small cages without social companions (Reite, 1987). Similarly, captive gorillas will show poor maternal care of newborns if alone, but will improve dramatically when at least the male is allowed to live with them (Nadler, 1980). Early separations from the mother can have both immediate and long-lasting effects. When infant rhesus monkeys are separated from their mother under experimental conditions, they can become hyperaggressive adults and not provide adequate care for their infants (e.g., Harlow, 1958). In pigtails, separations lasting only 10 days in infancy can result in juveniles and adolescents that are deficient in developing close friendships and social networks (Reite, 1987). In rhesus, early separations in infancy can compromise adult immunological responses (e.g., to Simian Immunodeficiency Virus challenges; Capitanio and Lerche, 1991).

Maestripieri and Carroll (2000) argue that the naturally occurring variation in maternal competence in macaques and mangabeys can serve as a model of child abuse in humans, as long as clear distinctions are made between abuse and neglect. Abuse has clear consequences for the infant, ranging from distress to injury and death. Even distress, which may be the mildest consequence of maternal abuse, however, can have long-lasting effects (Maestripieri and Carroll, 2000). Neglect is slightly harder to define than abuse but is evident when infants are abandoned. Risk factors for neglect of monkey infants include (1) maternal age, (2) mother's lack of experience, (3) infant age, and (4) infant's or mother's poor health. Poor maternal health or poor infant health can cause neglect of infants. Many argue that abandoning infants under conditions of poor health is an adaptive strategy (e.g., Fairbanks, 2000). Mothers are more likely to neglect their first offspring compared with those of subsequent births. Mothers with little or no prior infant-handling experience are more likely to neglect their offspring. Finally, newborns are at highest risk for neglect.

The risk factors for abuse in monkeys, in contrast to neglect, do not include parity, infant age, infant gender, or prior experience: "The primary risk factor for infant abuse appears to be genetic relatedness to another abusive individual" (Maestripieri and Carroll, 2000, p. 249). In fact, abusive monkey mothers have a distinctive temperamental profile that includes high anxiety, high aggressiveness to other adults, high protectiveness to infant, and a high vulnerability to stress. Abusive monkey mothers, either rhesus, pigtail, or mangabeys, abuse most of their infants. The mechanism of cross-generation transmission of abuse is not yet clear. There is some evidence that abuse is likely to be caused by both direct experience and observational learning (Berman, 1990; Fairbanks, 1989). Evidence of a genetic basis for impulsiveness and anxiety has led both Fairbanks (2001) and Maestripieri and Carroll (2000) to suggest that some temperamental factors associated with maternal style may be inherited.

Maternal abuse has consequences for the infant. Abused infants cry more as a direct consequence of abuse, and they cry more even when they are not being abused. Abuse increases the infant's tendency to cling to the mother, which may paradoxically cause more abuse. Abused infants are developmentally delayed in initiating play with peers, and they play less (Maestripieri and Carroll, 1998; Reite, 1987).

What are the Advantages of Good Parenting?

Reflections on maternal behavior across primates and across environments has caused serious reconsideration of "Mother Nature" (e.g., Hrdy, 1995, 2000), and the "Nurture Assumptions" (Fairbanks,

2000). There is not a maternal *instinct* for warm and caring attention to infants; that is, there is not an instinct to provide care to infants that is always responsive to their needs. Mothers tend to provide care in balance with meeting their own reproductive needs: Good mothers are ones that "adjust and withhold parental care according to rules that promote the mother's reproductive success, thus providing support for parental investment theory and contrary to the 'ideal mother' assumption" (Fairbanks, 2000, p. 23). However, when maternal conditions are poor or when the infant's probability of survival is low, then it can be advantageous to the mother to weigh her own survival against that of her infant. Therefore to cease investing any further energy into a current offspring in order to increase the mother's chances of survival to raise more (or healthier) offspring later is an expected outcome (Hrdy, 1995). For some species, a good mother is one that allows others to provide most of the care. For those species that typically produce twins, for example, it appears that a "cooperative breeding system is critical for offspring survivorship" (Wright, 1990, p. 96).

What are the consequences for the Old World monkey infant of being raised by mothers with different "maternal styles"? In general, protectiveness is thought to protect infants from potential dangers, including harassment from others (Maestripieri, 1994). Infants and juveniles of more protective mothers are more cautious in response to novelty (Fairbanks, 1996). Although these infants do have less risk from predation, they appear to be less able to cope with stressors, such as the loss of the mother (Hinde, 1987). Maternal style can include differences in abuse or rough handling, typically reflected in "rejection rates." Rejecting mothers have infants that show more enterprise (if they survive): The infants develop independence at an earlier age and are more resourceful (Fairbanks, 1996). Infants of rejecting mothers are more stressed, however, as they vocalize more and have more temper tantrums. Rejecting mothers, however, have adolescents that are rated as more bold (for males only, $r = .55$; Fairbanks, 1996). For daughters, it appears that the mothers' maternal style is the best predictor of their own maternal style with their offspring (Berman, 1990; Fairbanks, 1996).

Infant temperament and the maternal style experienced early in life interact in the attainment of dominance status, which is a measure of social success. High-reactive rhesus monkey infants reared with nurturant mothers attain high status in an adolescent peer group whereas high-reactive rhesus monkey infants reared with punitive mothers are lowest in dominance status (Scanlan, 1986). Schneider (1984) found that high-reactive nursery-reared rhesus infants and low-reactive mother-reared infants score highest on cognitive assessments when tested as juveniles even though there were no overall group differences based on rearing or on reactivity. In chimpanzees of the Tai Forest, there appears to be differential maternal investment in sons and daughters, based in part on maternal dominance rank. Mothers of high rank have a longer period of time between the birth of a son and the next offspring—which does decrease the mortality of sons of high-ranking mothers—whereas mother chimpanzees of low rank tend to invest more in their daughters (Boesch and Boesch-Achermann, 2000). Moreover, through their continuing support, mother chimpanzees of high status aid their sons in achieving high dominance status as well (Boesch and Boesch-Achermann, 2000).

Parenting can vary with ecological variables. In macaques and vervets, there is some variation in maternal style that is dependent on the environmental conditions. When the infant is at great risk, either from social aggression, from the introduction of a new male, or because the mother is of low status, then mothers tend to be more protective. Mothers also increase their protectiveness if they have lost a previous infant. In general, however, the degree of protectiveness is inversely related to interbirth intervals, so that less protectiveness correlates with increased fertility. If the mother is in good condition, that is, there is lots of food and she is healthy, then she will increase the rejection of her infant. Increasing rejection causes the infant to wean earlier, the mother begins estrus earlier, and she can have more offspring. In food-rich conditions, the infants mature more quickly and achieve independence earlier. In food-rich conditions, rejection is not related to infant mortality. However, when the mother is in poor or marginal condition, then increased rejection is related to increased infant mortality (Fairbanks, 1996). Changing the foraging demands on mothers, even in the laboratory, has an effect on mother–infant relations (Andrews and Rosenblum, 1993). Moreover, those infants that experienced changes in maternal responsiveness as a function of changing environmental demands were more reactive to stress as adolescents (Rosenblum, Coplan, Friedman, Bassoff, Gorman, and Andrews, 1994). The magnitude of the effect of environmental variables on maternal style or on infant outcome, however, is small in Old World monkeys (Fairbanks, 1996). The effect of changing environmental conditions is likely to vary by species.

CONCLUSIONS

There is no single "primate pattern" of parenting. Diversity, variability, and flexibility are among the most important characteristics of primate parenting. There is obviously a strong genetic basis for maternal behavior, but an equally strong influence of experience. It would be a mistake to expect any single variable to have an exclusive determination for parenting: "Maternal behavior is obviously so important to the survival of a species that it has been 'overdetermined'—that is, driven by multiple behavioral and physiological systems" (Coe, 1990, p. 178).

Maternal competence in primates can be simply defined as rearing an infant and incompetence defined as an infant requiring nursery rearing. Maternal competence in chimpanzees, expressed in interaction even with very young infants, reflects sensitive responsivity during which the mother engages in contingent behavior and encourages development of infant capacities (Bard, 1994a). These behaviors parallel those observed in intuitive parenting in humans (Papoušek and Papoušek, 1987). Necessary conditions for the emergence of adult competence in chimpanzees appear to be interaction with conspecifics of both same and different age classes. It appears that early experiences facilitate the development of cognitive, social, and reproductive competencies. These conditions, however, are not sufficient for the emergence of maternal competence in chimpanzees. Although early mother rearing provides many benefits, it is not a sufficient condition for the expression of maternal competence. The most important early experience for chimpanzees appears to be giving care to a younger individual, that is, direct hands-on exposure rather than receiving competent maternal care.

For chimpanzees, the role of early experience in maternal competence in adulthood is becoming clearer. For chimpanzees, being reared with their mothers provides a myriad of benefits. No argument is being offered that the experiences of early infancy are not critically important for cognitive, motor, emotional, and communicative development in chimpanzees. However, these experiences do not provide all the necessary experiences to promote maternal competence. Longitudinal research and remedial intervention strategies provide strong support for the thesis that direct hands-on experience with infants is required in order for chimpanzees to demonstrate maternal competence in adulthood.

There may be differences among primate species in terms of the necessary and sufficient conditions to demonstrate maternal competence in adulthood. In many primate species, maternal competence is neither instinctual (Rogers and Davenport, 1970) nor hormonally determined (Coe, 1990). It is clear that in rhesus monkeys, even abusive motherless ones, repeated exposure to infants results in improvements in maternal behavior (Ruppenthal, Arling, Harlow, Sackett, and Suomi, 1976). In rhesus monkeys, observation of another female exhibiting maternal care even without direct exposure is sufficient to promote maternal behavior (Dienske et al., 1980). Allomothering for rhesus juveniles has the advantage of increasing the survival of firstborn infants but no effect for survival for subsequent offspring (Berman, 1990). Maternal competence in rhesus monkeys requires passive acceptance without active rejection. In chimpanzees, however, there are many examples of females who have given birth to more than 10 infants and show no diminution of terror at the sight of their newborns. These are also examples of females who are very attentive to their newborns but do not have the sufficient skills to pick up and cradle their newborns. Maternal competence in chimpanzees requires active and positive behaviors.

There is not a single theoretical account, barring evolutionary theory, that can explain the diversity of parenting patterns in primates. Moreover, there is not a single theoretical account that explains or predicts the diversity of patterns of infant interactions with individuals other than the mother

(Caine, 1993; Chism, 2000; Maestripieri, 1994; Manson, 1999; Paul, 1999; Ross and MacLarnon, 2000; Silk, 1999; Snowdon, 1996; Wright, 1990). It is likely that there will not be a single theoretical account that explains the ontogeny of maternal competence in primates, because there is a similar pattern of diversity in maternal behavior across species. For some species, such as tamarins, mothers must learn to let others help in infant care. Rhesus mothers must learn to let infants cling. Chimpanzee mothers must learn to provide support for the infant, physically, emotionally, and communicatively.

The optimal or sensitive period of maximizing maternal competence appears to be the juvenile period rather than infancy. In fact, it appears in rats that parental behavior may be induced in juveniles merely by exposure to infants. The juvenile period "may represent a universally important time for the development of parental behavior" (Brunelli and Hofer, 1990, p. 373). The parenting behaviors that are frequently observed during the juvenile period often have a playful character, thus providing support for use of the term play mothering and support for the idea that play has an extremely important developmental function (e.g., Bruner, 1972).

Parenting in primates is diverse. Some prosimian mothers park their infants in nests, carry them in their mouth, and let them nurse and otherwise do not engage with their infants. In contrast, chimpanzee mothers provide cradling support and spend up to 15 min/hr interacting socially, communicatively, or didactically with their infants. Some New World monkey fathers play an important role in parenting infants, as do gorilla fathers. Consideration of the influence of monogamy or living in a harem group illuminates the manner in which social organization contributes to the behavioral expression of parenting. Cognitive influences on parenting, especially evident in the great apes, typically provide for flexibility and richness in parenting behaviors, making great ape parenting more similar to human parenting than that of other primates. The evolutionary risks, however, include greater dysfunction in parental behavior when learning environments are altered. The continuing influence of parents on older offspring, especially adolescents, requires more focused study. The manner in which independence is achieved is an important consideration. Evidence of the teaching of complex locomotor behaviors, tool use, hunting, and subtle food-searching patterns suggest that primate parents continue to influence offspring throughout development. As we develop new primate models of parenting, it will be important to consider emotional components of parenting with an emphasis on the positive aspects of bonding and attachment, and on investigation of the mechanisms underlying the reinforcing qualities of parenting. There is much that remains to be learned.

ACKNOWLEDGMENTS

Funding was provided by U.S. National Institutes of Health (NIH) grant RR-00165 to the Yerkes Regional Primate Research Center of Emory University, NIH grant RR-03591 to R. B. Swenson of the Yerkes Center, National Institute of Child Health and Human Development (NICHD) Intramural Research Program funds through the Laboratory of Comparative Ethology and S. J. Suomi, a Max-Planck Society stipend in cooperation with the Developmental Psychobiology project directed by H. Papoušek at the Max-Planck Institute for Psychiatry, NICHD-NRSA Research Fellowship HD-07105 to K. A. Bard, and NIH grant RR-06158 to K. A. Bard. The British Council sponsored a visit to the Primate Research Institute, Kyoto University to gather observations on the cross-cultural development of mutual gaze in chimpanzees in collaboration with Masako Myowa-Yamakoshi, Masaki Tomonaga and Tetsuro Matsuzawa. The Yerkes Center is fully accredited by the American Association for Accreditation of Laboratory Animal Care. I thank my research assistants, Kelly McDonald, Yvette Veira, Kathy Gardner, and Josh Schneider, for all their work with the chimpanzees, and I thank N. Johns for finding every reference that I asked for in writing in 1995 chapter. Maria O'Neill was an enormous help with the referencing for this substantially revised version. Special appreciation is extended to Marc Bornstein, Steve Suomi, Mechthild Papoušek, and to the memory of Hanuš Papoušek.

REFERENCES

Adamson, L., and Bakeman, R. (1984). Mother's communication acts: Changes during infancy. *Infant Behavior and Development, 7,* 467–487.

Ainsworth, M. D. S. (1967). *Infancy in Uganda: Infant care and the growth of love.* Baltimore: Johns Hopkins University Press.

Ainsworth, M. D., and Bell, S. M. (1970). Attachment, exploration, and separation; Illustrated by the behavior of one-year-olds in a strange situation. *Child Development, 41,* 49–67.

Alberts, S. (1987). Parental care in captive siamangs (*Hylobates syndactylus*). *Zoo Biology, 6,* 401–406.

Altmann, J. (1980). *Baboon mothers and infants.* Cambridge, MA: Harvard University Press.

Altmann, J., Altmann, S. A., Hausfater, G., and McCuskey, S. A. (1977). Life history of yellow baboons: Physical development, reproductive parameters, and infant mortality. *Primates, 18,* 315–330.

Altmann, S. (1962). A field study of the sociobiology of rhesus monkeys, *Macaca mulatta. Annals of the New York Academy of Science, 102,* 338–435.

Altmann, S. (1967). *Social communication among primates.* Chicago: Chicago University Press.

Andrews, M. W., and Rosenblum, L. A. (1993). Assessment of attachment in differentially reared infant monkeys (*Macaca radiata*): Response to separation and a novel environment. *Journal of Comparative Psychology, 107,* 84–90.

Bales, K., Dietz, J., Baker, A., Miller, K., and Tardif, S. D. (2000). Effects of allocaregivers on fitness of infants and parents in callitrichid primates. *Folia Primatologica, 71,* 27–38.

Balsamo, E., Bradley, R. J., Bradley, D. M., Pegram, G. V., and Rhodes, J. M. (1972). Sleep ontogeny in the chimpanzee: From birth to two months. *Electroencephalography and Clinical Neurophysiology, 33,* 41–46.

Bard, K. A. (1991). Distribution of attachment classifications in nursery chimpanzees. *American Journal of Primatology, 20,* 171.

Bard, K. A. (1992). Intentional behavior and intentional communication in young free-ranging orangutans. *Child Development, 63,* 1186–1197.

Bard, K. A. (1993). Cognitive competence underlying tool use in free-ranging orangutans. In A. Berthelet and J. Chavaillon (Eds.). *The use of tools by human and nonhuman primates* (pp. 103–117). Oxford, England: Oxford University Press.

Bard, K. A. (1994a). Evolutionary roots of intuitive parenting: Maternal competence in chimpanzees. *Early Development and Parenting, 3,* 19–28.

Bard, K. A. (1994b). Very early social learning: The effect of neonatal environment on chimpanzees' social responsiveness. In J. J. Roeder, B. Thierry, J. R. Anderson, and N. Herrenschmidt (Eds.), *Current primatology: Vol. II. Social development, learning, and behavior* (pp. 339–346). Strasbourg, France: Université Louis Pasteur.

Bard, K. A. (1995a). Parenting in primates. In M. H. Bornstein (Ed.), *Handbook of parenting: Vol. 2. Biology and ecology of parenting* (pp. 27–58). Mahwah, NJ: Lawrence Erlbaum Associates.

Bard, K. A. (1995b). Sensorimotor cognition in young feral orangutans (*Pongo pygmaeus*). *Primates, 36,* 297–321.

Bard, K. A. (1996). *Responsive care: Behavioral intervention for nursery-reared chimpanzees. The 1996 ChimpanZoo Conference,* V. I. Landau (Ed). Tucson, AZ: ChimpanZoo, sponsored program of the Jane Goodall Institute.

Bard, K. A. (1998a). Neonatal neurobehavioral correlates of lateral bias and affect in infant chimpanzees (*Pan troglodytes*). *Developmental Neuropsychology, 14,* 471–494.

Bard, K. A. (1998b). Social-experiential contributions to imitation and emotion in chimpanzees. In S. Braten (Ed.), *Intersubjective communication and emotion in early ontogeny. Studies in emotion and social interaction* (2nd series, pp. 208–227). New York: Cambridge University Press.

Bard, K. A. (2000). Crying in infant primates: Insights into the development of crying in chimpanzees. In R. Barr, B. Hopkins, and J. Green (Eds.), *Crying as a sign, a symptom and a signal: Developmental and clinical aspects of early crying behavior* (pp. 157–175). London: MacKeith.

Bard, K. A., Fragaszy, D. M., and Visalberghi, E. (1995). Acquisition and comprehension of a tool-using behavior by young chimpanzees: Effects of age and modeling. *International Journal of Comparative Psychology, 8,* 47–68.

Bard, K. A., and Gardner, K. H. (1996). Influences on development in infant chimpanzees: Enculturation, temperament, and cognition. In A. E. Russon, K. A. Bard, and S. T. Park (Eds.), *Reaching into thought: The minds of the great apes* (pp. 235–256). Cambridge, England: Cambridge University Press.

Bard, K. A., Hopkins, W. D., and Fort, C. (1990). Lateral bias in infant chimpanzees (*Pan troglodytes*). *Journal of Comparative Psychology, 104,* 309–321.

Bard, K. A., Myowa-Yamakoshi, M., and Tomonaga, M. (2001). *Mutual gaze in chimpanzee mother–infant face-to-face interactions.* Unpublished manuscript.

Bard, K. A., Platzman, K. A., and Coffman, H. (1989). *Behavioral states in neonatal mother-reared chimpanzees (Pan troglodytes)*. Unpublished manuscript.

Bard, K. A., Platzman, K. A., Lester, B. M., and Suomi, S. J. (1992). Orientation to social and nonsocial stimuli in neonatal chimpanzees and humans. *Infant Behavior and Development, 15,* 43–56.

Bard, K. A., and Russell, C. L. (1999). Evolutionary foundations of imitation: Social, cognitive and developmental aspects of imitative processes in non-human primates. In J. Nadel and G. Butterworth (Eds.), *Imitation in infancy. Cambridge studies in cognitive perceptual development* (pp. 89–123). New York: Cambridge University Press.

Bard, K. A., Street, E., McCrary, C., and Boothe, R. (1995). The development of visual acuity in infant chimpanzees. *Infant Behavior and Development, 18,* 225–232.

Bennett, E. (1988). The occurrence of twins and accompanying behavioral changes in the banded langur (*Presbytis melalophos*). *Primates, 29,* 557–563.

Berman, C. M. (1990). Consistency in maternal behavior within families of free-ranging rhesus monkeys: An extension of the concept of maternal style. *American Journal of Primatology, 22,* 159–169.

Bernstein, J., Judge, P. G., and Ruehlmann, T. E. (1993). Sex differences in adolescent rhesus monkey (*Macaca mulatta*) behavior. *American Journal of Primatology, 31,* 197–210.

Bernstein, I. S., Ruehlmann, T. E., Judge, P. G., Lindquist, T., and Weed, J. L. (1991). Testosterone changes during the period of adolescence in male rhesus monkeys (*Macaca mulatta*). *American Journal of Primatology, 24,* 29–38.

Biben, M. (1992). Allomaternal vocal behavior in squirrel monkeys. *Developmental Psychobiology, 25,* 79–92.

Biben, M. (1994). Eye contact and vocal responsiveness in squirrel monkey infants and their caregivers. *Early Development and Parenting, 3,* 29–36.

Bingham, H. C. (1927). Parental play of chimpanzees. *Journal of Mammology, 8,* 77–89.

Bingham, H. C. (1932). Gorillas in a native habitat. *Carnegie Institute Washington Publication, 426,* 1–66.

Blersch, B. H., and Schmidt, C. R. (1992). Adoption of an additional infant by a western lowland gorilla (*Gorilla gorilla gorilla*). *Folia Primatologica, 58,* 190–196.

Boesch, C. (1991). Teaching among wild chimpanzees. *Animal Behaviour, 41,* 530–532.

Boesch, C., and Boesch, H. (1981). Sex differences in the use of natural hammers by wild chimpanzees: A preliminary report. *Journal of Human Evolution, 10,* 585–593.

Boesch, C., and Boesch, H. (1989). Hunting behavior of wild chimpanzees in the Tai National Park. *American Journal of Physical Anthropology, 78,* 547–573.

Boesch, C., and Boesch-Achermann, H. (2000). *The chimpanzees of the Tai Forest: Behavioural ecology and evolution.* Oxford, England: Oxford University Press.

Bolwig, N. (1980). Early social development and emancipation of *Macaca nemestrina* and species of *Papio. Primates, 21,* 357–375.

Bornstein, M. H. (1989). Sensitive periods in development: Structural characteristics and casual interpretations. *Psychological Bulletin, 105,* 179–197.

Bowlby, J. (1969). *Attachment and Loss: Vol. 1. Attachment.* New York: Basic Books.

Bowlby, J. (1973). *Attachment and Loss: Vol. 2. Separation.* New York: Basic Books.

Box, H. O. (1977). Quantitative data on the carrying of young captive monkeys (*Callitrix jacchus*) by other members of their captive groups. *Primates, 18,* 475–484.

Brazelton, T. B. (1984). Neonatal behavioral assessment scale. *Clinics in Developmental Medicine No. 88,* Philadelphia: Lippincott.

Brown, J. V., and Pieper, W. A. (1973). Non-nutritive sucking in great ape and human newborns. *American Journal of Physical Anthropology, 38,* 549–554.

Brown, K., and Mack, D. S. (1978). Food sharing among captive *Leontopithecus rosalia. Folia Primatologica, 29,* 268–290.

Brunelli, S. A., and Hofer, M. A. (1990). Parental behavior in juvenile rats: Environmental and biological determinants. In N. Krasnegor and R. Bridges (Eds.), *Mammalian parenting* (pp. 372–399). New York: Oxford University Press.

Bruner, J. (1972). Nature and uses of immaturity. *American Psychologist, 27,* 687–708.

Caine, N. (1986). Behavior during puberty and adolescence. In G. Mitchell and J. Erwin (Eds.), *Comparative primate biology: Vol. 2, Part A. Behavior conservation, and ecology.* New York: Liss.

Caine, N. (1993). Flexibility and co-operation as unifying themes in *Saguinus* social organization and behaviour: The role of predation pressures. In A. B. Rylands (Ed.), *Marmoset and tamarins: Systematics, behaviour, and ecology* (pp. 200–219). Oxford, England: Oxford University Press.

Capitanio, J. P., and Lerche, N. W. (1991). Psychosocial factors and disease progression in simian AIDS: A preliminary report. *AIDS, 5,* 1103–1106.

Capitanio, J. P., and Mason, W. A. (2000). Cognitive style: Problem solving by rhesus macaques (*Macaca mulatta*) reared with living or inanimate substitute mothers. *Journal of Comparative Psychology, 114,* 115–125.

Caro, T. M., and Hauser, M. (1992). Is there teaching in nonhuman animals? *Quarterly Review of Biology, 67,* 151–174.

Carpenter, C. R. (1964). *Naturalistic behavior of nonhuman primates.* University Park, PA: Pennsylvania State University Press.

Champoux, M., Byrne, E., DeLizio, R., and Suomi, S. J. (1992). Motherless mothers revisited: Rhesus maternal behavior and rearing history. *Primates, 33,* 251–255.

Charles-Dominique, P. (1977). *Ecology and behaviour of nocturnal primates. Prosimians of equatorial West Africa.* New York: Columbia University Press.

Chism, J. (1986). Development and mother–infant relations among captive patas monkeys. *International Journal of Primatology, 7,* 49–81.

Chism, J. (2000). Allocare patterns among cercopithecines. *Folia Primatologica, 71,* 55–66.

Clark, C. B. (1977). A preliminary report on weaning among chimpanzees of the Gombe National Park, Tanzania. In S. Chevalier-Skolnikoff and F. E. Poirier (Eds.), *Primate bio-social development: Biological, social and ecological determinants* (pp. 235–260). New York: Garland.

Coe, C. L. (1990). Psychobiology of maternal behavior in nonhuman primates. In N. Krasnegor and R. Bridges (Eds.), *Mammalian parenting* (pp. 157–183). New York: Oxford University Press.

Custance, D., and Bard, K. A. (1994). The comparative and developmental study of self-recognition and imitation: The importance of social factors. In S. T. Parker, M. Boccia, and R. W. Mitchell (Eds.). *Self-awareness in animals and humans: Developmental perspectives* (pp. 207–226). Cambridge, England: Cambridge University Press.

Custance, D., Whiten, A., and Bard, K. A. (1995). Can young chimpanzees (*Pan troglodytes*) imitate arbitrary actions? Hayes and Hayes (1952) revisited. *Behaviour, 132,* 837–859.

Davis, D., Fouts, R. S., and Hannum, M. E. (1981). The maternal behavior of a home-reared, language using chimpanzee. *Primates, 22,* 570–573.

Deag, J. M., and Crook, J. H. (1971). Social behavior and 'agonistic buffering' in the wild barbary macaque *Macaca sylvanus. Folia Primatologica, 15,* 183–200.

DeVore, I. (1963). Mother–infant relations in free-ranging baboons. In H. L. Reingold (Ed.), *Maternal behavior in mammals* (pp. 305–335) New York: Wiley.

DeVore, I. (1965). *Primate behavior: Field studies of monkeys and apes.* New York: Holt, Reinhart & Winston.

Dienske, H., and Vreeswijk, W. van (1987). Regulation of nursing in chimpanzees. *Developmental Psychobiology, 20,* 71–83.

Dienske, H., Vreeswijk, W. van, and Konig, H. (1980). Adequate mothering by partially isolated rhesus monkeys after observation of maternal care. *Journal of Abnormal Psychology, 89,* 489–492.

Dolhinow, P. (Ed.). (1972). *Primate Patterns.* New York: Holt, Rinehart & Winston.

Duijghuisen, J. A. H., Timmermans, P. J. A., Vochteloo, J. D., and Vossen, J. M. H. (1992). Mobile surrogate mothers and the development of explanatory behavior and radius of action in infant long-tailed Macaques (*Macaca fascicularis*). *Developmental Psychobiology, 25,* 441–459.

Fairbanks, L. A. (1988). Vervet monkey grandmothers: Interactions with infant grandoffspring. *International Journal of Primatology, 9,* 425–441.

Fairbanks, L. A. (1989). Early experience and cross-generational continuity of mother–infant contact in vervet monkeys. *Developmental Psychology, 22,* 669–681.

Fairbanks, L. A. (1990). Reciprocal benefits of allomothering for female vervet monkeys. *Animal Behaviour, 40,* 553–562.

Fairbanks, L. A. (1996). Individual differences in maternal style: Cause and consequences for mothers and offspring. In J. S. Rosenblat and C. T. Snowdan (Eds.). *Advances in the study of behavior* (Vol. 25, pp. 597–612). London: Academic Press.

Fairbanks, L. (2000). The nurture assumptions: Things your mother never told you. *American Journal of Primatology, 51, Supplement 1,* 23 (abstract).

Fairbanks, L. (2001). Individual differences in response to a stranger: Social impulsivity as a dimension of temperament in vervet monkeys (*Cercopithecus aethiops sabaeus*). *Journal of Comparative Psychology, 115,* 22–28.

Fairbanks, L. A., and McGuire, M. T. (1993). Maternal protectiveness and response to the unfamiliar in Vervet monkeys. *American Journal of Primatology, 30,* 119–129.

Field, T., Widmayer, S., Stringer, S., and Ignatoff, E. (1980). Teenage, lower-class, black mothers and their preterm infants. An intervention and developmental follow-up. *Child Development, 51,* 426–436.

Fimbel, C. C. (1992). Cross-species handling of Colobine infants. *Primates, 33,* 545–549.

Fleming, A. S. (1990). Hormonal and experimental correlates of maternal responsiveness in human mothers. In N. Krasnegor and R. Bridges (Eds.), *Mammalian parenting* (pp. 154–207). New York: Oxford University Press.

Fossey, D. (1979). Development of the Mountain gorilla (*Gorilla gorilla beringei*): The first thirty-six months. In D. Hamburg and E. McCown (Eds.), The great apes (pp. 138–184). New York: Benjamin/Cummings.

Fossey, D. (1983). *Gorillas in the mist.* Boston: Houghton Mifflin.

Fouts, R. S., Hirsch, A. D., and Fouts, D. H. (1982). Cultural transmission of a human language in a chimpanzee mother–infant relationship. In H. E. Fitzgerald, J. A. Mullins, and P. Gage (Eds.), *Child nurturance: Vol. 3. Studies of development in nonhuman primates.* New York: Plenum.

Fragaszy, D. M., and Bard, K. A. (1997). Comparisons of development and life history in *Pan* and *Cebus. International Journal of Primatology, 18,* 683–701.

Fritz, J. (1986). Resocialization of asocial chimpanzees. In K. Benirschke (Ed.), *Primates: The road to self-sustaining populations* (pp. 351–359). New York: Springer-Verlag.

Fritz, J. (1989). Resocialization of captive chimpanzees: An amelioration procedure. *American Journal of Primatology, Suppl. 1*, 79–86.

Fritz, J., and Fritz, P. (1985). The hand-rearing unit: Management decisions that may affect chimpanzee development. In C. E. Graham and J. A. Bowen (Eds.), *Clinical management of infant great apes* (pp. 1–34). New York: Liss.

Gagneux, P., Woodruff, D., and Boesch, C. (1997). Furtive mating in female chimpanzees. *Nature (London), 387*, 358–359.

Galdikas, B. M. F. (1979). Orangutan adaptation at Tanjung Puting Reserve: Mating and ecology. In D. Hamburg and E. McCown (Eds.), *The great apes* (pp. 194–233). New York: Benjamin/Cummings.

Galdikas, B. M. F. (1982). Wild orangutan birth at Tanjung Puting Reserve. *Primates, 23*, 500–510.

Goldizen, A. W. (1987). Tamarins and marmosets: Communal care of offspring. In B. B. Smuts, D. L. Cheney, R. M. Seyfarth, R. W. Wrangham, and T. T. Struhsaker (Eds.), *Primate Societies*. Chicago: University of Chicago Press.

Goodall, J. (1967). Mother–offspring relationships in chimpanzees. In D. Morris (Ed.), *Primate ethology* (pp. 287–346). London: Weidenfeld and Nicolson.

Goodall, J. (1986). *The chimpanzees of Gombe: Patterns of behavior*. Cambridge, MA: Harvard University Press.

Goosen, C., Schrama, A., Brinkhof, H., Schonk, J., and van Hoek, L. A. (1983). Housing conditions and breeding success of chimpanzees at the Primate Center TNO. *Zoo Biology, 2*, 295–302.

Gursky, S. (2000). Allocare in a nocturnal primate: Data on the spectral tarsier, *Tarsius spectrum*. *Folia Primatologica, 71*, 39–54.

Hall, K. R. L. (1962). The sexual, agonistic, and derived social behavior patterns of the wild chacma baboon, *Papio ursinus*. *Proceedings of the Zoological Society of London, 139*, 283–327.

Hannah, A. C., and Brotman, B. (1990). Procedures for improving maternal behavior in captive chimpanzees. *Zoo Biology, 9*, 233–240.

Hansen, E. W. (1966). The development of maternal and infant behavior in the rhesus monkey. *Behaviour, 27*, 107–149.

Harcourt, A. H. (1979). Social relations among adult female mountain gorillas. *Animal Behaviour, 27*, 251–264.

Harcourt, A. H., and Stewart, K. J. (1981). Gorilla male relationships: Can differences during immaturity lead to contrasting reproductive tactics during adulthood? *Animal Behaviour, 29*, 206–210.

Harlow, H. F. (1958). The nature of love. *American Psychologist, 13*, 673–685.

Harlow, H. F., and Harlow, M. K. (1965). The affectional systems. In A. Schrier, H. Harlow, and F. Stollnitz (Eds.), *The behavior of nonhuman primates* (Vol. II, pp. 287–334). New York: Academic.

Hausfater, G., and Hrdy, S. (Eds.). (1984). *Infanticide: Comparative and evolutionary perspectives*. New York: Aldine de Gruyter.

Higley, J. D., and Suomi, S. J. (1986). Parental behavior in non-human primates. In. W. Sluckin and M. Herbert (Eds.), *Parental behaviour* (pp. 152–207). Oxford, England: Blackwell.

Hinde, R. A. (1969). Analyzing the roles of the partners in a behavioral interaction: Mother–infant relations in rhesus macaques. *Annals of the New York Academy of Science, 159*, 651–657.

Hinde, R. (1987). Can nonhuman primates help us understand human behavior? In B. Smuts, D. L. Cheney, R. M. Seyfarth, R. W. Wrangham, and T. T. Struhsaker (Eds.), *Primate Societies* (pp. 413–420). Chicago: University of Chicago Press.

Hinde, R. A., and Simpson, M. J. A. (1975). Qualities of mother–infant relationships in monkeys. In *Parent-offspring relationships* (CIBA Foundation Symposium 33). Amsterdam: Elsevier.

Hinde, R. A., and Spencer-Booth, Y. (1967). The behaviour of socially living rhesus monkeys in their first two and a half years. *Animal Behaviour, 15*, 169–196.

Hinde, R. A., and Stevenson-Hinde, J. (1990). Attachment: Biological, cultural and individual desiderata. *Human Development, 33*, 62–72.

Hiraiwa-Hasegawa, M. (1990). Maternal investment before weaning. In T. Nishida (Ed.), *The chimpanzees of the Mahale Mountains*. Tokyo: University of Tokyo Press.

Hopf, A. (1981). Conditions of failure and recovery of maternal behavior in captive squirrel monkeys (*Saimiri*). *International Journal of Primatology, 2*, 335–349.

Hopkins, W. D., and Bard, K. A. (1993). Hemispheric specialization in infant chimpanzees (*Pan troglodytes*): Evidence for a relation with gender and arousal. *Developmental Psychobiology, 26*, 219–235.

Hopkins, W. D., and Bard, K. A. (2000). A longitudinal study of hand preferences in chimpanzees (*Pan troglodytes*). *Developmental Psychobiology, 36*, 292–300.

Horvat, J. R., and Kraemer, H. C. (1981). Infant socialization and maternal influence in chimpanzees. *Folia Primatologica, 36*, 99–110.

Hrdy, S. (1976). Care and exploitation of nonhuman primate infants by conspecifics other than the mother. In J. S. Rosenblatt, R. A. Hinde, E. Shaw, and C. Beer (Eds.), *Advances in the study of behavior* (Vol. 6, pp. 101–158). New York: Academic.

Hrdy, S. (1995). Natural-born mothers. *Natural History, 12*, 30–42.

Hrdy, S. B. (2000). *Mother nature: A history of mothers, infants, and natural selection*. New York: Pantheon.

Itani, J. (1959). Paternal care in the wild Japanese monkey, *Macaca fuscata fuscata*. *Primates, 2*, 61–93.

Jacobsen, C. F., Jacobsen, M. M., and Yoshioka, J.G. (1932). Development of an infant chimpanzee during her first year. *Comparative Psychology Monographs, 9*, 1–94.

Jay, P. C. (1962). Aspects of maternal behavior among langurs. *Annals of the New York Academy of Science, 102*, 468–476.

Jay, P. C. (1968). *Primates: Studies in adaptation and variability.* New York: Holt, Reinhart & Winston.

Johnson, L. D., Petto, A. J., and Sehgal, P. K. (1991). Factors in the rejection and survival of captive cotton-top Tamarins (*Saguinus oedipus*). *American Journal of Primatology, 25*, 91–102.

Joines, S. (1977). A training programme designed to induce maternal behavior in a multiparous female lowland gorilla (*Gorilla gorilla gorilla*) at the San Diego Wild Animal Park. *International Zoo Yearbook, 17*, 185–188.

Jolly, A. (1966). *Lemur behavior.* Chicago: University of Chicago Press.

Jolly, A. (1985). *The evolution of primate behavior* (2nd ed.). New York: Macmillian.

Kaufman, I. C., and Rosenblum, L. A. (1969). The waning of the mother–infant bond in two species of macaque. In B. M. Foss (Ed.), *Determinants of infant behavior IV.* London: Metheun.

Keiter, M. D., Reichard, T., and Simmons, J. (1983). Removal, early hand rearing, and successful reintroduction of an orangutan (*Pongo pygmaeus pygmaeus abelii*) to her mother. *Zoo Biology 2*, 55–59.

Kellog, W., and Kellog, L. A. (1933). *The Ape and the child.* New York: McGraw-Hill.

Kemps, A., Timmermans, P., and Vossen, J. (1989). Effects of mother's rearing condition and multiple motherhood on the early development of mother–infant interactions in java-macaques (*Macaca fascicularis*). *Behaviour, 111*, 1–4.

Keverne, E. B. (1992). Primate social relationships: Their determinants and consequences. In P. J. B. Slater, J. S. Rosenblatt, C. Beer, and M. Milinski (Eds.), *Advances in the study of behavior* (Vol. 21, pp. 1–37). New York: Academic.

King, M. C., and Wilson, A. C. (1975). Evolution at two levels in humans and chimpanzees, *Science, 188*, 107–146.

Klopfer, P. H., and Boskoff, K. J. (1979). Maternal behavior in prosimians. In G. A. Doyle and R. D. Martin (Eds.), *The study of prosimian behavior.* New York, Academic.

Kluver, J. (1933). *Behaviour mechanisms in monkeys.* Chicago: University of Chicago Press.

Kohler, W. (1925). *The mentality of apes.* London: Routledge and Kegan Paul.

Kohts, N. (1935). *Infant ape and human child.* Moscow: Scientific Memoirs of the Museum Darwinium.

Krasnegor, N., and Bridges, R. S. (1990). Future directions in research on mammalian parenting. In N. Krasnegor and R. S. Bridges (Eds.), *Mammalian parenting: Biochemical, neurobiological, and behavioral determinants* (pp. 485–488). New York: Oxford University Press.

Kummer, H. (1967). Triparite relations in hamadryas baboons. In S. Altmann (Ed.), *Social communication among primates.* Chicago: University of Chicago Press.

Lancaster, J. (1971). Play-mothering: The relations between juvenile females and young infants among free-ranging vervet monkeys (*Cercopithecus aethiops*). *Folia Primatologica, 15*, 161–182.

Lefebvre, L. (1985). Parent-offspring food sharing: A statistical test of the early weaning hypothesis. *Journal of Human Evolution, 14*, 225–261.

Leighton, D. R. (1987). Gibbons: Territoriality and monogamy. In B. Smuts, D. L. Cheney, R. M. Seyfarth, R. W. Wrangham, and T. T. Struhsaker (Eds.), *Primate Societies* (pp. 330–342). Chicago: University of Chicago Press.

Lin, A., Bard, K. A., and Anderson, J. A. (1992). Development of self-recognition in chimpanzees (*Pan troglodytes*). *Journal of Comparative Psychology, 106*, 120–127.

Maestripieri, D. (1993). Infant kidnapping among group-living rhesus macaques: Why don't mothers rescue their infants? *Primates, 34*, 211–216.

Maestripieri, D. (1994). Social structure, infant handling, and mothering styles in group-living Old World monkeys. *International Journal of Primatology, 15*, 531–553.

Maestripieri, D. (1995). Maternal encouragement in nonhuman primates and the question of animal teaching. *Human Nature, 6*, 361–378.

Maestripieri, D. (1999). The biology of human parenting: Insights from nonhuman primates. *Neuroscience and Biobehavioral Reviews, 23*, 411–422.

Maestripieri, D., and Call, J. (1996). Mother–infant communication in primates. *Advances in the Study of Behavior, 25*, 613–642.

Maestripieri, D., and Carroll, K. (1998). Child abuse and neglect: Usefulness of the animal data. *Psychological Bulletin, 123*, 211–223.

Maestripieri, D., and Carroll, K. (2000). Causes and consequences of infant abuse and neglect in monkeys. *Aggression and Violent Behavior, 5*, 245–254.

Manson, J. H. (1999). Infant handling in wild *Cebus capucinus*: testing bonds between females? *Animal Behaviour, 57*, 911–921.

Mason, W. A., and Mendoza, S. P. (1998). Generic aspects of primate attachments: Parents, offspring, and mates. *Psychoneuro endocrinology, 23*, 765–778.

McGrew, W. C. (1974). Patterns of plant food sharing by wild chimpanzees. *Contemporary Primatology*, 304–309.

McGrew, W. C. (1977). Socialization and object manipulation of wild chimpanzees. In S. Chevalier-Skolnikoff and F. E. Poirer (Eds.), *Primate bio-social development: Biological, social, and ecological determinants.* New York: Garland.

McKenna, J. J. (1979). The evolution of allomothering behavior among colobine monkeys: Function and opportunism in evolution. *American Anthropologist, 81*, 818–840.

Mehren, K. G., and Rapley, W. A. (1979). Reintroduction of a rejected orangutan infant to its mother. *Annual Proceedings of the American Association of Zoo Veterinarians 1978, 116*, 122–125.

Miller, L. C., and Nadler, R. D. (1981). mother–infant relations and infant development in captive chimpanzees and orangutans. *International Journal of Primatology, 2*, 247–261.

Mineka, S., Davidson, M., Cooke, M., and Keir, R. (1984). Observational conditioning of snake fear in rhesus monkeys, *Journal of Abnormal Psychology, 93*, 355–372.

Morris, D. (1967). *Primate Ethology*. Chicago: Aldine de Gruyter.

Nadler, R. (1980). Child abuse: Evidence from nonhuman primates. *Developmental Psychobiology, 13*, 507–512.

Nadler, R. (1983). Experiential influences on infant abuse of gorillas and some other nonhuman primates. In M. Reite and N. Caine (Eds.), *Child abuse: The nonhuman primate data*. New York: Liss.

Nankivell, B., Fritz, J., Nash, L., and Fritz, P. (1988). Competent maternal behavior by a hand-reared, resocialized, primiparous chimpanzee: A case history. *Laboratory Primate Newsletter, 27*, 5–8.

Napier, J. R., and Napier, P. H. (1967). *A handbook of living primates*. London: Academic.

Negayana, K., Negayana, T., and Kondo, K. (1986). Behavior of Japanese monkey (*Macaca fuscata*) mothers and neonates at parturition. *International Journal of Primatology, 7*, 365–387.

Nicolson, N. A. (1987). Infants, mothers and other females. In B. Smuts, D. L. Cheney, R. M. Seyfarth, R. W. Wrangham, and T. T. Struhsaker (Eds.), *Primate societies* (pp. 330–342). Chicago: University of Chicago Press.

Nicolson, N. A. (1991). Maternal behavior in human and nonhuman primates. In J. D. Loy and C. B. Peters (Eds.), *Understanding behavior: What primate studies tell us about human behavior*. New York: Oxford University Press.

Niemitz, C. (1979). Outline of the behavior of *Tarsius bancanus*. In G. Doyle and R. Martin (Eds.), *The study of prosimian behavior*. New York: Academic.

Nishida, T. (1968). The social group of wild chimpanzees in the Mahale Mountains. *Primates, 9*, 167–224.

Nishida, T. (1983). Alloparental behavior in wild chimpanzees of the Mahale Mountains, Tanzania. *Primates, 41*, 1–33.

Nishida, T. (1988). Development of social grooming between mother and offspring in wild chimpanzees. *Folia Primatologica, 50*, 109–123.

Nissen, H. W. (1931). A field study of the chimpanzee. *Comparative Psychology Monograph, 8*, 1–122.

Panksepp, J. (1986). The psychobiology of prosocial behaviors: Separation distress, play and altruism. In C. Zahn-Waxler, E. M. Cummings, and R. Jannotti (Eds), *Altruism and aggression: Biological and social origins* (pp. 19–57). Cambridge, England: Cambridge University of Press.

Papoušek, H., and Papoušek, M. (1987). Intuitive parenting: A dialectic counterpart to the infants' integrative capacities. In J. D. Osofsky (Ed.), *Handbook of infant development* (2nd ed., pp. 669–720). New York: Wiley.

Papoušek, H., Papoušek, M., Suomi, S. J., and Rahn, C. W. (1991). Preverbal communication and attachment: Comparative views. In J. L. Gewirtz and W. M. Kurtines (Eds.), *Intersections with attachment* (pp. 97–122). Hillsdale, NJ: Lawrence Erlbaum Associates.

Parker, S. T. (1990). Origins of comparative developmental evolutionary studies of primate mental abilities. In S.T. Parker and K. R. Gibson (Eds.), *"Language" and intelligence in monkeys and apes* (pp. 3–64). New York: Cambridge University Press.

Paul, A. (1999). The socioecology of infant handling in primates: Is the current model convincing? *Primates, 40*, 33–46.

Pereira, M. E., and Fairbanks, L. A (1993). *Juvenile primates: Life history, development and behavior*. New York: Oxford University Press.

Plooij, F. X. (1979). How wild chimpanzee babies trigger the onset of mother–infant play and what the mother makes of it. In M. Bullowa (Ed.), *Before speech: The beginning of interpersonal communication* (pp. 223–243). Cambridge, England: Cambridge University Press.

Plooij, F. X. (1984). *The behavioral development of free-living chimpanzee babies and infants*. Norwood, NJ: Ablex.

Preuschoft, H., Chivers, D. J., Brockelman, W. Y., and Creel, N. (Eds.). (1984). *The lesser apes: Evolutionary and behavioral biology*. Edinburgh, Scotland: Edinburgh University Press.

Price, E. C. (1992). The costs of infant carrying in captive cotton-top Tamarins. *American Journal of Primatology, 26*, 23–33.

Pryce, C. (1995). Determinants of motherhood in human and nonhuman primates: A biosocial model. In C. R. Pryce, R. D. Martin, and D. Skuse (Eds.), *Motherhood in human and nonhuman primates: Biosocial determinants* (pp. 1–15). Basle, Switzerland: Karger.

Pryce, C. R., Abbott, D. H., Hodges, J. K., and Martin, R. D. (1988). Maternal behavior is related to prepartum urinary estradiol levels in red-bellied Tamarin monkeys. *Physiology and Behavior, 44*, 717–726.

Pusey, A. (1990). Behavioral changes at adolescence in chimpanzees. *Behaviour, 115*, 203–246.

Quiatt, D. (1979). Aunts and mothers: Adaptive implications of allomaternal behavior of nonhuman primates. *American Anthropologist, 81*, 310–319.

Rajpurohit, L. S., and Mohnot, S. M. (1991). The process of weaning in Hanuman langurs (*Presbytis entellus entellus*). *Primates, 32*, 213–218.

Ransom, T. W., and Rowell, T. E. (1972). Early social development of feral baboons. In F. Poirer (Ed.), *Primate socialization* (pp. 105–144). New York: Random House.

Reite, M. (1987). Infant abuse and neglect: Lessons from the primate laboratory. *Child Abuse and Neglect, 11,* 347–355.

Reite, M., and Caine, N. (1983). *Child abuse: The nonhuman primate data.* New York: Liss.

Reynolds, V. (1965). Chimpanzees of the Budongo Forest. In I. DeVore (Ed.), *Primate behavior: Field studies of monkeys and apes* (pp. 368–424). New York: Holt, Reinhart & Winston.

Rheingold, H. L. (1963). *Maternal behavior in mammals.* New York: Wiley.

Rijt-Plooij, H. H. C., and Plooij, F. X. (1987). Growing independence, conflict, and learning in mother–infant relations in free-ranging chimpanzees. *Behaviour, 101,* 1–86.

Robinson, J. G., and Janson, C. H. (1987). Capuchins, squirrel monkeys, and atelines: Socioecological convergence with old world primates. In B. Smuts, D. L. Cheney, R. M. Seyfarth, R. W. Wrangham, and T. T. Struhsaker (Eds.), *Primate Societies* (pp. 69–82). Chicago: University of Chicago Press.

Rogers, C. M., and Davenport, R. K. (1970). Chimpanzee maternal behavior. *The Chimpanzee, 3,* 361–368.

Rosenblum, L. A. (1971). The ontogeny of mother–infant relations in macaques. In H. Moltz (Ed.), *Ontogeny of vertebrate behavior* (pp. 315–365). New York: Academic.

Rosenblum, L. A., Coplan, J. D., Friedman, S., Bassoff, T., Gorman, J. M., and Andrews, M. W. (1994). Adverse early experiences affect noradrenergic and serotonergic functioning in adult primates. *Biological Psychiatry, 35,* 221–227.

Rosenblum, L. A., and Harlow, H. (1963). Approach-avoidance conflict in the mother-surrogate situation. *Psychological Reports, 12,* 83–85.

Rosenblum, L. A., and Paully, G. S. (1984). The effects of varying environmental demands on maternal and infant behavior. *Child Development, 55,* 305–314.

Ross, C., and MacLarnon, A. (2000). The evolution of non-maternal care in anthropoid primates: A test of the hypotheses. *Folia Primatologica, 71,* 93–113.

Rothe, H., Darms, K., Koenig, A., Radespiel, U., and Juenemann, B. (1993). Long-term study of infant-carrying behavior in captive common marmosets (*Callithrix jacchus*): Effect of nonreproductive helpers on the parents' carrying performance. *International Journal of Primatology, 14,* 79–91.

Rowell, T. E. (1996). Forest-living baboons in Uganda. *Journal of the Zoological Society of London, 149,* 344–364.

Rowell, T., Hinde, R., and Spencer-Booth, Y. (1964). Aunt–infant interaction in captive rhesus monkeys. *Animal Behaviour, 12,* 219–226.

Rumbaugh, D. M. (1965). Maternal care in relation to infant behavior in the squirrel monkey. *Psychological Reports, 16,* 171–176.

Ruppenthal, G., Arling, G. L., Harlow, H. F., Sackett, G., and Suomi, S. (1976). A ten-year perspective of motherless-mother monkey behavior. *Journal of Abnormal Psychology, 85,* 341–349.

Russell, C. L., Bard, K. A., and Adamson, L. B. (1997). Social referencing by young chimpanzees (*Pan troglodytes*). *Journal of Comparative Psychology, 111,* 185–193.

Russon, A., and Galdikas, B. M. F. (1993). Imitation in ex-captive orangutans (*Pongo pygmaeus*). *Journal of Comparative Psychology, 107,* 147–161.

Sackett, G., and Ruppenthal, G. C. (1974). Some factors influencing the attraction of adult female macaque monkeys to neonates. In M. Lewis and L. A. Rosenblum (Eds.), *The effect of the infant on its caregiver* (pp. 163–185). New York: Wiley.

Sánchez, S., Peláez, F., Gil-Bürmann, C., and Kaumanns, W. (1999). Costs of infant-carrying in the cotton-top tamarin (*Saguinus oedipus*). *American Journal of Primatology, 48,* 99–111.

Santos, C. V., French, J. A., and Otta, E. (1997). Infant carrying behavior in Callitrichid primates: *Callithrix* and *Leontopithecus. International Journal of Primatology, 18,* 889–907.

Scanlan, J. M. (1986). *The inheritance of social dominance in rhesus monkeys.* Unpublished doctoral dissertation data, University of Wisconsin-Madison.

Schaller, G. (1963). *The mountain gorilla: Ecology and behavior.* Chicago: University of Chicago Press.

Schneider, M. L. (1984). *Neonatal assessment of rhesus monkeys (Macaca mulatta).* Unpublished master's thesis, University of Wisconsin-Madison.

Schrier, A., Harlow, H., and Stollnitz, F. (1965). *Behavior of nonhuman primates.* New York: Academic.

Seal, U. S., and Flesness, N. R. (1986). Captive chimpanzee populations—Past, present and future. In K. Benirschke (Ed.), *Primates: The road to self-sustaining populations* (pp. 47–55). New York: Springer-Verlag.

Seay, B., Hansen, E., and Harlow, H. F. (1962). Mother–infant separations in monkeys. *Journal of Child Psychology and Psychiatry, 3,* 123–132.

Silk, J. B. (1978). Patterns of food sharing among mother and infant chimpanzees at Gombe National Park, Tanzania. *Folia Primatologica, 29,* 129–141.

Silk, J. B. (1979). Feeding, foraging, and food sharing behavior of immature chimpanzees. *Folia Primatologica, 31,* 123–142.

Silk, J. B. (1999). Why are infants so attractive to others? The form and function of infant handling in bonnet macaques. *Animal Behaviour, 57,* 1021–1032.

Smuts, B., Cheney, D. L., Seyfarth, R. M., Wrangham, R. W., and Shruhsaker, T. T. (1987). *Primate Societies.* Chicago: University of Chicago Press.

Snowdon, C. T. (1996). Infant care in cooperatively breeding species. In P. J. B. Slater, J. S. Rosenblatt, C. Beer, and M. Milinski (Eds.), *Advances in the study of behavior* (Vol. 21, pp. 643–689). New York: Academic.

Starin, E. D. (1978). Food transfer by wild Titi monkeys (*Callicebus torquatas torquatus*). *Folia Primatologica, 30*, 145–151.

Strum, S. C. (1984). Why males use infants. In D. Taub (Ed.), *Primate paternalism* (Vol. 30, pp. 145–151). New York: Van Nostrand Reinhold.

Strum, S. C. (1987). *Almost human*. New York: Random House.

Struthers, E. J., Bloomsmith, M. A., and Alford, P. (1990). A case history of a decrement in maternal competence in a captive chimpanzee (*Pan troglodytes*). *Laboratory Primate Newsletter, 29*, 3–6.

Suomi, S. J. (1979). Differential development of various social relationships by rhesus monkey infants. In M. Lewis and L. Rosenblum (Eds.), *Genesis of behavior: Vol. 2. The child and family* (pp. 219–244). New York: Plenum.

Suomi, S. J. (1987). Genetic and maternal contributions to individual differences in rhesus monkey biobehavioral development. In N. A. Krasnegor, E. M. Blass, M. A. Hofer, and W. P. Smotherman (Eds.), *Perinatal development: A psychobiological perspective* (pp. 397–419). New York: Academic.

Suomi, S. J., and Levine, S. (1998). Psychobiology of intergenerational effects of trauma: Evidence from animal studies. In Y. Danieli (Ed.), *International handbook of multigenerational legacies of trauma* (pp. 623–637). New York: Plenum.

Tardif, S. D., Carson, R. L., and Gangaware, B. L. (1992). Infant-care behavior of non-reproductive helpers in a communal-care primate, the cotton-top Tamarin (*Saguinus oedipus*). *Ethology, 92*, 155–167.

Tardif, S. D., Harrison, M. L., and Simek, M. A. (1993). Communal infant care in marmosets and tamarins: Relations to energetics, ecology, and social organization. In A. B. Rylands (Ed.), *Marmosets and tamarins: Systematics, behavior, and ecology* (pp. 220–235). New York: Oxford University Press.

Tardif, S. D., Richter, C. B., and Carson, R. L. (1984). Effects of sibling-rearing experience on future reproductive success in two special of Callitrichidae. *American Journal of Primatology, 6*, 377–380.

Taub, D. M. (1984a). *Primate paternalism*. New York: Van Nostrand Reinhold.

Taub, D. M. (1984b). Male caretaking behavior among wild barbary macaques (*Macaca sylvanus*). In D. M. Taub (Ed.), *Primate paternalism* (pp. 20–55). New York: Van Nostrand Reinhold.

Taub, D. M., and Redican, W. K. (1984). Adult male–infant interactions in Old World monkeys and apes. In D. M. Taub (Ed.), *Primate paternalism* (pp. 377–406). New York: Van Nostrand Reinhold.

Thierry, B., and Anderson, B. (1986). Adoption in anthropoid primates. *International Journal of Primatology, 7*, 191–216.

Tilford, B. A., and Nadler, R. D. (1978). Male parental behavior in a captive group of lowland gorillas (*Gorilla gorilla gorilla*). *Folia Primatologica, 29*, 218–228.

Timmermans, P., and Vossen, J. (1996). The influence of repeated motherhood on periparturitional behavior in cynomologous macaques (*Macaca fascicularis*). *International Journal of Primatology, 17*, 277–296.

Tinklepaugh, O. L., and Hartman, C. G. (1932). Behavior and maternal care of the newborn monkey (*Macaca mulatta*). *Journal of Genetic Psychology, 40*, 257–286.

Tomasello, M., and Call, J. (1997). *Primate cognition*. Oxford, England: Oxford University Press.

Tomasello, M., Davis-Dasilva, M., Camak, L., and Bard, K. (1987). Observational learning of tool-use by young chimpanzees. *Human Evolution, 2*, 175–183.

Trevarthen, C. (1979). Communication and cooperation in early infancy: A description of primary intersubjectivity. In M. Bullowa (Ed.), *Before speech: The beginning of interpersonal communication* (pp. 321–347). Cambridge, England: Cambridge University Press.

Trivers, R. L. (1974). Parent-offspring conflict. *American Zoologist, 14*, 249–264.

Tronick, E., Als, H., and Adamson, L. (1979). Structure of early face-to-face communication interactions. In M. Bullowa (Ed.), *Before speech: The beginning of interpersonal communication* (pp. 349–372). Cambridge, England: Cambridge University Press.

van Elsacker, L., de Meurichy, W., Verheyen, R., and Walraven, V. (1992). Maternal differences in infant carriage in golden-headed lion tamarins (*Leontopithecus chrysomelas*). *Folia Primatologica, 59*, 121–126.

van Lawick-Goodall, J. (1968). The behaviour of free-living chimpanzees in the Gombe Stream Reserve. *Animal Behaviour Monographs, 1*, 161–31.

van Wulfften Palthe, T., and van Hooff, J. A. R. A. M. (1975). A case of the adoption of an infant chimpanzee by a suckling foster chimpanzee. *Primates, 16*, 231–234.

Visalberghi, E., and Fragaszy, D. (1990). Do monkeys ape? In S. T. Parker and K. R. Gibson (Eds.), *"Language" and intelligence in monkeys and apes: Comparative developmental perspectives* (pp. 247–273). New York: Cambridge University Press.

Vogt, J. L. (1984). Interactions between adult males and infants in prosimians and New World monkeys. In D. Taub (Ed.), *Primate paternalism* (pp. 346–376). New York: Van Nostrand Reinhold.

Walters, J. R. (1987). Transition to adulthood. In B. Smuts, D. L. Cheney, R. M. Seyfarth, R. W. Wrangham, and T. T. Shruhsaker (Eds.), *Primate societies* (pp. 358–369). Chicago: The University of Chicago Press.

Wamboldt, M. Z., Gelhard, R. E., and Insel, T. R. (1988). Gender differences in caring for infant *Cebuella pygmaea*: The role of infant age and relatedness. *Developmental Psychobiology, 21*, 187–202.

Whiten, A. (1999). Parental encouragement in *Gorilla* in comparative perspective: Implications for social cognition and the evolution of teaching. In S. T. Parker, R. W. Mitchell, and H. L. Miles (Eds.), *The mentalities of gorillas and orangutans: Comparative perspectives.* Cambridge, England: Cambridge University Press.

Whiten, A., Custance, D., Gomez, J. C., Teixidor, P., and Bard, K.A. (1996). Imitative learning of artificial fruit processing in children (*Homo sapiens*) and chimpanzees (*Pan troglodytes*). *Journal of Comparative Psychology, 110,* 3–14.

Whiten, A., and Ham, R. (1992). On the nature and evolution of imitation in the animal kingdom: Reappraisal of a century of research. In P. J. B. Slater, J. S. Rosenblatt, C. Beer, and M. Milinski (Eds.), *Advances in the study of behavior* (Vol. 21, pp. 239–283), New York: Academic.

Whitten, D. L. (1987). Infants and adult males. In B. Smuts, D. L. Cheney, R. M. Seyfarth, R. W. Wrangham, and T. T. Shruhsaker (Eds.), *Primate societies* (pp. 343–357). Chicago: University of Chicago Press.

Wood, D., Bruner, J., and Ross, G. (1976). The role of tutoring in problem-solving. *Journal of Child Psychology and Psychiatry, 17,* 89–100.

Wright, P. C. (1990). Patterns of parental care in primates. *International Journal of Primatology, 11,* 89–102.

Wright, R. (1972). Imitative learning of a flaked stone technology—The case of an orangutan. *Mankind, 8,* 296–306.

Yamomato, A. E., Box, H. O., Albuquerque, F. S., and Arruda, M. (1996). Carrying behaviour in captive and wild marmosets (*Callithrix jacchus*): A comparison between two colonies and a field site. *Primates, 37,* 297–304.

Yerkes, R. M. (1943). *Chimpanzees: A laboratory colony.* New Haven, CT: Yale University Press.

Yerkes, R. M., and Tomilin, M. I. (1935). Mother–infant relations in chimpanzees. *Journal of Comparative Psychology, 20,* 321–348.

Yerkes, R. M., and Yerkes, A. W. (1929). *The great apes.* New Haven, CT: Yale University Press.

Yogman, M. W. (1990). Male parental behavior in humans and nonhuman primates. In N. Krasnegor and R. Bridges (Eds.), *Mammalian parenting* (pp. 461–481). New York: Oxford University Press.

Yoshida, H., Norikoshi, K., and Kitahara, T. (1991). A study of the mother–infant relationships in chimpanzees (*Pan troglodytes*) during the first four years of infancy in Tama Zoological Park. *The Japanese Journal of Animal Psychology, 41-2,* 88–99.

Zeifman, D., Delaney, S., and Blass, E. (1996). Sweet taste, looking, and calm in 2- and 4-week-old infants: The eyes have it. *Developmental Psychology, 32,* 1090–1099.

Zuckerman, S. (1932). *The social life of monkeys and apes.* London: Routledge.

5

Psychobiology of Maternal Behavior in Human Beings

Carl M. Corter
Alison S. Fleming
University of Toronto

INTRODUCTION

In this chapter we focus on the interaction between psychological and physiological influences in the expression of maternal behavior in human mothers. It is organized around the premise that research on nonhuman maternal behavior provides a useful starting point for the examination of psychobiological influences in human maternal behavior. Research on nonhuman maternal behavior reveals that in even in "lower" animals, such as rodents, in which hormones exert clear and powerful influences, an animal's maternal behavior will not occur or will be masked by competing responses given dysfunctional ontogenetic and proximal experiences. Conversely, in human beings, the obvious importance of background and situational factors seems to mask the role of biological factors in early mothering; however, given a normative "healthy" psychological history and optimal current circumstances (e.g., healthy baby, supportive partner, and so forth), with sensitive assays and manipulations, it is possible to detect influences of physiological factors. As well, psychobiological processes involved in the control of normal mothering may be revealed by a growing variety of studies on human diversity and pathology. Examples include studies of how maternal behavior is influenced by pathologic physiological conditions as occur with endocrine disorders, brain damage, or use of illicit drugs. Systematic study of cultural universals in maternal behavior may also reveal areas in which biosocial factors exert an influence (Bornstein, 1991). This research is reviewed briefly in the next section in relation to the task of defining maternal behavior in the face of cultural variation (see also Harkness and Super, in Vol. 2 of this *Handbook*). Health factors in human maternal behavior represent another area in which psychobiological factors are receiving new attention, and some of this research is reviewed later in this chapter.

Whereas some reference is made to relevant research on fathers (see Parke, in Vol. 3 of this *Handbook*), the emphasis on mothers continues to reflect the state of the literature on psychobiological influences on both human and infrahuman parenting. It should be noted as well that this literature and this chapter also emphasize maternal behavior with infants rather than with older offspring. Thus in this chapter we seek to uncover the sensory, hormonal, and neural factors that regulate parental behavior in human beings with particular emphasis on mother–infant interactions during the early postpartum period. Because these factors exert different effects that are dependent on parents' prior experiences, the interactive effects of experience with these psychobiological factors are also discussed. The general psychobiological framework for this discussion is essentially the same as the framework adopted by Fleming and Li (in Vol. 2 of this *Handbook*) in the analysis of psychobiology of parenting in other mammals.

Although there is a rapidly growing literature on the psychobiological aspects of parenting effects, in which the physiological variables recorded are from the child (e.g., Hertsgaard, Gunnar, Erickson, and Nachmias, 1995; Larson, Gunnar, and Hertsgaard, 1991), the emphasis here is on parenting, not on parenting effects (see Collins, Maccoby, Steinberg, Hetherington, and Bornstein, 2000). In the complex bidirectional interaction of infant and mother, we place most emphasis on infant stimulus effects on maternal behavior and physiology. Nevertheless, a full account of maternal behavior requires framing in a dynamic systems account of the interactions and social ecology in which it is embedded.

The next section of this chapter considers general issues related to the psychobiology of human parenting, including the use of animal models, the complexities of defining maternal behavior across cultures, and different methodologies for examining psychobiological influences. The next section reviews the development of maternal behavior across pregnancy and parturition with emphasis on hormonal effects and their interactions with sensory effects of infant stimuli. Related issues of maternal mood and health are also discussed. The following section reviews how maternal behavior is maintained after parturition by short-term experience and a variety of sensory effects. In this section, infant adoption and prematurity are analyzed as potentially useful "preparations" for exploring the interaction of experience and psychobiological factors. The next section deals with sensory mechanisms in maternal behavior. The following section reviews long-term experience and psychobiological factors with particular reference to parity effects on maternal behavior. The last major section provides a systems perspective on physiological factors in maternal behavior with reference to interactional reciprocity between mother and infant as well as consideration of possible concordance in mechanisms that control the behavior of each partner. A brief discussion of intergenerational effects, from mother to daughter to daughter's offspring, is also included. The systems perspective is followed by consideration of some of the comparable findings on the psychobiology of parenting by fathers and implications for understanding the triadic system of infant–mother–father. Finally, a brief section on the role of the brain discusses how little is known about the psychobiology of maternal behavior in human beings compared with knowledge about some other species, and another includes a comparative analysis of some of the principal findings on hormonal and sensory effects in animal and human mothers. The rat is emphasized as an animal model of the psychobiology of maternal behavior because of the breadth and depth of research on this species and because many of the principles derived from this research have been shown to generalize to other mammalian species.

GENERAL ISSUES: ANIMAL MODELS, CULTURE, AND METHODOLOGY

Consideration of a number of general issues helps to place the examination of psychobiology and parenting in conceptual and methodological context. The application of animal models to the analysis of human maternal behavior has had a productive history and is a principal theme of this chapter. More recently, applied areas of research interest, such as maternal health–behavior relations are developing without particular reference to animal work. In addition, analyses of the human case necessarily include a systems perspective that embraces the complexity of human social ecology, as described in a later section on social systems perspectives. Thus the conceptualizations and research methods by which animal models are applied and tested in the human case need to take into account the social–cultural variations that partly define human parenting. In addition, the constraints on experimental research in the human case require different and more indirect methodologies than those that have been used to build knowledge about the psychobiology of maternal behavior in other species. Nonetheless, the animal model provides a very useful starting point in focusing on proximal factors and the interactions between physiological and experiential factors.

The Role of Animal Models in Understanding Human Mothering

Animal models have had a substantial impact on many theoretical approaches to understanding human maternal care and mother–infant relationships. In the past few decades, the broad metaphors provided by work on imprinting in the young of avian species influenced Bowlby's (1969) theory of attachment, and the work on maternal critical periods in goats (Klopfer, Adams, and Klopfer, 1964), provided some of the impetus for the theorizing of Klaus and Kennell (1976) about maternal care and bonding in the early postpartum period. In evolutionary and ethological analyses of parenting (e.g., Bjorklund, Yunger, and Pellegrini, in Vol. 2 of this *Handbook*; Daly, 1990; Hinde and Stevenson-Hinde, 1990), biological factors have been discussed in both phylogenetic and ontogenetic terms, and causality has been analyzed in terms of both proximal and distal causes. For example, Hinde (1984) showed that the concepts of inclusive fitness and reproductive success can be applied to issues varying from differential treatment of male and female offspring to conflicts between infant and mother around weaning, with the result that human parenting may be seen from perspectives beyond the usual psychological approaches. On the other hand, Hinde (1984) also pointed out that assuming applicability of broad animal models to the human case can be problematic. One such model is that continuous contact between mother and infant is a biological norm for human beings, as is the case for other primates. This particular model has some degree of empirical support; Blurton Jones (1972) presented a detailed comparative analysis of a number of factors—including infant behavior, composition of maternal milk, and fat deposits on infants—that led him to infer that the human mother–infant dyad was biologically prepared for carrying rather than caching the infant in a safe place while the mother forages. Nevertheless, it can be argued as well that human beings are also biologically prepared to use novel technological and social–cultural arrangements (e.g., monitors, carriers, nannies) to accomplish functions (such as protection of the infant) carried out in more limited ways by other species.

The "bonding" literature provides a lesson in the dialectics between ideas from the animal literature and medical practice. Klaus and Kennell (1976) originally propounded a complex model of multiple physiological and experiential influences on maternal behavior in the immediate postpartum period and beyond. The original impetus for research in this area came, however, from practical concerns around reducing separation between parents and high-risk infants in neonatal intensive care units and related efforts to humanize birthing and rooming arrangements for families. The hard science aspects of ideas relating to animal models and physiological factors probably contributed to an earlier acceptance of more humane medical practices, but these ideas may have been oversold and oversimplified. A number of critical reviews questioned conclusions about the long-term importance of early contact for the mother–infant relationship (Goldberg, 1983; Lamb, 1982). Nevertheless, much of the research in those reviews is limited to fairly nonspecific manipulations of "contact" between mother and newborn, and the research to date does not do justice to the complexity of the early outline of Klaus and Kennell of interplay among hormonal factors, experience, and sensory qualities of the infant. More recent literature on rooming-in practices for mother and infant and on skin-to-skin contact for low-birthweight (LBW) infants appears to take a more fine-grained, short-term perspective on the mother–infant dyad as a dynamic, regulated physical system that can be supported to benefit thermoregulation and lactation; a different sort of animal model is seen in related neonatal nursing practices labeled as kangaroo care (Anderson, 1991).

In some of the medical literature on maternal behavior, research has developed without particular reference to animal models. Examples of these areas include maternal health, health-related behaviors, and the capacity for effective parenting, and in these areas there is increasing emphasis on the psychobiological level of analysis. With respect to mental health and maternal depression, the interplay of physical factors such as fatigue, hormonal levels, and their interaction with experience and social context continue to attract attention as determinants of maternal behavior. A newer area for investigation is the analysis of intergenerational effects in physical health-related behavior with possible psychobiological mediation (e.g., Kandel and Udry, 1999). Recent animal work on intergenerational effects (e.g., Fleming, O'Day, and Kraemer, 1999), although obviously not health related, holds out the promise of useful exchanges between animal and human work on parenting effects across generations.

The animal model used here begins with experimental work on proximal factors that control maternal behavior; nevertheless, research reviewed in this chapter moves beyond a simple view of early interactional experiences between parent and infant to a broader systems perspective. The animal model is intended to provide a heuristic, comparative approach.

Defining Human Maternal Behavior: Cultural Relativity and Universality

A common biological-human core of parental care is necessary for survival and healthy development of the human infant. This core consists of multiple functions such as feeding, protecting, thermoregulating, grooming and cleaning, stimulating, regulating affect, and social communication (Bornstein, in Vol. 1 of this *Handbook*). Nevertheless, parenting is considerably more difficult to describe and measure in human beings than it is in rats. Human maternal behavior must be understood to involve feelings, cognitions, and beliefs, as well as overt motor patterns. Thus the particular behaviors the new mother displays depend on a variety of cultural, situational, and individual factors (Corter and Fleming, 1990).

A cross-cultural survey of mothering practices indicates that, although the biological mother is typically the primary caregiver and in that role usually breast-feeds her infant (Leiderman and Leiderman, 1977), there is enormous variability in how mothers interact with their infants. In some cultures, mothers provide infants with considerable tactile and kinesthetic stimulation by carrying them on their bodies for most of the day (Brazelton, 1977; Konner, 1977; Leiderman and Leiderman, 1977), and in others infants are left alone in a cradle for much of time (Caudill and Weinstein, 1969; Moss, 1967). In some colder climates, infants are swaddled and placed on cradle boards, in which case skin-to-skin contact is reduced, and in more tropical climates, infants are lightly clothed and free to move their limbs (Whiting, 1981). In North American culture, *en face* gazing and vocalizing to the infant are accepted as a normal part of the mother–infant relationship, but in other cultures, mothers do not vocalize directly to the infant (Tronick, 1987) or do not look *en face* at the infant (Brazelton, 1977).

Apart from variations in specific caregiving practices across cultures, there also appear to be general differences in emphasis on the basic functions of parents, such as soothing and stimulating. North American mothers place relatively more emphasis on stimulation, compared with Dutch mothers (Rebelsky, 1967) and Japanese mothers (Caudill and Weinstein, 1969; but see Bornstein, Azuma, Tamis-LeMonda, and Ogino, 1990).

Of course, maternal behaviors and beliefs are embedded in larger social systems, including family structures that vary across cultures. For example, Tronick, Morelli, and Ivey (1992), in examining social relationships of young children among the Efe foragers of Africa, found a model of multiple caregivers, even at the stage of infancy, that challenges usual dyadic models of maternal and parental care. To complicate the human case further, care is not only distributed in different ways across relationships, depending on the culture, but is also extended to and supported by technology and tools such as slings, swings, monitors, and webcams, as well as by other forms of the unique human capacity to modify the environment to provide shelter and inanimate stimulation to the young. Innovations in reproductive technologies such as *in vitro* fertilization will also add to the complexities of analyzing variations in parenting (e.g., Hahn and DiPietro, 2001).

Despite the range of cultural variation in early maternal behavior and surrounding social systems, universal patterns and common functions of human maternal behavior are suggested by a number of studies. The universality of these patterns is consistent with an influence of human biology on parenting (see Bornstein, 1991; H. Papoušek and M. Papoušek, in Vol. 2 of this *Handbook*). Bornstein, Tal, and Tamis-LeMonda (1991) studied everyday interactions of U.S., Japanese, and French mothers with their young infants. Across all three groups, mothers responded more to infants' vocalizations than to infants' looks. Particular maternal responses also tended to follow particular infant behaviors: Nurturant responses followed vocal distress, imitation followed nondistress vocalizations, and encouragement to the environment followed explorations. A universal response to vocal distress is expected and is no doubt tied to the necessity of ensuring the physical survival of the infant. The imitative response to infant vocalizations suggests another area of universality: mother–infant interactions that reflect and foreshadow the special human capacity for linguistic communication.

Speech adjustments to infants have been found across cultures and appear to be universal; these include prosodic features of higher pitch, slower tempo, and simple repeating contours (Papoušek, Papoušek, and Symmes, 1991). For older infants, lexical variation in maternal speech may also be keyed by infant interactive behaviors (Brousseau, Malcuit, Pomerleau, and Feider, 1996). Similarities in grammatical adjustments and repeated utterances have been found in Anglo-American and Japanese mothers' speech to infants (Fernald and Morikawa, 1993). These features appear to have a variety of effects on the infant relating to regulation of affect, arousal, and attention (Fernald, 1992); they also appear to be regulated in part by stimulus characteristics of the infant, including age. Research results suggesting a similar pattern of universal adjustments, along with some cultural variations, have been reported for maternal singing to infants. Trehub, Unyk, and Trainor (1993) found common qualities of voice tone in infant-directed singing, which could be recognized by adults outside the language–culture group. Bornstein et al. (1992) also showed possible universals in the contents of maternal speech across a number of cultures. In speaking to 5-month-old infants, mothers in Argentina, France, Japan, and the United States use both affect-salient and information-salient speech, but with a preponderance of speech relating to affect. By the time the infant is 13 months of age, mother's speech becomes more information salient, presumably in response to the growing cognitive sophistication of the older infant.

Whatever the commonalities and variations in patterns of maternal behavior, adaptive mothering necessarily involves behaving so as to ensure the infant's survival and healthy development; thus instrumental attitudes and behaviors (like nursing) that facilitate the infant's growth, as well as emotional–nurturant attitudes and behaviors that promote the infant's emotional development, comprise some of the more frequently used measures of maternal behavior in human beings.

Methodology

Although research on the physiology of human parenting has been stimulated by animal work, it has depended on very different research strategies from those usually found in animal studies. Whereas animal work usually involves observing behavior in the laboratory under relatively controlled environmental conditions and in animals with known and controlled prior experiences, human beings have heterogenous backgrounds and experiences and, in general, are observed under quite varied conditions, as in the home or hospital setting.

With respect to measurement, maternal behavior in animals is usually clearly defined by the species-typical behavioral repertoire exhibited by adults in response to infants. In human beings, by contrast, behavior is assessed in a wide variety of ways. In most of the studies reviewed here, maternal behavior was assessed in one of several ways: by assessments of physiological responses to infants and their cues, by use of either autonomic measures or endocrine measures; by hedonic or recognition responses to specific infant cues; by analysis of mothers' expressed feelings and attitudes measured by their responses in semistructured interviews or to attitude items on questionnaires; or by analysis of mothers' interactive behavior with their infants, by use of either ratings of general attributes across different behaviors, such as maternal "sensitivity," or coding of particular maternal behaviors. Sensitivity has been an ever-increasingly used measure of maternal responsiveness to infants (e.g., Atkinson et al., 2000; Gibson, Ungerer, McMahon, Leslie, and Saunders, 2000); in most cases, it is rated on the basis of direct observations of mother–infant interaction. It has the apparent advantage of transcending particular motor patterns of maternal behavior and thus would appear to offer more generality than some measures, but at the same time it suffers from the problem of whether rating judgments can be made across different cultural contexts and across different infants.

There are also clear differences in the animal and the human work in research design. Whereas the study of the physiology of parenting in animals tends to be invasive and involve surgical and other experimental manipulations, analogous human studies tend to use correlational, noninvasive strategies. For instance, to explore the role of hormonal factors in the regulation of human maternal behavior, studies may measure concentrations of biologically active hormones or their metabolites in blood plasma, saliva, or urine and correlate these with ongoing behavior (e.g., Worthman and Stallings, 1997). Alternatively, researchers may measure acute changes in hormones in response to the controlled presentation of stimuli or events, as in the presentation of cries or "stressors," or in response to the administration of other hormones or chemicals. Yet another strategy that has been adopted to determine the role of hormones in human behavior is to evaluate behavioral changes associated with natural changes in the reproductive cycle, for instance, across the menstrual cycle, puberty, the prepartum and the postpartum periods, or menopause. In some instances, as with the contraceptive pill, behavior may also be assessed in relation to the administration of exogenous hormones. Finally, in some cases in which endocrine disorders exist, as with the adrenogenital syndrome (involving overproduction of androgens by the fetal adrenal gland) or testicular-feminization syndrome (in which certain androgen receptors are absent), it is possible to compare the behavior of people suffering from the endocrine disorder with the behavior of siblings or other matched controls.

In general, the hormones that have been investigated most thoroughly in the context of parental behavior are the steroid hormones known to be elevated during human pregnancy or parturition or known to play a role in parental behavior in other animals. In the female, these include the steroid hormones, estrogens, and progesterone, produced by the placenta and ovaries; cortisol, produced by the fetal and maternal adrenal glands; and the protein hormones, prolactin and oxytocin, produced by the maternal pituitary gland. In the male, the testicular androgen, testosterone, has also been investigated.

In addition to correlating endocrine profiles and responses with behavior, physiological states and responses to discrete stimuli or during actual mother–infant interaction (e.g., Donovan and Leavitt, 1985) are assessed with indices of autonomic activity, including heart rate (HR), blood pressure, and galvanic skin response (GSR). In assessing parental responses, the presented stimuli are in general infant-related cues including cries, odors, video images, and the infant herself or himself. Different patterns of autonomic responses are assumed to have different meanings. Although there is debate regarding the mechanisms and the meaning of HR accelerations and decelerations in response to emotionally evocative stimuli, HR accelerations are generally assumed to reflect the salience of the stimulus to the subject or a preparatory response to that stimulus; decelerations are in general thought to reflect attention (see Furedy et al., 1989; Leavitt and Donovan, 1979). Donovan, Leavitt and Walsh (1997) showed the utility of more complex measures of HR change in analyzing mothers' sensitivity in detecting variants of infant cries. They found a three-phase HR response to cries with deceleration, acceleration, and deceleration. Mothers whose acceleration phase habituated most rapidly over repeated presentation of the cry were also more sensitive in detecting differences among cries. Another concept that is frequently raised when the meaning of HR accelerations or elevated GSR is discussed is the concept of arousal. Heightened autonomic activation is often interpreted to mean heightened arousal, "interest," "motivation," or even "defensive" arousal. Some investigators have suggested that physiological indices provide a better measure of underlying motivation than actual behavior does; for example, Jones and Thomas (1989) argued that HR changes in response to newborns provided a better measure of interest among new fathers than did behavioral indices. Unfortunately, such motivational and cognitive concepts often are not operationally defined. Thus they add little to our understanding of causation or mechanisms that control behavior.

Relative to the study of neuroanatomy of behavior in animals, which depends on invasive methodologies (including lesioning, stimulating and recording from neural structures deep within the brain), our understanding of functional neuroanatomy in human beings is in its infancy. Although human neuropsychology is a burgeoning field, most work has concentrated on the neuroanatomy of learning, memory, and cognition; very little is known about the neuroanatomy of human social behavior. The primary kinds of evidence relating brain to human behavior of any kind are derived from studies of people with known brain lesions that are due to head trauma, stroke, epilepsies, or other disease states (such as Alzheimer's or Parkinson's). Most psychological studies have focused on cognitive and, occasionally, emotional impairments; with the possible exception of early studies on temporal lobe (in the "temporal" cortex and subcortex) damage and sexual and aggressive behaviors, few studies have attempted to relate brain dysfunctions to dysfunctions in social behaviors. With the increased availability of the positron-emission-tomography scan and magnetic resonance imaging (MRI) technology, which provide information on parts of the brain that are active during ongoing behavior, we may eventually determine which brain systems are activated when infants or their cues are presented to parents or when parents interact with their infants.

Similarly, study of the neurochemistry of parenting can rarely depend, as it does in other animals, on the effects on behavior of the administration of controlled quantities of different drugs with known neurochemical properties; instead, the correlational approach that can, in theory, be adapted is to study populations of people with neurochemical disorders or who are substance abusers. Because of the problem of multiple drug dependence, as well as confounding social and nutritional variables associated with these populations, interpretation of these kinds of data is often problematic (see Jeremy, Jeruschiamowicz, and Bernstein, 1984; Mayes and Truman, in Vol. 4 of this *Handbook*).

In short, the study of the psychobiology of human parenting depends very heavily on correlational and multivariate strategies, which do not permit definitive causal analysis and which often use quite heterogeneous populations. However, with animal data as a backdrop and through the use of convergent analytic approaches, we may come closer to understanding psychobiological mechanisms of human parenting. Thus, in a heuristic strategy for moving between studies of animal and human mothering, research on rat mothers provides approaches to the analysis of more proximal and mechanistic features of human maternal behavior, as in the analysis of the role of hormones or of olfactory cues from the infant. Reciprocally, the work on human maternal behavior and its emphasis on the importance of psychological factors yields useful directions in animal research, including the examination of variables such as mothers' prior experiences and affective state.

DEVELOPMENT OF MATERNAL BEHAVIOR ACROSS PREGNANCY AND PARTURITION

Although there are large individual differences among mothers, there is some degree of normative change in attitudes and behavior over pregnancy. For instance, a number of studies have found that mothers experience heightened feelings and readiness to respond at approximately 20 weeks of gestation, at the time of the first fetal movements, and then once again at the parturition, with the birth of the baby (Corter and Fleming, 1990; Fleming and Corter, 1988; Gaffney, 1989). Similarly, Leifer (1977, 1980) observed that even mothers who initially have negative attitudes toward being pregnant generally come to possess positive ones at approximately 5 months into the pregnancy, when fetal movements are first detected. These results are also consistent with observations made by Bleichfeld and Moely (1984), who found that nulliparous but pregnant women show a more variable HR response to the pain cry of an unfamiliar baby than do nonpregnant women, who show either no change or a deceleration; in contrast, under some testing conditions, pregnant women show the same pattern of HR acceleration as that seen in new mothers. Despite these self-report and psychophysiological indications of heightened maternal feelings during pregnancy, some behavioral data suggest that pregnant women, compared with nonpregnant women, do not respond more maternally to unfamiliar infants in a waiting room situation and do not spend more time looking at pictures of infants or infant-related themes (Feldman and Nash, 1978); however, the stage of pregnancy at which women were assessed was unclear. Similar assessments very late in pregnancy may well produce a different outcome from first trimester assessments.

Even though maternal behavior may grow across pregnancy in some women, especially among less anxious mothers (Gaffney, 1989), there is evidence that for many mothers feelings of nurturance are not experienced prior to birth or even immediately after birth, but instead develop over the first few weeks (Leifer, 1980); in fact, mothers often report retrospectively that their first feelings of attachment did not occur until the first eye-to-eye contact or first infant smiles (Moss and Jones, 1977; Robson, 1967; Robson and Kumar, 1980; Trevathan, 1983). Fleming, Ruble, Flett, and Van Wagner (1990) found that positive feeling toward the infant continues to develop more or less linearly over the first postpartum year. Behaviorally, there is also considerable variability in maternal responsiveness at birth. Although there is some evidence that mothers who receive skin-to-skin contact with their infants spend time stroking and tactually stimulating them (Klaus, Kennell, Plumb, and Zuehkle, 1970; Trevathan, 1981, 1983), one study found that approximately 50% of mothers did not even touch their infants when they were first presented (Carek and Cappelli, 1981).

Hormonal Correlates of Maternal Behavior During Pregnancy and Postpartum

The influence of pregnancy hormones (those normally elevated during pregnancy) on maternal behavior has long been a topic of interest and research, but primarily among nonhuman species. Decades of research in rats and other mammals indicate that the hormonal milieu of parturition, that is, high levels of oxytocin, prolactin, and estradiol, with a decline of progesterone, provides a hormonal basis for maternal behavior (Bridges, 1990; Insel, 1990; Pryce, Martin, and Skuse, 1995; Rosenblatt, 1990; Rosenblatt, Olufowobi, and Siegel, 1998). In rats this same hormonal profile also increases mothers' attraction to infant cues, enhances the reinforcing value of pups, and results in marked changes in mothers' affective state (Fleming and Corter, 1995). A similar hormonal effect may also be present in human mothers (Fleming, Ruble, Krieger, and Wong, 1997). In pregnant women, feelings of attachment to the fetus grow during the pregnancy, an effect that is not related to changing levels of pregnancy hormones. However, mothers who experienced greater attachment to their new babies after birth underwent an increase from early to late pregnancy in their estradiol/progesterone ratio, whereas those with low attachment experienced a decrease in the estradiol/progesterone ratio over this same time period. Interestingly, this same change in hormonal profile was also associated with mothers' affective state; mothers with a greater shift in the estradiol to progesterone ratio across pregnancy also experienced greater postpartum well-being. Although well-being and attachment feelings were both related to hormones and to one another, further analyses indicated that hormones are related to attachment both indirectly, by altering mothers' affect, as well as directly. Hormones and well-being together explain 40% to 50% of the variance in mothers' attachment (Fleming, Ruble et al., 1997).

In addition to the hormones of pregnancy, postpartum hormones from the hypothalamic–pituitary–adrenal (HPA) axis may also play a role in mothers' response to their newborns. The HPA axis is a system richly studied in relation to reactivity to various social, behavioral, and psychological stimuli (Cacioppo et al., 1998; Dettling, Gunnar, and Donzella, 1999; Kirschbaum , Wust, and Hellhammer, 1992; McEwen, de Kloet, and Rostene, 1986; Smyth et al., 1998; Stansbury and Gunnar, 1994), and in a series of studies, Fleming and colleagues (Corter and Fleming, 1990; Fleming, Steiner, and Anderson, 1987) examined cortisol in relation to maternal behavior in the early postpartum period when cortisol levels are relatively high and mothers' emotional status is labile. The latter studies suggest a relation between cortisol levels on days 3 and 4 postpartum and mother–infant interactions:

Higher cortisol levels were significantly and strongly associated with maternal approach behaviors, positive maternal attitudes, or more vocally active infants. These hormone–behavior relations were, however, considerably stronger in mothers who felt positive toward infants or caregiving activities during their pregnancies. These results suggest that arousal or "engagement" state, indexed by cortisol, may interact with individual differences in mothers' attitudes to affect the infant–caregiver feedback system.

Furthermore, in a follow-up study (Fleming, Steiner, and Corter, 1997), new mothers were asked to complete a hedonics task, using a pleasantness scale to provide an attraction score to different odorants presented on a cotton substrate in a 1-pt Baskin-Robbins container. Others were "blind" to the contents of the container. Mothers also provided salivary samples for radioimmunoassay of salivary cortisol levels. Results showed that first-time mothers with higher cortisol levels were more attracted to their own infants' body odors and were better able to recognize their own infants' odors. Cortisol levels were not related to mothers' attitudes.

Finally, Stallings, Fleming, Corter, Worthman, and Steiner (2001) investigated cortisol and HR baselines and changes in response to infant cries and odors, along with affective responses, among women differing in parity and postpartum status. Mothers with higher circulating levels of cortisol and higher baseline HRs (before stimulus presentation) tend to be mothers who respond more sympathetically when they hear the infant cries. The positive association between cortisol levels and sympathetic responses is consistent with earlier findings of a positive association between cortisol and positive responses to infant odors in new mothers as well as with their responses to infants themselves (Fleming, Steiner, and Corter, 1997). In the study by Stallings et al. (2001), mothers with higher baseline cortisol levels were also more discriminating in their affective responses to pain, as opposed to hunger, cries, showing greater sympathy to the pain cry and less sympathy to the hunger cry, than did mothers with lower cortisol. Furthermore, mothers with higher baseline cortisol levels also had higher baseline HR responses, and both physiological measures showed a similar relation to sympathetic feelings. In contrast to the patterns of individual differences, there was little evidence of differential infant stimulus effects. That is, there were no differences in either hormones or HR in responses to cries versus odors. In fact, hormones underwent very little change with either stimulus. Thus individual differences in maternal physiology, perhaps as part of personality differences, seem to play a major part in affective responses to infant stimuli.

Research in infrahuman animals shows that hormones act in a variety of ways to augment maternal behavior: They alter the animal's affective state, they augment maternal attraction to offspring-related odors, they facilitate the effects of a brief maternal experience and they enhance the reinforcing effects of offspring. The literature on humans suggests that similar behavioral states are activated at parturition and during the early postpartum period, and these states may well be influenced by hormones. The following subsections discuss the effect of hormones on maternal feelings and attitudes. These psychological states influence how mothers respond to their infants, thus providing an indirect route by which hormones influence mothering. In some cases, these states may reflect relatively stable predispositions or "personality" and resultant associations between hormonal factors and responsiveness (see Stallings et al., 2001)

Maternal Emotion and Health

New mothers experience a change in affective state, and these mood changes may be hormonally mediated; mothers' moods, in turn, may influence the way they respond to their offspring. There is evidence that new mothers undergo mood fluctuations and intensifications during the early postpartum period reflected in postpartum "blues" and "lability." During this early postpartum period, some 40% to 80% of women have been reported to experience a mixture of tearfulness and anxiety, often alternating with periods of euphoria (Pitt, 1968; Stein, 1982). Moreover, approximately 20% of women continue to experience dysphoria through the first 3 postpartum months (Fleming, Ruble, Flett, and Shaul, 1988). Although it is widely assumed that the puerperal blues and depression are hormonally mediated, in fact the evidence is mixed, and to date no single hormone, neurotransmitter, or combination thereof has been consistently implicated. Nevertheless, a number of theories of the etiology of postpartum mood dysphoria have been proposed; most predict a relation between depression and the extent of prepartum-to-postpartum changes in circulating hormones. Cases have been made for a role for cortisol (Handley, Dunn, Baker, Cockshott, and Goulds, 1977; Handley, Dunn, Waldron, and Baker, 1980), β-endorphin (Newnham et al., 1984; Smith et al., 1990), and the female steroids, estrogen and progesterone (Nott, Franklin, Armitage, and Gelder, 1976; O'Hara, Schlechte, Lewis, and Wright, 1991; see also Steiner, 1992; Steiner, Fleming, Anderson, Monkhouse, and Boulter, 1986).

The lack of clear connection between postpartum clinical depression and psychobiological factors is also supported by a study of postpartum, clinically depressed mothers who had been breast-feeding (Misri, Sinclair, and Kuan, 1997). There was no connection in this sample between giving up breast-feeding and the onset of depression.

The absence of a clear hormonal effect on postpartum mood is not surprising; most studies use traditional linear correlation techniques, in which mood state is related to hormone level or to a change in hormone level. However, the true relation may not be so simple; it certainly is not in other animals. It is likely, for instance, that there exists an interaction between hormonal effects and background and situational factors, such that hormonal influences are expressed primarily as alterations in mood intensity, whereas background and situational factors determine the valence of the affect, whether positive or negative.

In contrast to the absence of any clear linear effect of parturitional hormones on postpartum mood, a variety of situational and experiential factors has been found to influence mothers' postpartum mood states (e.g., Belsky, Rovine, and Taylor, 1984; Cutrona, 1984; Hopkins, Marcus, and Campbell, 1984), the most notable and consistent being their prior experience with children (e.g., Fleming et al., 1988). Mothers with more childcare experience tend to be less depressed postpartum. Sosa, Kennell, Klaus, Robertson, and Urrutia (1980) reported that the presence of a supportive companion, or doula, during labor led to more alert and responsive maternal behavior with the newborn (stroking, smiling, talking) among Guatemalan mothers. Newton and Newton (1962) found that mothers who had positive interactions with their birth attendants were also more pleased with the first sight of their infant. Kennell and McGrath (1993) summarized positive findings from two clinical trials in which supportive companions were provided to women during labor; effects were seen in shorter labors and fewer obstetric and neonatal difficulties. They speculated that the association among anxiety, various difficulties in labor, and fetal distress may imply increased levels of some of the neurotransmitters released by the autonomic nervous system. This speculation is consistent with Lederman's (1984) report of correlations between plasma epinephrine levels and self-reported anxiety during labor. Some of these same associations might also mediate the connection between the presence of a doula and increased maternal responsiveness.

Regardless of the etiology of mothers' moods, maternal emotional states strongly influence the quality of their interactions with their offspring. Compared with more dysphoric mothers, at birth, happier mothers show more instrumental responding; at 1 and 3 months postpartum, happier mothers respond more contingently to their infants (e.g., talking or vocalizing to their infants when the infants vocalize) and are more affectionate altogether. At birth, they feel more attached to their newborn (Fleming, Ruble et al., 1997); at 4 to 6 months postpartum, they are more sensitive to variations in infant cries; and at 19 months postpartum, mothers who had been better adjusted during the first year showed more "affective sharing" and sociability (Donovan, Leavitt, and Walsh, 1998; Stein et al., 1991).

Beyond the emotional–maternal behavior link in animals and humans, there are other potential connections between the human mother's physical and mental health states and psychobiological dimensions with potential importance for her maternal behaviors and attitudes. For example, "tiredness" reported by mothers is connected to negative mood and reported health problems, and each of these variables may be associated with reduced or impaired maternal behavior. Tiredness may also be related to various contextual factors, such as lack of social support, which can have negative effects on mothering. Some of these potential connections were explored by Green and Kafetsios (1997) in a questionnaire study of 1,285 mothers at 6 weeks after delivery. The variable of reported health problems was positively related to the interrelated factors of negative mood, negative feelings about motherhood, and feelings of tiredness. However, feeling tired and depressed were more central factors in the constellation of associations than was health. In regression analyses, they both made independent contributions to the prediction of feelings about motherhood, whereas health did not. Tiredness and mood also were more highly correlated with contextual variables, such as lack of social support and difficultness of the baby. Thus, as in the case of hormonal differences among new mothers, the influence of health differences must be traced through other levels of analysis. Links among the levels may be dynamic and bidirectional. Tiredness, for example, can come from physical illness, relationship difficulties, mood declines, or a combination of such factors, and in turn can feed back into negative attitudes or behaviors, including challenges to effective parenting, or to partner relationships, or to both.

Finally, "health behaviors" on the part of parents may also be included as categories of parental behavior. Parental choices about smoking and caffeine intake have direct physiological effects on offspring and may be a conscious part of parents' roles (Gennaro and Fehder, 2000) as well as partially dependent on their early experience and physiology (e.g., Kandel and Udry, 1999).

Interactions Between Hormonal and Sensory Effects: Response to Infant Cues

Beyond emotional regulation, research on animals indicates that a second way hormones may act to facilitate early responsiveness to offspring is to alter the valence of pup-related cues—in particular odor cues; thus new mothers are more attracted to pup odors than are virgin animals, an effect that seems to be hormonally mediated (see Fleming and Li, in Vol. 2 of this *Handbook*). This subsection considers the human case and whether hormones have effects on mothers' responses to their newborn infants' odors.

Although human mothers are able to recognize their offspring based on their odors (Porter, Cernoch, and Balogh, 1985; Schaal, 1986; Schaal and Porter, 1991), whether new mothers are especially attracted to these odors and the extent of their influence on maternal emotional state and responsiveness has only recently been addressed. Fleming et al. (1993) asked groups of mothers of 2-day-old infants, 1-month-old infants, and female and male nonparent controls to rate the pleasantness of a variety of infant-related and noninfant odorants. Odors consisted of 2- to 3-day-old infants' T-shirts (worn for 8 to 12 hr), infant urine, infant feces, adult axillary odors, spice, and cheese. The primary findings showed that new mothers give higher hedonic ratings to the infants' T-shirts than do nonmothers, while not differing in response to other stimuli. A number of factors that are correlated with mothers' hedonic ratings of their own infants' T-shirt odors suggest the importance of early postpartum experience in this result. Mothers who gave positive ratings experienced, on the one hand, a shorter postpartum interval to their first extended contact and nursing of their infants and, on the other hand, also evidenced heightened maternal responsiveness, measured both behaviorally and by self-report. From these findings, it seems that new mothers show heightened attraction to the general body odors of infants, but this attraction varies as a function of early postpartum contact and experiences interacting with young.

Fleming, Steiner, and Corter (1997) showed that the postpartum hormone, cortisol, as well as experience, influenced responses to newborn baby odors. They assayed hedonic responses and salivary samples for progesterone, testosterone, and cortisol. In general, associations between cortisol and hedonics emerged only for primiparous mothers: Higher levels of cortisol predicted higher ratings of infants' T-shirt body odors and urine but was unrelated to control odorants. Maternal report of more prior experience with infants also predicted higher ratings. These patterns suggest that both cortisol and experience are tied to attraction to infant odors and further suggest that prior experience could mask hormonal effects on attraction because they were seen only in first-time mothers. Interestingly, for the measure of recognition of their own infants, which was also part of the design of the study, there was a positive correlation with cortisol levels, but in this case only for multiparous mothers.

Taken together, the results imply that hormones may indeed contribute to mothers' responses to their new infants by acting with respect to a variety of behavioral functions relating to affect, sensory effects, and so forth. However, the hormone that has most consistently been implicated in human beings, cortisol, is not thought to be important in other mammals that have been studied.

MAINTENANCE AND RETENTION OF MATERNAL BEHAVIOR: SHORT-TERM EXPERIENCE AND SENSORY EFFECTS

Although hormones may prime maternal behavior in both humans and other species, the maintenance and retention of maternal behavior depend on experience, including sensory input from the infant (Fleming, 1990).

Effects of Postpartum Experiences in the First 3 Months

As mothers gain experience with their infants during the first few postpartum months, most come to feel increasingly attached to them; they express more positive attitudes, become more efficient at tasks such as feeding (Thoman, Barnett, and Leiderman, 1971; Thoman, Turner, Leiderman, and Barnett, 1970), and are more attuned to infant signals (Sagi, 1981). In analyzing the importance of early experience in developing and maintaining maternal behavior, the effects of separation versus contact at birth on mothers' initial interactions with their babies is of interest. Gaulin-Kremer, Shaw, and Thoman (1977) looked at differences in mothers' first extended interactions. These investigators found that, the closer to parturition the first extended contact occurred, the more mothers held, talked to, and caressed their infants before actually nursing them. In general, however, the first extended contact did not occur until some hours after birth, and beyond the time when contact is supposed to be most critical according to Klaus and Kennell (1976). A number of other studies also suggest that the shorter the interval between birth and the mother's first extended contact with the infant, the stronger her later behavior. There is, for instance, an inverse relation between the interval to the first contact during the first day and the duration of maternal approach behavior (contact, hugging, talking to) at 3 to 4 days postpartum, although not at 6 weeks postpartum (Fleming et al., 1987). Short-term experience effects on early maternal responding have also been suggested by studies that vary the timing of mother–infant contact during the first postpartum days (e.g., Grossman, Thane, and Grossman, 1981). Contact effects have also been shown for fathers, but again not universally (Keller, Hildebrandt, and Richards, 1985; but see Palkovitz, 1985). Taken together, these studies indicate that additional contact may facilitate maternal behavior in first-time mothers of term infants, although the benefits appear to be short lived and occur only in some women.

Although there is little evidence of an association between hormones and behavior during the early postpartum period, there is some evidence that mothers who are breast-feeding, as opposed to bottle-feeding, feel and behave differently while feeding their infants and exhibit quite different patterns of autonomic responses to infant stimuli. At both 1 and 3 months postpartum, bottle-feeding mothers show fewer affectionate responses while feeding their infants than do mothers who are breast-feeding, although the former do not feel less close or nurturant (Fleming et al., 1988). Bernal and Richards (1970) also found that breast-fed babies are left alone less often, are fed for longer periods, and are responded to more contingently during feeding than are bottle-fed babies. These data suggest that in the actual feeding situation, breast-feeders are closer to their infants, but these differences may not be apparent during nonfeeding interactions and may result entirely from physical constraints associated with the two modes of feeding. There is some evidence, however, that differences between feeding modes may have implications beyond the feeding context.

Wiesenfeld, Malatesta, Whitman, Granrose, and Uili (1985) reported, for instance, that mothers who are bottle-feeding, as opposed to breast-feeding, show an augmented and sustained HR acceleration arousal response to black-and-white videotapes depicting their own infants' expressions, as well as overall higher baseline skin conductance responses. Although these psychobiological differences may reflect personality differences between breast- and bottle-feeding women, these authors argue that lactational hormones (e.g., prolactin, corticoids, oxytocin) could modify overall arousal levels. These observations are consistent with evidence from the rodent literature that lactation is associated with reduced responsivity to a variety of environmental cues (Stern, Goldman, and Levine, 1973; Stern and Levine, 1974; Thoman, Conner, and Levine, 1970). According to these data, it may well be that elevated arousal during the puerperium, which may underlie heightened maternal responsiveness in motivated mothers, may be disruptive to optimal behavior once some maternal experience has been acquired.

Adoption and Prematurity: Experience and Biological Preparation

In analyzing the interactions of experience and biology on mothers' interactions with their babies, a variety of other separation "preparations" may be relevant, beyond the studies of varying durations of contact for "normal" mother–infant dyads. These include observations on mothers who give up infants for adoption, surrogate mothers, and mothers with infants undergoing some medical treatments such as neonatal intensive care for prematurity. These topics are discussed elsewhere in this *Handbook* (see Brodzinsky and Pinderhughes and Goldberg and DiVitto, in Vol. 1 of this *Handbook*), although not from a psychobiological perspective. In general, these conditions may offer opportunities to examine the interaction of "biological preparation" and experience in the development of parental behavior. In considering the more specific psychobiological implications of these conditions, a number of questions may be asked. In some cases, empirical work has been done, but many of the questions remain largely unexplored. For instance, when women plan to give up infants for adoption shortly after birth, are the developmental changes in behavior during pregnancy altered by the plan (see Fischer and Gillman, 1991)? Do the experiences of giving birth and the immediate contact trigger behaviors and feelings that make it difficult to follow through on earlier decisions? Does the absence of extended experience with the infant and consequent absence of infant sensory input cause maternal behavior to wane? Are there experience effects on the behavior of adoptive mothers that parallel "pup-induction" effects in animal research (see Fleming and Li, in Vol. 2 of this *Handbook*)?

Also, from a psychobiological point of view, what is the pattern of changes in nurturant feelings experienced by mothers in relation to such factors as time awaiting a baby, whether they are aware of the baby's existence during gestational development or only at birth, duration of postpartum "uncertainty" when biological mothers can change their minds, whether they have other children, and so forth? As with biological mothers who give up their babies, adoptive mothers have a potential armament of cognitions that may protect them from the loss of the infant and that could affect their maternal feelings.

Questions about prematurity and parenting may also be asked from a psychobiological standpoint. Differences in maternal responsiveness to preterm infants have been reported in a number of studies (see Corter and Minde, 1987; Goldberg and DiVitto, in Vol. 1 of this *Handbook*, for reviews). To what extent do these differences in responsiveness reflect suboptimal infant stimulus qualities or lack of a normal hormonal profile in the mother whose pregnancy is terminated early? Such questions may complement the analysis of other crucial factors such as early experience, maternal interpretations, and the social context of the mother–infant dyad. In terms of sensory effects, the preterm infant presents differences in a number of stimulus dimensions including visual appearance (Maier, Holmes, Slaymaker, and Reich, 1984), cry characteristics (Frodi, Lamb, Leavitt, Donovan, Neff, and Sherry, 1978; Worchel and Allen, 1997), and delayed or weakened behaviors or even hyperresponsivity (e.g., Eckerman, Oehler, Hannan, and Molitor, 1993). Furthermore, medical treatment such as isolette care may prevent tactile and olfactory contact. Reduced contact or separation may exacerbate problems in caregivers' responses to the stimulus qualities of preterm infants; conversely, experience with these qualities can lead to more positive responses (e.g., Corter et al., 1978; Feldman, Weller, Leckman, Kuint, and Eidelman, 1999).

Prematurity is associated with, in addition to infant characteristics, maternal characteristics such as health and parity, as well as with altered hormonal states (Darne, McGarrigle, and Lachelin, 1987a). Darne, McGarrigle, and Lachelin (1987b) assayed saliva estriol, estradiol, and progesterone concentrations in the weeks preceding birth in a group of term mothers and reported that the estriol-to-progesterone ratio began to rise approximately 6 weeks before delivery from a ratio of less than 1 to nearly $1\frac{1}{2}$. Among mothers giving birth prematurely, the heightened ratio was found in those who went into labor with intact membranes, but was not present in mothers who went into preterm labor after prolonged rupture of the membranes. These investigators suggest that, in both the term case and the case of mothers with intact membranes who go into spontaneous preterm labor, increased fetal adrenal activity may trigger the hormonal changes in the mother (see Anderson, Lawrence, Davies, Campbell, and Turnbull, 1971). Thus it is possible that hormonal biochemical changes in the fetus (stimulus qualities) may contribute to the early delivery and thus to the sequelae of prematurity, which in turn alter maternal behavior, as noted earlier. In addition, the altered hormonal state of some mothers, such as those delivering after prolonged rupture of membranes, could contribute more directly to altered maternal behavior, although we have found no research investigating this question.

Sensory Mechanisms

A number of studies, previously reviewed, suggest that early contact can increase maternal approach behavior (e.g., Fleming et al., 1987). Unfortunately, few studies have analyzed the nature of these experience effects by determining what aspects of early interaction may be important for subsequent responsiveness. Observations indicate that mothers receive stimulation in multiple modalities when they hold, cradle, nurse, look at, and talk to their infants (Fleming, 1990) and come to individually recognize their infants based on their cues (as subsequently detailed).

Functions of infant cues.   Infant stimuli provide salient individual cues that mothers may come to recognize as an important part of the extended mother–infant attachment process. Infant stimuli may also serve a variety of other functions. They may alter maternal behavior by producing immediate changes in arousal or by producing longer-lasting motivational states that affect maternal behavior. For example, research on infant odor shows that the hedonic value of infant cues co-varies with hormonal state and higher maternal responsiveness as measured by direct interaction and attitude scales. A variety of other studies, subsequently reviewed, shows that infant cues have diverse effects on measures of physiological arousal, including HR, GSR, and self-report. In addition to the motivational effects, infant cues also serve the function of evoking specific maternal behavior patterns. These stimulus–response connections may be learned or may be species-typical patterns. For example, Klaus, Trause, and Kennell (1975) reported a stereotyped pattern of human maternal response during the first hours following birth, which they called the claiming response (see Trevathan, 1987); they argued that it is a species-typical pattern released by skin-to-skin contact with the baby. Stern (1974) suggested that the infant's gaze evokes species-typical exaggerations in maternal vocalization, facial expression, and gaze during face-to-face play. Another general function of infant stimulus effects is to inhibit or disrupt behavior of the mother that is incompatible with caregiving behavior. In speculation about human mothers, it has been said that part of the power of distal signals like the smile and the cry lies in their ability to disrupt noncaregiving behavior (e.g., home or office work/housework) as much as in their ability to directly evoke caregiving (Rheingold, 1969). Another important function of infant stimuli relates to the role of the infant in establishing rhythms, or a degree of reciprocity, in the flow of dyadic interaction. These sequences are seen as a foundation for species-typical patterns of emotional communication and language acquisition by the child (Trevarthan, 1985). Finally, infant stimuli provide information that evokes and directs maternal cognitions that in turn guide maternal behavior (see Brazelton, 1973; Parke, 1978). For example, crying signals a distressed state that the mother may interpret as requiring a response or not, depending on intensity, context, and other factors.

It should be noted that relatively little human research involves experimentally isolating infant stimulus effects within individual sensory modalities; instead, the stimuli are often multimodal, as in the case of naturalistic or videotaped study of infant cries, in which the stimulus is visual as well as auditory. Nevertheless, stimulus effects are reviewed below by modality, with particular reference to their arousing and motivating properties, which are often gauged by physiological measures such as HR and GSR.

Audition.   Given the biological necessity of continual proximity between infant mammals and their mothers, auditory communication is a crucial channel for motivating and directing proximity-promoting behaviors, especially for those that bring the mother and her young together. In contrast to the other distal channels, audition is subject to less interference than vision and is capable of conveying more complex and rapidly changing information than is olfaction (see Stallings et al., 2001). It is therefore not surprising that calling behavior in some form is characteristic of most young mammals, despite the wide variation in patterns of proximity maintenance—ranging from nesting, to caching, to carrying, to following by the young—and consequent differences in patterns of distal communication between parent and offspring.

The general adaptive functions of arousal and proximity maintenance seen in calling behavior by rodent young are also seen in crying behavior by human infants. For example, Boukydis and Burgess (1982) demonstrated GSR changes to audiotaped infant cries among female and male adults. Cries also produce HR changes, either acceleration or deceleration, depending on the adult population studied and on infant characteristics, such as whether the infant is the adult's own child or an unfamiliar infant (Bleichfeld and Moely, 1984; Donovan et al., 1997; Frodi and Lamb, 1980; Wiesenfeld and Malatesta, 1982). Other studies have gauged arousing effects in terms of subjective feeling. Thus, in the Boukydis and Burgess (1982) study, multiparous parents not only showed less GSR change to cries but also rated them as less piercing than primiparous parents or nonparents did. In addition, males rated themselves as more angry in response to the cries but did not differ from females in GSR response.

Murray's reviews (1979, 1985) of research on infant crying suggest that the motivational effects of crying are key to understanding parental response because the data do not fit a simple releaser model in which a particular pattern of parental behavior follows the cry. An alternative account is provided by Furedy et al. (1989), who suggested that the infant cry evokes a physiological preparatory response in mothers that in turn facilitates caregiving or nurturant behaviors. Consistent with this suggestion, they found that nulliparous females showed HR acceleration to videotapes of a crying infant. In contrast, males showed a deceleration pattern more characteristic of attention. In another model, crying activated motives of an altruistic nature in the parent. Hoffman (1975) argued that altruism is based on a universal, primitive empathic response to distress that is present even in young children (cf., Martin and Clark, 1982). On the other hand, Murray used the term *egoistic* to acknowledge motives that involve escape or avoidance of the cry as an aversive stimulus. Normally, altruistic motives must outweigh egoistic motives, or babies would be abandoned. However, in some cases, such as child abuse triggered by crying, the aversive qualities of the cry may outweigh its ability to inspire nurturant or altruistic feelings. Frodi and Lamb (1980) showed that child abusers responded to videotapes of crying infants with greater HR acceleration and higher ratings of aversion and less sympathy than did a control group of nonabusive parents. Murray (1985) also showed that normal experience may tip adults' responses from the egoistic to the altruistic. She found an inverse relation between urgency of the cry and sympathy among inexperienced adults. For experienced adults both mild and moderately urgent cries evoked sympathy, although an extremely urgent pain cry failed to produce sympathy even among this experienced group. Murray thus speculated that there may be an optimal range of infant distress; crying that is too prolonged or intense may evoke avoidance or aggression. Animal evidence along these lines was provided by the study of Bell, Nitschke, Bell, and Zackman (1974) that showed the disruptive effects of prolonged ultrasonic calling. Human evidence comes from a study by Papoušek and van Hofacker (1998) that showed that unusually persistent crying among infants aged 1 to 6 months was associated with a host of problems such as maternal depression and disturbed infant–mother relationships.

With regard to proximity promotion, Bell and Ainsworth (1972) found that the most common response to a crying infant was to pick it up; this response was also the most effective one, terminating crying in more than 80% of observed instances in naturalistic home observations of infant–mother dyads across the first year. Other proximity-increasing behaviors, such as approaching or entering the baby's room, were also noted, but did not always end in contact. These results extended observations on newborns in the hospital (Korner and Thoman, 1970), which showed that picking up a crying newborn and putting the baby to the shoulders is a most effective soothing technique. Similarly, Devore and Konner (1974) reported that crying is never ignored in hunter–gatherer societies, but contact is more continuous and crying is much less frequent.

Cultural differences suggest that the response to crying is subject to cognitive social learning principles. Rheingold (1969) observed that the crying infant "instructs" the parents by terminating the cry when an appropriate parental behavior has been emitted. Within culture, there may be considerable variability in the maternal response. Bell and Ainsworth (1972) found that the median number of cries ignored by mothers in their sample was 46%, with a range from 4% to 97%.

Not all cries are terminated by mere proximity or contact; those triggered by pain and hunger require other interventions. Some research has suggested that mothers can recognize "types" of cries from auditory properties alone and that this ability is acquired through experience (e.g., Russell, Mendelson, and Peeke, 1983; Stallings et al., 2001). Although other studies have not found such discriminations (Muller, Hollien, and Murry, 1974), research on nonhuman primates documents different types of calls within other species (Levine, Wiener, Coe, Bayart, and Hayashi, 1987; Newman, 1985) with different effects on maternal arousal and behavior.

In a novel approach to human research, Gustafson and Harris (1990) tested mothers of infants and nonmaternal females with pain and hunger cries in two paradigms. In the first, the mothers listened to one of the two cry types as they "baby-sat" a baby manikin. The type of cry had little impact on the nature of their behavior. Mothers and nonmothers did not differ markedly in their caregiving behavior, although mothers did put the manikin to their shoulder more often. In the second paradigm, the same women listened to a series of pain and hunger cries and tried to identify the cause from a list that included pain, hunger, anger, fright, sleepiness, and diaper discomfort. Responses showed that the cries were discriminable, but that intensity of distress was more salient than its cause. Although judgements about cause were inconsistent, particularly when the cry sample came from the middle of a crying bout, mothers were more accurate than nonmothers in discrimination. These findings and others (e.g., Lester, Boukydis, Garcia-Coll, Hole, and Peucker, 1992; Zeskind, Klein, and Marshall, 1992) suggest that the cry is a "graded signal" that broadcasts the infant's level of arousal by means of perceptual dimensions of pitch and pause patterns and is then interpreted by adults on the basis of contextual factors.

Recognition of a mother's own infant's cries versus other infants' cries has also been a focus in studies of human mothers. Valanne, Vuorenkowski, Partanen, Lind, and Wasz-Hockert (1967) and Formby (1967) showed that mothers could identify crying samples belonging to their own infants; Wiesenfeld and Malatesta (1982) showed that patterns of maternal HR change differed in response to audiotapes of their own versus another's baby, even though these tapes were presented without identification to the mothers. In the latter study, HR acceleration, interpreted as arousal preparatory to active coping, followed the mother's own infant's cries, whereas deceleration, interpreted as attention or passive coping, followed cries of other infants. Formby (1967) also reported findings consistent with preparatory arousal to the mother's own infant's cries. Mothers who roomed together in the hospital with their infants and with several other infant–mother pairs recorded how often they awakened and whether they did so in response to their own baby. During the first few nights, 58% of the reported awakenings were in response to own baby; thereafter the percentage rose to 96%.

There has been little research on the role of infant stimuli as inhibitors of responses incompatible with maternal behavior. One extreme case, which involved crying, was captured on a filmed record of an attempted infanticide in a New Guinea tribe in which the practice was relatively common (Schiefenhovel and Schiefenhovel, 1975). In this film, a mother abandoned her infant and covered it with leaves and branches at some distance from her hut. The infant cried lustily for hours, and the mother finally relented, retrieving her infant. She was reported to have changed her mind about giving up her baby. However, crying does not always prevent abuse or infanticide (Eisenberg, 1990).

With respect to the role of infant stimuli in guiding interaction sequences, infant crying is not part of synchronous sequences of positive interaction with the mother, although other types of infant vocalizations are. Nevertheless, the mother's successful soothing of her infant no doubt prepares both partners for positive interaction, and sensitive responses to the infant cry—that is, rapid responses that effectively terminate it—indicate a developing secure attachment relationship (Ainsworth, 1979).

Vision. Although vision plays a wide-ranging role in mother–infant interaction in human beings, no particular visually perceptible behavior of the infant predominates in the relationship in the same way that crying does. Instead, the sight of any number of infant behaviors ranging from arm and leg movements to yawning to smiling may cue maternal response. In addition, vision conveys information about physical states independently of movement or behavior. For example, individual differences in the physical attractiveness of infants may play a part in adults' responses to them (Hildebrandt and Fitzgerald, 1983), including feelings of affection and actual behavior, just as Lorenz (1943) speculated that the generally "babyish" appearance of young mammals contributes to motivating maternal care.

Visual stimuli from the infant have been shown to affect maternal behavior by means of the general adaptive functions of arousal, evocation of maternal behavior, recognition, and sequencing of interactive behaviors. As in the case of the research on auditory infant stimulus effects, most studies on visual stimuli assess effects behaviorally. Some researchers, however, have used physiological measures. The study of Wiesenfeld and Klorman (1978) demonstrated physiological arousal effects for parents at the sight of their own baby crying or smiling; HR first decelerated then accelerated as parents viewed silent videotapes of their 5-month-old infants. Leavitt and Donovan (1979) found that mothers of 3-month-old infants responded with HR acceleration when the gaze of an unfamiliar infant was directed toward them, but did not evidence this arousal pattern when the infant was looking away. At the behavioral level, the infant's gaze appears to evoke mother's gaze (Messer and Vietz, 1984) and thus leads to *en face* behavior between the two, which Klaus et al. (1975) have described as species-typical maternal behavior.

Stern (1974) suggested that the infant's gaze may have species-typical effects on maternal face-to-face "games." In longitudinal observations beginning when the infant was between 3 and 4 months of age, he observed that infant gaze led to elongated and exaggerated vocalization, facial expressions, and gazing by the mother. Furthermore, he reported that mothers could not duplicate these displays unless their babies were actually gazing at them. Nevertheless, Butterfield, Emde, Svejda, and Naiman (1982) did not find that eye opening by the infant, as a function of whether they had been given silver nitrate drops immediately following birth, affected the mother's visual attention to her baby in the recovery room following birth. In a sample of mothers at a birthing center in which eye prophylaxis was delayed, Trevathan (1987) found that eye-to-eye contact was common but differed significantly between Hispanic and non-Hispanic mothers.

Some writers have speculated about the "releaserlike" effects of the infant's smile or gaze, but, as in the case of crying, there is no one-to-one connection between an infant's smiles and a mother's response. Scanlon-Jones (1984) proposed that there is a genetic basis for the salience of the infant smile. She found that women showed better recognition memory for smiling faces of infants than men did; women and men did not differ in memory for infant faces with other expressions, suggesting that gender-stereotyped interest in babies was not a sufficient explanation for the results (see Frodi and Lamb, 1978).

Vision, as a channel for mutual face-to-face communication and gaze, is clearly important in sequences of interaction between infant and mother. Such sequences may be of unique importance in human beings because, as many writers have noted (e.g., Trevarthen, 1985), the abstract rules or regularities underlying these sequences may form a template for language acquisition. In cases in which either the infant (Fraiberg, 1975) or the mother (Adamson, Als, Tronick, and Brazelton, 1977) is blind, establishment of reciprocal patterns of play and communication are disrupted and delayed. For example, Adamson et al. (1977) described the case of a blind mother who on occasion disturbed her young infant by touching the face in an attempt to monitor the baby's facial behavior; during nursing the baby rooted to the mother's touch and lost contact with the nipple. Despite such problems, synchronous interactions are eventually established (Als, Tronick, and Brazelton, 1980) and may come more easily if the mother is multiparous (Fraiberg, 1975).

Olfactory–chemosensory cues. It is now well established that new mothers can recognize their own infants on the basis of olfactory cues; for example, they can discriminate their own infants' soiled T-shirts from the T-shirts of same-age infants (Porter, Cernoch, and McLaughlin, 1983; Schaal et al., 1980), requiring very little interaction with their infants to do so (Kaitz, Good, Rokem, and Eidelman, 1987; Porter et al., 1983). To determine whether new mothers are better than nonparents at learning about infant-related cues specifically or whether they are simply better able to learn in general, Fleming et al. (1993) compared mothers with nonmothers in their ability to recognize a set of infant-related and non-infant-related odors to which they had been preexposed. Groups of day 2 postpartum mothers and female and male nonparent controls were presented with a target stimulus and then asked to identify the target from among three similar stimuli. Stimuli consisted of an infant T-shirt (worn for 8 to 12 hr), axillary sweat, or body lotion. New mothers were also tested with their own infants' T-shirt. All groups recognized all the stimuli at better than chance performance (at all the temporal intervals used), and the groups did not differ. In the preexposure paradigm, mothers did no better at recognizing their own infants' odors than they did recognizing the odors of unfamiliar infants. Few variables were associated with recognition of the unfamiliar infant T-shirt, but a number of factors were associated with the mother's own infant odor recognition. For instance, in comparison with mothers who were incorrect, mothers who identified their own infants' odors on all three trials had experienced earlier and longer contact with their infants after birth, had spent more time in close proximal contact with their infants during interactions, and had more positive maternal feelings and attitudes. Although they do not indicate the direction of causality, these data suggest that mothers are no better than nonparents at recognizing either infant odors or other odors to which they have been preexposed, indicating that mothers are not especially primed to acquire this sort of information. However, these data also show that early postpartum experience may contribute to mothers' ability to recognize their own infants' odors and that this ability is related to other measures of maternal behavior. Finally, as indicated in the next section, recognition ability may relate to circulating hormones; the evidence shows that hormonal factors may also affect the arousing and attractive properties of infant odors.

Just as infant odors affect the mother–infant relationship, maternal odors are also important. The view of the mother–infant dyad as a bidirectional, mutual regulating system fits the evidence of odors' being important for both partners. Porter and Winberg (1999) reviewed literature on the role of maternal breast odors in the dyad. For the baby, breast odors may help in locating the breast, aid recognition, and alter state by initially quieting and then arousing the infant to cry if there is no opportunity to actually feed. The mother provides these sensory stimuli that alter the infant's behavior, which in turn feeds back into and alters the mother's behavior. Even the mother's role as odorant may be subject to bidirectional influences. Infant saliva is deposited on the nipples of rodent mothers and contributes to their functional role in guiding approach; melding of odors of mother and infant may also take place in the human case but has not yet been investigated. Porter and Winberg also suggest that infant preparedness to recognize the mother may contribute to early strengthening of maternal attachment to the infant by signaling to the mother that she is special.

Touch. Given the amount of time mothers spend in physical contact with their infants, it is surprising that so little attention has been directed to the role of this modality. One study that examined the role of touch (Kaitz, Lapidot, Bronner, and Eidelman, 1992) reported the surprising finding that mothers are able to recognize their infants based on the tactile characteristics of the dorsal surface of their hands, an effect that occurs after only a couple of hours of experience in interacting with the infant. Stack and Muir (1992) examined the infant's side of the interaction and found that adult touch appears to reduce the infant's negative emotional responses to the adult's still face and supports smiling and continued social interchange by the infant; it is possible that touch from the infant has the same supporting effect on a parent's emotional–motivational state and behavior toward the infant, particularly when the infant is distressed (see Levine and Stanton, 1990). A variety of arousing effects of tactile stimulation from the infant is experienced by mothers while breast-feeding, and the pleasures of touching a young baby's soft skin and fuzzy scalp are part of the everyday experience of most new parents.

In addition to touch as a general modality for attraction, recognition, and interaction, this modality has been a particular focus in the literature on maternal bonding (e.g., skin-to-skin contact, as noted earlier in this chapter) and breast-feeding. In the literature on both maternal bonding and breast-feeding there is little new empirical research, but there is continued interest. Touch is a key part of the sucking experience for the mother and for the breast-feeding interaction. Nevertheless, the connection between suckling and the milk ejection reflex and related oxytocin levels and the amount of milk released is not as clear in the human case as it is in the animal literature (See Wakerley, Clarke, and Summerlee, 1994, for a review); as an example, the human picture is muddied by conditioned response to the sight and the sound of the infant, which accompany touch. Furthermore, maternal anxiety and "nervous temperament," among other factors, may inhibit success. Although oxytocin has been shown to be a fairly direct link between suckling and milk release in other animals and has been proposed as a key to the onset of human parental behavior and attachment (Insel, 1997), there is not a clear enough link in humans to suggest oxytocin therapies for breast-feeding failures.

Overall, the findings on sensory effects show the potential value of considering how all the sensory modalities affect maternal behavior. There is clear evidence that particular modalities contribute to important functions such as arousal, attraction, and recognition in mother–infant interaction.

PARITY AS A MODERATOR OF PERINATAL EXPERIENCE AND SENSORY EFFECTS

In humans, as in other species, the long-term experiences and biological factors associated with parity and gender act to moderate the short-term effects of perinatal experience and the responses to infant stimuli. Postpartum effects of prior maternal experience, or other caregiving experiences with children, have been found in a variety of studies. For example, primiparous mothers who have more prior caregiving experiences report a stronger attachment to their infants, display more maternal self-confidence, and show higher levels of affectionate contact behaviors with their infants at 3 months postpartum (Deutsch, Ruble, Fleming, Brooks-Gunn, and Stangor, 1986; Fleming et al., 1987, 1988).

Consistent with demonstrated effects of prior experiences for primiparous mothers, comparisons between first-time and multiparous mothers indicate that having had an infant before has considerable impact on maternal attitudes and interactions. Prior maternal experience may buffer the multiparous mother from a variety of adverse situations found to influence the first-time mother and may mask other factors. Grossman et al. (1980) reported, for instance, that pregnancy, which was often experienced as a crisis period for primiparous mothers, was less problematic and less emotionally draining for multiparous women. They also found several strong predictors of adaptation to pregnancy and the postpartum period for primiparous mothers (e.g., prior experience with children), but there were very few significant predictors for multiparous mothers, indicating once again the overriding effects of parity.

The effects of parity favoring multiparous mothers occur primarily during the first few postpartum days and weeks, before first-time mothers have acquired experience. There is evidence, for instance, that multiparous women tend to be more maternally responsive to their newborns than primiparous mothers are (Robson and Kumar, 1980); they are more likely to respond—and more rapidly—to their own infants' cries (Bernal, 1972). They also show greater HR accelerations than do primiparous women to the cry of their own infant (Wiesenfeld and Malatesta, 1982). Bleichfeld and Moely (1984) found that experienced multiparous mothers showed greater HR accelerations than inexperienced women to any infant cry stimulus if the two groups were both nonpregnant or both pregnant but not if they were newly parturient. In line with changes in maternal attitudes and maternal behavior, more experienced mothers also became more responsive to infant cues. Parents and experienced nonparents (e.g., midwives) were better able than inexperienced women to identify different types of cries (Sagi, 1981; Wasz-Hockert, Partanen, Vuorenkowski, Michelson, and Valanne, 1964); they found infants' cries to be less aversive (Zeskind and Lester, 1978), and they responded to them in a more nurturant or caring fashion (Boukydis and Burgess, 1982; Zeskind, 1980). These results suggest that prior experience augments women's autonomic responsiveness to a salient infant cue in pregnant and nonpregnant states, whereas inexperienced women are less responsive. However, during the parturient period, when infant stimuli take on considerable salience and when hormonal effects may be present, prior experience does not appear to produce additional effects on arousal.

Not only are there parity effects on HR responses, there are also effects on more general arousal responses. According to Boukydis and Burgess (1982), primiparous mothers show higher skin potential response to the hunger cries of infants than do both nonparents and multiparous women. From these data, it could be that experienced mothers show lower arousal because they are less anxious about their own competence and about the baby than are inexperienced mothers (Thompson, Walker, and Crain, 1981), whereas for nonparents the infant cry produces less arousal because the cry stimulus is not as salient. Parity effects were also found in the study by Stallings et al. (2001) of the effects of cry types and odors on emotional, HR, and hormonal responses. Mothers clearly responded differentially to pain versus hunger cries reflected in the observation that the pain cry tended to elicit more intense sympathy and distress reactions than did the hunger cry; for feelings of sympathy, this response discrimination depended on the parity of the mothers—first-time mothers were equally sympathetic to pain and hunger cries, whereas the multiparous mothers were relatively unsympathetic to the hunger cries, but extremely responsive to the pain cries. There were no differences in the physiological indices as a function of cry type. Cortisol did vary as a function of parity, with higher levels shown by inexperienced, first-time mothers regardless of the stimulus cue or type presented. Hence parity affected both differential responsivity to cries and cortisol levels. However, the pattern of subjective emotional responses was not seen in nonpostpartum women; they were less sympathetic and less alert in response to cries than postpartum mothers were. Finally, in contrast to postpartum women, nonpostpartum women did not show differential sympathy to cry types, although they could distinguish between them.

As to mothers' responsiveness to the odor of their newborns, Schaal et al. (1980) found that parity did not augment the ability of new mothers to recognize the odors of their own babies although, as previously indicated, postpartum experience did. These data and those of Bleichfeld and Moely (1984) suggest that events associated with birth or the early postpartum period have a more powerful influence on heightened responses to infants' individual cues than does prior maternal experience. However, as indicated in the material reviewed previously, effects of parity favoring multiparous mothers may be stronger in early behavioral interactions with young infants.

Consistent with these observations, multiparous mothers are also less disrupted by periods of separation from their infants at birth; Seashore, Leifer, Barnett, and Leiderman (1973) found that, in comparison with multiparous women, primiparous women separated from their preterm babies undergo greater loss of self-confidence, an effect that apparently can be blocked if primiparous women have had prior experience caring for infants. In a subsequent study, Thompson et al. (1981) found that large parity differences in self-confidence seen at 1 to 2 days postpartum are considerably reduced by 4 to 6 weeks, after mothers have had experience.

Whereas many of the parity differences in behavior favoring multiparous mothers disappear after additional experience has been acquired (Bernal, 1972; Thoman et al., 1970b, 1971), other differences may emerge later. For instance, Belsky and colleagues (Belsky, Gilstrap, and Rovine, 1984; Belsky, Rovine, and Taylor, 1984) assessed primiparous and multiparous parents' attitudes and behaviors at four time points from the end of pregnancy through the first 9 months postpartum. They reported no parity differences in behavior during the first 3 months postpartum, when both groups are extremely attentive to their infants. Similarly, Kaitz, Chriki, Bear-Scharf, Nir, and Eidelman (2000) found no differences between primiparae and multiparae in either effectiveness of soothing their crying 2- to 3-day-old infants or in particular parental behaviors. The lack of difference for parents differing in parity held for comparisons among mothers and among fathers. Nevertheless, Belsky's research showed substantial differences by parity after 3 months, when the more immediate demands of frequent feeding and caregiving are lessened. In comparison with the more experienced mothers, primiparous mothers expressed more positive affect to their infants and showed a higher level of reciprocal interaction with them; they also provided more infant-directed vocalization and general stimulation, as well as more focused attention on the infants. At 10 to 11 months postpartum, primiparous mothers continued to be more attentive. In a study conducted by Donate-Bartfield and Passman (1985), mothers were led to believe that their infants were alone in a playroom and that the cries heard over an intercom were the cries of their own infants. Using latency to approach the playroom door as an index of responsiveness, primiparous mothers were found to respond significantly more rapidly than experienced mothers, in contrast to the longer latencies of response in the earlier postpartum period (Bernal, 1972).

Although we assume that parity influences maternal responsiveness largely by providing prior maternal experience and the opportunity to learn more optimal ways of interacting with babies and may thereby reduce feelings of inadequacy and anxiety, no studies have adequately addressed the relevant underlying mechanisms of the parity effects. For instance, in comparisons of mothers of different parity conditions, few studies control for age difference between multiparous and primiparous women. In a number of studies, maternal age has been shown to make a substantial contribution to variance in maternal behavior. Field (1980) and Jones, Green, and Kraus (1980) found that, compared with adult first-time mothers, 17- to 18-year-old mothers have less realistic expectations of their infants' development and are less responsive to newborns on some behavioral measures. Even among adult women, older mothers of term infants are more affectionately responsive than are younger mothers (Jones et al., 1980). In addition to considering age and experience as contributors to parity effects, it is also important to bear in mind that both age and parity effects may also reflect biological differences.

SOCIAL SYSTEMS PERSPECTIVES: DYADIC RECIPROCITY, CONCORDANCE, AND INTERGENERATIONAL EFFECTS

The analysis of the mother–infant dyad as a mutually regulated system with psychobiological linkages is seen in a number of lines of investigation. In some cases, a focus on bidirectionality reveals the interaction of complex developmental systems operating across both partners (e.g., Bornstein and Suess, 2000). In other cases, evolutionary analysis suggests that comparable mechanisms may be at work in both partners to regulate the relationship. In the latter regard, MacDonald (1992) concluded that the animal attachment model is not sufficient to account for parent–child relationships in human beings. He reviewed a range of findings to support the proposal that warmth and affection evolved as an independent motivational system in human beings and is important to pair bonding and extended parental investment in children, including that of the father. He also suggested that there are species-typical affectional behaviors and a built-in positive social reward value for affectionate interchanges, in contrast to the attachment system that is designed to avoid separation and associated negative emotions such as fear. The positive social reward value motivates both parental and infant behavior; MacDonald cites Panksepp's (1986, 1989) work to suggest that the reward system may lie in the limbic system and subcortical structures and may be based on opiod systems—systems that are now also known to exist in nonhuman mammals and that regulate parental motivation and behavior in those species.

The idea of corresponding mechanisms for infant and maternal behaviors and attachment relationships in particular has been outlined in some detail by Insel (1997; see also Feldman et al., 1999; Fleming et al., 1999). Insel's research builds on Bowlby's (1973) conceptualization of how separation and loss affect the human infant attachment relationship and Hofer's (1995) experimental research on pup–dam proximity and separation in rats. By manipulating the timing and the modalities of contact, Hofer had shown that different modalities influenced different aspects of pup behavior. Consistent with Bowlby's analysis, he also found differences in pup behavior between temporary and prolonged loss of contact. Insel extended Hofer's research by examining effects of loss of contact on the *mother* in rodents, finding support for corresponding patterns between infant and mother in response to separation. He also proposed the existence of parallel neurobiological systems within both the mother and offspring to explain these and other bonding phenomena. Specifically, he proposed that mating pair and parental bonding may relate to the neuropeptide oxytocin, which has been shown in his research, and that of others, to operate on both sides of mother–pup early interactions related to nursing and ultrasonic distress cries from the young.

Feldman et al. (1999) explored parts of this model in the human case by examining maternal attitudes in relation to the nature and duration of separation between new mothers and infants who were full term (FT), low birthweight (LBW) or very low birthweight (VLBW). Mothers of LBW infants had regular opportunities for contact with their healthy infants in the hospital but less opportunity than in the home. Mothers of VLBW infants had much less opportunity for contact because their infants were threatened by respiratory illness and were in intensive care. Interviews with the mothers yielded measures of preoccupation with the infant's safety and well-being, attachment representations (images, nicknames), and reported attachment behaviors. Attachment behaviors and representations showed a linear decrease with the increases in separation across the three groups (FT to LBW to VLBW). In contrast, preoccupations were higher among mothers of LBW infants compared with those of mothers of FT infants, but lowest among mothers of VLBW infants. The latter finding suggests support for the conceptual distinction between separation and loss; as previously noted, this distinction gained prominence in Bowlby's seminal work on human infant attachment but also appears in the patterns of separation effects on rodent maternal behavior reported by Insel (1997).

Feldman et al. suggested that elements of repression may contribute to the lack of preoccupation of mothers of VLBW infants because they are faced with prolonged fears about the survival of their babies. This parallels Bowlby's analysis of the role of defensive processes in infant cognition during loss. At the same time, Feldman et al. also speculated, as did Bowlby (1973), about the biological core of infant–mother attachment in relation to early separation. They suggested that separation associated with LBW may have some of its effects on maternal behavior by means of interference with normal delivery, touch, nursing, and caregiving and its oxytocin-releasing quality. At the same time, they point out that mothering a sick LBW baby will be a function of many other types of factors, including the stimulus qualities of the infant (previously reviewed in this chapter) and the mother's mood and personality.

Bornstein and Suess (2000) carried out a study that directly examined concordance between mother and infant in a comparable physiological process—vagal regulation. Their study was framed in a broad set of conceptual issues including the value of a joint analysis of mother and child physiological development (e.g., concordance) and the analysis of both individual developmental patterns (continuity or discontinuity) and individual differences (stability) in vagal function. They also cited a rapidly growing literature on the development of the vagal system and evidence that it is an important component of individual differences in emotion, temperament, information processing, and self-regulation in both children and adults. In general, Bornstein and Suess proposed that the joint analysis of mother and child vagal functioning may shed light on interwoven aspects of mother and child development by focusing on concrete psychobiological mediators of experiential and genetic interaction.

Bornstein and Suess did not examine vagal tone in direct mother–infant interaction. Instead, they took individual measures, for both mother and infant, of heart period (or interbeat intervals) and rhythmic changes in HR between breathing expiration and inspiration (respiratory sinus arrhythmia, or vagal, tone); both these measures were taken in resting state and in baseline-to-task changes. For the 2-month-old infant, the task was a standard visual habituation procedure. For the mother, the task was the Peabody Picture Vocabulary Test, Revised. There were a number of findings relevant to the psychobiology of mothering and its complex connections to the infant and the infant's development. For example, resting vagal tone in the mothers was higher at 2 months postpartum than at a 5-year follow-up, suggesting that the postnatal period is a time when high stress and little rest have effects on baseline maternal functioning. Individual differences among mothers were stable across the 5-year period in vagal tone and heart period measures, during both baseline and across the introduction of a challenging task. These results suggest stable predispositions in mothers' emotions, self-regulation, and the like, which may also affect their maternal behavior. Finally, Bornstein and Suess found concordance between the infant's and the mother's vagal tone changes from baseline to task but not during baseline alone. This is particularly noteworthy because their predictions had been the reverse. They expected concordance for the baseline tone measure on the basis of its being relatively directly connected to biological or genetic factors in the mother that might in turn contribute to the child's physiological functioning. In contrast, they did not expect concordance for the change-to-task measure because they assumed that it would be more subject to "the coordination of multiple systems (e.g., emotion, cognition, attention, and physiology) as well as environmental demand . . ." (Bornstein and Suess, 2000, p. 56), and further, that these multiple systems of mother and infant would not yet have had a chance to gel. The unexpected results suggest that a potentially important biological mediator of self-regulation and mutual regulation of infant and mother is influenced more by a complex array of interacting systems than by biology itself, even when the infant is 2 months of age.

There is also new research that illustrates how biology and experience may interact in intergenerational effects on development and parenting. Kandel and Udry (1999) showed that prenatal physiology may play a part in transmitting smoking by mothers to their daughters, beyond the obvious influences such as modeling once a daughter is old enough to learn by example. In an ambitious analysis of data collected on 471 mother–daughter pairs across four decades, they examined prenatal sera levels of cotinine (a nicotine metabolite) and testosterone as well as mothers' reported smoking prenatally and postnatally and daughters' smoking in adolescence and at 27 to 30 years of age. Sophisticated statistical testing of causal models showed that prenatal smoking and testosterone were linked and that testosterone independently contributed to adolescent daughters' smoking, which in turn predicted adult daughters' smoking. Interestingly, fathers' smoking did not link significantly to daughters' smoking. These findings suggest that mothers' prenatal smoking may alter testosterone levels that affect brain-behavior links that lead to smoking by their daughters. As adults, the daughters' smoking could in turn affect their offspring. Although the investigators could not rule out alternative, postnatal experiential or genetic explanations for these links, the evidence nevertheless demonstrates that psychobiological measures will be important in attempts to understand intergenerational systems effects on human maternal behavior.

The potential importance of biological factors is also reinforced by a review of literature on intergenerational transmission of child abuse by Buchanan (1998). In her analysis, biological factors were considered along with psychological, sociopolitical, and cultural factors to achieve a full understanding of the problem and to design effective interventions. In concrete biological terms, maternal disease, inherited disorder, and neurological impairment can contribute to abusive behavior and to direct physical damage to offspring, with both the mother's behavior and the child's biology then contributing to abuse in the next parental generation. Similarly, Francis, Champagne, Liu, and Meaney (1999) showed how early life events connect to health in adulthood by means of behavioral, endocrine, and neural mediators, with implications for cycles of abuse.

ONSET AND MAINTENANCE OF PATERNAL BEHAVIOR

In most mammals the mother is the primary caregiver during the early postnatal period and fathers play no role in the direct care of the young (see Rosenblatt and Snowdon, 1996). However, in some species this is not the case and the father shares in the caregiving (Brown, 1993; Elwood and Mason, 1994; Wang, Liu, Young, and Insel, 2000; Ziegler, 2000). In a few species, fathers are, in fact, the primary caregiver, with the mother mainly providing nutrition (Ziegler, 2000). Human fathers show variable involvement in the early nurturing of their infants. In some cultures, the father does not directly care for the young but he does provision the family; in others, the father takes a large role in the early parenting by carrying the babies, keeping them clean and warm, and sometimes feeding them (Parke, in Vol. 3 of this *Handbook*).

Questions about species distribution of care, between mates as well as in nonparental care, have been explored in the animal literature from a comparative, evolutionary standpoint (e.g., Maynard Smith, 1977; Webb, Houston, McNamara, and Szekely, 1999; Ziegler, 2000). Although at first glance, game-theoretic models of care distribution and reproductive fitness might seem too grossly simplified for the human case (e.g., Yamamura and Tsuji, 1993), Webb et al. (1999) examined ways of accounting for variations within species (e.g., both biparental and uniparental care in the same species and shifts from one form to another across time within mating pairs) that come closer to matching the variability in the human case. For example, one reason for variations in parental care "decisions" and distribution rests on individual differences in both parents (e.g, nest-building ability) as well as other members of the population. Thus blending of evolutionary analysis with some of the social ecology complexities of the human case could prove to be interesting.

A sophisticated evolutionary analysis of biological factors in rodent biparental care is found in research on Djungarian hamsters (Reburn and Wynne-Edwards, 1999). In this species, hormonal changes around the birth are similar in mothers and fathers, and fathers are active in sharing parenting at the time of birth by pulling the pups from the birth canal, licking away birth membranes, and eating the afterbirth. Fathers in a related species, Siberian hamsters, do not act parentally at birth and do not show the coupling with maternal hormonal changes, although they do eventually engage in parenting. These findings, from laboratory investigations, may reflect habitat differences and species adaptation. Djungarian hamsters actually originate in a colder part of Siberia than Siberian hamsters; Djungarian males remain in the burrow at the time of birth, perhaps as a contribution to temperature regulation. This propinquity in turn may have evolved along with genetic factors that control biparental care, including hormonal mediation.

At the level of direct parent interaction in humans, increasing attention has been paid to nurturance or parental responsiveness in the new father (Parke, in Vol. 3 of this *Handbook*), and some of this attention is aimed explicitly at psychobiological factors (Fleming, Corter, Stallings, and Steiner, in preparation; Storey, Walsh, Quintor, and Wynne-Edwards, 2000; see below). New fathers who are present at the delivery experience many of the same feelings of elation, nurturance, "engrossment," and pleasure described by new mothers (Greenberg and Morris, 1974; Parke and Sawin, 1975, 1977; Robson and Moss, 1970). A study comparing mothers and fathers in their nurturant feelings and attitudes on the day after their infants' births found no differences between mothers and fathers in how anxious, self-confident, or elated they felt. There were modest differences in their reported feelings of attachment to their infants and attraction to other children, feelings of tiredness, and depression, with mothers scoring higher on these dimensions (Fleming, Steiner, and Corter, in preparation). The largest differences were in parents' attitudes toward caregiving activities in general; fathers felt considerably more negative about detailed aspects of caring for an infant, despite never having had much caregiving experience. These negative feelings about caregiving before experiencing it may, indeed, contribute to the clear differences in the quality of later parenting exhibited by fathers and mothers. The same study showed that experience played a role in the gender differences in negative feelings about caregiving; males with more experience with infants before becoming fathers had less negative attitudes toward caregiving. Brophy-Herb, Gibbons, Omar, and Schiffman (1999) also found a potential experience effect for low-income fathers observed in a standardized teaching task for a sample of infants ranging from 1 to 16 months of age. Fathers who shared a residence with their infant were more sensitive in their interactions than were those who did not (perhaps comparable to "burrow effects" in hamsters), although a number of other parental behaviors were not associated with this differential. Also, among nonhuman primates, there is good evidence that, when fathering occurs, experience plays an important regulatory role. In marmoset monkeys, for instance, fathers spend more time carrying their infants than do mothers, and they do so earlier in life as juveniles and subadults with their younger siblings (Ziegler, 2000). In fact, in the absence of this earlier carrying experience, it is likely that the father would not show adequate paternal behavior when he has his first offspring. As with mothers, what the father learns when interacting with the young probably involves becoming habituated to the novelty of the young and becoming familiar with their various cues as well as developing more skillful ways of behaviorally interacting with the infants.

In any case, mothers and fathers are similar in some behavioral respects during the early postpartum period. Fathers show the same pattern of tactile response to their newborn infants as that shown by mothers, although it develops more slowly (Abbott, 1975), and during interaction with their newborns, they evidence HR and blood pressure increases characteristic of a preparatory response (Jones and Thomas, 1989). Fathers also show the same differential pattern of psychophysiological responses to infants' cries and smiles (Frodi, Lamb, Leavitt, Donovan, Neff, and Sherry, 1978). Fleming, Corter, Stallings, and Steiner (in preparation) also found that mothers and fathers do not differ in their attraction to infant odors. Both experience infant body odor more positively than do female nonparent controls, and for both the time in contact with the infant after the birth enhances the attraction. These data suggest that the attraction mothers are known to have for infant odors must be ascribable to situational or environmental influences, but the additional observation that for both mothers and fathers there is a significant relation between salivary cortisol and ratings of their own infants' T-shirts suggests that physiological factors may also affect attraction. Thus for both mothers and fathers high salivary cortisols are associated with high hedonic ratings.

There is also evidence in other biparental species that hormones in the father, as well as experiential factors, activate his paternal behavior. For instance, in the California mouse, paternal responsiveness, which is not present in the virgin male, increases during the mother's gestation (Gubernick and Nelson, 1989). However, this pattern occurs in only some fathers. Others show no interest in their young during the mother's gestation, but only respond to them once the young are born (Gubernick, Schneider, and Jeannotte, 1994); in other species, the onset of paternal responsiveness occurs only in interaction with the young and the mother (e.g., male meadow voles, Storey, Bradbury, and Joyce, 1994 and Storey and Joyce, 1995; gerbils, Brown, Murdoch, Murphy, and Moger, 1995; mice, Elwood, 1986; for a complete review, see Brown, 1993, and Ziegler, 2000). In many of these biparental species, the change in father's parental behavior is associated with an increase in his prolactin levels (Brown et al., 1995; Jones and Wynne-Edwards, 2000; Mota and Sousa, 2000; Reburn and Wynne-Edwards, 1999; Ziegler, Wegner, and Snowdon, 1996); in some cases, there also occurs a decrease in the male's testosterone levels (Brown et al., 1995; Reburn and Wynne-Edwards, 1999). Whether these hormonal changes are in response to pup-related cues or not, is often not known. Studies on gerbils by Brown (1993) indicate that, compared with virgin male gerbils, new gerbil fathers also exhibit elevated prolactin levels and reduced testosterone levels. In this species, pup stimulation per se, after a period of separation, does not produce a prolactin surge, as it does in the mother. Moreover, the postpartum reduction in testosterone in gerbils seems also not to be directly stimulated by the pups. A recent study by Reburn and Wynne Edwards (1999) compared the endocrine profiles of Djungarian and Siberian hamsters and found that higher postpartum levels of prolactin and lower levels of testosterone occurred in new Djungarian fathers. These fathers behave parentally immediately after birth, at the same time their hormones are changing. In common marmosets, both carrying males and subadults show elevations in prolactin, whereas noncarrying members of the group do not, suggesting an effect on prolactin of contact stimulation associated with the behavior.

For human fathers little was known about the endocrine profile until the recent study by Storey, Walsh, Quinton, and Wynne-Edwards (2000). These investigators studied groups of 8 to 12 couples at each of four time points, two prenatal and two postnatal. Endocrine measures were taken twice at each time point, once before and once after an interval when the parents either held the infant or a doll and were exposed to an audiotape of infant crying along with a videotape of infant nursing. Hence it was possible to obtain information on changes in baseline as a function of reproductive stage and in response to infant-related stimuli. Results were consistent with other biparental species and suggest hormonal priming in expectant or new fathers. Levels of cortisol, prolactin, and testosterone in the fathers showed patterned changes over time. Although the changes were less pronounced than those in women, there was suggestive evidence of links with paternal responsiveness. For example, testosterone generally dropped in fathers following the births of their infants, and those with the lowest levels showed more parental behavior. Lower paternal testosterone during pregnancy was also associated with more reports of symptoms consistent with "sympathetic pregnancy," such as fatigue and weight gain. The investigators also showed that cortisol changes in response to a tape of a newborn cry and a video on breast-feeding were similar in the mothers and the fathers. Finally, compared with less concerned men, fathers in the combined prenatal and postnatal groups who reported feeling concerned about baby's cries or who reported wanting to comfort the baby had higher prolactin levels and lower testosterone levels. These findings are preliminary but consistent with studies in other species, including nonhuman primates, in which there are regular changes across pregnancy in the hormonal profile of prolactin, estradiol, testosterone, and cortisol for both expectant mothers and fathers (see Ziegler, 2000).

In addition to finding male hormonal stage changes over pregnancy and birth and the suggestive evidence on male hormonal priming for responsiveness to infants, Storey et al. (2000) reported another finding paralleling some of the animal literature. In their study, correlations emerged in hormonal levels between mother and father pairs—strong evidence that there may be social systems effects within families on hormonal factors. In particular, both men's baseline cortisol levels and their situational changes in cortisol after test exposures to infant stimuli were associated with levels of estradiol, prolactin, and cortisol for their partners, at least during some stages. In other species, as previously noted, links between social systems effects and parental responsiveness have been found with the possibility of hormonal mediation. In the study of Storey et al. (2000), it is not clear whether the correlations might have implications for parental responsiveness to the infant. They interpreted their findings as reflecting a connection between male "physiological changes" and differences in "communication" among parent couples. This suggestion raises the possibility that the quality of marriage effects on children might include psychobiological mediators.

From these results and previous findings that showed a relation between cortisol and mothers' sympathetic responses to infant cries (Stallings et al., 2001), Fleming, Corter et al. (in preparation) used a considerably larger sample of fathers and nonfather controls to examine emotional and endocrine changes associated with a controlled presentation of infant cries, odors, or their combination. Similar to new mothers (Stallings et al., 2001), new fathers respond to infant cries with greater feelings of emotion than they do to infant odors, and these feelings are both positive and negative. In particular, fathers expressed greater sympathy, a greater need to respond, and greater alertness to cries; at the same time, they also felt more irritated and annoyed. Although earlier studies showed that parents experience infant body odors as more pleasant than other infant-neutral control stimuli

(Fleming, Corter, Surbey, Franks, and Steiner, 1995), more recent studies (Fleming, Corter et al., in preparation; Stallings et al., 2001) clearly show that odors do not produce a feeling of sympathy or nurturance in the recipient. These studies also show that fathers tend not to respond differentially to pain versus to hunger cries, in contrast to mothers' differential responses; fathers show the same level of sympathy, alertness, positive, and negative emotion to the two cry types. However, when action, as opposed to simple affect, is implied, a different pattern of effects was seen: Fathers expressed higher need to respond to the pain than to the hunger cries, and multiparous fathers expressed higher need to respond to the cries than did primiparous fathers.

In addition to producing an emotional response in fathers, the presentation of cries also had an effect on the fathers' hormones, which was independent of fathers' affective reactions. For instance, in fathers hearing cry stimuli, there were greater increases in testosterone from baseline to the first poststimulus assessment than in fathers not hearing cries, and this cry-induced change did not vary as a function of the fathers' parity. In contrast, with respect to prolactin, parity differences were very important. There was a decrease in prolactin levels from baseline to the poststimulus in primiparous fathers and an increase in the multiparous fathers. Hence multiparous fathers listening to cries showed a greater percentage of increase in prolactin levels than did primiparous fathers listening to cries or than did either group of fathers in the control conditions. For cortisol, there were greater elevations in cortisol in those hearing the cries than in fathers not hearing the cries; moreover, first-time fathers hearing the cry had higher cortisol levels than did multiparous fathers hearing the cry. In addition, there were no specific effects of the cry stimuli or of parity on fathers' HR responses, similar to the pattern in new mothers.

Although hormones were clearly affected by the presentation of the cry stimuli, when one considers how fathers responded affectively to those cries, a different pattern of hormone–affect relations can be seen. From the nonhuman animal studies of parental behavior and on our previous study of mothers, we predicted that nurturant and sympathetic responses in fathers would be associated with lower levels of circulating testosterone and elevations in prolactin and/or cortisol. These results show clearly that, not only do the cries produce some change in the fathers' hormones, but the endocrine states of the fathers before they hear the cries are also related to how they respond to those cries. Fathers with lower baseline testosterone levels (before they hear the cries) are more sympathetic and show a greater need to respond when presented with infant cries; as well, fathers with higher baseline prolactin levels are more positive and more alert in the face of infant cries. Analyses indicated further that the relation between hormones and affective responses to infant cries is not solely mediated by the effects of prior parental experience on hormones. In fact, the same testosterone–affect relation was found among nonfather males, most of whom had no prior parentallike experience and no recent contact with infants. These data, in combination with the findings that sympathy feelings are inversely associated with baseline testosterone, even when no infant stimuli are presented, suggest that among human fathers androgen levels at baseline are associated with a nurturant style and are predictive of responsiveness to infant cues. This pattern parallels the suggestive evidence on physiological baselines in mothers associated with "personality" differences in maternal nurturance (Stallings et al., 2001).

Among fathers in this study we also found experience effects that parallel some of those for mothers; these were seen in comparisons of fathers with nonfathers and more directly among fathers with differing amounts of experience. For example, fathers are more responsive to infant cues than are nonfathers; comparisons between fathers and nonfathers in their affective and physiological responses to the cries showed that fathers were more likely to experience sympathy or to be alerted by cry stimuli; they also had lower testosterone levels, both before and during the cries. Among fathers, those with more experience expressed both less sympathy and a greater need to respond to infant cries. With respect to experience effects on the hormonal response to the cries, there were large parity differences in reactivity or percentage of change from baseline to the first poststimulus test in prolactin, with multiparous fathers listening to the cries showing a greater percentage of increase in prolactin level than primiparous fathers listening to cries or either group of fathers in the control conditions. These effects are consistent with findings from nonhuman studies that show that prolactin release can be conditioned, in particular in mothers who have had more interactive experience with their offspring (Grosvenor and Mena, 1992). Whether a similar effect obtains in human fathers is, of course, not known, but is certainly suggested by these results. Finally, in terms of baseline levels of hormones, first-time (and less experienced) fathers had higher overall baseline testosterone and cortisol levels, but lower prolactin levels. The latter finding suggests that less experienced fathers are aroused by cry stimuli, and as a result may experience heightened "engagement" with the infant; this seems to also be true of the nonfather males presented with the cries, in which higher levels of cortisol were associated with greater alertness (Henry and Wang, 1998; Wang, 1997).

The issue as to whether the hormonal profile of new fathers precedes the birth and contact with the young or is based on infant-induced changes in the male's endocrinology cannot be answered by this study. However, it is likely that some aspect of experience with infants may well have affected the fathers' endocrine states. At two days postpartum, fathers, as opposed to nonfathers, have lower testosterone levels. Moreover, fathers with more prior interactive experience in caring for infants (as a result, usually, of having had a previous baby) have lower testosterone levels and higher prolactin levels than do fathers having their first baby and hence having less prior experience. Although some of these differences reflect age differences in the male and father populations, in which older males have lower testosterone levels than younger males, covarying age does not eliminate these experience–hormone relations in new fathers.

To get a better handle on the mechanisms through which becoming a father influences and is influenced by the infant stimulus and experience with infants, it would be necessary to assess first-time and multiparous fathers during their wives' pregnancies as well as after the infants' births, both before and after fathers have had the opportunity to hold their infants. As well, in future studies it will be necessary to obtain information from these fathers about other experiences they may have that could affect their endocrine levels.

In conclusion, it is notable that the human evidence to date suggests that in many respects experience and hormones work in similar ways in mothers and fathers. In addition, animal research and evolutionary speculation about parenting have become more complex in suggesting that a psychobiological perspective needs to look beyond the mother–infant attachment relationship to examine biological influences in what the human literature refers to as a family systems perspective. It thus appears that a psychobiological approach may help to understand the possibilities for *flexibility* in parenting that challenge stereotypical views of fathers and mothers.

ROLE OF THE BRAIN IN HUMAN MATERNAL BEHAVIOR

Surprisingly, there is virtually no research on the role of the nervous system in the regulation of human maternal behavior. A review of the literature reveals very little case reporting on parenting motivation or behavior in patients with brain damage. For example, MacLean (1990) reviewed hundreds of cases of psychomotor epilepsy and found good evidence for the role of the limbic system in regulating basic affects; however, he reports that none of the findings were suggestive of effects on "feelings or sentiments related to parental behavior" (p. 449). Moreover, in most studies involving mothers with brain damage or disorder, such as epilepsy, the focus has been almost exclusively on the effects of pregnancy seizures or of drugs taken by mothers on their infants' development (see Mayes and Truman, in Vol. 4 of this *Handbook*), with only a cursory allusion to the possible role of altered parenting in these mothers (e.g., Gaily, Kantola-Sorsa, and Granstrom, 1990). Similarly, with the exception of studies of parenting in postpartum psychotic or clinically depressed mothers (see Zahn-Waxler, Duggal, and Gruber, in Vol. 4 of this *Handbook*), no studies attempt to relate neurochemical dysfunction and maternal behavior.

Potential populations for analysis of links between neurochemical dysfunction and maternal behavior include mothers who abuse substances such heroine, cocaine, tranquilizers, or alcohol, or mothers, who because of psychiatric problems, are receiving antidepressants or neuroleptics (Field, 1984; James and Coles, 1991; Rodning, Beckwith, and Howard, 1991; Stein et al., 1991). These populations, in theory, could provide information on the involvement in maternal behavior of the opioids (e.g., heroine), the catecholamines (e.g., cocaine, antidepressants, neuroleptics), or the diazepines (e.g., tranquilizers). In reality, very little good information on the role of these neurochemical agonists and antagonists can be garnered from existing research. In general, drug dependence is associated with a host of other dependencies, as well as social and demographic factors, that make it difficult to establish how much of the variability in behavior is due to the specific drug and how much to these other factors or to drug interactions (e.g., James and Coles, 1991). Moreover, in most drug studies, populations are chronic abusers and thus are exposed to extreme pharmacologic levels. In cases in which drug intake is better controlled, it is usually when drugs are prescribed for treatment of affective disorders or psychoses, posing further problems in the interpretation of drug effects. Finally, the focus of most of the drug studies has been on the infant and effects of prenatal exposure and not on the quality of parenting by the mother.

In spite the dearth of evidence on the role of the brain in maternal behavior, there are scattered signs of promise in the use of neuroimaging techniques to investigate maternal responsiveness. In one example (Lorberbaum et al., 1999), functional MRI imaging was used in a pilot study of four experienced mothers listening to cries and white noise. The investigators recorded emotional reactions reported by the mothers and imaged functional activity in a number of areas of the brain, including the orbitofrontal cortex and the cingulate gyrus. Although the sample was too small to establish patterns, the methodology proved workable. In another preliminary study (Bremner et al., 1997) MRI anatomical imaging was used to estimate the volume of the hippocampus among adults with Post Traumatic Stress Disorder resulting from severe physical or sexual abuse during childhood (not necessarily early childhood or infancy). Reduced volume was found, suggesting that childhood abuse leads to long-term alterations of the brain as well as immediate effects on brain activity (Ito, Teicher, Glod, and Ackerman, 1998) and HPA activity (Hart, Gunnar, and Cicchetti, 1996). The speculative implication for parental behavior is that such long-term biological embedding may contribute to the intergenerational transmission of abusive behavior. Findings in the literature on rats support the notion that biological embedding in the brain based on early experience may explain later individual differences in mothering and intergenerational effects (Francis et al., 1999).

RAT AND HUMAN DATA ON MATERNAL BEHAVIOR CONTRASTED

As noted earlier, the research on maternal behavior in the rat is extensive and has yielded findings that are applicable to other mammalian species (Rosenblatt and Fleming and Li, in Vol. 2 of this *Handbook*). In the case of humans, comparisons with the rat are useful in a heuristic way, despite obvious differences in the maternal behavior of the two species. Both rat and human mothers undergo a change in affective state during the early postpartum period that may be hormonally mediated and that can influence early mother–infant interactions. In the case of the rat dam whose environment is homogeneous and who is bred for high yield, the postpartum affective state tends to be positive, showing little variability, and thus the undisturbed mother behaves nurturantly toward her offspring. It should be noted, however, that perturbations to the environment associated with C-section or artificially induced inclement weather conditions often result in cannibalism or abandonment of the litter (Leon, Croskerry, and Smith, 1978; Orpen and Fleming, 1987). Human mothers, on the other hand, are highly variable on a multitude of environmental and background factors and experience a wide range of emotional states postpartum; however, those exhibiting a more positive mood state tend also to exhibit more positive interactions with their offspring.

The research on sensory effects reveals that both rat and human mothers also develop an attraction to odors associated with offspring. In neither case is it known what the relevant odors may be, although excrement and urine products seem not to be involved. In the case of human beings, newborn infants possess a high concentration of glands that secrete sweat and sebum. Both types of secretions constitute rich sources for bacteria that rapidly colonize the neonatal skin surface and therefore constitute good sources of infant odorants (see Schaal and Porter, 1991). Although rat mothers show a preference for infant-related odors in the absence of explicit experience with those odors, it is also clear that with experience with pups their preferences are stronger and more long lasting. The human mother, in contrast, probably requires some experience with the infant for an attraction to infant odors to develop. Heightened attraction is associated with both earlier postpartum contact and with more time interacting proximally with the infant. Although it is tempting to conclude that the mother's attraction to infant odors promotes more rapid maternal attachment, as may be the case in rats, available data are purely correlational and do not address the issue of causality.

Both rat and human studies indicate that experiences during the early postpartum period may be important for the development of a longer-term attachment to the young. In rats, separation at birth results in a rapid loss of responsiveness, and a brief maternal experience results in a robust long-term retention of behavior. Human beings differ in that neither short-term separation from the infant nor brief additional contact with the infant exerts such profound long-term effects. For human mothers there does not appear to be a "sensitive period" during which contact must occur for normal development of attachment; instead, the development of behavior is a more gradual process, and even if experiences during the early postpartum period have an impact, they are by no means necessary for the development of mothers' attachment to their infants. Furthermore, life experiences and cognitive factors can alter the impact of immediate experience, as can be seen in parity effects or in cases of mothers who successfully give up their infants for adoption.

In addition, there is evidence that new human mothers, like rat mothers, learn about infant odor cues during the postpartum period: Rats learn about litter characteristics, and human mothers learn to recognize individual characteristics. This ability to learn about infant cues is not unique to either new mothers or to infant cues and can be demonstrated in nonparents as well. However, with that in mind, a mother's success at recognizing her own infant's odor may depend on processes that are quite different from those involved in either her recognition or other people's recognition of odors from an unfamiliar infant or from other sources. Like rat mothers that exhibit a robust conditioned odor preference only if odors are experienced during proximal mother–litter interactions, new human mothers recognize infants' odors if they experience them during earlier postpartum nursing and/or closer proximal mother–infant interactions.

Finally, there is good evidence that hormones mediate maternal behavior in rats and other mammals (Bridges, 1990; Insel, 1990; Keverne and Kendrick, 1990), but in the case of human beings the evidence is not so strong. Nevertheless, there is growing evidence showing a relation between behavioral measures and circulating cortisol in human mothers. These data are provocative and suggest some speculations and testable hypotheses regarding a role for this hormone (secreted by the adrenal gland) in the initiation of maternal behavior.

Elevated concentrations of cortisol (or possibly the pituitary hormone, the adrenocorticotropic hormone [ACTH], or indeed any of the related peptide hormones that rise at parturition along with ACTH) may function to create in the new mother a heightened state of arousal and susceptibility to environmental influences, which, depending on background and situational factors, may determine the valence of mother's mood and behavior to offspring (Corter and Fleming, 1990; Fleming and Corter, 1988). Thus high cortisol in association with positive background and situational factors (e.g., good health, social supports, healthy infant, prior maternal experience) is predicted to produce elevated mood and positive maternal behavior, whereas high cortisol in association with negative background and situational factors is predicted to have a negative impact on both mood and maternal behavior. In other words, high cortisol levels may amplify the effects of more psychological factors in producing either positive or negative effects on mood and behavior. Alternatively, or additionally, there is evidence that the adrenal hormones can influence olfactory function specifically (Goodspeed,

Gent, Catalanotto, Cain, and Zagraniski, 1986; Henken, 1975), as well as the impact of reinforcing stimuli in general; the pituitary–adrenal axis may also affect the ease with which experiences are acquired and retained (Dunn, 1984). Whether and how any or all of these processes are involved in maternal affect, maternal hedonics, maternal recognition, or maternal behavior have yet to be determined.

CONCLUSIONS

Many of the crucial functions that human parents serve for their infants (such as feeding, protection, thermoregulation, and grooming) are common in other species; this commonality supports the utility of a comparative approach to parenting and also suggests that biological factors may be important in human parenting. Research findings that appear to document cultural universals in parenting are also consistent with the possibility that biology plays a part. Such universals have been found in areas of parent–infant interaction that are particularly characteristic of human beings, for example, in the communicative adjustments adults make in vocalizing and singing to their infants. Although nurturance and affection for infants also appear to be universal across cultures, their concrete behavioral forms vary widely across cultures and across individuals within a culture. Despite suggestions that there may be human species-typical motor patterns of maternal behavior, such as *en face* gazing at the infant, there appear to be cultures in which these behaviors do not typically occur. Furthermore, the unique human capacities for flexible social interaction and technological adaptation mean that the basic functions of parenting can be distributed across relationships in different ways, depending on the particular family and culture, and that parenting behavior can be modified by use of slings, swings, monitors, and so forth.

Human flexibility makes it difficult to define maternal behavior in terms of a limited set of actions. A broader definition that includes maternal attitudes and feelings, as well as interactive behaviors, makes it possible to consider enough human research to examine the premise that experimental research on nonhuman maternal behavior can stimulate the exploration of the psychobiological basis of human maternal behavior. The methodology in much of the human research is correlational or descriptive. For example, measures of individual differences in hormonal concentrations have been related to maternal responsiveness, or groups differing in their parturitional status, and presumably in their hormonal profiles, have been compared. In theory, it would also be possible to carry out descriptive research examining the neurochemical and neuroanatomical correlates of parenting in clinical populations or by use of imaging techniques that could relate brain activity in different sites to parental behavior; however, very little of this type of research appears to have been done.

The area in which the greatest amount of relevant human knowledge has been gleaned is in the investigation of infant stimulus or sensory effects. As in the animal literature, cues in different sensory modalities can be examined to determine their functional roles in evoking and modulating parental behavior. For example, a large number of studies have looked at autonomic arousal, measured by HR and GSR, in response to infant cries; some of these studies have focused on comparisons between different groups of parents (e.g., abusive versus nonabusive), whereas others have focused on stimulus differences between different groups of infants (e.g., preterm versus term). In general, these studies suggest that there may be an optimal level of arousal in response to potent infant cues, such as the cry. Other modalities for infant sensory effects have also been examined, with some work on the visual modality and a small amount of recent work on olfaction and touch.

Infant sensory effects go beyond mere arousal. They are the basis of a variety of other functions including recognition of, and attraction to, the infant. Some studies of sensory effects demonstrate that new mothers have a remarkable ability to recognize their infants by sound, by odor, and even by touch. In addition, new mothers appear to be more attracted to infant odors compared with other adults, including mothers without young infants. These findings could be interpreted to indicate that new mothers are "biologically prepared" to respond to infant cues, but that interpretation must be qualified by the role that experience has been shown to play. The studies also show that both the accuracy of recognition and the degree of hedonic response to infant cues depend on amount of relevant experience with the infant following birth. Furthermore, new fathers also show more positive hedonic responses to infant cues than nonparents do, and their responses also vary with the degree of experience with their new infants. New evidence on both mothers and fathers suggests that responsiveness to infant cues may also be a function of individual differences in parental physiological states, which in turn may be part of parental "personality".

Both short-term experience following birth and developmental history of experience with children have been shown to affect maternal behavior, measured by attitudes and by interactive behaviors. Differences in experience may account for differences that have been found between primiparous and multiparous mothers in maternal attitudes such as self-confidence and in autonomic arousal to infant cues. Differences in experience may also contribute to differences in the behavior of mothers and fathers. From a psychobiological perspective, the most important aspects of experience effects are their potential interactions with sensory and hormonal effects. Such interactions have been clearly demonstrated in the animal research (see Fleming and Li, in Vol. 2 of this *Handbook*); the limited human research to date suggests similar interactions.

Postpartum mood affects maternal behavior and is clearly affected by situational and experiential factors. Surprisingly, an interactive influence of hormones has been harder to demonstrate. These difficulties could be due to the powerful and obscuring effects of psychological variables or to the search for linear relations between hormonal levels and mood. Nevertheless, there is limited evidence that cortisol plays a part in both postpartum mood and behavior. The animal research suggests a number of ways in which hormonal factors could influence behavior, but the preliminary findings on human parents will need further replication and extension to test for these possibilities. Similarly, animal research suggests that examination of the role of the brain in human parental behavior could be fruitful, but the corresponding human research has not been done.

Both biological and psychological factors influence human parenting in some ways that parallel the effects of these factors on parenting in other species. Thus it is clear that sensory factors and experience play a part in structuring human maternal behavior, and hormones appear to have a role as well. New findings suggest that these factors may interact to structure the parental behavior of fathers in similar fashion. The experimental work on maternal behavior in rats provides a useful starting place for the exploration of psychobiological factors in human maternal behavior.

In both animal and human investigations of the psychobiology of parenting, there is new research framed in social systems perspectives. The analysis of the mother–infant dyad as a mutually regulated system with psychobiological linkages is seen in a number of lines of investigation. In some cases, a focus on bidirectionality in the dyad reveals the interaction of complex developmental systems operating across both partners, including physiological mechanisms such as vagal functioning or the HPA axis. In addition, evolutionary analysis also suggests that comparable mechanisms may be at work in both partners to regulate the relationship. Finally, analysis of intergenerational effects on parenting and offspring, including mechanisms of biological embedding of earlier experiences, is a promising new area in both animal and human research. In the human case, there is a potential for new applications, including interventions that improve the health of offspring and that reduce the incidence of abuse.

ACKNOWLEDGMENTS

Support for our own research on human parenting has been provided by the Social Sciences and Humanities Research Council, and the Medical Research Council of Canada. Our animal research has been supported by the Medical Research Council of Canada and the Natural Sciences and Engineering Research Council of Canada.

REFERENCES

Abbott, L. (1975). *Paternal touch of the newborn: Its role in paternal attachment.* Boston, MA: Boston University School of Nursing.

Adamson, L., Als, H., Tronick, E., and Brazelton, T. (1977). The development of social reciprocity between a sighted infant and a blind infant and her parents. *Journal of the American Academy of Child Psychiatry, 16,* 194–207.

Ainsworth, M. (1979). Attachment as related to mother–infant interaction. *Advances in the study of behavior, 9,* 1–49. New York: Academic.

Als, H., Tronick, E., and Brazelton, T. (1980). Stages of early behavioral organization: The study of a sighted infant and a blind infant in interaction with their mothers. In T. Field, S. Goldberg, D. Stern, and A. Sostek (Eds.), *High-risk infants and children* (pp. 184–204). New York: Academic.

Anderson, A., Lawrence, K., Davies, K., Campbell, H., and Turnbull, A. (1971). Fetal adrenal weight and the cause of premature delivery in human pregnancy. *Journal of Obstetrics and Gynaecology of the British Commonwealth, 78,* 481–488.

Anderson, G. C. (1991). Current knowledge about skin-to-skin (kangaroo) care for preterm infants. *Journal of Perinatology, 11,* 216–226.

Atkinson, L., Niccols, A., Paglia, A., Coolbear, J., Parker, K. C. H., Poulton, L., Guger, S., and Sitarenios, G. (2000). A meta-analysis of time between maternal sensitivity and attachment assessments: Implications for internal working models in infancy/toddlerhood. *Journal of Social and Personal Relationships, 17,* 791–810.

Bell, R., Nitschke, W., Bell, N., and Zachman, T. (1974). Early experience, ultrasonic vocalizations and maternal responsiveness in rats. *Developmental Psychobiology, 7,* 235–242.

Bell, S., and Ainsworth, M. (1972). Infant crying and maternal responsiveness. *Child Development, 43,* 1171–1190.

Belsky, J., Gilstrap, B., and Rovine, M. (1984). The Pennsylvania Infant and Family Development Project, I: Stability and change in mother–infant interaction and father–infant interaction in a family setting at one, three and nine months. *Child Development, 55,* 692–705.

Belsky, J., Rovine, M., and Taylor, D. (1984). The Pennsylvania Infant and Family Development Project, III: The origins of individual differences in infant-mother attachment: Maternal and infant contributions. *Child Development, 55,* 718–728.

Bernal, J. (1972). Crying during the first 10 days of life and maternal responses. *Developmental Medicine and Child Neurology, 14,* 362–372.

Bernal, J., and Richards, M. P. (1970). The effects of bottle and breast feeding on infant development. *Journal of Psychosomatic Research, 14,* 247–252.

Bleichfeld, B., and Moely, B. E. (1984). Psychophysiological responses to an infant cry: Comparisons of groups of women in different phases of the maternal cycle. *Developmental Psychology, 20,* 1082–1091.

Blurton Jones, N. (1972). Comparative aspects of mother-child contact. In N. Blurton Jones (Ed.), *Ethological studies of child behaviour* (pp. 305–308). Cambridge, England: Cambridge University Press.

Bornstein, M. H. (1991). Approaches to parenting in culture. In M. H. Bornstein (Ed.), *Cultural approaches to parenting* (pp. 3–19). Hillsdale, NJ: Lawrence Erlbaum Associates.

Bornstein, M. H., Azuma, H., Tamis-LeMonda, C., and Ogino, M. (1990). Mother and infant activity and interaction in Japan and in the United States: A comparative microanalysis of naturalistic exchanges. *International Journal of Behavioral Development, 13,* 267–287.

Bornstein, M., and Suess, P. E. (2000). Child and mother cardiac vagal tone: Continuity, stability, and concordance across the first 5 years. *Developmental Psychology, 36,* 54–65.

Bornstein, M. H., Tal, J., Rahn, C., Galperin, C., Pêcheux, M., Lamour, M., Toda, S., Azuma, H., Ogino, M., and Tamis-LeMonda, C. (1992). Functional analysis of the contents of maternal speech to infants of 5 and 13 months in four cultures: Argentina, France, Japan, and the United States. *Developmental Psychology, 28,* 593–603.

Bornstein, M. H., Tal, J., and Tamis-LeMonda, C. S. (1991). Parenting in cross-cultural perspective: The United States, France, and Japan. In M. H. Bornstein (Ed.), *Cultural approaches to parenting* (pp. 69–90). Hillsdale, NJ: Lawrence Erlbaum Associates.

Boukydis, Z., and Burgess, R. (1982). Adult physiological response to infant cries: Effects of temperament of infant, parental status, and gender. *Child Development, 53,* 1291–1298.

Bowlby, J. (1969). *Attachment and loss: Vol. 1. Attachment.* London: Hogarth.

Bowlby, J. (1973). *Attachment and loss: Vol. 2. Separation: Anxiety and anger.* London: Hogarth.

Brazelton, T. B. (1973). Effect of maternal expectations on early infant behavior. *Early Child Development Care, 2,* 259–273.

Brazelton, T. B. (1977). Implications of infant development among Mayan Indians of Mexico. In P. H. Leiderman, S. R. Tulkin, and A. Rosenfeld (Eds.), *Culture and infancy: Variations in the human experience* (pp. 151–188). New York: Academic.

Bremner, J. D., Randall, P., Vermetten, E., Staib, L., Bronen, R. A., Mazure, C., Capelli, S., McCarthy, G., Innis, R. B., and Charney, D. S. (1997). Magnetic resonance imaging-based measurement of hippocampal volume in posttraumatic stress disorder related to childhood physical and sexual abuse—a preliminary report. *Biological Psychiatry, 41,* 23–32.

Bridges, R. S. (1990). Endocrine regulation of parental behavior in rodents. In N. A. Krasnegor and R. S. Bridges (Eds.), *Mammalian parenting: Biological, neurobiological, and behavioral determinants* (pp. 93–117). New York: Oxford University Press.

Bridges, R. S. (Ed.). (1990). *Mammalian parenting: Biochemical, neurobiological, and behavioral determinants* (pp. 260–280). New York: Oxford University Press.

Brophy-Herb, H. E., Gibbons, C., Omar, M. A., and Schiffman, R. F. (1999). Low-income fathers and their infants: Interactions during teaching episodes. *Infant Mental Health Journal, 20,* 305–321.

Brousseau, L., Malcuit, G., Pomerleau, A., and Feider, H. (1996). Relations between lexical–temporal features in mothers' speech and infants' interactive behaviours. *First Language, 16,* 41–59.

Brown, R. E. (1993). Hormonal and experiential factors influencing parental behaviour in male rodents: An integrative approach. *Behavioural processes, 23,* 89–102.

Brown, R. E., Murdoch, T., Murphy, P. R., and Moger, W. H. B. (1995). Hormonal responses of male gerbils to stimuli from their mate and pups. *Hormones and Behavior, 29,* 474–491.

Buchanan, A. (1998). Intergenerational child maltreatment. In Y. Danieli (Ed.), *International handbook of multigenerational legacies of trauma* (pp. 535–552). New York: Plenum.

Butterfield, P., Emde, R., Svejda, M., and Naiman, S. (1982). Silver nitrate and the eyes of the newborn: Effects on parental responsiveness during infant social interaction. In R. Emde and R. Harmon (Eds.), *The development of attachment and affiliative systems* (pp. 95–108). New York: Plenum.

Cacioppo, J. T., Berntson, G. G., Malarkey, W. B., Kiecolt-Glaser, J. K., Sheridan, J. F., Poehlmann, K. M., Burleson, M. H., Ernst, J. M., Hawkley, L. C., and Glaser, R. (1998). Autonomic, neuroendocrine, and immune responses to psychological stress: The reactivity hypothesis. *Annals of the New York Academy of Sciences, 840,* 664–673.

Carek, D. J., and Cappelli, A. J. (1981). Mothers' reactions to their newborn infants. *Journal of American Academy of Child Psychiatry, 20,* 16–31.

Caudill, W., and Weinstein, H. (1969). Maternal care and infant behavior in Japan and America. *Psychiatry, 32,* 12–43.

Collins, W. A., Maccoby, E. E., Steinberg, L., Hetherington, E. M., and Bornstein, M. (2000). Contemporary research on parenting. *American Psychologist, 55,* 171–173.

Corter, C., and Fleming, A. S. (1990). Maternal responsiveness in humans: Emotional, cognitive and biological factors. *Advances in the study of behavior, 19,* 83–136. New York: Academic.

Corter, C., and Minde, K. (1987). Impact of infant prematurity on family systems. In M. Wolraich (Ed.), *Advances in development and behavioral pediatrics* (Vol. 8, pp. 1–48). Greenwich, CT: Fawcett.

Corter, C., Trehub, S., Boukydis, C., Ford, L., Celhoffer, L., and Minde, K. (1978). Nurses' judgements of the attractiveness of premature infants. *Infant Behavior and Development, 1,* 373–380.

Cutrona, C. S. (1984). Social support and stress in the transition to parenthood. *Journal of Abnormal Psychology, 93,* 378–390.

Daly, M. (1990). Evolutionary theory and parental motives. In N. A. Krasnegor and R. S. Bridges (Eds.), *Mammalian parenting: Biochemical, neurobiological, and behavioral determinants* (pp. 25–39). New York: Oxford University Press.

Darne, J., McGarrigle, H., and Lachelin, G. (1987a). Increased saliva oestriol to progesterone ratio before idiopathic preterm delivery: A possible predictor for preterm labor? *British Medical Journal, 294,* 270–272.

Darne, J., McGarrigle, H., and Lachelin, G. (1987b). Saliva oestriol, oestradiol, oestrone and progesterone levels in pregnancy: Spontaneous labour at term is preceded by a rise in the saliva oestriol progesterone ratio. *British Journal of Obstetrics and Gynaecology, 94,* 227–235.

Dettling, A. C., Gunnar, M. R., and Donzella, B. (1999). Cortisol levels of young children in full-day childcare centers: Relations with age and temperament. *Psychoneuroendocrinology, 24,* 519–536.

Deutsch, F., Ruble, D. N., Fleming, A. S., Brooks-Gunn, J., and Stangor, C. (1986, April). *Becoming a mother: Information-seeking and self-definitional processes.* Paper presented at the annual meeting of the Eastern Psychological Association, New York.

Devore, I., and Konner, M. (1974). Infancy in a hunter–gatherer life: An ethological perspective. In N. White (Ed.), *Ethology and psychiatry.* Toronto: University of Toronto Press.

Donate-Bartfield, E., and Passman, R. (1985). Attentiveness of mothers and fathers to their babys' cries. *Infant Behavior and Development, 8,* 383–393.

Donovan, W. L., and Leavitt, L. A. (1985). Physiologic assessment of mother-infant attachment. *Journal of the American Academy of Child Psychiatry, 24,* 65–70.

Donovan, W. L., Leavitt, L. A., and Walsh, R. O. (1997). Cognitive set and coping strategy affect mothers' sensitivity to infant cries: A signal detection approach. *Child Development, 68,* 760–772.

Donovan, W. L., Leavitt, L. A., and Walsh, R. O. (1998). Conflict and depression predict maternal sensitivity to infant cries. *Infant Behavior and Development, 21,* 505–517.

Dunn, A. J. (1984). Effects of A.C.T.H. B-lipoprotein and related peptides on the central nervous system. In C. B. Nermeroff and A. J. Dunn (Eds.), *Peptides, hormones and behavior* (pp. 273–348). New York: Medical Science Books.

Eckerman, C. O., Oehler, J. M., Hannan, T. E., and Molitor, A. (1993, March). *Developmental emergence of social responsiveness in very-prematurely-born newborns*. Paper presented at the biennial meeting of the Society for Research in Child Development, New Orleans, LA.

Eisenberg, L. (1990). The biosocial context of parenting in human families. In N. A. Krasnegor and R. S. Bridges (Eds.), *Mammalian parenting: Biochemical, neurobiological, and behavioral determinants* (pp. 9–24). New York: Oxford University Press.

Elwood, R. W. (1986). What makes male mice parental? *Behavioral and Neural Biology, 46*, 54–63.

Elwood, R. W., and Mason, C. (1994). The couvade and the onset of paternal care: A biological perspective. *Ethological Sociobiology, 15*, 145–156.

Feldman, R., Weller, A., Leckman, J., Kuint, J., and Eidelman, A. (1999). The nature of the mother's tie to her infant: Maternal bonding under conditions of proximity, separation and potential loss. *Journal of Child Psychology and Psychiatry, 40*, 929–939.

Feldman, S. S., and Nash, S. C. (1978). Interest in babies during young adulthood. *Child Development, 49*, 617–622.

Fernald, A. (1992). Meaningful melodies in mothers' speech to infants. In H. Papoušek, V. J., Jürgens, and M. Papoušek (Eds.), *Nonverbal vocal communication: Comparative and developmental approaches* (pp. 262–282). Cambridge, England: Cambridge University Press.

Fernald, A., and Morikawa, H. (1993). Common themes and cultural variations in Japanese and American mothers' speech to infants. *Child Development, 64*, 637–656.

Field, T. (1980). Interactions of preterm and term infants with their lower and middle-class teenage and adult mothers. In T. Field, S. Goldberg, D. Stern, and A. Sostek (Eds.), *High-risk infants and children* (pp. 113–132). New York: Academic.

Field, T. (1984). Early interactions between infants and their postpartum depressed mother. *Infant Behavior and Development, 7*, 517–522.

Field, T., Sandberg, D., Garcia, R., Vega-Lahr, N., Goldstein, S., and Guy, L. (1985). Pregnancy problems, postpartum depression and early mother-infant interactions. *Developmental Psychology, 21*, 1152–1156.

Fischer, S., and Gillman, I. (1991). Surrogate motherhood: Attachment, attitudes and social support. *Psychiatry, 54*, 13–20.

Fleming, A. S. (1990). Hormonal and experiential correlates of maternal responsiveness in human mothers. In N. A. Krasnegor and R. S. Bridges (Eds.), *Mammalian parenting: Biochemical, neurobiological, and behavioral determinants* (pp. 184–208). New York: Oxford University Press.

Fleming, A. S., and Corter, C. (1988). Factors influencing maternal responsiveness in humans: Usefulness of an animal model. *Psychoneuroendocrinology, 13*, 189–212.

Fleming, A. S., and Corter, C. (1995). Psychobiology of maternal behavior in nonhuman mammals. In M. H. Bornstein (Ed.), *Handbook of parenting: Vol. 2. Biology and ecology of parenting* (pp. 59–85). Mahwah, New Jersey: Lawrence Erlbaum Associates.

Fleming, A. S., Corter, C., Franks, P., Surbey, M., Schneider, B. A., and Steiner, M. (1993). Postpartum factors related to mother's attraction to newborn infant odors. *Developmental Psychobiology, 26*, 115–132.

Fleming, A. S., Corter, C., Stallings, J., and Steiner, M. (In preparation). Testosterone and prolactin are associated with emotional responses to infant cues in new fathers.

Fleming, A. S., Corter, C., Surbey, M., Franks, P., and Steiner, M. (1995). Postpartum factors related to mother's recognition of newborn infant odors. *Journal of Reproductive and Infant Psychology, 13*, 197–210.

Fleming, A. S., Morgan, H. D., and Walsh, C. (1996). Experiential factors in postpartum regulation of maternal care. *Advances in the Study of Behavior, 25*, 295–332.

Fleming, A. S., O'Day, D., and Kraemer, G. W. (1999). Neurobiology of mother–infant interactions: experience and central nervous system plasticity across development and generations. *Neuroscience and Biobehavioral Reviews, 23*, 673–685.

Fleming, A. S., Ruble, D. N., Flett, G. L., and Shaul, D. (1988). Postpartum adjustment in first-time mothers: Relations between mood, maternal attitude, and mother-infant interactions. *Development Psychology, 24*, 71–81.

Fleming, A. S., Ruble, D. N., Flett, G. L., and Van Wagner, V. (1990). Postpartum adjustment in first-time mothers: Changes in mood and mood content during the early postpartum months. *Developmental Psychology, 26*, 137–143.

Fleming, A. S., Ruble, D., Krieger, H., and Wong, P. Y. (1997). Hormonal and experiential correlates of maternal responsiveness during pregnancy and the puerperium in human mothers. *Hormones and Behavior, 31*, 145–158.

Fleming, A. S., Steiner, M., and Anderson, V. (1987). Hormonal and attitudinal correlates of maternal behavior during the early postpartum period. *Journal of Reproductive and Infant Psychology, 5*, 193–205.

Fleming, A. S., Steiner, M., and Corter, C. (1997). Cortisol, hedonics, and maternal responsiveness in human mothers. *Hormones and Behavior, 32*, 85–98.

Fleming, A. S., Steiner, M., and Corter, C. (In preparation). Hormonal correlates of parental responsiveness.

Formby, D. (1967). Maternal recognition of infant's cry. *Developmental Medicine and Child Neurology, 9*, 293–298.

Fraiberg, S. (1975). The development of human attachments in infants blind from birth. *Merrill-Palmer Quarterly, 21*, 315–334.

Francis, D. D., Champagne, F. A., Liu, D., and Meaney, M. J. (1999). Maternal care, gene expression, and the development of individual differences in stress reactivity. *Annals of the New York Academy of Sciences*. Socioeconomic status and health in industrial nations: Social, psychological, and biological pathways, *896*, 66–84.

Frodi, A. M., and Lamb, M. E. (1978). Sex differences in responsiveness to infants: A developmental study of psychophysiological and behavioral responses. *Child Development, 49*, 1182–1188.

Frodi, A. M., and Lamb, M. E. (1980). Child abusers' responses to infant smiles and cries. *Child Development, 51*, 238–241.

Frodi, A. M., Lamb, M. E., Leavitt, L., Donovan, W. L., Neff, C., and Sherry, D. (1978). Fathers' and mothers' responses to the faces and cries of normal and premature infants. *Developmental Psychology, 14*, 490–498.

Furedy, J., Fleming, A. S., Ruble, D., Scher, H., Daly, J., Day, D., and Loewen, R. (1989). Sex differences in small-magnitude heart-rate program to sex use and input related stimuli: A psychophysiological approach. *Physiology and Behavior, 46*, 903–905.

Gaffney, K. F. (1989). Maternal–fetal attachment in relation to self-concept and anxiety. *Maternal–Child Nursing Journal, 15*, 91–101.

Gaily, E., Kantola-Sorsa, E., and Granstrom, M. (1990). Specific cognitive dysfunction in children with epileptic mothers. *Developmental Medicine and Child Neurology, 32*, 403–414.

Gaulin-Kremer, E., Shaw, J. L., and Thoman, E. B. (1977, March). *Mother–infant interaction at first prolonged encounter. Effects of variation in delay after delivery.* Paper presented at the meeting of the Society for Research in Child Develop-2 ment, New Orleans, LA.

Gennaro, S., and Fehder, W. (2000). Health behaviors in postpartum women. *Family and Community Health, 22*, 16–26.

Gibson, F., Ungerer, J. A., McMahon, C. A., Leslie, G. I., and Saunders, D. M. (2000). The mother–child relationship following in vitro fertilisation (IVF): Infant attachment, responsivity, and maternal sensitivity. *Journal of Child Psychology and Psychiatry and Allied Disciplines, 41*, 1015–1023.

Goldberg, S. (1983). Parent–infant bonding: Another look. *Child Development, 54*, 1355–1382.

Goodspeed, R. B., Gent, J. F., Catalanotto, F. I., Cain, W. S., and Zagraniski, R. T. (1986). Corticosteriods in olfactory dysfunction. In H. L. Meiselman and R. S. Rivlin (Eds.), *Clinical measurement of taste and smell* (pp. 514–518). New York: Macmillan.

Green, J., and Kafetsios, K. (1997). Positive experiences of early motherhood: Predictive variables from a longitudinal study. *Journal of Reproductive and Infant Psychology, 15*, 141–157.

Greenberg, M., and Morris, N. (1974). Engrossment: The newborn's impact upon the father. *American Journal of Orthopsychiatry, 44*, 520–531.

Grossman, F. K., Eichler, L. S., Winickoff, S. A., Anzalone, M. K., Gofseyeff, M. H., and Sargent, S. P. (1980). *Pregnancy, birth, and parenthood.* San Francisco: Jossey-Bass.

Grossman, K., Thane, K., and Grossman, K. (1981). Maternal tactual contact of the newborn after various conditions of mother–infant contact. *Developmental Psychology, 17*, 158–169.

Grosvenor, C. E., and Mena, F. (1992). Regulation of prolactin transformation in the rat pituitary. *CIBA Foundation Symposium, 168*, 69–80.

Gubernick, D., and Alberts, J. (1989). Postpartum maintenance of paternal behaviour in the biparental California mouse, *Peromyscus californicus. Animal Behaviour, 37*, 656–664.

Gubernick, D. J., and Nelson, R. J. (1989). Prolactin and paternal behavior in the biparental California mouse, *Peromyscus californicus. Hormones and Behavior, 23*, 203–210.

Gubernick, D., Schneider, K. A., and Jeannotte, L. A. (1994). Individual differences in the mechanism underlying the onset and maintenance of paternal behavior and the inhibition of infanticide in the monogamous biparental California mouse, *Peromyscus californicus. Animal Behavior, 46*, 539–546.

Gubernick, D., Worthman, C., and Stallings, J. (In preparation). Hormonal correlates of fatherhood in men: A preliminary study.

Gustafson, G., and Harris, K. (1990). Women's responses to young infants' cries. *Developmental Psychology, 26*, 144–152.

Hahn, C., and DiPietro, J. A. (2001). In vitro fertilization and the family: Quality of parenting, family functioning, and child psychosocial adjustment. *Developmental Psychology, 37*, 37–48.

Handley, S. L., Dunn, T. L., Baker, S. M., Cockshott, C., and Goulds, S. (1977). Mood changes in the puerperium and plasma tryptophan and cortisol. *British Medical Journal, 2*, 18–22.

Handley, S. L., Dunn, T. L., Waldron, G., and Baker, J. M. (1980). Tryptophan, cortisol and puerperal mood. *British Journal of Psychiatry, 136*, 498–508.

Hart, J., Gunnar, M., and Cicchetti, D. (1996). Altered neuroendocrine activity in maltreated children related to symptoms of depression. *Developmental Psychopathology, 8*, 210–214.

Henken, R. I. (1975). The role of adrenal corticosteroids in sensory processes. In H. Blaschko, G. Savers, and A. D. Smith (Eds.), *The handbook of physiological endocrinology* (Vol. 6, pp. 209–230). Baltimore: Williams and Wilkins.

Henry, J. P., and Wang, S. (1998). Effects of Early Stress on Adult Affiliative Behavior. *Psychoneuroendocrinology, 23*, 863–875.

Hertsgaard, L., Gunnar, M. R., Erickson, M. F., and Nachmias, M. (1995). Adrenocortical responses to the strange situation in infants with disorganized/disoriented attachment relationships. *Child Development, 66,* 1100–1106.

Hildebrandt, K., and Fitzgerald, H. (1983). Mothers' responses to infant physical appearance. *Infant Mental Health Journal, 2,* 56–61.

Hinde, R. A. (1984). Biological bases of the mother–child relationship. In J. Call, E. Galenson, and R. Tyson (Eds.), *Frontiers of infant psychiatry* (Vol. 2, pp. 284–294). New York: Basic Books.

Hinde, R. A., and Stevenson-Hinde, J. (1990). Attachment : Biological, cultural, and individual desiderata. *Human Development, 33,* 62–72.

Hofer, M. A. (1995). An evolutionary perspective on anxiety. In S. P. Rose and R. A. Glick (Eds.), *Anxiety as a symptom and a signal* (pp. 17–38). Hillsdale, NJ: Analytic Press.

Hoffman, M. (1975). Developmental synthesis of affect and cognition and its implications for altruistic motivation. *Developmental Psychology, 11,* 607–622.

Hopkins, J., Marcus, M., and Campbell, S. B. (1984). Postpartum depression: A critical review. *Psychological Bulletin, 95,* 498–515.

Insel, T. R. (1990). Oxytocin and maternal behavior. In N. A. Krasnegor and R. S. Bridges (Eds.), *Mammalian parenting: Biochemical, neurobiological, and behavioral determinants* (pp. 260–280). New York, Oxford University Press.

Insel, T. R. (1997). A neurobiological basis of social attachment. *American Journal of Psychiatry, 154,* 726–735.

Ito, Y., Teicher, M. H., Glod, C. A., and Ackerman, E. (1998). Preliminary evidence for aberrant cortical development in abused children: A quantitative EEG study. *Journal of Neuropsychiatry and Clinical Neuroscience, 10,* 298–307.

James, M. E., and Coles, C. D. (1991). Cocaine abuse during pregnancy: Psychiatric considerations. *General Hospital Psychiatry, 13,* 399–409.

Jeremy, R. J., Jeruschiamowicz, R., and Bernstein, V. J. (1984). Dyads at risk: Methadone-maintained women and their four-month-old infants. *Child Development, 55,* 1141–1154.

Jones, F. A., Green, V., and Krauss, D. R. (1980). Maternal responsiveness of primiparous mothers during the postpartum period: Age differences. *Pediatrics, 65,* 579–584.

Jones, J. S., and Wynne-Edwards, K. E. (2000). Paternal hamsters mechanically assist the delivery, consume amniotic fluid and placenta, remove fetal membranes, and provide parental care during the birth process. *Hormones and Behavior, 37,* 116–125.

Jones, J. S., and Wynne-Edwards, K. E. (in press). Midwifery by males in a naturally biparental hamster. *Animal Behavior.*

Jones, L. C., and Thomas, S. A. (1989). New father's blood pressure and heart rate: Relationships to interaction with their newborn infants. *Nursing Research, 38,* 237–241.

Kaitz, M., Chriki, M., Bear-Scharf, L., Nir, T., and Eidelman, A. I. (2000). Effectiveness of primiparae and multiparae at soothing their newborn infants. *The Journal of Genetic Psychology, 161,* 203–215.

Kaitz, M., Good, A., Rokem, A. M., and Eidelman, A. I. (1987). Mother's recognition of their infants by olfactory cues. *Developmental Psychobiology, 20,* 587–591.

Kaitz, M., Lapidot, P., Bronner, R., and Eidelman, A. (1992). Parturient women can recognize their infants by touch. *Developmental Psychology, 28,* 35–39.

Kandel, D. B., and Udry, J. R. (1999). Prenatal effects of maternal smoking on daughter's smoking: Nicotine or testosterone exposure? *American Journal of Public Health, 89,* 1377–1383.

Keller, W., Hildebrandt, K., and Richards, M. (1985). Effects of extended father–infant contact during the newborn period. *Infant Behavior and Development, 8,* 337–350.

Kennell, J. H., and McGrath, S. (1993, March). *Effects of environment on perinatal behavior: Perinatal effects of labor support.* Paper presented at the meeting of the Society for Research in Child Development, New Orleans, LA.

Keverne, E. B., and Kendrick, K. M. (1990). Neurochemical changes accompanying parturition and their significance for maternal behavior. In N. A. Krasnegor and R. S. Bridges (Eds.), *Mammalian parenting: Biochemical, neurobiological, and behavioral determinants* (pp. 281–304). New York: Oxford University Press.

Kirschbaum, C., Wust, S., and Hellhammer, D. (1992). Consistent sex differences in cortisol responses to psychological stress. *Psychosomatic Medicine, 54,* 648–657.

Klaus, M. H., and Kennell, J. H. (1976). *Maternal–infant bonding.* St. Louis, MO: Mosby.

Klaus, M. H., Kennell, J. H., Plumb, N., and Zuehkle, S. (1970). Human maternal behavior on first contact with her young. *Pediatrics, 46,* 187–192.

Klaus, M. H., Trause, M., and Kennell, J. H. (1975). *Does human maternal behavior after birth show a characteristic pattern? Parent–infant interaction.* (CIBA Foundation, Symposium, No. 33, pp. 69–85). Amsterdam: Elsevier.

Klopfer, P. H., Adams, D. K., and Klopfer, M. S. (1964). Maternal imprinting in goats. *Proceedings of the National Academy of Sciences, U.S.A., 52,* 911–914.

Konner, M. (1977). Infancy among the Kalahari Desert San. In P. H. Leiderman, S. R. Tulkin, and A. Rosenfeld (Eds.), *Culture and infancy: Variations in human experience* (pp. 287–328). New York: Academic.

Korner, A., and Thoman, E. (1970). Visual alertness in neonates as evoked by maternal care. *Journal of Experimental Child Psychology, 10,* 67–68.

Lamb, M. (1982). Early contact and mother–infant bonding: One decade later. *Pediatrics, 70,* 763–768.

Larson, M. C., Gunnar, M. R., and Hertsgaard, L. (1991). The effects of morning naps, car trips, and maternal separation on adrenocortical activity in human infants. *Child Development, 62*, 362–372.

Leavitt, L. A., and Donovan, W. L. (1979). Perceived infant temperament, locus of control, and maternal physiological response to infant gaze. *Journal of Research in Personality, 13*, 276–278.

Lederman, R. P. (1984). *Psychosocial adaptation in pregnancy.* Englewood Cliffs, NJ: Prentice-Hall.

Leiderman, P., and Leiderman, M. (1977). Economic change and infant care in an East African agricultural community. In P. H. Leiderman, S. R. Tulkin, and A. Rosenfeld (Eds.), *Culture and infancy: Variations in human experience.* New York: Academic.

Leifer, M. (1977). Psychological changes accompanying pregnancy and motherhood. *Genetic Psychological Monographs, 95*, 55–96.

Leifer, M. (1980). *Psychological effects of motherhood: A study of first pregnancy.* New York: Praeger.

Leon, M., Croskerry, P. G., and Smith, G. K. (1978). Thermal control of mother–young contact in rats. *Physiology and Behavior, 21*, 793–811.

Lester, B. M., Boukydis, C. F. Z., Garcia-Coll, C. T., Hole, W., and Peucker, M. (1992). Infant colic: Acoustic cry characteristics, maternal perception of cry and temperament. *Infant Behavior and Development, 15*, 15–26.

Levine, S., and Stanton, M. (1990). The hormonal consequences of mother–infant contact. In K. Barnard and T. B. Brazelton (Eds.), *Touch: The foundation of experience* (pp. 165–194). Madison, CT: International Universities Press.

Levine, S., Wiener, S., Coe, C., Bayart, F., and Hayashi, K. (1987). Primate vocalization: A psychobiological approach. *Child Development, 58*, 1408–1419.

Lorberbaum, J. P., Newman, J. D., Dubno, J. R., Horwitz, A. R., Nahas, Z., Teneback, C., Johnson, M. R., Lydiard, R. B., Ballenger, J. C., and George, M. S. (1999). *Feasibility of using fMRI to study mothers responding to infant cries.* [On-line]. Available: http://www.musc.edu/psychiatry/fnrd/babycry.htm.

Lorenz, K. (1943). Die angeborenen Formen moglicher Erfahrung [Innate forms of practical experience]. *Zeitschrift für Tierpsychologie, 5*, 243–409.

MacDonald, K. (1992). Warmth as a developmental construct: An evolutionary analysis. *Child Development, 63*, 753–773.

MacLean, P. (1990). *The triune brain in evolution: Role in paleocerebral functions.* New York: Plenum.

Maier, R., Holmes, D., Slaymaker, F., and Reich, J. (1984). The perceived attractiveness of preterm infants. *Infant Behavior and Development, 7*, 403–414.

Martin, G., and Clark, R. (1982). Distress crying in neonates: Species and peer specificity. *Developmental Psychology, 18*, 3–9.

Maynard Smith, J. (1977). Parental investment: A prospective analysis. *Animal Behaviour, 25*, 1–9.

McEwen, B. S., de Kloet, E. R., and Rostene, W. (1986). Adrenal steroid receptors and actions in the nervous system. *Physiological Review, 66*, 1121–1188.

Mcnamara, J. M., Szekely, T., Webb, J. N., and Houston, A. I. (2000). A dynamic game-theoretic model of parental care. *Journal of Theoretical Biology, 205*, 605–623.

Messer, D., and Vietz, P. (1984). Timing and transitions in mother–infant gaze. *Infant Behavior and Development, 7*, 167–181.

Misri, S., Sinclair, D. A., and Kuan, A. J. (1997). Breast-feeding and postpartum depression: Is there a relationship? *Canadian Journal of Psychiatry, 42*, 1061–1065.

Moss, H. (1967). Sex, age and state as determinants of mother–infant interaction. *Merrill-Palmer Quarterly, 128*, 19–36.

Moss, H. A., and Jones, S. J. (1977). Relations between maternal attitudes and maternal behavior as a function of social class. In P. H. Leiderman, S. R. Tulkin, and A. Rosenfeld (Eds.), *Culture and infancy* (pp. 439–468). New York: Academic.

Mota, M. T., and Sousa, M. B. C. (2000). Prolactin levels of fathers and helpers related to alloparental care in common marmosets, *Callithrix jacchus. Folia Primatologica, 71*, 22–26.

Muller, E., Hollien, H., and Murry, T. (1974). Perceptual response to infant crying: Identification of cry types. *Journal of Child Language, 1*, 175–179.

Murray, A. (1979). Infant-crying as an elicitor of parental behavior. An examination of two models. *Psychological Bulletin, 86*, 191–215.

Murray, A. (1985). Aversiveness is in the mind of the beholder: Perception of infant crying by adults. In B. Lester and C. Boukydis (Eds.), *Infant crying* (pp. 217–240). New York: Plenum.

Newman, J. (1985). The infant cry of primates: An evolutionary perspective. In B. Lester and C. Boukydis (Eds.), *Infant crying* (pp. 307–324). New York: Plenum.

Newnham, J. P., Dennett, P. M., Ferron, S. A., Tomlin, S., Legg, C., Bourne, G. L., and Rees, L. H. (1984). A study of the relationship between circulating E-endorphin-like immunoreactivity and postpartum "blues." *Clinical Endocrinology, 20*, 169–177.

Newton, N., and Newton, M. (1962). Mothers' reactions to their newborn babies. *Journal of the American Medical Association, 181*, 206–210.

Nott, P. N., Franklin, M., Armitage, C., and Gelder, M. (1976). Hormonal changes and mood in the puerperium. *British Journal of Psychiatry, 128*, 379–383.

O'Hara, M. W., Schlechte, J. A., Lewis, D. A., and Wright, E. J. (1991). Prospective study of postpartum blues: Biological and psychosocial factors. *Archives of General Psychiatry, 48*, 801–806.

Orpen, B. G., and Fleming, A. S. (1987). Experience with pups sustains maternal responding in postpartum rats. *Physiology and Behavior, 40,* 47–54.

Palkovitz, R. (1985). Fathers' birth attendance, early contact, and extended contact with their newborns: A critical review. *Child Development, 56,* 392–406.

Panksepp, J. (1986). The psychobiology of prosocial behaviors: Separation distress, play, and altruism. In C. Zahn-Waxler, E. Cummings, and R. Ianotti (Eds.), *Altruism and aggression* (pp. 19–57). Cambridge, England: Cambridge University Press.

Panksepp, J. (1989). The psychobiology of the emotions. In H. Wagner and A. Manstead (Eds.), *Handbook of social psychophysiology* (pp. 5–26). Chichester, England: Wiley.

Papoušek, M., Papoušek, H., and Symmes, D. (1991). The meanings of melodies in motherese in tone and stress languages. *Infant Behavior and Development, 14,* 415–440.

Papoušek, M., and von Hofacker, N. (1998). Persistent crying in early infancy: A non-trivial condition of risk for the developing mother–infant relationship. *Child: Care, Health, and Development, 24,* 395–424.

Parke, R. D. (1978). Parent–infant interaction: Progress, paradigms, and problems. In G. Sackett (Ed.), *Observing behavior: Vol. 1. Theory and applications in mental retardation* (pp. 69–94). Baltimore: University Park Press.

Parke, R. D., and Sawin, D. (1975, March). *Infant characteristics and behavior as elicitors of maternal and paternal responsivity in the newborn period.* Paper presented at the meeting of the Society for Research in Child Development, Denver, CO.

Parke, R. D., and Sawin, D. (1977, March). *The family in early infancy: Social interactional and attitudinal analyses.* Paper presented at the meeting of the Society for Research in Child Development, New Orleans, LA.

Pitt, B. (1968). "Atypical" depression following childbirth. *British Journal of Psychiatry, 114,* 1325–1335.

Porter, R. H., Cernoch, J. M., and Balogh, R. D. (1985). Odor signatures and kin recognition. *Physiology and Behavior, 34,* 445–448.

Porter, R. H., Cernoch, J. M., and McLaughlin, F. (1983). Maternal recognition of neonates through olfactory cues. *Physiology and Behavior, 30,* 151–154.

Porter, R., and Winberg, J. (1999). Unique salience of maternal breast odors for newborn infants. *Neuroscience and Biobehavioral Reviews, 23,* 439–449.

Pryce, C. R. (1993). The regulation of maternal behavior in marmosets and tamarins. *Behavioural Processes, 30,* 201–224.

Pryce, C. R. (1995). Determinants of motherhood in human and non-human primates: A biosocial model. In C. R. Pryce, R. D. Martin, and D. Skuses (Eds.), *Motherhood in human and nonhuman primates—Biosocial determinants.* Basle, Switzerland: Karger.

Pryce, C. R., Martin, R. D., and Skuse, D. (Eds.). (1995). *Motherhood in human and nonhuman primates: Biosocial determinants* (Vol. 8). Basle, Switzerland: Karger.

Rebelsky, F. G. (1967, June). Infancy in two cultures. *Netherlands Tijdschrift voor de Psychologie en Haar Grensgebieden,* 379–385.

Reburn, C. J., and Wynne-Edwards, K. (1999). Hormonal changes in males of a naturally biparental and a uniparental mammal. *Hormones and Behavior, 35,* 163–176.

Rheingold, H. L. (1969). The social and socializing infant. In D. Goslin (Ed.), *Handbook of socialization theory and research* (pp. 779–790). Chicago: Rand McNally.

Robson, K. S. (1967). The role of eye-to-eye contact in maternal–infant attachment. *Journal of Child Psychology and Psychiatry, 87,* 13–25.

Robson, K. S., and Kumar, R. (1980). Delayed onset of maternal affection after childbirth. *British Journal of Psychiatry, 136,* 347–353.

Robson, K. S., and Moss, H. A. (1970). Patterns and determinants of maternal attachment. *Journal of Pediatrics, 77,* 976–985.

Rodning, C., Beckwith, L., and Howard, J. (1991). Quality of attachment and home environments in children prenatally exposed to PCP and cocaine. *Development and Psychopathology, 3,* 351–366.

Rosenblatt, J. S. (1990). Landmarks in the physiological study of maternal behavior with special reference to the rat. In N. A. Krasnegor and R. S. Bridges (Eds.), *Mammalian parenting: Biochemical, neurobiological and behavioral determinants* (pp. 40–60). New York: Oxford University Press.

Rosenblatt, J. S., Olufowobi, A., and Siegel, H. I. (1998). Effects of pregnancy hormones on maternal responsiveness, responsiveness to estrogen stimulation of maternal behavior, and the lordosis response to estrogen stimulation. *Hormones and Behavior, 33,* 104–114.

Rosenblatt, J. S., and Snowdon, C. S. (1996). Parental care: Evolution, mechanisms, and adaptive significance. *Advances in the Study of Behavior, 25,* 317–362. New York Academic.

Russell, M. J., Mendelson, T., and Peeke, H. V. (1983). Mothers' identification of their infants' odors. *Ethology and Sociobiology, 4,* 29–41.

Sagi, A. (1981). Mothers' and non-mothers' identification of infant cries. *Infant Behavior and Development, 41,* 37–40.

Scanlon-Jones, S. (1984). Adult recipients of infant communications: A sex difference in the salience of early "social" smiling. *Infant Behavior and Development, 7,* 211–221.

Schaal, B. (1986). Presumed olfactory exchanges between mother and neonate in humans. In J. LeCamus and R. Campon (Eds.), *Ethologie et psychologie de l'enfant* [Infant ethology and psychology]. Toulouse, France: Privat.

Schaal, B., Montagner, H., Hertling, E., Bolzoni, D., Moyse, A., and Quichon, R. (1980). Les stimulations olfactives dans les relations entre l'enfant et la mére [Olfactory stimuli in the infant-mother relationship]. *Reproduction, Nurturance and Development, 20*, 843–858.

Schaal, B., and Porter, R. H. (1991). "Microsmatic humans" revisited: The generation and perception of chemical signals. *Advances in the Study of Behavior, 20*, 135–199.

Schiefenhovel, V. G., and Schiefenhovel, W. (1975). *Vorgange bei der Geburt eines Madchens und Anderung der Infantizid-Absicht* [Occurrences during the birth of a girl and modification of intentions of infanticide]. Human Etrologischer Filmarchiv der Max-Planck-Gesellschaft [Human Ethology Film Archive of the Max-Planck-Institute].

Seashore, M., Liefer, A., Barnett, C., and Leiderman, P. (1973). The effects of denial of early mother-infant interactions on maternal self-confidence. *Journal of Personality and Social Psychology, 26*, 369–378.

Smith, R., Cubis, J., Brinsmead, T. L., Singh, B., Owens, P., Chan, E., Hall, C., Adler, R., Lovelock, M., Hurt, D., Rowley, M., and Nolan, M. (1990). Mood changes, obstetric experience and alterations in plasma cortisol, beta-endorphin and corticotrophin releasing hormone during pregnancy and the puerperium. *Journal of Psychosomatic Research, 34*, 53–69.

Smyth, J., Ockenfels, M. C., Porter, L., Kirschbaum, C., Hellhammer, D. H., and Stone, A. A. (1998). Stressors and mood measured on a momentary basis are associated with salivary cortisol secretion. *Psychoneuroendocrinology, 23*, 353–370.

Sosa, R., Kennell, J., Klaus, M., Robertson, S., and Urrutia, J. (1980). The effect of a supportive companion on perinatal problems, length of labor, and mother–infant interaction. *New England Journal of Medicine, 303*, 597–600.

Stack, K., and Muir, D. (1992). Adult tactile stimulation during face-to-face interaction modulates five-month-old's affect and attention. *Child Development, 63*, 1509–1525.

Stallings, J., Fleming, A. S., Corter, C., Worthman, C., and Steiner, M. (2001). The effects of infant cries and odors on sympathy, cortisol, and autonomic responses in new mothers and nonpostpartum women. *Parenting: Science and Practice, 1*, 71–100.

Stansbury, K., and Gunnar, M. R. (1994). Adrenocortical activity and emotion regulation. *Monographs of the Society for Research in Child Development, 59* (2–3), 108–134, 250–283.

Stein, A., Gath, D. H., Bucher, J., Bond, A., Day, A., and Cooper, P. J. (1991). The relationship between post-natal depression and mother–child interaction. *British Journal of Psychiatry, 158*, 46–52.

Steiner, M. (1992). Female specific mood disorders. *Clinical Obstetrics and Gynecology, 35*, 594–611.

Steiner, M., Fleming, A. S., Anderson, V., Monkhouse, E., and Boulter, G. E. (1986). A psychoneuroendocrine profile for postpartum blues? In L. Dennerstein and J. Fraser (Eds.), *Hormones and behavior* (pp. 327–335). Amsterdam: Elsevier.

Stein, G. (1982). The maternity blues. In I. F. Brockington and R. Kumar (Eds.), *Motherhood and mental illness* (pp. 119–154). London: Academic.

Stern, D. (1974). Mother and infant at play: The dyadic interaction involving facial, vocal, and gaze behaviors. In M. Lewis and L. Rosenblum (Eds.), *The effects of the infant on its caregiver* (pp. 187–214). New York: Wiley.

Stern, J. M., Goldman, L., and Levine, S. (1973). Pituitary–adrenal responsiveness during lactation in rats. *Neuroendocrinology, 12*, 179–191.

Stern, J. M., and Levine, S. (1974). Psychobiological aspects of lactation in rats. In D. F. Swabb and J. P. Schade (Eds.), *Integrative hypothalamic activity: Progress in brain research* (Vol. 41, pp. 20–29). Amsterdam: Elsevier.

Storey, A. E., Bradbury, C. G., and Joyce, T. L. (1994). Nest attendance in male meadow voles: The role of the female in regulating male interactions with pups. *Animal Behaviour, 47*, 1037–1046.

Storey, A. E., and Joyce, T. L. (1995). Pup contact promotes paternal responsiveness in male meadow voles. *Animal Behaviour, 49*, 1–10.

Storey, A. E., and Walsh, C. J. (1994). Are chemical cues as effective as pup contact for inducing paternal behaviour in meadow voles? *Behaviour, 131*, 139–151.

Storey, A. E., Walsh, C. J., Quinton, R. L., and Wynne-Edwards, K. E. (2000). Hormonal correlates of paternal responsiveness in new and expectant fathers. *Evolution and Human Behavior, 21*, 79–95.

Thoman, E. B., Barnett, C. R., and Leiderman, P. H. (1971). Feeding behaviors of newborn infants as a function of parity of the mother. *Child Development, 42*, 1471–1483.

Thoman, E. B., Conner, R. L., and Levine, S. (1970). Lactation suppresses adrenal corticosteroid activity and aggressiveness in rats. *Journal of Comparative and Physiological Psychology, 70*, 364–369.

Thoman, E. B., Turner, A. M., Leiderman, H., and Barnett, C. R. (1970). Neonate–mother interactions: Effects of parity on feeding behavior. *Child Development, 41*, 1103–1111.

Thompson, E. T., Walker, L. O., and Crain, H. C. (1981). *Effects of parity and time on maternal attitudes in the neonatal period*. Unpublished manuscript, University of Texas at Austin.

Trehub, S., Unyk, A., and Trainor, L. J. (1993). Maternal singing in cross-cultural perspective. *Infant Behavior and Development, 16*, 285–295.

Trevarthen, C. (1985). Facial expressions of emotion in mother–infant interaction. *Human Neurobiology, 4*, 21–37.

Trevathan, W. R. (1981). Maternal touch at first contact with the newborn infant. *Developmental Psychobiology, 14*, 549–558.

Trevathan, W. R. (1983). Maternal "en face" orientation during the first hours after birth. *American Journal of Orthopsychiatry, 53*, 92–99.

Trevathan, W. R. (1987). *Human birth*. New York: Aldine de Gruyter.

Tronick, E. Z. (1987, March). *An interdisciplinary view of human intuitive parenting behaviors and their role in interactions with infants.* Paper presented at the meeting of the Society for Research in Child Development, Baltimore.

Tronick, E. Z., Morelli, G. A., and Ivey, P. K. (1992). The Efe forager infant and toddler's pattern of social relationships: Multiple and simultaneous. *Developmental Psychology, 28,* 568–577.

Turnbull, A. C., Flint, A. P. F., Jeremy, J. Y., Patten, P. T., Keirse, M., and Anderson, A. B. (1974). Significant fall in progesterone and rise in estradiol levels in human peripheral plasma before onset of labour. *Lancet, 101,* 101–104.

Valanne, E., Vuorenkowski, V., Partanen, T., Lind, J., and Wasz-Hockert, O. (1967). The ability of human mothers to identify the hunger cry signals of their own new-born infants during the lying-in period. *Experientia, 23,* 768–769.

Wakerley, J. B. Clarke, G., and Summerlee, A. J. S. (1994). Milk ejection and its control. In E. Knobil and J. Neill (Eds.), *The physiology of reproduction* (2nd ed., pp. 2283–2321). New York: Raven.

Wang, Z. X., Liu, Y., Young, L. J., and Insel, T. R. (2000). Hypothalamic vasopressin gene expression increases in both males and females postpartum in a biparental rodent. *Journal of Neuroendocrinology, 12,* 111–120.

Wang, S. (1997). Traumatic stress and attachment. *Acta Physiologica Scandinavica, 161,* 164–169.

Wasz-Hockert, O., Partanen, T., Vuorenkowski, V., Michelsson, K., and Valanne, E. (1964). Effect of training on ability to identify preverbal vocalizations. *Developmental Medicine and Child Neurology. 6,* 397–402.

Webb, J. N., Houston, A. I., McNamara, J. M., and Szekely, T. (1999). Multiple patterns of parental care. *Animal Behaviour, 58,* 983–993.

Whiting, J. W. (1981). Environmental constraints on infant care practices. In R. H. Munroe, R. L. Munroe, and B. B. Whiting (Eds.), *Handbook of cross-cultural human development* (pp. 155–178). New York: Garland.

Wiesenfeld, A., and Klorman, R. (1978). The mother's psychophysiological reactions to contrasting affective expressions by her own and an unfamiliar infant. *Developmental Psychology, 14,* 294–304.

Wiesenfeld, A., and Malatesta, C. Z. (1982). Infant distress: Variables affecting responses of caregivers and others. In L. W. Hoffman, R. Gandelman, and H. R. Schiffman (Eds.), *Parenting: Its causes and consequences* (pp. 123–139). Hillsdale, NJ: Lawrence, Erlbaum Associates.

Wiesenfeld, A. R., Malatesta, C. Z., Whitman, P. B., Granrose, C., and Uili, R. (1985). Psychophysiological response of breast-and bottle-feeding mothers to their infants' signals. *Psychophysiology, 22,* 79–86.

Willcox, D. L., Yovich, J. L., McColm, S. C., and Schmitt, L. H. (1985). Changes in total and free concentrations of steroid hormones in the plasma of women throughout pregnancy. Effects of medroxyprogesterone acetate in the first trimester. *Journal of Endocrinology, 107,* 293–300.

Worchel, F. F., and Allen, M. (1997). Mothers' ability to discriminate cry types in low-birthweight premature and full-term infants. *Children's Health Care, 26,* 183–195.

Worthman, C. M., and Stallings, J. F. (1997). Hormone measures in finger-prick blood spot samples: New field methods for reproductive endocrinology. *American Journal of Physical Anthropology, 104,* 1–21.

Yamamura, N., and Tsuji, N. (1993). Parental care as a game. *Journal of Evolutionary Biology, 6,* 103–127.

Zeskind, P. S. (1980). Adult responses to cries of low and high risk infants. *Infant Behavior and Development, 3,* 167–77.

Zeskind, P. S., Klein, L., and Marshall, T. (1992). Adults' perceptions of experimental modifications of durations of pauses and expiratory sounds in infant crying. *Developmental Psychology, 28,* 1153–1162.

Zeskind, P. S., and Lester, B. M. (1978). Acoustic features and auditory perceptions of the cries of newborns with prenatal and perinatal complications. *Child Development, 49,* 580–589.

Ziegler, T. E. (2000). Hormones associated with non-maternal infant care: A review of mammalian and avian studies. *Folia Primatologica, 71,* 6–21.

Ziegler, T. E., Wegner, F. H., and Snowdon, C. T. (1996). Hormonal responses to parental and nonparental conditions in male cotton-top tamarins, *Saguinus oedipus,* a New World primate. *Hormones and Behavior, 30,* 287–297.

6

Intuitive Parenting

Hanuš Papoušek
Mechthild Papoušek
University of Munich

INTRODUCTION

Parenting is a complex, multifactorial, and dynamic phenomenon, often too difficult to study without reductionistic restrictions to experimental approaches. Therefore evidence of new factors that may contribute to parenting tests the limits of scientific patience, particularly if acknowledging its relevance also necessitates the conclusion that a central aspect has been overlooked in the wealth of accumulated findings. This seems to be true in the case of intuitive parenting. Conversely, intuitive parenting appears most effective in relation to infancy, a developmental period that still seems to hide sources of surprise and to demand full scientific attention.

To understand how much attention to pay to intuitive processes in parenting, it helps to return to the beginnings of its relatively short history, in the 1970s. By that time, psychological, sociocultural, ecological, and clinical factors that influence parental roles in child development had been well documented. In contrast, biological determinants and functional mechanisms of parental conduct concerning early infancy were relatively underresearched, and gaps in knowledge were bridged with speculative concepts.

Human parents seemed to differ from other mammalian parents mainly in their access to a cultural heritage, and their behavioral repertoire seemed to be fully controllable by individuals' rational decisions, cultural traditions, or the recommendations of cultural institutions. Only affective bonding and expressions of internal feelings seemed to occupy a position between innate and cultural determinants. The lists of infant needs, commonly considered in contemporary theoretical concepts, did not then include more than the autonomic, nutritional, general hygienic, and emotional. Without a sufficient scientific justification, emotions were viewed as independent of or even antagonistic toward processes that characterize human thought.

At the same time, infancy research consistently pointed to weak aspects in then contemporary theoretical interpretations. Little attention was paid to the ontogeny of symbolic communication, although in an evolutionary perspective the ability to create symbols for any part of the external environment, to construct an abstract internal world of symbols, to freely explore their potential variations and combinations, and to assign them individual or social value had brought about powerful means of biological adaptation, connected with strong intrinsic motivators. Our interest in parenting was motivated by findings about the early integrative competencies of infants. Because of exceptionally advantageous circumstances, we were able to investigate early learning and problem solving in long-term daily experimental arrangements (H. Papoušek, 1967, 1977). These experiments led to a conception of infant integration of experience resulting not only from perceptual input but also from interactions with environmental events. Those studies brought early evidence about biologically related aspects of parenting.

Infants appeared to manifest predispositions, not only for early learning about how to cope with environmental events and for conceptualizing newly acquired modes of coping, including simple numerical concepts (H. Papoušek, 1969), but also for making their engagement in coping processes with resulting failures and successes evident to social environment, even when no social partner was visible. The repertoire of observed infant cues, such as visual attention and exploration, brow knitting, facial and vocal expressions of either displeasure or pleasure, hand gestures, or changes in general movements, did not reach beyond what was once interpreted as expressions of emotions. However, these cues proved convincingly related to the course of learning and problem solving and allowed observers to estimate the course of coping with experimental tasks and/or to adjust the duration or the arrangement of their experiments so as to facilitate infant coping. Together with the span of infant attention, those cues also indicated a strong intrinsic motivation in infants to explore and manipulate the environment. Special experimental modifications confirmed that the infant's intrinsic motivation exceeded effects of environmental rewards (H. Papoušek, 1967; 1969).

In general, infants' integrative competencies seemed to depend on innate predispositions, on account of their early postpartum functioning, and to correspond to fundamental needs for accumulating and processing of information. Studies of infant competence showed that integrative capacities quickly developed under the influences of maturation, accumulated experience, and experimental facilitation. Although infants were interacting with a nonsocial, physical environment during experiments, they still tended to display communicative cues, meaningful to observers. The experimenter was often in the position of a teacher inasmuch as the infant's achievement also depended on the experimenter's attention to the infant's behavioral/emotional state and on optimal arrangements of learning tasks.

Laboratory findings of that sort naturally raised the question of whether and how infants utilize their integrative predispositions in everyday life conditions and whether parents utilize didactic strategies to influence infants' achievements in learning. Careful analyses of home situations showed that, in the absence of social partners, naturalistic situations seldom offer learning situations in which infants could detect, conceptualize, and control contingent events. In contrast, such opportunities were plentiful during caregivers' interactions with infants (H. Papoušek and M. Papoušek, 1984). Studies of parent–infant interactions were facilitated by the availability of modern audiovisual documentation and its adjustment for microanalytic purposes in the combination of videorecording with sonographic and spectral analyses of vocal utterances. New methods soon made it evident that a considerable part of caregiving consisted of nonconscious interventions and that caregivers were unaware of their potential contributions to infant competencies, even though in many cases obvious adjustments to infant constraints or facilitatory interventions could be profitably interpreted as didactic forms of support.

Pilot microanalytic studies of early interactions indicated that infants' predispositions for integrative and communicative competencies might have a counterpart in parental predispositions to provide adequate support. At the same time, these studies opened a new experimental approach to research on biological determinants of human parenting, a matter of increasing interest in the interdisciplinary community of infancy researchers in which developmentalists from psychology, biology, medicine, and linguistics (among other fields) were trying to improve their understanding of early human development. Comparisons of parenting between human beings and other species were expected to elucidate universals pointing to genetic determinants and adaptive relevance during evolution on the one hand and species-specific forms of human parenting absent in animal models on the other. As in the interpretation of morphological development, a better understanding of human evolution promised further progress in concepts of behavioral development, including the problems of human parenting (Bjorklund, Yunger, and Pelligrini, in Vol. 2 of this *Handbook*).

Next to the theoretical and the clinical significance of this work, sociological changes in traditional forms of family life accelerated a better understanding of parenting. In the main sections of this chapter, we discuss contributions of methodological approaches, comparative studies, and attention to nonconscious regulatory processes to research on human parenting.

THE POSITION OF HUMAN PARENTING IN A COMPARATIVE VIEW

When mammals appeared on the stage of evolution, they brought about structural innovations in the brain, interrelated to functional innovations in the forms of reproduction and care for progeny. In spite of rich modifications occurring during the evolution of individual mammalian species, the main principles of those innovations have remained universal to all mammals. In contrast to the "reptilian brain" (roughly corresponding to the corpus striatum and lower structures in the human brain), the limbic system appeared in "the mammalian brain" and enabled more effective control of emotions together with new forms of nursing and care for progeny, such as retrieving, nest building, carrying infants, and vocal calls for maintaining contact between mothers and pups (MacLean, 1973, 1990; Rosenblatt, in Vol. 2 of this *Handbook*). A corresponding counterpart was selected in terms of coevolution on the side of infantile behaviors, including sucking, social bonding, shorter or longer periods of dependence on parental care, separation calls, and, last but not least, playfulness.

During 100 million years of evolution, the "old mammalian brain" of rodents and rabbits has gained a third level of circuits in newer species, corresponding to the neocortex of primates and human beings in particular. One important aspect of this evolutionary change was the shift from chemical signals as the basis of communication in older mammalian species to visual and vocal signals in primate communication. This development dated back to the appearance of the Zeuxis, the first apelike arboreal mammal, approximately 30 million years ago, and it included the gradual emergence of symbolic competence culminating in humans. The consequences of this exchange were far reaching because communication generally represents a very important means of biological adaptation and is narrowly related to parenting.

For instance, higher levels of visual perception increased the significance of observational learning and, in connection with progress in eye–hand coordination, learning through exploratory manipulation and imitation. In contrast to rodent pups, primate infants profit from these circumstances, particularly if their parents support or at least tolerate infant exploration and imitation, such as in the case of tool use in chimpanzees (Bard, in Vol. 2 of this *Handbook*, van Lawick-Goodall, 1967; Matsuzawa, 1993).

The beginning of the protohuman line with specific human features in primate evolution is easier to trace in relation to upright walking than to the emergence of speech. The history of bipedalism— distinctly evident in fossil skeletons of *Australopithecus afarensis* (Johanson and White, 1979) from $3^{1}/_{2}$ million years ago—first seemed to be of little relevance to the history of human parenting so long as bipedalism was viewed as a consequence of tool use (Darwin, 1871). However, that view was revised after the discovery of *afarensis* fossils because the earliest recognized stone tools from Olduvai Gorge were only approximately 2 million years old. That discrepancy led anthropologists to alternative interpretations and reconsiderations of biological determinants, such as demographic propagation and care for progeny. Lovejoy (1981) suggested that the biologically disadvantageous form of upright walking might have resulted from a mere genetic mutation, which, however, secondarily proved advantageous for carrying dependent offspring and for intense parenting. The fact that the span between two births is much shorter in humans (three years in nomadic hunters–gatherers) than in other primates (six to seven years in wild chimpanzees) increased the plausibility of Lovejoy's arguments. Moreover, disadvantages in slow locomotion forced close social cooperation and communication.

Merely indirect morphological evidence, such as the structure of the upper vocal tract (Lieberman, 1984) or changes of the skull that are due to the enlargement of frontal and parietal lobes and particularly poles of the temporal lobes, indicated the emergence of human intellect, memory, symbolic competence, and language. The most recent hypotheses, independently elaborated by geneticists and linguists, suggest that all present variants of *Homo sapiens sapiens* had a common African ancestor, dated at 200,000 years ago. According to those hypotheses, racial differences in human populations were caused by negligible genetic differences in comparison with the major, presumably unique, biologically significant genetic mutations that brought about self-consciousness, language, and culture.

Together with upright walking that freed the upper extremities for tasks other than locomotor activities, the morphological evolution of hand and fingers, their fine innervation, and their rich representation in the neocortex also distinctly differentiated human beings from other primates, including chimpanzees. Fine manipulation of small objects probably facilitated gathering and hunting; however, it also played a crucial role in the evolution of human communication, particularly in the fast and rich repertoire of gestures (as evident in the perfection of sign languages), in instrumental communication across wider distances (as in drumming), and most importantly, in the permanent symbolic coding of information as in writing or its precursors in the earliest "calendars" or "numerical accounts" (Haarmann, 1990).

Anthropological research, comparative research in biology, and research on behavioral development profited from one other's progress. Behavioral similarities between human and nonhuman species helped to highlight universals in regulation that were the more obvious the more relevant aspects of biological adaptation they concerned. They also helped to show animal models for experimental analyses of human behaviors. Dissimilarities drew attention to species-specific means of adaptation and to the limits of generalizations from findings in animal models to concepts of human behaviors. It is advisable for us to keep those limits in mind when attempting to interpret human parenting. The fundamental functions of parenting were extensively studied in laboratory rats and cats, that is, in easily available laboratory animals. Studies by Rosenblatt and his group (Rosenblatt, 1975; in Vol. 2 of this *Handbook*), for instance, substantially enriched our knowledge of genetic and environmental contributions to maternal behavior, developmental changes in the roles of individual perceptual systems, interrelations between maternal and infantile predispositions, and the universality with which, for instance, crouching necessary in rat mothers for nursing pups was elicitable with infant cue signals—even in males and in spite of their inability to nurse. Yet the evolutionary distance between rats and humans was too large to allow general conclusions about human parenting without verification in closer species, and in primates in particular.

Occasionally comparative research was confounded by the use of available laboratory animals for experimental studies. Although traditional examples, such as frogs, pigeons, rats, cats, dogs, and rhesus monkeys, represent different evolutionary levels and directions, they could not satisfactorily represent the broad territory of comparative sciences with its vast amount of field observations on parenting and its adaptations to ecological circumstances. The importance of studies on mother–infant bonding and effects of maternal deprivation in rhesus monkeys became widely known; however, students of human development seemed unaware of variations in the many monkey species and were incautious in acknowledging rhesus monkeys as adequate models for analyses of human parenting. Squirrel monkeys, tamarins, or vervets seemed to be closer to humans in terms of vocal communication in which the use of representational signals has been documented (Seyfarth, Cheney, and Marler, 1980; Winter, Ploog, and Latta, 1966).

The most adequate comparisons between humans and their phylogenetically closest relatives among apes, chimpanzees (*Pan troglodytes*), and particularly their pygmy variety, called bonobos (*Pan paniscus*), were not yet available. Bonobos are similar to human beings in genetic and immunological parameters, in intelligence, in symbolic communication (de Waal, 1988), in the use of affect for social pacification, and in sexual behavior, independent of estrus (de Waal, 1987). Even then, of course, the species-specific involvement of verbal communication and sociocultural impact remained limited to direct investigations in human subjects.

These comparative views made us aware of several substantial aspects that had not previously been satisfactorily considered in studies of human parenting. First, with respect to the universality and adaptive significance of parental care for progeny among mammals, it seemed improbable that human parenting evolved without a set of genetically determined predispositions concerning not only universal physiological functions, such as lactation, but also specific integrative and communicative capacities. The fact that these capacities are known to depend on sociocultural learning does not contradict such an expectation so long as the hypothesis could not be excluded that even the processes of cultural integration and sociocultural learning are to some degree based on innate predispositions.

Second, among those specific aspects of human adaptation, potentially interrelated with parental care, speech acquisition attracted particular attention. On the one hand, the biological roots of speech are evident in nonhuman animals: for instance, the fundamental steps toward abstraction and concept formation in rats (Tolman, 1949) or pigeons (Herrnstein and Loveland, 1964), the nonvocal elements of symbolic abstraction in honeybees (von Frisch, 1965), a small number of "words" in monkey vocalizations (Seyfarth et al., 1980; Winter et al., 1966), the nonvocal signing on a humanlike level in chimpanzees (Gardner and Gardner, 1969), and the capacity for understanding human speech in bonobos (Savage-Rumbaugh, 1990). On the other hand, it was evident from cross-cultural adoptions that young human infants learn their first language, or mother tongue, from their social environment. It was not known, however, to what degree and in which ways caregivers influence speech acquisition in infants, although from a biological view, a coevolution of matching predispositions for an adaptively relevant competence in infants and in parents is predictable.

Third, the question of biological predisposition for human parenting was appealing for general theoretical and clinical reasons. Interactional behaviors are mostly interpreted as expressions of emotional bonding, and little attention is paid to their communicative aspects or their significance for cognitive development of infants. This was particularly true about vocal, facial, and gestural displays in infants; all such displays were viewed as expressions of affective states, in spite of Bühler's (1934) postulate that every such signal not only expresses internal feelings, but also always represents the contextual situation and is addressed to the social environment as an appeal that is expected to be answered. Correspondingly, failures in mother–infant interactions were viewed as disturbances in emotional bonding; causes were expected in the history of early emotional experience of mothers, and hardly any attention was paid to the history of preceding hands-on experience in baby care or to predispositions for establishing adequate communication with preverbal infants.

At the same time, H. Papoušek and M. Papoušek (1978) suggested a revision of contemporary approaches and recommended increased attention be paid to intuitive forms of parenting. The difficult task of demonstrating innate components in intuitive parenting could not be solved in direct experimental ways in humans. Therefore indirect criteria of innateness had to be considered: for instance, the universality of a given behavioral pattern across parental genders, ages, cultures, and eventually across species; the early emergence of such pattern during ontogeny; the involvement of the pattern in biologically relevant means of adaptation; or the evidence of a nonconscious control in the regulation of such patterns.

METHODOLOGICAL APPROACHES TO THE STUDY
OF HUMAN PARENTING

In the early 1970s, new methods of audiovisual documentation brought analyses of observable behaviors to perfection in several points relevant to studies of human parenting (H. Papoušek and M. Papoušek, 1987; M. Papoušek and H. Papoušek, 1981): (1) Filming that required a disturbing intensity of illumination was replaced with videorecording that was more comfortable, less intrusive, and more amenable to computer-aided evaluation. (2) Consequently, former paper-and-pencil protocols and their automated versions that required instant and hardly revisable categorization of observed behaviors before registration were replaced with a kind of documentation that could be evaluated after observations. Reduplicated and consecutive evaluations by independent evaluators or, eventually, by experts from diverse disciplines became possible, as did revisions in categorization, provoked by conceptual innovations. (3) Frame-by-frame analyses of playback allowed exact measures of duration, latency, or sequential order in observed behaviors (in terms of 20 or 40 ms in European systems and 16.6 or 33.3 ms in U.S. systems). Moreover, individual frames could be exactly identified with the help of inserted time codes or computer-generated numbering. (4) Records of two interacting partners and/or selected contextual circumstances could be combined in forms of split-screen videotaping for exact sequential analysis. (5) As soon as it was experimentally proved that young infants would perceive and recognize videorecorded persons in playback (H. Papoušek and M. Papoušek, 1974), the effects of selected parental behaviors could be experimentally verified in stimulus-response (S-R) type experiments. Conversely, playback with selected infant behaviors could be used for verification of parental responsiveness to infant cues (M. Papoušek, 1989). Further, the development of this responsiveness before parenthood could be studied in children (Haekel, 1985; Kestermann, 1982; H. Papoušek and M. Papoušek, 1987).

Methodological progress brought with it conceptual enrichment in several important directions concerning the biological origins of human parenting. For instance, measures of latency facilitated identification of nonconscious, intuitive patterns in parental behaviors (H. Papoušek and M. Papoušek, 1987). Participation of nonconscious regulation in behavioral patterns and their early emergence in ontogeny indicate genetic determination. For this reason, it was especially helpful that the new methodology extended studies of parenting to ages before parenthood and to subjects without infants to bring to the laboratory.

Because parent–infant interactions are so complex, it is often difficult to show convincingly the presence and the effectiveness of observed behavioral sequences with the help of linear statistical methods. For instance, infants' hand gestures almost always appear entangled in ever-changing combinations with vocal and facial displays. However, specifically modified experimental designs in which subjects were exposed to isolated patterns of hand gestures (Kestermann, 1982) or vocal sounds (M. Papoušek, 1989) demonstrated their effects conclusively.

The history of transition from classical S-R studies of one-way effects of stimulation in standardized laboratory situations to studies of parent–infant interactions brought about serious general problems in terms of statistical evaluations. Interrelations among interacting partners and contextual circumstances were multidirectional and could hardly be standardized or narrowed so that selected aspects could be measured and others disregarded. Conversely, attempts to capture the complexity of interacting subsystems with the help of linear mathematical models met increasing opposition from theoreticians of dynamic systems. However, predictions at the price of exaggerated simplification of complex phenomena did not seem less problematical. Since the 1970s, application of dynamic systems theory and nonlinear mathematical models in research on human parenting has not been easy inasmuch as at least two premises have been difficult to fulfill: reliable knowledge of all regulatory factors involved in the observed system and the difficulty of quantifying the effects of those factors with sufficient exactness in sufficiently large populations.

THE ROLE OF NONCONSCIOUS REGULATION IN HUMAN LIFE

Pilot recordings of parent–infant dialogues in home situations revealed frequent behavioral sequences that parents use in order to gain and maintain infant attention or display models for infant vocalization, even when parents were unaware of them and unable to control them voluntarily. Researchers today pay considerable attention to nonconscious cognition and behavioral regulation (Hoffmann, 1993;

Kihlstrom, 1987; Lewicki, 1986) and attribute to them crucial roles, for instance, in the achievement of top performances of champions in sport or in musical virtuosity. Yet, even nowadays intuitive, nonconscious processes are often viewed as inferior rather than complementary to rational decision making and as mere relics of animal regulation that should be inhibited during cultural integration.

However, in the 1970s it was not commonly accepted that biological survival or intelligent coping with complex life situations could only partly be accomplished on the basis of logical thinking and rational, conscious decisions. To define and explain human consciousness was difficult, although it had been the focus of philosophical speculation since the first Greek schools of philosophy. In humans, consciousness is related to intentionality, for instance, and to anticipatory images (James, 1890/1981), to imaginations (Wundt, 1893), or to cortical functions of the "second signaling system" (verbal representation) (Pavlov, 1927). The clinical significance of disturbances in competitive interrelations between conscious and subconscious ego processes became a central issue in Freud's (1911/1975) psychoanalytical model of human psychopathology. However, all neuroscientific attempts to locate a neuronal "ego," a phantom interposed between afferent and efferent impulses, assumed in all concepts of mind failed.

Interest in consciousness increased again in connection with studies of hemispheric lateralization in the brain. According to recent definitions, consciousness is a capacity to show higher-order cognitive processes, typical human emotions, self-recognition, and freely creative thought (Bogen and Bogen, 1969; Preilowski, 1979); this capacity requires an interaction of the full capacities of both halves of the brain. Each hemisphere is independently self-conscious and possesses a complex cognitive system that includes internal models of self and environment, plans, concepts of goals and errors, and the capacity to change strategies in response to environmental feedback (Sperry, 1985). Thought need not be solely linguistic (Joseph, Gallagher, Holloway, and Kahn, 1984), but may consist of nonverbal components, for instance, spatial, pictorial, or imaginary. The verbal self utilizes language and the integrative power of words to organize experience and make it socially accessible; it attributes causes, logical relations, or hierarchical structures to experience, expresses it in verbal, communicable symbols, and creates a sense of conscious reality (Gazzaniga and LeDoux, 1978; MacKay and MacKay, 1982). Surgical patients in whom the speech-dominant hemisphere has been selectively anesthetized with sodium amytal (Wada technique) are capable of procedural learning in nonverbal tasks (how to do things) but incapable of declarative learning (how to name things). After anesthesia, they are unaware of any learned experience, but in adequate tests demonstrate nonconsciously the effects of procedural learning (Gaddes, 1985).

The speed of behavioral regulation is yet another relevant aspect of consciousness. According to neurophysiologists (Vander, Sherman, and Luciano, 1990), a minimum of 500-ms cortical activation is necessary for adults to become aware of stimulation and capable of reporting it. To coordinate an adequate motor response takes even more time, in line with complexity of the response. Many circumstances in human life (for instance, muscle activities involved in the production of speech, instrumental music, or dance) require much faster regulation. Such fast forms of regulation are possible only on the level of nonverbal, intuitive coordination.

Intuitive behaviors can be based on innate predispositions and function as preconscious during the preverbal age. In adults, focused attention may lead to conscious awareness and control of intuitive behaviors, albeit at the price of slower decision making. Conversely, some fast complex acts have to be learned from scratch and guided by slow, rational control, based on verbal information; later, however, they can be automated during training to the level of fast, nonconsciously performed patterns. Thus, at present, mind and consciousness are mostly considered as holistic attributes of organismic, self-regulating systems that reach various degrees of complexity because of structural differences in those systems and, particularly, because of participation of the verbal system.

The category of intuitive behaviors includes a rich repertoire of adaptive activities lying between very fast and rigid innate reflexes and relatively slow, highly flexible, often culturally determined, rational behaviors. Their biological significance is obvious; they enable human beings to cope with novel situations for which rational or cultural models have not yet been acquired (such as during infancy and childhood), and they allow faster, cognitively less strenuous coping with one situation while leaving enough attention free for coping with other situations at the same time (such as when adults interact with babies). Thus, for instance, a scientist might solve demanding logical problems while occupied with automated sport or home activities. Similarly, a parent can enjoy a 20-min interchange with an infant while constantly answering infant signals with meaningful, emotionally highlighted interventions and at the same time paying attention to potential environmental dangers.

The scientific landscape of the 1970s has been briefly outlined in order to explain the relevance of questions raised in relation to human parenting, the gaps in knowledge, and the complexity of emerging problems that necessitated some concentration of attention on central problems of intuitive parenting. Both their relevance and their complexity may be illustrated in the role of parenting in the development of human communication.

THE PREVERBAL INFANT AS AN OBJECT OF INTUITIVE PARENTING

Polar differences between neonates and parents in the amount of integrated life experience and communicative capacity lend interactions between both partners a clear character of potential didactic situations in which parents may function as teachers. Studies of early integrative development confirm that infants are capable of learning and cognition and that in learning situations infants display didactically relevant feedback cues about their momentary state of alertness or the course of their coping with the learning situations (H. Papoušek, 1967, 1969). Professional teachers attentively perceive such pupil cues and adjust the amount, complexity, and timing of learning materials, according to those cues. Parents, and caregivers in general, are capable of reading various cues in infant behaviors as communicative signals and answering them in dialogic ways. While doing so, they also make themselves contingent on infant behaviors and controllable in a positive sense inasmuch as they offer infants opportunities for training integrative processes. Thus the infant's communicative development appears to be closely related to the development of integrative abilities, and both aspects of infant development appear to relate to the repertoire of parental interventions.

Learning how to communicate represents perhaps the most important developmental process that takes place during infancy. The process concerns both physiological functions of the organism and complex integrative capacities and is affected by innate predispositions just as it is by sociocultural factors. During the initial absence of speech signals, any observable component of infant behavior may function as a communicative signal as far as the caregiver is capable of processing it as such; it may also serve as an intentional communicative signal as soon as the infant has detected its contingent effects on the caregiver and has learned the rules of its use. Although nobody can explain anything about verbal communication to preverbal infants in words, infants will typically learn a spoken language in speaking families or a sign language in signing families. However, if the communicative circumstances are too difficult, they may surpass the limits of infant integrative competence and cause behavioral disorders (H. Papoušek and M. Papoušek, 1992).

At the beginning, the neonate lacks even the capacity to prolong or segment expiration for the purposes of vocal sounds, except crying. Infant cries function from the very beginning in a fully developed, innate form lasting up to 1 or 2 s, and qualify for long-distance signaling of the neonate's distress (Morton, 1977; Wolff, 1969). The human cry is comparable with the distress or separation cries that characterize mammalian neonates with considerable universality (Newman, 1985). Although it need not be learned in initial form, crying may be learned by human infants as an intentional communicative signal during their second half-year; crying's original tonic character then modifies into phasic forms, typical for short and fast means of communication (Papoušek, Papoušek, and Koester, 1986).

Conversely, speech-related vocal sounds have to be learned from the scratch, involve subsystems of neuromotor control other than crying, are inversely related to crying in infant interactions with social environment, and distinctly depend on environmental factors (M. Papoušek and H. Papoušek, 1991). The first level of expertise is achieved when initial fundamental voicing (quasi-resonant sounds, according to Oller, 1980) develops into prolonged, euphonic "cooing sounds" when the infant is approximately 8 weeks of age and allows the infant to practice modulations of pitch contours—the earliest modulation available for vocal interchanges during quiet, stress-free waking states. In 1-year-old children, gliding transitions between "squealing" and "growling" registers of voice cover one or two entire octaves (M. Papoušek, 1994a).

During the exploratory stage of precanonical sound production, infants explore and expand their control of pitch, loudness, timbre, resonance, and duration in vocal sounds affected by morphological changes of the upper vocal tract and rhythmic segmentation of expiration. During the infant's second half-year—the canonical stage—canonical syllables (Oller, 1980) appear in infant vocalization, and a steep increase in their frequency together with their new, distinct pattern of reduplicated and variegated babbling lends them the character of a developmental milestone (Locke, 1990; Oller and Eilers, 1992; M. Papoušek, 1994a; M. Papoušek and H. Papoušek, 1991). This milestone seems to depend on the maturation of innate predispositions as it appears in deaf infants, too. However, a distinct delay in its appearance in deaf infants in comparison with hearing infants indicates a learning deficit that is due to a lack of both auditory feedback available to hearing infants and facilitating parental interventions (Oller and Eilers, 1988).

Reduplicated canonical syllables bring about the potential of protowords and are soon followed by the appearance of the first words. Up to this point, the infant's vocal development corresponds to procedural learning of relevant phonetic subroutines. Parallel to the control of universal articulatory features and the phonology of the mother tongue, the infant also learns a number of other skills, such as taking turns between vocalizing and listening, integration of sound production and sound perception, and imitation of vocal sounds (Anderson, Vietze and Dokecki, 1977; M. Papoušek, 1994a; M. Papoušek and H. Papoušek, 1991; Užgiris, 1981). Thus the integrative competence of human infants develops beyond the universal mammalian scope in the direction of human-specific forms of communication under sociocultural influences.

Rather early in an infant's life, playful variations become evident in infant vocalizations and participate in vocal development with an increasing frequency; they are particularly evident in infant monologues (Lewis, 1936; M. Papoušek and H. Papoušek, 1981). Although playfulness is rather universal in mammalian infants, including phylogenetically old species, human playfulness seems to have reached a specifically high level of adaptation in association with verbal representation. Whereas in other mammals play mostly concerns practicing innate behavioral patterns, such as skills that serve foraging or predation (Eibl-Eibesfeldt, 1967), humans can playfully process and modify any part of reality and any part of internal representations of reality in any thinkable way, independent of physical or behavioral limits. While doing so, they typically revisit existing concepts about objects of play, modify their premises, recombine them, or bring them into new relations with a freedom that may lead to surprising discoveries, humorous qualities, or artistic creations.

The significance of playfulness for cognitive development has been stressed in psychology (e.g., Piaget, 1962), among others. Huizinga (1955) saw in it the roots of human culture. The freedom in regulation of playful behaviors represents an early expression of the freedom in decisions and creations of values that von Bertalanffy (1968) pointed to as a human-specific phenomenon. The early emergence of playfulness during human ontogeny and its relation to communicative development indicates its adaptive significance in relation to species-specific aspects of human integrative competence (H. Papoušek, 1979; Papoušek, Papoušek and Harris, 1987). From this point of view, the human vocal tract is the first naturalistic toy and musical instrument, allowing for early practicing of specific mental operations and calling for special attention in infancy research (M. Papoušek and H. Papoušek, 1981).

The brief survey of early communicative development points to aspects that have nourished interest in examining the role of intuitive parenting in the process of speech acquisition. The evidence of biological roots in the infant's specific competence for learning a mother tongue from sociocultural environment naturally leads to the necessity of elucidating parental predispositions for mediating those environmental determinants.

INTUITIVE PARENTING IN RELATION TO EARLY COMMUNICATIVE DEVELOPMENT

Important adaptive behaviors have been secured during evolution not only by selection of genetically determined predispositions, but in many cases also by coevolution of supportive or complementary behavioral counterparts in the social environment. This seems to be true of early communicative development in human beings: Biological parents are not the only exclusive supporters, although they may be the most adequate caregivers of offspring for both biological and cultural reasons. Predispositions for supportive interventions concerning communicative development are universal across caregivers' genders, ages, and cultures. Yet here they are discussed with the focus on predispositions in maternal populations, in which they have been studied most frequently.

Special attention is paid to the following aspects of parenting: (1) assessment of the infant's momentary behavioral/emotional state and interventions intended to maintain state within convenient limits, (2) support for the acquisition of general procedural skills enabling dialogic interchanges, (3) support for the acquisition of specific procedural skills necessary for the production and subtle modification of vocal sounds, and (4) support for the declarative use of vocal sounds in verbal symbols (naming, attribution of meanings, categorical generalization of meanings, abstraction). Not all of these features are equally valid to the preverbal period of communication, which is the main concern of this chapter; however, it is not always easy to separate the listed aspects, because the premises for discriminating developmental transitions among individual periods, observable in communicative development, are not yet reliably known and are certainly difficult to study in human infants.

Interventions Regarding Behavioral States

When parents have doubts about their infant's momentary state of alertness or mood during interactions, they usually test either the responsiveness or the muscle tone in the infant, particularly in the perioral area and in the hands. Parents stimulate with various visual or auditory stimuli, trying to open the infant's mouth while slightly pushing the infant's chin toward the chest or trying to open the infant's palm with a finger (H. Papoušek and M. Papoušek, 1979). Elicited responses provide differential information. Visual attention may increase and be combined with smiles or pleasurable vocal sounds or it may remain unchanged, and eventually decrease, and the infant turns away. It may be easy to open the infant's mouth or palm without any resistance in sleepy infants, whereas alert infants tend to respond with gentle finger play, hungry infants with sucking movements and attempts to bring the parent's finger into the mouth, satiated infants with firmer mouth closing, and infants upset because of some discomfort with firm, sometimes spastic, grasps.

Hand gestures of that sort can appear spontaneously and serve as observable cues independent of testing. Their effects on parents are difficult to separate from other simultaneous cues during parent–infant interaction; however, in specifically designed experiments, a selective variation of hand gestures in pictures of infants elicited expected patterns of intuitive responses. The quality and the latency of responses depended significantly on the ages of the subjects and their amounts of hands-on experience in babycare (Kestermann, 1982; H. Papoušek and M. Papoušek, 1987). Although these individuals were unaware of the real elicitors and wrongly believed they were responding to some facial cues, their responses confirmed the presence of a nonconscious predisposition for adequate responses to hand gestures. Parents have also been known to tend to affect the infant's behavioral state, sometimes with the use of interesting stimulation (Wolff, 1987), other times with more general vestibuloproprioceptive stimulation produced by lifting the infant upright (Korner and Thoman, 1972) or with various forms of rhythmical tapping or stroking (Koester, Papoušek, and Papoušek, 1989). Parents do not intervene as long as the infant quietly sleeps or is fully awake, but they do tend to restore one of these two states if the infant becomes upset and fussy or passive and drowsy.

Support for General Dialogic Skills

During the preverbal stage, infants learn that vocal interchanges play a particularly significant role in interaction and that they are to be used in dialogical forms that assume (among other things) establishment of mutual visual attention and turn taking between listening and vocalizing. Visual contact is a particularly important prerequisite for human communication (Robson, 1967). The possibility of displaying instructive models of sound production to infants depends on good visual availability of parents' facial behaviors, on the distance between the parent's face and the infant's eyes, and on the proper orientation of the face, at best in a face-to-face position, with parallel vertical axes of both faces, at a distance of ~23 cm. During the infant's first postpartum months, limits are given by developmental constraints in infant vision and head control; thus adjustments can be expected only by caregivers.

Unconsciously, parents carry out those adjustments whenever they see a chance for dialogue, as demonstrated in mothers of newborns, even in cases in which mothers were convinced that newborn infants could not see anything (Schoetzau and Papoušek, 1977). The tendency to talk to newborns is probably based on a biological predisposition, which is due to its universality (Rheingold and Adams, 1980). In addition to adjustments in face orientation and distance, parents also "reward" infants with "greeting responses" for achieving visual contact (H. Papoušek and M. Papoušek, 1979). Greeting responses consist of a slight retroflexion of the head, raised eyebrows, broadly opened eyes, and half-open mouth. They belong to the earliest contingent events that infants experience in procedural learning. The striking effort in parents to achieve and maintain direct visual contact with the infant is one of the species-specific features of intuitive parenting, as it is not known in other animals, including primates (Papoušek, Papoušek, Suomi, and Rahn, 1991). In other than human animals, direct eye-to-eye contact functions as a warning signal, mostly followed by aggressive threat or attack. Even in gorillas, chimpanzees, and bonobos, mothers very attentively observe the environment when nursing or holding an alert young baby. Direct visual contacts occur incidently; however, mothers do not use special strategies to achieve or maintain them, neither do they adjust their face-to-face distance and reinforce achieved contacts with greeting responses.

The smooth temporal coordination of speaking and listening turns, which is characteristic of dialogues between adult humans, requires reciprocal adjustments of vocal and visual cues. Such adjustments largely depend on the coordination of visual behaviors, for instance, on signs of visual attention while listening to the speaker, looking away while speaking, and brief visual contact with the listener while yielding a turn (Rutter and Durkin, 1987). Infants seem not to be able to accomplish true turn taking before the end of their second year (Schaffer, Collis, and Parsons, 1977). In other aspects, however, fine temporal coordinations have been reported much earlier and have been considered typical of early parent–infant interactions.

Synchrony, rhythmicity, and reciprocity in interactional behaviors attracted much interest among infancy researchers as soon as statistical models for evaluation were available. These findings led to appealing concepts, for instance, of a "mutual dance" or "affective reciprocity" (Tronick, Als, and Brazelton, 1980), "affect attunement" (Stern, 1985), "vocal congruence" or "coordinated inter-personal timing" (Beebe, Alson, Jaffe, Feldstein, and Crown, 1988), and a number of others. Some authors have argued, however, that only selected items were analyzed (temporal parameters of gaze or vocal sounds) without sufficient respect for situational contexts and with a tacit assumption that both interacting partners participated in comparable ways. According to these authors, early reciprocity is often an illusion resulting from maternal readiness to be guided by the infant and from her ability to predict infant behaviors and frame them so as to create seemingly reciprocal sequences (Collis and Schaffer, 1975; Kaye and Fogel, 1980; M. Papoušek, 1995). Kaye and Wells (1980) demonstrated, in studies on neonatal sucking and maternal "jiggling," that the finely attuned turn taking resulted from sensitive maternal adjustments to the infant's spontaneous sucking patterns.

Long before the infant has learned adequate turn taking, parents provide turn-taking frames themselves, open or close infant turns while responding to concurrent infant behaviors, encourage infant vocalization, and pause whenever the infant seems ready to vocalize (M. Papoušek, 1994a). Parents do so intuitively and usually show a remarkable consistency and a rich repertoire of vivid displays of pleasure in face and voice for this purpose. Thus they also regularly offer attractive contingent events; infants can detect these contingencies and learn how to control them on their own from the first months onward because of their aforementioned capacity for instrumental learning. Interactional turn-taking frames also become ritualized in sequences within early idiosyncratic games, for instance, in tickling games or peekaboo, and within vocal play (Papoušek, Papoušek and Harris, 1987), including vocal matching (M. Papoušek and H. Papoušek, 1989).

Rather typically, interactional behaviors engage more than one perceptual modality (Sullivan and Horowitz, 1983). Parents combine auditory, visual, tactile, and proprioceptive modes in dialogues with their infants in variable, although not random, patterns that still await systematic analysis. Aspects to be considered are the effects on infant attention and alertness, the potential significance for identification of the partner, and a compensatory function in the case of perceptual handicap. For instance, repetitive, respectively ritualized combinations may familiarize or identify the caregiver or the ethnic or cultural environment from which the caregiver comes. Occasionally, they may facilitate the introduction of a new caregiver. A stable caregiver may use variations in repetitive patterns to reinforce and maintain infant attention, which is known to remain at a high level under the influence of familiar and slightly varying stimulation (McCall and Kagan, 1967). Other, more radical variations are used by caregivers intuitively to influence the infant's behavioral state. The multimodal character of interactions may hypothetically secure a compensatory alternative in case one modality is lost or severely disturbed. For instance, sudden loss of hearing may be partly compensated for by the perception of visual cues in facial displays or hand gestures (Erting, Prezioso, and Hynes, 1990).

Support for Specific Procedural Skills in Vocal Production

Even though newborns are far from competent conversational partners and are incapable of understanding words, they provoke adults to talk to them. Not only do biological parents do so (Parke and O'Leary, 1976), but both female and male strangers address speech to newborns equally (Rheingold and Adams, 1980). The tendency to talk to infants is also universal across cultures, according to Anglo–German (Parke, Grossmann, and Tinsley, 1981), Anglo–Spanish (Blount and Padgug, 1977), and American–Dutch comparisons (Snow, De Blauw, and van Roosmalen, 1979). This universal intuitive tendency becomes particularly interesting if the following circumstances are considered:

(1) Caregivers' child-directed speech is categorically different from adult-directed speech (Fernald and Simon, 1984).

(2) The differences between both forms of speech are universal among caregivers across gender, age, and culture (Fernald et al., 1989; Papoušek and Hwang, 1991). Moreover, a cross-modal universality has recently been indicated when analogous differences between child-directed and adult-directed signing were found in deaf mothers who used American Sign Language (Erting et al., 1990).

(3) Caregivers are typically unaware of those differences and their significance; no cultural traditions or institutions are known to have developed to consciously promote care for the use of such a special register.

(4) Transitions from adult-directed to child-directed speech are fast, unquestionable, and discontinuous, like transitions between two languages in bilingual persons.

(5) The structure and the quality of child-directed speech change with time in correlation with the development of communicative competence in infants, whereby the caregiver holds a lead in the direction of the next developmental progress (M. Papoušek, 1994a, 1994b).

These circumstances indicate biologically selected predispositions in the regulation of child-directed speech that seem to serve the purpose of social support for the development of species-specific communicative capacities in the progeny. Particularly, the fifth point deserves full attention inasmuch as it points to an intuitive didactic competence in caregivers and, consequently, the existence of a biologically determined precursor of didactics (H. Papoušek and M. Papoušek, 1978, 1982)—supposed to be a primarily cultural institution. The adaptive character of this didactic process can be tested, for instance, in relation to two developmental phases during speech acquisition—the periods before and after the appearance of canonical syllables, interpretable as milestones marking the transition from predominant procedural learning of how to produce vocal sounds to the onset of declarative learning of how to name things, persons, and events.

With respect to aforementioned limits in integrative capacities of newborns and young infants and to constraints in the production of vocal sounds, infants would be helped didactically in the best way with simple, easily processible models that encourage prolongation of expirium and utilization of pitch contours that they can modulate earlier than other phonetic elements. Child-directed speech is predominantly characterized by corresponding features: linguistic simplicity and a specific utilization of expanded, strikingly melodic prosodic contours. Both parents—indeed, caregivers in general—tend to reduce the average duration of utterances (Fernald and Simon, 1984; Garnica, 1977; Papoušek, Papoušek, and Bornstein, 1985; Phillips, 1973). Both mothers and fathers most frequently use one-syllable utterances toward 3-month-old infants; in two thirds of utterances prosodic features are favored on account of semantic significance (Papoušek, Papoušek, and Bornstein, 1985). Elongated vowels (Ratner, 1984; Snow, 1977) with increased participation of pitch contours and/or rhythmicity (Ferguson, 1964; Stern and Gibbon, 1979) give parental utterances the character of a pleasant melody.

Moreover, both male and female caregivers use a higher average pitch (by three to four semitones) in child-directed speech in comparison with adult-directed speech (Papoušek, Papoušek, and Haekel, 1987). Fernald and Simon (1984) found a significant increase in average pitch from 203 to 247 Hz in 24 mothers speaking to an adult observer versus to a newborn, but no increase when mothers were asked to simulate "motherese" without newborns present. Jacobson, Boersma, Fields, and Olson (1983) asked adults to read a text for children under four conditions: baseline, to a pretended but absent child, to a present child, and to a present infant. The average fundamental frequency significantly and gradually increased across these conditions and reached the highest level both in females and males with an infant present. The adaptive significance of this regulation is unclear; it might help the infant discriminate to whom caregivers are going to talk.

The simplified structure of parental utterances, prolongation of vowels, highlighting with expressive pitch contours, and the face-to-face position at a short distance allow the parent to display an elementary vocal repertoire in very distinct and easily observable models. This opportunity is almost unique in human life inasmuch as it relates to the infant's limited locomotion and depends on the infant's being held by the parent. Therefore the delay in locomotion, because of which human infants are commonly viewed as altricial, may be advantageous, pointing an adaptive way toward precocity in communicative capacities.

Microanalyses of interchanges between parents and infants have elucidated a high frequency of short episodes in which the infant is encouraged to imitate attractively displayed models of vocal sounds (M. Papoušek and H. Papoušek, 1989). Infant imitations are rewarded with parental expressions of pleasure and are embedded by parents into dialoguelike sequences that include matching responses and models for turn taking. Parental responses to vocal signals from infants may act as contingent events and offer plenty of opportunities in which infants may learn how to control and conceptualize such contingencies. Thus parental predispositions supportively affect not only procedural skills for production of vocal sounds, but also integrative processes in general, including transmodal matching of perception and production of vocal sounds. It is assumed that procedural learning dominates in the development of integrative capacities in preverbal infants until they reach the age of approximately 6 or 7 months. Until that time, parental didactic interventions almost exclusively concern procedural skills in infants.

Support for the Declarative Use of Vocal Symbols

When an infant is approximately 6 or 7 months of age, the production of vocal sounds reaches the level at which the infant can produce not only distinct syllables, but also consecutive chains of syllables during one prolonged expirium. Auditorily, the achievement is marked by the appearance of reduplicated, canonical syllables in infant babbling (Locke, 1990; Oller and Eilers, 1992). Parents seem to be provoked by the appearance of canonical syllables to use new strategies in intuitive didactic support: They take reduplicated syllables, bisyllables in particular, for potential protowords and start modeling words based on them (Papoušek, 1994a). This is the beginning of the declarative use of vocal symbols.

However, the use of declarative symbols has already been prepared by the use of categorical symbols at the preverbal level at which pitch contours in child-directed speech function as early carriers of categorical messages (M. Papoušek, 1994b; Papoušek, Papoušek, and Bornstein, 1985). Thus, in addition to what has already been said about pitch contours, at least two more aspects deserve attention: their role as categorical signals and their universality across stress versus tonal languages.

In cultures that use stress languages, prosodic pitch contours of adult-directed speech are mainly used for linguistic stress and intonation; they carry syntactic, semantic, and/or affective meanings. Most commonly, they give sentences the meanings of statements, questions, warnings, threats, and the like. During preverbal infancy, melodic contours are not yet as closely tied to the linguistic content of utterances as in adult speech. Infants, in turn, can modify pitch contours earlier than they can other phonetic elements, and they can discriminate and process pitch contours earlier than they can linguistic information. This seems to be the reason for using pitch contours in highly expressive forms as carriers of the earliest categorical messages in child-directed speech (Papoušek, Papoušek, and Symmes, 1991).

Unlike adult-directed speech, in which melodic contours are complex and highly variable, in child-directed speech one contour carrying a categorical message may repeat several times across utterances with varying verbal content as if to facilitate infant processing of informational input. The potential high variability of melodic contours is reduced: Papoušek and colleagues (1985, 1986) identified six prototypes in individual caregivers. The content of categorical messages relates to the situational context and to infant coping with the given situation. Thus, for instance, the messages may mean that the infant should activate integrative functions or reduce superfluous arousal because help is available, or that coping should either continue, as adequate, or stop, as inadequate.

The meaning of the message is carried by the prototypical forms of melodic contour and/or their combinations and can be graded by acoustic features of the contour. In general, gradations in the direction of wide range and high peaks in fundamental frequency, high average pitch, steep slope in rising or falling contours, and brief duration accentuate messages calling for activation of coping mechanisms or conveying high degrees of emotional engagement. Changes of acoustic features in the direction of low peaks and narrow range in fundamental frequency, low average pitch, flat slopes in contours, and prolonged duration accentuate comforting and soothing messages and convey low degrees of emotional engagement (Papoušek, Papoušek, and Symmes, 1991).

The use of melodic contours to carry preverbal prototypical messages seems understandable in stress languages because the other roles of modulations in fundamental frequency are reduced in adult-directed speech. Conversely, in tonal languages, melodic patterns play a crucial role in semantic differentiation of words. For instance, in Mandarin Chinese, one syllable can have four very different lexical meanings, according to the tone pattern. This circumstance seems to leave less freedom for yet another tonal variation in child-directed speech and raises the question of potential cultural differences in the expression of biological predispositions (H. Papoušek and M. Papoušek, 1991). Comparisons of child-directed speech between European American and Mandarin Chinese mothers (Papoušek, Papoušek, and Symmes, 1991) show that the aforementioned biological predispositions are universal even across stress and tone languages, at least in this case, and that Mandarin Chinese mothers even tend to violate phonological tone rules in favor of child-directed prototypical melodic messages (Papoušek and Hwang, 1991). Only minor differences are detectable in the degree of melodic expansion. Striking similarities in melodic contours across parental gender and language groups do not preclude interindividual variations in pitch excursions, duration of contours, or steepness of slope. These variations are individually stable (H. Papoušek and M. Papoušek, 1987) and thus may enable the infant to identify individual caregivers.

When speechlike vocal symbols take the lead in declarative learning, melodic gestures remain in function, and their frequency does not decrease (M. Papoušek, 1994b). They acquire new roles in segmenting the stream of speech into linguistically meaningful units, in highlighting phonological contrasts, the relevance of the first protowords and then the first referential words (Fernald and Mazzie, 1991; M. Papoušek, 1994b), and in linking focus of visual and auditory attention to objects of verbal communication (M. Papoušek, 1994a).

The extent of changes in intuitive parenting that are related to the appearance of reduplicated, canonical syllables is remarkable and, in most aspects, discontinuous. Some of these changes precede canonical syllables and seem to facilitate their development, for instance, in idiosyncratic games. Mothers introduce rhythmical games, including rhythmical stimulation in various modalities, at an age when infants are just about to start rhythmical kicking (Thelen, 1981) or rhythmical hand activities. Mothers combine infant movements with elements of vocal communication and thus frame them in pleasurable games as if to make the future significance of rhythms evident to infants. According to linguists (Holmgren, Lindblom, Aurelius, Jalling, and Zetterström, 1986; Locke, 1990), the mastery of rhythmical patterns is crucial for the onset of canonical babbling and for speech inasmuch as canonical syllables are considered the minimal rhythmic unit of most languages of the world (Oller and Eilers, 1992).

Other changes follow the appearance of canonical syllables and seem to utilize the newly opened area of support, namely, the acquisition of names for vital parts of environment. Corresponding changes have been documented, for instance, in the semantic content of maternal utterances, now related to objects of joint attention and declarative learning. Mothers increasingly direct or follow infant attention to objects within the infant's intimate environment. They help establish joint attention, joint action, and, finally, joint reference. Similarly, object play significantly increases at this time (M. Papoušek and H. Papoušek, 1991; M. Papoušek, 1993; 1994a, 1994b).

Thus, the main interactional transformation in maternal and infantile behaviors occurs at the beginning of canonical syllables, when the infant is between 7 and 11 months of age. Before it, mothers temporarily introduce rhythmic (idiosyncratic) games, whereas after it, mothers increasingly introduce word models in interactional contexts (M. Papoušek and H. Papoušek 1991; M. Papoušek, 1994a). The appearance of canonical syllables opens the stage for cultural influence. At the same time, the infant starts crawling and meeting new forms of cultural support and the first cultural limits to incipient independence. Babyishness, play face, and smile still secure sufficient tolerance in the social environment. However, the time is approaching when this biological basis of protection will disappear and when it will be increasingly urgent for the child to rely on adequate achievements in cultural integration. The biological case for necessary support in this direction is evidently based on apt timing.

CONCLUSIONS

The concept of intuitive parenting arose from interdisciplinary approaches with major contributions of developmental psychology, biology, and systems theory. While taking biological roots of human behaviors into consideration, students of parenting try to detect species-specific predispositions that differentiate primates from other mammals and humans from other primates. They do so for several theoretical and clinical reasons, the main one being to bridge gaps in our knowledge of regulatory factors and their functional roles in biological and cultural adaptation. This knowledge is a *sine qua non* for contemporary attempts to substitute outmoded behavioristic models of parenting with dynamic models of self-regulating, interactional systems (Fogel, 1990); the application of dynamic models requires a reliable quantification of all regulatory factors. The present concept of intuitive parenting cannot entirely cover such a requirement; it only demonstrates how serious gaps are still to be overcome. Additional theoretical aspects have been indicated in this chapter in relation to the interpretation of human evolution, to the altricity/precocity issue, and to the question of innate predispositions for speech acquisition and for its support from social environment.

Observations providing a database for theoretical reconsiderations have, of course, accumulated under circumstances that have been in focus of increasing attention among clinicians. To clinicians, it is of utmost importance to understand intrinsic motivators of human development and the functional significance of behavioral patterns observable in parent–infant interactions; their better understanding may facilitate detection of pathogenetic deviations. Potential origins of interactional and communicative disorders related to intuitive parenting have been discussed elsewhere (H. Papoušek and M. Papoušek, 1983, 1992; M. Papoušek, 2000); nevertheless, they elucidate the necessity of extending concepts of such disorders beyond the framework of emotional attachment in both diagnostic and therapeutic terms.

Moreover, educational psychologists may also find it interesting that intuitive parenting provides a window on those didactic interventions that have been selected by Nature during the process of evolution rather than prescribed by some cultural institution (H. Papoušek and M. Papoušek, 1989). Interestingly, the primary parental didactics are based on a dialogic interchange (including musical and playful elements) rather than on some systematic stimulation. The mechanisms of contingent rewards, instrumental learning, or associative conditioning may be involved but subsumed within complex interactions between two actively and spontaneously interacting partners and within a changing environmental context. Thus both the infant and the mother jointly contribute to developing competencies in the child, as Bornstein (1985) put it.

The parent—and the caregiver in general—is biologically predisposed as the more experienced partner to lead the infant toward a fundamental sociocultural integration and, for this purpose, toward the acquisition of a proper cultural communication. The dialogic character of this lead is evident in the respect to intrinsic motivations in infants on the one hand and to their developmental constraints in behavioral regulation on the other. The dosage and the complexity of didactic interventions are adjusted according to feedback cues in infant behaviors. Efforts for eliciting and maintaining infant communication are obvious. Expressions of emotions are often involved, sometimes as mere feelings to share, very often, though, as means serving to or resulting from communicative interchanges and sharing of information. Intuitive caregiving aims not only at hygienic, autonomic, and emotional needs of infants, but also at the needs to be together with someone, to share experience, to acquire adequate means of communication, and to create novel symbols—needs that seldom appear in the literature on children.

Some aspects of intuitive parenting have met increased attention in research, but might cause misunderstanding. For instance, the universality of behavioral tendencies that were formerly considered as solely maternal might lead to a narrow-minded conclusion that it is easy to replace the mother. Similarly, the effective functioning of nonconsciously displayed patterns of intuitive parenting might cause an underestimation of cultural achievements in the care of progeny. Misinterpretations of these types should be rejected as oversimplifications similar to the former either–or simplifications of concepts of maturation, learning, or emotional bonding. At a time of doubts about the value of family, when the newborn can expect parental divorce with a higher probability than the birth of a sibling, any simplification in concepts of parenting may be inappropriate. However, novel aspects of parenting merit the full attention of researchers and further study in all related disciplines.

ACKNOWLEDGMENTS

The preparation of this manuscript was kindly supported by the Alexander von Humboldt Foundation. The authors gratefully acknowledge Marc Bornstein's editorial recommendations and linguistic supervision.

REFERENCES

Anderson, B. J., Vietze, P., and Dokecki, P. R. (1977). Reciprocity in vocal interactions of mothers and infants. *Child Development, 48*, 1676–1681.

Beebe, B., Alson, D., Jaffe, J., Feldstein, S., and Crown, C. (1988). Vocal congruence in mother–infant play. *Journal of Psycholinguistic Research, 17*, 245–259.

Blount, B. G., and Padgug, E. J. (1977). Prosodic, paralinguistic, and interactional features of parent–child speech: English and Spanish. *Journal of Child Language, 4*, 67–86.

Bogen, J. E., and Bogen, G. M. (1969). The other side of the brain I, II, III. *Bulletin of the Los Angeles Neurological Society, 34*, 73–105; 135–162; 191–220.

Bornstein, M. H. (1985). How infant and mother jointly contribute to developing cognitive competence in the child. *Proceedings of the National Academy of Sciences U.S.A. 82*, 7470–7473.

Bühler, K. (1934). *Sprachtheorie* [The theory of language]. Jena, Germany: Fischer.

Collis, G. M., and Schaffer, H. R. (1975). Synchronization of visual attention in mother–infant pairs. *Journal of Child Psychology and Psychiatry, 16*, 315–320.

Darwin, C. (1871). The descent of man. London: Murray.

de Waal, F. B. M. (1987). Tension regulation and nonreproductive functions of sex among captive bonobos (*Pan paniscus*). *National Geographic Research, 3*, 318–335.

de Waal, F. B. M. (1988). The communicative repertoire of captive bonobos (*Pan paniscus*), compared to that of chimpanzees. *Behavior, 106*, 183–251.

Eibl-Eibesfeldt, I. (1967). Concepts of ethology and their significance in the study of human behavior. In H. W. Stevenson, E. H. Hess, and H. L. Rheingold (Eds.), *Early behavior: Comparative and developmental approaches* (pp. 127–146). New York: Wiley.

Erting, C. J., Prezioso, C., and Hynes, M. O. (1990). The interactional context of deaf mother–infant communication. In V. Volterra and C. Erting (Eds.), *From gesture to language in hearing and deaf children* (pp. 97–106). Berlin: Springer-Verlag.

Ferguson, C. A. (1964). Babytalk in six languages. *American Anthropologist, 66*, 103–114.

Fernald, A., and Mazzie, C. (1991). Prosody and focus in speech to infants and adults. *Developmental Psychology, 27*, 209–221.

Fernald, A., and Simon, T. (1984). Expanded intonation contours in mothers' speech to newborns. *Developmental Psychology, 20*, 104–113.

Fernald, A., Taeschner, T., Dunn, J., Papoušek, M., Boysson-Bardies, B., and Fukui, I. (1989). A cross-language study of prosodic modifications in mothers' and fathers' speech to preverbal infants. *Journal of Child Language, 16*, 977–1001.

Fogel, A. (1990). The process of developmental change in infant communicative action: Using dynamic systems theory to study individual ontogenies. In J. Colombo and J. Fagen (Eds.), *Individual differences in infancy: Reliability, stability, prediction* (pp. 341–358). Hillsdale, NJ: Lawrence Erlbaum Associates.

Freud, S. (1911/1975). Formulierungen über die zwei Prinzipien des psychischen Geschehens [Formulations on the two principles of mental functioning]. In *Studienausgabe* [Essays]. (Vol. III, pp. 17–24). Frankfurt: Fischer Verlag.

Gaddes, W. H. (1985). *Learning disabilities and brain function. A neuropsychological approach* (2nd ed.). New York, Berlin, Heidelberg, Tokyo: Springer-Verlag.

Gardner, R. A., and Gardner, B. T. (1969). Teaching sign language to a chimpanzee. *Science, 165*, 664–672.

Garnica, O. K. (1977). Some prosodic and paralinguistic features of speech to young children. In C. Snow and C. Ferguson (Eds.), *Talking to children: Language input and acquisition* (pp. 63–88). Cambridge, England: Cambridge University Press.

Gazzaniga, M., and LeDoux, J. (1978). *The integrated mind*. New York: Plenum.

Haarmann, H. (1990). *Universalgeschichte der Schrift* [Universal history of handwriting]. Frankfurt: Campus Verlag.

Haekel, M. (1985). Greeting behavior in 3-month-old infants during mother–infant interactions (Abstract). *Cahiers de Psychologie Cognitive, 5*, 275–276.

Herrnstein, R. J., and Loveland, D. H. (1964). Complex visual concept in the pigeon. *Science, 146*, 549–551.

Hoffmann, J. (1993). Unbewusstes Lernen—eine besondere Lernform? [Unconscious learning—a special form of learning?]. *Psychologische Rundschau, 44,* 75–89.

Holmgren, K., Lindblom, B., Aurelius, G., Jalling, B., and Zetterström, R. (1986). On the phonetics of infant vocalization. In B. Lindblom and R. Zetterstöm (Eds.), *Precursors of early speech. Wenner-Gren International Symposium Series* (Vol. 44, pp. 51–63). New York: Stockton.

Huizinga, J. (1955). *Homo ludens.* Boston: Beacon.

Jacobson, J. L., Boersma, D. C., Fields, R. B., and Olson, K. L. (1983). Paralinguistic features of adult speech to infants and small children. *Child Development, 54,* 436–442.

James, W. (1981). The principles of psychology (Vol. II). Cambridge, MA: Harvard University Press. (Original work published 1890).

Johanson, D. C., and White, T. D. (1979). A systematic assessment of early African hominids. *Science, 203,* 321–330.

Joseph, R., Gallagher, R. E., Holloway, W., and Kahn, J. (1984). Two brains, one child: Interhemispheric information transfer deficits and confabulatory responding in children aged 4, 7, 10. *Cortex, 20,* 317–331.

Kaye, K., and Fogel, A. (1980). The temporal structure of face-to-face communication between mothers and infants. *Developmental Psychology, 16,* 454–464.

Kaye, K., and Wells, A. J. (1980). Mother's jiggling and the burst–pause pattern in neonatal feeding. *Infant Behavior and Development, 3,* 29–46.

Kestermann, G. (1982). Gestik von Säuglingen: Ihre kommunikative Bedeutung für erfahrene und unerfahrene Bezugspersonen [Infant gesticulation: Its communicative significance for experienced and inexperienced caregivers]. Unpublished doctoral dissertation, University of Bielefeld, Germany.

Kihlstrom, J. F. (1987). The cognitive unconscious. *Science, 237,* 1445–1452.

Koester, L. S., Papoušek, H., and Papoušek, M. (1989). Patterns of rhythmic stimulation by mothers with three-month-olds: A cross-modal comparison. *International Journal of Behavioural Development, 12,* 143–154.

Korner, A. F., and Thoman, E. B. (1972). The relative efficacy of contact and vestibular stimulation in soothing neonates. *Child Development, 43,* 443–453.

Lewicki, P. (1986). *Nonconscious social information processing.* New York: Academic.

Lewis, M. M. (1936). *Infant speech. A study of the beginning of language.* New York: Harcourt, Brace.

Lieberman, P. (1984). *The biology and evolution of language.* Cambridge, MA: Harvard University Press.

Locke, J. L. (1990). Structure and stimulation in the ontogeny of spoken language. *Developmental Psychobiology, 23,* 621–643.

Lovejoy, C. O. (1981). The origin of man. *Science, 211,* 341–350.

MacKay, D. M., and MacKay, V. (1982). Explicit dialogue between left and right half of split-brains. *Nature (London), 295,* 690.

MacLean, P. D. (1973). *A triune concept of brain and behavior.* Toronto: University of Toronto Press.

MacLean, P. D. (1990). *The triune brain in evolution. Role in paleocerebral functions.* New York: Plenum.

Matsuzawa, T. (1993, July). *Cognitive development in stone-tool use by wild chimpanzees and human children in Guinea.* Keynote presentation at the 12th biennial meeting of The International Society for the Study of Behavioural Development, Recife, Brazil.

McCall, R. B., and Kagan, J. (1967). Attention in the infant: Effects of complexity, contour, perimeter, and familiarity. *Child Development, 38,* 939–952.

Morton, E. S. (1977). On the occurrence and significance of motivation-structural rules in some bird and mammal sounds. *American Naturalist, 111,* 855–869.

Newman, J. D. (1985). The infant cry of primates: An evolutionary perspective. In B. M. Lester and C. F. Z. Boukydis (Eds.), *Infant crying: Theoretical and research perspectives* (pp. 307–323). New York: Plenum.

Oller, D. K. (1980). The emergence of the sounds of speech in infancy. In G. H. Yeni-Komshian, J. F. Kavanagh, and C. A. Ferguson (Eds.), *Child Phonology: Vol. 1. Production* (pp. 93–112). New York: Academic.

Oller, D. K., and Eilers, R. E. (1988). The role of audition in infant babbling. *Child Development, 59,* 441–449.

Oller, D. K., and Eilers, R. E. (1992). Development of vocal signaling in human infants: Toward a methodology for cross-species vocalization comparisons. In H. Papoušek, U. Jürgens, and M. Papoušek (Eds.), *Nonverbal vocal communication: Comparative and developmental approaches* (pp. 174–191). New York: Cambridge University Press.

Papoušek, H. (1967). Experimental studies of appetitional behavior in human newborns and infants. In H. W. Stevenson, E. H. Hess, and H. L. Rheingold (Eds.), *Early behavior: Comparative and developmental approaches* (pp. 249–277). New York: Wiley.

Papoušek, H. (1969). Individual variability in learned responses during early post-natal development. In R. J. Robinson (Ed.), *Brain and early behavior. Development in the fetus and infant* (pp. 229–252). London: Academic.

Papoušek, H. (1977). Entwicklung der Lernfähigkeit im Säuglingsalter [Development of learning capabilities in infancy]. In G. Nissen (Ed.), *Intelligenz, Lernen und Lernstörungen* [Intelligence, learning and learning disabilities] (pp. 75–93). . Berlin: Springer-Verlag.

Papoušek, H. (1979). From adaptive responses to social cognition: The learning view of development. In M. H. Bornstein and W. Kessen (Eds.), *Psychological development from infancy: Image to intention* (pp. 251–267). Hillsdale, NJ: Lawrence Erlbaum Associates.

Papoušek, H., and Papoušek, M. (1974). Mirror image and self-recognition in young human infants: I. A new method of experimental analysis. *Developmental Psychobiology, 7*, 149–157.

Papoušek, H., and Papoušek, M. (1978). Interdisciplinary parallels in studies of early human behavior: From physical to cognitive needs, from attachment to dyadic education. *International Journal of Behavioural Development, 1*, 37–49.

Papoušek, H., and Papoušek, M. (1979). Early ontogeny of human social interaction: Its biological roots and social dimensions. In M. von Cranach, K. Foppa, W. Lepenies, and D. Ploog (Eds.), *Human ethology: Claims and limits of a new discipline* (pp. 456–478). Cambridge, England: Cambridge University Press.

Papoušek, H., and Papoušek, M. (1982). Integration into the social world: Survey of research. In P. M. Stratton (Ed.), *Psychobiology of the human newborn* (pp. 367–390), London: Wiley.

Papoušek, H., and Papoušek, M. (1983). Interactional failures: Their origins and significance in infant psychiatry. In J. D. Call, E. Galenson, and R. L. Tyson (Eds.), *Frontiers of infant psychiatry* (pp. 31–37). New York: Basic Books.

Papoušek, H., and Papoušek, M. (1984). Learning and cognition in the everyday life of human infants. In J. S. Rosenblatt (Ed.), *Advances in the study of behavior* (Vol. 14, pp. 127–163). New York: Academic.

Papoušek, H., and Papoušek, M. (1987). Intuitive parenting: A dialectic counterpart to the infant's integrative competence. In J. D. Osofsky (Ed.), *Handbook of infant development* (2nd ed., pp. 669–720). New York: Wiley.

Papoušek, H., and Papoušek, M. (1989). Intuitive parenting: Aspects related to educational psychology. In B. Hopkins, M.-G. Pecheux, and H. Papoušek (Eds.), Infancy and education: Psychological considerations. *European Journal of Psychology of Education, 4* (2, Special Issue), 201–210.

Papoušek, H., and Papoušek, M. (1991). Innate and cultural guidance of infants' integrative competencies: China, the United States, and Germany. In M. H. Bornstein (Ed.), *Cultural approaches to parenting* (pp. 23–44). Hillsdale, NJ: Lawrence Erlbaum Associates.

Papoušek, H., and Papoušek, M. (1992). Beyond emotional bonding: The role of preverbal communication in mental growth and health. *Infant Mental Health Journal, 13*, 43–53.

Papoušek, H., Papoušek, M., and Koester, L. S. (1986). Sharing emotionality and sharing knowledge: A microanalytic approach to parent–infant communication. In C. E. Izard and P. Read (Eds.), *Measuring emotions in infants and children* (Vol. 2, pp. 93–123). Cambridge, England: Cambridge University Press.

Papoušek, H., Papoušek, M., Suomi, S., and Rahn, C. (1991). Preverbal communication and attachment: Comparative views. In J. L. Gewirtz and W. M. Kurtines (Eds.), *Intersections with attachment* (pp. 97–122). Hillsdale, NJ: Lawrence Erlbaum Associates.

Papoušek, M. (1989). Determinants of responsiveness to infant vocal expression of emotional state. *Infant Behavior and Development, 12*, 505–522.

Papoušek, M. (1993, March). *Stages in child-directed speech: Relation to stages in the infant's interactional vocal repertoire.* Paper presented at the 60th meeting of the Society for Research in Child Development, New Orleans, LA.

Papoušek, M. (1994a). *Vom ersten Schrei zum ersten Wort: Anfänge der Sprachentwicklung in der vorsprachlichen Kommunikation* [From the first cry to the first word: origins of language acquisition in preverbal communication]. Bern, Germany: Huber.

Papoušek, M. (1994b). Melodies in caregivers' speech: A species-specific guidance toward language. In H. Papoušek (Ed.), Intuitive parenting: Comparative and clinical approaches. *Early Development and Parenting, 3* (1, Special Issue), 5–17.

Papoušek, M. (1995). Origins of reciprocity and mutuality in prelinguistic parent–infant dialogues. In I. Marková, C. Graumann, and K. Foppa (Eds.), *Mutualities in dialogue* (pp. 58–81). Cambridge England: Cambridge University Press.

Papoušek, M. (2000). Persistent crying, parenting, and infant mental health. In J. D. Osofsky, and H. E. Fitzgerald (Eds.), *WAIMH handbook of infant mental health: Vol. IV. Infant mental health in groups at high risk* (pp. 415–453). New York: Wiley.

Papoušek, M., and Hwang, S.-F. C. (1991). Tone and intonation in Mandarin babytalk to presyllabic infants: comparison with registers of adult conversation and foreign language instruction. *Applied Psycholinguistics, 12*, 481–504.

Papoušek, M., and Papoušek, H. (1981). Musical elements in the infant's vocalizations: Their significance for communication, cognition, and creativity. In L. P. Lipsitt (Ed.), *Advances in Infancy Research* (Vol. 1, pp. 163–224). Norwood, NJ: Ablex.

Papoušek, M., and Papoušek, H. (1989). Forms and functions of vocal matching in interactions between mothers and their precanonical infants. *First Language, 9*, 137–158.

Papoušek, M., and Papoušek, H. (1991). Preverbal vocal communication from zero to one: Preparing the ground for language acquisition. In M. E. Lamb and H. Keller (Eds.), *Infant development: Perspectives from German-speaking countries* (pp. 299–328). Hillsdale, NJ: Lawrence Erlbaum Associates.

Papoušek, M., Papoušek, H., and Bornstein, M. H. (1985). The naturalistic vocal environment of young infants: On the significance of homogeneity and variability in parental speech. In T. Field, and N. Fox (Eds.), *Social perception in infants* (pp. 269–297). Norwood, NJ: Ablex.

Papoušek, M., Papoušek, H., and Haekel, M. (1987). Didactic adjustments in fathers' and mothers' speech to their three-month-old infants. *Journal of Psycholinguistic Research, 16*, 491–516.

Papoušek, M., Papoušek, H., and Harris, B. J. (1987). The emergence of play in parent–infant interactions. In D. Görlitz and J. F. Wohlwill (Eds.), *Curiosity, imagination, and play: On the development of spontaneous cognitive and motivational processes* (pp. 214–246). Hillsdale, NJ: Lawrence Erlbaum Associates.

Papoušek, M., Papoušek, H., and Symmes, D. (1991). The meanings of melodies in motherese in tone and stress languages. *Infant Behavior and Development, 14*, 414–440.

Parke, R. D., Grossmann, K., and Tinsley, B. R. (1981). Father–mother–infant interaction in the newborn period: A German–American comparison. In T. Field (Ed.), *Culture and early interactions* (pp. 95–113). Hillsdale, NJ: Lawrence. Erlbaum Associates.

Parke, R. D., and O'Leary, S. E. (1976). Family interaction in the newborn period: Some findings, some observations, and some unresolved issues. In K. Riegel and J. Meacham (Eds.), *The developing infant in a changing world* (Vol. 2, pp. 653–663). The Hague: Mouton.

Pavlov, I. P. (1927). *Conditioned reflexes*. London: Oxford University Press.

Phillips, J. (1973). Syntax and vocabulary of mothers' speech to young children: Age and sex comparisons. *Child Development, 44*, 182–186.

Piaget, J. (1962). *Play, dreams, and imitation in childhood*. New York: Norton.

Preilowski, B. (1979). Consciousness after complete surgical section of the forebrain commissures in man. In I. Steele Russel, M. W. van Hof and G. Berlucchi (Eds.), *Structure and function of cerebral commissures* (pp. 411–420). London: Macmillan.

Ratner, N. B. (1984). Patterns of vowel modification in mother–child speech. *Journal of Child Language, 11*, 557–578.

Rheingold, H. L., and Adams, J. L. (1980). The significance of speech to newborns. *Developmental Psychology, 16*, 397–403.

Robson, K. (1967). The role of eye-to-eye contact in maternal–infant attachment. *Journal of Child Psychology and Psychiatry and Allied Disciplines, 8*, 13–25.

Rosenblatt, J. S. (1975). Prepartum and postpartum regulation of maternal behavior in the rat. In M. O'Connor (Ed.), *Parent–infant-interaction* (pp. 17–37). Amsterdam: Elsevier.

Rutter, R., and Durkin, K. (1987). Turn-taking in mother–infant interaction: An examination of vocalizations and gaze. *Developmental Psychology, 23*, 54–61.

Savage-Rumbaugh, E. S. (1990). Language acquisition in a nonhuman species: Implications for the innateness debate. *Developmental Psychobiology, 23*, 599–620.

Schaffer, H. R., Collis, G. M., and Parsons, G. (1977). Vocal interchange and visual regard in verbal and preverbal children. In H. R. Schaffer (Ed.), *Studies in mother–infant interaction* (pp. 291–324). London: Academic.

Schoetzau, A., and Papoušek, H. (1977). Mütterliches Verhalten bei der Aufnahme von Blickkontakt mit dem Neugeborenen [Maternal behaviour during establishment of eye contact with the newborn]. *Zeitschrift für Entwicklungspsychologie und pädagogische Psychologie, 9*, 231–239.

Seyfarth, R. M., Cheney, D. L., and Marler, P. (1980). Vervet monkey alarm calls: Semantic communication in a free-ranging primate. *Animal Behaviour, 28*, 1070–1094.

Snow, C. E. (1977). The development of conversation between mothers and babies. *Journal of Child Language, 4*, 1–22.

Snow, C. E., De Blauw, A., and van Roosmalen, G. (1979). Talking and playing with babies: The role of ideologies of child-rearing. In M. Bullowa (Ed.), *Before speech: The beginning of interpersonal communication* (pp. 269–289). Cambridge, England: Cambridge University Press.

Sperry, R. (1985). Consciousness, personal identity, and the dicided brain. In D. F. Benson and E. Zaidel (Eds.), *The dual brain* (pp. 11–26). New York: Guilford.

Stern, D. N. (1985). *The interpersonal world of the infant*. New York: Basic Books.

Stern, D. N., and Gibbon, J. (1979). Temporal expectancies of social behaviors in mother–infant play. In E. B. Thoman (Ed.), *Origins of the infant's social responsiveness* (pp. 409–429). Hillsdale, NJ: Lawrence. Erlbaum Associates.

Sullivan, J. W., and Horowitz, F. D. (1983). Infant intermodal perception and maternal multimodal stimulation: Implications for language development. In L. P. Lipsitt and C. K. Rovee-Collier (Eds.), *Advances in infancy research* (Vol. 2, pp. 183–239). Norwood, NJ: Ablex.

Thelen, E. (1981). Rhythmical behavior in infancy: An ethological perspective. *Developmental Psychology, 17*, 237–257.

Tolman, E. C. (1949). There is more than one kind of learning. *Psychological Review, 56*, 144–155.

Tronick, E. Z., Als, H., and Brazelton, T. B. (1980). Monadic phases: A structural descriptive analysis of infant-mother face-to-face interaction. *Merrill-Palmer Quarterly, 26*, 3–24.

Užgiris, I. C. (1981). Two functions of imitation during infancy. *International Journal of Behavioural Development, 4*, 1–12.

van Lawick-Goodall, J. (1967). *My friends the wild chimpanzees*. Washington, DC: National Geographic Society.

Vander, A. J., Sherman, J. H., and Luciano, D. S. (1990). *Human physiology. The mechanisms of body functions* (5th ed.). New York: McGraw-Hill.

von Bertalanffy, L. (1968). *General systems theory: Foundations, development, applications*. New York: Braziller.

von Frisch, K. (1965). *Tanzsprache und Orientierung der Bienen* [Dance language and orientation of bees]. Berlin: Springer.

Winter, P., Ploog, D., and Latta, J. (1966). Vocal repertoire of the squirrel monkey (Saimiri sciureus), its analysis and significance. *Experimental Brain Research, 1*, 359–384.

Wolff, P. H. (1969). The natural history of crying and other vocalizations in early infancy. In B. Foss (Ed.), *Determinants of infant behavior* (Vol. 4, pp. 81–109). London: Methuen.

Wolff, P. H. (1987). *The development of behavioral states and the expression of emotions in early infancy: New proposals for investigation*. Chicago, London: University of Chicago Press.

Wundt, W. (1893). Grundzuege der physiologischen Psychologie [Characteristics of physiological psychology] (Vol. II, 4th ed.). Leipzig: Engelmann.

PART II

SOCIAL ECOLOGY
OF PARENTING

7

Maternal and Dual-Earner Employment Status and Parenting

Adele Eskeles Gottfried
California State University, Northridge
Allen W. Gottfried
Kay Bathurst
California State University, Fullerton

INTRODUCTION

Research on maternal employment has proliferated over the past 50 years. Interest in the role of maternal employment and parenting has been coincident with the consistent increase in families with employed mothers over this period of time (Gottfried, Bathurst, and Gottfried, 1994). Cohen and Bianchi (1999) reported that women's labor force participation gave evidence of a steady, linear upward trend from 1971 to 1997. The U.S. Government Bureau of Labor Statistics reported that in 1999, for families with children under the age of 18 years, in 64.1% of the families both mothers and fathers were employed, whereas in 29.1% only fathers were employed, indicating that traditional family employment roles are in the minority. Even in families with children under the age of 6 years, the percentage of traditional families is in the minority, comprising only 36.9%, and when the youngest child is between 6 and 17 years of age the percent declines to 22.6% (U.S. Bureau of Labor Statistics, 2000). Whereas maternal employment was a minority phenomenon of 43% in 1975 (Hayghe, 1990), it is now the norm for mothers to be employed. These demographic trends correspond to other reports of maternal and dual-earner employment (Bond, Galinsky, and Swanberg, 1998). In the Fullerton Longitudinal Study the percentage of employed mothers increased from 36.2% when children were 1 year of age to 83% by the time children were 17 years old. Interestingly, although dual-earner families constitute the norm demographically, they continue to be nontraditional in that they deviate from the single- (male) earner, two-parent family that has dominated cultural expectations and developmental theory (Gottfried, Gottfried, Bathurst, and Killian, 1999).

In this chapter we focus on theory and research regarding maternal and dual-earner employment and parenting, including an overview of historical and central issues; major theories, themes, and perspectives; early and contemporary research defining three distinct phases; practical implications of the research; and future directions. Consideration is given to parental involvement, parenting processes by which maternal and dual-earner employment impinge on children's development; longitudinal research; employed parents' attitudes toward parenting and employment; child developmental and cultural concerns; family adaptations; and changes in conceptions of adults' gender-based roles and responsibilities.

HISTORICAL CONSIDERATIONS AND CENTRAL ISSUES REGARDING MATERNAL AND DUAL-EARNER EMPLOYMENT AND PARENTING

Historically, the research on maternal employment and parenting can be divided into three general sequential phases, which also define the central issues in this field of study. Phase 1 can best be described as the period of looking for direct effects of maternal employment on children's development. It began with an empirical question guided by the expectation that maternal employment would be detrimental to children's development because of maternal absence during the time mother was working (Gottfried, Gottfried, and Bathurst, 1995). The empirical question was whether maternal employment was detrimental to children. In this early research, the issue of maternal employment and parenting was reduced to the direct comparison of the children of employed and nonemployed mothers, usually without examination of parenting directly, and the implication was that any difference between the groups was due to the impact that employment had on the maternal role (Gottfried, 1988). Hence parenting was not examined as a complex variable that was related to employment on the one hand and children's development on the other. Rather, the maternal employment variable was typically divided into the employed versus nonemployed groups, and comparisons among children were made. Early research on maternal employment often reflected negative expectations of the impact of maternal employment on parenting and consequently on children's development. Many studies expected to detect detriment to children (e.g., Hand, 1957). Maternal absence through employment was believed to be deprivational, and research was designed to test the maternal deprivation perspective (Burchinal, 1963; Nye, Perry, and Ogles, 1963). Psychoanalytic theory provided a foundation for this perspective because the mother was considered to be of unparalleled importance to her child's psychological development (Bretherton, 1993; Cohler and Paul, in Vol. 3 of this *Handbook*).

This expectation of detriment to children caused by maternal employment has not been borne out by research. A conclusion that may be drawn is that maternal employment per se is neither facilitative nor detrimental to parenting and children's development. This conclusion is based on extensive empirical data across research studies and exhaustive reviews of research (Etaugh, 1974; Gottfried and Gottfried, 1988a; Gottfried et al., 1995, 1999; Hoffman, 1989; Lerner, 1994; Zaslow, Rabinovich, and Suwalsky, 1991). Not only did early Phase 1 research fail to consider the multifaceted role of parenting, the research did not account for heterogeneity within the employed- and the nonemployed-mother groups, such as family socioeconomic status, maternal occupational status and work hours, number of children in the home, mothers' and fathers' involvement, home environment, and maternal well-being, which could be responsible for differences between the groups when they were obtained (Gottfried et al., 1995).

Inasmuch as researchers increasingly saw the need to move beyond the direct effects approach of Phase 1 research, the research entered Phase 2, which characterizes the trend of current research. The research within this phase is predicated by the view, resulting from Phase 1 work, that maternal employment is embedded within the complex network of cultural, developmental, environmental, family, and socioeconomic factors. To understand fully the role of maternal employment in parenting and children's development, these factors need to be taken into account. Phase 2 concerns delineating the maternal employment variable into more refined issues and can be characterized as adopting a mediational viewpoint. This means that any effect of maternal employment on children's development is conceived to be due to the mediation of parenting and/or environmental variables that intervene between work variables on the one hand and children's development on the other. Hence, it has replaced the direct-effects approach that guided the research issues of Phase 1, in which it was expected that maternal employment would have a direct impact on children's development.

In contrast, Phase 2 research is concerned with the processes that mediate between maternal employment and children's development, and therefore maternal employment is viewed as playing an indirect role in children's development, with the influential variable being parenting. Variables such as family socioeconomic status, mothers' work hours and occupational status, maternal attitudes toward employment and parenting, role division between employed mothers and fathers, paternal involvement, and the quality of home environment play a dominant role in researchers' formulation of hypotheses and models to test (e.g., Hoffman and Youngblade, 1999; Lerner, 1994).

Whereas Phase 2 research has contributed to our knowledge about the role played by parental employment in family functioning and children's development, it continues to perpetuate adverse views of the impact of maternal employment. For example, themes such as maternal stress and role strain have been two such variables studied (e.g., Barling, 1990; Repetti and Wood, 1997b). Although this approach has contributed to an increased understanding of the indirect manner in which work roles and conditions may have an impact on children through parenting, its focus on work stress and role strains also serves to limit new conceptualizations of the role of maternal employment in parenting and children's development. It is important for the definition of research issues to advance beyond this perspective because, when research is framed to focus on stress, then attention is not being paid to the positive and adaptive functions of maternal and dual-earner employment with regard to parenting and children's development.

We advance the view that the field needs to enter Phase 3. In this phase, it is proposed that the field of maternal employment research will make additional headway when new research questions are formed in which maternal and dual-earner employment are conceptualized positively and in which families are viewed as adapting. New definitions of parenting roles between mothers and fathers are implicitly being developed by the families themselves, and greater attention needs to be paid to this in relation to maternal and dual-earner employment and parenting and children's development.

Our goal in this chapter is to present what we see as the most salient contemporary issues in the investigation of maternal and dual-earner employment with regard to parenting. Our conclusions will suggest taking a new approach to investigating maternal and dual-earner employment in relation to parenting and, ultimately, children's development. It is our view that the bottom line in the study of the impact of maternal and dual-earner employment on parenting concerns the welfare of children and their development. Implications and applications must be made with regard to enhancing the potential for facilitating the positive growth of children.

THEMES AND PERSPECTIVES REGARDING MATERNAL AND DUAL-EARNER EMPLOYMENT AND PARENTING

There are no overarching theories that pervade this field. Rather, the literature is characterized by many themes and perspectives. Several theoretical perspectives have been delineated, including the following: maternal deprivation, compensation, developmental impingement, and adaptation (Gottfried and Gottfried, 1994; Gottfried et al., 1994, 1995, 1999). The *maternal deprivation* perspective posits that when the mother is no longer the primary caregiver deprivation occurs and children's development suffers as a consequence. This perspective was derived from the psychoanalytic view of family functioning in which the mother–child relationship is regarded as being of unparalleled significance in the child's psychological development (Bretherton, 1993). With regard to maternal and dual-earner employment, the maternal deprivation view played an influential role in the early research in which maternal employment was conceptualized as a form of maternal absence that was due to employment, and hence the child was deprived of being with the mother while she was at work (Burchinal, 1963; Nye, Perry, and Ogles, 1963). Today, few studies discuss maternal absence that is due to employment, albeit the legacy of this approach continues to exist in the form of an underlying skepticism that maternal employment, even if the norm, is still not optimal.

The *compensation* perspective typically takes the form that father's increased involvement that is due to mother's employment serves to make up for mother's absence when she is at work. Certainly, the data strongly support a pattern of increased paternal involvement in dual-earner families (Gottfried et al., 1995, 1999, and in this chapter). However, the compensation perspective continues to operate under the presumption of deficit; that is, special family effort is required for overcoming the presumed deficit resulting from mothers being at work instead of being at home with their children. Rather than viewing families with employed mothers as different, perhaps because of their values about societal and family roles, gender-role definitions that may be more egalitarian (Deutsch, 1999), or seeing the father's increase in shared childcare responsibilities as a choice of the couple, the father's involvement is viewed as a response to the mother's work rather than an input to the decision to work. Alternatives to this view need to be considered. Research on attitudinal and ideological selection factors that influence parents' choices regarding employment and family roles, and the resulting impact on children's development, has not yet been conducted. Such attitudes have been studied contemporaneously or subsequent to parental employment, but not as precursors to the decision for mothers to be employed or to maintain a dual-earner home.

Another perspective pertaining to maternal and dual-earner employment is *developmental impingement*, which emerged from work on redefined or nontraditional families that includes maternal and dual-earner employment (Gottfried and Gottfried, 1994). The developmental impingement perspective includes four basic tenets: (1) There is no presumption of deficit, detriment, or benefit to children being reared in families with alternative structures. (2) The developmental level and other characteristics (e.g., gender, culture) of the child must be taken into account because the impact of certain variables may differ across such factors. (3) The impact of any alternative family form must be examined across a broad array of developmental outcomes to determine its generalizability and pervasiveness. This was recommended because many studies used a single outcome measure of children's development at a single point in time, and, if the findings were negative, explicit statements about detriment were made based on limited evidence. Hence multivariate and longitudinal studies can best address the breadth and the cross-time developmental aspects of effects. (4) A related concern is the need to generalize results across ecological levels and to examine, for example, extrafamilial societal influences that may have a spectrum of possible outcomes (e.g., positive, negative, none). In the maternal and dual-earner employment research, the developmental impingement perspective is beginning to accrue support. There is increasingly more maternal and dual-earner research on lower- and middle-socioeconomic status groups, varying cultural groups, and internationally (Gottfried et al., 1994, 1999). The developmental impingement perspective was an impetus to our proposal of examining family adaptations regarding maternal and dual-earner families (Gottfried et al., 1995, 1999).

Another perspective concerns *family adaptations* regarding maternal employment and dual-earner families (Gottfried et al., 1994, 1995, 1999; Spain and Bianchi, 1996). Family adaptation concerns practices and changes that support effective family functioning; for example, increased father participation, greater participation of children in housework, greater independence training of young children, nontraditional work schedules and alternating schedules of mothers and fathers, work flexibility, and others. Adaptation requires a change in perspective from deficit and compensation to neutrality consistent with the developmental impingement perspective.

Other perspectives have been proposed as well, including the mediation perspective (e.g., Hoffman and Youngblade, 1999), which views parenting behaviors as being the causal factors between maternal work on the one hand and children's development on the other; the lifespan contextual view (Lerner, 1994), in which maternal employment is but one process in the context of a multiplicity of processes that interact with children's development throughout the lifespan; contributions from work and sociology literature, including work and family interaction such as spillover of effects from work to family or family to work (e.g., satisfaction or stress in either work or family may have an impact on the other realm) (Edwards and Rothbard, 2000); gender-based versus egalitarian views of family roles that may influence mothers' and fathers' child involvement and division of household labor (Coltrane, 1996; Deutsch, 1999); ecological approaches that include time use (Richards and Duckett, 1994) and monitoring (Crouter and Head, in Vol. 3 of this *Handbook*; Crouter, Helms-Erikson, Updegraff, and McHale, 1999); and job conditions such as family friendly business policies and programs (Hughes and Galinsky, 1988; Levine and Pittinsky, 1997), work schedules (Presser, 1988, 1999), and job complexity (Greenberger, O'Neil, and Nagel, 1994; Parcel and Menaghan, 1994; Ryu and Mortimer, 1996). Each of these has made a contribution to our understanding of the complex interweave of variables among work, parenting, and ultimately children's development. These factors may not be mutually exclusive inasmuch as aspects in one area may have an impact on another. For example, changes in father involvement with children as related to mothers' employment may simultaneously indicate changes in role definitions and also have implications for the developmental impingement model in which children's increased exposure to fathers may be beneficial. A multiplicity of theories and perspectives characterizes the field, which presents a future challenge to integrating these approaches.

CLASSICAL AND MODERN RESEARCH: MATERNAL AND DUAL-EARNER EMPLOYMENT AND PARENTING

The research continues to defy coming to neatly packaged conclusions. Findings of studies often provide contrary evidence regarding the impact of maternal and dual-earner employment on parenting because contextual variables alter family situations, different variables are chosen for study, and populations differ, for example. Regardless, there are certain generalizations that can be made, and these will be advanced. As research issues have advanced in complexity, so too have the methods used.

Phase 1

Early Phase 1 research used a univariate or direct-effects approach. Children of employed and nonemployed mothers were compared as to their development without a control for the many other concomitant or confounding factors that may mediate the relation between maternal employment and children's development (Gottfried, 1988). However, by the 1980s it was widely recognized that samples of employed and nonemployed mothers in research studies may differ in various ways, such as socioeconomic status, occupational status, family size, or marital status. Direct comparisons of children are inadequate because differences between the groups could be attributable to these confounded factors, and not to maternal employment per se (Bronfenbrenner and Crouter, 1982; Gottfried, Gottfried, and Bathurst, 1988; Hoffman, 1984). Factors such as these should be controlled in statistical analyses to reduce the impact of confounded variables when one is attempting to study unique aspects of maternal employment status. Because there have been, by now, many thorough reviews examining whether children's development in various domains is related to maternal employment, in this chapter we do not seek to repeat them (Etaugh, 1974; Gottfried et al., 1995; Gottfried and Gottfried, 1988a, 1988b; Hoffman, 1974, 1984, 1989; Lerner, 1994; Rubenstein, 1985; Zaslow et al., 1991). In this chapter we focus on issues that are specifically pertinent to parenting and children, and inasmuch as the contemporary research is dominated by a Phase 2 approach, we concentrate on this. It is important to note that, across research and reviews of this area, there is consensus that maternal employment per se is not detrimental to children. Rather, the literature indicates that maternal employment is embedded within a complex network of cultural, socioeconomic, environmental, family, gender-role, and work factors. The key to understanding maternal employment and its relation to parenting is to study the processes and contexts within which maternal employment exists.

Phase 2

Virtually all contemporary research in the developmental literature pertaining to maternal and dual-earner employment, parenting, and children's development can be categorized as Phase 2 work. Although not always possible, multivariate longitudinal research (that is, multiple measures over time) is a necessity in this area, as in many other areas of developmental science. As Gottfried and Gottfried (1988a) indicated, longitudinal research provides the means whereby the consistency, patterns, and magnitudes of relations across time, ages, and developmental domains can be addressed. A multivariate approach is requisite to provide replicability of relations across different measures of the same constructs and across measures of different constructs (see Gottfried et al., 1988, 1995). Cross-time measures within and across domains of development are required for establishing generalizability of significant effects. Findings of statistical significance obtained at one time only, rather than across time, may be unreliable or spurious. Certain issues can be addressed only through longitudinal research, such as the existence of "sleeper effects" (effects that do not emerge contemporaneously, but emerge over time), timing of employment onset and offset, and stability and change of employment and family processes. These issues of continuity, generalizability, and stability have been addressed in results of individual longitudinal studies (Galambos, Petersen, and Lenerz, 1988; Goldberg and Easterbrooks, 1988; Gottfried et al., 1988; Gottfried and Gottfried, 1988b; Hock, DeMeis, and McBride, 1988; Lerner and Galambos, 1988; and Owen and Cox, 1988).

The issue of causality in studies of maternal employment needs special attention. Frequently, when a statistical finding about differences between employed and nonemployed groups is significant, the finding is interpreted as showing the "effect" of maternal employment on children. However, the research is inherently associational, as maternal employment is not a randomly assigned variable. Selective factors create the groups, and maternal employment may covary with other deterministic factors. This research requires multivariate analyses with appropriate controls. Even when appropriate controls are made and significant findings emerge, these should not necessarily be taken as causal relations. Certainly, still unaccounted for variables may affect the results.

In this section we address issues in contemporary research regarding maternal employment and parenting, including the mediation model concerning the role of maternal and dual-earner employment parenting behaviors and family environments; mothers' and fathers' child involvement; maternal attitudes concerning satisfaction with work and parenting roles; the developmental impingement model including the effects of child age, gender, socioeconomic status, and culture; family–work-related issues such as work hours and schedules, job flexibility, and role definitions and sharing. It is important to note here that, whereas the earlier chapter on maternal and dual-earner employment status and parenting (Gottfried et al., 1995) is indeed pertinent, in this chapter we do not seek to duplicate the issues and findings presented in the first. Hence, the reader is directed to the earlier chapter that provides the integration up to that point.

Mediation Models Concerning Parenting in Maternal and Dual-Earner Employment

This line of research has contributed to our understanding of parenting processes that intervene between work and children's development. The research generally tests the view that maternal employment and children's development are linked through intervening parenting processes. Whereas many studies suggest mediation of effects from maternal employment to parenting to children's development, not many studies have actually tested the models statistically. Overall, research supports the view that any impact of maternal employment would occur because of parenting (Barling, 1990; Beyer, 1995; Gottfried et al., 1988, 1995; MacEwen and Barling, 1991).

Using regressions and path analyses, Hoffman and Youngblade (1999) found that several mediation analyses supported the links from mothers' employment status to parenting styles and from parenting styles to children's outcomes, indicating that the extent to which maternal employment was linked to more optimal parenting styles, was, in turn, related to better academic and social outcomes in children, particularly for the lower-socioeconomic status families. For third- and fourth-grade children of lower- and middle-socioeconomic status African American, European American, and Latin American families, Hoffman and Youngblade (1999) found that mothers' mood mediated between employment and parenting style, and that parenting style related to children's development, but that these relations varied with the socioeconomic status of the family. In the lower-socioeconomic status families, maternal employment was significantly and inversely related to mothers' depressed mood. The working mothers were less depressed, and, in turn, depressed mood was positively related to both authoritarian and permissive parenting, but negatively related to authoritative parenting. Hence less depressed mothers were significantly more authoritative and significantly less authoritarian and permissive with their children. Morale (satisfaction with life) was found to mediate between maternal employment and positive mother–child interaction, whereby employed working class mothers had more positive morale and this in turn related to more positive interactions. A specific mediation path was also found for working class mothers of boys, in which maternal employment was inversely related to depressed mood, which was in turn inversely related to authoritative parenting. Hence working class mothers of boys who were less depressed also used more authoritative parenting. More authoritative parenting was related to more positive academic and social behaviors, whereas more authoritarian behaviors were related to less positive child outcomes in these areas for those of lower-socioeconomic status.

In the middle-socioeconomic status sample, associations emerged between maternal employment and parenting behaviors; however, maternal employment was not significantly associated with maternal mood, indicating that it was not a mediator between employment and parenting in these analyses. Hoffman and Youngblade (1999) also reported a number of significant associations between maternal employment and parenting behavior in their sample, suggesting that in general, employed mothers used less authoritarian control, less permissiveness, and more authoritative styles. Married employed mothers held higher educational expectations for their children. Whereas the reasons for differences in mediation found between the lower- and the middle-socioeconomic status families with regard to these findings is not immediately apparent, it may be that middle-socioeconomic status mothers are buffered from the effects of mood because they have more available resources, possibly resulting in an absence of relation to their employment status. Adding to this possibility is the difference in sample composition between middle- and lower-socioeconomic status mothers inasmuch as the middle-socioeconomic status mothers were all married and the lower-socioeconomic status sample consisted of married and single mothers. These findings are good examples of the importance of the contextual variables that need to be accounted for (Lerner, 1994).

Other research has supported a mediation model of the impact of maternal employment on children's development. Using structural equation modeling, Crouter, Bumpus, Maguire, and McHale (1999) found that high levels of work pressure were associated with heightened feelings of role overload for both mothers and fathers of adolescents. High role overload predicted greater parent–child conflict associated with lower adolescent psychological well-being. Moreover, fathers' work pressure predicted both their own and mothers' feelings of role overload, whereas mothers' work pressure predicted only their own overload, not their spouses'. Hence, fathers' work pressure appears to be shared by mothers, but not the reverse. Findings of Ex and Janssens (1998), using exploratory LISREL analyses, indicated that, in a Dutch sample, daughters' gender-role attitudes were indirectly related to maternal employment through childrearing patterns. The more a mother worked, the less she used a conformist childrearing style relating to more nontraditional attitudes of her daughter. Traditional attitudes held by mothers contributed to a greater emphasis on daughters' conformity and daughters' attitudes were more traditional. These findings suggest a complex interlinking among maternal employment, traditional and nontraditional attitudes and childrearing patterns, and traditionality of daughters' attitudes.

Lerner and Galambos (1988) sought to examine mediating factors between role satisfaction and child outcome. They found that parent–child interaction was affected by role satisfaction, and that this in turn related to child difficulty in employed and nonemployed mothers. When mothers in the New York Longitudinal Study were more satisfied with their role, they evidenced lower levels of maternal rejection; maternal rejection was positively related to child difficulty (a temperament variable). Their findings suggest that parental role satisfaction affects children's behavior through its impact on parent–child interaction.

Whitbeck et al. (1997), using structural equation modeling, found that, for both mothers and fathers living in rural areas, aspects of work and/or economic strain affected parenting behaviors, which in turn contributed to adolescents' self-efficacy. Fathers whose work allowed autonomy and self-direction were more likely to use inductive or reasoning-oriented parenting techniques and avoided using harsh parenting, such as losing one's temper or physical punishment, whereas fathers' economic pressures were related to less use of inductive parenting and greater harshness. Whereas neither fathers' working conditions nor economic strain related directly to adolescents' sense of mastery and control, the use of inductive parenting techniques and avoidance of harsh punishment techniques were predictive of adolescents' positive self-efficacy. For mothers, economic hardship, but not working conditions, predicted less use of inductive and greater harshness of parenting, which were in turn related to adolescents' mastery and control.

Parental Involvement

Mothers. The question that has been addressed in this area is whether and how employment may have an impact on the involvement of mothers with their children. Current data reveal that there is not a great deal of difference in the amount of time that mothers spend with their children or in the types of activities engaged in, regardless of maternal employment status, and explanations focus on the change in patterning of time-use choices by mothers and families in homes in which the mothers are employed and nonemployed.

Bianchi (2000) found that children's time with mothers changed little from 1981 to 1997 despite the increase in maternal employment and single parenting. Whereas employed mothers spent less time with their children than nonemployed mothers did, Bianchi (2000) concluded that the differences between the groups was not dramatic (ranging from 82% to 92% as much time as employed mothers across the studies reviewed), and that this difference has remained stable over time. In two-parent homes, the amount of time fathers spent with children increased from 1965 to 1998 to counteract any decrease in mothers' time spent with children that was due to their employment. Bianchi (2000) asserted that employed mothers have reoriented their time commitments and spend less time in volunteer work, get less sleep, and engage in less free and leisure time to try to balance paid work and child involvement. This explanation is an example of family adaptation to maternal employment. Bianchi (2000) also proposed that there is less difference in the activities of children of employed and nonemployed mothers now than in the past, as it is widely accepted for nonemployed as well as employed mothers to place children in nonmaternal care settings (Clarke-Stewart and Allhusen, in Vol. 3 of this *Handbook*). As family incomes rise, children engage in more out-of-home activities than in the past. In addressing the question of why there are so few negative outcomes of maternal employment, Bianchi (2000) asserted that there has been reallocation of mothers' time and priorities, delegation of family work to others, increased preschool enrollment for children of employed and nonemployed mothers, and redefinition of parenting roles.

Data reported by Bond et al. (1998) were consistent with those of Bianchi (2000) in that they found that over the period of 1977 to 1997 there was no difference in the total amount of time that employed mothers spent in caring for and doing things with their child on workdays, and concluded that mothers have preserved the time they have with children on workdays despite longer work hours. Employed mothers' time spent with children on nonwork days increased from 1977 to 1997, although not significantly. Fathers' time involvement with children on workdays and days off increased significantly over that interval. Nevertheless, working mothers were more likely to take care of sick children on workdays than fathers were, and mothers also spent more time than fathers in caring for their children on work and nonwork days. The authors concluded that both mothers and fathers sacrifice personal time to maintain their care for their children.

Further supporting the absence of difference between the involvement and parenting behaviors of employed and nonemployed mothers, DeMeis and Perkins (1996) found little difference in the caregiving behaviors of employed and nonemployed mothers of young children (with the youngest child in the family less than 5 years old). The only significant difference that emerged was that homemaker mothers were more likely than employed mothers to watch educational TV with their children. They concluded that the mothering role of employed and nonemployed mothers included the same range of childcare activities and that this may reflect the efforts that employed mothers make to fulfill their mothering role. This conclusion is consistent with that of Bianchi (2000). Galinsky and Swanberg (2000) came to a similar conclusion in their research by indicating that mothers preserved the amount of time they spent with their children while decreasing the amount of time they spent on household chores and their own personal activities. Fathers increased the amount of time they spent on child and household chores and reduced their free-time activities. This is another example of family adaptation and role balance that occurs in homes with employed mothers. A study of German mothers whose children were either at home or in childcare centers (Ahnert, Rickert, and Lamb, 2000) generalizes this finding cross nationally by showing that the overall time spent in caregiving with toddlers did not differ, but patterning of time did, with the mothers who used childcare providing more communication, soothing, proximity, and emotional exchanges with their children in the evenings than did mothers of home-only toddlers. Stith and Davis (1984) compared the interactions of mothers of 5- to 6-month-old infants and childcare providers on a number of interaction variables and found no differences between employed and nonemployed mothers in sensory stimulation. Both employed and nonemployed mothers were superior to caregivers in providing contingent socially mediated stimulation. Employed mothers were also superior to the caregivers in providing sensory stimulation.

In addition to the research reviewed in the current work, in our previous chapter we discussed maternal involvement in relation to proximal home environment to which children are exposed (Gottfried et al., 1995). Overall, as consistent with the present review, the overview in that chapter indicated that employed mothers were involved with their children, with some differences in patterns of interaction between employed and nonemployed mothers and their children. For example, employed mothers made more attempts at training toileting and dressing skills and held higher educational aspirations for their children (Gottfried et al., 1995). Overall, the evidence clearly shows that employed mothers are as capable of providing nurturing and stimulating environments for their children as are nonemployed mothers.

Fathers. There has been a great deal of evidence documenting the increase in fathers' involvement with their children when mothers are employed. The literature continues to provide consistent and overwhelming evidence that fathers are more involved in childcare and activities with their children when mothers are employed, and this involvement increases the more hours that mothers are employed (Bonney, Kelley, and Levant, 1999; Deutsch, Lussier, and Servis, 1993; Fagan, 1998; Hoffman and Youngblade, 1999; Grych and Clark, 1999; NICHD Early Child Care Research Network, 2000). This has been a reliable finding across the different research groups and across socioeconomic status and ethnicities represented in the cited studies. It has also been found that fathers' involvement decreases as the fathers' work hours increase (Bonney et al., 1999). Hence there is evidence that there is role balance between mothers and fathers in dual-earner families, although mothers still provide more of the care (Gottfried et al., 1995, 1999).

In current research, some interesting patterns have been obtained. Beitel and Parke (1998) found that for first-time parents of 3- to 5-month-old infants, fathers' level of sole responsibility in parenting their infants was related to mothers' employment, whether it was treated as a categorical variable or the number of work hours was examined when mothers were at work. Hence infants were cared for by their fathers when mothers were at work. In contrast, when mothers were home, the amount of time fathers spent with their infants did not differ by maternal employment status. Fathers' work hours were inversely related to their sole and joint responsibility for their infants. There was also evidence that fathers' levels of involvement were affected by mothers' and fathers' attitudes toward that involvement, with greater involvement related to more favorable attitudes. This latter finding is supported by Deutsch et al. (1993), who found that fathers of 3- to 8-month-old infants were more likely to be engaged in childcare if the wife's attitudes were more nontraditional or feminist.

Grych and Clark (1999) found that fathers were more sensitive and responsive in their interactions with their infants when their wives worked part time or were nonemployed. This can be related to an earlier finding by Goldberg and Easterbrooks (1988), who found that fathers were less sensitive (emotional support and quality of assistance) in interacting with their toddlers in a puzzle-solving task when their wives were employed full time compared with those working part time or not working. Goldberg and Easterbrooks (1988) attributed this to fathers' increase in childcare responsibilities. It is also possible that fathers are not used to juggling multiple roles, and this is more likely to occur more when mothers' work involvement is greater. However, when children were kindergartners, Goldberg and Easterbrooks (1988) found no differences in fathers' authoritative childrearing attitudes or reports of their own emotional experiences during the week. The possibility that degree of sensitivity in father–child interaction is related to child age should be examined in the literature inasmuch as young children require more intensive involvement in physical care than older children, and this itself may serve as a stressor for fathers. The developmental impingement model would suggest this as a possibility as well.

Crouter, Helms-Erikson et al. (1999) found that, in dual-earner families of elementary school-age children, fathers were more knowledgeable about their children's daily experiences (activities, whereabouts, and companions) when their wives worked longer hours, whereas mothers' knowledge did not differ with regard to work hours. Furthermore, all parents were more knowledgeable about the same-gender and the younger children. This indicates that, as mothers' employment intensity increases, fathers appear to be brought into the family to a greater extent, and, consistent with the findings reported above for mothers' involvement, they are equally knowledgeable regardless of their work intensity. The developmental impingement model is further supported by differences in age and gender found.

Mothers' and fathers' workplace situations may also relate to father involvement. For example, Berry and Rao (1997) found that, as fathers in dual-earner families engaged in more child-related events that interfered with work roles, they experienced more stress. Casper and O'Connell (1998) found that, for dual-earner families with children under the age of 5, the more hours a husband is not at work during the interval his wife is working, the more likely he is to care for the children. When parents work different shifts and when both spouses work nonday shifts, fathers are more likely to care for their children than when both parents work day shifts. When both spouses work part time and when mothers work part time and husbands work full time, fathers are more likely to provide childcare than are fathers in families in which both spouses work full time. Furthermore, during the period of economic recession of 1990–1991 there was a sharp increase in the use of fathers as child-care providers as unemployment climbed, which decreased as unemployment declined. Therefore both father availability and economic factors play a role in fathers' childcare. Glass (1998) reported that fathers of 6- to 12-month-old infants were more likely to provide childcare when mothers worked fewer than 20 hr/week, families had lower incomes, one parent worked an evening or night shift, and fathers worked fewer hours. When mothers' work hours increased, couples looked for nonparental care. Here, a complex interplay of availability and work hours appear to be operating in fathers' provision of childcare with young children in dual-earner households. This highlights the balance of roles that occurs within dual-earner families.

Hoffman and Youngblade (1999) studied whether fathers' involvement is facilitative of children's scholastic outcomes through their gender attitudes. They found that higher father participation in routine childcare tasks was related to higher academic achievement. Using a mediational analysis, they found that, as mothers' employment increased fathers' involvement in childcare, daughters were more likely to adopt less gender-based views of their competence, which related to their sense of competence and academic achievement. Hence fathers who provide childcare may be serving as nontraditional role models that serve to raise daughters' future possibilities in what may have been traditionally considered male roles.

Overall, the increased involvement of fathers with their children is supported by demographic as well as child developmental literature. Even if the increase may have been a response to family needs, the outcomes for children appear to be favorable. In addition to having a greater exposure to their fathers, children's development is likely to be positively affected, as noted in this chapter and by Tamis-LeMonda and Cabrera (1999), who reported that from infancy through adolescence, higher involvement of children with fathers is associated with a host of favorable affective and cognitive outcomes.

The Fullerton Longitudinal Study: Mothers' and Fathers' Involvement and the Developmental Impingement Perspective

The Fullerton Longitudinal Study has focused on the cross-time investigation of maternal employment, family environment, and children's development from infancy through adolescence (Gottfried et al., 1988, 1994). It was initiated with 130 healthy 1-year-old infants and their families with not less than 80% of the participants returning for any assessment. The sample represents a wide range of the middle-class as measured by the Hollingshead Four Factor Index of Social Status (Gottfried, 1985; Hollingshead, 1975), ranging from semiskilled workers through professionals. Developmental assessments were conducted every 6 months from the ages 1 through 3.5 years and yearly from age 5 years through adolescence. Throughout the course of this investigation, numerous developmental assessments across intellectual, cognitive, affective, social, academic, motivational, and behavioral adjustment domains were conducted as well as assessment of the proximal home environment and involvement of mothers and fathers with their children in families in which the mothers were employed and not employed. Having a longitudinal study of children from ages 1 through 17 years affords us the opportunity to determine if there are any differences in patterns of parental involvement between employed and nonemployed mother families. At the initiation of the study 36.2% of mothers were employed, and by the time the children reached the age of 17 years, 83% of the mothers were employed. The overwhelming majority of mothers were employed by the end of their children's adolescence, and therefore in data analyses over the course of the study, the comparison of employed and nonemployed mothers is based on an increasingly larger employed group and an increasingly smaller nonemployed group. This itself represents an aspect of the developmental impingement perspective with regard to the changing of maternal roles to which the children were exposed during their childhood.

With regard to fathers' involvement, we detected differences related to maternal employment status from early childhood through adolescence, and the patterning of these findings is supportive of the developmental impingement model. When mothers were employed, fathers were shown to be more involved with their children (childcare, playing, nurturing, stimulating) when their children were 6 years old, which was predicted from mothers' employment status when their children were 5 years old (Gottfried et al., 1988). The findings (Gottfried et al., 1994) continued to show that fathers were significantly more involved with their 8- to 12-year-old children when mothers were employed. When analyzed contemporaneously (i.e., maternal employment status at age 8 years with father involvement at the same age, and so on through the age of 12 years), it was found that fathers spent significantly more time with children at the ages of 8 and 12 years. With regard to sharing activities with their children, fathers shared significantly more activities with their 8-year-old sons in employed-mother families, whereas there were no significant differences in activities spent with daughters regardless of maternal employment status. Prospective analyses (i.e., earlier maternal employment status with subsequent father involvement) showed that, when mothers were employed in previous years, fathers were subsequently more involved with their children through the age of 12 years compared with those in homes in which mothers were nonemployed. When mothers were employed when children were 3.5 and 6 years of age, fathers spent significantly more time with their 8-year-old children; likewise, when mothers were employed when children were 3.5 and 8 years of age fathers spent significantly more time with their 12-year-old children. Across the contemporaneous and prospective analyses, the increased time that fathers spent with children when mothers were employed was primarily on weekdays. There were no significant differences obtained regarding children's gender in these analyses. These findings showed that subsequent patterns of increased paternal involvement with children were established earlier during the children's preschool years. When mothers entered the work force earlier, fathers established increased time involvement with their children, and this pattern continued into preadolescence.

We have continued to examine fathers' time involvement with their adolescent children at the ages of 13 through 17 years as related to maternal employment status by using both contemporaneous and prospective analyses. Whereas contemporaneous analyses showed an absence of significance in the time fathers spent with adolescents regardless of maternal employment status on both weekdays and weekends, prospective analyses indicated that earlier maternal employment continued to result in significantly greater father time involvement with their adolescents. When mothers were employed when children were 3.5 years, fathers spent significantly more time with their adolescents at the ages of 13, 14, 15, and 17 years, with near significance occurring in the same direction when their adolescents were 16 years of age. These results occurred for both weekday and weekend time spent with adolescents, and these results occurred for boys and girls. When mothers were employed when children were 8 years old, fathers spent significantly more weekday time with their 14- and 17-year-old adolescents, and when maternal employment occurred when children were 10 years old, fathers were significantly more involved with their 14-year-old adolescents on weekdays. In these analyses at adolescence, the sample was restricted to both biological parents in the home to ensure family structure consistency. These results are significant inasmuch as they indicate that the earlier a mother is employed, the more likely the father is to establish a pattern of increased time involvement with their children, which is consistent through the end of their children's adolescence. This occurred most consistently when children were of preschool age and extended through the age of 17 years, although maternal employment when children were aged 8 and 10 years was also related to increased paternal involvement, but not thereafter. Perhaps it is within the children's preschool years that it is optimal to establish a consistent pattern of increased father time involvement inasmuch as this period is increasingly the beginning of school years for children (e.g., Bianchi, 2000) and children of employed mothers are more likely to be in preschool (Hofferth and Sandberg, 1998). Our findings may also indicate that mothers' employment when children are young results in or is concomitant with a stronger commitment of both mothers and fathers for fathers to be more involved with their children. These data provide convincing support for the developmental impingement model inasmuch as the patterning of experience of children with fathers is different depending on the time at which mothers are employed, and children are more likely to receive more father involvement consistently over time when mothers are employed earlier. Additionally, these findings also underscore the unique role that longitudinal data play in examining maternal and dual-earner employment as related to parenting. Had we had only contemporaneous or cross-sectional data, we would have come to very different conclusions about fathers' involvement during their children's adolescence in relation to maternal employment. Having a history of maternal employment with father involvement data permitted the evaluation of long-term trends and detecting consistencies across time.

Regarding mothers, in analyses when children were ages 1 though 12 years (Gottfried et al., 1988, 1994), the homes and parenting provided by employed and nonemployed mothers did not differ significantly with respect to stimulation, nurturing, parent–child interactions, and family climate across the age range and the numerous and varied environmental measures previously described. For the most part, the environments in the homes of employed and nonemployed mothers were equivalent regarding these aspects. The few significant differences that were obtained indicated that employed mothers had higher educational attitudes during early childhood and encouraged greater independence training for their infants. Regarding time spent with children from the ages 8 through 12 years, regardless of maternal employment status, mothers' time spent with children was not significantly different whether considered contemporaneously or prospectively, with the exception of employed mothers who reported spending more time with their sons at the ages of 8 and 12 years, but no differences with daughters in relation to maternal employment status in contemporaneous analyses. Regarding mothers' time involvement with their adolescents at the ages of 13 through

17 years, there were no significant differences, regardless of maternal employment status in either contemporaneous or prospective analyses. Overall, these data are consistent with those reported by Bianchi (2000), Bond et al. (1998), and DeMeis and Perkins (1996) regarding maternal involvement.

We also examined the amount of time parents spent with children over the years from ages 8 through 17 years. It was not possible to statistically analyze employed-mother versus nonemployed-mother homes as to these differences over time because only one mother never worked at all over this period. However, visual inspection of the data revealed that for both mothers and fathers in employed-mother and nonemployed-mother homes, there was a continuous decrease in the amount of time spent with children on both weekdays and weekends across this age span. This finding is supported by others who reported a progressive decrease in parental time and childcare involvement from childhood through adolescence (Galinsky, 1999; DeLuccie, 1996; Higgins and Duxbury, 1994; Lerner and Abrams, 1994). It may be that researchers must redefine parental involvement during adolescence. Earlier dimensions of parental involvement such as childcare and time spent with children in activities may decrease in relevance during adolescence (Steinberg and Silk, in Vol. 1 of this *Handbook*.) Perhaps there are more subtle forms of parental involvement that are more distal and less proximal, such as monitoring (Crouter and Head, in Vol. 3 of this *Handbook*), overseeing, or the initiation of help seeking by adolescents. Is it possible that adolescents in dual-earner families may seek their parents' help differentially relative to those in single-earner families? Such questions have yet to be examined, but may result in new views of parental involvement.

Maternal Satisfaction with Employment and Parenting

Gottfried et al. (1995) concluded that research indicates that satisfaction with one's role as an employed or a nonemployed mother is significant to furthering an understanding of maternal employment. Role satisfaction is associated with more favorable maternal mental health and child-related outcomes. Research continues to support this link between mothers' satisfaction with their employment roles relating favorably to family and child characteristics. For example, Kim and Honig (1998) found that in highly educated, stable homes of Korean immigrant families in the United States, maternal satisfaction with employment was positively related to child resilience. Windle and Dumenci (1997) found that in dual-earner families with children, higher levels of parental and occupational stress were related to less marital satisfaction and family cohesion.

In the Fullerton Longitudinal Study, we studied maternal attitudes toward the dual responsibilities of parenting and employment as related to children's development and family environment when the children were 5 through 17 years old. The scale we developed included items pertaining to perceptions of ability to handle the dual responsibilities of work and parenting, satisfaction with employment, reason for employment (financial, personal satisfaction), ability to coordinate work and family responsibilities, positive emotional and stress spillover from employment to home, and worry about their child. Higher scores on the scale indicated more positive perceptions of the ability to handle dual responsibilities, more work satisfaction, and less stress and worry.

In earlier research (Gottfried et al., 1988), findings indicated that whereas mothers' attitudes toward the dual responsibilities of parenting and employment were not pervasively related to home environment or children's development, they did exhibit some significant, albeit low, correlations indicating that when employed mothers held more positive attitudes children (5 years old) had higher interest and participation in school, greater academic intrinsic motivation in reading (7 years old), higher reading and writing achievement (7 years old), and fewer reported behavior problems (5 and 7 years old); and their environments were somewhat more stimulating (5 years old), there was more maternal involvement (5 and 7 years old), and more democratic family regulation (7 years old). Overall, whereas attitudes toward the dual responsibilities of employment and parenting did not relate to most of the developmental and the environmental variables that were measured in the Fullerton Longitudinal Study, they did relate in a consistent manner to school-related behavior, child behaviors, and limited aspects of the home environment.

When the children were 11 through 17 years old, mothers' attitudes toward the dual responsibilities of parenting and employment were measured at each assessment with a highly reliable scale we developed based on the maternal attitude findings when children were ages 5 and 7 years. This scale consists of 15 items measuring the same construct as that for ages 5 and 7 years regarding mothers' perceptions about their ability to meet the dual responsibilities of parenting and employment. Higher scores represented more positive attitudes, less stress, and less worry. Factor analyses indicated a single factor. Coefficient alphas conducted at each age were strong, ranging from .76 to .84. Cross-time correlations were also conducted to determine stability reliability of the instrument, showing that attitudes showed substantial stability from one year to the next, with correlations at contiguous years ranging from .68, $p < .001$, to .76, $p < .001$.

Thus far in our analyses, we have correlated maternal attitudes with work variables on the one hand, and a thorough range of developmental outcomes and family environment on the other. Work conditions included mothers' and fathers' work flexibility, work hours during the week and weekend, occupational status, and socioeconomic status. Development included academic achievement, intellectual functioning, academic motivation, self-esteem, and behavior problems, and environmental measures included emotional climate of the home and parent–child relationships. Hence our strategy was to ascertain the degree to which maternal attitudes were related to work conditions on the one hand, and developmental and environmental outcomes on the other. Correlations were all conducted partialing socioeconomic status to be sure that significant results were independent of social status. Zero-order and partial correlations were virtually identical, and the partial correlations are reported here. Correlations are combined across child gender as patterns were similar for boys and girls.

Regarding work conditions, mothers' attitudes toward the dual responsibilities of employment and parenting were significantly more positive when their work schedules were more flexible at every age, with r ranging from .31, $p < .05$, to .57, $p < .001$. Furthermore, as the number of work hours during the week increased, mothers' attitudes became more negative at every age, with correlations ranging from $-.29$, $p < .05$, to $-.71$, $p < .001$. The strongest correlation between attitudes and work hours was when the children were 11 years old. Maternal attitudes did not correlate significantly with fathers' work conditions. Hence, when mothers' jobs were more flexible and when mothers worked fewer hours, their satisfaction with dual responsibilities of parenting and employment were more positive.

In relation to children's development, maternal attitudes were significantly correlated with behavior problems, as measured by the Parent Report version of the Child Behavior Checklist. These correlations were significant and negative when the children were from the ages of 13 to 17 years, indicating that, when mothers had more favorable attitudes, their children had fewer behavior problems. Significant correlations ranged from $-.30$, $p < .01$, to $-.41$, $p < .001$. This is consistent with the findings obtained earlier when the children were 5 and 7 years old. There were no other significant patterns of correlations between maternal attitudes and child outcomes. Hence the few relations found earlier with some educationally relevant developmental outcomes were not obtained during adolescence.

Regarding the relations between maternal employment attitudes and environmental outcomes, some interesting patterns were obtained. When mothers had more positive attitudes, using the Family Environment Scale (administered when the children were 12, 14, 16, and 17 years old) (Moos and Moos, 1994), there was greater family cohesion (ages 12, 14, and 16 years), with r ranging from .23, $p < .05$, to .29, $p < .01$, and less family conflict (ages 12, 16, and 17 years), r ranging from $-.33$, $p < .01$, to $-.21$, $p < .05$. By use of the Parent–Child Relationship Inventory (administered when the children were 15 and 16 years old), when mothers reported greater emotional and practical support in the parenting role, greater satisfaction with parenting, greater involvement (i.e., positive attitude toward interest in their child's activities, level of knowledge of the child, and time spent with the child), and were more effective in setting limits with their child they had more favorable attitudes toward employment and parenting, with r ranging from .22, $p < .05$, to .50, $p < .001$.

Overall, these patterns reveal a network of relations with maternal employment attitudes showing that mothers are more satisfied with the dual responsibilities of employment and parenting when their work is characterized by more flexibility and fewer work hours and when the home environments evidence more cohesion, less conflict, more support for parenting, and more satisfaction in the parenting role. Our future analyses will be directed at determining causal relations between work variables, maternal attitudes, child behavior problems, and environment.

Specific Developmental and Contextual Issues

Gender.   There has been great interest in whether maternal employment has a differential impact on boys and girls. Whereas in early literature there was concern that middle-socioeconomic status boys were vulnerable to detrimental effects of maternal employment, this has not been substantiated by subsequent and longitudinal research, as indicated by a paucity of gender differences (Gottfried and Gottfried, 1988a). The most consistent finding regarding child gender in the maternal employment literature has been for daughters to have more egalitarian gender-role concepts and higher aspirations (Gottfried et al., 1995; Hoffman and Youngblade, 1999; Nelson and Keith, 1990; Wright and Young, 1998). A particularly interesting finding was reported by Wolfer and Moen (1996): Daughters of African American mothers were more likely to stay in school longer the more years their mothers worked during childhood and preadolescence. For daughters of European American mothers, the duration of staying in school was not related to mothers' employment. Here, not only is gender important, but ethnicity is as well. For African American daughters, perhaps mothers' work serves as a particularly important stimulus to lengthening their education.

Career development.   A relatively new focus in the research regarding maternal employment and child outcomes has been with regard to how maternal employment may relate to career choices or employment of adolescents. Castellino, Lerner, Lerner, and von Eye (1998) found that young adolescents (mean age of 11.8 years) had higher career aspirations when their mothers had higher occupational statuses and higher education. Structural equation modeling showed that maternal employment and education directly influenced adolescent career trajectories both at the beginning and the end of sixth grade. In the Fullerton Longitudinal Study, Gottfried (2000) found that adolescents were more satisfied with their own employment when their mothers were employed and had higher occupational status and education and when fathers had greater job flexibility. Mothers' and fathers' occupational statuses were positively related to children's cognitive and academic performance and to more intellectually and educationally stimulating home environments in analyses from early childhood through the age of 12 years (Gottfried et al., 1988, 1994). These findings are consistent with those of Castellino et al. (1998) and suggest that parental occupational status may ultimately affect children's career paths through school achievement.

Ryu and Mortimer (1996) found that mothers' but not fathers' intrinsic and extrinsic work values significantly influenced girls' extrinsic work values, whereby mothers' intrinsic values were negatively related and their extrinsic values were positively related to daughters' extrinsic work values but unrelated to daughters' intrinsic values. Sons' intrinsic and extrinsic values were influenced by the supportiveness of both parents. Zick and Allen (1996) found that adolescent daughters, but not sons, were more likely to be employed when their mothers were employed. Whereas these studies do not identify the specific parenting linkages between parental employment on the one hand and adolescent career development on the other, they do suggest that parents' employment has an impact on these aspects, and further work would be important in this area.

Socioeconomic status and culture.   The developmental impingement perspective and contextual views (Gottfried et al., 1999; Lerner, 1994) would both indicate the necessity for examining socioeconomic status and cultural factors in relations among parental employment, parenting, development, and environments. Evidence suggests benefits of maternal employment for children within lower-socioeconomic status families (Cherry and Eaton, 1977; Gottfried et al., 1995; Heyns, 1982; Hoffman and Youngblade, 1999; Rieber and Womack, 1968; Zaslow and Emig, 1997). An issue that is as yet unresolved is the impact of mothers' employment on families that are moving from welfare to work. Wilson, Ellwood, and Brooks-Gunn (1995) cautioned that the change may produce new stressors such as schedule changes. Zaslow and Emig (1997) suggested that when the effects of mandatory welfare-to-work programs are examined, attention should be paid to outcomes that may occur when mothers involuntarily work, as when they move from welfare to work, as opposed to studies of lower-socioeconomic status families in which the mothers are employed voluntarily. Although specific parenting mechanisms linking maternal employment and children's development in less advantaged families have yet to be specifically elucidated, such factors as relieving economic strain, better resources to facilitate home environments and opportunities, as well as role satisfaction and parental well-being should be considered.

Ethnic variation is also important to study. McLoyd (1993) suggested that maternal employment in African American families is more central to the economic well-being of these families than is the employment of European American wives and therefore may be more positively accepted. In African American families, work is viewed as compatible with maternal and marital roles (Bridges and Etaugh, 1994; McLoyd, 1993). Another study indicating the important effect of culture was conducted by Moorehouse and Sanders (1992). In middle-socioeconomic status European American and working class Mexican American families, more academically competent elementary school children saw their parents as having more positive feelings about their work. However, more competent children in labor class Mexican American families viewed their mothers' feelings about work as more negative. Moorehouse and Sanders concluded that children in these families may be exposed to aspects of their parents' work they find undesirable. Lerner and Noh (2000) noted that the significance of work in the family differs across cultural groups, depending on such factors as the level of employment, education, and consistency with the gender roles of the family.

Internationally, there was an increase in maternal employment from 1970 to 1990 (Engle and Breaux, 1998). As reviewed in Gottfried et al. (1999), the emergent literature on maternal employment in developing and third world countries is often focused on issues relevant to child survival, health, and growth. Gottfried et al. (1995) and Engle and Breaux (1998) indicated that the role of cultural factors is important to consider as the values of particular countries are likely to have an impact on maternal employment phenomena such as fathers' involvement. Komarraju (1997) found that the interactions of mothers and fathers in single- and dual-earner homes in India were no different, indicating that mothers were still perceived as the primary caregivers of infants and fathers remained at a distance. In cultures with more adherence to traditional gender-defined roles, fathers' participation in childcare did not show the same trends of increased involvement with maternal employment, as reported for India (Chowdhury, 1995; Sekaran, 1992) and Malaysia (Peng, 1993). Peng (1993) reported that 23% of Malaysian women were forced to leave the labor force because of lack of adequate childcare. On the other hand, research with Latin families (Herrera and DelCampo, 1995; Valdez and Coltrane, 1993; Ybarra, 1982) and families in Sweden (Sandqvist, 1992) and Singapore (Yuen and Lim, 1992) shows increased father involvement associated with maternal employment. In comparing first-time mothers of infants, Pascual, Haynes, Galperin, and Bornstein (1995) found that higher education and occupational status predicted fewer work hours for Argentinian mothers but greater work hours for mothers in the United States. Hence specific cultural issues are important to consider as factors moderating these relations.

Specific work issues. A plethora of work-related variables has been examined in relation to parenting, and processes regarding work–family interactions have been advanced across a wide and varied literature (e.g., Edwards and Rothbard, 2000; Frederiksen-Goldsen and Sharlach, 2000; Galinsky and Swanberg, 2000), including spillover from work to family and from family to work; compensation representing efforts to offset dissatisfaction in one domain by seeking satisfaction in another; segmentation or separating the spheres of work and family; resource drain, which refers to transferring resources such as time from one area to another; congruence or similarity between family and work; work–family conflict, in which meeting the needs of work and family are incompatible with each other (role strain, time conflicts); and role gain. Of those proposed, the two that have been given substantially more attention in the parenting literature have been schedule flexibility and work hours and role strain. Gottfried et al. (1995) reviewed aspects of schedule flexibility and role strain that may have an impact on parenting, and a broad conclusion was that when the work schedule flexibility is limited and incompatible role demands are made, parental stress can be expected to increase. The extent to which this stress is likely to have an impact on parenting and children's development is a question that is increasingly being examined in the mediation models previously described. Additionally, research continues to support the need for work flexibility as an important variable for working parents and children. As an example, in our own data, parents were more positive in their attitudes regarding being able to handle the dual responsibilities of work and parenting when they had more flexible work schedules and fewer employment hours. Other research supports this conclusion as well (Fredriksen-Goldsen and Sharlach, 2000; Galambos and Walters, 1992). Levine and Pittinsky (1997) reviewed surveys that indicated that work schedule flexibility is considered essential to job satisfaction by large percentages of both men and women, and, whereas employers generally view job flexibility as an accommodation for working mothers, it is now becoming important to recruiting and retaining working fathers as well and to their work productivity. According to the U.S. Bureau of Labor Statistics (1998), parents with children under the age of 18 years were more likely to work a flexible schedule than were workers with no children under the age of 18 years (28.9% compared with 26.8%, respectively). Regarding role strain, research shows that work stress appears to have an impact on the well-being of mothers (Duxbury and Higgins, 1994; Galinsky and Swanberg, 2000; Schwartzberg and Dytell, 1996) and interactions with preschoolers (Repetti and Wood, 1997a). Overall, regarding work schedules and work hours, there is no optimal number of work hours nor any one type of schedule that has been established to recommend to employed parents in dual-earner families. Rather, individual circumstances determine these, and favorable or adverse aspects of work conditions would be expected to be related to parenting through work–family processes that mediate between employment and parenting.

PRACTICAL CONSIDERATIONS REGARDING MATERNAL AND DUAL-EARNER EMPLOYMENT AND PARENTING

It is important to reassure parents that work per se is not a detriment to children's development at any age. It is the success to which parents are able to manage the demands of work and family and provide quality parenting and environments for their children by which children's development is likely to be affected. To the extent that parenting itself is efficacious and to the extent that conditions in the workplace and family either support or stress the families, then parenting is likely to be influenced, which in turn is likely to have an impact on children's development.

The most obvious practical consideration is for the provision of childcare and afterschool care. It is beyond the realm of this chapter to review childcare options. However, in dual-earner families, fathers can be expected to provide part of the childcare, particularly when the mothers work more hours. Parents need to be concerned about types and quality of childcare, and such organizations as the National Association for the Education of Young Children (http://www.naeyc.org) may be a resource for helping to choose suitable care. Quality childcare is essential for facilitating the family adaptations and positive outcomes of maternal and dual-earner employment.

Another practical implication of this look at maternal and dual-earner employment and parenting is that job flexibility is probably the most important job characteristic to seek in combining work and family. This is borne out by the literature, which shows more favorable attitudes and the ability to handle dual roles when work hours are more controllable. Identifying family friendly work conditions and work settings (Frederiksen-Goldsen and Sharlach, 2000; Galinsky and Swanberg, 2000; Heymann, 2000; Hughes and Galinsky, 1988; Spalter-Roth, R. M., 1996) is a practical concern. It is important for supervisors to be supportive of mothers' and fathers' desires to exercise flexible work options and to help provide conditions that reduce work stress. Job searches by working parents may include flexibility and supportiveness as factors.

Finally, although not a practical suggestion, it may be heartening for parents to know that, in a study of children's perceptions of their parents' work, Galinsky (1999) found that children had many positive perceptions of their parents. For example, with regard to feeling important and loved there was no difference in children's view, regardless of mothers being employed or nonemployed.

As has been suggested (Gottfried et al., 1995), applications of research concerning maternal and dual-earner employment and parenting must be made to the societal arena. It is not sufficient for the academic community alone to be aware of the findings of this enormous body of research on maternal and dual-earner employment, parenting, and children's development. Top priority needs to be given to disseminating the results of research accurately, and with contemporary data, in textbooks; to professionals in allied fields, such as attorneys, judges, teachers, and pediatricians, who work with families routinely; and to the media for the public. It is up to families to decide whether to adopt new patterns or follow traditional ones, but it is ultimately important for all families to be viewed impartially and fairly.

CONCLUSIONS

Maternal and dual-earner employment has by now amassed a considerable body of literature that results in a few generalizable conclusions. Aside from the by now familiar conclusion that maternal employment is not detrimental to children's development and that any effects that are due to mothers' employment can be understood only through parenting and environmental processes that mediate between mothers' employment on the one hand and children's development on the other, it is apparent that work-related stress is not desirable as it impinges on parenting processes, whereas at the other end of the continuum a greater sense of well-being in mothers and fathers is more favorable. This conclusion may be similar to that for any family, regardless of maternal employment. Any situation that enhances stress is likely to affect parenting (Gottfried et al., 1999), and when parents feel self-efficacious they are likely to engage in more positive parenting with their child. Along with this finding is the reality of the demographics, that maternal employment is the norm, even among mothers with infants and young children. With the pervasiveness of this phenomenon and the general lack of negative outcomes that are due to employment, and indeed some positive results, it appears that it is time to stop considering maternal employment as a separate genre of family. It needs to become integrated into the mainstream of family research. It should be included regularly as a contextual variable to better refine and understand parenting processes in general, and not isolated as a separate phenomenon. Hence it is our recommendation that in future parenting research all studies collect sample characteristic data on the employment status of the families, just as one would collect data on the socioeconomic status, child gender, marital status, and other characteristics. Hence parental employment status would become integrated within the literature and naturally analyzed along with other family processes that are being studied.

The major future direction to be advanced here, however, is with regard to initiating Phase 3 research. It is time to look at maternal and dual-earner employment with a fresh perspective concerning the changes and competencies that exist and how they relate to parenting and children's development. For example, there is an increasing body of literature from psychology and sociology focusing on the development of equality between male and female roles (Berry and Rao, 1997; Coltrane, 1996; Deutsch, 1999; Levine and Pittinsky, 1997; Potuchek, 1997). Indeed, employed parents are redefining and renegotiating their roles to become coproviders to their children. This research has done much to raise our awareness of these issues, but it has not gone far enough because it has thus far not been related to parenting and children's development. This is a major research focus that needs to be implemented.

Another area that has been overlooked is the impact of employment on the competencies that mothers attain as a result of their work and how this may have an impact on both their parenting and children's development. Across the literature, there has been no systematic study of the positive characteristics of mothers that result from their employment and how they might relate to mothers' parenting and their children's development, whereas the literature has continued to focus on the stress produced by work schedules, work hours, occupying dual roles, and the like. Are there aspects of the mother herself that change for the better as a result of employment? Certainly the increased independence of mothers, assertiveness, negotiating skills, insights into work and organizations, ability to work with others, and exposure of mothers to a more diverse world outside of the home setting are all aspects of work that may have a significant impact on the mothers' parenting and their children's development, and these could apply across all social strata. This view needs to be conceptualized into a new research agendum. Now is the time to reorient the focus to examining the positive strengths of maternal and dual-earner employment for parenting and, ultimately, children's development. Furthermore, delineating causal pathways between these variables needs to be accomplished as well, a trend that has already begun in Phase 2.

Another aspect of competencies of maternal and dual-earner families, which we have elaborated earlier (Gottfried et al., 1995, 1999), concerns the family adaptations that are often made. For example, the greater involvement of fathers with their children when mothers are employed, job flexibility, and nontraditional work schedules may be all be considered family adaptations. It is possible that with new forms of work, such as telecommuting, family adaptations will become even more diverse and entrenched. The degree to which these families are initially different, or changed by work, is as yet undetermined, and selective factors may also add to the issue of family adaptation.

It is our view that, unless we transcend the search for adverse circumstances of maternal employment and enter Phase 3 research by reconceptualizing the issues into those of maternal as well as paternal contributions to the family through their dual parenting and employment roles, the field will move no further toward understanding the interplay among parental employment, parenting, and children's development. We would like to see that understanding enlarged.

ACKNOWLEDGMENTS

We thank the California State Universities, Northridge and Fullerton; Thrasher Research Foundation; Spencer Foundation; the Society for the Psychological Study of Social Issues (Division 9 of the American Psychological Association); and AMC Theaters for supporting our research. The continuing interest of the children and families in the Fullerton Longitudinal Study is deeply appreciated.

REFERENCES

Ahnert, L., Rickert, H., and Lamb, M. E. (2000). Shared caregiving: Comparisons between home and child care settings. *Developmental Psychology, 36*, 339–351.

Barling, J. (1990). *Employment, stress, and family functioning*. New York: Wiley.

Beitel, A. H., and Parke, R. D. (1998). Paternal involvement in infancy: The role of maternal and paternal attitudes. *Journal of Family Psychology, 12*, 268–288.

Berry, J. O., and Rao, J. M. (1997). Balancing employment and fatherhood: A systems perspective. *Journal of Family Issues, 18*, 386–402.

Beyer, S. (1995). Maternal employment and children's academic achievement: Parenting styles as mediating variables. *Developmental Review, 15*, 212–253.

Bianchi, S. M. (2000, March). *Maternal employment and time with children: Dramatic change or surprising continuity?* 2000 Presidential Address, Population Association of America, Los Angeles.

Bond, J. T., Galinsky, E., and Swanberg, J. E. (1998). *The 1997 national study of the changing workforce*. New York: Families and Work Institute.

Bonney, J. F., Kelley, M. L., and Levant, R. F. (1999). A model of fathers' behavioral involvement in child care in dual-earner families. *Journal of Family Issues, 13*, 401–415.

Bretherton, I. (1993). Theoretical contributions from developmental psychology. In P. G. Boss, W. J. Doherty, R. LaRossa, W. R. Schumm, and S. K. Steinmetz (Eds.), *Sourcebook of family theories and methods: A contextual approach* (pp. 275–297). New York: Plenum.

Bridges, J. S., and Etaugh, C. (1994). Black and white college women's perceptions of early maternal employment. *Psychology of Women Quarterly, 18*, 427–431.

Bronfenbrenner, U., and Crouter, A. C. (1982). Work and family through time and space. In S. B. Kamerman and C. D. Hayes (Eds.), *Families that work: Children in a changing world* (pp. 39–83). Washington, DC: National Academy Press.

Burchinal, L. G. (1963). Personality characteristics of children. In F. I. Nye and L. W. Hoffman (Eds.), *The employed mother in America* (pp. 106–124). Chicago: Rand McNally.

Castellino, D. R., Lerner, J. V., Lerner, R. M., and von Eye, A. (1998). Maternal employment and education: Predictors of young adolescent career trajectories. *Applied Developmental Science, 2*, 114–126.

Casper, L. M., and O'Connell, M. (1998). Work, income, the economy, and married fathers as child-care providers. *Demography, 35*, 243–250.

Cherry, F. F., and Eaton, E. L. (1977). Physical and cognitive development in children of low-income mothers working in the child's early years. *Child Development, 48*, 158–166.

Chowdhury, A. (1995). Employed mothers and their families in India. *Early Child Development and Care, 113*, 65–75.

Cohen, P. N., and Bianchi, S. M. (1999, December). Marriage, children, and women's employment: What do we know? *Monthly Labor Review, 122*, 22–31.

Coltrane, S. (1996). *Family man.* New York: Oxford University Press.

Crouter, A. C., Bumpus, M. F., Maguire, M. C., and McHale, S. M. (1999). Linking parents' work pressure and adolescents' well-being: Insights into dynamics in dual-earner families. *Developmental Psychology, 35*, 1453–1461.

Crouter, A. C., Helms-Erikson, H., Updegraff, K., and McHale, S. (1999). Conditions underlying parents' knowledge about children's daily lives in middle childhood: Between- and within-family comparisons. *Child Development, 70*, 246–259.

DeLuccie, M. (1996). Predictors of paternal involvement and satisfaction. *Psychological Reports, 79*, 1351–1359.

DeMeis, D. K., and Perkins, H. W. (1996). "Supermoms" of the Nineties: Homemaker and employed mothers' performance and perceptions of the motherhood role. *Journal of Family Issues, 17*, 777–792.

Deutsch, F. M. (1999). *Halving it all: How equally shared parenting works.* Cambridge, MA: Harvard University Press.

Deutsch, F. M., Lussier, J. B., and Servis, L. J. (1993). Husbands at home: Predictor of paternal participation in childcare and housework. *Journal of Personality and Social Psychology, 65*, 1154–1166.

Duxbury, L., and Higgins, C. (1994). Work–family conflict: A comparison by gender, family type, and perceived control. *Journal of Family Issues, 15*, 449–467.

Edwards, J. R., and Rothbard, N. P. (2000). Mechanisms linking work and family: Clarifying the relationship between work and family constructs. *Academy of Management Review, 25*, 178–200.

Engle, P. L., and Breaux, C. (1998). *Fathers' involvement with children: Perspectives from developing countries.* (Social Policy Rep., Vol. 12, No. 1, pp. 1–21). Ann Arbor, MI: Society for Research in Child Development.

Etaugh, C. (1974). Effects of maternal employment on children: A review of recent research. *Merrill-Palmer Quarterly, 20*, 71–98.

Ex, C. T. G. M., and Janssens, J. M. A. M. (1998). Maternal influences on daughters' gender role attitudes. *Sex Roles, 38*, 171–186.

Fagan, J. (1998). Corrrelates of low-income African-American and Puerto Rican fathers' involvement with their children. *Journal of Black Psychology, 24*, 351–367.

Fredriksen-Goldsen, K. I., and Scharlach, A. E. (2000). *Families and work: New directions in the twenty-first century.* New York: Oxford University Press.

Galambos, N. L., Petersen, A. C., and Lenerz, K. (1988). Maternal employment and sex typing in early adolescence: Contemporaneous an longitudinal relations. In A. E. Gottfried and A. W. Gottfried (Eds.), *Maternal employment and children's development: Longitudinal research* (pp. 155–189). New York: Plenum.

Galambos, N. L., and Walters, B. J. (1992). Work hours, schedule inflexibility, and stress in dual-earner spouses. *Canadian Journal of Behavioral Science, 24*, 290–302.

Galinsky, E. (1999). *Ask the children: What America's children really think about working parents.* New York: Morrow.

Galinsky, E., and Swanberg, J. E. (2000). Employed mothers and fathers in the United States: Understanding how work and family life fit together. In J. L. Haas, P. Hwang, and G. Russell (Eds.), *Organizational change and gender equity: International perspectives on fathers and mothers at the workplace* (pp. 15–28). Thousand Oaks, CA: Sage.

Glass, J. (1998). Gender liberation, economic squeeze, or fear of strangers: Why fathers provide infant care in dual-earner families. *Journal of Marriage and the Family, 60*, 821–834.

Goldberg, W. A., and Easterbrooks, M. A. (1988). Maternal employment when children are toddlers and kindergartners. In A. E. Gottfried and A. W. Gottfried (Eds.), *Maternal employment and children's development: Longitudinal research* (pp. 121–154). New York: Plenum.

Gottfried, A. E. (1988). Maternal employment and children's development: An introduction to the issues. In A. E. Gottfried and A. W. Gottfried (Eds.), *Maternal employment and children's development: Longitudinal research* (pp. 3–8). New York: Plenum.

Gottfried, A. E. (2000, February). *Developmental aspects of adolescent employment in the family setting.* Presented at the Annual Faculty Poster and Creative Activities Fair, California State University, Northridge.

Gottfried, A. E., Bathurst, K., and Gottfried, A. W. (1994). Role of maternal and dual-earner employment status in children's development: A longitudinal study from infancy through early adolescence. In A. E. Gottfried and A. W. Gottfried (Eds.), *Redefining families: Implications for children's development* (pp. 55–97). New York: Plenum.

Gottfried, A. E., and Gottfried, A. W. (1988a). *Maternal employment and children's development: Longitudinal research.* New York: Plenum.

Gottfried, A. E., and Gottfried, A. W. (1988b). Maternal employment and children's development: An integration of longitudinal findings with implications for social policy. In A. E. Gottfried and A. W. Gottfried (Eds.), *Maternal employment and children's development: Longitudinal research* (pp. 269–287). New York: Plenum.

Gottfried, A. E., and Gottfried, A. W. (1994). Impact of redefined families on children's development: Conclusions, conceptual perspectives, and social implications. In A. E. Gottfried and A. W. Gottfried (Eds.), *Redefining families: Implications for children's development* (pp. 221–229). New York: Plenum.

Gottfried, A. E., Gottfried, A. W., and Bathurst, K. (1988). Maternal employment, family environment, and children's development: Infancy through the school years. In A. E. Gottfried and A. W. Gottfried (Eds.), *Maternal employment and children's development: Longitudinal research* (pp. 11–58). New York: Plenum.

Gottfried, A. E., Gottfried, A. W., and Bathurst, K. (1995). Maternal and dual-earner employment status and parenting. In M. H. Bornstein (Ed.), *Handbook of Parenting: Vol. 2. Biology and Ecology of Parenting* (pp. 139–160). Mahwah, NJ: Lawrence Erlbaum Associates.

Gottfried, A. E., Gottfried, A. W., Bathurst, K., and Killian, C. (1999). Maternal and dual-earner employment: Family environment, adaptations, and the developmental impingement perspective. In M. Lamb (Ed.), *Parenting and child development in "nontraditional" families* (pp. 15–37). Mahwah, NJ: Lawrence Erlbaum Associates.

Gottfried, A. E. (1985). Measures of socioeconomic status in child development research: Data and recommendations. *Merrill-Palmer Quarterly, 32,* 85–92.

Greenberger, E., O'Neil, R., and Nagel, S. K. (1994). Linking worplace and homeplace: Relations between the nature of adults' work and their parenting behaviors. *Developmental Psychology, 30,* 990–1002.

Grych, J. H., and Clark, R. (1999). Maternal employment and development of the father–infant relationship in the first year. *Developmental Psychology, 35,* 893–903.

Hand, H. (1957). Working mothers and maladjusted children. *The Journal of Educational Sociology, 30,* 245–246.

Hayghe, H. V. (1990). Family members in the work force. *Monthly Labor Review, 113,* 14–19.

Herrera, R. S., and DelCampo, R. L. (1995). Beyond the superwoman syndrome: Work satisfaction and family functioning among working-class, Mexican American women. *Hispanic Journal of Behavioral Sciences, 17,* 49–60.

Heymann, J. (2000). *The widening gap.* New York: Basic Books.

Heyns, B. (1982). The influence of parents' work on children's school achievement. In S. B. Kamerman and C. D. Hayes (Eds.), *Families that work: Children in a changing world* (pp. 229–267). Washington, DC: National Academy Press.

Higgins, C., and Duxbury, L. (1994). Impact of life-cycle stage and gender on the ability to balance work and family responsibilities. *Family Relations, 43,* 144–151.

Hock, E., DeMeis, D., and McBride, S. (1988). Maternal separation anxiety: Its role in the balance of employment and motherhood in mothers of infants. In A. E. Gottfried and A. W. Gottfried (Eds.), *Maternal employment and children's development: Longitudinal research* (pp. 191–229). New York: Plenum.

Hofferth, S. L., and Sandberg, J. (1998). *Changes in American children's time: 1981–1997.* Unpublished manuscript, University of Michigan, Ann Arbor.

Hoffman, L. W. (1974). Effects of maternal employment on the child: A review of the research. *Developmental Psychology, 10,* 204–228.

Hoffman, L. W. (1984). Maternal employment and the young child. In M. Perlmutter (Ed.), *The Minnesota Symposia on Child Psychology: Vol. 17. Parent–Child interactions and parent–child relations in child development* (pp. 101–127). Hillsdale, NJ: Lawrence Erlbaum.

Hoffman, L. W. (1989). Effects of maternal employment in the two-parent family. *American Psychologist, 44,* 283–292.

Hoffman, L. W., and Youngblade, L. M. (1999). *Mothers at work: Effects on children's well-being.* New York; Cambridge University Press.

Hollingshead, A. B. (1975). *Four factor index of social status.* Unpublished manuscript, Yale University, Department of Sociology, New Haven, CT.

Hughes, D., and Galinsky, E. (1988). Balancing work and family lives: Research and corporate applications. In A. E. Gottfried and A. W. Gottfried (Eds.), *Maternal employment and children's development: Longitudinal research* (pp. 233–268). New York: Plenum.

Kim, K., and Honig, A. S. (1998). Relationship of maternal employment status and support for resilience with child resilience among Korean immigrant families in the United States. *Early Child Development and Care*, *141*, 41–60.

Komarraju, M. (1997). The work–family interface in India. In S. Parasuraman and J. H. Greenhaus (Eds.), *Integrating work and family: Challenges and choices for a changing world* (pp. 104–114). Westport, CT: Quorum Books.

Lerner, J. V. (1994). *Employed mothers and their families*. Newbury Park, CA: Sage.

Lerner, J. V., and Abrams, L. A. (1994). Developmental correlates of maternal employment influences on children. In C. B. Fisher and R. M. Lerner (Eds.), *Applied developmental psychology* (pp. 174–206). New York: McGraw-Hill.

Lerner, J. V., and Galambos, N. L. (1988). The influences of maternal employment across life: The New York Longitudinal Study. In A. E. Gottfried and A. W. Gottfried (Eds.), *Maternal employment and children's development: Longitudinal research* (pp. 59–83). New York: Plenum.

Lerner, J. V., and Noh, E. R. (2000). Maternal employment influences on early adolescent development: A contextual view. In R. D. Taylor and M. C. Wang (Eds.), *Resilience across contexts: Family, work, culture, and community* (pp. 121–145). Mahwah, NJ: Lawrence Erlbaum Associates.

Levine, J. A., and Pittinsky, T. L. (1997). *Working fathers: New strategies for balancing work and family*. New York: Harcourt, Brace.

MacEwen, K. E., and Barling, J. (1991). Effects of maternal employment experiences on children's behavior via mood, cognitive difficulties, and parenting behavior. *Journal of Marriage and the Family*, *53*, 635–645.

McLoyd, V. C. (1993). Employment among African-American mothers in dual-earner families: Antecedents and consequences for family life and child development. In J. Frankel (Ed.), *The employed mother and the family context* (pp. 180–226). New York: Springer.

Moorehouse, M. J., and Sanders, P. E. (1992). Children's feelings of school competence and perceptions of parents' work in four socio-cultural contexts. *Social Development*, *1*, 185–200.

Moos, R. H., and Moos, B. S. (1994). *Family Environment Scale manual*. Palo Alto, CA: Consulting Psychologists Press.

Nelson, C., and Keith, J. (1990). Comparisons of female and male early adolescent sex role attitude and behavior development. *Adolescence*, *25*, 183–203.

NICHD Early Child Care Research Network. (2000). Factors associated with fathers' caregiving activities and sensitivity with young children. *Journal of Family Psychology*, *14*, 200–219.

Nye, F. I., Perry, J. B., and Ogles, R. H. (1963). Anxiety and anti-social behavior in preschool children. In F. I. Nye and L. W. Hoffman (Eds.), *The employed mother in America* (pp. 3–17). Chicago: Rand McNally.

Owen, M. T., and Cox, M. J. (1988). Maternal employment and the transition to parenthood. In A. E. Gottfried and A. W. Gottfried (Eds.), *Maternal employment and children's development: Longitudinal research* (pp. 85–119). New York: Plenum.

Parcel, T. L., and Menaghan, E. G. (1994). *Parents' jobs and children's lives*. New York: Aldine de Gruyter.

Pascual, L., Haynes, O. M., Galperin, C. Z., and Bornstein, M. (1995). Psychological determinants of whether and how much new mothers work: A study in the United States and Argentina. *Journal of Cross-Cultural Psychology*, *26*, 314–330.

Peng, T. N. (1993). Maternal employment and child care. In C. H. Keng (Ed.), *Securing our future: Proceedings of the conference on children—our future* (pp. 251–255). Malaysia: University of Malaya, Child Development Centre.

Potuchek, J. L. (1997). *Who supports the family? Gender and breadwinning in dual-earner marriages*. Stanford, CA: Stanford University Press.

Presser, H. B. (1988). Shift work and child care among young dual-earner American parents. *Journal of Marriage and the Family*, *50*, 133–148.

Presser, H. B. (1999). Toward a 24-hour economy. *Science*, *284*, 1778–1779.

Repetti, R. L., and Wood, J. (1997a). Effects of daily stress at work on mothers' interactions with preschoolers. *Journal of Family Psychology*, *11*, 90–108.

Repetti, R. L., and Wood, J. (1997b). Families accommodating to chronic stress: Unintended and unnoticed processes. In B. H. Gottlieb (Ed.), *Coping with chronic stress* (pp. 191–220). New York: Plenum.

Richards, M. H., and Duckett, E. (1994). The relationship of maternal employment to early adolescent daily experience with and without parents. *Child Development*, *65*, 225–236.

Rieber, M., and Womack, M. (1968). The intelligence of preschool children as related to ethnic and demographic variables. *Exceptional Children*, *34*, 609–614.

Rubenstein, J. L. (1985). The effects of maternal employment on young children. In F. J. Morrison, C. Lord, and D. Keating (Eds.), *Applied Developmental Psychology*, (Vol. 2, pp. 99–128). New York: Academic.

Ryu, S., and Mortimer, J. (1996). The "occupational linkage hypothesis" applied to occupational value formation in adolescence. In J. T. Mortimer and M. D. Finch (Eds.). *Adolescents, work, and family* (pp. 167–190). Thousand Oaks, CA: Sage.

Sandqvist, K. (1992). Sweden's sex-role scheme and commitment to gender equality. In S. Lewis, D. N. Izraeli, and H. Hootsmans (Eds.), *Dual-earner families: International perspectives* (pp. 80–98). Newbury Park, CA: Sage.

Schwartzberg, N. S., and Dytell, R. S. (1996). Dual-earner families: The importance of work stress and family stress for psychological well-being. *Journal of Occupational Health Psychology*, *1*, 211–223.

Sekaran, U. (1992). Middle-class dual-earner families and their support systems in urban India. In S. Lewis, D. N. Izraeli, and H. Hootsmans (Eds.), *Dual-earner families: International perspectives* (pp. 46–61). Newbury Park, CA: Sage.

Spain, D., and Bianchi, S. M. (1996). Balancing act: Motherhood, marriage, and employment among American women. New York: Russell Sage Foundation.

Spalter-Roth, R. M. (1996). *What works: The Working Women Count Honor Roll: A selection of programs and policies that make work better.* Washington, DC: U.S. Department of Labor, Women's Bureau.

Stith, S. M., and Davis, A. J. (1984). Employed mothers and family day-care substitute caregivers: A comparative analysis of infant care. *Child Development, 55*, 1340–1348.

Tamis-LeMonda, C. S., and Cabrera, N. (1999). *Perspectives on father involvement: Research and policy.* (Social Policy Rep., Vol. 13, No. 2, pp. 1–25). Ann Arbor, MI: Society for Research in Child Development.

U.S. Bureau of Labor Statistics. (1998). Workers on flexible and shift schedules in 1997 [On-line]. Available: http://stats.bls.gov/newsrels.htm.

U.S. Bureau of Labor Statistics. (2000). Employment characteristics of families in 1999 [On-line]. Available: http://stats.bls.gov/newsrels.htm.

Valdez, E. O., and Coltrane, S. (1993). Work, family, and the Chicana: Power, perception, and equity. In J. Frankel (Ed.), *The employed and the family context* (pp. 153–179). New York: Springer.

Whitbeck, L. B., Simons, R. L., Conger, R. D., Wickrama, K. A. S., Ackley, K. A., and Elder, G. H. Jr. (1997). The effects of parents' working conditions and family economic hardship on parenting behaviors and children's self-efficacy. *Social Psychology Quarterly, 60*, 291–303.

Wilson, J. B., Ellwood, D. T., and Brooks-Gunn, J. (1995). Welfare-to-work through the eyes of children. In P. L. Chase-Lansdale and J. Brooks-Gunn (Eds.), *Escape from poverty: What makes a difference for children* (pp. 63–86). New York: Cambridge University Press.

Windle, M., and Dumenci, L. (1997). Parental and occupational stress as predictors of depressive symptoms among dual-income couples: A multilevel modeling approach. *Journal of Marriage and the Family, 59*, 625–634.

Wolfer, L. T., and Moen, P. (1996). Staying in school: Maternal employment and the timing of black and white daughters' school exit. *Journal of Family Issues, 17*, 540–551.

Wright, D. W., and Young, R. (1998). The effects of family structure and maternal employment on the development of gender-related attitudes among men and women. *Journal of Family Issues, 19*, 300–314.

Ybarra, L. (1982). When wives work: The impact on the Chicano family. *Journal of Marriage and the Family, 44*, 169–178.

Yuen, E. C., and Lim, V. (1992). Dual-earner families in Singapore: Issues and challenges. In S. Lewis, D. N. Izraeli, and H. Hootsmans (Eds.), *Dual-earner families: International perspectives* (pp. 62–79). Newbury Park, CA: Sage.

Zaslow, M. J., and Emig, C. A. (1997). When low-income mothers go to work: Implications for children. *The Future of Children: Welfare to Work, 7*, 110–115.

Zaslow, B. A., Rabinovich, B. A., and Suwalsky, J. T. D. (1991). From maternal employment to child outcomes: Preexisting group differences and moderating variables. In J. V. Lerner and N. L. Galambos (Eds.), *Employed mothers and their children* (pp. 237–282). New York: Garland.

Zick, C. D., and Allen, C. R. (1996). The impact of parents' marital status on the time adolescents spend in productive activities. *Family Relations, 45*, 65–71.

8

Socioeconomic Status and Parenting

Erika Hoff
Brett Laursen
Florida Atlantic University
Twila Tardif
The Chinese University of Hong Kong

INTRODUCTION

Parenting differs across socioeconomic strata. Our primary goals in this chapter are to describe how and why this is so. We begin the chapter by reviewing the history of research on socioeconomic status (SES) and parenting, including the political and the scientific trends that have shaped that research. We follow with a discussion of definitional and methodological issues that complicate conducting and synthesizing research in this area. We then turn to the literature that describes the relations between SES and parenting, reviewing evidence that the goals parents have for their children, the nature of the emotional relationship parents establish with their children, and the particular practices parents use in rearing their children all vary as a function of SES. As we move through the literature on differences in parenting that are associated with SES, we describe potential sources of those differences. One concern is to distinguish influences on parenting that derive from external factors associated with SES from influences on parenting that derive from characteristics of individuals that differ according to SES. Another concern is to identify, from the cluster of interrelated variables that SES comprises, the specific factors that cause or contribute to particular differences in parenting. To foreshadow our conclusion, the evidence suggests that both external and internal factors influence parenting and that multiple causal variables work, separately and in concert, to effect SES-related differences in parenting. Parents from different socioeconomic strata rear their children differently partly in response to the different circumstances in which they live and partly because they are themselves different sorts of people with different ways of interacting with the world. Educational, occupational, and financial factors all work to create SES-related differences in parents' circumstances and characteristics, with educational factors appearing to carry the greatest share of the variance. Finally, we consider some of the interpretive issues and limitations of the current literature, and how, given both its findings and its limitations, the literature on SES and parenting might be applied to improving child welfare.

HISTORICAL CONSIDERATIONS IN THE STUDY
OF SES AND PARENTING

Research on SES and parenting has, historically, been motivated both by the applied child welfare goal of improving the circumstances of children's lives and also by the more basic research goal of documenting how parental values and behaviors vary as a function of social status. The history of research on SES and parenting reflects the waxing and waning of political and scientific interest in pursuing these goals.

A 1936 White House conference on child health and protection announced the results of a survey of 3,000 U.S. families, documenting the conditions of children's early lives. It reported SES-related differences in aspects of parenting as diverse as the likelihood that parents served their children spinach and the likelihood that the parents read books on childcare (Anderson, 1936). This conference report not withstanding, the child welfare motive remained a minor theme in research on SES and parenting for the next two decades. Then, in the 1960s, a heightened awareness of social inequalities across North America and Western Europe provided impetus for new research on disadvantaged children. In the United States, for instance, the War on Poverty was launched to eradicate some of the worst consequences of low-income living conditions and was accompanied by an infusion of funds for research aimed at better understanding the developmental sequelae of SES. By the end of the next decade, however, research on SES was on the wane.

The near demise of research on SES and parenting can be traced to several factors. First, against a background of general unease with the notion of social stratification that prevailed during the 1970s and beyond, findings of SES-related differences in parenting and the attendant interpretation that lower-SES parents were to blame for their children's difficulties were unpopular and controversial. Second, SES and ethnicity were confounded, which made it difficult to disentangle issues of race from issues of lower-SES parenting. Also, scientific interest turned from seeking explanations of variation in development to seeking explanations of universal aspects of development. Research on individual and group differences was supplanted by research on normative growth and developmental trajectories. Recently, however, has the child welfare motive regained currency among research scientists (e.g., Collins, Maccoby, Steinberg, Hetherington, and Bornstein, 2000; Garcia Coll et al., 1996). In addition, the narrower view that implicated lower-SES parents in their children's difficulties has been supplanted by a broader view that includes forces outside the family (e.g., poverty, prejudice, schools, neighborhoods) as sources of SES-related differences in child development. As a consequence, SES now enjoys legitimacy as a contextual variable in studies of both parenting and child well-being (DeGarmo, Forgatch, and Martinez, 1999; Glasgow, Dornbush, Troyer, and Steinberg, 1997; Gutman and Eccles, 1999).

Another strand in the early research on SES and parenting, which was dominant during the 1940s and 1950s, consisted of studies that sought to document the differences associated with SES in a manner similar to anthropologists' descriptions of cultural differences (e.g., Mead, 1928, 1930; Whiting and Child, 1953). *Middletown* was the landmark for all subsequent research of this type. This longitudinal investigation by Lynd and Lynd (1929, 1937) carefully documented social stratification in a typical U.S. town and concluded that one aspect of life that varied with social status was childrearing. For example, the working class mothers interviewed ranked "strict obedience" as their most important childrearing goal, whereas the group referred to as "business class" ranked "independence" as equal to obedience in importance. In the research that followed, the effects of parenting practices on children were not of primary concern. The focus was rather on understanding parents and contextual factors that influenced them. It was in this vein that Kohn (1963, 1969) proposed that SES-associated differences in parent–child relationships stem from differences in parents' child-rearing values that, in turn, stem from differences in parents' occupational conditions. Kohn argued that blue-collar jobs fostered authoritarian childrearing because these jobs require obedience and conformity, whereas white-collar occupations fostered authoritative parenting because those occupations require initiative and independent thinking. The hypothesis that the workplace operates as a socializing agent in parents' lives remains current (e.g., Menaghan and Parcel, 1991), and the role of culture, ethnicity, and SES are still topics of considerable research interest (e.g., Harkness and Super, in Vol. 2 of this *Handbook*; Leyendecker, Carlson, Asencio, and Miller, in Vol. 4 of this *Handbook*; Harwood, Schoelmerich, Ventura-Cook, Schulze, and Wilson, 1996; McAdoo, in Vol. 4 of this *Handbook*; Sigel, McGillicuddy-De Lisi, and Goodnow, 1992).

DOMAINS OF INVESTIGATION IN THE STUDY OF SES AND PARENTING

Research on SES and parenting has been shaped also by theoretical shifts in developmental psychology. Changes in the way developmental psychology viewed parenting has prompted changes in the design and selection of research variables. Early work focused on parents as agents of socialization and on aspects of parenting that were thought to influence social and personality development. In the 1930s and 1940s, weaning and toilet training were of great concern, as were aggression and sex play, the latter of which often fell under the heading of "impulse control" (Bronfenbrenner, 1958). Through the 1950s, "responsibility training," or the demands for independence that parents placed on children, was the focus of attention (e.g., Ericson, 1963). These aspects of parenting were considered important to socialization, and it is clear that socialization was of interest because it was thought to hold the key to explaining SES-associated differences in children's achievement. For example, Davis and Havighurst (1946, p. 707) concluded that "middle-class children are subjected earlier and more consistently to the influences which make a child an orderly, conscientious, responsible, and tame person." Scientific trends shifted in the 1960s, and interest in specific behaviors such as weaning and toilet training gave way to interest in more global dimensions of parenting and child outcomes (see Maccoby, 1992, and Maccoby and Martin, 1983, for reviews).

Changing social and political attitudes were another cause of a shift of focus in parenting research in the 1960s. Because a major goal of the War on Poverty was to remedy the poor academic performance of low-SES children, research focused on how experiences with their parents prepared children for schooling (Slaughter-Defoe, 1995). SES-associated differences in mother–child interaction (and their consequences for cognitive development), along with differences in the strategies mothers used in teaching and conversing with their children, received the greatest attention. The concern was not with the content of what mothers taught their children but with the cognitive developmental value of the processes of interaction. An important early influence on this work was the work of the British sociolinguist Bernstein, who argued that families from different socioeconomic strata use language differently and their children acquire different communicative abilities as a result (e.g., Bernstein, 1970). Bernstein articulated this position in somewhat different ways in different writings, but in essence his view was that language carries more of a communicative burden in lower-SES homes than in higher-SES homes because roles are fixed in lower-SES homes but flexible in higher-SES homes, where they therefore need to be negotiated. Although that particular explanation of SES-related differences in language use is not well supported by evidence (Gecas, 1979), it is clear that there are SES-associated differences in how mothers use language in talking to their children (e.g., Hoff-Ginsberg, 1991; 1998). This literature is reviewed in the section on parenting practices.

The study of the relation between SES and parenting is, to a degree, a search for a moving target. Over time, some SES-related differences in parenting change because culturally prescribed beliefs about parenting change. Parents are influenced by theories of child development, but parents in higher socioeconomic strata change more and change more rapidly in response to theory changes than parents in lower socioeconomic strata, thus altering the SES-related differences (Bronfenbrenner, 1958). During the period from 1930 to 1955, according to Bronfenbrenner, higher-SES parents exerted greater pressure on their children than lower-SES parents, as evidenced by earlier weaning and toilet training. In the later years of this period, the direction of the difference reversed, with higher-SES parents being more lenient than lower-SES parents.

Not all aspects of parenting seem equally susceptible to the influence of prevailing theory, however. During the same period, two SES-associated differences remained stable. First, higher-SES parents were consistently more likely to use psychological techniques of discipline, including reasoning and appeals to guilt, whereas lower-SES parents were more likely to use physical punishment. Second, higher-SES parents had more equalitarian relationships with their children than lower-SES parents. These differences continued in the decades that followed (Gecas, 1979; Hess, 1970). Thus it appears that some aspects of parent behavior are more a function of characteristics of the parents than they are a function of the prevailing expert advice.

METHODOLOGICAL CONSIDERATIONS IN THE STUDY OF SES AND PARENTING

Defining and Measuring SES

SES is a multifaceted variable, which has been defined and measured in different ways by different researchers. One basic definitional issue is whether SES is a discrete or a continuous variable. In general, the use of the term *social class* implies discrete categories of people who are similar in their levels of education, income, occupational status, and housing. In contrast, the term *socioeconomic status* connotes a more continuous variable. Although social class and SES have been used interchangeably to describe basic differences associated with education, occupation, and income, we avoid the confusion that follows from the conflation of terms and adopt the contemporary preference for SES, with the exception that in reporting findings we use the terminology of the original studies.

SES has been measured by a single indicator (e.g., occupation *or* education), by multiple indicators (e.g., occupation *and* education), and by composite indices based on some combination of the multiple variables that define SES (e.g., a weighted sum of occupation and education). The most widely used composite measures have been the Hollingshead indexes (Hollingshead, 1957, 1975; Hollingshead and Redlich, 1958). The Hollingshead's Four Factor Index of Social Status is based on maternal and paternal occupation and education; the Two Factor index is based on paternal occupation and education.

A general disadvantage to composite indices are that they obscure the source of SES effects. For this reason, Entwisle and Astone (1994) argued for separately measuring household income, parental education, and family structure. These measures index three types of resources that are important to children: (1) financial capital, or the ability to buy the things children need, (2) human capital, or the ability to communicate high academic aspirations and concrete help in achieving those aspirations, and (3) social capital, or the ability of parents to provide connections to the larger community (Coleman, 1988). There are other approaches as well. Because occupational prestige is stable (Hauser, 1994; Otto, 1975), it may be a better indicator of long-term income than direct measures of household finances. Parent education is also stable, and, of all the socioeconomic variables, maternal education has been found to be most strongly associated with parenting (Alwin, 1984; Richman, Miller, and LeVine, 1992; Wright and Wright, 1976). The use of these and other measures permits assessment of the relative impact of each individual indicator (Burns, Homel, and Goodnow, 1984; DeGarmo et al., 1999). Accumulating evidence indicates that different indicators of SES bear different relations both to parenting and to child outcomes. As a consequence, the various indicators of SES should not be considered interchangeable. We return to this topic when we consider the interpretive issues that the literature on SES and parenting presents.

Defining and Measuring Parenting

As we have already seen, parenting has been conceptualized in different ways at different times. Darling and Steinberg (1993) argued for distinguishing three aspects of parenting: goals, styles, and practices. Other work argues that beliefs should also be considered as a distinct component of parenting (see Sigel and McGillicuddy-De Lisi, in Vol. 3 of this *Handbook*). These categories capture meaningful distinctions among different components of parenting and thus provide a useful device for organizing the literature. Each of these aspects of parenting poses formidable measurement challenges, some specific to the goal of comparing parenting across different socioeconomic strata.

Parental beliefs include what parents expect the course of development to look like and what parents see as their own role in their children's development. Goals are the outcomes toward which parents direct their efforts. The measurement of parental beliefs and goals has been accomplished using open-ended interviews, multiple-response questionnaires, and hypothetical scenarios. Extensive reviews of parental beliefs and the instruments that have been used to measure them are available elsewhere (Goodnow, in Vol. 3 of this *Handbook*; Goodnow and Collins; 1990; Holden and Buck, in Vol. 3 of this *Handbook*; Holden and Edwards, 1989; Okagaki and Divecha, 1993; Sigel and McGillicudy-De Lisi, in Vol. 3 of this *Handbook*). One difficulty with many of these instruments is that they depend heavily on verbal skills. As a result, observed SES-related differences in beliefs and goals may be artifacts of differential responding to the instruments themselves (Holden and Edwards, 1989).

Parenting style consists of the attitudes about children that parents communicate to their own children and the emotional climate in which these attitudes are expressed. Most of the research on parenting style begins with Baumrind's (1967) typology, which describes parents in terms of three qualitatively different types defined as a function of the control they exert over their children: authoritative, authoritarian, or permissive. Control, in this system, is the willingness of parents to socialize their children and the manner in which they attempt to integrate children into the family and society (Darling and Steinberg, 1993). Subsequent to Baumrind's work, Maccoby and Martin (1983) proposed a revised scheme in which parenting style was conceptualized as a function of two dimensions: the number and type of demands parents make of children and the level of responsiveness parents display toward children. This system yielded four styles: two of which were approximately equivalent to the authoritative and authoritarian styles of Baumrind's system, and two additional categories, indulgent and neglectful, which superceded Baumrind's permissive category. Authoritative parents are high on demandingness and high on responsiveness; authoritarian parents are high on demandingness and low on responsiveness; indulgent parents are low on demandingness and high on responsiveness, and neglectful parents are low on both demandingness and responsiveness. Although Baumrind's system remains the benchmark for research on SES and parenting, the newer four-category system has enjoyed widespread acceptance among contemporary scholars.

Parenting styles have been measured both by direct observation and, more commonly, by questionnaires administered to or interviews of parents and children. Parent and child reports tend to be quite different. Some have argued that child reports may be more accurate and more relevant than parent reports because children are less susceptible than parents to biases that stem from social desirability and because perceptions of parenting experienced are a better predictor of child outcomes than perceptions of parenting expressed (Gonzales, Cauce, and Mason, 1996; Paulson, 1994). An interesting but unexplored issue is whether SES affects the accuracy of reports of parenting style or the discrepancy between child and parent reports. Arguments that higher-SES parents are more susceptible to social desirability biases (see Graves and Glick, 1978; Pine, 1992) would predict SES-related differences in the validity of these measures.

Parenting practices cover a large domain, including behaviors parents produce in interactions with their children, the kinds of home environments parents create for children, and the connections to the world outside the home that parents both enable and permit. One can measure practices by asking parents what they do, by asking them what they would do in hypothetical situations, or by observing them. Direct observation can use behavior checklists, time sampling, or more detailed coding schemes applied to audio or videotape records of interaction. One checklist instrument that has been widely used in the study of SES and parenting is the Home Observation for Measurement of the Environment (HOME) (Caldwell and Bradley, 1984; see also Bradley, in Vol. 2 of this *Handbook*). Based on home observations and interviews with parents, the index was designed to assess the adequacy of children's early developmental environments. Of particular interest here is the fact that it was developed with the aim of replacing social class designations as an index of the quality of home environments.

As a means of assessing parenting practices, interview and self-report techniques may have many of the same problems of dependence on verbal skills as techniques for assessing beliefs and goals. Additionally, the possibility that parental estimations of their own behavior may vary as a function of SES is suggested by evidence that SES affects how parents report on their children's behavior. Specifically, lower-SES parents appear to overestimate their children's comprehension vocabularies (Fenson, et al., 1994; Reznick, 1990). Direct observation avoids such problems. Concern has been raised, however, that the effects of being observed may be different at different SES levels, potentially creating SES-associated differences in measures of parenting in which no differences actually exist (e.g., Graves and Glick, 1978; Pine, 1992). It has been argued both that higher-SES mothers may feel more comfortable around researchers and be less inhibited and, alternatively, that they may be more likely to "put on a show" for the researchers than lower-SES mothers. The available evidence, however, does not support either contention (Field and Ignatoff, 1981; Graves and Glick, 1978). Mothers do interact more with their children when they know they are being observed, but the effect does not differ as a function of SES.

The measurement technique selected should fit the aspect of parenting being measured. Hypothetical scenarios are best reserved for the measurement of parental goals and beliefs. Because such instruments tap parents' intentions and aspirations, they are excellent tools for understanding parental attitudes, even if the measures produced have little relation to actual parent behaviors. Styles are better captured with interviews or questionnaires, and when children are old enough to participate, they should be regarded as a source of information equal to or better than parents. With respect to measuring practices, direct observation, including the use of videotape, produces the richest data, but cannot capture the larger picture regarding how parents structure their children's days (e.g., the frequency of trips to the zoo, visitors to the home). Thus interviews and questionnaires may be a necessary supplement to observational methods, depending on the nature of the practices of interest.

RESEARCH ON SES AND PARENTING

Consonant with our earlier definition of parenting, our review of the research on SES and parenting is organized into subsections on parenting beliefs and goals, parenting styles, and parenting practices. In the final subsection we consider how beliefs, styles, and practices are related, and whether and how SES moderates those associations. Virtually all of the research reviewed in this chapter concerns parents, and most of it is limited to mothers. Parenting roles are also filled by fathers (Kohn, 1979; Parke, in Vol. 3 of this Handbook), grandmothers (Stevens, 1984), childcare providers (Greenbaum and Landau, 1979; Tardif, 1993), and older siblings (Harkness and Super, 1992; Whiting and Edwards, 1988; Zukow-Goldring, in Vol. 3 of this *Handbook*) to a degree that varies widely across socioeconomic and cultural groups. Our understanding of these variations is hampered by limited empirical evidence, however, and we do not address them here.

SES and Parenting Beliefs and Goals

The developmental outcomes parents expect and desire for their children and the roles parents see for themselves in achieving those outcomes vary as a function of SES. Parents from different strata expect different developmental timetables. In general, and across cultures, higher-SES mothers give earlier age estimates for children's attainment of developmental milestones and higher estimates of young children's capacties than do lower-SES mothers (Mansbach and Greenbaum, 1999; Ninio, 1988; von der Lippe, 1999). Some SES-related differences in expected timetables, however, appear to reflect cultural differences. In general, higher-SES parents expect earlier mastery of whatever skills the mainstream culture values than do lower-SES parents. For instance, in both Japanese and U.S. samples, higher-SES mothers expected their children to master school-related skills at a younger age than did lower-SES mothers; in Japanese samples, higher-SES mothers also expected earlier mastery of social skills (Hess, Kashiwagi, Azuma, Price, and Dickson, 1980). In another study, mothers in the United States, China, Hong Kong, and Japan were asked to estimate the age at which toddlers achieve 39 developmental milestones. Across these four cultures, mothers with higher levels of education estimated that their children felt emotions, were able to say their first sounds and first words, and were able to "think" earlier than did mothers with lower levels of education. In contrast, mothers with lower levels of education expected that their children would be toilet trained and able to greet adults with polite forms of address and say "thank you" earlier than did mothers with higher levels of education (Tardif, Au, Wellman, and Nakamura, 2000).

These latter differences in expectation coincide with SES-related differences in parents' values. For example, asked to describe how they would like their toddlers to behave if left with a stranger in a doctor's waiting room, lower-SES mothers rated proper demeanor, which included obedient, respectful, and quiet behavior, as more important than did higher-SES mothers (Harwood, 1992; Harwood, Miller, and Lucca Irizarry, 1995). The preference of lower-SES mothers for proper behavior may be a specific example of a more general preference among lower-SES parents for conformity to societal prescriptions. It has been repeatedly observed in different cultures that parents from lower socioeconomic strata value conformity in their children whereas parents from higher socioeconomic strata want their children to be self-directed (e.g., Alwin, 1984; Holden, 1995; Kohn, 1979; Luster, Rhoades, and Haas, 1989; Pearlin and Kohn, 1966; Tudge, Hogan, Snezhkova, Kulakova, and Etz, 2000; Wright and Wright, 1976). As mentioned earlier, Kohn (1963, 1969) speculated that differences in the kinds of jobs that parents hold produce differences in the characteristics they value in children.

Finally, there are SES-related differences in the beliefs parents hold about their role in achieving the outcomes they value. Lower-SES parents believe they have less control over the outcome of their children's development than do higher-SES parents (Elder, Eccles, Ardelt, and Lord, 1995; Luster and Kain, 1987). These differences in self-efficacy beliefs, in turn, result in differences in goals and practices (Brody, Flor, and Gibson, 1999). We return to this topic after we review the literature on SES-related differences in parenting styles and parenting practices.

SES and Parenting Styles

Different parenting styles create different emotional climates in the home (Darling and Steinberg, 1993). Scholars have long argued that parenting style varies as a function of SES, and considerable evidence supports this assertion. As early as 1958, Bronfenbrenner (1958, p. 420) concluded that "parent–child relationships in the middle-class are consistently reported as more acceptant and equalitarian, while those in the working-class are oriented toward maintaining order and obediance." Parenting styles in higher-SES homes have been described as democratic (Hoffman, 1963) and child centered (Sears, Maccoby, and Levin, 1957), in contrast to the authoritarian and parent-centered style that characterizes lower-SES homes.

Baumrind's (1967) authoritative, authoritarian, and permissive typology was derived from a primarily well-educated, middle-SES, North American sample. When parenting style has been examined in more diverse samples, it is clear that the prevalence of these styles varies as a function of social stratum. Analyses of a large, diverse sample of adolescents in California revealed that families with higher parental education tended to be lower in authoritarian and permissive parenting and higher in authoritative parenting than families with lower parental education (Dornbusch, Ritter, Leiderman, and Roberts, 1987). Similar findings emerged from an exclusively African American sample, in which maternal education was associated with child-centered parenting (Bluestone and Tamis-LeMonda, 1999). Additional evidence corroborating the association between SES and parenting style comes from research conducted in Egypt, where mothers with low levels of education displayed and reported less authoritative parenting than did mothers with higher levels of education (von der Lippe, 1999), and from research conducted in China, where a composite SES score derived from maternal and paternal occupation and education correlated positively with authoritative parenting by mothers and fathers and correlated negatively with authoritarian parenting by mothers (Chen, Dong, and Zhou, 1997).

Although fewer studies of SES-related differences in parenting style have used the expanded typology of Maccoby and Martin (1983), the research that has been conducted suggests that the prevalence of these categories also varies as a function of SES. Reports from several thousand U.S. adolescents indicate that parent education is positively correlated with authoritative parenting and negatively correlated with authoritarian parenting, while also revealing that parent education is positively correlated with indulgent parenting and negatively correlated with neglectful parenting (Glasgow et al., 1997).

SES and Parenting Practices

Parenting practices may be understood in terms of the roles parents play in their children's lives (e.g., interactive partner, manager) (Parke and Buriel, 1998) or in terms of the socialization goal toward which practices are directed (Darling and Steinberg, 1993). Although we have adopted the former approach in this review, it is important to note that there is little consensus on how best to conceptualize parenting practices. Regardless of the system adopted, however, direct interaction with children is a central aspect of parenting, and there is a large body of observational research on SES-related differences in parent–child interaction, particularly focusing on how mothers interact with their young children (see Hoff-Ginsberg and Tardif, 1995, for review). Our summary is divided into two subsections, the first on verbal properties of interaction and the second on direct control practices used in interaction. These are followed by a brief overview of SES-related differences in the way parents control children by managing their home environments and their experiences outside the home.

Verbal interaction.   A substantial body of evidence indicates that both the amount and the nature of verbal interaction that takes place between parents and children differ as functions of SES. With respect to amount, several studies have found that higher-SES mothers address more speech to their children than do lower-SES mothers (Brody, 1968; Dunn, Wooding, and Herman, 1977; Feiring and Lewis, 1981; Field and Pawlby, 1980; Greenberg and Formanek, 1974; Heath, 1983; Hess and Shipman, 1965; Hoff-Ginsberg, 1992, 1998; Ninio, 1980; Schachter, 1979; Tulkin and Kagan, 1972). Similar trends have been observed in families with adolescent sons (Jacob, 1974). Relatedly, the responsivity subscale of the HOME inventory, which is heavily loaded with indices of verbal responsivity, is positively related to parental education and, less robustly, to occupation (Caldwell and Bradley, 1984).

With respect to the content of verbal interaction, higher-SES children who hear more speech also hear speech that contains a greater variety of words, greater syntactic complexity, and a larger proportion of conversation-eliciting questions (Hoff-Ginsberg, 1991, 1998; Snow et al., 1976). Both the quantity and the quality of speech have positive relations to language development (Bornstein, Haynes, and Painter, 1998; Huttenlocher, Haight, Bryk, Seltzer, and Lyons, 1991), which suggests that higher-SES children are provided a better database from which to learn language than lower-SES children. More educated mothers also provide more explicit information when they talk to their children than do less educated mothers. Findings from several different ethnic groups reveal that more educated mothers engage in more explicit teaching of object labels than do less educated mothers (Brophy, 1970; Hammer and Weiss, 1999; Lawrence and Shipley, 1996; Ninio, 1980; Reger, 1990).

In addition, middle-class mothers have been found to talk about causality with their children more than working-class mothers (Brophy, 1970; Sigel, McGillicuddy-De Lisi, and Johnson, 1980).

In general, there are more SES-associated differences on language measures than on nonverbal measures of how parents interact with their children across a wide range of child ages and across ethnic groups. (Hoff-Ginsberg and Tardif, 1995). For example, college-educated mothers who talk more to their children than high school-educated mothers do not spend more time in joint (verbal and nonverbal) attention with their children (Hoff-Ginsberg, 1991). More educated African American mothers who talk more and engage in more verbal games with their children do not differ from less educated African American mothers in nonverbal measures of involvement in play (Hammer and Weiss, 1999). Some have suggested that the high level of verbal activity that characterizes middle-SES Western mothers' interactions reflects their belief that babies are "separate individuals with whom communication is possible and necessary" (Snow, De Blauw, and Van Roosmalen, 1979, p. 270). Certainly some lower-SES caregivers are explicit about their views that there is no point in talking to very young children, and no doubt their behavior is in part a reflection of this belief (Heath, 1983). Other factors are implicated as well. Residential density affects the amount of talk addressed to children (Evans, Maxwell, and Hart, 1999), and this external source of influence may play a role in SES-related differences. An internal source of SES-related differences in the amount of talk addressed to children may be general levels of talkativeness; higher-SES mothers also talk more than lower-SES mothers in conversation with adults (Hoff-Ginsberg, 1991, 1992).

Direct control practices.   In interacting with young children, lower-SES mothers have consistently been found to be more controlling, restrictive, and disapproving than higher-SES mothers. Across cultures, and in laboratory settings and home observations, lower-SES mothers devote proportionately more talk to directing child behavior than higher-SES mothers (Budwig and Chaudary, 1996; Hart and Risley, 1992; 1995; Hoff-Ginsberg, 1991; 1998; Pomerleau, LaCroix, Malcuit, and Seguin, 1999; Reger, 1990; Tardif, 1993). Findings from the home observation data of the Berkeley Growth Study show that lower-SES mothers granted their children less autonomy, were less equalitarian, less cooperative, more restrictive, and more punitive and intrusive than higher-SES mothers (Bayley and Schaefer, 1960). Similar findings emerged from an observational study of fathers and young children (Woodworth, Belsky, and Crnic, 1996). Data from the HOME inventory show that more educated parents are less restrictive and less punitive with children from infancy through the age of 6 years (Caldwell and Bradley, 1984). These findings extend to the use of physical forms of discipline: Lower-SES parents practice corporal punishment to a greater degree than higher-SES parents (Clarke-Stewart, VanderStoep, and Killian, 1979; Straus and Stewart, 1999). SES-related differences in direct control strategies appear with older children as well. During middle childhood, harsh punishment is more frequently found in the lower socioeconomic strata than in the upper strata (Bronfenbrenner, 1970; Straus, Gelles, and Steinmetz, 1980). Data from the Iowa Youth and Families Project indicate that parental education is more strongly related to the use of harsh discipline than is family income, particularly with boys (Simons, Whitbeck, Conger, and Chyi-In, 1991). Financial strain and economic hardship exacerbate these trends (Gutman and Eccles, 1999).

Managerial control.   Not all parenting involves direct interaction between parent and child. Parenting also consists of indirect or managerial control exercised through the experiences parents provide their children and the physical environments they create for their children (Parke and Buriel, 1998). Data from the HOME inventory suggest that, for parents of infants and preschool children, education and, to a lesser degree, paternal occupation are positively related to the provision of appropriate play materials, variety of daily stimulation, and organization of the environment (e.g., regular outings and trips to the doctor and to the grocery store) (Caldwell and Bradley, 1984). With 9-year-old boys, indices of SES predicted how children spent their time at home: Maternal education was positively related to the amount of time spent in skill activities such as homework and reading for fun and negatively related to the amount of time spent watching television (DeGarmo et al., 1999). Parents also may coordinate participation in the larger community, through activities such as clubs, private lessons, sports teams, and church-related activities. Middle-class mothers have been found both to participate in these activities as volunteers more than working-class mothers and also to involve their children in more of these activities (O'Donnell and Stueve, 1983). The same study found that maternal employment was not associated with mothers' level of involvement as volunteers.

Monitoring, or the degree to which parents know their children's whereabouts, is another managerial aspect of parenting that is particularly relevant for older children (see Crouter and Head, in Vol. 3 of this *Handbook*). The research on SES and parental monitoring is sparse, but where indices of SES have been included as variables in studies of monitoring their relations tend to be weak. Self-reported monitoring by mothers was found not to be related to perceived economic stress (Klein, Forehand, Family Health Project Research Group, 2000), and child-reported parental monitoring was not associated with a composite measure of SES (Jacobson and Crockett, 2000). One study suggests that education is positively related to levels of monitoring for fathers, but not for mothers, and offers the explanation that mothers' behavior may be more scripted than fathers' (Crouter, Helms-Erikson, Updegraff, and McHale, 1999).

In sum, the research makes clear that children from different socioeconomic strata experience different parenting, but some aspects of parenting appear to be more susceptible to the influence of SES than others. A large component of the SES-related differences in parenting can be attributed to SES-related differences in parents' styles of verbal interaction. In comparison, SES-related differences in nonverbal interaction are fewer. Another pervasive difference is the tendency of lower-SES parents to be more controlling and more punitive than higher-SES parents. Lower-SES parents take less of a role in arranging activities outside the home for their children, but they are not necessarily less aware of what their children are doing than higher-SES parents. For those aspects of parenting that differ as a function of SES, external stressors such as financial strain and residential crowding contribute to but do not fully explain the differences.

Relations Among Parenting Beliefs, Styles, and Practices

At the theoretical level, it has been argued that parenting styles and parenting practices are an expression of parents' goals, values, and beliefs (Darling and Steinberg, 1993). As we have seen in the review of the literature, however, parental styles and practices are also influenced by contextual support and personal characteristics of the parent (see also Belsky, 1984). If we look to the literature for empirical data on the role of beliefs in SES-related differences in parenting styles and practices, we find evidence for three types of relations: Sometimes beliefs serve as mediators, linking SES to the associated styles and practices; sometimes beliefs serve as moderators, altering the relation between other beliefs and practices; and sometimes beliefs are causally irrelevant to practices.

An example of beliefs as mediators comes from an examination of the links among parents' SES, values, childrearing beliefs, and actual parenting behavior (Luster et al., 1989). In this study, SES was inversely related to the extent to which parents value conformity, which, in turn, was related to their beliefs about control and discipline, which, in turn, predicted observers' ratings of maternal involvement and warmth. Higher-SES mothers were more apt to value self-direction in their children and display warmth and involvement, whereas lower-SES mothers tended to believe that babies should not be spoiled and therefore treated them in a less warm and supportive manner (Luster et al., 1989). Self-efficacy can also be a parenting belief with a mediating effect, linking SES to parenting goals and practices. As discussed earlier, lower-SES parents are less likely than higher-SES parents to believe they have influence over their child's outcomes and, as a result, are less likely to endorse positive outcomes as childrearing goals and less likely to engage in "competence promoting parenting" (Brody et al., 1999).

An example of beliefs as moderators of the association between SES and parenting practices and styles is the finding that childrearing beliefs are more closely linked to childrearing behaviors among middle-class mothers than among working-class mothers (Tulkin and Cohler, 1973).

Among middle-class mothers, attitudes concerning reciprocity were related to how physically close mothers stayed to their infants; attitudes concerning children's expression of aggression were related to how frequently mothers issued prohibitions. The significant associations between attitudes and behavior were fewer in the working-class sample. Again, self-efficacy has been invoked as an explanation. In this case, it is argued that working-class mothers do not feel that they have much influence over their children's development and therefore have less reason to put their beliefs into practice.

Last, there are examples of SES-related differences in parenting practices that are not a function of beliefs. With respect to verbal interaction, the evidence suggests that mothers' own inclinations toward talkativeness, not just maternal theories about children as conversational partners, accounts for SES-related differences (Hoff-Ginsberg, 1991). As another example, data from the Iowa Youth and Families Project show that the use of harsh parenting is predicted by father's education but that belief in the use of physical discipline is not. Across that entire sample, parent beliefs in discipline and concurrent parent use of harsh discipline are correlated, but the connection between parental education and harsh discipline is direct, not mediated by beliefs (Simons et al., 1991).

INTERPRETIVE ISSUES AND METHODOLOGICAL LIMITATIONS IN RESEARCH ON SES AND PARENTING

Research on SES and parenting has the potential to contribute to a better understanding of how SES influences parents and of how SES and parenting jointly and independently influence children. One of the primary goals of this line of inquiry is to provide a framework for interventions designed to improve the outcomes of low-achieving lower-SES children. In this regard, the utility of the extant literature is limited by several methodological factors including (1) the difficulty of isolating the effects of SES when other variables operate both to influence parenting and to restrict representative sampling and participation, (2) the difficulty of delineating the source of effects attributed to SES, (3) the difficulty of separating effects that are the product of SES from effects that are the product of other correlated variables, and (4) the difficulty of determining which of the statistically significant SES effects are meaningful.

Identifying When SES Affects Parenting

SES is not a completely deterministic variable or set of variables. A host of other factors also influence parenting (Belsky, 1984), making it difficult to isolate the variance accounted for by SES. This problem is exacerbated by the fact that both SES and parenting behaviors are confounded with the willingness of parents to participate in research. Recruiting lower-SES participants is much more difficult than recruiting higher-SES participants, and attrition rates are much higher for lower-SES participants when they are recruited (Spoth, Goldberg, and Redmond, 1999). It is probably also true that parents who are committed to their parenting role join and continue in research on parenting at greater rates than do uninterested parents, although we know of no evidence on this score. Systematically different participation and attrition rates threaten the validity and generalizability of research on the relation between SES and parenting.

Another concern related to sampling arises when one is trying to draw a single conclusion from multiple studies that differ in the range of socioeconomic strata investigated. Some of the studies reviewed in this chapter address the relation of SES to parenting by comparing extremely low-SES groups to mid-SES groups. Other studies compare midrange groups to higher-range groups. Still other studies treat SES as a continuous variable, with considerable variation in the range of strata sampled and the degree to which extreme strata are represented. The differences in parenting that appear when very low-SES groups are compared with higher-SES groups often do not appear when comparing groups in the middle and the higher ranges of the SES continuum. Similarly, if the range of SES is restricted, effects of SES may not appear when SES is included in a linear regression model. Furthermore, because SES does not necessarily capture a continuum of experience, there may be parenting phenomena specific to particular groups that are not linearly related to SES. For all these reasons, it is perilous to extrapolate from differences observed between groups at one end of the SES continuum to the entire range, and it is correspondingly perilous to conclude from an absence of SES effects across its range that extremes, such as extreme poverty, have no effect.

Unpacking SES

There are two views with respect to how SES operates to influence parenting. One is that SES is a convenient proxy for a host of specific factors that bear individual relations to parenting (Bronfenbrenner, 1958). The alternative view is that SES operates as a single, coherent variable that broadly affects most aspects of the daily lives of parents and children in a manner that cannot be meaningfully reduced to the sum of its parts (Featherman, Spenner, and Tsunematsu, 1988). In support of the first view, studies that have separately considered the variables that make up SES have found that different components of SES often have different associations with different aspects of parenting. As examples, data from the HOME scale reveal that family income predicts the home learning environment but that maternal education predicts both the home learning environment and warmth (Klebanov, Brooks-Gunn, and Duncan, 1994). Data from the Oregon Divorce Study similarly show that maternal education, occupation, and income each has a different relation both to parenting and to child outcome (DeGarmo et al., 1999).

If we consider each of the components of SES in turn, education is most reliably associated with differences in parenting, and this is true across different cultures and ethnic groups (Kelley, Sanchez-Hucles, and Walker, 1993; Laosa, 1980; Menaghan and Parcel, 1991; Tardif, 1993; Wright and Wright, 1976). Education is a robust variable that affects outcomes including the nature of talk to children, the nature of discipline practices, and, more globally, the style of parenting. Occupation is also associated with parenting (e.g., DeGarmo et al., 1999; Menaghan and Parcel, 1991), and some of the effects of education appear to be mediated by occupation (Menaghan and Parcel, 1991). Finally, income is less reliably associated with parenting, but that may be because income operates in a nonlinear fashion that most studies fail to capture. Specifically, low income and poverty may exert a debilitating influence on parenting, but once a certain threshold is reached, additional income may not produce commensurate benefits. For example, some factors associated with very low-income levels, such as living in unsafe neighborhoods, present parents with unique challenges and concerns that may prompt more strictness (Bartz and Levine, 1978; Garbarino and Kostelny, 1993; Goodnow and Collins, 1990). Additionally, financial stress, or the perception of financial distress, appears to have negative effects on the ability to parent (Elder, Van Nguyen, and Caspi, 1985; Gutman and Eccles, 1999; Lempers, Clark-Lempers, and Simons, 1989; McLoyd, 1990, 1998). The effects of income may also be obscured by individual differences in the ability of parents to cope with financial stress. For instance, among the chronically depressed, financial stress was associated with less sensitive parenting, but among mothers who were not depressed, income was unrelated to sensitivity (NICHD Early Child Care Research Network, 1999). Thus poverty or financial stress may be viewed as a risk factor for poor parenting, but otherwise it appears that income differences are neither necessary nor sufficient causes of differences in parenting.

The alternative view holds that SES is more than the sum of its constituent parts. If SES operates as a coherent, irreducible force, then different socioeconomic strata may be likened to different cultures. Some have argued that cultures create different "developmental niches" for children by virtue of three sources of influence: (1) the physical and social settings that they provide, (2) the prescribed customs of childcare, and (3) the psychological characteristics of the adult caregivers (Super and Harkness, 1986). Evidence suggests that each of these dimensions varies as a function of SES: (1) Income and family structure differences create SES-related differences in the physical and social settings; (2) SES-related patterns of parenting are handed down across generations (Simons et al., 1991); and (3) SES-related differences in parenting are caused by psychological characteristics of the adult caregivers, including verbal IQ (Borduin and Henggeler, 1981; Hess, 1970), the level of complexity with which parents think about development and parenting (McGillicuddy-De Lisi, 1982; Sameroff and Feil, 1985), self-efficacy (Luster and Kain, 1987), and mental health (Kohn, 1969, 1977; Sameroff and Fiese, 1992). Whether these findings provide evidence for the single-variable view of SES is an empirical question. If the variables that compose SES operate separately, then the influence of SES on parenting should be limited to these distinct components of SES. If SES influences are the product of the unique set of experiences associated with being a member of a group that shares these attributes, then group membership should offer additional power in predicting parenting beyond that of the constituent components combined.

Correlates of SES

Several variables that do not define SES are correlated with SES, including ethnicity, single parenting, parent age, and family size. Each of these has its own relation to parenting (see Harwood et al., in Vol. 4 of this *Handbook*; McAdoo, in Vol. 4 of this *Handbook*; Weinraub, Horvath, and Gringlas, in Vol. 3 of this *Handbook*). Although it is clear that there are effects of SES that are independent of these associated variables (Burns et al., 1984; Eisenberg, 1990; Hammer and Weiss, 1999; Harwood et al., 1996; Havighurst, 1976; Hess and Shipman, 1965; Hoff-Ginsberg, 1991, 1998; Lambert, Hamers, and Frasure-Smith, 1979), the degree to which confounded factors contribute to SES-related effects is often difficult to discern.

Another concern with respect to interpreting the literature on SES and parenting pertains to the direction of causality. In our discussion, we have assumed that correlations indicate the influence of SES on parenting, not the other way around. If, however, we consider parenting as one component of coping and performing competently in the world, and if we allow that there may be across domain individual differences in competence and coping skills, then SES may be the product of an individual's overall level of functioning, of which parenting is but one manifestation. Perhaps the most important point to be made, in summary, is that the mechanisms of causality underlying relations between SES and parenting remain unspecified.

Identifying Meaningful Effects of SES on Parenting

In addition to the problem of locating the effects of SES on parenting, there is the problem of deciding which effects matter. Ultimately, what matters is not whether there are statistically significant differences in parenting among groups that differ in SES, but rather whether the differences among groups are meaningful. Although research on SES and parenting is guided by a research literature that articulates aspects of parenting that affect child development, we have a limited understanding of the effects of parenting on child outcomes across contexts that vary as a function of SES. As a consequence, it is difficult to identify with any certainty the SES-related differences in parenting that matter for children. The problem is compounded by the manner in which SES is treated as a variable and the ways in which effects of SES are reported. Although some studies are designed to explicitly consider SES-related differences, SES is treated as a nuisance variable in most research on parenting, and its association with parenting is often not reported or is statistically controlled. Furthermore, when group differences are detected, failure to describe the magnitude of the effect frequently limits the practical significance of the findings (McCartney and Rosenthal, 2000). Because vote-counting reviews of the literature (such as this one) contain a host of well-documented limitations (Hedges and Olkin, 1985), at the end of the day, we must confess that although it is our impression that the differences we have described are meaningful in terms of their impact on the lives of children, we are unable to quantify our assertion.

APPLICATIONS OF RESEARCH ON SES AND PARENTING

Although the foregoing limitations are serious, the problems of low-SES children are also serious and cannot await a perfect science. One of the motives that has spurred research on how parenting differs as a function of SES is the goal of increasing the chances for educational and occupational success of children from lower socioeconomic strata, or, put less optimistically, scholars have sought ways to minimize the presumed association between low SES and suboptimal parenting. Thus it seems relevant to consider what implications the literature on SES and parenting has for improving the daily lives and developmental trajectories of lower-SES children.

There is, however, a logically prior question concerning the legitimacy of prescribing how parents should raise their children. An argument against such a prescription is that it entails an arrogant and classist judgment that some ways of parenting are better than others and that the practices deemed better invariably reflect the values of the dominant culture (see Pine, 1992). The fact that educated academics regard authoritative parenting as the preferable style and that high levels of education are associated with being an authoritative parent and with being a research scientist may be an example of this imposition of values by a higher-SES group on a lower-SES group. A related concern is the fact that the values attached to outcomes may vary as a function of SES. Although some outcomes, for example, the death of a child, are universally regarded as bad, others, for example, teen pregnancy, may not be. One potential solution is to allow that different values and practices may be appropriate adaptations to the social conditions that prevail within socioeconomic strata, while at the same time recognizing that some manners of parenting may better prepare children for participation in particular social niches (Laosa, 1980). This analysis suggests that generalizations from the literature should be limited to studies that identify aspects of parenting that are associated with universally valued outcomes, such as mental health, reproductive success, and successful socialization as a member of one's culture. There is no doubt, however, that most research in the area of SES and parenting is aimed at identifying aspects of parenting that are associated with positive outcomes as defined by the majority culture, such as avoiding public assistance and succeeding in school.

In addition to the difficulty of identifying appropriate goals for the application of research on SES and parenting, it is difficult to identify the types of parenting that should be promoted in the service of those goals if, as some have argued, the effects on children of different types of parenting are different for different groups. One possibility raised by Darling and Steinberg (1993) is that the effects of practices differ depending on parenting style. This hypothesis bears empirical investigation. Within the realm of the effects of style, it has been suggested that authoritarian style may be more beneficial than an authoritative style in the sorts of environments in which poor children live (Baumrind, 1972). This thesis failed to receive support, however, from a large study of U.S. adolescents that indicated that, regardless of SES and ethnicity, authoritative parenting was the best predictor of positive outcomes (Steinberg, Dornbusch, and Brown, 1992; Steinberg, Mounts, Lamborn, and Dornbusch, 1991; Steinberg, in this *Handbook*). That said, it does seem to be the case that factors other than parenting play a greater role in affecting child outcomes in some groups, and possibly in some social strata, than others. That is, although the nature of parenting effects is constant across groups, their magnitude is not. In some cases, parenting may matter less in low-SES groups, because a lack of adequate space, nutrition, and physical health are the limiting factors on development or because other relationships, such as those with peers, have relatively greater influence (Steinberg et al., 1992). In other cases, parenting may matter more in low-SES groups, because differences in the lower range of environmental support are more important to development than differences above a certain threshold of adequacy. In support of this latter contention, SES has been found to moderate the heritability of verbal IQ: In lower-SES homes, the environment accounts for a greater proportion of the variance than in higher-SES homes (Rowe, Jacobson, and Van den Oord, 1999).

These difficulties notwithstanding, some applied implications have been drawn from studies of SES and parenting. Implications have been drawn in cases in which the same aspects of parenting both reliably differ as functions of SES and reliably have effects on children. The robust findings

(1) that lower-SES parents are less verbally responsive, more frequently use harsh punishment, and are more authoritarian than higher SES parents and (2) that positive child outcomes are associated with high verbal responsiveness, less harsh discipline, and with authoritative child rearing underlie the view that warmth, neuturance, and contingent responsiveness should be encouraged in lower SES parents (National Research Council and Institute of Medicine, 2000). There is another, less optimistic implication in the literature—this one from investigations of the underlying sources of SES-related differences in parenting. The evidence suggests that these differences have roots outside the person, both in current circumstance and past personal experience. Specifically, parenting that is associated with positive child outcomes is associated with high levels of parental education and with an absence of financial strain, and, also, the parenting one does is related to the parenting one has received. For instance, mothers' provision of high-quality parenting is related to their own mothers' levels of education and to the presence of two parents in their home when they were children (Menaghan and Parcel, 1991). As another example, the practice of harsh parenting is transmitted across generations even when belief in harsh parenting is not (Simons et al., 1991). These findings imply that there will be limits to the efficacy of parental intervention because intervention does not target the real causes of parenting style or practices. It is, therefore, a testament to the quality of the programs that exist and to the motivation of parents who participate that parental invtervention efforts have the influence that they do (see National Research Council and Institute of Medicine, 2000).

FUTURE DIRECTIONS FOR RESEARCH ON SES AND PARENTING

There are gaps in the literature on SES and parenting, and there is relevant territory that has barely been explored. As the varying lengths of the different sections in this chapter reveal, research on the relation of SES to parenting is uneven in its coverage of the domain of parenting. There are a number of studies of SES-related differences in mother–child interaction with young children and in parenting styles with adolescents. Much less is known about SES-related differences in how fathers and other caregivers interact with children, and, with the exception of work on parenting style, relatively little is known about how SES affects the parenting of children in middle childhood and adolescence.

Another relatively unexplored topic concerns the extent to which SES-related differences in parenting are findings about parenting per se or are more general findings about SES-related differences in behavior. Several sources argue that the SES-related differences in parents' behavior with their children derive from internal characteristics that are not specifically related to parenting and that parenting behaviors are a function of more general behavioral inclinations. As examples, there may be SES-related differences in the overt expression of aggression that parallel the SES-related differences in the use of physical punishment (Zigler, 1970) and SES-related differences in general volubility that parallel SES-related differences in the amount of talk addressed to children (Hoff-Ginsberg, 1991). For other SES-related differences in parenting, such as in controlling child behavior and in the tendency toward an authoritarian style, it would be interesting and enlightening to know whether these SES-related differences in the manner of parent–child interaction and the quality of parent–child relations have counterparts in SES-related differences in adults' manner of interaction with other adults and in the quality of their other close relationships. It should not be surprising if such parallels exist. After all, there is little reason to expect that the factors that define SES and predict parenting behavior (i.e., education, occupation, and income) should affect only parenting and have no influence on other behaviors.

More work is needed in identifying the causal pathways that link components of SES to parents' personality and beliefs, to parenting style and practices, and to child outcomes. Identifying the first linkages, between SES and characteristics of parents and their behavior, is necessary for understanding how SES influences parents. Identifying the second linkages, between parenting and child outcome, is crucial for intervention. Right now, we know more about the relations between SES and parenting and between SES and child outcomes than we do about the extent and manner in which the effects of SES on child outcome are mediated by parenting.

Practically unexplored territory is the relation between SES and parenting across cultures. Culture itself is a strong influence on parenting (Bornstein, 1991; Harkness and Super, in Vol. 2 of this *Handbook*). There is also evidence that culture can moderate the effects of SES (Gutierrez, Sameroff, and Karrer, 1988; Harwood et al., 1996). For example, among Anglo Americans, lower-SES mothers were more concerned with their children's proper demeanor and higher-SES mothers were more concerned with their children's self-maximization (Harwood, et al., 1996). Among Puerto Rican mothers, in contrast, mothers were primarily concerned with proper demeanor regardless of SES. Despite the potential significance of culture as a variable affecting the relation between SES and parenting, most of the literature reviewed in this chapter concerned North American parents and North American conceptions of SES. Cross-cultural extensions of this work replicate North American findings, which suggests a certain universality to some relations: More educated parents use language differently and are less authoritarian and more authoritative in their dealings with their children across a wide variety of cultural contexts.

Because cross-cultural extensions tend to seek replication, we do not know what relations between SES and parenting may exist elsewhere but not in North America. The research strategy of replication holds the danger of reifying North American constructs as universal constants and glosses over particulars that may be central to the rest of the world's population. Truly cross-cultural work will require a reexamination of the definitions of both SES and parenting. The components that define SES and parenting and the components that create variability in SES and in parenting may be different in different cultures. Certainly, the mean, the range, and the shape of the distribution of SES differ across cultures. Cross-cultural research is needed to complete the descriptive account of the relation of SES to parenting, and such research also holds the promise of shedding new light on how and why parents' experiences and the circumstances in which parents operate affect how they parent.

CONCLUSIONS

In this chapter we asked how and why one's SES influences the way in which one parents. Our first step in answering this question was to describe the SES-associated differences in parenting that have been observed. Although no summary can do justice to the complexity of parenting and its relation to SES, the literature suggests that, on average, lower-SES parents (1) are more concerned that their children conform to societal expectations, (2) create a home atmosphere in which it is clear that parents have authority over children, and (3) are punitive when that authority is countermanded. In everyday interaction with their children, lower-SES parents are more directive of their children's behavior and less conversational than are higher-SES parents. In contrast, higher-SES parents (1) are more concerned that their children develop initiative, (2) create a home atmosphere in which children are more nearly equal participants and in which rules are discussed as opposed to laid down, and (3) are less apt to be punitive, and especially less likely to resort to harsh physical punishment. In everyday interaction, higher-SES parents are less directive and more conversational than are lower-SES parents.

Our second step in addressing how SES influences parenting was to identify the source of the SES-associated differences in parenting that have been observed. One way in which we posed that question was by asking whether SES-associated differences in parenting derive from external factors associated with SES or from internal characteristics of adults that differ according to their SES. There is evidence of both sources of influence. As an example of an internal characteristic, parents in different socioeconomic strata have different communicative styles, and these styles are reflected in the way they interact with their children (Crouter and McHale, 1993; Hoff-Ginsberg, 1991, 1994,

1998; Laosa, 1980). As an example of an external influence, contemporary "expert" advice affects the behavior of higher-SES parents before it affects the behavior of lower-SES parents (Bronfenbrenner, 1958). However, the distinction between internal and external factors may be somewhat artificial because internal characteristics of adults may have sources in SES-related experiences such as education or occupation.

Another way that the question of how SES exerts its influence was addressed involved unpacking SES and reconceptualizing it. When examined separately, the multiple factors that make up SES bear different relations to parenting behaviors. For example, education and occupation have been implicated as sources of influence on parents' values and on their communicative styles (e.g., Hoff-Ginsberg 1991, 1994, 1998; Luster et al., 1989). Low income, particularly at poverty levels, has a general debilitating effect on parenting. Even so, the multiple variables that make up SES are interrelated. Education affects income and occupation, and family income affects opportunities for education. It is not unusual that one variable, typically education, is used as a proxy for SES, which renders its causal role is inseparable from the effects of correlated SES variables. One challenge for future research is to collect sufficient data on the various components of SES to be able to formulate and test more precise hypotheses about the specific and global effects of SES on parenting.

A third issue, briefly touched on in this chapter, concerns the practical implications of the observed relations between SES and parenting. In deriving practical implications from the literature, there is tension between the disinterested scientific stance, which seeks to describe and understand SES-related differences in parenting, and the applied goal of bettering the prospects of lower-SES children. There is also tension between the immediacy of children's needs and the current limitations of the literature. It is not clear when it is legitimate to try to change parenting, nor does the literature provide certainty with respect to what changes one would try to make. Another finding with relevance for application is that in addition to its being a response to external circumstances and expressions of childrearing beliefs and values, parenting is also a reflection of the persons who parent. Aspects of parenting behavior that have origins beyond current SES may be relatively difficult to change.

In sum, the literature on SES and parenting suggests that the effects of SES on parenting are both profound and pervasive. Parents in different socioeconomic strata have had different experiences that make them different people. Parents in different socioeconomic strata also operate in different environmental contexts. Via paths of influence that are imperfectly understood, these differences in parents and in the circumstances in which they behave as parents result in differences in the goals parents have, the emotional climates of childrearing that they create, and the parenting practices they use.

ACKNOWLEDGMENTS

Brett Laursen received support for the preparation of this chapter from the U. S. National Institute of Child Health and Human Development (R29-HD33006).

REFERENCES

Alwin, D. F. (1984). Trends in parental socialization values: Detroit, 1958–1983. *American Journal of Sociology, 90*, 359–381.

Anderson, H. E. (1936). *The young child in the home*. Report of the Committee on the Infant and Preschool Child, White House Conference on Child Health and Protection. New York: Appleton-Century.

Bartz, K. W., and Levine, E. S. (1978). Childrearing by Black parents: A description and comparison to Anglo and Chicano parents. *Journal of Marriage and the Family, 40*, 709–719.

Baumrind, D. (1967). Child care practices anteceding three patterns of preschool behavior. *Genetic Psychology Monographs, 75*, 43–88.

Baumrind, D. (1972). An exploratory study of socialization effects on Black children: Some Black–White comparisons. *Child Development, 43*, 261–267.

Bayley, N., and Schaefer, E. S. (1960). Relationships between socioeconomic variables and the behavior of mothers toward young children. *Journal of Genetic Psychology, 96*, 61–77.

Belsky, J. (1984). The determinants of parenting: A process model. *Child Development, 5*, 83–96.

Bernstein, B. B. (1970). A socio-linguistic approach to social learning. In F. Williams (Ed.), *Language and poverty* (pp. 25–61). Chicago: Markham.

Bluestone, C., and Tamis-LeMonda, C. S. (1999). Correlates of parenting styles in predominantly working- and middle-class African American mothers. *Journal of Marriage and the Family, 61*, 881–893.

Borduin, C. M., and Henggeler, S. W. (1981). Social class, experimental setting, and task characteristics as determinants of mother–child interaction. *Developmental Psychology, 17*, 209–214.

Bornstein, M. H. (1991). *Cultural approaches to parenting*. Hillsdale, NJ: Lawrence Erlbaum Associates.

Bornstein, M. H., Haynes, M. O., and Painter, K. M. (1998). Sources of child vocabulary competence: A multivariate model. *Journal of Child Language, 25*, 367–393.

Brody, G. F. (1968). Socioeconomic differences in stated maternal child-rearing practices and in observed maternal behavior. *Journal of Marriage and the Family, 30*, 656–660.

Brody, G. H., Flor, D. L., and Gibson, N. M. (1999). Linking maternal efficacy beliefs, developmental goals, parenting practices, and child competence in rural single-parent African American families. *Child Development, 70*, 1197–1208.

Bronfenbrenner, U. (1958). Socialization and social class through time and space. In E. E. Maccoby, R. M. Newcomb, and E. L. Harley (Eds.), *Readings in social psychology* (pp. 400–425). New York: Holt, Rinehart & Winston.

Bronfenbrenner, U. (1970). Two worlds of childhood: U.S. and U.S.S.R. New York: Russell Sage Foundation.

Brophy, J. E. (1970). Mothers as teachers of their own preschool children: The influence of socioeconomic status and task structure on teaching specificity. *Child Development, 41*, 79–94.

Budwig, N., and Chaudhary, N. (1996). Hindi-speaking caregivers' input: Towards an integration of typological and language socialization approaches. In A. Stringfellow, D. Cahana-Amitay, E. Hughes, and A. Zukowski (Eds.), *Proceedings of the 20th annual Boston University conference on language development* (pp. 135–145). Somerville, MA: Cascadilla.

Burns, A. Homel, R., and Goodnow, J. (1984). Conditions of life and parental values. *Australian Journal of Psychology, 36*, 219–237.

Caldwell, B. M., and Bradley, R. H. (1984). *Home observation for measurement of the environment*. Little Rock, AK: University of Arkansas.

Chen, X., Dong, Q., and Zhou, H. (1997). Authoritative and authoritarian parenting practices and social and school performance in Chinese children. *International Journal of Behavioral Development, 21*, 855–873.

Clarke-Stewart. K. A., VanderStoep, L. P., and Killian, G. A. (1979). Analysis and replication of mother–child relations at two years of age. *Child Development, 50*, 777–793.

Coleman, J. S. (1988). Social capital in the creation of human capital. *American Journal of Sociology, 94* (Suppl.), S95–S120.

Collins, W. A., Maccoby, E. E., Steinberg, L., Hetherington, E. M., and Bornstein, M. H. (2000). Contemporary research on parenting. *American Psychologist, 55*, 218–232.

Crouter, A. C., Helms-Erikson, H., Updegraff, K., and McHale, S. M. (1999). Conditions underlying parents' knowledge about children's daily lives in middle childhood: Between- and within-family comparisons. *Child Development, 70*, 246–259.

Crouter, A. C., and McHale, S. M. (1993). The long arm of the job: Influences of parental work on childrearing. In T. Luster and L. Okagaki (Eds.), *Parenting: An ecological perspective* (pp. 179–202). Hillsdale, NJ: Lawrence Erlbaum Associates.

Darling, N., and Steinberg, L. (1993). Parenting style as context: An integrative model. *Psychological Bulletin, 113*, 487–496.

Davis, A., and Havighurst, R. J. (1946). Social class and color differences in child-rearing. *American Sociological Review, 11*, 698–710.

DeGarmo D. S., Forgatch, M. S., and Martinez, C. R., Jr. (1999). Parenting of divorced mothers as a link between social status and boys' academic outcomes: Unpacking the effects of socioeconomic status. *Child Development, 70*, 1231–1245.

Dornbusch, S. M., Ritter, P. L., Leiderman, P. H., Roberts, D. F., and Fraleigh, M. J. (1987). The relation of parenting style to adolescent school performance. *Child Development, 58*, 1244–1257.

Dunn, J., Wooding, C., and Herman, J. (1977). Mothers' speech to young children: Variation in context. *Developmental Medicine and Child Neurology, 19*, 629–638.

Eisenberg, A. (1990, March). *Task effects on social class and ethnic variation in mother–child communication*. Paper presented at the meetings of the Southwestern Society for Research in Human Development, Dallas, TX.

Elder, G. H., Jr., Eccles, J. S., Ardelt, M., and Lord, S. (1995). Inner-city parents under economic pressure: Perspectives on the strategies of parenting. *Journal of Marriage and the Family, 57*, 771–784.

Elder, G. H., Van Nguyen, T., and Caspi, A. (1985). Linking family hardship to children's lives. *Child Development, 56*, 361–375.

Entwisle, D. R., and Astone, N. M. (1994). Some practical guidelines for measuring youth's race/ethnicity and socioeconomic status. *Child Development, 65*, 1521–1540.

Ericson, M. C. (1963). Child-rearing and social status. *American Journal of Sociology, 68*, 190–192.

Evans, G. W., Maxwell, L. E., and Hart, B. (1999). Parental language and verbal responsiveness to children in crowded homes. *Developmental Psychology, 35*, 1020–1023.

Featherman, D. L., Spenner, K. I., and Tsunematsu, N. (1988). Class and the socialization of children: Constancy, change, or irrelevance? In E. M. Heatherington, R. M. Lerner, and M. Perlmutter (Eds.), *Child development in life-span perspective* (pp. 67–90). Hillsdale, NJ: Lawrence Erlbaum Associates.

Feiring, C., and Lewis, M. (1981). Middle-class differences in mother–child-interaction and the child's cognitive development. In T. M. Field, A. M. Sostek, P. Vietze, and P. H. Leiderman (Eds.), *Culture and early interactions* (pp. 63–91). Hillsdale, NJ: Lawrence Erlbaum Associates.

Fenson, L., Dale, P. S., Reznick, J. S., Bates, E., Thal, D. J., and Pethick, S. J. (1994). Variability in early communicative development. *Monographs of the Society for Research in Child Development*, (Serial No. 242).

Field, T., and Ignatoff, E. (1981). Videotaping effects on the behaviours of low income mothers and their infants during floor-play interactions. *Journal of Applied Developmental Psychology*, 2, 227–235.

Field, T., and Pawlby, S. (1980). Early face-to-face interactions of British and American working- and middle-class mother–infant dyads. *Child Development, 51*, 250–253.

Garcia Coll, C. Lamberty, G., Jenkins, R., McAdoo, H. P., Crnic, K., Wasik, B. H., Vasquez Garcia, H. (1996). An integrative model for the study of developmental competencies in minority children. *Child Development, 67*, 1891–1914.

Garbarino, J., and Kostelny, K. (1993). Neighborhood and community influences on parenting. In T. Luster and L. Okagaki (Eds.), *Parenting: An ecological perspective* (pp. 203–226). Hillsdale, NJ: Lawrence Erlbaum Associates.

Gecas, V. (1979). The influence of social class on socialization. In W. R. Burr, R. Hill, F. I. Nye, and I. L. Reiss (Eds.), *Contemporary theories about the family* (pp. 365–404). New York: Free Press.

Glasgow, K. L., Dornbusch, S. M., Troyer, L., and Steinberg, L. (1997). Parenting styles, adolescents' attributions, and educational outcomes in nine heterogeneous high schools. *Child Development, 68*, 507–529.

Goodnow, J. J., and Collins, W. A. (1990). *Development according to parents: The nature, sources, and consequences of parents' ideas*. Hillsdale, NJ: Lawrence Erlbaum Associates.

Gonzales, N. A., Cauce, A. M., and Mason, C. A. (1996). Interobserver agreement in the assessment of parental behavior and parent–adolescent conflict: African American mothers, daughters, and independent observers. *Child Development, 67*, 1483–1498.

Graves, Z. R., and Glick, J. (1978). The effect of context on mother–child interaction: A progress report. *The Quarterly Newsletter of the Institute for Comparative Human Development*, 2, 41–46.

Greenbaum, C. W., and Landau, R. (1979). The infants' exposure to talk by familiar people: Mothers, fathers, and siblings in different environments. In M. Lewis and L. A. Rosenblum (Eds.), *The child and its family* (pp. 67–89). New York: Plenum.

Greenberg, S., and Formanek, R. (1974). Social class differences in spontaneous verbal interactions. *Child Study Journal, 4*, 145–153.

Gutierrez, J., Sameroff, A. J., and Karrer, B. M. (1988). Acculturation and SES effects on Mexican-American parents' concepts of development. *Child Development, 59*, 250–255.

Gutman, L. M., and Eccles, J. S. (1999). Financial strain, parenting behaviors, and adolescents, achievement: Testing model equivalence between African American and European American single- and two-parent families. *Child Development, 70*, 1464–1476.

Hammer, C. S., and Weiss, A. L. (1999). Guiding language development: How African American mothers and their infants structure play interactions. *Journal of Speech, Language, and Hearing Research*, 42, 1219–1233.

Harkness, S., and Super, C. (1992). Parental ethnotheories in action. In I. E. Sigel, A. V. McGillicuddy-De Lisi, and J. J. Goodnow (Eds.), *Parental belief systems: The psychological consequences for children* (2nd ed., pp. 373–391). Hillsdale, NJ: Lawrence Erlbaum Associates.

Hart, B., and Risley, T. R. (1992). American parenting of language-learning children: Persisting differences in family–child interactions observed in natural home environments. *Developmental Psychology*, 28, 1096–1106.

Hart, B., and Risley, T. R. (1995). *Meaningful differences in the everyday experience of young American children*. Baltimore: Brookes.

Harwood, R. L. (1992). The influence of culturally derived values on Anglo and Puerto Rican mothers' perceptions of attachment behavior. *Child Development, 63*, 822–839.

Harwood, R. L., Miller, J. G., and Lucca Irizarry, N. (1995). *Culture and attachment: Perceptions of the child in context*. New York: Guilford.

Harwood, R. L., Schoelmerich, A.,Ventura-Cook, E., Schulze, P. A., and Wilson, S. P. (1996). Cultural and class influences on Anglo and Puerto Rican mothers' beliefs regarding long-term socialization goals and child behavior. *Child Development, 67*, 2446–2461.

Hauser, R. M. (1994). Measuring socioeconomic status in studies of child development. *Child Development, 65*, 1541–1545.

Havighurst, R. J. (1976). The relative importance of social class and ethnicity in human development. *Human Development, 19*, 56–64.

Heath, S. B. (1983). *Ways with words: Language, life, and work in communities and classrooms*. New York: Cambridge University Press.

Hedges, L. V., and Olkin, I. (1985). *Statistical methods for meta-analysis*. New York: Academic.

Hess, R. D. (1970). Social class and ethnic influences upon socialization. In P. H. Mussen (Ed.), *Carmichael's manual of child psychology* (3rd ed., Vol. 2, pp. 457–557). New York: Wiley.

Hess, R. D., and Shipman, V. C. (1965). Early experience and the socialization of cognitive modes in children. *Child Development, 36,* 869–886.

Hess, R. D., Kashiwagi, K., Azuma, H., Price, G. G., and Dickson, W. P. (1980). Maternal expectations for mastery of developmental tasks in Japan and the United States. *International Journal of Psychology, 15,* 259–271.

Hoff-Ginsberg, E. (1991). Mother–child conversation in different social classes and communicative settings. *Child Development, 62,* 782–796.

Hoff-Ginsberg, E. (1992). How should frequency in input be measured? *First Language, 12,* 233–245.

Hoff-Ginsberg, E. (1994). Influences of mother and child on maternal talkativeness. *Discourse Processes, 18,* 105–117.

Hoff-Ginsberg, E. (1998). The relation of birth order and socioeconomic status to children's language experience and language development. *Applied Psycholinguistics, 19,* 603–630.

Hoff-Ginsberg, E., and Tardif, T. (1995). Socioeconomic status and parenting. In M. H. Bornstein, (Ed.), *The handbook of parenting: Vol. 2. Biology and ecology of parenting* (pp. 161–188). Mahwah, NJ: Lawrence Erlbaum Associates.

Hoffman, M. L. (1963). Personality, family structure, and social class as antecedents of parental power assertion. *Child Development, 34,* 869–884.

Holden, G. W. (1995). Parental attitudes towards child caring. In M. H. Bornstein (Ed.), *Handbook of parenting, Vol. 3: Status and social conditions of parenting* (pp. 359–392). Mahwah, NJ: Lawrence Erlbaum Associates.

Holden, G. W., and Edwards, L. A. (1989). Parental attitudes toward child rearing: Instruments, issues, and implications. *Psychological Bulletin, 106,* 29–58.

Hollingshead, A. (1957). *Two-factor index of social position.* Unpublished manuscript, Yale University, Department of Sociology, New Haven, CT.

Hollingshead, A. (1975). *The four-factor index of social status.* Unpublished manuscript, Yale University, Department of Sociology, New Haven, CT.

Hollingshead, A. B., and Redlich, F. C. (1958). *Social class and mental health.* New York: Wiley.

Huttenlocher, J., Haight, W., Bryk, A., Seltzer, M., and Lyons, T. (1991). Early vocabulary growth: relation to language input and gender. *Developmental Psychology, 27,* 236–248.

Jacob, T. (1974). Patterns of family conflict and dominance as a function of child age and social class. *Developmental Psychology, 10,* 1–12.

Jacobson, K. C., and Crockett, L. J. (2000). Parental monitoring and adolescent adjustment: An ecological perspective. *Journal of Research on Adolescents, 10,* 65–97.

Kelley, M. L., Sanchez-Hucles, J., and Walker, R. (1993). Correlates of disciplinary practices in working- to middle-class African-American mothers. *Merrill-Palmer Quarterly, 39,* 252–264.

Klebanov, P. K., Brooks-Gunn, J., and Duncan, G. J. (1994). Does neighborhood and family poverty affect mothers' parenting, mental health, and social support? *Journal of Marriage and the Family, 56,* 441–455.

Klein, K., Forehand, R., and Family Health Project Research Group (2000). Family processes as resources for African American children exposed to a constellation of sociodemographic risk factors. *Journal of Clinical Child Psychology, 29,* 53–65.

Kohn, M. L. (1963). Social class and parent–child relationships: An interpretation. *American Journal of Sociology, 68,* 471–480.

Kohn, M. L. (1969). *Class and conformity: A study in values.* Homewood, IL: Dorsey.

Kohn, M. L. (1997). *Class and conformity: A study in values* (2nd ed.). Chicago: University of Chicago Press.

Kohn, M. L. (1979). The effects of social class on parental values and practices. In D. Reiss and H. A. Hoffman (Eds.), *The American family: Dying or developing* (pp. 45–68). New York: Plenum.

Lambert, W. E., Hamers, J., and Frasure-Smith, N. (1979). *Child-rearing values: A cross-national study.* New York: Praeger.

Laosa, L. M. (1980). Maternal teaching strategies in Chicano and Anglo-American families: the influence of culture and education on maternal behavior. *Child Development, 51,* 759–765.

Lawrence, V., and Shipley, E. (1996). Parental speech to middle- and working-class children from two racial groups in three settings. *Applied Psycholinguistics, 17,* 233–255.

Lempers, J. D., Clark-Lempers, D., and Simons, R. L. (1989). Economic hardship, parenting, and distress in adolescence. *Child Development, 60,* 25–39.

Luster, T., and Kain, E. L. (1987). The relation between family context and perceptions of parental efficacy. *Early Child Development and Care, 29,* 301–311.

Luster, T., Rhoades, K., and Haas, B. (1989). The relation between parental values and parenting behavior: A test of the Kohn hypothesis. *Journal of Marriage and the Family, 51,* 139–147.

Lynd, R. S., and Lynd, H. M. (1929). *Middletown: A study in American culture.* New York: Harcourt, Brace.

Lynd, R. S., and Lynd, H. M. (1937). *Middletown in transition: A study in cultural conflicts.* New York: Harcourt, Brace.

Maccoby, E. E. (1992). The role of parents in the socialization of children: An historical overview. *Developmental Psychology, 28,* 1006–1017.

Maccoby, E. E., and Martin, J. A. (1983). Socialization in the context of the family: Parent–child interaction. In P. H. Mussen (Series Ed.) and E. M. Hetheringten (Vol. Ed.), *Handbook of child psychology* (4th ed., Vol. 4, pp. 1–102). New York: Wiley.

Mansbach, I. K., and Greenbaum, C. W. (1999). Developmental maturity expectations of Israeli fathers and mothers: Effects of education, ethnic origin, and religiosity. *International Journal of Behavioral Development, 23,* 771–797.

McCartney, K., and Rosenthal, R. (2000). Effect size, practical importance, and social policy for children. *Child Development, 71,* 173–180.

McGillicuddy-De Lisi, A. V. (1982). Parental beliefs about developmental processes. *Human Development, 25,* 192–200.

McLoyd, V. (1990). The impact of economic hardship on Black families and children: Psychological distress, parenting, and socioecomotional development. *Child Development, 61,* 311–346.

McLoyd, V. (1998). Socioeconomic disadvantage and child development. *American Psychologist, 53,* 185–204.

Mead, M. (1928). *Coming of age in Samoa.* New York: Morrow.

Mead, M. (1930). *Growing up in New Guinea.* New York: Morrow.

Menaghan, E. G., and Parcel, T. L. (1991). Determining children's home environments: The impact of maternal characteristics and current occupational and family conditions. *Journal of Marriage and the Family, 53,* 417–431.

National Research Council and Institute of Medicine (2000). *From neurons to neighborhoods: The science of early childhood development.* Committee on Integrating the Science of Early Childhood Development. J. P. ShonKoff and Deborah A. Phillips (Eds.), Board on Children Youth, and Families, Commission on Behavioral and Social Sciences and Education. Washington, DC: National Academy Press.

NICHD Early Child Care Research Network (1999). Chronicity of maternal depressive symptoms, maternal sensitivity, and child functioning at 36 months. *Developmental Psychology, 35,* 1297–1310.

Ninio, A. (1980). Picture-book reading in mother–infant dyads belonging to two subgroups in Israel. *Child Development, 51,* 587–590.

Ninio, A. (1988). The effects of cultural background, sex, and parenthood on beliefs about the timetable of cognitive development in infancy. *Merrill-Palmer Quarterly, 34,* 369–388.

O'Donnell, L., and Stueve, A. (1983). Mothers as social agents: Structuring the community activities of school aged children. *Research in the Interweave of Social Roles: Jobs and Families, 3,* 113–129.

Okagaki, L., and Divecha, D. J. (1993). Development of parental beliefs. In T. Luster and L. Okagaki (Eds.), *Parenting: An ecological perspective* (pp. 35–68). Hillsdale, NJ: Lawrence Erlbaum Associates.

Otto, L. B. (1975). Class and status in family research. *Journal of Marriage and the Family, 37,* 315–332.

Parke, R. D., and Buriel, R. (1998). Socialization in the family: Ethnic and ecological perspectives. In W. Damon (Series Ed.) and N. Eisenberg (Vol. Ed.), *Handbook of child psychology: Vol. 3. Social, emotional, and personality development* (5th ed., pp. 463–552). New York: Wiley.

Paulson, S. E. (1994). Relations of parenting style and parental involvement with ninth-grade students' achievement. *Journal of Early Adolescence, 14,* 250–267.

Pearlin, L. I., and Kohn, M. L. (1966). Social class, occupation, and parental values: A cross-national study. *American Sociological Review, 31,* 466–479.

Pine, J. (1992). Commentary on: How should frequency in input be measured? *First Language, 12,* 245–249.

Pomerleau, A, LaCroix, V., Malcuit, G., and Seguin, R. (1999, April). *Content of mother's speech, child's language, and cognitive development in different socioeconomic groups: A longitudinal study.* Paper presented at the meeting of the Society for Research in Child Development, Albuquerque, NM.

Reger, Z. (1990). Mothers' speech in different social groups in Hungary. In G. Conti-Ramsden and C. Snow (Eds.), *Children's language* (Vol. 7, pp. 197–222). Hillsdale, NJ: Lawrence Erlbaum Associates.

Reznick, J. S. (1990). Visual preference as a test of infant word comprehension. *Journal of Applied Psycholinguistics, 11,* 145–165.

Richman, A. L., Miller, P. M., and LeVine, R. A. (1992). Cultural and educational variations in maternal responsiveness. *Developmental Psychology, 28,* 614–621.

Rowe, D. C., Jacobson, K. C., and Van den Oord, E. J. C. G. (1999). Genetic and environmental influences on vocabulary IQ: Parental education level as moderator. *Child Development, 70,* 1047–1275.

Sameroff, A. J., and Feil, L. A. (1985). Parental concepts of development. In I. E. Sigel (Ed.), *Parental belief systems: The psychological consequences for children* (pp. 83–105). Hillsdale, NJ: Lawrence Erlbaum Associates.

Sameroff, A. J., and Fiese, B. H. (1992). Family representations of development. In I. E. Sigel, A. V. McGillicuddy-DeLisi, and J. J. Goodnow (Eds.), *Parental belief systems: The psychological consequences for children* (2nd ed., pp. 347–369). Hillsdale, NJ: Lawrence Erlbaum Associates.

Schachter, F. (1979). *Everyday mother talk to toddlers.* New York: Academic.

Sears, R. R., Maccoby, E., and Levin, H. (1957). *Patterns of child rearing.* Evanston, IL: Row, Peterson.

Sigel, I. E. (1992). The belief–behavior connection: A resolvable dilemma? In I. E. Sigel, A. V. McGillicuddy-De Lisi, and J. J. Goodnow (Eds.), *Parental belief systems: The psychological consequences for children* (2nd ed., pp. 433–456). Hillsdale, NJ: Lawrence Erlbaum Associates.

Sigel, I. E., McGillicuddy-De Lisi, A. A., and Goodnow, J. J. (Eds.) (1992). *Parental belief systems: The psychological consequences for children* (2nd ed.), Hillsdale, NJ: Lawrence Erlbaum Associates.

Sigel, I. E., McGillicuddy-De Lisi, A. A., and Johnson, J. E. (1980). *Parental distancing, beliefs, and children's representational competence within the family context*. Princeton, NJ: Educational Testing Service.

Simons, R. L., Whitbeck, L. B., Conger, R. D., and Chyi-In, W. (1991). Intergenerational transmission of harsh parenting. *Developmental Psychology, 27*, 159–171.

Slaughter-Defoe, D. T. (1995). Revisition the concept of socialization: Caregiving and teaching in the 90s—A personal perspective. *American Psychologist, 50*, 276–286.

Snow, C. E., Arlman-Rupp, A., Hassing, Y., Jobse, J., Joosten, J., and Vorster, J. (1976). Mothers' speech in three social classes. *Journal of Psycholinguistic Research, 5*, 1–20.

Snow, C. E., De Blauw, A., and Van Roosmalen, G. (1979). Talking and playing with babies:

Spoth, R., Goldberg, C., and Redmond, C. (1999). Engaging families in longitudinal preventive intervention research: Discrete-time survival analysis of socioeconomic and social–emotional risk factors. *Journal of Consulting and Clinical Psychology, 67*, 157–163.

Steinberg, L., Dornbusch, S. M., and Brown, B. B. (1992). Ethnic differences in adolescent achievement: An ecological perspective. *American Psychologist, 47*, 723–729.

Steinberg, L. Mounts, N. S., Lamborn, S. D., and Dornbusch, S. (1991). Authoritative parenting and adolescent adjustment across varied ecological niches. *Journal of Research on Adolescence, 1*, 19–36.

Stevens, J. H. (1984). Black grandmothers and black adolescent mothers' knowledge about parenting. *Developmental Psychology, 20*, 1017–1025.

Straus, M. A., Gelles, R. J., and Steinmetz, S. K. (1980). *Behind closed doors: Violence in the American family*. Beverly Hills, CA: Sage.

Straus, M. A., and Stewart, J. H. (1999). Corporal punishment by American parents: National data on prevalence, chronicity, severity, and duration, in relation to child and family characteristics. *Child and Family Psychology Review, 2*, 55–70.

Super, C. M., and Harkness, S. (1986). The developmental niche: A conceptualization at the interface of child and culture. *International Journal of Behavioral Development, 9*, 545–569.

Tardif, T. (1993). *Adult-to-child speech and language acquisition in Mandarin Chinese*. Unpublished doctoral dissertation, Yale University, New Haven, CT.

Tardif, T., Au, E. P. K., Wellman, H. M., and Nakamura, K. (2000, June). *Adults' theories of children's minds in three cultures*. Paper presented at the 30th Annual Meeting of the Jean Piaget Society, Montreal, Canada.

Tudge, J. R. H., Hogan, D. M., Snezhkova, I. A., Kulakova, N. N., and Etz, K. E. (2000). Parents' child-rearing values and beliefs in the United States and Russia: The impact of culture and social class. *Infant and Child Development, 9*, 105–121.

Tulkin, S. R., and Cohler, B. J. (1973). Childrearing attitudes and mother–child interaction in the first year of life. *Merrill-Palmer Quarterly, 19*, 95–106.

Tulkin, S. R., and Kagan, J. (1972). Mother–child interaction in the first year of life. *Child Development, 43*, 31–41.

von der Lippe, A. L. (1999). The impact of maternal schooling and occupation on child-rearing attitudes and behaviours in low income neighbourhoods in Cairo, Egypt. *International Journal of Behavioral Development, 23*, 703–729.

Whiting, J., and Child, I. (1953). *Child training and personality*. New Haven, CT: Yale University Press.

Whiting, B. B., and Edwards, C. P. (1988). *Children of different worlds: The formation of social behavior*. Cambridge, MA: Harvard University Press.

Woodworth, S., Belsky, J., and Crnic, K. (1996). The determinants of fathering during the child's second and third years of life: A developmental analysis. *Journal of Marriage and the Family, 58*, 679–692.

Wright, J. D., and Wright, S. R. (1976). Social class and parental values for children: A partial replication and extension of the Kohn thesis. *American Sociological Review, 41*, 527–537.

Zigler, E. (1970). Social class and the socialization process. *Review of Educational Research, 40*, 87–110.

9

Culture and Parenting

Sara Harkness
Charles M. Super
University of Connecticut-Storrs

At birth, your child will be divine, closer to the world of the gods than to the human world. Having just arrived from heaven, your infant should be treated as a celestial being. Provide the attention that a god deserves, and address your child with the high language suitable to a person of higher rank. You should hold your newborn high, for gods and members of higher rank should always be elevated relative to their inferiors. For the first 210 days (or 105 days, depending on region and status), never put your baby down on the ground or floor, which is too profane for a god. Until then, your baby should be carried at all times.

—Diener (2000, p. 105)

INTRODUCTION

These words of advice to Balinese parents, taken from *A World of Babies: Imagined Childcare Guides for Seven Societies*, use a charming fiction to illustrate a profound truth: Parenting is culturally constructed. As DeLoache and Gottlieb (2000) illustrate, parents in different cultures receive many different kinds of guidance about how to rear children properly, whether in the form of books of advice or simply in training by example. Until fairly recently, such advice has been largely accepted as basic truth within its own cultural context; but as cultural worlds collide, merge, and struggle to maintain a sense of their own identity, it is becoming ever more difficult to uphold a sense of certainty about the "right" ways to bring up children. In this context, paying attention to culture as a dimension of parenting can help answer some enduring questions: *What is the nature and extent of variability in normative parenting? What are the social, historic, or economic causes of cultural differences in parenting? How are cultural beliefs and values related to parenting practices? What are the effects on children of different cultural approaches to parenting, both in the immediate sense and over the longer course of development?*

In this chapter we review the development of research on culture and parenting, beginning with classic anthropological studies and continuing on to the current flowering of culturally oriented research within and across several disciplines and subdisciplines. In the first section we review classical ethnographic studies of whole cultures, carried out by anthropologists from the end of the nineteenth century to roughly the 1950s. During the latter part of this period—beginning in the 1930s—the "culture and personality" school accorded special attention to parenting because of its perceived importance to socialization and enculturation, concepts shared with the burgeoning child development movement of that era. Thus, in the second section, we consider the work of researchers who saw children's culturally shaped experience as the medium of culture transmission and thereby the production of culturally specific adult personality patterns. In the third part of the chapter we discuss systematic cross-cultural analyses for their distinctive contribution to understanding parenting as it varies in different cultures; this literature, with its attendant methodology, reached its heyday in the 1960s but continues to be produced up to the present. Recognition of the limitations of analyses based on disparately collected ethnographic data led to the mounting of comparative field studies of parents and children, notably by the Whitings and their colleagues, and we discuss the substance and significance of this work. We then turn to more recent research that has attempted a closer integration of the general Whiting paradigm with advances in cognitive, developmental, and systems theories; current research on parental ethnotheories is in part an outgrowth of this integration. Interestingly, the present wide-ranging efforts to understand culture and parenting by anthropologists, developmental scientists, educators, and health professionals is reminiscent of the press for interdisciplinary synthesis more than half-century ago, following the purely descriptive ethnographic studies, with which the story really starts.

CLASSICAL STUDIES: ETHNOGRAPHY AS SCIENCE AND ART

Classical studies of parenting from a cultural perspective come from the genre of the ethnography, literally the "writing" of a cultural group. No matter what theoretical perspective the ethnographer pursued, a faithful description of customs and practices throughout the lifespan was attempted. In an early example from Radcliffe-Brown's (1932/1964, p. 76) study of the Andaman Islanders, based on field work carried out from 1906 to 1908, we find the following summary of parenting practices for young children:

> We may turn now to the duties to one another of parents and children. During their infancy the children are in the care of the mother. Children are, however, such favourites with the Andamanese that a child is played with and petted and nursed not only by his own father and mother but by everyone in the village. A woman with an unweaned child will often give suck to the children of other women. Babies are not weaned till they are three or four years old.
>
> Before the children can walk, they are carried about by the mother, and sometimes by the father or other persons, in a bark sling (called *ciba* in *Aka-Jeru*). . . . After they can walk the children generally accompany their mothers in their expeditions near the camp for firewood or vegetables. When they are not with their mothers they amuse themselves with games in the village or on the beach. All the children of the coast villages learn to swim when they are very young, in fact almost as soon as they learn to walk, and many of their games are conducted in the water.

In these classic studies, descriptions of informal customary practices such as those given in the preceding summary are often interwoven with detailed documentation of more formal practices such as birth rituals, naming ceremonies, or rites of passage. The importance of documenting not only formal practices but also the "apparently trivial contacts of everyday life" is highlighted in Firth's (1936/1966, p. 125) discussion of kinship among the Tikopia, residents of a remote Pacific island whom he studied in the 1920s:

In ethnographic lists of the "functions of kin" the reciprocal relations between parents and children are usually most ill-defined. They are more difficult to classify and enumerate than are the periodic devoirs to be rendered by kin outside this circle. Here, above all, the investigator's personal observation of behaviour must supplement and give perspective to the statements received from his informants, since from them it is impossible to obtain any adequate explicit formulation of the actual conditions. For accuracy of presentation, it is necessary to give actual examples of what seem to be trivial incidents, but which in reality form the substance of the kinship pattern.

Ethnographic studies raise the basic question of validity: Is the anthropologist's characterization of not only specific customs and practices but also of their meaning really correct? Anthropological studies of culture and parenting have differentially identified with scientific or humanistic disciplines. Malinowski (1936/1966, pp. vii–viii) in the Preface to *We, the Tikopia*, praised Firth's work while expressing doubts about both mathematical and literary models in the analysis of ethnographic data:

> On the one hand, we have the application of mathematics, in fact calculus with integrals and differential equations, to facts as elusive and essentially unmathematical as belief, sentiment, or social organization. On the other hand, attempts are made to analyze cultures in terms of Schismogenesis, or to define the individual and singular 'genius' of each particular society as Apollonian, Dionysian, or Paranoid, and the like. Under the deft touch of another writer the women of one tribe appear masculine, while in another males develop feminine qualities almost to the verge of parturition.

The unnamed other writers to whom Malinowski was referring here were Ruth Benedict and Margaret Mead, whose work on "patterns of culture" laid the foundations for the culture and personality school of anthropology in which parenting played a central theoretical role. Benedict and Mead's approach has been called "configurationist" in that it sought to find general patterns of order across many domains of a society's functioning. In this view, personality and culture were seen as inseparable. In Benedict's (1932, p. 24) evocative phrase, culture was imagined as "individual psychology thrown large upon the screen, given gigantic proportions and a long time span." In contrast to Malinowski, Benedict and Mead were not primarily concerned with how these unique cultural configurations may have arisen; rather, they focused their efforts on understanding how culture affected the individual person, especially how cultural patterns are expressed in childrearing, and how different cultural situations affect persons of differing dispositions. In *Patterns of Culture*, the classic statement of the configurationist approach, Benedict (1934/1959, pp. 2–3) sets forth clearly her view of childhood socialization and development as a process of cultural assimilation:

> The life-history of the individual is first and foremost an accommodation to the patterns and standards traditionally handed down in his community. From the moment of his birth the customs into which he is born shape his experience and behaviour. By the time he can talk, he is the little creature of his culture, and by the time he is grown and able to take part in its activities, its habits are his habits, its beliefs his beliefs, its impossibilities his impossibilities. Every child that is born into his group will share them with him, and no child born into one on the opposite side of the globe can ever achieve the thousandth part. There is no social problem it is more incumbent upon us to understand than this of the role of custom. Until we are intelligent as to its laws and varieties, the main complicating facts of human life must remain unintelligible.

Benedict is best known for her formulation of single themes that characterized entire cultures–the calm "Apollonian civilization" of the Pueblo Indians in the American Southwest and the frenzied "Dionysian" culture of the Kwakiutl of Vancouver Island in Canada. However, Benedict was not unaware of the issue of cultural integration, and her later work, *The Chrysanthemum and the Sword* (Benedict, 1946), addressed the question of how to reconcile apparently contradictory images of Japanese culture. In describing the cultural construction of childhood in Japan, Benedict (1946, pp. 253–254) pointed out that cultural integration over the lifespan can take different forms—which, in typical fashion, she presented in vivid metaphorical terms:

> Japanese babies are not brought up in the fashion that a thoughtful Westerner might suppose. American parents, training their children for a life so much less circumspect and stoical than life in Japan, neverthe- less begin immediately to prove to the baby that his own little wishes are not supreme in this world. We put him immediately on a feeding schedule and sleeping schedule, and no matter how he fusses before bottle time or bed time, he has to wait. A little later his mother strikes his hand to make him take his finger out of his mouth or away from other parts of his body. His mother is frequently out of sight and when she goes out he has to stay behind. He has to be weaned before he prefers other foods, or if he is bottle fed, he has to give up his bottle. There are certain foods that are good for him and he must eat them. He is punished when he does not do what is right. What is more natural for an American to suppose than that these disciplines are redoubled for the little Japanese baby who, when he is a finished product, will have to subordinate his own wishes and be so careful and punctilious an observer of such a demanding code?
>
> The Japanese, however, do not follow this course. The arc of life in Japan is plotted in opposite fashion to that in the United States. It is a great shallow U-curve with maximum freedom and indulgence allowed to babies and to the old.

Benedict's portrayal of childrearing practices by parents and others is both detailed and thematic, emphasizing how fear of social ridicule or ostracism is inculcated through teasing and other practices starting at an early age. For the most part, however, she did not ascribe to particular childrearing practices particular outcomes for adult personality: The main argument, rather, was to create a sense of the multiple experiences over the course of childhood that create distinctive meaning systems in adulthood.

Although Benedict did not articulate specifically by what developmental mechanisms the child becomes a "creature of his culture," her younger colleague Mead proposed a theoretical app- roach that resonates with present-day conceptualizations: Cultural environments "communicate" ways of thinking, feeling and behaving to the growing child. LeVine (1973, p. 54) described this formulation:

> The transmission of culture from generation to generation is, in Mead's view, a process of communication in which many aspects of the growing individual's cultural environment relay the same messages to him, messages reflecting the dominant configurations of his culture. He acquires his "cultural character" by internalizing the substance of these consistent messages. The first set of messages is transmitted to him by his parents in infancy and early childhood. They enter into communication with him by making certain (culturally approved) reactions to his cries, his performance of bodily functions, his attempts to move and grasp; much of this communication is nonverbal and implicit. It lays a basis for the later transmission of the same underlying messages in a thousand other ways, some of them explicit, as the child increasingly participates in the various aspects of adult culture. Child rearing is fundamental in the acquisition of cultural character, but it is only the first of many formative experiences, each reinforcing the other in communicating cultural configurations to the individual.

In Mead's work, we find the first sustained descriptions of child and family life in other cultures. Not only was the focus of her research novel in anthropology, so also was her incorporation of psychological methods for the study of individuals and their behavior. Under the guidance of her mentor, Franz Boas (who had started his own career studying in Wundt's experimental psychology laboratory in Leipzig), Mead essentially developed a new kind of ethnography, one which sought to understand culture through its impact on developing individuals. Parenting appears in these accounts as it serves the larger purpose of accomplishing this goal. Although there is little information on parents *per se* in Mead's *Coming of Age in Samoa* (Mead, 1928/1968), her monograph on the Manus, *Growing Up in New Guinea* (Mead, 1930/1966, p. 29), provides a wealth of material on mothers and fathers, including vivid portrayals such as the following account of how small children are encouraged to become competent in their marine environment:

> The next step in water proficiency is reached when the child begins to punt a large canoe. Early in the morning the village is alive with canoes in which the elders sit sedately on the centre platforms while small children of three punt the canoes which are three or four times as long as the children are tall. At first glance this procession looks like either the crudest sort of display of adult prestige or a particularly conspicuous form of child labour. The father sits in casual state, a man of five feet nine or ten, weighing a hundred and fifty pounds. The canoe is long and heavy, dug out of a solid log; the unwieldy outrigger makes it difficult to steer. At the end of the long craft, perched precariously on the thin gunwales, his tiny brown feet curved tensely to keep his hold, stands a small brown baby, manfully straining at the six foot punt in his hands. He is so small that he looks more like an unobtrusive stern ornament than like the pilot of the lumbering craft. Slowly, with a great display of energy but not too much actual progress, the canoe moves through the village, among other canoes similarly manned by the merest tots. But this is neither child labour nor idle prestige hunting on the part of the parents. It is part of the whole system by which a child is encouraged to do his physical best.

Contrary to the common stereotype of anthropological accounts invariably putting other cultures in a favorable light compared with our own, Mead also documented cultural patterns supporting severe child maltreatment. Among the Mundugumor, a group of cannibals in the isolated interior of New Guinea, Mead (1972, p. 205) found a culture that seemed at the opposite pole from the mountain-dwelling Arapesh who lived not so far away:

> The Mundugumor contrasted with the Arapesh in every conceivable way. Fierce possessive men and women were the preferred type; warm and cherishing men and women were culturally disallowed. A woman who had the generosity to breastfeed another woman's infant simply did not find another husband when she was widowed. Both men and women were expected to be positively sexed and aggressive. In general, both rejected children and, where the children that were allowed to survive were concerned, adult men and women strongly favored children of the opposite sex. In Arapesh the women were kept away from the gardens for their own protection, because yams dislike anything to do with women. In Mundugumor people copulated in gardens belonging to someone else, just to spoil their yams.

In this context, Mead (1972, p. 206) encountered practices of infanticide that were truly wrenching:

> Most difficult of all for me to bear was the Mundugumor attitude toward children. Women wanted sons and men wanted daughters, and babies of the wrong sex were tossed into the river, still alive, wrapped in a bark sheath. Someone might pull the bark container out of the water, inspect the sex of the baby, and cast it away again. I reacted so strongly against the set of the culture that it was here that I decided that I would have a child no matter how many miscarriages it meant. It seemed clear to me that a culture that so repudiated children could not be a good culture, and the relationship between the harsh culturally prescribed style and the acts of individuals was only too obvious.

The cultural patterns of parenting and other behavior that Mead and Benedict described were not supposed to be equally true of all individuals in a cultural group: Indeed, a significant part of their thinking and writing addressed the issue of cultural goodness or poorness of fit for individuals of differing dispositions. Benedict (1934) even went so far as to propose that mental illness itself might be a cultural construction, and Mead was concerned about the question of how individuals of differing temperaments would relate to the dominant ethos of their cultures. As she summarized this thinking later (Mead, 1972, p. 219), "there are a limited number of temperamental types, each of which is characterized by an identifiable cluster of inborn personality traits, and . . . these several types are systematically related to one another. If this was so, it seemed clear that an individual whose temperament was incompatible with the type (or types) emphasized in the culture in which he was born and reared would be at a disadvantage—a disadvantage that was systematic and predictable for that culture." In this formulation, we see a precursor to more recent conceptualizations of temperament and "goodness of fit" at the cultural level (Lerner, Rothbaum, Boulos, and Castellino, in Vol. 2 of this *Handbook*; Super and Harkness, 1986b; Thomas and Chess, 1977).

Given Mead and Benedict's concern about how individual variation in temperament or disposition relates to culture, it is ironic that their work has been criticized primarily on the grounds that they overgeneralized about the dominance of particular cultural patterns, suggesting a level of internal homogeneity which could be easily disputed with nonconforming data. Jahoda (1982, p. 82), summarizing this perspective, goes as far as to conclude that Benedict's contribution, "while highly influential at the time, is today mainly of historical interest." Mead and Benedict themselves contributed to the perception of their analyses as oversimplified, by offering sweeping generalizations even while documenting individual differences and cultural "inconsistencies" in their ethnographic reports. The fact that Mead and Benedict were not able to create a satisfactory balance between the discovery of cultural patterns and exceptions to these patterns, however, should not deter us today from reassessing the importance of their work for current theory and research.

The problem of cultural patterns that Mead, Benedict, and other anthropologists grappled with is analogous to the challenge of explaining parental behavior in relation to personality, beliefs, or attitudes. Behavioral research has foundered on the discovery that general beliefs or attitudes are often not good predictors of behavior in particular instances. More recently, however, developmentalists have realized that trying to understand parental behavior *without* reference to beliefs is equally fruitless (Goodnow and Collins, 1990), and cognitive anthropologists have recognized the importance of "thematicity" (the repetition of the same idea in a variety of contexts) in cultures as an organizer of behavior (Quinn and Holland, 1987). Freed from the overly concrete requirement of total "consistency" between parental beliefs and behavior, researchers in culture and parenting are now beginning to appreciate culturally structured ways of understanding the world and the self that are expressed in behavior. Mead's and Benedict's work on patterns of culture and their interactions with individuals of differing dispositions can be seen as a generative early formulation of this approach.

In summary, classical ethnographic studies characteristically included chapters on culture and parenting, and these concerned both the formal marking of developmental events by parents and informal parenting behavior in everyday settings. While emphasizing general cultural patterns over individual or subgroup differences, these anthropological studies recognized individual differences and, to varying extents, attempted to incorporate them into cultural analyses. Given their concern with both accurate description of reality and the evocation of more abstract themes in culture, it is not surprising that anthropologists have been divided among themselves about whether to consider their field as science or as art. A retrospective look at the work of Mead and Benedict, two leading figures in early studies of culture and parenting, suggests that the dichotomy is by no means clear cut: Far from abandoning science for adventures of the imagination in exotic cultures, both Mead and Benedict were dedicated to scholarly research on the behavior and thought of individual parents and children in cultural context. Mead and Benedict established a new focus in ethnography, oriented to understanding not why cultures differ from each other, but how culture influences individual development in the context of the family. This concern, developed in the culture and personality school, resulted in a flowering of research on culture and parenting.

CULTURE, PARENTING, AND PERSONALITY: THE SEARCH FOR DEVELOPMENTAL PROCESSES

A primary concern of anthropological studies in the culture and personality school that reached its zenith in the 1950s and 1960s was to understand the actual processes through which culture is transmitted from one generation to the next. Anthropologists turned to Freudian theory, to learning theory, and to cognitive approaches in their attempts to relate culturally structured childhood experiences to the customs, behavior, or belief systems characteristic of adults or of the society as a whole. Freudian concepts were particularly popular and were used for a variety of purposes: for example, in analyses of family life in non-Western societies as related to the Oedipus conflict (Cohler and Paul, in Vol. 3 of this *Handbook*; Malinowski, 1927/1966; Spiro, 1982), in theories about the effects of infant swaddling practices on adult personality (Gorer and Rickman, 1949), and in the creation of cultural–psychiatric profiles for entire communities (DuBois, 1944/1961; Kardiner, 1939, 1945). Jahoda (1982) suggested that Freudian theory was attractive to anthropologists interested in the psychological aspects of their data because it dealt with domains, such as envy and its cultural expressions, that are evident in everyday life but largely ignored by academic personality theory. Freudian theory provided a framework for relating apparently distinct aspects of a culture, for example Hindu belief systems related to bodily cleanliness and the control of instinctual impulses (Carstairs, 1957). In this drive to relate seemingly disparate aspects of a culture to a single organizing principle, we see another expression of the same idea that motivated Benedict and Mead in proposing "patterns of culture."

A subtheme in these studies, anticipating current scientific interest in home–school relations, was the labeling of childrearing customs as "education." Studies based on this perspective focused on the detailed description of processes through which adult culture is transmitted to children and how educational practices in turn reflect the demands of adult life (for a collection of this literature and a bibliography, see Middleton, 1970; Jahoda, 1982). Parents were seen as playing a primary role in this training; in fact, as Middleton (1970) pointed out, the separation of "formal" education (i.e., schooling) from more general training in the values and meaning systems of a culture is characteristic of only literate societies. In preliterate societies, researchers noted that most of what children need to be taught is accomplished at home under the tutelage of parents or other familiar elders. An early, oft-cited example of this approach is Fortes's (1938/1970) ethnographic study of education among the Tallensi of northern Ghana. Fortes found that the Tallensi people themselves considered parents' role as educators to be in the nature of a religious duty, and the idea of education was a frequent topic of discussion. According to his informants, observation and imitation were thought to be the most important means of learning, and education was "regarded as a joint enterprise in which parents are as eager to lead as children to follow" (Fortes, 1938/1970, p. 23). The child who learned quickly, in this culture, was characterized as having "very good eyes," an evident reference to the ability to transfer seeing to doing. Practice was also considered important; thus, fathers would customarily buy their 7- to 8-year-old sons small bows so they could learn marksmanship in play with their friends.

Although "education" continues to be a useful way to frame the role of parents and others in transmitting cultural knowledge, the processes of teaching and learning are not always straightforward. Spiro's (1953) essay on "Ifaluk ghosts" posed an important problem: How can we explain the maintenance, across generations, of customs that in and of themselves seem aversive? The case in point was a set of beliefs held by residents of a small atoll in the Pacific Ocean concerning the existence of malevolent ghosts whose influence was experienced in a multitude of contexts in everyday life, from strange noises on the roof to the occurrence of illness. Spiro reviewed the psychological theories available at that time (the 1950s), and concluded that, although learning theory could not explain the acquisition of such cultural knowledge, a combination of cognitive and Freudian perspectives could. Beliefs in malevolent ghosts, Spiro suggested, derived from certain specific childhood experiences such as the daily cold-water bath that infants were subjected to; and later, the abrupt transition from the generally coddled status of infancy (aside from the baths) to the relatively neglected place of the next-to-youngest child in toddlerhood. Such experiences, Spiro (1953, in Hunt, 1967, p. 245) proposed, led the child to "develop the hypothesis that their world is threatening and, therefore, predispose them to believe in these threatening ghosts." Furthermore, Spiro suggested that Freud's theory of anxiety (that it is caused by unaccepted hostile feelings) could explain how beliefs in ghosts persisted into adulthood: Hostile thoughts could be attributed not to the self but to the ghosts.

Studies of parenting and adult customs or personality were featured in the culture and personality school with a variety of different rationales. Thus, for example, LeVine (1960) analyzed differences in political behavior among the Gusii and the Nuer of Africa, both pastoral "stateless societies" of

Africa, as they related to father–child relationships in each group. Whereas the Nuer had strong traditions of egalitarianism that made it difficult for them to accept new roles (such as judge) conferred by
the British colonial government, the Gusii were authoritarian and were quite willing to judge and mete
out punishments to their fellow tribesmen. LeVine related these differences at the level of political life
to culturally prescribed relationships between fathers and sons, drawing from psychological theories
of the development of authoritarian values as rooted in early childhood experience in the family.
Essentially, he proposed, patterns for social relationships among adults of differing status were socialized by childhood experience in the family. Thus, Evans-Pritchard's (1953, in Hunt, 1967, p. 196)
characterization of Nuer father–infant relationships indicated a nurturing, nonpunitive orientation:

> ... the father also takes an interest in his infant children, and one often sees a man nursing his child while
> the mother is engaged in the tasks of the home. Nuer fathers are proud of their children and give much
> time to them, petting and spoiling them, giving them titbits, playing with them and teaching them to
> talk: and the children are often in the byres with the man. I have never seen a man beat his child or lose
> his temper with him, however aggravating he may be. When a father speaks crossly to his child, as he
> does if, let us say, the child goes to the edge of a river or among the cattle, where he may be injured, it
> is evident that the child is not afraid of his loud words and obeys from affection rather than fear.

In contrast, as LeVine (1960, in Hunt, 1967, p. 197) noted:

> Among the Gusii, fathers rarely take care of infants, as most mothers have daughters or sisters aged five
> to eleven who are charged with the responsibility of caretaking in her absence. If there is no such child
> caretaker (*omoreri*), the mother's co-wife or mother-in-law helps her out in this regard, but the father's
> role in infant care is minimal. Nor do fathers spend much time with their children, play with them, or
> act otherwise nurturant. On the contrary, the Gusii father tends to be aloof and severe, being called in by
> the mother primarily when the child needs to disciplined. Fathers threaten their sons with punishment,
> and administer harsh beatings with wooden switches, explicitly intending to make the sons fearful and
> therefore obedient. The mother and older siblings help to exaggerate the punitive image of the father by
> warning the child of the dire paternal punishments which await him if he does wrong. At the end of his
> son's initiation ceremony the father ritually promises not to beat him any more, as an acknowledgment
> of his maturity. Most Gusii men recall a thrashing by the father for neglect of cattle-herding as one their
> outstanding childhood experiences.

LeVine's analysis of father–son relationships and political values and behavior among the Nuer
and Gusii was notable in its comparative cross-cultural approach. In contrast, the more typical studies
of this era drew from psychological theories to explain relationships between child life and adult
customs that the author had studied in a single field site (see Jahoda, 1982, for discussion of this
literature). However, these studies, no matter how richly documented or theoretically persuasive,
shared the disadvantage that causal relations that seemed reasonable in the context of one culture
might not hold up in others. What was needed was a systematic cross-cultural approach to the study
of childrearing and adult culture, in which hypothesized relations could be tested across a wide
variety of societies. Such an approach was developed by John W. M. Whiting and his colleagues.

CROSS-CULTURAL STUDIES OF CULTURE AND PARENTING: THE SEARCH FOR GENERAL PRINCIPLES

By the 1950s, anthropologists had compiled a considerable body of information on traditional cultures around the world. Whiting and Child (1953) proposed a framework that could be used to test
hypotheses about parenting practices in the production and transmission of culture across samples
of societies drawn from this ethnographic universe. Building on the ideas of Kardiner (1939, 1945),

Whiting and Child suggested that cultures can be thought of as consisting of "antecedent" and "consequent" components, linked to each other in a causal sequence with childrearing practices at the center. In a later formulation (Whiting, 1981, p. 155), this theory postulated that

(1) Features in the history of any society and in the cultural environment in which it is located influence
(2) the customary methods by which infants (and children) are cared for in that society, which have
(3) enduring psychological and physiological effects on the members of that society, which are manifested in
(4) the cultural projective-expressive systems of the society and the physiques of its members.

In this formulation, the physical ecology, cultural history, and "maintenance systems" (e.g., economy, social and political structure) form the structures to which parenting must adapt; these in turn shape children's development, promoting culture-specific patterns of personality, including anxieties, conflicts, and defensive systems. An innovative aspect of this model is that it did not demand direct information on adult personality, which was generally not available in the ethnographic literature; rather, the psychological outcomes of culturally specific parenting practices were to be measured indirectly through "expressive systems," such as art, ceremonial forms, religions, and other belief systems.

The study by Whiting and Child (1953) of childrearing and beliefs about the causes of illness, based on a sample of 75 societies described in the ethnographic literature, was the first major application of this approach. Drawing from a synthesis of psychoanalytic and behaviorist theory as recommended by Dollard and Miller (1950), the authors proposed that the concept of fixation should be differentiated into positive and negative types. At the cultural expressive system level, they suggested, widely shared areas of anxiety derived from harsh early socialization practices (negative fixation) would be expressed in beliefs about illness, whereas customary therapeutic practices were proposed as cultural expressions of positive fixation. Their cross-cultural analysis showed that strict socialization practices (for example, early weaning) were associated with attributions of patient responsibility for illness; on the other hand, permissive rearing practices were not associated with any particular pattern of illness beliefs. Whiting and Child viewed these findings as support for the power of negative fixations in later psychological functioning, but disconfirming the effects of positive fixation.

Whiting and his colleagues were creative in both their theoretical formulations of relations between childrearing variables and adult outcomes and in the measures they devised to test these relations by using the available ethnographic literature, some of which was conveniently organized in the Human Relations Area Files (HRAF). Their studies of mother–infant sleeping arrangements and adolescent initiation rites provide a case in point (Burton and Whiting, 1961; Whiting, Kluckhohn and Anthony, 1958). Cross-cultural research established a pattern of co-occurrence between polygyny or a nomadic lifestyle, extended mother–child co-sleeping arrangements, and later adolescent circumcision ceremonies. Whiting and his colleagues explored a variety of possible psychological mediators to link these cultural practices, including the formation of Oedipal rivalry and the development (in boys) of cross-sex identity—either of which was supposed to be resolved through the adolescent initiation ceremonies that are intended to inculcate adult male roles. Following this line of reasoning, they suggested that societies that had extended mother–infant sleeping arrangements but *lacked* initiation ceremonies would have customs reflecting men's continuing "female" subidentity in such practices as the couvade or male pregnancy symptoms (Burton and Whiting, 1961; Munroe and Munroe, 1971). All these hypothesized relations were supported by statistical tests of significance; but so were other, entirely different explanatory models that did not invoke psychological mediating variables at all (e.g., Cohen, 1964; Young, 1965). Although the cross-cultural evidence on parenting practices for young children and the "expressive systems" of adult society could be supported in the formal sense of tests of significance, the hypotheses and means of testing them seemed far fetched to some. As LeVine (1970, pp. 596–597) stated;

Customs like child-rearing practices and the variety of cultural behavior patterns with which they have been hypothetically linked tend to be associated with many other customs, and these multiple associations lend themselves to a variety of interpretations, some of them sociological or ecological rather than psychological. In the welter of multiple connections... it is all too easy to find support of simple causal hypotheses by limiting one's investigation to a few variables rather than looking at the larger structure of relations in which they are embedded.

As Jahoda (1982) has pointed out, however, the cross-cultural method in itself could be applied to a wide variety of different questions about relations between parenting and culture. The cross-cultural study by Barry, Child, and Bacon (1959) of economic subsistence patterns and childrearing practices in a worldwide sample of 104 societies is a prominent example. Societies were rated in terms of the degree to which they depended on the accumulation and the storage of food. At one extreme were societies based on hunting and gathering societies, in which daily efforts at foraging, fishing, or hunting provide food for immediate consumption. At the other end of the distribution were societies based on pastoralism or agriculture, where animals must be faithfully tended, and crops must be planted, tended, stored, and used planfully until the next harvest. The authors argued that, in societies with high food accumulation, there would be a need for adults who would be responsible, conservative, and willing to defer to seniors to ensure survival of the group. Societies characterized by low food accumulation, on the other hand, would need adults who could exercise initiative and imagination in finding food for the day. The results confirmed expectations: Societies high in food accumulation tended to have stronger socialization for obedience and responsibility, whereas low-accumulation societies encouraged achievement, self-reliance, and independence in children. The association between subsistence type and socialization practices was so consistent that Barry, Child, and Bacon (1959, in Ford, 1967, p. 254) concluded that "a knowledge of the economy alone would enable one to predict with considerable accuracy whether a society's socialization pressures were primarily toward compliance or assertion."

Barry, Child, and Bacon's study of subsistence types and "socialization pressures" has assumed the status of a classic in anthropology: On the basis of their work, social anthropologists do indeed predict (with considerable accuracy) the type of parenting styles that will be encountered in small-scale non-Western, traditional societies. Our field research in a "high food-accumulation society," the Kipsigis of Kenya, illustrates the general pattern: Children are socialized to be responsible and obedient, and they do a great deal of responsible work, for example, cow herding, agricultural tasks, help with food preparation, and infant care (Harkness and Super, 1985, 1991, 1992). The general association between economic subsistence and child socialization is also reflected in changes documented among the !Kung, a traditional hunting-and-gathering society now undergoing the transition to a sedentary agricultural lifestyle (Draper and Cashdan, 1988): Whereas !Kung children living in the bush are granted a longer period of infancy and are expected to do little work until well into adolescence, adults living in sedentary agricultural settlements attempted to train their children to help out with the ongoing work of the household. Part of the reason for this is that, in societies such as the Kipsigis or the sedentary !Kung, there is a great deal of work to do, and everyone needs to help out to support the household economy; the nomadic !Kung, on the other hand, were traditionally a "leisure society" in which little daily expenditure of effort was required to supply the needs of families. Thus the extremely high correlation between economy and "socialization pressure" is attributable, at least in part, to the necessary involvement of children as workers in certain kinds of economies—those that are intermediate between the most ancient form of human subsistence and the most modern.

But what of modern societies, in which not only food but all sorts of other material goods are accumulated and stored? According to the hypothesis under consideration, such societies should be characterized by even stronger socialization pressures toward compliance as opposed to assertion. Research on parenting in such societies—including those of the United States—suggests a complex picture in which the idea of Barry et al. is relevant: Socialization for compliance may be characteristic of economically poorer social groups in which there is greater uncertainty about the family's ability to accumulate the necessary goods, whereas in more economically privileged groups the emphasis again shifts to training for independence and risk taking.

COMPARATIVE FIELD STUDIES OF PARENTS AND CHILDREN

In addition to problems of interpretation already discussed, a major drawback of the cross-cultural method was that it involved no direct measures of individuals (LeVine, 1973). Furthermore, the ethnographic information available for different cultures frequently was not comparable, and information on childrearing in particular was apt to be missing altogether. The Six Culture Study, initiated in the early 1950s by John and Beatrice Whiting and their associates, was designed to overcome these problems without giving up the wider database that cross-cultural research uniquely afforded. Six cultures in different areas of the world were chosen for detailed field studies of children's "learning environments" and social behavior. A standardized set of procedures was developed for gathering information on the physical and the social environments of daily life, parenting practices, and child behavior from early to middle childhood.

The Six Culture Study was, by the account of the investigators, the first systematic observational study of children in other cultures (Whiting and Whiting, 1975). For the first time, researchers now had access to quantitative as well as qualitative data that could be directly compared across similar samples of children in a worldwide array of cultural settings. Three other characteristics of this research contributed to the Six Culture Study as a model for subsequent work. One was the deliberate combination of various researcher perspectives. Traditionally, anthropological fieldwork was carried out by lone researchers who, by virtue of their sex, age, and marital status (usually single) were not easily granted access to some aspects of the culture, particularly the intimacies of family life. Most of the Six Culture teams, consequently, were married couples (the exception being Leigh Minturn in the Rajput study). The Whitings were also concerned about the "insider" perspective on behavior as it might contrast to the interpretations of cultural "outsiders." The behavior observation system developed by the Whitings, accordingly, stipulated that the observer be a member of the community who could appropriately interpret the meaning and intentions of social behavior.

A second notable aspect of the Six Culture Study was the choice of sample communities, which differed considerably from traditional ethnographic research sites. The six cultures chosen included five subsistence farming communities and, notably, an American middle-socioeconomic suburban community. The farming communities varied in terms of general societal complexity (e.g., degree of occupational specialization, centralized government) as well as in household structure; but all would be at the high end of the "food accumulation" dimension defined by Barry et al. (1959). The inclusion of these communities (especially the American sample), however, raised a new issue that anthropologists had traditionally not faced—namely, the question of "representativeness." Whereas the societies traditionally studied by anthropologists had been either too small or too unknown to provoke this question, readers of the Six Culture Study reports might reasonably ask to what extent the parenting practices and child behavior of communities such as "Orchard Town," a Boston suburb, could be said to be typical of the whole political–cultural entity to which they belonged.

The Whitings' answer to this question (often discussed with students, although never published) constitutes a third contribution of this research. Representativeness, according to the Whitings, should not be a concern of cross-cultural research; rather, *each community* is analyzed both internally (e.g., the relations between variables such as family type and social behavior of children) and in relation to the other sample communities. The question of representativeness does not arise, although readers can, on the basis of the extensive ethnographic information provided, make their own inferences about generalizability to other families or communities in the same cultural or political area. In essence, the approach developed in the Six Culture Study made it possible to collect systematic field data designed to test general hypotheses about relations among sociocultural organization, parenting practices, and child behavior and development. Rather than seeking generalizability across populations, this approach sought to make generalizations across *types* of families or communities.

The Six Culture Study resulted in several publications (Minturn and Lambert, 1964; Whiting, 1964; Whiting, Child, and Lambert, 1966; Whiting and Edwards, 1988), but its most important theoretical findings were first presented in *Children of Six Cultures: A Psycho-cultural Analysis* (Whiting and Whiting, 1975). In this work, the Whitings addressed the question of how children's social behavior is affected by the cultural environments in which they are reared. Extensive analysis of observational data collected on samples of children in each community led to the identification of two dimensions of contrast: Dimension A contrasted nurturance and responsibility to dependence and dominance, and Dimension B distinguished social–intimate behavior from authoritarian–aggressive behavior. In each case, the six cultures could be divided into two equal and contrasting sets, with variation in societal complexity corresponding to Dimension A, whereas household type (nuclear versus extended) covaried with Dimension B.

The Whitings's analysis of Dimension A is particularly revealing of links among socioeconomic structure, parenting practices, and the development of social behavior in children. The fact that children's social behavioral profiles in the different cultural communities differed from each other demanded an explanation, and, using the model for psychocultural research developed previously, the Whitings sought answers in the economic and social environments of childrearing and family life. Whiting and Whiting (1975, p. 71), stated in discussing Dimension A,

> According to the model adopted for this study, there should be some contrast in the maintenance systems— for example, the social, economic, and political structures—of the two sets of cultures that impels parents to press children toward being nurturant–responsible on the one hand or dependent–dominant on the other. It is not assumed that parents do so in any conscious way, though this might be the case in some instances, but rather that different daily life routines dictated by different sets of environmental and historical factors impel parents to interact with children in different ways, to assign different tasks, and to reward and punish different ways of behaving. It is also true that the methods of socialization adopted by different cultures prepare the children for the adult roles that they must assume when they grow up.

"Cultural complexity" was identified as the construct whose covariation with Dimension A offered the most explanatory power. As Whiting and Whiting (1975, p. 71) stated,

> Simpler societies, lacking superordinate authority, . . . , require a high degree of cooperation within the family, the extended family, the lineage, or the micro-community. Complex societies, on the other hand, with a multiplicity of roles and a hierarchical structure should train their children to be competitive and achievement-oriented. Egoistic–dominance and attention-seeking is consonant with such training. Even to seek help to gain one's ends is not incompatible with a hierarchical system.

Variations in level of cultural complexity, although they may suggest the need for different kinds of social roles and behavior, do not provide an explanation of the *mechanisms* of influence, as the Whitings noted. To address this question, they turned to the study of children's daily routines, particularly the tasks that parents assign to children in different cultural settings. Women's work load emerged as a powerful predictor of children's tasks and consequently of the kinds of social behavior children would receive the most training for. In complex societies, many household tasks are taken care of by technology (e.g., providing running water, grinding flour) or by specialists outside the home (e.g., kindergartens to provide childcare and early education); in simpler societies, on the other hand, these functions are often carried out by mothers—and their child helpers. Overall, children in the three more complex societies had fewer chores than children in simple agricultural societies, and children in Orchard Town had the fewest of all. Children in Nyansongo (a Gusii agricultural community in Kenya) were expected to help with the care of younger siblings, herd the cows, collect firewood, fetch water from the river, and help with gardening and food preparation, whereas their peers in Orchard Town were expected mainly to help by cleaning their own rooms and setting the table for dinner.

As the Whitings (Whiting and Whiting, 1975, p. 103) perceived, it is not only the *amount* of work that parents ask of their children that is important for the formation of social behavior; the *nature* of children's tasks is also significant:

> Both the number and the type of chores expected of the children of a culture are positively related to the cultural evaluation on Dimension A, as measured by the social behavior of the children. It is evident that carrying wood and water, the preparation and cooking of food, gardening, caring for animals, and caring for younger siblings, particularly infants, are more likely to be performed by children of simpler cultures than by children of the more complex societies. It is our interpretation that the performance of these tasks provides one of the mechanisms by which children learn to be nurturant–responsible. All of these chores are intimately related to the daily life of a child aged 3 to 10 and must give him or her a feeling of personal worth and competence.

The typical chores of children in communities like Orchard Town embody rather different cultural messages (Whiting and Whiting, 1975, p. 106):

> By contrast, in urban or semi-urban, nonagricultural communities like Orchard Town the tasks assigned to children are less clearly related to the economy and welfare of the child or the child's family and probably seem more arbitrary to the child. Picking up toys or making one's own bed are egoistic, for the benefit of the child. The need for having clothes hung up, bureau drawers tidy, or the bed smoothed out neatly is probably not immediately clear, nor are the consequences of negligence obviously serious. Washing dishes and setting the table are more closely associated with the family as a whole, but the chore may seem less important if the mother uses the respite from work to sit and talk to her husband. Interestingly, housecleaning tasks, of all the chores analyzed, are least related to Dimension A.

The Whitings's analysis of societal complexity, women's work load, children's household tasks, and the development of social behavior made effective use of John Whiting's (1981) theoretical model linking aspects of cultural maintenance systems to the environments of child life, but went beyond the model in relating these features of the cultural environment to individual behavioral and developmental outcomes in both parents and children. It also led to Beatrice Whiting's novel formulation of culture as a "provider of settings" and of parents as organizers of settings for their children's development, an idea elaborated in a sequel volume, *Children of Different Worlds: The Formation of Social Behavior* (Whiting and Edwards, 1988, p. 35):

> Our theory holds that patterns of social behavior are learned and practiced in interaction with various types of individuals in a variety of settings. In part, the effect of culture on these patterns in childhood is a direct consequence of the settings to which children are assigned and the people who frequent them. Socializing agents orchestrate children's participation in these learning environments by assigning children to some and proscribing others. Our theory holds that the power of parents and socializers to mold social behavior lies primarily in the assignment of boys and girls to different settings where they interact with different categories of individuals.

This perspective on the role of parents as socializing agents represents a notable departure from psychological literature focused on parent–child interaction: In essence, Whiting and Edwards proposed, parents have a greater effect through their "assignment" of children to different settings insofar as these settings determine the whole array of interactions that children experience. Children, however, according to this approach, are not the only ones whose behavior is shaped by their settings of daily life—parents themselves are also assigned by their cultures to different settings with their own distinctive profiles of personnel and activities. The effects of environmentally or culturally mandated parental settings were also analyzed as they relate to parental behavior. Fathers' involvement in the care of young children, for example, was found to vary dramatically among the societies studied, and this variation appears to be mediated by the more general division of labor between husband

and wife, their degree of emotional intimacy or aloofness, and associated living arrangements. In societies such as sub-Saharan groups where husband and wife customarily eat and sleep apart and have separate spheres of responsibility, fathers' involvement with the care of infants was found to be minimal or even culturally proscribed; in societies characterized by high intimacy and sharing of work roles, on the other hand, fathers shared childcare tasks with their wives. Thus, as Whiting and Edwards demonstrated, cultures assign settings to parents that in turn facilitate or discourage particular kinds of parenting behavior.

The settings of mothers' own lives were found to contribute to three different behavioral "maternal profiles." As with the previous analysis of child behavior, Whiting and Edwards found that mothers' behavior in a wide variety of cultural settings could be categorized into a fairly limited set of groupings: in this case, nurturance, training, control, and sociability. Cultural differences in the relative frequencies of these behaviors formed the basis for suggesting three different styles of mothers: the "training mother," found in all the sub-Saharan agricultural societies; the "controlling mother," found in other agricultural communities of the Philippines, Mexico, and north India is a region, and the "sociable mother," found only in the American community of Orchard Town. Whiting and Edwards (1988, p. 95) description of the African training mothers is particularly striking in its contrast with American parenting styles:

> The Ngeca mothers [in a community outside Nairobi] we interviewed are typical: they believe that they should train a child to be a competent farmer, herdsman, and child nurse and that a child from age 2 on should be assigned chores that increase in complexity and arduousness with age. They punish their children for failure to perform these tasks responsibly or for stubbornly refusing to do what their elders request of them. They allow much of their children's learning to occur through observation and imitation; only occasionally do they instruct them explicitly. Moreover, mothers seldom praise their children lest they become proud, a trait that is unacceptable. They allow the major rewards for task performance to be intrinsic.

The sociable mothers of Orchard Town contrasted to the other mothers not in the proportion of controlling behavior (which, as for the mothers of the middle group, was highest in occurrence), but rather in the fact that "sociability" ranked *second* among these mothers, whereas it was third or fourth in frequency among the two other groups. Whiting and Edwards explained this behavioral profile as partly an expression of the mothers' own social isolation from other adults in the separate nuclear family dwellings of an American suburb—children, in this view, were the only available partners for social interaction. They also noted that the Orchard Town mothers were providing training for later success in school and thus for successful life in a complex, literate, and competitive society.

The Whitings' most active period of research on culture and childrearing spanned four decades, and during this time they also trained several generations of anthropologists and psychologists in empirical methods for the cross-cultural study of children and families. Current approaches to culture and parenting reflect this educational legacy in interaction with more recent other theoretical developments. In addition, other approaches to culture and parenting are evident in this now rapidly growing field of study.

RECENT TRENDS: CONCEPTUAL ISSUES
IN CULTURE AND PARENTING

Over the past two decades, increasing interest in cross-cultural approaches to human development and a rising concern with the family have converged to produce a literature specifically concerned with culture and parenting. The emergence of this field is manifested in, among other things, several edited volumes on this topic (Bornstein, 1991, 1995; LeVine, Miller, and West, 1988), including two devoted to fathers (Hewlett, 1992; Lamb, 1981), as well as special issues or sections in scholarly journals (*Newsletter of the International Society for the Study of Behavioral Development*, 2001;

Special Issue: Social and emotional development: A cross-cultural perspective, 1998; Special Section: Developmental Psychology in China, 2000). The literature on culture and parenting intersects with related scholarship focusing on cultural images of childhood (Hwang, Lamb, and Sigel, 1996), cultural practices as contexts for development (Goodnow, Miller, and Kessel, 1995), and the cultural construction of the child (Harkness, Raeff, and Super, 2000). Likewise, increasing interest in parental belief systems has helped focus new attention the role of culture in their formation, expression, and developmental consequences (Harkness and Super, 1996; Sigel and McGillicuddy-De Lisi, in Vol. 3 of this *Handbook*; Sigel, McGillicuddy-De Lisi, and Goodnow, 1992). The relation between cross-cultural studies of culture and parenting and issues in minority child development in the United States is also illustrated in new studies (Greenfield and Cocking, 1994; LeVine et al., 1994), and these studies complement recent work on ethnic and minority families in the United States (e.g., Deater-Deckard, Dodge, Bates and Pettit, 1996; Garcia-Coll and Garrido, 2000; Pachter, 2000).

Parenting as "A Lifetime of Changing Relationships"

The growth of new scholarship in culture and parenting has provided a context for revisiting several abiding theoretical issues. Cross-cultural approaches to parenting have highlighted the fact that parenting involves, in Townsend's (2000) words, "a lifetime of relationships." Among fathers in Botswana whom Townsend studied, for example, biological fatherhood may not even be acknowledged by fathers themselves until the establishment of social fatherhood through the lengthy process of establishing a marriage. In the meantime, maternal grandfathers are the "social fathers" in terms of both the child's identity and support and care. Arrangements like this seem less unusual today as we experience wide varieties of parental arrangements within the United States and other postindustrial societies. As Townsend (2000, p. 343) pointed out, "Men's responsibilities to children, and to the well-being of future generations, are not, however, restricted to a narrowly defined paternal role. Before we decide what men should do for their children we must know what they actually do." The same principle, as Townsend notes, pertains to mothers whose biological and social roles may intertwine over a lifetime of relationships with their own children, their grandchildren, and other people related to them in through a variety of kinshiplike relationships. A similar point is evident in Minturn's (1993) and Seymour's (1980) longitudinal studies of women in India, and this perspective is further buttressed by studies of sibling relationships across the lifespan (Nucholls, 1994). Although lifespan theorists have long made the point that development continues past childhood, research on parenting relationships across the lifespan has been slow to catch up (see Zarit and Eggebeen, in Vol. 1 of this *Handbook*), because of, at least in part, a shared cultural model in the United States of parenting as a task related to the care of young dependent children. In this regard, studies of other groups that do not share this cultural model support a widening of focus that is ultimately more realistic for our own culture as well.

Conceptualizing Relations Between Cultural Variability and Socioeconomic Differences

An enduring issue for cross-cultural research is how variability in socioeconomic status (SES) may intersect with cultural differences, and this question has been examined in recent research. Richman, Miller, and LeVine (1992) compared cross-cultural differences in maternal responsiveness to their infants with intracultural variability related to mother's education. Their cross-cultural comparison of rural African mothers (belonging to the Gusii ethnic group of Kenya) and middle-SES U.S. mothers showed two contrasting styles of responsiveness, with the U.S. mothers talking and looking at their infants more whereas the Gusii mothers held and touched their babies more. As Richman et al. (1992, pp. 616–617) comment, "We interpret this as showing that the Gusii mothers seek to quiet and soothe their babies, whereas the American mothers pursue a style in which verbal interaction and stimulation of the baby play an important part." The Gusii mothers had little schooling

(2 to 3 years), compared with the U.S. sample in which the average length of mothers' schooling was 14 to 15 years, raising the possibility that the cultural differences between the two groups could be due at least in part to maternal differences in education. Intracultural variability among a sample of Mexican mothers in the city of Cuernavaca supports this hypothesis: Years of schooling were found to be correlated with more talking and looking and less holding of the infant, and these differences became more pronounced with the infant's increasing age. The authors suggest that the mechanism for this replication of cross-cultural by intracultural variability is mothers' exposure to norms of discourse in school that may override traditional cultural scripts for mother–child interaction.

Although there are evidently some similarities between the parenting styles of less educated mothers in Western societies and maternal behavior in traditional non-Western cultures, it is also clear that cultural differences remain after schooling has been taken into account. Harwood and her colleagues (Harwood, Schölmerich, and Schulze, 2000; Harwood, Schölmerich, Ventura-Cook, Schulze, and Wilson, 1996) have compared long-range socialization goals held by Puerto Rican and Anglo (i.e., Americans of European descent) mothers. In general, they find that the Anglo mothers talk most about goals for their children related to "self-maximization" (development of one's talents, self-confidence, and independence) in contrast to the Puerto Rican mothers who spoke most about "proper demeanor" (including respectfulness and the appropriate performance of role obligations). Comparisons of middle-SES and blue-collar mothers within each sample revealed a pattern of differences that seemed to capture both the differing realities of these two socioeconomic groups and the dominant cultural models of each sample. For example, the blue-collar Anglo mothers used the "self-maximization" category less in talking about goals for their children, and when they did talk about it, there was a sense of an "American dream" that they themselves had not managed to achieve. For the Puerto Rican mothers, in contrast, the cultural emphasis on "proper demeanor" was more strongly evident among the blue-collar mothers; for middle-SES mothers, the development of proper demeanor was accompanied by more frequent mention of other kinds of goals, including self-maximization. Harwood et al. (2000. p. 49) concluded, "It therefore appears that socioeconomic status functions in both the Anglo and Puerto Rican groups as a locus for the transformation of broad cultural constructs into more specific group concerns and that these broad transformations reflect an awareness of and a patterned response to broad-level cultural constructs."

Dimensions of Cultural Variability in Parenting: The Individualistic–Collectivistic Construct

As research on culture and SES differences indicates, some themes in parenting behavior and thinking cut across cultures. One attempt to capture these transcultural themes is represented in the contrast between individualism (or independence) and collectivism (or interdependence) (Triandis, 1995). Kagitçibasi (1980a) has discussed several explanations for the popularity of the individualistic–collectivistic (I/C) concept, including its close correlation with economic development at the national level and its appeal as a single dimension that can be universally applied. Although this concept appears to capture important elements of variability, however, Kagitçibasi (1980, p. 9) cautioned against its overuse: "There is a danger that Individualism/Collectivism is too readily used as an explanation for every behavioral variation between so-called individualistic and collectivistic cultures—an all-purpose construct. If Individualism/Collectivism is used to explain everything, it may explain nothing."

Research illustrates the problems inherent in the attempt to fit many different aspects of cultural difference into this one construct. For example, "interdependent" parenting styles in Asia have been linked to children's school success, whereas they have been used to explain Mexican immigrant children's problems in adaptation to U.S. schools (Kagitçibasi, 1996b; Greenfield and Cocking, 1994). Predictions of parental behavior based on the similar dichotomies have also produced mixed results. For example, Bornstein, Tal, and Tamis-LeMonda (1991) studied variations in maternal behavior with infants in three different cultural settings: New York City, Paris, and Tokyo. General cultural orientations in the three settings were predicted to result in particular patterns of mother–infant interaction in each setting: For example, the American cultural emphasis on encouraging autonomy was predicted to result in a greater emphasis on didactic stimulation of infant attention to the object world, whereas French and Japanese mothers, with more social orientations, were expected to promote more attention to themselves in dyadic interactions. Results supported some predictions while disconfirming others: although American mothers engaged in significantly higher rates of object stimulation than the French or Japanese, rates of social stimulation were equal among the American and Japanese mothers, and (contrary to expectations) lower among the French mothers.

Research using the I/C framework has led some investigators to conclude that *all* societies are characterized by expressions of both individualism and collectivism, and the question then becomes not how to categorize societies into one type or the other, but how to conceptualize the ways that individualistic and collectivistic values and beliefs are interwoven and instantiated (Greenfield and Cocking, 1994; Harkness et al., 2000). Killen and Wainryb (2000), for example, noted that in the Druze culture of Israel, in which male authority dominates in the family and the community contexts, wives and daughters acquiesce partly out of fear of being seriously harmed by their husbands and fathers and that they consider this arrangement unfair. Boys and men, in contrast, expect to have more power in making independent decisions for themselves and their daughters. Killen and Wainryb (2000, p. 16) came to the following conclusion:

> It appears that (at least for certain types of interaction in the family) males are conceptualized as autonomous and as legitimately making personal choices. Males are accorded entitlements due to them mostly by those in subordinate positions; women are regarded as dependent on their roles and duties in the system.
>
> In sum, these findings illustrated how concerns with autonomy are not absent from traditional societies but are played out differently for individuals in different roles and positions, resulting in a complex interweaving of independence and interdependence. Furthermore, the perspectives and judgments of those in subordinate positions reflect the struggles and conflicts characteristic of the interplay between opposing orientations in cultures. This is especially noteworthy given that collectivistic societies are presumed to be characterized by coherence and harmony.

Research within the Western industrialized world has also revealed complex relations among presumably individualistic parental ideas in different cultures. Harkness, Super, and van Tijen (2000) studied Dutch and American parents' descriptions of their young children. They found several significant differences in the proportions of different kinds of descriptors used by each group: whereas the U.S. parents more frequently described their children as smart, self-confident, and as leaders, the Dutch parents described their children more in terms of being sociable, enterprising, and strong willed. With the exception of "sociable," each of these descriptors seems to belong in the individualistic category, yet the differential ways they are combined reflect different parental beliefs about the nature of the child and what characteristics may be seen as most desirable. Furthermore, although the two groups of parents were similar in the extent to which they described their children as independent or dependent, an analysis of how parents talked about these qualities revealed important differences in their meanings. The Dutch parents found dependent behavior normal in young children, whereas the U.S. parents tended to see such behavior as "clingy" and worrisome in that it suggested the child was experiencing some kind of problem. Likewise, whereas the Dutch parents had a benign interpretation of independent behavior as "pushing out the boundaries," the U.S. parents often saw their children as conflicted between a desire to pull away and to hang on.

Kagitçibasi (1996a, 1996b), writing from her Turkish cultural perspective, suggested that a basic problem in Western conceptualizations of independence is that it confounds two distinct dimensions: agency and separateness. Agency is concerned with the degree to which individuals have control over their own circumstances, whereas separateness is the extent to which individuals live in close physical and social proximity to each other. As a visitor to the U.S., Kagitçibasi observed that the

American commitment to socialization for independence seems to require that mothers "let go" of their toddlers—surely an early age at which to expect separation! In Kagitçibasi's model of family relationships, however, this would not be necessary for the development of individuals who could make their own decisions. Kagitçibasi proposes the idea of the "autonomous relational self" as a product of families which encourage independent decision making while expecting family members to remain close to each other over the life course. This kind of cultural self, she suggests, is more likely to be found in societies that are in a process of transition from traditional to modern (and, we would note, also may be more typical of continental European societies). It is important to note that Kagitçibasi's model does not put all societies on a single developmental pathway, but rather suggests a different (and in her view, more adaptive) resolution to the universal human needs for agency and connectedness.

Reprise: Subsistence Systems and Parenting Revisited

As noted earlier in this chapter, the Whiting model proposed that childrearing is systematically related to the ways that the child's environment of daily life is shaped by physical, economic, and social characteristics of the society—its subsistence systems. Recent formulations have revisited the question of how these may influence the environment of childrearing. LeVine's formulation of "parental goals" proposes a broad-reaching theory of the relations among subsistence patterns and health conditions, the organization of parenting strategies, and child health and development (LeVine, 1974; LeVine et al., 1988; Richman et al., 1992). He suggests that "what parents want for their children" can be conceptualized in terms of a universal hierarchy of goals, ranging from ensuring basic survival to the acquisition of economic capabilities, and finally to the attainment of locally relevant cultural values. In traditional agrarian societies with high infant mortality rates such as have been prevalent in sub-Saharan Africa, he argues, parents' caregiving behavior is organized by the most basic goal of ensuring survival past infancy. This approach is part of a "quantitative" strategy of bearing as many children as possible in order that at least some will survive to adulthood and care for aging parents. In urbanized industrial societies with low infant mortality rates, on the other hand, LeVine and his colleagues suggest that parents take a "qualitative" approach and their goals are oriented around the child's acquisition of skills and cultural values. The different parental goals are expressed in differential rates of "proximal" caregiving behavior (such as holding the baby) versus "distal" behavior (talking to the baby) (Richman et al., 1992).

Research in diverse cultural settings, however, suggests that the relations between sociocultural context and parental goals are complex. Welles-Nyström (1988), for example, described a high level of parental anxiety about infant survival among Swedish mothers in a society characterized by the lowest mortality rates in the world. New (1988), likewise, noted that Italian patterns of infant care seem to be more oriented to meeting basic physical needs than would be expected in a modern postindustrial society according to LeVine's theory. The findings of Whiting and Edwards on "maternal profiles," discussed earlier in this chapter, suggest that parents in diverse societies are concerned about their children's behavioral development, although they focus their efforts on encouraging different *kinds* of behavior.

Hewlett and his colleagues have also revisited the question of cultural determinants of parenting in research on infant care and development among the Aka (a foraging group) and the Ngandu (an agricultural society) of central Africa (Hewlett, Lamb, Shannon, Leyendecker, and Schölmerich, 1998). Because these two groups share the same general environment—the tropical forest—and have similar infant and child mortality rates, they provide a useful case study for focusing on the relations between subsistence type and infant care. The study of Hewlett et al. included behavior observations of both infants aged 3 to 4 months and 9 to 10 months and their care providers (mothers, fathers, and other adults) in both cultural groups. A principal finding was that the Aka babies were more often sleeping or drowsy, were held and fed more, and were generally in closer proximity to the care provider, whereas the Ngandu pattern of infantcare included being alone more but also being more stimulated by their care providers. Overall, the Aka infant–adult interactions were more proximal in comparison with the more distal pattern of Ngandu care. To put this another way, the Aka babies were being held more, either in a sling or the caregiver's lap. Devices for holding or carrying the baby also differed: Aka babies were carried in slings on the left side of the caregiver's body, whereas Ngandu babies were tied on the back; Aka babies were minimally dressed in a waist cord and had no devices to be kept safely in, whereas Ngandu babies were more fully dressed, and parents made small chairs, beds, or mats for them to lie on. The authors review several possible explanations for this cultural difference in holding the baby, including LeVine's theory previously described, as well as mothers' work loads and cultural ideologies, and find none of them adequate. In contrast, Hewlett et al. (1998, p. 660) suggest, "Whatever the reason for the observed differences between the Aka and the Ngandu, the data presented in this article suggest that there may be a forager pattern of infant care."

This interpretation recalls the long-established differentiation between hunting-and-gathering societies and agricultural societies over a wide range of childrearing practices, as suggested by the work of Barry et al. (1959), discussed earlier in this chapter. In addition, the specific topic of infant carrying practices was a focus of cross-cultural study on the role of climate as a determinant of such practices (Whiting, 1981). As Konner's discussion of this work (1981, pp. 25–26) makes clear, the climate hypotheses was put forth by Whiting as a challenge to the then accepted wisdom that cultural subsistence types (e.g., foraging in contrast to agricultural) were the sole determinants of cultural practices regarding infant carrying:

> ...there are extensive variations of carrying method of young infants in nonindustrial societies, and these have been closely studied by J. Whiting.... Variations include almost constant carrying in a sling at the mother's side, back, or front, with or without direct skin contact; some carrying with some time in a crib, cradle, or hammock, or on a blanket on the ground or floor; very little or no carrying, with infant tied in a cradleboard or swaddled tightly. These variations were found to be systematically related to the ecological conditions of the society into which the infant was born, with climate having the most powerful influence.... *Thus Whiting questions whether hunting–gathering is a necessary or sufficient condition for close physical contact and sling carrying* [italics added]. However, the two exceptions he mentions to the generalization about cold-climate societies are the Eskimo and the Yahgan of Patagonia, both of whom have close physical contact and both of whom are nontropical, nonmounted, "classical" hunter–gatherers. This suggests that hunting–gathering may be a sufficient condition for close contact, although not a necessary one. In any case, since the great majority of the events of human evolution took place in tropical regions, the inference that early humans had close physical contact, probably with use of a sling, is still likely to be sound. Such carrying is also characteristic of many nonforaging nonindustrial societies in tropical regions. Thus societies of the middle range run the gamut from close contact in a sling to little or no contact in a tightly tied cradleboard. It is likely that the two variables of level of subsistence organization and, perhaps more important, ambient temperature would together explain much of the variation in carrying method. It may be correct to say that leaving behind the hunting-gathering mode of subsistence permitted, but did not cause, a decrease in the use of direct contact in a sling as the principal carrying method.

Thus the search for general explanations of cultural differences in parenting continues, and in some cases the conclusions of earlier work are rediscovered and elaborated. Now, as earlier, the most useful explanatory frameworks are likely to be found somewhere between universalistic claims on the one hand and an ideological commitment to the total uniqueness and incomparability of each society on the other.

CULTURE, PARENTING, AND THE NICHES OF DEVELOPMENT

In addition to theories focused on the relations between culture and parenting, there is a need for frameworks that provide a way of thinking about parenting as a culturally constructed interface between the larger environment and the development of children. Whereas some research has focused on *why* parenting varies across cultures, other studies have sought to understand *how* parenting works as part of a cultural and developmental system. Although studies in culture and parenting have been conducted within several different disciplinary paradigms, they share a common set of assumptions. First, the importance of settings for both parents and children is recognized. The settings of daily life not only define the parameters of experience, they also embody important cultural meanings. Cultural communities provide an array of normative and possible settings, from types of dwellings and household groups to expectable activities for parents and children of different ages and sexes. Parents choose from among the possibilities available to them to create settings of development for their children. The process of "choosing settings" is an ongoing one that is renegotiated in response to the changing needs of parents themselves, children, and the changing environment. Second, the activities that routinely take place within different settings are key to understanding parents' cultural construction of child life and development. Activities, routines, or cultural practices involved in the care and rearing of children instantiate cultural themes of importance to parents, and in this way they communicate cultural messages. Third, the meanings inherent in both settings and activities for particular cultural groups seem to be characterized by a high level of thematicity, in that the same ideas or images (e.g., "independence" for American middle-SES parents) are expressed in a variety of contexts. Furthermore, the ways that parents organize settings and activities for their children, interact with them, and talk about them are clearly part of an integrated system, although one that may require frequent adjustments to keep the various elements in harmony with each other. Finally, parenting is mediated not only by the cultural experiences of parents themselves but also by characteristics of individual children.

These ideas about culture and parenting have been formalized in several cultural and ecological frameworks. Of particular relevance to the study of culture and parenting are the "ecocultural niche" and the "developmental niche." The ecocultural niche framework has been proposed by Weisner, Gallimore, and their colleagues to study adaptation processes at the family level, including families of differing lifestyles in California as well as families who have young children with developmental delays (Gallimore, Weisner, Kaufman, and Bernheimer, 1989; Weisner and Garnier, 1992; Weisner, Matheson, and Bernheimer, 1996). Although these two groups of families might seem to have little in common, both have faced challenges in maintaining a lifestyle consistent with their own cultural belief systems—the first group because their orientations differ consciously from mainstream American culture, and the second because of difficulties associated with rearing a child with special needs. These two groups of challenged families provide particularly clear evidence of the fact that families are active participants in the construction of their own cultural settings rather than simply replicators of the wider culture around them. Weisner, Gallimore, and their colleagues have argued that understanding how daily routines are affected by ecocultural features in the larger society, how parents interpret and cope with these features, and how they construct sustainable daily routines is central to understanding and supporting families.

In contrast to a focus on families, the developmental niche elaborated by Super and Harkness is a theoretical framework for studying how the child's microenvironment of daily life is culturally shaped (Harkness and Super, 1992; Super and Harkness, 1986a, 1999). The developmental niche is conceptualized in terms of three components or subsystems, each of which relates centrally to parents: (1) the physical and social settings of the child's life, (2) culturally regulated customs and practices of childcare and childrearing, and (3) the psychology of the caregivers. These three subsystems (Super and Harkness, 1986a, p. 552)

...share the common function of mediating the individual's developmental experience within the larger culture. Regularities in the subsystems, as well as thematic continuities from one culturally defined developmental stage to the next, provide material from which the child abstracts the social, affective, and cognitive rules of the culture, much as the rules of grammar are abstracted from the regularities of the speech environment. The three components of the developmental niche form the cultural context of child development.

Three "corollaries" have been proposed to capture dynamic aspects of the developmental niche. First, three components interact with each other as a system, with homeostatic mechanisms to seek consonance among them. Second, the niche is an "open system" in that each component also interacts independently with elements in the larger culture. Finally, the niche and the organism adapt to characteristics of the other, although there may be discordance between the two at various historical or developmental moments.

The Developmental Niche and the Cultural Organization of Sleep

The concept of the developmental niche is illustrated by a growing literature on cultural variation in family sleeping arrangements (Abbott, 1992; Caudill and Plath, 1966; Lozoff, Wolf, and Davis, 1984; Morelli, Rogoff, Oppenheim, and Goldsmith, 1992; New and Richman, 1995; Shweder, Jensen, and Goldstein, 1995; Super and Harkness, 1982; Wolf, Lozoff, Latz, and Paludetto, 1996). The organization of sleep, including the determination of places and partners for sleeping and the scheduling of sleep, is an interesting aspect of cultural practice in that sleep is generally a private rather than public activity, but one that is nevertheless highly structured by cultures and relatively resistant to change. Parents play a primary role in the assignment of settings and routines for sleep, thus perpetuating a cycle of culture transmission within the privileged context of the family.

Empirical research has documented a wide variety of culturally normative physical and social settings for sleep, which represent customary practices that reflect more general parental and cultural belief systems. Caudill and Plath, who considered the question of "Who sleeps by whom?" in a classic study of Japanese cosleeping arrangements, open with the comment (Caudill and Plath, 1996, p. 344): "If a third of life is passed in bed, with whom this time is spent is not a trivial matter. As ethnologists, we expect co-sleeping customs to be consonant with major interpersonal and emotional patterns of family life in a culture, and at the same time to reflect cross-cultural differences." As their study showed, sleeping arrangements among urban Japanese families were one important index of the individual's developmental niche as it changed over the lifespan; in fact, changes in sleeping arrangements are good indicators of how developmental change is recognized by parents in culturally appropriate ways. For example, the Japanese children in their cross-sectional sample coslept with parents up to the age of approximately 13 to 15 years, at which time cosleeping declined rapidly—suggesting that puberty marked a culturally recognized shift to more independent sleeping. In another example of how changes in sleeping arrangements mark larger developmental shifts, Super and Harkness (1982) found that, with the birth of the next child, the (now) second-to-youngest child in Kipsigis families of rural Kenya continued to cosleep with the mother and other young siblings, but was put to sleep at the mother's back instead of her front. This change was coordinated with several others such as the termination of breast-feeding and back-carrying, which together constituted a fundamental shift in the child's physical and social settings of daily life.

Customs of care involving sleeping arrangements are supported by emotional commitments by parents. For example, Mayan mothers studied by Morelli et al. (1992, p. 608) expressed strong disapproval of the American middle-SES custom of putting infants to sleep alone, an arrangement that they regarded as "tantamount to child neglect." Similarly, an Appalachian woman of eastern Kentucky asked rhetorically, "how can you expect to hold onto them in later life if you begin by pushing them away?" (Abbott, 1992, p. 34). Views like this demonstrate clearly that customs regarding sleeping arrangements instantiate culturally central ideas about family relationships and the proper course of human development. These ideas—which form part of the psychology of the caregivers—are linked in turn to pervasive cultural themes such as "independence" for American middle-SES families or the nurturing of interdependence in other cultures such as the Japanese. Sleeping arrangements also are strongly mandated by cultural customs, upheld by elders or by "expert" specialists such as pediatricians and psychologists.

As with other aspects of the niche, these variations have consequences for the developing child. There is ample experimental evidence that cosleeping, at least in the North American context, yields a different pattern of "quiet" and "active" sleep than does sleeping alone (Mosko, Richard, McKenna, Drummond, and Mukai, 1997), although there remains disagreement on the public health implications of such findings. When cosleeping takes place as part of a larger set of parental choices, the behavioral differences may be broader. Within North American culture, Elias, Nicolson, Bora, and Johnston (1986) found a higher rate and longer duration of breast-feeding for infants who coslept. Super and Harkness (1982) found that, cross culturally, among the Kipsigis of Kenya, traditional methods of back-carrying by a sibling caregiver during the daytime and cosleeping with the mother at night yielded a significantly different developmental course of sleep. In this context, babies napped more during the day and continued to wake up at intervals of approximately three hours at night through the age of 8 months. However, contrasts with U.S. babies' typical sleep patterns were found to be even greater in a study of middle-SES Dutch families (Super et al., 1996). In interviews, parents in these families emphasized the importance of a regular and restful schedule for children's development. Sleep was considered especially important for growth and for maintaining a calm, cheerful, and well-regulated state. Correspondingly, the Dutch parents did encourage more sleep and a more regular schedule for bedtime and meal times, and their infants and young children slept more, and more regularly, than U.S. babies at similar ages. The contrast in total sleep per 24 hours at 6 months of age—2 hours more for the Dutch babies—is especially striking as it is about twice the difference between U.S. and Kipsigis babies on this measure.

Parental Ethnotheories

As the research on the cultural organization of sleep indicates, parents' cultural belief systems, or ethnotheories, play a powerful role in shaping parental behavior. Much recent research has focused on relations among parents' cultural beliefs and children's development, including studies of emotional development, parenting styles, and social and emotional adjustment or maladjustment (Special Issue: Social and Emotional Development: A Cross-Cultural Perspective, 1998). Asian cultures have also received special attention, in part because of the observation that children from Asian families tend to perform very well in school (Special Section: Developmental Psychology in China, 2000). One example of this work is the study by Cole and Tamang (1998) of differences between Chhetri-Brahmin and Tamang children in Nepal with regard to their ideas about emotional displays in hypothetical challenges. The authors reasoned that cultural differences related to religious traditions (Hindu versus Tibetan Buddhism) would be manifested in parents' socialization of their children's emotional expression. Specifically, they hypothesized that the ethos of Chhetri-Brahmin life, with its emphasis on self-awareness and discipline, would be reflected in children's early understanding of "masking" emotion; in contrast, the Tamang children, reared in a more egalitarian society that emphasized the importance of maintaining a calm and peaceful mind, would have different ideas about emotion regulation and expression. Interviews with the children's mothers showed cultural differences in mothers' preferred socialization practices, with most of the Chhetri-Brahmin mothers reporting that they taught their children about emotion display, in contrast to the Tamang mothers who thought that children would learn on their own. The Tamang mothers also favored cajoling and comforting a young child who expressed anger toward themselves, in contrast to reprimanding as endorsed by the Chhetri-Brahmin mothers. Differences in the children's choice of masking in the hypothetical challenge situations were dramatic, with from 40% to 70% of the Chhetri-Brahmin children reporting masking whereas virtually none of the Tamang children did. In a nice touch of ecological validation, the Tamang mothers reported knowing their child's emotional state to a later age.

The study of Cole and Tamang is noteworthy in that it focuses on a progression of ideas—from cultural belief systems, to parental beliefs regarding the socialization of children, to the ideas of children themselves. Other studies have combined a focus on cultural beliefs with behavioral measures. For example, Gaskins (1995), in a study of the socialization of play in a traditional Mayan community of Mexico, found that these parents held beliefs about child development that contrasted strongly with American middle-SES beliefs—specifically, the Mayan parents believed that development is internally generated, and the idea of stimulating the infant's development through play was not encouraged. Patterns of infant exploratory play appeared to be in harmony with these parental beliefs: Mayan babies spent the same amount of time playing with objects as American infants, but the quality of their play was relatively undifferentiated.

A particularly interesting challenge in the study of culture and parenting is how parents' responses to individual differences among children are culturally shaped. Chen, Rubin, and their colleagues have studied differences between Chinese and Canadian children's behavioral inhibition, parental response to this behavioral constellation, and children's development (Chen, Rubin, and Li, 1995; Chen, Rubin, and Sun, 1992). They found that at the age of 2 years, the Chinese children in their sample were more inhibited than the Canadian children, but the mothers in each sample responded differently, with the Chinese mothers of inhibited children having more warm and accepting attitudes whereas the Canadian mothers of such children were more punitive (Chen et al., 1998). In school, Chinese children who were shy and sensitive did better academically and were rated higher by their teachers and peers, in contrast to the shy Canadian children who did worse in general (Chen, Rubin, Li, and Li, 1999; Chen, Rubin, and Ki, 1995). This research provides strong evidence for the importance of cultural meanings of behavioral inhibition as they affect children's developmental trajectories across several kinds of social contexts (Rubin, 1998, p. 612):

> Given that the majority of the world's inhabitants do not reside in culturally "Westernized" countries, the cross-cultural work on behavioral inhibition bears careful note. From the example of a single individual characteristic, social inhibition, one can begin to understand the significance of culture in determining the "meanings" of social and emotional behavior and development at all levels of social complexity. Clearly, child development is influenced by multiple factors. Within any culture, children are shaped by the physical and social settings within which they live, culturally regulated customs and child-rearing practices, and culturally based belief systems (Harkness and Super, 1995). The bottom line is that the psychological "meaning" attributed to any given social behavior is, in large part, a function of the ecological niche within which it is produced. If a given behavior is viewed as acceptable, then parents (and significant others) will attempt to encourage its development; if the behavior is perceived as maladaptive or abnormal, then parents (and significant others) will attempt to discourage its growth and development. . . . All in all, then, it would appear most sensible for the international community of child development researchers not to generalize to other cultures their own culture-specific theories of normal and abnormal development.

CONCLUSIONS

In this chapter we reviewed research concerned with the dual, interactive issues of parenting and culture. From early roots in ethnographic studies, studies of parents in the context of culture have grown to occupy an important place in developmental thinking that complements cross-cultural research on children. Four central issues have occupied the attention of researchers in this area, and the progress of the field can be measured in part through their evolving formulations. First, in regard to the question of universality and cultural variation in parenting, our knowledge base grew geometrically in the second half of the twentieth century, even as the unique features of cultures barely discovered by outside observers have succumbed to the inevitable forces of global ecological, economic, and social change. The history of the quest for causal explanations of cultural variation in parenting, a second major issue, is to some extent the history of cultural anthropology and developmental psychology in microcosm: Early cultural diffusionist conceptualizations gave way to the formulation of "patterns of culture," to be succeeded in turn by psychological (especially Freudian) and functionalist frameworks. Recent explanatory models for the causes of cross-cultural differences in parenting behavior range from global theories of contrasting value orientations to more discrete analyses of how individual parents are enculturated. The communicative function of cultural parenting practices, the third major issue, has been recognized since the early days of research in this field. Formulations such as those of Benedict and Mead sound surprisingly modern; the newest approaches, in their emphasis on fine-grained analysis of parental behavior, elaborate more than they innovate. In contrast, analyses of the developmental effects of culturally constituted parenting, the fourth issue, have shifted from long-term sequelae for adult personality and cultural "expressive systems" to immediate or short-term effects on the development of specific behaviors such as object play, performance on cognitive tests, or social orientation to the caregiver. In this change of focus, the basic question has changed from how to explain culture to how to explain development.

At a more abstract level, we can see the history of research in culture and parenting as a creative tension, at best a dialogue, between the drive for clarity, concreteness, and universality on the one hand, and for synthesis, thematicity, and the understanding of cultural uniqueness on the other. Among the first group, we could list, for example, Malinowski, with his dedication to the collection of "solid, scientific" information; the Whitings' cross-cultural research on discrete behavioral sequences; and current psychological research analyzing parenting "variables" across different cultural settings. In the second category are studies of "patterns of culture" and interpretive approaches to the study of parenting as a cultural meaning system. Both approaches are necessary for the further development of the field. Without concrete empirical data, comparison and generalization are impossible; without analysis of how discrete behaviors relate more broadly to cultural systems, interpretation must remain speculative at best.

Future directions for the field of culture and parenting will include continuing progress toward synthesizing these two approaches. In order to accomplish this goal, however, we must first abandon the unfortunate tendency to discard the products of earlier thinking and research, and instead rediscover the information and insights that are our intellectual heritage. Second, we need to collect data on cultural beliefs, practices, and the settings of child development in a more detailed and systematic manner in order to inform findings on individual behavior in varying cultural contexts. This continues to be difficult in that it requires the combination of strategies traditionally associated with two different disciplines, psychology and anthropology. If we can accomplish this task, we will be well on our way to meeting a third central challenge, that of reconceptualizing culture in relation to development. Culture, as we are becoming increasingly aware, is not a static entity but rather a dynamic system that is constantly in the process of reconstruction and renegotiation in the context of individual lives. Rather than consider cultural "effects" on parenting, thus, we could more realistically turn our attention to how culture is created across the lifespans of individuals in families and communities. This approach, the developmental study of culture, should lead to a better understanding of how parents in a variety of contexts come to think, feel, and act they way they do.

ACKNOWLEDGMENTS

Preparation of this chapter was supported in part by a grant from the Spencer Foundation. All statements made and views expressed are the sole responsibility of the authors.

REFERENCES

Abbott, S. (1992). Holding on and pushing away: Comparative perspectives on an Eastern Kentucky child-rearing practice. *Ethos, 20,* 33–65.

Barry, H. I., Child, I. L., and Bacon, M. K. (1959). Relations of child training to subsistence economy. *American Anthropologist, 61,* 51–63.

Benedict, R. (1932). Configurations of culture in North America. *American Anthropologist, 34,* 1–27.

Benedict, R. (1959). *Patterns of culture.* Boston: Houghton Mifflin. (Original work published 1934.)

Benedict, R. (1934). Anthropology and the abnormal. *Journal of General Psychology, 10,* 59–82.

Benedict, R. (1946). *The chrysanthemum and the sword: Patterns of Japanese culture.* Boston: Houghton Mifflin.

Bornstein, M. H. (Ed.). (1991). *Cultural approaches to parenting.* Hillsdale, NJ: Lawrence Erlbaum Associates.

Bornstein, M. H. (Ed.). (1995). *Handbook of parenting.* Mahwah, NJ: Lawrence Erlbaum Associates.

Bornstein, M. H., Tal, J., and Tamis-LeMonda, C. (1991). Parenting in cross-cultural perspective: The United States, France, and Japan. In M. H. Bornstein (Ed.), *Cultural approaches to parenting* (pp. 69–90). Hillsdale, NJ: Lawrence Erlbaum Associates.

Burton, R., and Whiting, J. W. M. (1961). The absent father and cross-sex identity. *Merrill-Palmer Quarterly, 7,* 85–95.

Carstairs, G. M. (1957). *The Twice-Born.* London: Hogarth.

Caudill, W., and Plath, D. W. (1966). Who sleeps by whom? Parent–child involvement in urban Japanese families. *Psychiatry, 29,* 344–366.

Chen, X., Hastings, P. D., Rubin, K. H., Chen, H., Cen, G., and Stewart, S. L. (1998). Child-rearing attitudes and behavioral inhibition in Chinese and Canadian toddlers: A cross-cultural study. *Developmental Psychology, 34,* 677–686.

Chen, X., Rubin, K. H., and Ki, B. (1995). Social and school adjustment of shy and aggressive children in China. *Development and Psychopathology. 7,* 337–349.

Chen, X., Rubin, K. H., Li, B., and Li, D. (1999). Adolescent outcomes of social functioning in Chinese children. *International Journal of Behavioral Development, 23,* 199–223.

Chen, X., Rubin, K. H., and Li, Z. (1995). Social functioning and adjustment in Chinese children: A longitudinal study. *Developmental Psychology, 31,* 531–540.

Chen, X., Rubin, K. H., and Sun, Y. (1992). Social reputation and peer relationships in Chinese and Canadian children: A cross-cultural study. *Child Development, 63,* 1336–1343.

Cohen, Y. (1964). *The transition from childhood to adolescence.* Chicago: Aldine.

Cole, P., and Tamang, B. L. (1998). Nepali children's ideas about emotional displays in hypothetical challenges. *Developmental Psychology, 34,* 640–646.

Deater-Deckard, K., Dodge, K. A., Bates, J. E., and Pettit, G. S. (1996). Physical discipline among African American and European American mothers: Links to children's externalizing behaviors. *Developmental Psychology, 32,* 1065–1072.

DeLoache, J., and Gottlieb, A. (2000). *A world of babies: Imagined childcare guides for seven societies.* Cambridge, England: Cambridge University Press.

Diener, M. (2000). Gift from the gods: A Balinese guide to early child rearing. In J. G. DeLoache and A. Gottlieb (Eds.), *A world of babies: Imagined childcare guides for seven societies* (pp. 97–116). Cambridge, England: Cambridge University Press.

Dollard, J., and Miller, N. E. (1950). *Personality and Psychotherapy.* New York: McGraw-Hill.

Draper, P., and Cashdan, E. (1988). Technological change and child behavior among the !Kung. *Ethnology, 27,* 339–365.

DuBois, C. (1961). *The people of Alor.* New York: Harper. (First published 1944 by University of Minnesota Press, Minneapolis, MN.)

Elias, M. F., Nicolson, N. A., Bora, C., and Johnston, J. (1986). Sleep/wake patterns of breast-fed infants in the first 2 years of life. *Pediatrics, 77,* 322–329.

Firth, R. (1966). *We, the Tikopia: Kinship in primitive Polynesia.* Boston: Beacon. (First published 1936 by G. Allen and Unwin, London.)

Ford, C. S. (Ed.). (1967). *Cross-cultural approaches: Readings in comparative research.* New Haven, CT: HRAF Press.

Fortes, M. (1938/1970). Social and psychological aspects of education in Taleland. *Africa, 11*(Suppl.).

Gallimore, R., Weisner, T., Kaufman, S. Z., and Bernheimer, L. P. (1989). The social construction of ecocultural niches: Family accommodation of developmentally delayed children. *American Journal on Mental Retardation, 94,* 216–230.

Garcia-Coll, C., and Garrido, M. (2000). Minorities in the United States: Sociocultural context for mental health and developmental. In A. J. Sameroff and M. Lewis (Eds.), *Handbook of developmental psychopathology* (2nd ed., pp. 177–195). New York: Kluwer Academic/Plenum.

Gaskins, S. (1995). How Mayan parental theories come into play. In S. Harkness and C. M. Super (Eds.), *Parents' cultural belief systems: Their origins, expressions, and consequences.* New York: Guilford.

Goodnow, J. J., and Collins, W. A. (1990). *Development according to parents: The nature, sources, and consequences of parents' ideas.* Hillsdale, NJ: Lawrence Erlbaum Associates.

Goodnow, J. J., Miller, P. J. and Kessel, F. (Eds.). (1995). *New directions for child and adolescent development: Vol. 67. Cultural practices as contexts for development.* San Francisco: Jossey-Bass.

Gorer, G., and Rickman, J. (1949). *The people of great Russia.* London: Cresset.

Greenfield, P. M., and Cocking, R. R. (Eds.). (1994). *Cross-cultural roots of minority child development.* Hillsdale, NJ: Lawrence Erlbaum Associates.

Harkness, S., Raeff, C., and Super, C. M. (Eds.). (2000). *New directions for child and adolescent development: Vol. 87. Variability in the social construction of the child.* San Francisco: Jossey-Bass.

Harkness, S., and Super, C. M. (1985). Child–environment interactions in the socialization of affect. In M. Lewis and C. Saarni (Eds.), *The socialization of emotions* (pp. 21–36). New York: Plenum.

Harkness, S., and Super, C. M. (1991). East Africa. In H. R. Hiner and J. M. Hawes (Eds.), *Children in comparative and historical perspective: An international handbook and research guide* (pp. 217–240). Westport, CT: Greenwood.

Harkness, S., and Super, C. M. (1992). The developmental niche: A theoretical framework for analyzing the household production of health. *Social Science and Medicine. 38* (2), 217–226.

Harkness, S., and Super, C. M. (1992). The cultural foundations of fathers' roles: Evidence from Kenya and the United States. In B. S. Hewlett (Ed.), *The father's role: Cultural and evolutionary perspectives* (pp. 191–211). New York: Aldine de Gruyter.

Harkness, S., and Super, C. M. (1995). Culture and parenting. In M. H. Bornstein (Ed.), *Handbook of parenting, Vol. 2. Biology and ecology of parenting* (pp. 211–234). Mahwah, NJ: Lawrence Erlbaum Associates.

Harkness, S., and Super, C. M. (Eds.). (1996). *Parents' cultural belief systems: Their origins, expressions, and consequences.* New York: Guilford.

Harkness, S., Super, C. M., and van Tijen, N. (2000). Individualism and the "Western mind" reconsidered: American and Dutch parents' ethnotheories of the child. In S. Harkness, C. Raeff, and C. M. Super (Eds.), *New directions in child development: Vol. 87. The social construction of the child: Understanding variability within and across contexts.* San Francisco: Jossey-Bass.

Harwood, R. L., Schölmerich, A., and Schulze, P. A. (2000). Homogeneity and heterogeneity in cultural belief systems. In S. Harkness, C. Raeff, and C. M. Super (Eds.), *New directions in child development: Vol. 87. The social construction of the child: Understanding variability within and across contexts.* San Francisco: Jossey-Bass.

Harwood, R. L., Schölmerich, A., Ventura-Cook, E., Schulze, P. A., and Wilson, S. P. (1996). Culture and class influences on Anglo and Puerto Rican mothers' beliefs regarding long-term socialization goals and child behavior. *Child Development, 67,* 2446–2461.

Hewlett, B. S. (Ed.). (1992). *Father–child relations: Cultural and evolutionary contexts.* New York: Aldine de Gruyter.

Hewlett, B. S., Lamb, M. E., Shannon, D., Leyendecker, B., and Schölmerich, A. (1998). Culture and early infancy among Central African foragers and farmers. *Developmental Psychology, 34,* 653–661.

Hunt, R. (Ed.). (1967). *Personalities and cultures: Readings in psychological anthropology.* New York: Natural History Press.

Hwang, C. P., Lamb, M. E., and Sigel, I. E. (Eds.). (1996). *Images of childhood.* Mahwah, NJ: Lawrence Erlbaum Associates.

Jahoda, G. (1982). *Psychology and anthropology: A psychological perspective.* New York: Academic.

Kagitçibasi, C. (1980). Individualism and collectivism. In J. W. Berry, M. H. Segall, and C. Kagitçibasi (Eds.), *Handbook of cross-cultural psychology: Vol. 3. Social Behavior and Applications* (pp. 1–50). Needham Heights, MA: Allyn and Bacon.

Kagitçibasi, C. (1996a). The autonomous-relational self: A new synthesis. *European Psychologist, 1,* 180–186.

Kagitçibasi, C. (1996b). *Family and human development across cultures: A view from the other side.* Hillsdale, NJ: Lawrence Erlbaum Associates.

Kardiner, A. (1939). *The individual and his society.* New York: Columbia University Press.

Kardiner, A. (1945). *The psychological frontiers of society.* New York: Columbia University Press.

Killen, M., and Wainryb, C. (2000). Independence and interdependence in diverse cultural contexts. In S. Harkness, C. Raeff, and C. M. Super (Eds.), *New directions in child development: Vol. 87. The social construction of the child: Understanding variability within and across contexts.* San Francisco: Jossey-Bass.

Konner, M. J. (1981). Evolution of human behavior development. In R. H. Munroe, R. L. Munroe, and B. B. Whiting (Eds.), *Handbook of cross-cultural human development* (pp. 3–52). New York: Garland.

Lamb, M. (Ed.). (1981). *The role of the father in child development* (2nd ed.). New York: Wiley.

LeVine, R. A. (1960). The internalization of political values in stateless societies. *Human Organization, 19,* 51–58.

LeVine, R. A. (1970). Cross-cultural study in child psychology. In P. Mussen (Ed.), *Carmichael's manual of child psychology* (3rd ed., Vol. 2, pp. 559–612). New York: Wiley.

LeVine, R. A. (1973). *Culture, behavior, and personality.* Chicago: Aldine.

LeVine, R. A. (1974). Parental goals: A cross-cultural view. *Teachers College Record, 76,* 226–239.

LeVine, R. A., Dixon, S., LeVine, S., Richman, A., Leiderman, P. H., Keefer, C. H., and Brazelton, T. B. (1994). *Child care and culture: Lessons from Africa.* Cambridge, England: Cambridge University Press.

LeVine, R. A., Miller, P. M., and West, M. M. (Eds.). (1988). *New directions for child development: Vol. 40. Parental behavior in diverse societies.* San Francisco: Jossey-Bass.

Lozoff, B., Wolf, A., and Davis, N. (1984). Co-sleeping in urban families with young children in the United States. *Pediatrics, 74,* 171–182.

Malinowski, B. (1966). *The father in primitive psychology.* New York: Norton. (Originally published 1927.)

Malinowski, B. (1966). Preface. In R. Firth (Ed.), *We, the Tikopia: Kinship in primitive polynesia* (pp. i–xiii). Boston: Beacon. (First published 1966 by Allen and Unwin, London.)

Mead, M. (1968). *Coming of age in Samoa: A psychological study of primitive youth for western civilization.* New York: Dell. (Originally Published 1928.)

Mead, M. (1972). *Blackberry winter: My earlier years.* New York: Simon and Schuster.

Mead, M. (1966). *Growing up in New Guinea: A comparative study of primitive education.* New York: Morrow. (Originally Published 1930.)

Middleton, J. (Ed.). (1970). *From child to adult: Studies in the anthropology of education.* New York: Natural History Press.

Minturn, L. (1993). *Sita's daughters: Coming out of purdah*. New York: Oxford University Press.

Minturn, L., and Lambert, W. W. (1964). *Mothers of six cultures: Antecedents of child rearing*. New York: Wiley.

Morelli, G. A., Rogoff, B., Oppenheim, D., and Goldsmith, D. (1992). Cultural variation in infants' sleeping arrangements: Questions of independence. *Developmental Psychology, 28*, 604–613.

Mosko, S., Richard, C., McKenna, J., Drummond, S., and Mukai, D. (1997). Maternal proximity and infant CO_2 environment during bedsharing and possible implications for SIDS. *American Journal of Physical Anthropology, 103*, 315–328.

Munroe, R. L., and Munroe, R. H. (1971). Male pregnancy symptoms and cross-sex identity in three societies. *Journal of Social Psychology, 84*, 11–25.

New, R. (1988). Parental goals and Italian infant care. In R. A. LeVine, P. M. Miller and M. M. West (Eds.), *New directions for child development: Vol. 40. Parental behavior in diverse societies*. San Francisco: Jossey-Bass.

New, R. S., and Richman, A. L. (1995). Maternal beliefs and infant care practices in Italy and the United States. In S. Harkness and C. M. Super (Eds.), *Parents' cultural belief systems: Their origins, expressions, and consequences*. New York: Guilford.

Newsletter of the International Society for the Study of Behavioral Development. (2001), *1*(38).

Nucholls, C. W. (Ed.). (1994). *Siblings in South Asia: Brothers and sisters in cultural context*. New York: Guilford.

Pachter, L. M. (Ed.). (2000). *Child health in the multicultural environment*, Report of the thirty-first Ross roundtable on critical approaches to common pediatric problems. Columbus, Ohio: Ross Products Division, Abbott Laboratories.

Quinn, N., and Holland, D. (1987). Culture and cognition. In D. Holland and N. Quinn (Eds.), *Cultural models in language and thought* (pp. 3–42). Cambridge, England: Cambridge University Press.

Radcliffe-Brown, A. R. (1964). *The Andaman Islanders*. New York: Free Press of Glencoe. (Originally Published 1932.)

Richman, A., Miller, P., and LeVine, R. (1992). Cultural and educational variations in maternal responsiveness. *Developmental Psychology, 28*, 614–621.

Rubin, K. H. (1998). Social and emotional development from a cultural perspective. *Developmental Psychology, 34*, 611–615.

Seymour, S. (1980). Patterns of childrearing in a changing Indian town. In S. Seymour (Ed.), *The transformation of a sacred town: Bhubaneswar, India*. Boulder, CO: Westview.

Shweder, R. A., Jensen, L. A., and Goldstein, W. M. (1995). Who sleeps by whom revisited: A method for extracting the moral goods implicit in practice. In J. J. Goodnow, P. J. Miller, and F. Kessel (Eds.), *New directions for child development: Vol. 67. Cultural practices as contexts for development* (pp. 21–39). San Francisco: Jossey-Bass.

Sigel, I. E., McGillicuddy-De Lisi, A. V., and Goodnow, J. J. (Eds.). (1992). *Parental belief systems: The psychological consequences for children* (2nd ed.). Hillsdale, NJ: Lawrence Erlbaum Associates.

Special Issue: Social and emotional development: A cross-cultural perspective. (1998). K. H. Rubin (Ed.). *Developmental Psychology, 34*(4).

Special Section: Developmental Psychology in China. (2000). T. Tardif and X. Miao (Eds.). *International Journal of Behavioral Development, 24*(1).

Spiro, M. E. (1953). Ghosts: An anthropological inquiry into learning and perception. *Journal of Abnormal and Social Psychology, 48*, 376–382.

Spiro, M. E. (1982). *Oedipus in the Trobriands*. Chicago: University of Chicago Press.

Super, C. M., and Harkness, S. (1982). The infant's niche in rural Kenya and metropolitan America. In L. L. Adler (Ed.), *Cross-cultural research at issue* (pp. 47–56). New York: Academic.

Super, C. M., and Harkness, S. (1986a). The developmental niche: A conceptualization at the interface of child and culture. *International Journal of Behavioral Development, 9*, 545–569.

Super, C. M., and Harkness, S. (1986b). Temperament, culture, and development. In R. Plomin and J. Dunn (Eds.), *The study of temperament: Changes, continuities, and challenges* (pp. 131–150). Hillsdale, NJ: Lawrence Erlbaum Associates.

Super, C. M., and Harkness, S. (1999). The environment as culture in developmental research. In T. Wachs and S. Friedman (Eds.), *Measurement of the environment in developmental research* (pp. 279–323). Washington, DC: American Psychological Association.

Super, C. M., Harkness, S., van Tijen, N., van der Vlugt, E., Dykstra, J., and Fintelman, M. (1996). The three R's of Dutch child rearing and the socialization of infant arousal. In S. Harkness and C. M. Super (Eds.), *Parents' cultural belief systems: Their origins, expressions, and consequences* (pp. 447–466). New York: Guilford.

Thomas, A., and Chess, S. (1977). *Temperament and development*. New York: Brunner/Mazel.

Townsend, N. W. (2000). Male fertility as a lifetime of relationships: Contextualizing men's biological reproduction in Botswana. In C. Bledsoe, S. Lerner, and J. I. Guyer (Eds.), *Fertility and the male life-cycle in the era of fertility decline* (pp. 343–364). New York: Oxford University Press.

Triandis, H. (1995). *Individualism and collectivism*. Boulder, CO: Westview.

Weisner, T. S., and Garnier, H. (1992). Nonconventional family life-styles and school achievement: A 12-year longitudinal study. *American Educational Research Journal, 29*, 605–632.

Weisner, T. S., Matheson, C. C., and Bernheimer, L. P. (1996). American cultural models of early influence and parent recognition of developmental delays: Is earlier always better than later? In S. Harkness and C. M. Super (Eds.), *Parents' cultural belief systems: Their origins, expressions, and consequences* (pp. 496–532). New York: Guilford.

Welles-Nyström, B. (1988). Parenthood and infancy in Sweden. In R. A. LeVine, P. M. Miller and M. M. West (Eds.), *New directions for child development: Vol: 40. Parental behavior in diverse societies.* San Francisco: Jossey-Bass.

Whiting, B. B. (Ed.). (1964). *Six cultures: Studies of child rearing.* New York: Wiley.

Whiting, B. B., and Edwards, C. P. (1988). *Children of different worlds: The formation of social behavior.* Cambridge, MA: Harvard University Press.

Whiting, B. B., and Whiting, J. W. M. (1975). *The children of six cultures: A psychocultural analysis.* Cambridge, MA: Harvard University Press.

Whiting, J. W. M. (1981). Environmental constraints on infant care practices. In R. H. Munroe, R. L. Munroe, and B. B. Whiting (Eds.), *Handbook of cross-cultural human development* (pp. 155–180). New York: Garland.

Whiting, J. W. M., and Child, I. L. (1953). *Child training and personality: A cross-cultural study.* New Haven, CT: Yale University Press.

Whiting, J. W. M., Child, I. L., and Lambert, W. W. (1966). *Field guide to a study of socialization.* New York: Wiley.

Whiting, J. W. M., Kluckhohn, R., and Anthony, A. A. (1958). The function of male initiation ceremonies at puberty. In E. E. Maccoby, T. M. Newcomb, and E. L. Hartley (Eds.), *Readings in social anthropology* (pp. 359–370). New York: Holt.

Wolf, A. W., Lozoff, B., Latz, S., and Paludetto, R. (1996). Parental theories in the management of young children's sleep in Japan, Italy, and the United States. In S. Harkness and C. M. Super (Eds.), *Parents' cultural belief systems: Their origins, expressions, and consequences.* New York: Guilford.

Young, R. W. (1965). *Initiation ceremonies.* Indianapolis, IN: Bobbs-Merrill.

10

Environment and Parenting

Robert H. Bradley

University of Arkansas at Little Rock

INTRODUCTION

When plowing through the now hundreds of studies that deal with parent–child interactions, one can easily lose sight of how potent the immediate social and physical environment can be in shaping parental interactions with their children. Most studies focus at the group level on rather molar kinds of parenting processes, such as warmth, demandingness, and restrictiveness. But scenes from recent movies such as *Life Is Beautiful* and *Schindler's List*, which depict parents struggling against the horrors of Nazi internment camps in World War II, stand in vivid contrast to the placid (somewhat disembodied) representations of parenting found in most scholarly journals. These celluloid depictions of anguished parents groping to find ways to provide safe and nurturant care under extraordinarily challenging conditions—granted the artistic license of the moviemakers—make abundantly clear just how powerful surroundings can be in affecting what parents do. Who can forget the tortured agony of Sophie Zawistoska as she faced *the choice* regarding the most basic of parenting acts: staying with one's child in a time of peril!

Snippets from TV footage showing dazed parents trying to care for their children amidst the filth and fear of makeshift camps during the genocidal conflicts in Kosovo and Bosnia provide equally stiking (and quite real) evidence of how physical surroundings have an impact on what parents do in their role as parents; so, too, do the near-hopeless faces of African parents as they stumble, starving, into temporary shelters and foodbanks in search of nourishment and respite in the face of war and famine. Often forgotten in the face of imminent death is securing even basic protective health care for children with wasted immune systems.

The impact of the environment, the social and the physical surroundings, on what parents do and how often they do it is not well documented, whether the circumstances of family life be stressful or ordinary. There are nonetheless some revealing accounts in the anthropological literature. Notable is Scheper-Hughes' (1989) wrenching portrayal of home life in Alto do Cruzeiro, the largest shantytown in Bom Jesus da Mata, located in northeast Brazil. Like many third world shantytowns, Alto do Cruzeiro exudes chronic poverty, high mortality, marital instability, and disconnection from kin. Scheper-Hughes makes clear how the physical surroundings and the social actions that compose the home environments of Alto children are shaped by the larger economic, cultural, and historical forces present in urban Brazil today. The point of her article is that these conditions produce mothers who do not care. On average, the women of Alto experience 9.5 pregnancies, 3.5 child deaths, and 1.5 stillbirths. The women face child disease and death with fatalism and stoicism. They identify infants who have the strength and will to survive, then nurture them. To others they attribute a "will to die" or the kind of "child sickness" that cannot be cured—angels awaiting flight to heaven. These infants are viewed with indifference, often revulsion, and are allowed to die. Most of the infants die at home and are buried with little ceremony in unmarked graves, a form of passive infanticide to which mothers have been socialized by other women in the community and even by the church. Scheper-Hughes (1989, p. 117) concludes that "Frequent child death remains a powerful shaper of maternal thinking and practice. In the absence of firm expectation that a child will survive, mother love as we conceptualize it (whether in popular terms or in the psychobiological notion of maternal bonding) is attenuated and delayed with consequences for infant survival."

In affluent societies, adults tend to have substantially more control over their day-to-day lives and surroundings than is the case of adults in Bom Jesus de Mata. As a result, surroundings do not typically afford the level of challenge described by Scheper-Hughes—with perhaps the near-inevitable kinds of parenting actions that such challenges evoke. Be that as is may, there is substantial evidence that the environment, even in far less challenging conditions, acts to shape parenting behaviors. For example, in a recent study, Evans, Maxwell, and Hart (1999) found that parents who lived in crowded homes spoke in less complex sentences with their children, compared with parents who lived in uncrowded homes. Parents in crowded homes were also less verbally responsive. These effects obtained even when researchers controlled for the family's overall socioeconomic status (SES). A somewhat cheerier example can be found in the research conducted by Brown, Burton, and Sweaney (1998). They noted that over the past several decades there has been a move back to putting front porches on houses. This design change enables parents to spend more time interacting with their children and watching them play outdoors.

The physical and social settings in which families live constitute part of what Super and Harkness (in Vol. 2 of this *Handbook*) call the developmental niche. The developmental niche of families regulates the microenvironment for children. The impact of the developmental niche can also be seen in differences in sleep patterns between Kokwet infants from Kenya and infants living in urban America (Super and Harkness, 1986). Kokwet babies generally sleep with their mothers and are rarely left alone. American babies, by contrast, generally sleep in their own beds, often in their own rooms. The physical environment of mats, cribs, and chairs and the social environment of caregivers and companions provide the structure for the infant's emerging skills (i.e., they set the opportunities and incentives for infant action). In effect, the setting determines what the infant can see, hear, and do.

Neither the experiences of a child nor the actions of parents is precisely determined by their developmental niches. Culture and class help to shape and define what parents do and who parents are; but the environment parents create for their children does not exclusively reflect these macrolevel ecological factors either. Parenting also reflects what the neighborhood and the community afford. Moreover, as Belsky's (1984) model of parenting shows, parenting is a complex function of many factors, including the parent's own history and personality and the characteristics of the child being parented. Both parent and child are active constructors of their environments as well as responders to what the environment affords (Ford and Lerner, 1992; Wachs, 1992, 2000). The actual process of parenting involves numerous moment-to-moment exchanges with child and environment.

What constitutes the parenting environment? It seems useful to think of the environment for parenting as including all the social and physical phenomena within the home (Wachs, 1992; Wapner, 1987; Wohlwill and Heft, 1977). However, it is probably counterproductive to confine the concept of the parenting environment to a particular place, even though the concepts of parenting and home are semantically linked. In a child's mind, or in a parent's mind, what constitutes "home" will probably not refer exclusively to those events, objects, and actions within the four walls of a particular residence (or within the property lines that define a place of residence). Indeed, Lawrence and Low (1990) cite studies done in several cultures that demonstrate that the social boundaries of households do not necessarily coincide with the physical boundaries of dwellings. Home experiences may include any number of events that are seen as connected to home and family but not co-terminus with the physical boundaries of a place. A walk around the block with Dad, a visit to the local library with Mom, or an argument between Mom and Dad in the car on the way to visit Grandma may all be strongly associated with the network of acts and events that comprise a child's home life. A recent visit to the Oglala Sioux reservation in Pine Ridge made abundantly clear that, for some children, home can be an idea connected to several residences simultaneously. By the same token, the concept of the parenting environment as fully divorced from any place of residence is probably not useful either because the idea of home is generally associated with identifiable places. For both parent and child, many of the ideas and attitudes connected to "home" have their roots in scenes, episodes, and "scripts" which emanate from particular concrete places where family activities occur (Abelson, 1981).

The concept of the parenting environment might best be defined as phenomena emanating from the family setting. The boundaries of the parenting environment become somewhat permeable and expansive, a boundary of meaning not bricks or fences. Such an expansive definition is consistent with the position of social anthropologists who contend that the social boundaries of household units do not necessarily coincide with the physical boundaries of their dwellings (Altman, 1977; Lawrence and Low, 1990). Such an expansive definition seems more appropriate when one considers the actual living conditions of many families (e.g., families living out of a car or shelter, parents sharing dual custody, children who spend large amounts of time at their parents' sides in places other than home such as fields and workplaces). The concept of the parenting environment as not fully confined to a place becomes useful because the role of parent tends to change from that of direct provider and teacher (most of which may well occur within the four walls of the home residence) to that of mentor, guide, and arranger of experiences (some of which almost certainly occur outside the four walls of the residence) (Fagot and Kavanaugh, 1993; Maccoby and Martin, 1983). It is perhaps not surprising that the most commonly used measures of the home environment tend to include activities outside the child's residence that are directed or enabled by the parent (Bradley, 1999).

The parenting environment is best understood not only on the basis of activities and objects it contains or generates but on the basis of its *instrumentality* for childcare and childrearing (Korosec-Serafty, 1985). For individual parents, there is a sense of boundary to the spaces where parenting takes place, but what actually constitutes the boundary varies across parents and time, depending on an array of cultural, familial, personal, and child factors (Belsky, 1984; Bronfenbrenner, 1979, 1999). In effect, what is appropriated to the idea of the parenting environment is the meaning of the acts, objects, and places connected to parental caregiving. Different families may utilize different geographic settings to be part of the parenting environment (e.g., the street, the backyard, the zoo, a museum, the neighborhood park). The parenting environment encompasses the locations where the activities of caregiving take place; it is empirically defined (Rapoport, 1985).

My purpose in this chapter is to describe how the opportunities, constraints, and challenges within the environment provide a context in which parents pursue goals in their role as caregivers, to detail the primary tasks that parents are required to carry out to facilitate their children's development and to discuss how aspects of the social and physical environment can affect how a parent attempts to carry out these tasks, to present a view of parents as conscious actors in dealing with the needs of their children, to delineate how aspects of the surrounding environment affect the process of parenting, to describe how parents use structural features of the residence and resources within the community to accomplish the goals of caregiving, and to discuss complexities and limitations in research on parenting and the environment. Less attention will be given to bidirectional influences involved in parent and child behavior and to relationships with the broader ecology.

THE TASKS OF PARENTING

To understand how the physical and social environment affects parenting, it is first necessary to specify the kinds of critical tasks performed by parents that are directed at promoting child well-being. The fact is, what adults do in their role as parents has changed over the centuries, a function of technological, social, and economic adjustments. There is also substantial diversity in what parents do in their role as parents and how they do it both within and across cultures. Nonetheless, the primary goal of parenting is much the same despite these differences; that is, parents must do what is necessary to enable their children to become competent, caring adults who are able to function well within society (Maccoby and Martin, 1983). For any place and any era, attaining the goal is no mean feat. This seemingly innocuous generic prescription requires a plethora of specific parenting actions carried out over a lengthy period of time fitted to a particular child's needs and executed within the boundaries of the resources and constraints present.

We recently constructed a system for organizing the tasks of parenting (Bradley and Caldwell, 1995). It derives from systems theory and is organized around the concept that parents help to regulate the course of their children's development (Sameroff, 1995). Central to our framework is the notion that optimal parenting is best conceived of as a set of regulatory acts aimed at helping children adapt to the environment and successfully exploit the opportunities it affords (Saegert and Winkel, 1990). Such a concept seems in keeping with ecological developmental theories that place value on person–environment fit as the basic way of ensuring maximum adaptiveness and optimal development. Moreover, the notion that parents are regulators of person– (child–) environment fit connects with the idea from developmental systems theory that human beings are phylogenetically advanced, self-constructing organisms that actively engage their environments (Ford and Lerner, 1992). This framework is also consonant with the idea that children are conscious agents who are active in adapting to their environments (Lewis, 1997). From this basic notion, five basic regulatory tasks (or functions) performed by parents were identified: 1) sustenance, 2) stimulation, 3) support, 4) structure, and 5) surveillance.

The first three regulatory functions derive from what is known about human needs and arousal systems. Specifically, Maslow and Murphy (1954) contend that human beings need environments that promote survival, provide information (including enlistment of attention), and affirm worth. Relatedly, Ford and Lerner (1992) identify three major domains of organismic functioning, each with its own arousal processes: 1) biological–physical-activity arousal, 2) cognitive–attention arousal, and 3) social–emotional arousal (Ford and Lerner, 1992). For complex living systems such as human beings, the task of maintaining internal unity is quite complicated because of the large number of component subsystems involved and the elaborateness of their organization (Ford and Lerner, 1992; Wachs, 2000). To deal with the child's individuality and complexity, parents must perform other functions that ensure that the direct inputs designed to sustain, stimulate, and emotionally support the child are maximally fitted to the child's current needs, proclivities, and competencies—hence, structure and surveillance. The exact character of each of the five for a given parent–child dyad will tend to operate along the lines of stabilized central attractors as part of a family system (Wachs, 2000), some stronger, some weaker, depending on parental personality, child behavioral style, and the environment.

Sustenance

"The growth, health, and functioning of the human body as a physical entity requires the ability to collect and use appropriate material/energy forms and to protect against potentially damaging ones" (Ford and Lerner, 1992, p. 103). We call sustenance parenting acts and conditions that are designed to promote biological integrity. Parents must provide adequate nutrients, shelter, and conditions for the maintenance of health to ensure both survival and the level of biological integrity needed for physical and psychological development (Pollitt, 1988). Parents must also protect children from pathogenic conditions such as pollutants, passive cigarette smoke, and exposure to heavy metals (Evans, Kliewer, and Martin, 1991; Jacobson, Jacobson, Padgett, Brummitt, and Billings, 1992; Tong and McMichael, 1992).

There is not yet a great deal of information on how conditions in the social and physical environment affect what parents do to provide sustenance to their children. Part of the lack of research on the topic may stem from the fact that many of the answers seem obvious and, in some cases, trivial. That is, in conditions of danger or want, parents will take whatever actions necessary to provide for basic needs such as food and shelter or to remove a child from exposure to toxic substances. However, the few studies that are available suggest that parental actions are not so easy to predict. Early studies suggested that in times of food shortage, women and children are likely to suffer more from undernutrition than men because men consume a higher proportion of available food. Later studies observed that this pattern was more true of societies having a high degree of gender inequality (Safilios-Rotschild, 1980; Schofield, 1974; Zeitlin, 1996). There is also evidence that food deprivation does not always disproportionately affect children and that the burden of food shortage does not always fall equally on children of all ages. For example, Leonard (1991) actually found that caloric stress was greater on adults than on children among Andean agriculturalists, in which all able-bodied individuals participated in agriculturally related activities to the greatest extent possible. Wandel and Holmboe-Ottesen (1992) found that in Tanzania the burden fell heavier on preschool-age children than on older children because the older children were needed to help with the harvest. By contrast, McDonald, Sigman, Espunosa, and Newman (1994) found that in Kenya infants may not suffer as much during food shortages as do older children. In effect, although food availability is known to affect how much parents feed children, there is no consistency in the response of parents to food shortage. Moreover, cultural beliefs can have an impact on parental decisions with respect to feeding practices even when there is adequate food. For example, in Nigeria, there is a reticence to give food to children who do not directly contribute to family survival for fear that children may become spoiled (Zeitlin, 1996). Likewise, in Nicaragua, where the belief is prevalent that children will eat when they are hungry, mothers tend not to offer extra food to their young children, even in times of food shortage (Engle, Zeitlin, Medrano, and Garcia, 1996).

Although severe economic hardship is implicated in both health and nutritional status (Bradley and Whiteside-Mansell, 1997), there is little evidence that economic status affects the decision to breast-feed (Basiotix, Hirschman, and Kennedy, 1996). There is also little evidence that it affects the nutritional value of diets given to young children once other key sociodemographic factors were controlled (U.S. Department of Commerce, 1999).

Natural physical hazards can also affect what parents do in relation to their children. To reduce the risks, Ache parents living in Paraguay put limits on infant locomotion and exploratory behavior (Kaplan and Dove, 1987).

Stimulation

To ensure competence and continued effort toward life-enhancing goals, the environment must provide sensory data that engage attention and provide information (i.e., stimulation). There is an abundance of both psychological theory and empirical data to buttress the significance of stimulation for cognitive, psychomotor, and social development (Horowitz, 1987). Development in every domain of competency requires a manageable amount of meaningful information (Caldwell, 1968; Ford and Lerner, 1992).

Although children appear to benefit from exposure to a variety of stimulating objects and events (Bradley and Caldwell, 1976; Caldwell, 1968; Elardo, Bradley, and Caldwell, 1975; Kagan, 1984; Wohlwill, 1974), it does not appear true that more stimulation is always better. For example, exposure to chronic noise leads to elevated blood pressure, a condition that does not result in habituation when exposure is continued (World Health Organization, 1980). Wachs has accumulated evidence that noise levels in the home are negatively correlated with cognitive development in young children

(Wachs, 1992). Older children also seem to be negatively affected by high noise levels in the home, although these effects are somewhat difficult to gauge because older children may also be exposed to high levels of noise at school (Heft, 1979). Noise may have both direct and indirect effects on children: direct in the sense that it disturbs their concentration and coping, indirect in the sense that it disturbs others with whom they interact. Children may cope with overstimulation by trying to filter out the unwanted stimuli; but the strategy may backfire in that they filter indiscriminately.

There is relatively little data on how often children are exposed to stimulating objects, events, and experiences, much less how rates of exposure vary as a function of different environmental conditions. Bradley, Corwyn, McAdoo, and Garcia Coll (2001) recently examined the frequency with which children were exposed to common objects and conditions in the home environment by using data from the National Longitudinal Survey of Youth (NLSY). The data showed that 63% of European American infants not living in poverty had at least 10 books and 67% had parents who read to them at least three times a week. The figures were substantially less for members of other ethnic groups and for children living in poverty; only 25% of Hispanic American infants living in poverty had parents who read to them at least three times a week. Approximately 1/3 of infants from all groups had at least 3 push or pull toys. Over 93% of nonpoor European American preschoolers had at least 10 books in the home; over 60% of nonpoor preschoolers from other ethnic groups did as well. In all ethnic and socioeconomic groups, over 70% of preschool-age children were exposed to at least 3 hr of TV per day, and the majority had access to a record or tape player. Once children became of school age, parents reduced the number of times per week they read to children (less than 50% in all groups read to their children three or more times per week); but, except among poor African American and Hispanic American children, at least 50% of all households contained 10 or more books that were age appropriate for elementary school-age children. Almost half of the European American and Asian American households with incomes above poverty level also had musical instruments for children of elementary school age; and almost half the families in both these groups also subscribed to a daily newspaper. For 4 year old children, similar figures on the number of books present in the home and the number of times parents read to children emerged in the National Household Education Survey (NHES). In both surveys, there were differences between poor and nonpoor children in terms of the number of exposures to stimulating objects and events in the home, including direct efforts by the parents to teach school relevant competencies (albeit the vast majority of parents in all groups stated that they spent time in such activities). Relatedly, Hart and Risley (1995), in a detailed microanalytic study of children's exposure to parental language, found that middle-SES parents spoke to their children far more often than did blue-collor or poor parents. These differences corresponded to differences in vocabulary attainment for the three groups of children.

Li and Rao (2000) recently examined how parents of Chinese preschoolers in Beijing, Hong Kong, and Singapore assisted their children in attaining literacy skills. The majority of parents in all three cities (69% to 83%) believed that reading early was important and that storytelling was a useful way to help children learn Chinese literacy skills. However, many parents in Beijing (68%), Hong Kong (75%), and Singapore (86%) did not set aside a definite time to read to their children, although the majority in each city (56% to 73%) taught their children to read at home. The majority of children in Beijing (66%) and Hong Kong (76%) also had a chance to see their parents read each day; the figure for Singapore was 48%. Approximately one half of the parents in Hong Kong and Singapore also taught their children to write Chinese characters, but only approximately one third of the parents in Beijing did. Approximately 60% of parents in all three cities set up reading corners in the house but there tended to be more children's books available in Beijing households (62% had at least 30) than in Hong Kong (83% had fewer than 30) or Singapore (76% had fewer than 30).

The nature of parental employment also affects the kinds of stimulation parents provide their children. Parents who have jobs with greater substantive complexity and self-direction tend to value ideational flexibility and put less stress on conformity for family members (Schooler, 1999). The tend to engage in more intellectually demanding leisure activities and discourse with their children. They also take a more open-ended approach to problem solving and promote a self-directed orientation.

For decades, researchers have discussed SES differences in the rates at which children are exposed to potentially stimulating objects and experiences in the home environment. As well, they have posited the reasons for such differences, including parental knowledge and belief systems, stress, and limited access to resources (Bradley and Whiteside-Mansell, 1997). Evans et al. (1999) found that parents living in crowded conditions also tend to speak in less complex ways to their children than do parents from similar SES backgrounds who live in uncrowded conditions. These researchers suggest that coping with stress may also contribute to these parenting differences.

The socioeconomic conditions of the neighborhood also appear to affect the level of stimulation parents provide children, albeit the data do not show a consistent relation to either the quality of stimulation found in the home or to child achievement (Klebanov, Brooks-Gunn, Chase-Lansdale, and Gordon, 1997). The precise mechanisms linking neighborhood poverty and social disorganization to parenting practices are not clear, but residing in affluent, well-organized neighborhoods might set positive norms for parenting and might reinforce sanctions against neglectful parenting.

The NLSY and the NHES studies also provide information on what parents expose their children to outside the home. Between 60% and 80% of infants from all ethnic and SES groups are taken to the grocery store at least once a week. Approximately 50% to 60% of nonpoor mothers reported taking their preschoolers to some type of museum at least once a year; the figures for poor mothers were approximately 10% to 15% lower. Almost half of the nonpoor European American mothers indicated that they had taken their school-age children to the library in the past month. For the other groups, the figures ranged from approximately one fourth to one third. Generally less than 25% reported having taken their children to a concert within the past month, although the figures for African Americans were closer to one third. Approximately 15% to 25% of families also reported taking their children to the zoo, with Hispanic Americans reporting the highest rate of attendance. Over 60% of nonpoor European Americans stated that they provided some type of lessons for their school-age children, with figures ranging from 24% to 46% in other groups. Over 85% of nonpoor European American fathers reported spending some time outdoors with their children at least once a week, with figures ranging from 47% to 75% in other groups. In all ethnic groups, the figures were lower for poor families, except for taking children to the zoo.

In a recent study of 10 to 15 year-old children living in the United States, Bradley, Corwyn, Caldwell et al. (2000) found that 70% to 75% had two or more pictures on their bedroom walls, at least two types of reference materials, at least two board games, and at least two pieces of equipment useful for physical development or sports. Over 50% had 20 or more developmentally appropriate books, access to a musical instrument, and lived in a house in which the family received a daily newspaper. Less (approximately 40%) had access to home computers. Approximately 70% of the parents stated that they had discussed current events with the adolescent during the previous two weeks, and approximately 60% reported regular participation in church activities. Slightly less than half of the adolescents had been to a museum, a live musical or theater performance, or an organized sporting event accompanied by another family member during the previous year. Less than half reported regularly engaging in an outdoor activity with their fathers, but approximately 80% reported going on a family trip during the previous year. Although specific percentages of those involved in each activity were not reported by SES group, there was a correlation between SES and involvement in these activities.

In the United States, poor children are exposed to potentially stimulating objects and events at lower rates than nonpoor children were. There are a few exceptions, such as zoo attendance, but the general pattern is the same for all major ethnic groups. Indeed, Bradley, Corwyn, McAdoo, and Garcia Coll et al. (2001) found a proportional poverty effect for all types of objects and experiences across ethnic groups. In their cross-cultural review of studies involving use of the Home Observation for Measurement of the Environment (HOME) inventory, Bradley, Corwyn, and Whiteside-Mansell (1997) found SES differences in the variety and the amount of stimulation available to children of all ages in most countries. For example, scores on the HOME inventory for members of the lower caste systems in India were less than half those typically reported in the United States (Kurtz, Borkowski, and Deshmukh, 1987).

Consistent with findings by Evans et al. (1999) pertaining to parental language input to children, the findings of Bradley and Caldwell (1984) showed that crowding was related to the infant's access to learning materials and to variety in stimulation, even when other family demographic factors were controlled. Likewise, MacKinnon, Brody, and Stoneman (1982) and Bradley, Elardo, Rosenthal, and Friend (1984) found that single-parent households scored lower in stimulation on the HOME inventory than did two-parent households, even with other family demographic factors controlled. Bradley, Caldwell, Rock, Hamrick, and Harris (1988) and Bradley, Corwyn, Caldwell et al. (2000) reported moderate correlations between household crowding and HOME subscale scores related to stimulation for children in middle childhood and adolescence, although they did not control for other demographic factors. They also reported correlations between the same HOME subscale scores and marital status, but the correlations were somewhat weaker.

Among the more interesting findings pertaining to environmental effects on parenting are those stemming from cross-cultural comparisons in which the focus is not so much on cultural belief systems as on geographic differences and differences in access to resources. For example, compared with American parents, Israeli parents are less likely to include children in their recreational hobbies and less likely to spend time teaching their children motor skills, the latter partly owing to the fact that most such skills are learned in the neighborhood from peers. Because of working conditions and religious practices, Israeli children are also less likely to be taken to the theater or shopping (Jacobson et al., 1995). Israeli households tend to be smaller than American households; thus there tends to be fewer material possessions aimed at children present in the home. Dubrow, Jones, Bozoky, and Adam (1996) found that children from Jamaica and St. Vincent Island rarely had access to personal musical instruments nor did they take many trips of greater than 50 miles.

Support

Optimal social–emotional development depends on having an environment that responds to human social and emotional needs (Bretherton and Waters, 1985). Such acts and conditions we call support. Some acts of support are given in anticipation of unexpressed needs; others follow expressed needs. Emotions function to prepare human beings to take action in their own best interest (Grinker et al., 1956). Parents must assist in enlisting and modulating the motivational properties of emotions to help ensure optimal fit with environmental demands.

There is substantial evidence that development is more nearly optimal in an environment that is responsive in the sense that a child's requests for assistance are dealt with in a timely, predictable, and satisfying way (Ainsworth, 1973; Bowlby, 1969; Rotter, Chance, and Phares, 1972). Responsive care supports goal-directed (positively motivated) behavior. There is evidence that optimal emotional development also requires positive affirmation of personal worth. That is, to be supportive, the environment must be reinforcing (in a proactive sense) as well as responsive (in a reactive sense). More recently, Rohner (1986) marshaled evidence from several large cross-cultural studies showing that warm, supportive relationships help promote good adjustment, a sense of well-being, good health, and a wealth of other positive developmental outcomes. Lerner (1984) claims that involvement in sustained, mutually supportive arrangements is one of the five chief factors that facilitate a sense of continuity in a person's development. Finally, a supportive environment is one that provides guidance or direction for adequate functioning in other environments. Hostile, inconsistent parenting leads to socially incompetent behavior such as aggression whereas warm, responsive parenting leads to competence (Pettit, Dodge, and Brown, 1988). There is also evidence that parenting that relies on aversive methods to control children's behavior leads to suboptimal functioning and involvement with antisocial peers (Dishion, Patterson, Stoolmiller, and Skinner, 1991; Power and Chapsieski, 1986).

There is also evidence that children benefit from positive affirmation of worth (Roberts, 1983). That is, to be supportive, parents must be reinforcing (in a proactive sense) as well as responsive (in a reactive sense). How worth is affirmed varies substantially from culture to culture. In some societies worth is closely tied to individual accomplishments or status; in others, it is more strongly tied to collective commitments and involvement. Finally, a supportive environment is one that provides guidance or direction for adequate functioning in other environments. At its base, support is motivational preparation for encountering other environments (e.g., in the sense that a secure attachment allows a child to more freely explore the environment, Ainsworth, 1973).

As is the case with stimulation, there is relatively little documented in terms of how often parents offer various types of support to their children. Relatedly, not much is known with precision regarding how various aspects of the social and physical environment change the rate at which parents provide supportive actions and conditions for their children. Indeed, although much research has been done on particular aspects of support (e.g., maternal responsiveness), less is known about the actual frequency of such acts than is known about the frequency of such things as TV watching, toy availability, and trips to museums or libraries. It is difficult to perform the kind of exhausting documentation of supportive behaviors such as Hart and Risley (1995) accomplished with language input.

There are some data available on parental supportiveness from the NLSY (Bradley, Corwyn, McAdoo, and Garcia Coll, 2001). However, because of the way data were recorded on the HOME short form, these data are more like proxies for the frequency of parental behavior than actual counts of those behaviors. To be specific, data collectors only recorded such things as whether the parent spoke with a child at least twice, not how many times the parent spoke, and only recorded whether the parent ever caressed, kissed, or hugged a child, not how many times each happened during the course of the interview. Even so, the data are revealing. For example, approximately 90% of all parents spoke to their infants at least twice during the hour-long visit and 70% to 80% responded verbally to something the infant said. Approximately 80% to 85% of nonpoor mothers carressed, kissed, or hugged their infants; the figures for poor mothers were approximately 10% to 15% less, with poor African American mothers having the lowest rate (64%). Approximately 25% of African American mothers restricted their infants during the interview whereas only 12% of Asian mothers did (European American and Hispanic American mothers were intermediate). Less than 5% of nonpoor European American, Hispanic American, and Asian American mothers spanked their infants during the interview, compared with almost 9% of African American mothers. The figures for poor mothers in every group was higher (3% to 5%). All the rates of spanking observed during the home visit were relatively low; more than half of the mothers from all ethnic groups reported spanking their children at least once during the previous week. Indeed, approximately 40% of poor European American and poor African American families reported spanking their children at least three times. The figures for Hispanic American and Asian American families were approximately 10% lower. There were notable differences between poor and non-poor families in both European American and African American families but not in Hispanic American families.

The situation for preschool-age children was similar to that observed for infants. Of mothers who were not poor, 90% conversed with their children at least twice during the visit; the figures for poor mothers were approximately 5% to 10% lower. Approximately the same percentages of mothers responded to their children's questions. Approximately 60% of non-poor European American, Hispanic American, and Asian American mothers caressed, kissed, or hugged their children during the hour-long visit; the figures for African American mothers and for all poor mothers were lower (32% to 48%). Fewer than 5% of nonpoor mothers spanked their children during the visit as opposed to approximately 8% of poor mothers. However, between 5% and 10% of nonpoor mothers physically restricted their preschoolers; closer to 10% of poor mothers did. Approximately 60% to 80% of mothers from all ethnic groups admitted spanking their preschoolers during the previous week, but there were notable ethnic and family income differences in the rates. Asian Americans were the least likely to spank, African Americans the most.

Approximately 70% to 75% of nonpoor mothers encouraged their school-age children to talk during the visit (figures were approximately 10% less for poor mothers), and approximately 80% to 90% of nonpoor mothers answered their children's questions (approximately 7% less for poor mothers). Likewise, 80% to 95% of mothers showed generally positive feelings toward the child, with poor mothers lower than nonpoor mothers by 5% to 10%. Parents reported spanking school-age children less than they did preschoolers. Over 60% of European American and Asian American mothers from nonpoor families reported that they had not spanked their children during the past week; for African Americans approximately 50% said they had (the figures for Hispanics were intermediate).

Information on the amount of social and emotional support offered to children ten years of age and older is very sparse. There were no direct observations of these behaviors as part of the NLSY. What information there is comes by means of maternal report. More than 70% of nonpoor European American and Asian American mothers claimed to have expressed affection to their children seven or more times during the past week (in effect, daily). The figures for nonpoor Hispanic Americans and African Americans were 54% and 41%, respectively. In all ethnic groups, there was a substantial family income differential. Approximately 75% of nonpoor European American mothers stated that they had praised their children at least three times during the previous week. The figures were approximately 10% less in the other ethnic groups studied. The figures for poor families also tended to be lower than for nonpoor, most notably among Hispanic Americans.

Direct observations of parent–child interactions were included as part of the study of 10 to 15 year old children by Bradley, Corwyn, Caldwell et al. (2000). During an hour-long home visit, less than 6% of parents (representing five different ethnic groups) made derogatory comments about the adolescent, and almost all (97%) maintained a positive demeanor when speaking to the adolescent. Over 80% of the parents encouraged the adolescent to contribute to the conversation and responded appropriately to the adolescent's comments and questions. Almost 3/4 of the parents spontaneously mentioned a particular strength in the adolescent during the visit. Almost 90% of the parents stated that they allowed the adolescent some privacy while at home and stated that they allowed the adolescent to express disagreements without resorting to a harsh reprisal. Only approximately 25% of the parents said they lost their temper with the adolescent during the previous week. Scores on the acceptance and responsivity subscale of HOME were correlated moderately with both family income and maternal education.

The link between low family income (or low SES) and less nurturant, more hostile interactions between parents and children has been amply documented (Bradley and Whiteside-Mansell, 1997). The stresses connected to low SES and financial hardship have been linked to maternal distress and low self-efficacy which in turn seem to lead to neglectful, insensitive, and even hostile behavior on the part of parents (Brody et al., 1994; Brody, Flor, and Gibson, 1999; Conger et al., 1992; Conger, Patterson, and Ge, 1995; DeGarmo, Forgatch, and Martinez, 1999; McLoyd, 1998) (see the subsection on Poverty for a more complete treatment of this issue).

When appropriate adaptations cannot be made to residential conditions, the impact on parenting is frequently negative. For instance, there is evidence that crowding may increase tensions between family members and may make adults less responsive and less vocally stimulating to children (Wachs, 1992; Wachs and Camli, 1991). Evans and Lepore (1992) posited three major mechanisms that can adversely affect behavior in crowded situations: 1) behavioral constraint (i.e., density interferes with goal attainment and thereby causes frustration), 2) diminished control (i.e., density exposes people to situations over which they have little perceived control, leading to learned helplessness), and 3) overload or arousal (excessive stimulation from density overloads the sensory system). Although the research to support each of these mechanisms is limited in terms of precise applicability to parenting behaviors, the broader literature on stress reactions suggests that high density in the household could lead to both intrusive, hostile actions and to social withdrawal on the part of parents. Supportive of that hypothesis is a study by Bradley and Caldwell (1984). They found that household crowding was related to parental acceptance (lack of restrictiveness and punishment) of infants, even when they controlled for other family demographic factors. Caldwell and Bradley (1984) also reported a negative correlation between crowding and parental warmth for preschool age children, albeit they did not control for other family demographic variables. Likewise, Bradley, Corwyn, Caldwell et al. (2000) found that household crowding was related to parental acceptance and responsivity for teenagers, but they did not control for other demographic factors. In the study of adolescents, there was not a significant relation for African Americans.

MacKinnon et al. (1982) and Bradley et al. (1984) found that single-parent households scored lower in acceptance and responsiveness on the HOME inventory than did two-parent households, even with other family demographic factors controlled. Likewise, Black, Dubowitz, and Starr (1999) found that the presence of a father in the home was correlated with the total HOME inventory score in African American families with 3-year old toddlers, with maternal education and age controlled. Bradley et al. (1988) and Bradley, Corwyn, Caldwell et al. reported that paternal presence was associated with parental responsiveness during both middle childhood and adolescence. Paternal presence was also associated with the use of harsh punishment during middle childhood—again, the researchers did not control for other demographic factors.

There have been relatively few studies, beyond those pertaining to paternal presence or marital status, that examine the relation between family configuration and the quality of parental nurturance. There is anecdotal evidence that the presence of siblings can have effects on what parents do, but only a few studies. In one such study, Harris and Morgan (1991) found that the more brothers girls have, the more attention they get from their fathers. Crnic and Greenberg (1990) found that daily hassles (including dealing with sibling conflicts) contributed to lowered satisfaction with parenting, even though they were not associated with maternal sensitivity and engagement as assessed in a laboratory mother–child interaction paradigm.

Although they did not assess parenting behaviors per se, recent Stoneman, Brody, Churchill, and Winn (1999) suggest that frequent residential moves may undermine parental care. Specifically, they found that frequent moves increased conflict between caregivers and siblings. They specifically identified feelings of social isolation among mothers who moved often, a factor that had previously been associated with parental neglect (Burke, Chandy, Dannerbeck, and Watt, 1998).

Structure

Although children need sustenance, stimulation, and support for optimal growth and development, there is also evidence that the relation between these inputs and either growth or development is not constant. Receiving equal amounts of these inputs does not seem to result in equal amounts of "good" growth and development (Wachs, 2000). The arrangement of inputs may be as crucial to development as amount is. In sum, optimal parenting consists not only of ensuring that sufficient amounts of stimulation, sustenance, and support reach a child but of configuring or structuring a child's encounters with those direct inputs so that "fit" is achieved (Ford and Lerner, 1992). What fits one child's needs may not be suitable at all for another child. A good example may be seen in the differential responsiveness of preterm infants and infants prenatally exposed to drugs. Such biologically vulnerable infants are often overwhelmed by levels of stimulation that are quite comfortable for normal babies (Friedman and Sigman, 1996).

Parenting activities that involve the control and organization of objects, events, policies, and social encounters through time and space are called structure. Examples of areas of child functioning that require substantial parental structuring include learning. There is evidence that the number of objects a person can deal with effectively at any one point in time increases with age during childhood (Kuhn, 1992). Children also have fewer well-developed cognitive strategies for remembering and dealing with information and are therefore more dependent on instructional or other environmental aids to assist them in problem solving (Bjorklund, 1990). Learning is easier in the absence of distracting stimuli (Wohlwill and Heft, 1977). Children's cognitive development is enhanced not only by the type and amounts of stimuli children receive but how parents organize the physical and temporal features of the environment (Bradley and Caldwell, 1976). Particularly revealing are the studies of language development that show that parental "scaffolding" of children's early language experiences (i.e., providing a predictable referential and social context for communicative exchanges) contributes significantly to language acquisition (Bruner, 1983).

Structure within the physical environment can also be helpful. Having distinctive, well situated landmarks can enable children to orient themselves and to move throughout the environment with greater facility (Head, Bradley, and Rock, 1990; Weinstein and David, 1987). A study done among the Ache in Eastern Paraguay showed that parents react to physical hazards by restricting children's locomotion and freedom to explore (Kaplan and Dove, 1987). Crowded conditions in the home often make it difficult for children to organize things for themselves and to make maximum use of persons and objects in the environment. Crowded conditions limit exploration and impede sophisticated play. In the long run, crowding also appears to lead to lower achievement and heightened aggressiveness (Evans et al., 1991). Unfortunately, research shows that parents tend to provide less supervision in crowded homes and may involve themselves less intensively with their children (Bradley and Caldwell, 1984; Wachs, 1992). They are also more apt to send their children out to play (Gove, Hughes, and Galle, 1979). On the other hand, Bradley, Corwyn, Caldwell et al. (2000) found only a marginal correlation between household crowding and family efforts to regulate adolescent behavior. Crowded conditions (most particularly, physical crowding among dwellings) can also have an impact on what parents do to assist their children's needs. In Japan, because most families live in close quarters, there is typically very little space contiguous to the house for children to engage in outdoor play. Thus parents typically have to arrange for children (or permit, in the case of older children) to go to parks, playgrounds, and game halls for recreation.

The importance of structuring the environment can also be seen in terms of its relation to child health. Parental management practices such as the use of car restraints result in fewer injuries (Christerphersen, 1989). In an effort to protect their children from the physical danger and lure of gangs and drugs present in the inner city, parents use a variety of strategies, including keeping children inside the home, walking them to the school bus or school, restricting their children's associations within the neighborhood, and enrolling them in afterschool programs (Halpern, 1992; Hans, Musick, and Jagers, 1988; Jarrett, 1997).

Structure is important for socio-emotional functioning as well. When circumstances are appraised as uncontrollable, anxiety results (Lazarus, 1993). For example, high household density increases the level of state anxiety and leads to maladaptive behavior (Evans et al., 1991). Relatedly, there appears to be heightened emotional reactivity during times of externally imposed change such as changes in daycare arrangements, transitions to school, and residential moves (Coddington, 1972; Rice, 1992). Finally, there is substantial evidence from environmental psychology that physical arrangements in homes, daycare centers, and schools affect both the likelihood that people will engage in certain activities and their comfort in doing so (Moore, 1986).

Unfortunately, there is almost no information on how much time parents spend structuring the environment for their children. Nor is there much information on what kinds of environmental modifications parents make, other than some relatively gross estimates on the amount of time parents allow children to watch TV. Data from the NLSY (Bradley, Corwyn, McAdoo, and Garcia Coll, 2001) indicates that less than 20% of nonpoor European American parents restrict their preschool children to fewer than 3 hr of TV watching per day, the rates being even lower in other ethnic groups and lower for poor than for nonpoor families in all ethnic groups. Data from the National Household Education Survey essentially confirm these figures, granted the data were collected in a somewhat different form.

Beyond the general findings that high-SES parents tend to provide more effective scaffolding for their children's learning (Sigel, 1982) and that poor homes are more often characterized by household disorganization (Bradley and Whiteside-Mansell, 1997), there is not much in the literature pertaining to specific ways that aspects of the social and physical enviroment affect parents efforts to structure the environments of their children.

The quality and resources available in the neighborhood and community affect the kinds of regulatory strategies parents use and, ultimately, children's social competence (O'Neil and Parke, 1997). Parents use different approaches to supervision and impose different rules, depending on what the neighborhood affords. Parents indirectly influence their children's social behavior by serving as an interface between their children and the social institutions available in the community (e.g., clubs, social organizations, religious organizations). With younger children, parents also serve as a facilitator of interactions with peers (Bhavnagari and Parke, 1991). The larger the parent's own friendship network, the more likely they could put their children in contact with potential playmates and friendship networks (Homel, Burns, and Goodnow, 1987; Oliveri and Reiss, 1987).

Surveillance

To be effective in the management of inputs to a system, the regulatory apparatus designed to control the system must monitor both the system and its context. This important regulatory function performed by parents (or their proxies) is called surveillance. It involves "keeping track of" the whereabouts and activities of the child and the child's surrounding circumstances. Most commonly, surveillance has been thought of as keeping track of the child and of environmental conditions to which the child is exposed with the goal of protecting the child from harm (Darling and Steinberg, 1993; Lozoff, 1989; Patterson, DeBarsyshe, and Ramsey, 1989; Peterson, Ewigman, and Kivlahan, 1993; U.S. Department of Health and Human Services, 1991). Garbarino (1988) and Garbarino and Kostelny (in Vol. 5 of this *Handbook*) offer a compelling case that parental failure to provide adequate supervision is responsible for a sizable proportion of children's injuries. There is also evidence that parental monitoring relates to substance abuse, juvenile delinquency, risky sexual behavior, and school achievement for children in middle childhood and adolescence (Brown, Mounts, Lamborn, and Steinberg, 1993; Coombs and Landsverk, 1988; Crouter, MacDermid, McHale, and Perry-Jenkins, 1990; Dishion and McMahon, 1998; Dornbusch, Ritter, Leiderman, Roberts, and Fraleigh, 1987; Loeber and Dishion, 1983; Loeber and Stouthamer-Loeber, 1986; Metzler, Noell, Biglan, Ary, and Smolkowski, 1994; Patterson et al., 1989), albeit, lately researchers have raised questions concerning how parental monitoring actually functions in inhibiting undesirable behavior (Kerr and Stattin, 2000). Moreover, surveillance also includes observations of the child and the environment designed to determine how much the physical and social environment affords the child for productive and enjoyable engagements.

There is very little research on how specific social and physical aspects of the environment affect parental monitoring. The setting, in the classic sense used by Barker (1978), almost certainly has an influence on how and to what extent parents monitor their children. Each setting, because of the particular persons, objects, and activities it contains, exerts different pressures on a parent to maintain visual and/or physical contact with a child, pressures that vary according to the child's age, competence, and proclivities. Closer proximity is required at the state fair or the shopping mall than in the neighborhood park. In chaotic resource-poor settings, such as those in the Brazilian shantytowns described by Scheper-Hughes, monitoring a child can be extraordinarily difficult. Research in the area of injury prevention provides clues as to how parents adjust the amount of monitoring and supervision provided to children to varying environmental conditions. Peterson et al. (1993) asked parents how much time they felt it was appropriate to leave their children alone in different settings both inside and outside the home (e.g., living room, bathroom, yard, driveway, near a street with lots of traffic, near a street with little traffic). Parents recommended that children be supervised most closely in those situations that pose the most imminent dangers and they advocated less supervision as children get older. The study did not assess how closely parents actually monitor children in these various situations, but the findings support the notion that the more hazards present in the environment, the more a parent is likely to closely monitor and supervise children. Furthermore, anecdotes shared by parents indicate that their own level of monitoring inside or outside the home depends on their appraisal of the level of danger and difficulty posed by the setting. Parents living in the barrios of Los Angeles and parents living in housing projects in Philadelphia responded "no" to the following item on the HOME Inventory: "Child has visited a friend by himself/herself during past week." When asked why, the common response was, "It's too dangerous." In the same Philadelphia household, the grandmother sat patiently at the rear window of the apartment watching her two preschool-age grandchildren as they played immediately in back of the apartment during the visit used to collect information for the HOME. Qualitative data reported by Jarrett (1997) on children living in dangerous neighborhoods indicated that parents monitored their children both by keeping their children home more often and by chaperoning their children when they left the home.

Part of what determines how much and what kind of monitoring parents do relates to whether there are others available to keep track of the children. In families in which there other kith and kin to help parents monitor the children, the burden of monitoring particular children is distributed across these networks of adults and older children. There is evidence that the risk of injury is higher in single-parent households (Rivara and Mueller, 1987). Likewise, in stable neighborhoods where families know each other well and there is a high degree of social integration, monitoring is distributed across members of the community. Steinberg, Darling, and Fletcher (1995) have found that social integration benefits only children whose families live in neighborhoods characterized by good parenting. These findings connect to the classic sociological notions of social integration within communities and social capital available to children and families (see Furstenberg and Hughes, 1997, for a discussion of this issue).

Does careful attention to these five parenting tasks promote positive adaptation in children? The most straightforward answer is this: The research is incomplete. However, there is suggestive evidence. For example, Bradley et al. (1994) conducted a study of 243 premature, low-birthweight children living in chronic poverty. The purpose was to determine whether the availability of protective factors in the home environment of children at the age of one year and at the age of three years increased the probability of resiliency. Resiliency was operationalized as being in good to excellent health, being within the normal range for growth, not being below clinically designated cutoffs for maladaptive behavior on the Child Behavior Checklist, and having an IQ of 85 or greater. Six home environment factors were considered potentially protective: 1) low household density, 2) the availability of a safe play area, 3) parental acceptance or lack of punitiveness, 4) parental responsivity, 5) the availability of learning materials, and 6) variety of experiences. The first two would be classified under the sustenance category; the second two under the support category; and the final two under the stimulation category. Of the children with three or more protective factors present in the home, 15% at the age of one year were classified as resilient. By contrast, only 2% of children with two or fewer protective factors were classified as resilient. Similarly, 20% of children with three or more protective factors present in the home at the age three years were classified as resilient, whereas only 6% of children with two or fewer protective factors were resilient (Bradley et al., 1994). Not surprisingly, the structural aspects of the environment (e.g., low density and physical safety) were related to the process elements (e.g., parental responsivity and parental acceptance).

TRANSACTIONS BETWEEN PEOPLE AND THEIR ENVIRONMENTS: THE CONTEXTS OF PARENTING

Most studies of persons and their environments have focused on the environment as a separate entity, a kind of independent variable capable of effecting change within the human organism. Such an approach is not fully consonant with transactional theories of human behavior and development, currently the most widely accepted view of environment–development relations (Ford and Lerner, 1992; Gottlieb, 1991; Johnston, 1987; Sameroff, 1983, 1995; Wachs, 2000). In the transactional view, person and environment constantly define and transform each other over time as aspects of a unitary whole (Lerner, Rothbaum, Boulos, and Castellino, in Vol. 2 of this *Handbook*). Individuals are conceived as being active *in* their environments and goal oriented with respect to their environments.

The transactional view of human development grew out of psychobiological notions concerning adaptation to the environment for purposes of survival. More recent explications of the transactional view make clear that the relation of person and environment is not limited to issues of biological survival (Ford and Lerner, 1992). Human beings are portrayed as selectors of options within the constraints and opportunities afforded by the environment—what Saegert and Winkel (1990) refer to as the opportunity structure model. To this basic notion, Kaplan and Kaplan (1989) added the idea of the restorative and expansive experiences of the environment.

The concept of person/environment transactions moves in the direction of examining the environment in terms of how it is used or constructed by parents and children. Consider the issue of physical safety for purposes of illustrating the transactive entity. One can take account of the actual physical conditions or circumstances of the environment in terms of the risk for harm present. The quantification of this analysis can then be related to some aspect of human behavior or development. However, the person evaluates risk using subjective criteria and may determine not to take action because the environment is perceived to be more dangerous than it is (the parent who keeps a 10-year old child behind locked doors despite the fact that the neighborhood crime rate is not that high) or less dangerous than it is (the parent who allows an adolescent to attend a concert in an area of town with a high-crime rate). These transactions can also be related to various aspects of behavior and development. Holden (1985) has studied how parents take action to reduce accidents through verbally structuring the environment proactively to divert attention from potentially dangerous conditions and to direct children toward activities that match their capacities.

Parents are seen as active agents in the home environment. Parents experience, arrange, and use themselves and other elements within the environment for purposes of achieving different parenting goals (Wapner, 1987). Sometimes their use is proactive (such as when they introduce a toy to a child for the purpose of helping the child learn a new skill), sometimes reactive (such as when they remove a toy from a child when the toy poses a danger to the child). Parents' actions constitute a major part of the child's environment. So do their nonactions. There are times when lack of action on the part of a parent is deliberate (e.g., the parent does not wish to interfere with a child's ongoing play). At other times a lack of action may represent a lack of concern, a lack of awareness, or a lack of capacity (e.g., failure to respond to a child's call for help, not interfering with a child's play because the child is out of sight). In effect, from the standpoint of the child, the environment derives meaning both from what it contains (by way of actions and objects) and from what it lacks.

ENVIRONMENTAL CONDITIONS AND THEIR RELATION TO PARENTING

Human beings appear to be adapted such that they can carry out most of their daily functions in more or less the same way within a broad range of environmental conditions. Within these broad ranges, small modifications, in particular action sequences, are made to suit conditions, but the impetus to act and the character of the action pattern directed toward a particular goal remain largely unaffected. However, there are some aspects of the environment that, if encountered in an extreme range, cause marked changes in attitude and behavior. As stated earlier, intense background noise can be very disturbing and beyond a person's ability to cope effectively (World Health Organization, 1980). Likewise, traumatizing social circumstances (e.g., the Nazi internment camps mentioned at the beginning of this chapter or chronic, serious spousal abuse) can overcome a parent's capacity to parent effectively. There are some aspects of the environment that have something akin to a "dose-response effect" on most people (e.g., the amount of conversation a person is exposed to probably stands in direct proportion to their listening and talking behavior). In effect, most aspects of the surrounding environment appear to have a compelling quality at only extreme levels (e.g., temperature, background noise, war, chronic abuse), whereas others appear to have a compelling quality throughout the range encountered (e.g., the amount of particular activities directed at us by others). This section of the chapter is devoted to an examination of how social, ambient, built, and community environments affect parenting behavior.

Social Conditions

Researchers have long argued that it is easier to provide nurturant and stimulating care for children if the parent has access to social support and is not confronted with aversive social conditions (Bradley and Corwyn, 1999). Both MacKinnon et al. (1982) and Bradley et al. (1984) found that single-parent mothers had lower HOME scores and married mothers, even when they controlled for other relevant demographic characteristics. Coresidence with a grandmother had less consistent effects (Spieker and Bensley, 1994; Unger and Cooley, 1992; Whiteside-Mansell, Pope, and Bradley, 1996). The findings pertaining to coresidence with a grandmother stand somewhat in contrast to the generally positive correlations found between social support and positive parenting (Bradley, Caldwell, Rock, Casey, and Nelson, 1987; Wandersman and Unger, 1983). The discrepancy may indicate that young mothers do not always perceive the help from their own mothers as truly supportive (i.e., without accompanying demands and stresses).

The specific findings pertaining to spousal support are consistent with the more general findings pertaining to social support. That is, spousal support is associated with greater involvement and more nurturant care in both mothers (Cummings, 1994; Olsen, Martin, and Halverson, 1999) and fathers (Bonney, Kelley, and Levant, 1999; Coley and Chase-Lansdale, 1999; NICHD Early Child Care Research Network, 2000). The findings pertaining to social support are also consistent with findings on coparenting relationships. Specifically, Belsky, Putnam, and Crnic (1997) found that unsupportive coparenting was associated with less responsive parenting on the part of both mothers and fathers. Research on paternal alcohol abuse is also consistent with findings on low social support. Specifically, HOME scores were lower among families in which fathers abused alcohol, even when there was careful matching by area of residence (Noll, Zucker, Curtis, and Fitzgerald, 1989).

The presence of siblings in a family can also affect how parents treat a particular child. For example, the strain of dealing with sibling conflict can lead to harsher, more restrictive parenting (Crnic and Greenberg, 1990), albeit mothers and fathers tend to respond differently to squabbles between siblings. Mothers tend to try coaching more than fathers do, whereas fathers tend to directly intervene more often (McHale, Updegraff, Tucker, and Crouter, 2000). Harris and Morgan (1991) even found that fathers give daughters more attention if they also have sons.

The Ambient Environment

Theoretically, a person's attitude about any environment depends on the resources the environment contains, the quality of information the environment affords, and the type of sensory–proprioceptive stimuli resident in the environment (Ford and Lerner, 1992; Kaplan, 1983). Unfortunately, the impact of these ambient surrounding conditions on parenting practices is not well researched. Moreover, because environmental psychology represents an amalgam of largely unrelated disciplines, each with its own research traditions, the field does not offer a fully coherent view of how ambient environmental conditions influence parental behavior (Stokols, 1995). Thus one must look to the broader literature on contextual environmental effects to draw inferences.

Esthetic conditions seem to influence how supportive an environment is perceived to be. For example, Kaplan (1983) found that people judge their housing as friendlier, more supportive, and much more attractive when trees and woods are visible nearby. Vegetation appears to have a psychologically restorative quality to it, fostering both a sense of fascination and the perception of orderliness. By contrast, the degree of residential density, crowding within residences, and deterioration of property has been linked to fear of crime on the part of adults living in the neighborhood (Taylor and Brower, 1987). This fear leads to restricted outdoor activity and avoidance of certain areas (Gates and Rohe, 1987; Kail and Kleinman, 1985); it also leads to handgun ownership (Hassinger, 1985). The physical decay and "incivilities" in a community (e.g., graffiti, vandalism, and dilapidated buildings) move residents to either become more active in neighborhood associations or to leave the neighborhood in search of safer, friendlier surroundings (Stokols, 1995). Anecdotal accounts suggest that these esthetic conditions affect the kinds of stimulating out-of-residence experiences offered children, the kinds of structuring of children's activities provided, and the level and type of surveillance afforded.

Wachs (1989) contends that there is a cluster of environmental conditions, including high noise levels, high density living conditions, lack of physical and temporal structure in the home, and unpredictable changes in the family environment that lead to maladaptive behavior on the part of both parent and child. He lumps these conditions under the heading of environmental chaos. According to Wachs (2000), these chaotic conditions tend to increase both individual distractibility and family conflict. Ackerman, Kogos, Youngstrom, Schoff, and Izard (1999) reported that family instability led to increased conflict among family members and parents' negative emotionality.

Direct and indirect effects. It seems likely that the ambient environment affects parenting behavior both directly and indirectly. Because ambient conditions affect the parent's own stress level, they probably directly affect parental actions aimed at providing emotional support to children as well. Ambient stressors tend to be chronic and intractable environmental conditions that, although not urgent, are negatively valued and place adaptive demands on people (Lazarus, 1981). When parental coping fails, that parent may develop more pervasive feelings of helplessness and a generalized tendency to give up in the face of obstacles (Cohen, Evans, Stokols, and Krantz, 1986). According to Evans et al. (1991), aversive ambient circumstances can produce a general malaise that includes allergic reactions, fatigue, and lethargy. Unfortunately, it can also lead to child maltreatment (Garbarino and Kostelny, 1992).

The surrounding environment affects parenting indirectly by its influence on the child and other members of the household. For example, loud background noises may disturb a child in many ways, causing parents to provide some type of "stimulus shelter." Very cold temperatures or dangerous neighborhood surroundings may make children resist going outside to play, causing changes in caregiving behavior.

Climate. Wheeler (1993) speculated that bipedal locomotion conferred a distinct advantage on early hominids as they began to exploit the more open, drier habitats of the African savannah some 5 to 7 million years ago. He concluded that "bipedalism significantly decreased early hominids' dependence on shade, allowing them to forage in the open for longer periods and at higher temperatures. Bipedalism also greatly reduced the amount of drinking water they needed for evaporative cooling through sweating" (p. 66). The accuracy of Wheeler's analysis notwithstanding, the care with which the calculations were done makes clear the belief of anthropologists and biologists concerning the effect of climatic conditions on behavior. The effect of climate on parenting practices has been investigated to only a limited degree. Whiting (1981) demonstrated that climate, apart from cultural history, constrains infantcare practices in Europe, Africa, and Asia. The temperature of the coldest month of the year was the most important factor in determining whether infants were carried in cradles versus a sling or shawl. These carrying practices also affected mother–infant contact and parenting behaviors. For example, Tronick, Thomas, and Daltabuit (1994) observed that the practice of tightly swaddling infants in high-altitude cold climates, while acting to maintain body warmth and to conserve calories, also resulted in restricting the infant's motor activity and the mother's provision of stimulation. Not surprisingly, there is also evidence for seasonal variations in the onset of motor milestones in those regions where there are distinct seasonal changes in temperature. Hayashi (1990) found a consistent periodic relation between mean monthly temperature in Osaka and the onset of rolling, creeping, grasping a foot, and grasping a toy. Relatedly, Benson (1993) found that if the window of locomotor onset occurs during winter, experiential factors associated with the winter may limit opportunities for mobility, including heavier clothing that restricts movement, fewer daylight hours for outdoor play, and restriction to a smaller play area inside the house.

As children get older, they are often allowed greater autonomy in keeping with their increased competence. Accordingly, out-of-home activities increase. Climatic conditions directly affect the amount and the type of parental monitoring and involvement with children (seasonal variations, mean annual rainfall, mean temperature). Employment and schooling patterns are also connected to seasonal and climatic conditions. Crouter and McHale (1993) found that seasonal variations in employment patterns, for example, related to parent–child involvement, parental monitoring, and children's involvement in activities.

Whiting (1981, p. 155) postulated that "(1) Features in the history of any society and in the natural environment in which it is situated influence . . . (2) the customary methods by which infants (and children) are cared for in that society, which have . . . (3) enduring psychological and physiological effects on the members of that society, which are manifested in . . . (4) the cultural projective–expressive systems of the society and the physiques of its members." In a survival culture such as the Embus of Kenya, for example, the focus of infantcare is on protecting the child from harm rather than on development of competencies such as language; therefore, the infant is usually carried on the parent's back and is rarely spoken to (Sigman et al., 1988).

The Built Environment

Human beings respond not only to their general surroundings but also to the specific places they inhabit. The elements of physical settings may influence behavior directly by facilitating certain activities and obstructing others (Weinstein and David, 1987). What parents tend to do with their children (from play arrangements to sleeping arrangements to the use of control techniques) is partly determined by the physical features of the residence (i.e., size, number of rooms, proximity of certain spaces to others, acoustical properties). For example, in Kenya, among the Embu community, children spend very little time inside their homes, which are situated such that they open onto communal areas. When children become mobile, they join other children from the community outside to play or to perform chores. As a result, children do not tend to be in close proximity to their parents; thus they are not very likely to engage in verbal exchanges with adults. By contrast, Egyptian homes tend to be quite small; and they are not arranged so that they open onto communal areas. Toddlers spend most of their time within the residence or immediately outside it. Because of their close proximity to adult family members, Egytian toddlers tend to have their verbalizations responded to with high frequency (Wachs et al., 1992).

Physical settings communicate symbolic messages about the intentions and values of the adults who control the settings. There is evidence that children's bedrooms and playrooms reflect gender biases and that boys and girls respond differently to these environments (Rheingold and Cook, 1975). A number of child development specialists and residential designers have provided guidelines about how residences can be adapted to meet the needs of children, such as placing fixtures at appropriate heights, scaling down the size of tables and counters, providing accessible storage areas, and the like (Johnson, 1987). There are also recommendations on how to organize spatially well-defined areas so as to encourage task engagement and exploration (Weinstein and David, 1987). For example, Golbeck (1985) found that rooms with clear landmarks and boundaries make it easier for children to plan and carry out goal-directed activities. Berenson (1967) found that placing a mirror near the bed of emotionally disturbed girls resulted in increased efforts to maintain a good appearance and promoted more positive behavior. Such adaptations affect not only the child's attitude and actions but the parent's as well. For example, if the house is arranged so that children's play areas are near the center of the home, near where adults tend to be present while at home, adults tend to provide closer supervision and more involvement (Johnson, 1987). From her survey of 25 homes considered to have excellent physical environments for young children and from the literature on child development, Johnson (1987) provided the following design guidelines for residential dwellings: (1) play areas should be near the main living areas of the home; (2) create a series of small activity pockets that encourage a variety of different types of play activities; (3) store equipment and materials so that children have easy access; (4) attempt to scale and position fixtures, shelves, racks, and coat hooks so that they are usable by children; (5) establish closed or semiclosed spaces where children and retreat and rest from social activity; (6) establish sufficient open space for construction and large motor activities; (7) construct an "indoor" gymnasium; and (8) establish outdoor play spaces and equipment that can accommodate a variety of play activities.

Ecosystem models postulate a measure of equilibrium between the inhabitants of a building and the form of the building. Human beings adapt their buildings to their behavioral needs or functional requirements. The Efe foragers of Zaire live in small camps where they typically arrange their huts in a semicircle around the camp's perimeter, creating a communal space in which most day-to-day in-camp activities occur. This allows for young children to be cared for by many different members of the community and for mothers and fathers to go about their daily foraging tasks with relative ease (Tronick, Morelli, and Ivey, 1992).

When a building or arrangement of buildings ceases to accommodate behavioral requirements, people seek to correct the problem through construction, renovation, or moving to a different building. Conversely, people also change their behavior to fit the physical environment, especially when it presents limitations. It seems clear that adults, in their roles as parents, make numerous adjustments in the home environment to accommodate the needs of children: from preparing a nursery to "baby-proofing" the household, from acquiring child-size furniture to rearranging the furnishings and decorations of a child's room, from constructing outdoor play areas to acquiring play materials, from ensuring accessibility to household items to ensuring privacy (Weinstein and David, 1987). Adjustments are made in the physical features of the home and in the rules that govern social interactions. In the case of privacy, for example, it appears that families more often ensure it through rules than through direct manipulation of the physical environment (Altman, 1977). Some adjustments are made for the convenience of household members, others to accomplish developmental goals parents have for children. In almost all cases, however, they are designed to change the behavior of either parent or child. Wachs (1988) found that parents made more objects available to children with high activity levels so as to keep them occupied. Although the adjustments made to household arrangements, regulations, and furnishings are designed to have a particular effect on behavior, there has been little research on whether such effects typically emerge. In a small study on toys, Quitlitch and Risley (1973) found that pickup sticks and checkers facilitate cooperation, whereas clay and gyroscopes facilitate isolated play. There have also been studies suggesting that boys are provided objects that direct them away from home whereas girls are provided objects that direct them toward home (Weinstein and David, 1987).

The Community and Material Environment: Access to Resources

Bronfenbrenner (1979, 1999) offers compelling arguments that what goes on in the family environment is affected by the community context in which the family resides. Neighborhood and community contexts afford families a variety of resources that they can use to provide opportunities for learning and pleasure. Brooks-Gunn, Duncan, and Aber (1997) present substantial evidence regarding the lack of resources available in many poor neighborhoods and the implications that has for family functioning and child well-being. Changing technologies, changing patterns of employment, and governmental efforts to increase leisure and cultural opportunities have led to major changes in the ways family members spend time that is not committed to work, to routine family maintenance functions, or to education (Roberts, 1983; Veal, 1987). The U.S. Bureau of the Census estimated that, in 1997, 39% of all women over the age of 7 years in the United States spent some of their leisure time in exercise walking (24% of men), 25% of women and 24% of men went swimming, 21% of men and 16% of women went bicycle riding, 21% of men and 17% of women went camping, 23% of men and 10% of women went fishing, 4% of men and 3% of women went skiing, and 10% of women and 14% of men went boating (U.S. Department of Commerce, 1999). These figures (and others like them), albeit highly aggregated, provide some clues concerning how parents spend their leisure time, including time spent with children in using home and community resources. Given that even higher percentages of children ages 7 to 17 years took part in activities such as camping, swimming, and boating than was the case with adults, the availability of outdoor recreational facilities would appear to induce parents to afford such experiences to their children.

Although the statistics from the U.S. Bureau of the Census include children over the age of 7 years, the actual participation rates of children in the various activities is hard to estimate. The statistics also do not make clear the extent to which parents and children participate together in these activities. The most useful data come from recent surveys conducted by the National Center for Educational Statistics (1992). Approximately one third of children 3 to 5 years of age are involved in arts and crafts activities with family members at least three times a week; the percentage drops to 17% by the age 8 years. Over half of the children 3 to 5 years of age are involved in games or sports three or more times a week, with approximately 40% to 45% of children at the ages 6 to 8 years. Slightly over half the children not enrolled in nursery school or kindergarten watch educational TV with family members at least three times a week. However, once children enter kindergarten the percentage drops dramatically, with only 19% of third graders reported as watching educational TV with family members at least three times a week.

Access to a TV and to other types of communication equipment changes the behavior of both parents and children. However, it is not clear precisely what other activities TV and video watching replace or under what conditions they replace them (Huston, Wright, Marquis, and Green, 1999). What is clear is that there are both developmental trends and gender differences in the habits of children pertaining to TV.

Another way of estimating the scope and pattern of leisure pursuits is to track the amount of money spent on various activities and materials used for leisure and to track attendance figures for various recreational and cultural activities. The U.S. Bureau of the Census estimated that 57,800,000 people attended baseball games in 1997; 17,800,000 attended football games; and 12,300,000 attended hockey games. There were 275.3 million visits made to national parks, monuments, historical and archeological sites, and other national recreational areas. The National Association of State Park Directors estimated that on an average day 736,897 people visited a state park or recreational area. Total recreational expenditures (based on 1987 constant dollars) rose from $91.3 billion in 1970 to $257.3 billion in 1990, which represents an increase from 5% to 8% of total consumption. In 1996 the amounts included $23.2 billion for books and maps, $26.5 billion for magazines, newspapers, and sheet music, $38.1 billion for nondurable toys and sports supplies, $45.4 billion for wheel goods, sports, and photographic equipment, $89.7 billion for video and audio products, computer equipment, and musical instruments, $22.1 billion for spectator amusements such as movies, theaters, and spectator sports, and $46.2 billion for commercial participant amusements like dancing, golf, bowling, skating, sightseeing buses, casino gambling, and billiard parlors (U.S. Department of Commerce, 1999). Children are estimated to influence purchases of approximately $200 billion annually, especially in areas such as (1) snacks, toys, and hobby supplies; (2) items for the home such as furniture and stereos; and (3) items for the family such as vacations and recreation (McNeal, 1992). Again, unfortunately, such aggregated statistics provide only suggestive evidence regarding the ways children spend their recreational time and how parents avail themselves of community and material opportunities on behalf of their children. In addition, there are only a few categories of participation and expenditure that specifically refer to children (e.g., boys' club memberships, number of sporting goods purchased for persons less than 14 years of age, number of "juvenile" books sold).

After reviewing the literature on leisure activities in America, Holman and Epperson (1984, p. 278) concluded that "With the possible exception of adolescents . . . and young, unmarried adults . . . the family is the center of most people's leisure activities." The nature and placement of many of the activities included in the British study suggests that children are likely participants. There is also evidence that family decisions regarding where to go on vacation, whom to visit, and what to buy are influenced by the characteristics of children within the family (Crompton, 1981; Gelfand,

1992; Howard and Madrigal, 1990; McNeal, 1992). However, there remains little information on (1) children's actual levels of participation in most particular activities, (2) the parent's role in determining which activities children engage in, and (3) the amount of involvement of parents with their children in these activities.

Relatively little is known about parents' actual use of community cultural and recreational services such as libraries, museums, playgrounds, youth clubs, and parks (see the subsection on Stimluation for some limited summary figures). According to Roberts (1983), educational and youth services facilities do not play a prominent role in the lives of children in middle childhood and adolescence. Moreover, the generally low levels of use of museums and other cultural facilities makes it clear that they are not routinely used by parents for the benefit of their children (U.S. Department of Commerce, 1999). Research indicates that some cultural institutions such as libraries and museums are actively involved in trying to get parents to participate along with their children (Cammack, 1993; Monsour, 1993; Russell, 1991; Sonderquist, 1991). However, neighborhoods and communities offer vastly different recreational and cultural opportunities for families (Roberts, 1983), with poor and rural communities typically offering less by way of major cultural and recreational facilities.

What does seem clear is this: (1) Parents adjust their own leisure time pursuits to incorporate their children (Horna, 1989); (2) mothers play the dominant role in decisions concerning young children's participation in various out-of-home activities (Howard and Madrigal, 1990); (3) father-headed families have more active recreational pursuits than do mother-headed families (Murphy, Alpert, Christman, and Wiley, 1988); (4) parents' sports participation decreases as the number of their children increases (Horna, 1989); (5) parents with young children spend more time in sedentary activities at home (Horna, 1989); (6) dual-career families read more to their children and take them more often to special events, whereas traditional families spend more time just playing with their young children (United Media Enterprises, 1982); and (7) children tend to mimic the reading and TV watching behaviors and attitudes of their parents (Dorr et al., in Vol. 5 of this *Handbook*; Neuman, 1986).

There are notable cultural, SES, regional, and national differences in the rates and types of partici-pation in various out-of-home recreational and cultural activities for family members (Hendry, 1979; Hutchinson, 1987, 1988; Roberts, 1983). In a study of how African-Americans, Caucasians, and Hispanic-Americans used Chicago's public parks, for example, Hutchinson (1987) found significant differences not only in the types of activity, but also in the age, gender, size, and social composi-tion of activity groups. Hutchinson (1988, p. 24) concluded that "leisure and recreation behavior among Hispanics is structured so as to preserve the particular characteristics of their neighborhood and family system, while black and white activities emphasize the individual. Public recreation facilities occupy a special position in the Hispanic community, and appear much less important to the activities of whites and blacks." He also argued that Black–White differences in the use of recreational facilities tend to be minimal once SES is taken into consideration. Most of the differ-ences appear attributable to differential access to recreation resources (Garcia Coll et al., in Vol. 4 of this *Handbook*). However, Asian Americans tend to use certain recreational facilities (e.g., ball parks) less often than other ethnic groups even when such facilities are available, partly owing to a belief that there are more long-term opportunities in other areas (Bradley, Corwyn, Caldwell et al., 2000; Leong, Chao, and Hardin, 2000). Although there is evidence for mean differences in the use of community services among various cultural and community groups, there is also evidence that families within each cultural group vary considerably in both their capacity and inclination to avail themselves of community resources (Garcia Coll, in Vol. 4 of this *Handbook*; Leong et al., 2000; Murphy et al., 1988; United Media Enterprises, 1982).

Toys. What goes on in the family environment is also affected by the materials available within the home for recreation and learning (Bradley and Tedesco, 1982; Wachs and Gruen, 1982). In the past century, toys have become a major contributor to child learning and acculturation (Gottfried and Brown, 1986; Sutton-Smith, 1985). The amount of money spent on toys, audio–visual and computer equipment, musical equipment, and sports equipment has tripled (even as calculated in constant dollars) since 1970 (U.S. Department of Commerce, 1999). Children are becoming knowledgeable shoppers and are having a major impact on parent's purchasing decisions (McNeal, 1992; Toor, 1992; Zimmerman, 1992).

It is reasonably clear how much parents are spending on the purchase of toys, equipment, and other learning and educational materials for children—albeit, that does not fully equate with the child's actual access to such materials. Some of the mechanisms whereby toys and other materials contribute to development are also becoming better understood (Bradley, 1985; Gottfried and Brown, 1986; Wachs and Gruen, 1982). However, much remains unclear regarding how parents make available and use these materials with children beyond the fact that there appear to be social class, gender, and cultural differences in their use (Grusec and Lytton, 1988). This is an exceedingly important area for future research because children spend so much of their time with toys and equipment while in the home (Sutton-Smith, 1985) and because the types of toys and equipment (and presumably the child's involvement with them) is evolving rapidly (Gelfand, 1992).

COMPLEXITIES AND LIMITATIONS IN STUDIES OF PARENTING AND THE ENVIRONMENT

The idea of person–environment fit has long been a staple in ecological–developmental psychology (Ford and Lerner, 1992; Wachs, 2000). Fit pertains to environmental requirements and child needs and capabilities. The concept of fit has broader meaning too as applied to the parenting environment. Parents function as providers and arrangers of children's experiences and as mediators of those experiences for the child. A parent may also have to operate as a moderator of experiences coming from other family members, the community, and society at large. It is a commanding agendum. Because the process of parenting is complex, researching the process is difficult. This section is devoted to addressing some additional issues that complicate our understanding of the environment and its relation to parenting.

Direct and Indirect Environmental Effects

Understanding the relation of parenting to the environment is complicated because the environment tends to have both direct and indirect effects on parents as members of a family system. Some aspects of the environment can directly affect parenting whereas others affect parenting indirectly by first affecting the child. A good example of an indirect effect is when a child is bullied or victimized by peers (Crick and Grotpeter, 1995, 1996). Once a parent finds out about the victimization, there are likely to be efforts to deal with the emotional upheaval (support), to provide information on how to combat the victimization (stimulation), and to offer some type of protection (sustenance). When a child changes in reaction to the environment (e.g., starts running in the direction of an exciting event), the parent's behavior changes in reaction to the child's actions (e.g., running after the child to ensure the child's safety or enjoyment or to increase the amount of monitoring or instruction). Encountering incessant loud noises (a street jackhammer) may cause the parent to wince and become irritable toward the child (a direct effect) while at the same time it requires the parent to comfort and protect the startled and frightened child (an indirect effect).

Interactions Among Environmental Factors

People do not experience their environments as isolated elements. Any one event or circumstance is experienced in the context of other objects, situations, and happenings both in time and across time. The "effect" of one element on parent or child behavior is likely to be conditioned by the presence and pattern of the other elements in the contemporaneous surround and in one's personal history of experiences. It is rare, however, that studies have examined the moderating effect of one aspect of the environment on others. For example, there is a literature that indicates that children's cognitive–motivational behavior is enhanced by the availability of toys and learning materials (Gottfried, 1990). There is also a literature that speaks to the value of parental structuring in learning situations (Feuerstein, 1979). However, there is very little information on what happens when appropriate structure is provided in the context of lots of learning materials versus when the materials are available but little structure is provided. In one such study, Parks and Bradley (1991) found that the effect of toys on infant's development depended on the level of parental involvement with the child. Having lots of toys provided children a developmental advantage; so did having parents who were actively involved in encouraging developmental advances. However, children who had both lots of toys and actively involved parents accrued a developmental advantage that was greater than the sum of the two experiences.

Difficulties in Estimating Specific Environmental Effects

It may be difficult to estimate the impact of a particular environmental factor on parenting (or on children's development) because there is a high degree of co-occurence among certain environmental events and circumstances. Some sets of co-occurences reflect a more general set of ecological circumstances such as poverty (high crime, more single-parent families, more household crowding, greater likelihood of exposure to environmental toxins) or area of residence (isolation from neighbors, lack of access to culturally enriching events and facilities, more frequent encounters with "nature"). Few researchers have examined specific aspects of the environment as part of a compound. Thus the importance of some environmental factors has been overestimated. By the same token, research on broader aspects of the family ecology (e.g., poverty) has also not always recognized that the "effect" of poverty is not simply a function of not having money. Poverty represents an amalgam of environmental conditions (e.g., families lack productive employment, find it harder to stay together, live more often in crowded unsafe conditions, lack access to good health care, educational facilities and cultural events, and are subject to greater stresses). Being in poverty may also reflect a parent's characteristics and behaviors as well as it produces them (Bradley and Whiteside-Mansell, 1997).

A related problem in predicting the effects of environnmental conditions is that the effect of some conditions may tend not to occur until a parent has accumulated substantial experience with the condition. To date there is little research on the cumulative effects for most physical and social circumstances—the research on chronic noise, continuous crowding, and persistent poverty being among the few exceptions.

Among the most difficult features of environment–behavior relations to predict are those involving conditions of disturbance, catastrophe, or chaos. Such relations tend not to be linear—indeed, they may quite irregular; and outcomes may seem well out of proportion to the precipitating event (Little, 1999). One of the principles of dynamic systems theory is that minor adjustments in one component of a system can result in major shifts in a second (Prigogine and Stengers, 1984). For example, a single incident of harrassment at a playground or ball field may induce a formerly active mother to quit involving her children in organized sports activities altogether.

Another reason it is hard to estimate the impact of particular features of the environment on people because not all people respond the same to environmental circumstances in the same way. The issue of person–environment interaction has been treated extensively with regard to the impact of the environment on children's development (Wachs and Plomin, 1992). Rutter and Pickles (1992) argued that person–environment interactions are quite commonplace; but relatively few have been verified, perhaps because it requires extreme 'environmental circumstances to change the developmental course for most individuals (McCall, 1992). It may also be that the designs and analytic procedures used to detect interactions are weak (Cronbach, 1992) or that we may be insensitive to the many forms that an interaction may take (Rutter and Pickles, 1992). As an illustration of the latter, consider the work of Magnusson (1988), where discusses dynamic interaction models of behavior in which person mediating variables, person reaction variables, and situations are all considered simultaneously. Magnusson also discusses the differences between within-situation (in which individual behavior is constantly being influenced by ongoing situation cues) interactions and between-situation interactions (in which the individual moves from situation to situation and reacts to each).

Additionally, it may be difficult to accurately estimate environmental effects because of what Wachs (1992, 2000) terms person–environment covariation. Covariation refers to the process whereby persons with different characteristics either actively of passively elicit different types of experiences from their environments (e.g., brighter children often receive more instructional opportunities, more attentive parents receive more positive feedback from their children). Scarr and McCartney (1983) discuss how children tend to produce their own environments and how the nature of those influences on the environment tends to change with age.

Finally, and perhaps most fundamentally, it may be difficult to accurately estimate environmental effects because humans are conscious actors in their own lives (Lewis, 1997). As Wallenius (1999) has argued, "No goals or environmental settings are isolated units in a person's life. The psychological significance of situations and settings depends on their relationships to the individual's overall life situation and plans (p. 132)." Parenting goals are enormously diverse. Therefore what is quite disruptive to one parent's plans may be of little moment to another parent, if that second parent does not share the same goals. Transactional theories make clear the reciprocal, bidirectional nature of person–environment relations (Stokols, 1995). If the environment does not fit a parent's plans, then that parent may formulate a new plan that includes making the environment more amenable to the realization of the parent's goals.

The Hidden Door

In the classic C. S. Lewis (1994) book *The Lion, the Witch, and the Wardrobe*, children find their way into the magic land of Narnia behind a secret door at the back of a wardrobe. Although the world of Narnia is a fantasy world, Lewis' tale reminds us that children always bring with them a universe, part fantasy, part reality, that parents must confront. Part of the world that children bring with them is benign, even amusing; that part exerts very little force on parental action. However, other parts can be quite challenging; and those parts call upon parents to act so as to ensure the well-being of the child (Masten and Coatsworth, 1998). Part of the social and physical environment that children bring with them to the table of family action is shared with other family members (such as the conditions of poverty and household crowding discussed earlier in this chapter). Part is unique to the child and comes to parents only indirectly. Developmental research is only beginning to treat how parents respond the majority of opportunities and adversities children face in their daily lives.

For a few of the major environmental challenges children face, a literature on how parents need to respond to children's needs is emerging. Consider, just for starters, one of the more dramatic, war trauma. Although children's reactions to the experience of war vary as functions of age, the specific nature of their exposures, and the reactions of adults around them, children frequently display symptoms that fall under the label of posttraumatic stress disorder. Relatively little is known about efficacious treatments for posttraumatic stress disorder, but therapeutic interventions aimed at dealing with stress reactions, assistance with grieving, and encouragement to maintain planful behavior have been recommended (Macksoud and Aber, 1996). Although one could reasonably assume that parents would attempt to be nurturant and protective under such adverse conditions, there are no data on what mothers and fathers actually do. Bearing in mind that the parents themselves are being exposed simultaneously to the devasting conditions of war, it seems likely that they too will suffer severe stress, undermining their ability to respond optimally to their children's needs.

Although the milieu of violence that pervades some urban communities has occasionally been dubbed "a war zone" (Garbarino, 1999), children in the United States and most affluent nations do not face actual conditions of war. A far more commonplace difficulty for children to deal with is marital conflict. Davies and Cummings (1998) offer a functionalist perspective on emotion regulation as it relates to spousal conflict and child adjustment. They hypothesize that greater interparental conflict elicits heightened emotional reactivity in children and suggest that parents could help children deal with such reactions by calming the child, having the child witness warmth and conflict resolution, plus minimizing actual exposures to conflict. Johnson and Lieberman (1999) point to the value of parents becoming "emotion coaches" for their children under such circumstances, helping them to deal with feelings of anger, resentment, and loss of control. Sadly, there is evidence that some parents attempt to forge an alliance with their children against the other parent, which only exaccerbates the child's difficulties with emotion regulation. Shifflett and Cummings (1996) describe a program designed to educate parents with regard to how they should deal with divorce and parental conflict. It describes what parents should and should not do in front of their children (e.g., avoid criticizing the other parent in front of the child). Unfortunately, the literature on divorce suggests that parents may well not tend to respond in the ways considered most beneficial to children's well-being. Indeed, children of divorce often describe their families as emotionally distant and disorganized (Holdnack, 1992). In general it seems that whenever circumstances put parents themselves under stress and erodes their support, there is a tendency for the parent to become emotionally distant, disorganized, and neglectful; illustrative examples are responses to spousal death (the death of the other parent) (Saler and Skolnick, 1992) and to spousal suicide (Cerel, Fristad, Weller, and Weller, 2000).

Quite different from dealing with confict within the home is dealing with conflict and victimization from outside the home. In the latter case, parents are not dealing simultaneously with their own grief and trauma—but they may also be less aware of what their children are actually experiencing. Crick and Grotpeter (1995, 1996) and Crick, Casas, and Ku (1999) have explored the prevalence and consequences of both relational and physical victimization by peers. According to research by Coie and Dodge (1998), the incidence of peer victimization tends to be quite high during early and middle childhood and there is evidence that the same children tend to be victims for extended periods of time. Such a situation points to the need for parental monitoring, emotional support, and perhaps instruction in how to develop needed social skills. However, there is little information on what parents tend to do or even how often they are aware of their child's treatment by peers.

The variety of challenging events that children face (and that parents have to deal with) are legion: from dramatic and potentially devasting events, like school shootings, to relatively mundane but not necessarily inconsequential events, like not getting chosen for the ball team or the cheer leading squad. Little is known about the number of such incidences children typically face or how parents respond to them. Likewise, even for rather commonplace ongoing circumstances, like the threat of drugs or violent games and music, little is known about what parents actually do. Indeed, there tends to be disagreement between parents and children regarding parental actions. Most parents state that they monitor what their children watch on TV and listen to on the stereo. They also state that they talk with their children about drugs and alcohol. However, children report far less parental attention to these issues than do parents (Global Strategy Group, 2000). Thus parents react to both particular environmental events and general social circumstances that involve their children, but precisely what they do and how it affects their children's well-being is largely undetermined.

From anecdote we know that parents continually respond to the particular environmental challenges and opportunities their children face: from the requirement to take naps at kindergarten to the chance to run for third-grade hall monitor to the opportunity afforded by an appointment to Annapolis. The value of carefully examining parental responses to significant environmental challenges and opportunities faced by children—and ultimately the effect of those responses on child well-being—may be less obvious than seems true at first glance. Parents who tend to be thoughtful, sensitive, and organized in their treatment of children's ordinary needs and the ordinary events of the day are likely to bring those same talents and dispositions to bear on environmental challenges as well. However, the study of stressful life events shows that significant challenges have the power to induce emotion disregulation and its accompanying exaggerated (sometimes maladaptive) responses (in both parent and child). Within the confines of intimate family relationships, such events and their emotional aftermath can lead to a kind of spiraling escalation of behavior of the kind described by dynamic systems theorists as turbulence (Prigogine and Stengers, 1984). Small events induce rapid, sometimes unpredictable, changes in behavior—rather like the spewing and churning of water as it moves from a broad placid streambed through a narrow mountain gorge. Turbulent actions and reactions of the kind described by dynamic systems theorists are probably less rare than is generally recognized—at least that is what anecdotal evidence from rather commonplace occurrences would suggest. Illustrative of such turbulent encounters are the differences one might see in the exchanges between parent and child during the normal course of nightly homework versus the exchanges one might see when the homework assignment is perceived as overwhelming or too frought with significance (a big test); likewise the difference between mundane parent–child discussions related to the child's peers and the discussions that may occur moments or hours after a child has been beaten up by the neighborhood gang or has experienced a serious betrayal of friendship. In sum, we don't know much about how parents tend to manage the five tasks of parenting described earlier in this chapter as they pertain to these myriad, sometimes very potent, environmental circumstances. Those aspects of parenting largely remain behind a hidden door.

CONCLUSIONS

Understanding the effects of the environment on parenting and on children's development is difficult because of the multiplicity of influences on environmental action and the complexity of environmental action itself. Wachs (2000) has argued that none of the current theories offer a sufficient explanation for parental actions or their effects on children's development. Likewise, Little (1999) has argued that one of the primary problems facing ecological theorists is how to address both natural and social phenomena within a single explanatory framework. Garling (1998) goes a step further and argues that there is as yet no consensus on how the environment should even be conceptualized. Nonetheless, it appears that the objects and the materials available to parents in their place of residence, conditions present in the area surrounding the place of residence, and other facilities in the nearby community play an integral role in how parents parent.

Parents not only use what is in the environment to assist them in parenting; but they respond personally to the physical features and organizational arrangements of the home and to the objects and materials available in the neighborhood and more distant geographic areas. Importantly, parents react to the opportunities and adversities that their children encounter both at home and away. These aspects of the environment affect parenting directly; and they affect parenting indirectly through their impact on the child's behavior. Most parents seem able to adapt to what the environment affords by way of opportunities and constraints; thus they carry out the routines of parenting more or less unabated. However, as environmental conditions become extreme, parental behavior tends to become more constrained or irregular and unpredictable. It may not follow an adaptive path. A maladaptive response to environmental conditions is particularly likely if parents face a "pileup" of adverse environmental conditions. Research on risk factors has amply demonstrated that as the number of risk conditions increases, the likelihood of a bad develomental outcome for children increases in kind (Sameroff, 1995). The exact same analysis has not been applied to parental actions, but the linkage is likely the same. Fortunately, if most aspects of the parenting environment are supportive of adaptive parenting, the presence of a single negative condition may well be buffered. In general, if the environment does not afford parents what they need to carry out the parenting role as they see it, most parents will attempt to adapt their surroundings or attempt to acquire needed materials so that there is a better fit between the goals they have in their roles as parents and what the environment affords.

Parents use the environment to help regulate the behavior and development of children. They use it to provide sustenance, stimulation, and emotional support to children. They also use the environment to help structure the child's experiences and they monitor both child and environment to ensure optimal fit between what the environment affords the child and what the child needs. Unfortunately, too little is known about how the environment is actually used to carry out these basic regulatory functions and too little is known about how the environment can be used to help facilitate children's development (Miller, Shim, and Holden, 1998). Most of the information available on how the environment is used is either of a highly aggregated nature or is limited to a single point in time on a very narrow sample—there are, of course, some notable exceptions. The available research paints the picture of parenting in broad strokes. It suggests that the physical and social environment affects parents in terms of what it affords them by way of opportunities and structures for constructive parental actions, what it demands from them in order to function adaptively as parents, and how much it depletes them in terms of time, resources (both energy and material), and the motivation for productive engagement with their children and the environment at large. Most of the details about these processes and their consequences remain to be determined.

Finally, there continues to be something of a bias in the child development literature with most of the attention devoted to the social environments of children, despite the fact that children tend to spend substantial amounts of time in exchanges with nonanimate aspects of their surroundings (Wachs, 1989). The pattern of these experiences and how they relate to children and parents remains a critical area of needed attention. Research needs to be conducted with appreciation for the complexity of environmental action and the natural confounding of circumstances in people's lives.

REFERENCES

Abelson, R. (1981). Psychological status of the script concept. *American Psychologist, 36*, 715–729.

Ackerman, B. P., Kogos, J., Youngstrom, E., Schoff, K., and Izard, C. (1999). Family instability and problem behaviors of children from economically disadvantaged families. *Developmental Psychology, 35*, 258–268.

Ainsworth, M. D. S. (1973). The development of infant–mother attachment. In B. M. Caldwell and H. N. Riccuiti (Eds.), *Review of child development research* (Vol. 3, pp. 1–94). Chicago: University of Chicago Press.

Altman, I. (1977). Privacy regulation: Culturally universal or culturally specific? *Journal of Social Issues, 33*, 66–84.

Barker, R. G. (1978). *Habitats, environments, and human behavior*. San Francisco: Jossey-Bass.

Basiotix, P. P., Hirschman, J. D., and Kennedy, E. T. (1996). Economic and sociodemographic determinants of "health eating" as measured by the USDA's health eating index. *Consumer Interests Annual, 42*, 81–87.

Belsky, J. (1984). The determinants of parenting: A process model. *Child Development, 55*, 83–96.

Belsky, J., Putnam, S., and Crnic, K. (1997). Coparenting, parenting, and early emotional development. *New Directions in Child Development, 74*, 45–56.

Benson, J. B. (1993). Season of birth and onset of locomotion, Theoretical and methodological implications. *Infant Behavior and Development, 16*, 69–81.

Berenson, B. (1967). Considerations for behavioral research in architecture. In C. W. Taylor, R. Bailey, and C. H. H. Branc (Eds.), *Second national conference on architectural psychology*. Salt Lake City: University of Utah.

Bhavnagari, N., and Parke, R. D. (1991). Parents as direct facilitators of children's peer relationships: Effects of age of child and sex of parent. *Journal of Personal and Social Relationships, 8*, 423–440.

Bjorklund, D. (Ed.). (1990). *Children's strategies: Contemporary views of cognitive development*. Hillsdale, NJ: Lawrence Erlbaum Associates.

Black, M. M., Dubowitz, H., and Starr, R. H. (1999). African American fathers in low income, urban families: Development, behavior, and home environment of their three-year-old children. *Child Development, 70*, 967–978.

Bonney, J. F., Kelley, M. L., and Levant, R. F. (1999). A model of fathers' behavioral involvement in child care in dual-earner families. *Journal of Family Psychology, 13*, 401–415.

Bowlby, J. (1969). *Attachment and loss: Vol. 1. Attachment*. New York: Basic Books.

Bradley, R. H. (1985). Social–cognitive development and toys. *Topics in Early Childhood Special Education, 5*, 11–30.

Bradley, R. H. (1999). The home environment. In S. L. Friedman and T. D. Wachs (Eds.), *Measuring environment across the life span* (pp. 31–58). Washington, DC: American Psychological Association.

Bradley, R. H., and Caldwell, B. M. (1976). The relation of infants' home environments to mental test performance at fifty-four months: A follow-up study. *Child Development, 47*, 1172–1174.

Bradley, R. H., and Caldwell, B. M. (1984). The HOME Inventory and family demographics. *Developmental Psychology, 20*, 315–320.

Bradley, R. H., and Caldwell, B. M. (1995). Caregiving and the regulation of child growth and development: Describing proximal aspects of caregiving systems. *Developmental Review, 15*, 38–85.

Bradley, R. H., Caldwell, B. M., Rock, S. L., Casey, P. H., and Nelson, J. (1987). The early development of low birthweight infants: Relationship to health, family status, family context, family process, and parenting. *International Journal of Behavioral Development, 10,* 1–18.

Bradley, R. H., Caldwell, B. M., Rock, S. L., Hamrick, H. M., and Harris, P. T. (1988). Home observation for measurement of the environment: Development of a HOME Inventory for use with families having children 6 to 10 years old. *Contemporary Educational Psychology, 13,* 58–71.

Bradley, R. H., and Corwyn, R. (1999). Parenting. In C. Tamis-LaMonda and L. Balter (Eds.), *Child psychology: A handbook of contemporary issues* (pp. 339–362). New York: Garland.

Bradley, R. H., Corwyn, R. F., McAdoo, H. P., and Garcia Coll, C. (2000). *The home environments of children in the United States,* Part I: Variations by age, ethnicity, and poverty status. *Child Development.*

Bradley, R. H., Corwyn, R. F., Caldwell, B. M., Whiteside-Mansell, L., Wasserman, G. A., Mink, I. T. (2000). Measuring the home environments of children in early adolescence. *Journal of Research on Adolescence, 10,* 247–289.

Bradley, R. H., Elardo, R., Rosenthal, D., and Friend, J. H. (1984). A comparative study of the home environments of infants from single-parent and two-parent black families. *Acta Paedologica, 1,* 33–46.

Bradley, R. H., and Tedesco, L. (1982). Environmental correlates of mental retardation. In J. Lachenmeyer and M. Gibbs (Eds.), *Psychopathology in childhood* (pp. 155–188). New York: Gardner.

Bradley, R. H., and Whiteside-Mansell, L. (1997). Children in poverty. In R. T. Ammerman and M. Hersen (Eds.), *Handbook of prevention and treatment with children and adolescents* (pp. 13–58). New York: Wiley.

Bradley, R. H., Whiteside, L., Mundfrom, D. J., Casey, P. H., Kelleher, K. J., and Pope, S. K. (1994). The contribution of early intervention and early caregiving experiences to resilience in low birthweight, premature children living in poverty. *Journal of Clinical Child Psychology, 23,* 425–434.

Bretherton, I., and Waters, E. (1985). *Growing points of attachment theory. Monographs of the Society for Research in Child Development, 50* (No. 209).

Brody, G. H., Flor, D., and Gibson, N. M. (1999). Linking maternal efficacy beliefs, developmental goals, parenting practices, and child competence in rural single-parent African American families. *Child Development, 70,* 1197–1208.

Brody, G. H., Stoneman, Z., Flor, D., McCrary, C., Hastings, L., and Conyers, O. (1994). Financial resources, parent psycho-logical functioning, parent co-caregiving and early adolescent competence in rural two-parent African-American families. *Child Development, 65,* 590–605.

Bronfenbrenner, U. (1979). *The ecology of human development.* Cambridge, MA: Harvard University Press.

Bronfenbrenner, U. (1999). Environments in developmental perspective: Theoretical and operational models. In S. L. Friedman and T. D. Wachs (Eds.), *Measuring environment across the life span* (pp. 3–30). Washington, DC: American Psychological Association.

Brooks-Gunn, J., Duncan, G. J., and Aber, J. L. (Eds.). (1997). *Neighborhood poverty* (Vol. 2). New York: Sage.

Brown, B. B., Burton, J. R., and Sweaney, A. L. (1998). Neighbors, households and front porches, New urbanist community tool or mere nostalgia? *Environment and Behavior, 30,* 579–600.

Brown, B. B., Mounts, N., Lamborn, S. D., and Steinberg, L. (1993). Parenting practices and peer group affiliation in adolescence. *Child Development, 64,* 467–483.

Bruner, J. S. (1983). *Child's talk.* New York: Norton.

Burke, J., Chandy, J., Dannerbeck, A., and Watt, J. W. (1998). The parental environment cluster model of child neglect: An integrative conceptual model. *Child Welfare, 76,* 389–405.

Caldwell, B. M. (1968). On designing supplementary environments for early child development. *BAEYC Reports, 10,* 1–11.

Caldwell, B. M., and Bradley, R. H. (1984). *Home observation for measurement of the environment.* Little Rock, AR: University of Arkansas.

Cammack, N. (1993). Res's lending center is a roaring success. *American Libraries, 24,* 428–431.

Cerel, J., Fristad, J. A., Weller, E. B., and Weller, R. A. (2000). Suicide-bereaved children and adolescents: II. Parental and family functioning. *Journal of the American Academy of Child and Adolescent Psychiatry, 39,* 437–444.

Christerphersen, E. R. (1989). Injury control. *American Psychologist, 44,* 237–241.

Coddington, R. D. (1972). The significance of life events as etiologic factors in the diseases of children. II. A study of a normal population. *Journal of Psychosomatic Research, 16,* 7–18.

Cohen, S., Evans, G. W., Stokols, D., and Krantz, D. S. (1986). *Behavior, health, and environmental stress.* New York: Plenum.

Coie, J. D., and Dodge, K. A. (1998). Aggression and antisocial behavior. In N. Eisenberg (Ed.), *Handbook of child psychology* (pp. 799–862). New York: Wiley.

Conger, R., Conger, K., Elder, G., Lorenz, F., Simolns, R., and Whitbeck, L. (1992). A family process model of economic hardship and adjustment of early adolescent boys. *Child Development, 63,* 526–541.

Conger, R., Patterson, G. R., and Ge, X. (1995). It takes two to replicate: A mediational model for the impact of parents, stress on adolescent adjustment. *Child Development, 66,* 80–97.

Coley, R. L., and Chase-Lansdale, P. L. (1999). Stability and change in paternal involvement among urban African-American fathers. *Journal of Family Psychology, 13,* 416–435.

Coombs, R. H., and Landsverk, J. (1988). Parenting styles and substance abuse during childhood and adolescence. *Journal of Marriage and the Family, 50*, 473–482.

Crick, N. R., Casas, J. F., and Ku, H. (1999). Relational and physical forms of peer victimization in preschool. *Developmental Psychology, 35*, 376–385.

Crick, N. R., and Grotpeter, J. K. (1995). Relational aggression, gender, and social–psychological adjustment. *Child Development, 66*, 710–722.

Crick, N. R., and Grotpeter, J. K. (1996). Children's treatment by peers: Victims of relational and overt aggression. *Development and Psychopathology, 8*, 367–380.

Crnic, K., and Greenberg, M. T. (1990). Minor parenting stresses with young children. *Child Development, 61*, 1628–1637.

Crompton, J. L. (1981). Dimensions of the social group role in pleasure vacations. *Annals of Travel Research, 8*, 550–568.

Cronbach, L. J. (1992). Emerging views on methodology. In T. D. Wachs and R. Plomin (Eds.), *Conceptualization and measurement of the organism-environment interaction* (pp. 87–104). Washington, DC: American Psychological Association.

Crouter, A. C., MacDermid, S. M., HcHale, S. M., and Perry-Jenkins, M. (1990). Parental monitoring and perceptions of children's school performance and conduct in dual- and single-earner families. *Developmental Psychology, 26*, 649–657.

Crouter, A. C., and McHale, S. M. (1993). Temporal rhythms in family life: Seasonal variation in the relation between parental work and family processes. *Developmental Psychology, 29*, 198–205.

Cummings, M. (1994). *Children and marital conflict: The impact of family dispute and resolution.* New York: Guilford.

Darling, N., and Steinberg, L. (1993). Parenting style as a context. An integrative model. *Psychological Bulletin, 113*, 487–496.

Davies, P. T., and Cummings, M. (1998). Exploring children's emotional security as a mediator of the link between marital relations and child adjustment. *Child Development, 69*, 124–139.

DeGarmo, D. S., Forgatch, M. S., and Martinez, C. R. (1999). Parenting of divorced mothers as a link between social status and boys' academic outcomes: Unpacking the effects of socioeconomic status. *Child Development, 70*, 1231–1245.

Dishion, T. J., and McMahon, R. J. (1998). Parental monitoring and the prevention of adolescent problem behavior: A conceptual and empirical formulation. *Clinical Child and Family Psychology Review, 1*, 61–75.

Dishion, T. J., Patterson, G. R., Stoolmiller, M., and Skinner, M. L. (1991). Family, school, and behavioral antecedents to early adolescent involvement with antisocial peers. *Developmental Psychology, 27*, 172–180.

Dornbusch, S. M., Ritter, P. L., Leiderman, P. H., Roberts, D. F., and Fraleigh, M. J. (1987). The relation of parenting style to adolescent school performance. *Child Development, 58*, 1244–1257.

Durbrow, E., Jones, E., Bozoky, S. J., and Adam, E. (1996, August). *How well does the HOME Inventory predict Caribbean children's academic performance and behavior problems?* Poster session presented at the Fourteenth Biennial Meeting of the International Society for the Study of Behavioural Development, Quebec, City, Canada.

Elardo, R., Bradley, R. H., and Caldwell, B. M. (l975). The relation of infants' home environments to mental test performance from six to thirty-six months: A longitudinal analysis. *Child Development, 46*, 71–76.

Engle, P., Zeitlin, M., Medrano, Y., and Garcia, L. (1996). Growth consequences of low-income Nicaraguan mothers' theories about feeding one year olds. In S. Harkness and C. Super (Eds.), *Parents' cultural belief systems* (pp. 428–446). New York: Guilford.

Evans, G. W., Kliewer, W., and Martin, J. (1991). The role of the physical environment in the health and well being of children. In H. E. Schroeder (Ed.), *New directions in health psychology: Assessment* (pp.127–157). New York: Hemisphere.

Evans, G. W., Maxwell, L. E., and Hart, B. (1999). Parental language and verbal responsiveness to children in crowded homes. *Developmental Psychology, 35*, 1020–1023.

Fagot, B. I., and Kavanaugh, K. (1993). Parenting during the second year: Effects of children's age, sex, and attachment classification. *Child Development, 64*, 258–271.

Feuerstein, R. (1979). *The dynamic assessment of retarded performers. The learning potential assessment device, theory, instruments, and techniques.* Baltimore, MD: University Park Press.

Ford, D. H., and Lerner, R. M. (1992). *Developmental systems theory, an integrative approach.* Newbury Park, CA: Sage.

Friedman, S. L., and Sigman, M. D. (1996). Past, present, and future directions in research on the development of low-birthweight children. In L. S. Friedman and M. D. Sigman (Eds.). *The psychological development of low birthweight children* (pp. 3–22). Norwood, NJ: Ablex.

Furstenberg, F. F., and Hughes, M. E. (1997). The influence of neighborhoods on children's development: A theoretical perspective and a research agenda. In J. Brooks-Gunn, G. J. Duncan, and J. L. Aber (Eds.), *Neighborhood poverty: Context and consequences for children* (Vol. 2, pp. 23–47). New York: Sage.

Garbarino, J. (1988). Preventing childhood injury: Developmental and mental health issues. *American Journal of Orthopsychiatry, 58*, 25–45.

Garbarino, J. (1999). The effects of community violence on children. In L. Balter and C. Tamis-LeMonda (Eds.), *Child psychology, A handbook of contemporary issues* (pp. 412–425). New York: Garland.

Garbarino, J., and Kostelny, K. (1992). Child maltreatment as a community problem. *Child Abuse and Neglect, 16*, 455–464.

Garcia Coll, C. T. (1990). Developmental outcomes of minority infants: A process-oriented look at our beginnings. *Child Development, 61*, 270–289.

Garling, T. (1998). Introduction—Conceptualizations of human environments. *Journal of Environmental Psychology, 18,* 69–73.

Gates, L., and Rohe, W. (1987). Fear and reaction to crime: A revised model. *Urban Affairs Quarterly, 22,* 425–453.

Gelfand, M. (1992). Children's video: Play it again. *Discount Merchandiser, 32*(5), 38–41.

Global Strategy Group. (2000). *Talking with teens: The YMCA Parent and Teen Survey final report* [On-line]. Available: www.globalstrategygroup.com.

Golbeck, S. L. (1985). Spatial cognition as a function of environmental characteristics. In R. Cohen (Ed.), *The development of spatial cognition.* Hillsdale, NJ: Lawrence Erlbaum Associates.

Gottfried, A. E. (1990). Academic intrinsic motivation in young elementary school children. *Journal of Educational Psychology, 82,* 525–538.

Gottfried, A. W., and Brown, C. (1986). *Play interactions.* Lexington, MA: Lexington Books.

Gottlieb, G. (1991). Experiential canalization of behavioral development: Theory. *Developmental Psychology, 27,* 4–13.

Gove, W. R., Hughes, M., and Galle, V. (1979). Overcrowding in the home: An empirical investigation of its possible pathological consequences. *American Sociological Review, 44,* 59–80.

Grinker, R. R., Korchin, S. J., Bosowitz, H., Hamburg, D. A., Sabshin, M., Persky, H., Chevalier, J. A., and Borad, F. A. (1956). A theoretical and experimental approach to problems of anxiety. *AMA Archives of Neurology and Psychiatry, 76,* 420–431.

Grusec, J. E., and Lytton, H. (1988). *Social development, History, theory, and research.* New York: Springer-Verlag.

Halpern, R. (1992). The role of after-school programs in the lives of inner-city children: A study of the "Urban Youth Network." *Child Welfare, 71,* 215–233.

Hans, S., Musick, J., and Jagers, R. (1988, August). *Family factors affecting the competence of low-income black kindergarteners.* Report to the Spencer Foundation. Chicago, IL: Department of Psychiatry, University of Chicago.

Hassinger, J. (1985). Fear of crime in public environments. *Journal of Architectural Planning Research, 2,* 289–300.

Harris, K. M., and Morgan, S. P. (1991). Fathers, sons, and daughters: Differential paternal involvement in parenting. *Journal of Marriage and Family, 53,* 531–544.

Hart, B., and Risley, T. (1995). *Meaningful differences in the everyday experience of young American children.* Baltimore, MD: Brookes.

Hayashi, K. (1990). Correlation between temperature and gross motor development [Letter to the editor]. *Developmental Medicine and Child Neurology, 32,* 832–834.

Head, D., Bradley, R. H., and Rock, S. L. (1990). Using home environment measures with visually impaired children. *Journal of Visual Impairment and Blindness, 84,* 377–380.

Heft, H. (1979). Background and focal environmental conditions of the home and attention in young children. *Journal of Applied Social Psychology, 9,* 47–69.

Hendry, L. B. (1979). *Adolescence and leisure.* London: Lepus Books.

Holden, G. (1985). How parents create a social environment via proactive behavior. In T. Garling and J. Valsiner (Eds.), *Children within environments: Toward a psychology of accident prevention* (pp. 193–216). New York: Plenum.

Holdnack, J. A. (1992). The long-term effects of parental divorce on family relationships and the effects on adult children's self-concept. *Journal of Divorce, 15,* 137–155.

Holman, T. B., and Epperson, A. (1984). Family and leisure: A review of the literature with research recommendations. *Journal of Leisure Research, 16,* 277–294.

Homel, R., Burns, A., and Goodnow, J. (1987). Parental social networks and child development. *Journal of Personal and Social Relationships, 4,* 159–177.

Horna, J. L. (1989). The leisure component of the parental role. *Journal of Leisure Research, 21,* 228–241.

Horowitz, F. D. (1987). *Exploring developmental theories: Toward a structural/behavioral model of development.* Hillsdale, NJ: Lawrence Erlbaum Associates.

Howard, D. R., and Madrigal, R. (1990). Who makes the decision: The parent or the child? The perceived influence of parents and children on the purchase of recreation services. *Journal of Leisure Research, 22,* 244–258.

Huston, A. C., Wright, J. C., Marquis, J., and Green, S. B. (1999). How young children spend their time: Television and other activities. *Developmental Psychology, 35,* 912–925.

Hutchinson, R. (1987). Ethnicity and urban recreation: Whites, blacks, and Hispanics in Chicago's public parks. *Journal of Leisure Research, 19,* 205–222.

Hutchinson, R. (1988). A critique of race, ethnicity, and social class in recent leisure–recreation research. *Journal of Leisure Research, 20,* 10–30.

Jacobson, J. L., Jacobson, S. W., Padgett, R. J., Brummitt, G. A., and Billlings, R. L. (1992). Effects of prenatal PCB exposure on cognitive processing efficiency and sustained attention. *Developmental Psychology, 28,* 297–306.

Jacobson, J. L., Jacobson, S. W., Greenbaum, S. S., Gornish, K., Ella, S., and Billings, R. L. (1995, July). *Validity of the elementary version of the HOME Inventory in two cultures.* Paper presented at the Tenth Biennial Meeting of the International Society for the Study of Behavioural Development, Jyvaskyla, Findland.

Jarrett, R. (1997). Bringing famlies back in: Neighborhood effects on child development. In J. Brooks-Gunn, G. J. Duncan, and J. L. Aber (Eds.), *Neighborhood poverty* (Vol. 2, pp. 48–64). New York: Sage.

Johnson, L. C. (1987). The developmental implications of home environments. In C. S. Weinstein and T. G. David (Eds.), *Spaces for children: The built environment and child development* (pp. 139–158). New York: Plenum.

Johnson, V. K., and Lieberman, A. F. (1999, April). *Protecting 3–5-year-old children from the effects of witnessing domestic violence: The role of mothers as "emotion coaches."* Paper presented at the biennial meeting of the Society for Research in Child Development, Albuquerque, NM.

Johnston, T. D. (1987). The persistence of dichotomies in the study of behavioral development. *Developmental Review, 7,* 149–182.

Kagan, J. (1984). *The nature of the child.* New York: Basic Books.

Kail, B., and Kleinman, P. (1985). Fear, crime, community organization, and limitations on daily routines. *Urban Affairs Quarterly, 20,* 400–408.

Kaplan, R. (1983). A model of person–environment compatibility. *Environment and Behavior, 15,* 311–332.

Kaplan, H., and Dove, H. (1987). Infant development among the Ache of Eastern Paraguay. *Developmental Psychology, 23,* 190–198.

Kaplan, R., and Kaplan, S. (1989). *The experience of nature: A psychological perspective.* New York: Cambridge University Press.

Kerr, M., and Stattin, H. (2000). What parents know, how they know it, and several forms of adolescent adjustment: Further support for a reinterpretation of monitoring. *Developmental Psychology, 36,* 366–380.

Klebanov, P. K., Brooks-Gunn, J., Chase-Lansdale, P. L., and Gordon, R. A. (1997). Are neighborhood effects on young children mediated by features of the home environment? In J. Brooks-Gunn, G. J. Duncan, and J. L. Aber (Eds.), *Neighborhood poverty* (Vol. 1, pp. 119–145). New York: Sage.

Korosec-Serafty, P. (1985). Experience and use of the dwelling. In I. Altman and C. Werner (Eds.), *Home environments* (pp. 65–86). New York: Plenum.

Kuhn, D. (1992). Cognitive development. In M. H. Bornstein and M. E. Lamb (Eds.), *Developmental psychology: An advanced textbook* (3rd ed., pp. 211–272) Hillsdale, NJ: Lawrence Erlbaum Associates.

Kurtz, B. E., Borkowski, J. G., and Deshmukh, D. (1987). Metamemory and learning in Maharashtrian children: Influences from home and school. *Journal of Genetic Psychology, 149,* 363–376.

Lawrence, D. L., and Low, S. M. (1990). The built environment and spatial form. *Annual Review of Anthropology, 19,* 453–505.

Lazarus, R. S. (1981). The stress and coping paradigm. In E. Eisendforfer, D. Cohen, A. Kleinman, and P. Maxim (Eds.), *Models for clinical psychopathology* (pp. 177–244). New York: Spectrum.

Lazarus, R. S. (1993). From psychological stress to emotions: A history of changing outlooks. *Annual Review of Psychology, 44,* 1–21.

Leonard, W. R. (1991). Age and sex differences in the impact of seasonal energy stress among Andean agriculturists. *Human Ecology, 19,* 351–369.

Leong, F. T., Chao, R. K., and Hardin, E. E. (2000). Asian American adolescents: A research review to dispel the model minority myth. In R. Montemayor, G. Adams, and T. Gullotta (Eds.), Adolescent diversity in ethnic, economic, and cultural contexts (pp. 174–207). Thousand Oaks, CA: Sage.

Lerner, R. M. (1984). *On the nature of human plasticity.* New York: Cambridge University Press.

Lewis, C. S. (1994). *The lion, the witch, and the wardrobe.* New York: Harper Collins.

Lewis, M. (1997). *Altering fate.* New York: Guilford.

Li, H., and Rao, N. (2000). Parental influences on Chinese literacy development: A comparison of preschoolers in Beijing, Hong Kong, and Singapore. *International Journal of Behavioral Development, 24,* 82–90.

Little, P. E. (1999). Environments and environmentalisms in anthropological research: Facing a new millennium. *Annual Review of Antropology, 28,* 253–284.

Loeber, R., and Dishion, T. J. (1983). Early predictors of male delinquency: A review. *Psychological Bulletin, 94,* 68–99.

Loeber, R., and Stouthamer-Loeber, M. (1986). Family factors as correlates and predictors of juvenile conduct problems and delinquency. In M. Tonry and N. Morris (Eds.), *Crime and justice: An annual review of research* (Vol. 7, pp. 29–149). Chicago: University of Chicago Press.

Lozoff, B. (1989). Nutrition and behavior. *American Psychologist, 44,* 231–236.

Maccoby, E. E., and Martin, J. A. (1983). Socialization in the context of the family: Parent–child interaction. In P. H. Mussen (Series Ed.), E. M. Hetherington (Ed.), *Handbook of child psychology: Vol. 4. Socialization, personality, and social development* (4th ed., pp. 1–102). New York: Wiley.

MacKinnon, C., Brody, G., and Stoneman, Z. (1982). The effects of divorce and maternal employment on the home environments of preschool children. *Child Development, 53,* 1392–1399.

Macksoud, M. S., and Aber, J. L. (1996). The war experience and psychosocial development of children in Lebanon. *Child Development, 67,* 70–88.

Magnusson, D. (1988). *Individual development from an interactional perspective.* Hillsdale, NJ: Lawrence Erlbaum Associates.

Maslow, A., and Murphy, G. (1954). *Motivation and personality.* New York: Harper.

Masten, A. S., and Coatsworth, J. D. (1998). The development of competence in favorable and unfavorable environments. *American Psychologist, 53*, 205–220.

Mayes, L. C., Bornstein, M. H., Chawarska, K., Haynes, O. M., and Granger, R. H. (1996). Impaired regulation of arousal in 3-month-old infants exposed prenatally to cocaine and other drugs. *Development and Psychopathology, 8*, 29–42.

McCall, R. B. (1992). So many interactions, so little evidence. Why? In T. D. Wachs and R. Plomin (Eds.), *Conceptualization and measurement of the organism–environment interaction* (pp. 142–161). Washington, DC: American Psychological Association.

McDonald, M., Sigman, M., Espinosa, M., and Neuman, C. (1994). Effect of a temporary food shortage on children and their mothers. *Child Development, 65*, 404–415.

McHale, S. M., Updegraff, K. A., Tucker, C. J., and Crouter, A. C. (2000). Step in or stay out? Parents, roles in adolescent siblings, relationships. *Journal of Marriage and Family, 62*, 746–760.

McLoyd, V. C. (1998). Socioeconomic disadvantage and child development. *American Psychologist, 53*, 185–203.

McNeal, J. U. (1992). The littlest shoppers. *American Demographics, 14*(2), 48–53.

Metzler, C. W., Noell, J., Biglan, A., Ary, D., and Smolkowski, K. (1994). The social context for risky sexual behavior among adolescents. *Journal of Behavioral Medicine, 17*, 419–438.

Miller, P. C., Shim, J. E., and Holden, G. W. (1998). Immediate contextual influences on maternal behavior: Environmental affordances and demands. *Journal of Environmental Psychology, 18*, 387–398.

Monsour, M. (1993). Interiors showcase: New facilities for children. *American Libraries, 24*, 301–303.

Moore, G. T. (1986). Effects of spatial definition of behavior settings on children's behavior: A quasi-experimental field study. *Journal of Environmental Psychology, 6*, 205–231.

Murphy, J. K., Alpert, B. S., Christman, J. V., and Wiley, E. S. (1988). Physical fitness in children: A survey method based on parental report. *American Journal of Public Health, 78*, 708–710.

National Center for Educational Statistics. (1992). *Home activities of 3- to 8-year olds* (NCES Publication No. 92-004). Washington, DC: U.S. Department of Education, Office of Educational Research and Improvement.

NICHD Early Child Care Research Network. (2000). Factors associated with father's caregiving acativities and sensitivity with young children. *Journal of Family Psychology, 14*, 200–219.

Neuman, S. B. (1986). Television, reading, and the home environment. *Reading Research and Instruction, 25*, 173–183.

Noll, R. B. l., Zucker, R. A., Curtis, W. J., and Fitzgerald, H. E. (1989, April). *Young male offspring of alcoholic fathers: Early developmental and cognitive findings.* Paper presented at the biennial meeting of the Society for Research in Child Development, Kansas City, MO.

Oliveri, M. E., and Reiss, D. (1987). Social networks of family members: Distinctive roles of mothers and fathers. *Sex Roles, 17*, 719–736.

Olsen, S. F., Martin, P., and Halverson, C. F. (1999). Personality, marital relationships, and parenting in two generations of mothers. *International Journal of Behavioral Development, 23*, 457–476.

O'Neil, R., and Parke, R. D. (1997). *Objective and subjective features of children's neighborhoods: Relations to parental regulatory strategies and children's social competence.* Unpublished manuscript.

Parks, P., and Bradley, R. H. (1991). The interaction of home environment features and their relation to infant competence. *Infant Mental Health Journal, 12*, 3–16.

Patterson, G. R., DeBaryshe, B. D., and Ramsey, E. (1989). A developmental perspective on antisocial behavior. *American Psychologist, 44*, 329–335.

Peterson, L., Ewigman, B., and Kivlahan, C. (1993). Judgments regarding appropriate child supervision to prevent injury: The role of environmental risk and child age. *Child Development, 64*, 934–950.

Pettit, G. S., Dodge, K. A., and Brown, M. M. (1988). Early family experience, social problem solving patterns, and children's social competence. *Child Development, 59*, 107–120.

Pollitt, E. (1988). A critical review of three decades of research on the effect of chronic energy malnutrition on behavioral development. In B. Schureh and M. Scrimshaw (Eds.), *Chronic energy depletion: Consequences and related issues.* Luzanne: IDECC—Nestle Foundation.

Power, T. G., and Chapieski, M. L. (1986). Childrearing and impulse control in toddlers: A naturalistic investigation. *Developmental Psychology, 22*, 271–275.

Prigogine, I., and Stengers, I. (1984). *Order out of chaos.* Toronto, Ontario, Canada: Bantam.

Quitlitch, H. R., and Risley, T. R. (1973). The effects of play materials on social play. *Journal of Applied Behavior Analysis, 6*, 573–578.

Rapoport, A. (1985). Thinking about home environments, A conceptual framework. In I. Altman and C. M. Werner (Eds.), *Home environments* (pp. 255–286). New York: Plenum.

Rheingold, H. L., and Cook, K. V. (1975). The contents of boys' and girls' rooms as an index of parents' behavior. *Child Development, 46*, 459–464.

Rice, E. F. (1992). *Human development: A life-span approach.* New York: MacMillan.

Rivara, F. P., and Mueller, B. A. (1987). The epidemiology and causes of childhood injuries. *Journal of Social Issues, 43*, 13–31.

Roberts, K. (1983). *Youth and leisure*. London: Allen and Unwin.

Rohner, R. (1986). *The warmth dimension*. Beverley Hills, CA: Sage.

Rotter, J. B., Chance, J., and Phares, E. (1972). *Social learning theory of personality*. New York: Holt, Rinehart & Winston.

Russell, I. (1991). Hands on fun. *Leisure Management, 11*(2), 26–28.

Rutter, M., and Pickles, A. (1992). Person–environment interactions: Concepts, mechanisms, and implications for data analysis. In T. D. Wachs and R. Plomin (Eds.), *Conceptualization and measurement of the organism-environment interaction* (pp. 105–141). Washington, DC: American Psychological Association.

Saegert, S., and Winkel, G. H. (1990). Environmental psychology. *Annual Review of Psychology, 41*, 441–477.

Safilios-Rotschild, C. (1980). The role of family: A neglected aspect of poverty. In *Implementing programmes of human development* (World Bank staff working paper No. 403). Washington, DC: World Bank.

Saler, L., and Skolnick, N. (1992). Childhood parental death and depression in adulthood: Roles of surviving parent and family environment. *American Journal of Orthopsychiatry, 62*, 504–516.

Sameroff, A. J. (1983). Developmental systems: Contexts and evolution. In P. H. Mussen (Series Ed.) and W. Kessen (Ed.), *Handbook of child psychology: Vol. 1. History, theory, and methods* (4th ed., pp. 237–294). New York: Wiley.

Sameroff, A. J. (1995). General systems theory and developmental psychopathology. In D. Chiccheti and D. Cohen (Eds.), *Developmental psycholpathology: Vol. 1. Theory and method* (pp. 659–695). New York: Wiley.

Scarr, S., and McCartney, K. (1983). How people make their own environments. *Child Development, 54*, 424–435.

Scheper-Hughes, N. (1989). Death without weeping. *Natural History, 98*(10), 8–16.

Schofield, S. (1974). Seasonal factors affecting nutrition in different age groups and especially preschool children. *Journal of Developmental Studies, 11*, 22–40.

Schooler, C. (1999). The workplace environment: Measurement, psychological effects, and basic issues. In S. L. Friedman and T. D. Wachs (Eds.), *Measuring environment across the life span* (pp. 229–248). Washington, DC: American Psychological Association.

Shifflett, K., and Cummings, E. M. (1996). Mixed message resolution and children's responses to interadult conflict. *Child Development, 67*, 437–448.

Sigel, I. E. (1982). The relationship between parental distancing strategies and the child's cognitive behavior. In L. M. Laosa and I. E. Sigel (Eds.), *Families as learning environments for children* (pp. 47–86). New York: Plenum.

Sigman, M., Neumann, C., Carter, E., Cattle, D. J., D'Souza, S., and Bwibo, N. (1988). Home interactions and development of Embu toddlers in Kenya. *Child Development, 59*, 1251–1261.

Sonderquist, S. (1991). ARKS: Adults reading kids stuff—realizing an ideal. *American Libraries, 22*, 264–265.

Spieker, S. J., and Bensley, L. (1994). Roles of living arrangements and grandmother social support in adolescent mothering and infant attachment. *Developmental Psychology, 30*, 102–111.

Steinberg, L., Darling, N. E., and Fletcher, A. C. (1995). Authoritative parenting and adolescent adjustment: An ecological journey. In P. Moen, G. H. Elder, and K. Luscher (Eds.), *Examining lives in context: Perspectives on the ecology of development* (pp. 423–466). Washington, DC: American Psychological Association.

Stokols, D. (1995). The paradox of environmental psychology. *American Psychologist, 50*, 821–837.

Stoneman, Z., Brody, G. H., Churchill, S. L., and Winn, L. L. (1999). Effects of residential instability on Head Start children and their relationships with older siblings: Influences of child emotionality and conflict between family caregivers. *Child Development, 70*, 1246–1262.

Super, C. M., and Harkness, S. (1986). The developmental niche: A conceptualization at the interface of child and culture. *International Journal of Behavioral Development, 9*, 545–569.

Sutton-Smith, B. (1985). *Toys as culture*. New York: Gardner.

Taylor, R. B., and Brower, S. (1987). Home and near home territories. In I. Altman and C. Werner (Eds.), *Home environments* (pp. 183–212). New York: Plenum.

Tong, S., and McMichael, A. J. (1992). Maternal smoking and neuropsychological development in childhood: A review of the evidence. *Developmental Medicine and Child Neurology, 34*, 191–197.

Toor, M. (1992, April 9). Is the game over for toys? *Marketing*, pp. 18–19.

Tronick, E. Z., Morelli, G. A., and Ivey, P. K. (1992). The Efe forager infant and toddler's pattern of social relationships: Multiple and simultaneous. *Developmental Psychology, 28*, 568–577.

Tronick, E. Z., Thomas, R., and Daltabuit, M. (1994). The Quechua Manta pouch: A cargiving practice for buffering the Peruvian infant against the multiple stressors of high altitude. *Child Development, 65*, 1005–1013.

Unger, D. G., and Cooley, M. (1992). Partner and grandmother contact in Black and White teen parent families. *Journal of Adolescent Health, 13*, 546–552.

United Media Enterprises. (1982). *Report on leisure in America. Where does the time go?* New York: United Media Enterprises.

U. S. Department of Commerce, Bureau of the Census. (1999). *Statistical abstract of the United States 1999*. Washington, DC: Author.

U. S. Department of Health and Human Services. (1991). *Healthy people 2000* (DHHS Publication No. PHS 91-50212). Washington, DC: U.S. Government Printing Office.

Veal, A. J. (1987). *Leisure and the future*. London: Allen and Unwin.

Wachs, T. D. (1988). Relevance for physical environmental influences for toddler temperament. *Infant Behavior and Development, 11,* 431–445.

Wachs, T. D. (1989). The nature of the physical micro-environment: An expanded classification system. *Merrill-Palmer Quarterly, 35,* 399–402.

Wachs, T. D. (1992). *The nature of nurture.* Newbury Park, CA: Sage.

Wachs, T. D. (2000). *Necessary but not sufficient.* Washington, DC: American Psychological Association.

Wachs, T. D., and Camli, O. (1991). Do ecological or individual characteristics mediate the influence of the physical environment upon maternal behavior? *Journal of Environmental Psychology, 11,* 249–264.

Wachs, T. D., and Gruen, G. (1982). *Early experience and human development.* New York: Plenum.

Wachs, T. D., and Plomin, R. (Eds.). (1992). *Conceptualization and measurement of the organism–environment interaction.* Washington, DC: American Psychological Association.

Wachs, T. D., Sigman, M., Bishry, Z., Moussa, W., Jerome, N., Newmann, C., Bwibo, N., and McDonald, M. A. (1992). Caregiver–child interaction patterns in two cultures in relation to nutritional intake. *International Journal of Behavioral Development, 15,* 1–18.

Wallenius, M. (1999). Personal projects in everyday places: Perceived supportiveness of the environment and psychological well-being. *Journal of Environmental Psychology, 19,* 131–143.

Wandel, M., and Holmboe-Ottesen, G. (1992). Food availability and nutrition in seasonal perspective: A study from the Rukwa region in Tanzania. *Human Ecology, 20,* 89–107.

Wandersman, L. P., and Unger, D. G. (1983, March). *Interaction of infant difficulty and social support in adolescent mothers.* Paper presented at the biennial meeting of the Society for Research in Child Development, Detroit, MI.

Wapner, S. (1987). A holistic, developmental, systems-oriented environmental psychology: Some beginnings. In D. Stokols and I. Altman (Eds.), *Handbook of environmental psychology* (Vol. 2, pp. 1433–1465). New York: Wiley.

Weinstein, C. S., and David, T. G. (1987). *Spaces for children.* New York: Plenum.

Wheeler, P. (1993). Human ancestors walked tall, stayed cool. *Natural History, 102*(8), 65–67.

Whiteside-Mansell, L., Pope, S., and Bradley, R. H. (1996). Patterns of parenting behavior in young mothers. *Family Relations, 45,* 273–284.

Whiting, J. M. (1981). Environmental constraints on infant care practices. In R. H. Munroe, R. L. Munroe, and B. B. Whiting (Eds.), *Handbook of cross-cultural human development* (pp. 155–180). New York: Garland.

Wohlwill, J. (1974, July). *Environmental stimulation and the development of the child: How much and what kind.* Paper presented at the Conference on Environment and Cognitive Development, Arad, Israel.

Wohlwill, J. F., and Heft, H. (1977). The physical environment and the development of the child. In D. Stokols and I. Altman (Eds.), *Handbook of environmental psychology* (Vol. 1, pp. 281–328). New York: Wiley.

World Health Organization. (1980). *Environmental health criteria 12, Noise.* Geneva, Switzerland.

Zeitlin, M. (1996). My child is my crown: Yoruba parental theories and practices in early childhood. In S. Harkness and C. Super (Eds.), *Parents' cultural belief systems* (pp. 407–427). New York: Guilford.

Zimmerman, R. M. (1992). Today's children make shopping more than child's play. *Retail Control, 60*(1), 21–25.

11

Developmental Systems Perspective on Parenting

Richard M. Lerner
Fred Rothbaum
Shireen Boulos
Tufts University
Domini R. Castellino
Duke University

INTRODUCTION

Parenting is both a biological and a social process (Tobach and Schneirla, 1968). *Parenting* subsumes a set of behaviors involved across life in the relations among organisms, who are usually conspecifics and typically members of different generations. The social interactions involved in parenting provide resources across the generational groups and function in regard to domains of survival, reproduction, nurturance, and socialization. Especially in neotenous and paedomorphic species, such as human beings (Gould, 1977; Lerner, 1984), parenting by members of an older generation of members of a younger generation affords reproductive success; learning across an extended childhood—to fit within each generation's current and, potentially, future ecological niche; and intergenerational connectivity and interdependency. Connectivity and interdependency can extend both generations' capacity to function successfully in new niches.

Within the younger generation, this capacity to function in new arenas accrues as a consequence of the actualization of the high level of plasticity present at relatively early portions of the ontogenies of members of the younger group (Hebb, 1949; Lerner, 1984; Schneirla, 1957; Tobach, 1981). The actualization of the younger generation's potential for plasticity can maintain or enhance the quality of life of the older generation. That is, because of the connectivity maintained by the older generation, members of this group are provided with the skills and resources attained, developed, or controlled by the younger generation. At this writing, the widespread availability of personal computers, the Internet and the World Wide Web, e-mail, and other electronic means of communication (e.g., cell phones) are the latest example of such a contribution by younger generations. Often members of the older generation learn and benefit from their children's proficiency with these new media.

Thus, parenting is a complex process, involving much more than a mother or father providing food, safety, and succor to an infant or child. Parenting involves bidirectional relationships between members of two (or more) generations, can extend through the respective lifespans of these groups, may engage all institutions within a culture (including educational, economic, political, and social ones), and is embedded in the history of a people (Ford and Lerner, 1992). Moreover, *diversity* is a key substantive feature of parenting behavior. Diversity arises because of the temporal variation that constitutes history and the variation of culture and of its institutions that exist in different physical and designed ecological niches. In addition, there is variation within and across generations in strategies for and behaviors designed to fit with these niches. Focus on the breadth of this variation, rather than on central tendencies, is necessary in order to understand parenting adequately.

Parenting involves multiple levels of organization that change in and through integrated, mutually interdependent or "fused" relationships occurring over both ontogenetic and historical time (Lerner and Lerner, 1987; Tobach and Greenberg, 1984). This understanding of parenting may be usefully embedded in a developmental systems theory of human development (Ford and Lerner, 1992; Lerner, 1998b, 2002-a; Thelen and Smith, 1998), for example, bioecological theory (Bronfenbrenner, in press; Bronfenbrenner and Morris, 1998) or developmental contextualism (Lerner, 1986, 1995, 1996, 1998b). Accordingly, in this chapter we use these two instances of developmental systems theory to discuss the integrated and dynamic relationships involved in parenting.

We first present an overview of developmental systems theory and discuss ideas from instances of this perspective (i.e., from developmental contextual and bioecological perspectives) pertinent to parenting. Developmental systems theory focuses on the dynamic, or fused, and changing *relations* between developing people and their contexts and, as such, stresses these relations, as compared with the "elements," the child and her or his parent(s), involved in them. Both of the instances of developmental systems theories that we discuss focus on these relations as they are embedded in the actual ecology of human development. We explain that this emphasis on dynamic relations has important implications for research (e.g., involving an emphasis on multilevel, dynamic interaction effects—as opposed to either unilevel or main effects) and, as well, lends itself to a discussion of the application of developmental systems-predicated research to issues of policies or programs that may be used to promote positive development. As such, we conclude our presentation with recommendations for future research and a discussion of implications of a developmental systems theory for applications aimed at enhancing the contributions of parents to the healthy development of children and adolescents.

DEVELOPMENTAL SYSTEMS THEORY

Since its inception as a field of study within psychology, dating at least to the work of G. Stanley Hall (e.g., 1904; see Cairns, 1998; Dixon and Lerner, 1999), scholars of human development have been interested in understanding the environment, setting, ecology, or context of human development (Bronfenbrenner, 1977, 1979, in press; Bronfenbrenner and Morris, 1998). This interest has been motivated by both theoretical issues—ranging from ones steeped in biological (e.g., evolutionary) ideas about the sources of human development (e.g., Haeckel, 1876; Hall, 1904) to models seeking to identify the environmental stimulus conditions believed to shape human development (e.g., Watson, 1914, 1928; and see Bijou, 1976, and Bijou and Baer, 1961, 1965, for later versions of this viewpoint) and, as well, by concerns about how to apply ideas about human development to improve behavior in schools, families, work sites, and other key contexts of human life (e.g., see Cairns, 1998; McCandless, 1967, 1970).

In the latter two decades of the twentieth century, the emergence of dynamic, developmental systems perspectives about human development (e.g., Baltes, Lindenberger, and Staudinger, 1998; Brandtstädter, 1998, 1999; Elder, 1998; Fischer and Bidell, 1998; Ford and Lerner, 1992; Gottlieb, 1992, 1997; Lerner, 1998a, 1998b, 2002-a; Magnusson, 1995, 1999a, 1999b; Magnusson and Stattin, 1998; Sameroff, 1983; Thelen and Smith, 1994, 1998; Wapner and Demick, 1998) and the applications of developmental science to social policies and intervention programs aimed at promoting positive development that it has spawned (e.g., Fisher and Lerner, 1994; Lerner, in 2002-b; Lerner, Fisher, and Weinberg, 1997, 2000a, 2000b; Roth, Brooks-Gunn, Murray, and Foster, 1998), have provided additional theoretical and societal impetus to understand the integrative relations that exist between developing individuals and their changing, multilevel context (i.e., their biological, individual behavioral–psychological, social relational, familial, institutional, community, cultural, and historical/temporal levels of organization).

For example, as illustrated by most of the chapters in Volume 1 of the fifth edition of the *Handbook of Child Psychology* (Damon, 1998), a volume titled *Theoretical Models of Human Development* (Lerner, 1998a), the interest and, arguably, the power of these instances of contemporary developmental theories resided in their ability to transcend a unidimensional portrayal of the developing person. The person depicted in the newer theories is not seen exclusively from the vantage point of cognitions, or emotions, or stimulus–response connections; for example, see Piaget (1970), Freud (1949), and Bijou and Baer (1961), respectively. Rather, the individual is "systemized." The newer theories conceive of development as embedded within an integrated matrix of variables derived from multiple levels of organization.

Within this developmental systems view, children and parents are fused, both structurally and functionally, in a multilevel system involving biological through sociocultural and historical tiers of organization (Lerner, in 2002-a). Parents, as individuals in the developmental system, and the behaviors associated with the enactment of their caregiving role—parenting—are influenced by and simultaneously influence other levels of the developmental system. This dynamism means that the focus of developmental inquiry should be on the relations in this system, that is, on parents and parenting (on structure and function) as moderators of (dynamic interactors with) other levels in the developmental system *and* on multiple levels of the developmental system as moderators of parents and parenting.

Although all instances of developmental systems theory previously noted share these attributes, we have noted that two perspectives within this theoretical family—Bronfenbrenner's (in press; Bronfenbrenner and Morris, 1998) bioecological theory and Lerner's (e.g., 1995, 1996, 1998b, 2002-a) developmental contextual model—suggest themselves as useful in discussing extant research pertinent to parenting and to proposing ideas for future research and application. The applicability of the bioecological and the developmental contextual models derives from the explicit attention they have paid to the import of the parent–child relationship in texturing the ontogenies of individuals across the lifespan. Accordingly, we discuss both of these instances of developmental systems theory and generate from them ideas for research and application pertinent to the dynamic character of parent–child relations.

We underscore, however, that we do not present these two instances of developmental systems theory in order to raise or reconcile issues that discriminate the concepts or integrative utility of the two perspectives. To the contrary, our purpose is to illustrate that different instances of developmental systems theory may use different concepts or distinct vocabularies but, nevertheless, point to the same dynamic relations among individuals and other levels of organization, including temporality, in constituting the basic process of human development and, as such, of parenting.

DEVELOPMENTAL CONTEXTUALISM AND PARENTING

Developmental contextualism asserts that human beings are active rather than passive. As well, developmental contextualism stresses that the world around the developing person—both the physical and the social ecology of human life—is active also. All levels vary in dynamic interaction with historical changes, a temporality that provides a change component to human life.

Accordingly, developmental contextualists, like all developmental systems theorists, see the basic process of development as involving the integration, or fusion (Tobach and Greenberg, 1984), of these instances or these "levels" (the person and the context, or ecology) of human development.

Specifically, then, in developmental contextualism the integration of the actions of people in and on their world and the actions of the world on people shapes the quality of human behavioral and psychological functioning (Brandtstädter, 1998, 1999; Brandtstädter and Lerner, 1999; Lerner and Busch-Rossnagel, 1981). Developmental contextualism stresses that the source of these actions is the *dynamic* interaction between nature and nurture.

Biological (organismic) characteristics of the individual affect the context (e.g., adolescents who look differently as a consequence of contrasting rates of biological growth, earlier versus later maturation, elicit different social behaviors from peers and adults; Brooks-Gunn, 1987; Lerner, 1987; Petersen, 1988) and, at the same time, the contextual variables in the organism's world affect its biological characteristics (e.g., girls growing up in nations or at times in history with better health care and nutritional resources reach puberty earlier than girls developing is less advantaged contexts; Katchadourian, 1977; Tanner, 1991). Accordingly, scholars who use this approach seek to identify how variables from the levels involved in these relations fit together dynamically (that is, in a reciprocally interactive way) to provide bases for behavior and development.

As subsequently noted, a goodness or poorness of fit between a person's attributes of individuality (e.g., a person's temperamental characteristics) and the presses for or demands placed on the person for particular behaviors (e.g., by parents or other significant people in a person's life) may be established because the individual has characteristics that act on the environment and, at the same time, this individual lives in an environment that acts on her or his characteristics (Chess and Thomas, 1984, 1999; Lerner and Lerner, 1983, 1989; Thomas and Chess, 1977). These two components of the developmental system may interact to promote either adaptive or unhealthy outcomes. Of course, *any* instance of fit may result in either positive or negative outcomes, depending on the characteristics extant across the other levels of the developmental system at a given point in time (Bronfenbrenner and Morris, 1998; Elder, 1998). However, given that the individual is at the center of these reciprocal actions (or dynamic interactions), she or he, through her or his actions, is a source of her or his own development (Lerner, 1982; Lerner and Busch-Rossnagel, 1981; Lerner and Walls, 1999). In short, in developmental contextualism, there is a "third source" of development—the individual (see, for example, Schneirla, 1957).

The fused character of the interactions among levels in the developmental system envisioned within developmental contextualism constitutes an instance of a probabilistic epigenetic conception of developmental process (Gottlieb, 1970, 1983, 1992, 1997). Developmental changes are probabilistic in respect to normative outcomes because of variation in the *timing* of the biological, psychological, and social factors (or levels) that provide interactive bases of ontogenetic progressions (e.g., Schneirla, 1957; Tobach, 1981). This probabilistic character of both the directions and the outcomes of development involved in this version of epigenesis provides a basis for plasticity in development. This plasticity derives from the probabilistic (yet causal) interaction among levels and makes both continuity, discontinuity, or both, a probabilistic feature of developmental change across life periods.

A Developmental Contextual View of Parenting

How does developmental contextualism lend itself to understanding parenting? The model of the developmental system envisioned within developmental contextualism, presented in Figure 11.1, enables us to address this question. As shown in this figure, the inner and the outer worlds of a child are fused and dynamically interactive. In addition, of course, the same may be said of the parent depicted in the figure and, in fact, of the parent–child relationship. Each of these foci—child, parent, or relationship—is part of a larger, enmeshed system of fused relations among the multiple levels that compose the ecology of human life (Bronfenbrenner, 1979).

For instance, illustrated in Figure 11.1 is the idea that both parent and child are embedded in a broader social network, and each person has reciprocal reactions with this network. This set of relationships occurs because both the child and the parent are much more than just people playing

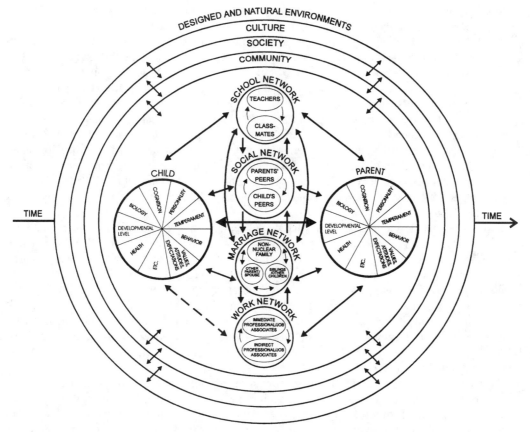

FIGURE 11.1. The developmental contextual view of human development: Person–context relations (e.g., involving parents and children and interpersonal and institutional networks) are embedded in and influenced by specific community, societal, cultural, and designed and natural environments, all changing interdependently across time (with history).

only one role in life. The child may also be a sibling, a peer, and a student; the parent may also be a spouse, a worker, and an adult child. All of these networks of relationships are embedded within a particular community, society, and culture. And, finally, all of these relationships are continually changing across time and history. Simply, for all portions of the system of person–context or biology–environment relations envisioned in developmental contextualism, change across time is an integral, indeed inescapable, feature of human life.

Thus Figure 11.1 illustrates also that within and among each of the networks depicted one may conceive of bidirectional relationships existing among the people populating the network. A child's behavior may function, in a sense, like a small pebble thrown into a quiet lake. It can prompt a large ripple. In turn, of course, the reverse of this possibility can occur. Events in settings lying far beyond the child–parent relationship can influence it. For instance, the resources in a community for child daycare during the parent's working hours, the laws (e.g., regarding tax exemptions) or social programs available in a society supporting daycare, and the cultural values regarding families who place their infants in daycare, all *exert* an impact on the quality of the parent–child relationship.

The child–parent relationship and the social networks in which it is located are embedded in still larger community, societal, cultural, and historical levels of organization. These relations are illustrated also in Figure 11.1. Moreover, the arrow of time—history—cuts through all the systems.

Ontogenetic time is interrelated, in which the individual, by virtue of age, is placed within the flow of generations in the family. In turn, the context is differentiated in regard to the flow of events that comprise history. Phenomena pertinent to parent–child relations (e.g., the influence of a difficult child on the parent–child relationship) vary in regard to the vicissitudes of the context operational at a given point in history (e.g., the presence of a drought, the outbreak of war, the availability of health care for children, or the presence of governmental programs to support single teenage parents).

The temporal component of the model underscores the idea that, as with the people populating the social systems, change is always occurring. Diversity within time is created as changes across time (across history) introduce variation into all the levels of organization involved in the system shown in Figure 11.1. As such, the nature of parent–child relationships, of family life and development, and of societal and cultural influences on the child–parent–family system are influenced by both "normative" and "nonnormative" historical changes (Baltes, 1987; Baltes et al., 1998) or, in other words, by "evolutionary" (i.e., gradual) and "revolutionary" (i.e., abrupt; Werner, 1957) historical changes.

In sum, then, the developmental contextual model depicts the presence and fused interrelation of development across all levels of the developmental system. People develop, the family changes from one having infants and young children to one having teenagers to an "empty nest." In the latter case, the children have left the home of their parents to live elsewhere and, very likely, to start their own families. Similarly, communities, societies, and cultures change (Elder, 1974; Elder, Modell, and Parke, 1993; Garbarino, 1992; Hernandez, 1993), and all are affected by alterations in the natural and human-designed physical ecology—a physical world that also changes (Bronfenbrenner, 1979). This system of multiple, interconnected, or "fused" (Tobach and Greenberg, 1984) levels comprises a complete depiction of the integrated organization involved in the developmental contextual view of human development (Lerner, 1986, 1991, 1995, 1996, 1998b).

The dynamic, multilevel perspective about human development presented in the model displayed in Figure 11.1 provides a frame for understanding how parents and parenting provide bases of human development. They do so *not* through their sole, main, or direct effects on children but, instead, through their embeddedness in a dynamic, multilevel system. As such, neither parents nor parenting are alone responsible for the development of children. Systems effects must be understood, and variables from any level of analysis may be, for a given behavioral development at a given point in time, integral in providing the significant variance that drives the system forward. In fact, given the stress in developmental contextualism on the "third source" of development, on the child as a source of her or his own development, the child may play a major role in influencing the actions of the parents that are striving to influence her or him.

Child Effects and Parenting

Given the role of the individual (e.g., the child) as a producer of her or his own development, one implication of developmental contextualism for the understanding of parenting is through the creation of "child effects." How we behave and think as adults—and especially as parents—is very much influenced by our experiences with our children. Our children rear us as much as we do them. The very fact that we are parents makes us different adults than we would be if we were childless. However, more important, the specific and often special characteristics of a particular child influence us in very unique ways. How we behave toward our children depends quite a lot on how they have influenced us to behave. Such child influences are termed child effects.

Child effects emerge largely as a consequence of a child's individual distinctiveness. All children, with the exception of genetically identical (monozygotic) twins, have a unique genotype, that is, a unique genetic inheritance. Similarly, no two children, including monozygotic twins, experience precisely the same environment. As we have noted, all human characteristics, be they behavioral or physical, arise from a probabilistic epigenetic interrelation of genes and environment (Gottlieb, 1970, 1983, 1991, 1992, 1997).

Child effects elicit a "circular function" (Schneirla, 1957) in individual development: Children stimulate differential reactions in their parents, and these reactions provide the basis of feedback to the child, that is, return stimulation that influences their further individual development. The bidirectional child–parent relationships involved in these circular functions underscore the point that children (and adolescents and adults) are producers of their own development and that individuals' relations to their contexts involve bidirectional exchanges (Lerner, 1982; Lerner and Busch-Rossnagel, 1981). The parent shapes the child, but part of what determines the way in which parents do this is children themselves.

Children shape their parents—as adults, as spouses, and of course as parents per se—and in so doing children help organize feedback to themselves, feedback that contributes further to their individuality and thus starts the circular function all over again (that is, returns the child effects process to its first component). Characteristics of behavioral or personality individuality allow the child to contribute to this circular function. However, this idea of circular functions needs to be extended; that is, in and of itself, the notion is mute regarding the specific characteristics of the feedback (e.g., its positive or negative valence) that children will receive as a consequence of their individuality. In other words, to account for the specific character of child–context relations, the circular functions model needs to be supplemented; this is the contribution of the goodness-of-fit model.

The Goodness-of-Fit Model

Just as children bring their characteristics of individuality to a particular social setting, there are demands placed on children by virtue of the social and the physical components of the setting. These demands may take the form of attitudes, values, or stereotypes that are held by others in the context regarding the person's attributes (either their physical or behavioral characteristics); the attributes (usually behavioral) of others in the context with whom the children must coordinate, or fit, their attributes (also, in this case, usually behavioral) for adaptive interactions to exist; or the physical characteristics of a setting (e.g., the presence or absence of access ramps for people with motor disabilities), which require the child to possess certain attributes (again, usually behavioral abilities) for the most efficient interaction within the setting to occur. The child's individuality in differentially meeting these demands provides a basis for the specific feedback she or he gets from the socializing environment.

For example, considering the demand "domain" of attitudes, values, or stereotypes, teachers and parents may have relatively individual and distinct expectations about behaviors desired of their students and their children, respectively. Teachers may want students who show little distractibility, but parents might desire their children to be moderately distractible, for example, when they require their children to move from watching television to dinner or to bed. Children whose behavioral individuality was either generally distractible or generally not distractible would thus differentially meet the demands of these two contexts. Problems of adjustment to school or to home might thus develop as a consequence of a child's lack of match (or goodness of fit) in either or both settings.

Thomas and Chess (1977, 1980, 1981) and Lerner and Lerner (1983, 1989) asserted that, if a child's characteristics of individuality provide a good fit (or match) with the demands of a particular setting, adaptive outcomes will accrue in that setting. Those children whose characteristics match most of the settings within which they exist should receive supportive or positive feedback from the contexts and should show evidence of the most adaptive behavioral development. In turn, of course, poorly fit, or mismatched, children—those whose characteristics are incongruent with one or most settings—should show alternative developmental outcomes. Such characteristics of individuality involve what the children do, why the children show a given behavior, and/or how the children do whatever they do.

This last characteristic of individuality raises the example of the temperamental pattern associated with the child's behavior (Chess and Thomas, 1984, 1999; Thomas and Chess, 1977).

There is evidence pertinent to circular functions that relates to individual differences in children's temperament.

Temperament and Tests of the Goodness-of-Fit Model

Much of the research literature supporting the use of the goodness-of-fit model is derived from the New York Longitudinal Study (NYLS) of Thomas and Chess (1977; Chess and Thomas, 1996, 1999). Within the NYLS data set, information relevant to the goodness-of-fit model exists as a consequence of the multiple samples present in the project. The NYLS core sample was composed of 133 middle-socioeconomic, mostly European American children of professional parents, who were followed from infancy through young adulthood. In addition, a sample of 98 New York City Puerto Rican children of blue-collar parents was followed for approximately nine years. Each sample was studied from at least the first month of life onward. Although the distribution of temperamental attributes in the two samples was not different, the import of the attributes for psychosocial adjustment was quite disparate.

Two examples may suffice to illustrate this distinction. Both relate to the concept of "easy" versus "difficult" temperament (Chess and Thomas, 1984, 1999; Thomas and Chess, 1977). Chess and Thomas (1984, 1999) explained that there are attributes of temperament that afford "difficulty" for caregiving, that is, they do not match with, or fit, the caregiver's demands, and this lack of good fit may be associated with distinct types of parental and family relations. For instance, temperamentally difficult children may be those who, because they are moody and biologically arrhythmic, do not fit with the preferences, expectations, or schedules of caregivers; by contrast, children with easy temperaments (e.g., rhythmic children who have a positive mood) may fit more with caregiver preferences, expectations, or schedules. However, the point of the examples we provide is that a child's temperament ease or difficulty does not "reside" in the child but rather in the dynamic relations involving the child, the parent, and the larger ecology of human development. What may be difficult in one setting and/or a predictor of negative developmental outcomes, may be irrelevant or, instead, a predictor of positive outcomes under different conditions of the developmental system.

Accordingly, to illustrate the dynamic interactional embeddedness of the functional significance of temperamental individuality let us consider first the impact of low regularity or rhythmicity of behavior, particularly in regard to sleep–wake cycles. The Puerto Rican parents studied by Thomas and Chess (1977; Thomas, Chess, Sillen, and Mendez, 1974) were quite permissive. No demands in regard to rhythmicity of sleep were placed on the infant or child. Indeed, the parents allowed the child to go to sleep at any time the child desired and permitted the child to awaken at any time as well. The parents molded their schedule around the children. Because parents were so accommodating there were no problems of fit associated with an arrhythmic infant or child. Indeed, neither within the infancy period nor throughout the first five years of life did arrhythmicity predict adjustment problems. In this sample arrhythmicity remained continuous and independent of adaptive implications for the child (Korn, 1978; Thomas et al., 1974). In the predominantly European American, middle-socioeconomic families, however, strong demands for rhythmic sleep patterns were maintained. Thus an arrhythmic child did not fit with parental demands, and, consistent with the goodness-of-fit model, arrhythmicity was a major predictor of problem behaviors both within the infancy years and through the first five years of life (Korn, 1978; Thomas et al., 1974).

It should be emphasized that there are at least two ways of viewing this finding. First, we may note that, consistent with the idea that children influence their parents, sleep arrhythmicity in their children resulted in problems in the parents—for example, through their reports of stress, anxiety, and anger (Thomas et al., 1974; Chess and Thomas, 1984, 1996, 1999). Such an effect of child temperament on the parent's own level of adaptation has been reported in other data sets; for instance, infants who had high thresholds for responsiveness to social stimulation, and thus were not easily soothed by their mothers, evoked intense distress reactions in their mothers and a virtual cessation of maternal caregiving behaviors (Brazelton, Koslowski, and Main, 1974). Thus it is possible that the presence of such child effects in the NYLS sample could have altered previous parenting styles in a way that constituted negative feedback ("negative parenting") to the child that was associated with the development of problem behaviors.

A second interpretation of this finding arises from the fact that problem behaviors in the children were identified initially on the basis of parental report. Thus it may be that, irrespective of any problem behavior evoked in the parent by the child and/or of any altered parent–child interactions that thereby ensued, one effect of the child on the parent was to increase the probability of the parent's labeling the child's temperamental style as problematic and so reporting it to the NYLS staff psychiatrist. Unfortunately, the current analysis of the NYLS data does not allow us to discriminate between these obviously nonmutually exclusive possibilities.

However, what the data in the NYLS do allow us to indicate is that the parents in the middle-socioeconomic sample took steps to change their arrhythmic children's sleep patterns; and as most of these arrhythmic children were also adaptable and because temperament may be modified by person–context interactions, low rhythmicity tended to be discontinuous for most children. That the parents behaved to modify their children's arrhythmicity is also an instance of a child effect on its psychosocial context. That is, the child "produced" in her or his parents alterations in parental caregiving behaviors regarding sleep. That these child effects on the parental context fed back to the child and influenced the child's further development is consistent with the previously noted finding that sleep arrhythmicity was discontinuous among these children.

Thus, in the predominantly European American, middle-socioeconomic sample, early infant arrhythmicity tended to be a problem during this time of life but proved to be neither continuous nor predictive of later adjustment problems. In turn, in the Puerto Rican sample, infant arrhythmicity was not a problem during this time of life, but it was continuous and—because in the Puerto Rican context it was not involved in poor fit—it was not associated with adjustment problems in the child in the first five years of life. Of course, this is not to say that the parents in the Puerto Rican families were not affected by their children's sleep arrhythmicity; as with the parents in the middle-socioeconomic families, it may be that the Puerto Rican parents had problems that were of fatigue and suffered marital or work-related problems that were due to irregular sleep patterns produced in them as a consequence of their child's sleep arrhythmicity; however, again, the data analyses in the NYLS do not indicate this possible child effect on the Puerto Rican parents.

The data do allow us to underscore the importance of considering fit with the demands of the psychosocial context of development, in that they indicate that arrhythmicity did begin to predict adjustment problems for the Puerto Rican children when they entered the school system. Their lack of a regular sleep pattern interfered with their getting sufficient sleep to perform well in school and, in addition, often caused them to be late to school (Korn, 1978; Thomas et al., 1974). Thus, before the age of 5 years, only one Puerto Rican child presented a clinical problem diagnosed as a sleep disorder. However, almost 50% of the Puerto Rican children who developed clinically identifiable problems between the ages of 5 and 9 years were diagnosed as having sleep problems.

Another example may be given of how the differential demands existing between the two family contexts provide different presses for adaptation. This example pertains to differences in the demands of the families' physical contexts. As noted by Thomas et al. (1974), as well as Korn (1978), overall there was a very low incidence of behavior problems in the Puerto Rican sample children in their first five years of life, especially when compared with the corresponding incidence among the core sample children. However, if a problem was presented at this time among the Puerto Rican sample, it was most likely to be a problem of motor activity. In fact, across the first nine years of their lives, of those Puerto Rican children who developed clinical problems, 53% presented symptoms diagnosed as involving problematic motor activity. Parents complained of excessive and uncontrollable motor activity in such cases. However, in the core sample only one child (a child with brain damage) was characterized in this way.

We may note here that the Puerto Rican parents' reports of "excessive and uncontrollable" activity in their children does constitute, in this group, an example of a child effect on the parents. That is, a major value of the Puerto Rican parents in the NYLS was child "obedience" to authority (Korn, 1978).

The type of motor activity shown by the highly active children of these Puerto Rican parents evoked considerable parental distress, given their perception that their children's behavior was inconsistent with what would be shown by obedient children (Korn, 1978).

In the Puerto Rican sample the families usually had several children and lived in small apartments. Even average motor activity therefore tended to impinge on others in the setting. Moreover, and as an illustration of the embeddedness of the child–temperament–home–context relation in the broader community context, we may note that the Puerto Rican parents were reluctant to let their children out of the apartment because of the actual dangers of playing on the streets of East Harlem, perhaps especially for children with high activity levels.

In the predominantly European American, middle-socioeconomic sample, however, the parents had the financial resources to provide large apartments or houses for their families. There were typically suitable play areas for the children both inside and outside the home. As a consequence, the presence of high activity levels in the home of the core sample did not cause the problems for interaction that they did in the Puerto Rican group. Thus, as Thomas, Chess, and Birch (1968) and Thomas et al. (1974) emphasize, the mismatch between temperamental attribute and physical environmental demand accounted for the group difference in the import of high activity level for the development of behavioral problems in the children.

Chess and Thomas (1999) reviewed other data from the NYLS and from independent data sets that tested their temperament–context, goodness-of-fit model. One very important study they discuss was conducted by de Vries (1984), who studied the Masai tribe living in the sub-Sahara region of Kenya at a time when a severe drought was beginning. After obtaining temperament ratings on 47 infants, aged 2 to 4 months, de Vries identified from within his sample the 10 infants with the easiest temperaments and the 10 with the most difficult temperaments. Five months later he returned to the tribal area, a time when 97% of the cattle herd had died from the drought. Given that the basic food supply was milk and blood, both derived from the tribe's cattle, the level of starvation and death experienced by the tribe was enormous. de Vries located the families of seven of the easy babies and six of the difficult ones. The families of the other infants had moved in order to try to escape the drought. Of the seven easy babies, five had died. All of the difficult babies had survived.

Chess and Thomas (1999) suggested two reasons for this dramatic finding. First, difficult infants cried loudly and frequently; the easy babies cried less loudly and less frequently. Parents fed the difficult babies either to stop their excessive crying or because they interpreted the cries as signals of extreme hunger. Alternatively, there may be a cultural reason for the survival of the difficult infants, one that would not have emerged to affect behavior during a time of plentiful food, when both easy and difficult babies could have been soothed easily when crying because of hunger. Chess and Thomas suggest that the parents, under the nonnormative historical conditions of the drought, saw the difficult babies not as a problem to be managed but as an asset to the survival of the tribe. As a consequence, the parents might have actually chosen "for survival these lusty expressive babies who has more desirable characteristics according to the tribes cultural standards" (Chess and Thomas, 1999, p. 111).

Accordingly, the parent–child relation, embedded in the developmental system at a time of non-normative natural environment disaster, led to a switch in the valence, or meaning, of difficulty and resulted in a dramatic differences in adaptive developmental outcome (survival or death). In turn, among the core NYLS sample, living under "privileged" conditions in New York City, difficult babies comprised 23% of the "clinical," behavior problem group (10 babies) but only 4% (4 cases) of the nonclinical sample (Thomas et al., 1968, p. 78). Thus Chess and Thomas (1999) stress that the relationship between child and the parent, a relation interactive with the multiple levels of the developmental system, including the physical ecology, culture, and history, must be the frame of reference for understanding the role of temperament in parent–child relationships and in the enactment and outcomes of parenting.

A similar conclusion may be derived from the research of Super and Harkness (1981). Studying the Kipsigis tribe in either the rural village of Kokwet, Kenya or in the urban setting of Nairobi, Kenya,

Super and Harkness (1981) found that sleep arrhythmicity had different implications for mother–infant interactions. Rural Kipsigis is an agricultural community, and the tribe assigns primary (and in fact virtually exclusive) caregiving duties to the mother who, even if she is working in the fields (or is socializing, sleeping, or the like), keeps the infant in close proximity to her (either on her shoulder or within a few feet of her). Sleep arrhythmicity in such a context is not a dimension of difficulty for the mother because, whenever the infant awakes she or he can be fed or soothed by the mother with little disruption of her other activities. By contrast, however, Kipsigis living in Nairobi are not farmers but office workers, professionals, and the like. In this context, they cannot keep the infant close to them at all times and, as a consequence, Super and Harkness (1981) found that sleep arrhythmicity is a sign of difficulty and is associated with problems for the mother and for her interactions with the infant.

Conclusions Regarding the Goodness-of-Fit Model

The tests of the goodness-of-fit model that we have reviewed enable us to underscore the key implication of developmental contextualism for the study of parenting. At any given point in ontogenetic and historical time, neither children's attributes per se nor the features of their context (e.g., the demands of their parents regarding temperamental style) per se are the key predictors of their adaptive functioning. Instead, the *relation* among the child, the parent, and the other levels of organization within the developmental system is most important in understanding the character of parenting and of the role of the ecology of human development on a child's ontogeny. This relationism, this dynamism, constitutes the basic process of human development (Lerner, 1991).

In essence, then, the developmental contextual model specifies that scholarship pertinent to parenting should focus on the relational process of human development, and should do so by integrating, across time, the study of the actions of the child and the actions of the parent and of the broader context (e.g., through notions such as the goodness-of-fit model). A comparable, four-dimensional prescription for scholarship about parenting—a call for focus on process, person, context, and time—is found in Bronfenbrenner's bioecological theory of development. Accordingly, to enable us to specify in richer detail the implications of developmental systems theory for research and applications pertinent to parenting, we consider Bronfenbrenner's model.

BRONFENBRENNER'S BIOECOLOGICAL THEORY

Throughout the 1970s and 1980s, Bronfenbrenner made several contributions to understanding the importance of the context of human development. In his 1979 book, *The Ecology of Human Development*, Bronfenbrenner explained the importance for human ontogeny of the interrelated ecological levels, conceived of as nested systems, involved in human development. Each of the ecological systems he described was explained to have an important impact on the child, the parent, the family, and in fact on the quality of life in society.

Bronfenbrenner (1977, 1979) described the microsystem as the setting within which the individual was behaving at a given moment in her or his life and the mesosystem as the set of microsystems constituting the individual's developmental niche within a given period of development. In addition, the exosystem is composed of contexts that, although not directly involving the developing person (e.g., the workplace of a child's parent), have an influence on the person's behavior and development (e.g., as may occur when the parent has had a stressful day at work and as a result has a reduced capacity to provide quality caregiving to the child). Finally, the macrosystem is the superordinate level of the ecology of human development; it is the level involving culture, macroinstitutions (such as the federal government), and public policy. The macrosystem influences the nature of interaction within all other levels of the ecology of human development (Garbarino, Vorrasi, and Kostelny, in Vol. 5 of this *Handbook*).

Bronfenbrenner's (1979) formulation had a broad impact on the field of human development, promoting considerable interest through the 1980s in the role of the ecological system in texturing the life course of individuals. Yet, by the end of that decade and into the 1990s, Bronfenbrenner indicated that he was not pleased with the nature of his contribution to either theory, research, or policy applications pertinent to enhancing the ecology of a child's life to promote the child's positive development. For instance, Bronfenbrenner (1989, p. 188) made the following observation:

> Existing developmental studies subscribing to an ecological model have provided far more knowledge about the nature of developmentally relevant environments, near and far, than about the characteristics of developing individuals, then and now . . . . The criticism I just made also applies to my own writings . . . . Nowhere in the 1979 monograph, nor elsewhere until today, does one find a parallel set of structures for conceptualizing the characteristics of the developing person.

Bronfenbrenner believes, as do other theorists drawn to developmental systems notions of human functioning, that *all* the levels of organization involved in human life are linked integratively in the constitution of the course of individual ontogeny. Although his 1979 book made an enormous contribution to such a conception of human development by giving scholars conceptual tools to understand and to study the differentiated but integrated levels of the context of human development, Bronfenbrenner recognized that his theory would be incomplete until he included in it the levels of individual structure and function (biology, psychology, and behavior) fused dynamically with the ecological systems he described. Accordingly, Bronfenbrenner and his colleagues (e.g., Bronfenbrenner, in press; Bronfenbrenner and Ceci, 1993, 1994a, 1994b; Bronfenbrenner and Morris, 1998) have, for more than a decade, worked to integrate the other levels of the developmental system, starting from biology, psychology, and behavior, into the model of human development he was formulating. The span of the levels he seeks to synthesize in his model—biology through the broadest level of the ecology of human development—accounts for the label, bioecological, he attaches to the model. In short, then, Bronfenbrenner (in press; Bronfenbrenner and Morris, 1998) has sought to bring the features of the developing person into the ecological system he has elaborated.

Thus, as Bronfenbrenner describes it, the defining properties of the model that has emerged from this scholarship involves four interrelated components: (1) The developmental *process*, involving the fused and dynamic relation of the individual and the context; (2) the *person*, with an individual repertoire of biological, cognitive, emotional, and behavioral characteristics; (3) the *context* of human development, conceptualized as the nested levels, or systems, of the ecology of human development he has depicted (Bronfenbrenner, 1977, 1979); and (4) *time*, conceptualized as involving the multiple dimensions of temporality that Elder (1998) explains are part of life course theory. These dimensions include "life" or "ontogenetic" time (one's age from birth to death), "family" time (one's location within the flow of prior and succeeding generations), and "historical" time (the social and cultural system that exists in the world when one is born and the changing circumstances regarding this system that occur during one's life) (Elder, 1998).

The Process–Person–Context–Time Model

Together, the four components of Bronfenbrenner's formulation of bioecological theory constitute a Process–Person–Context–Time (PPCT) model for conceptualizing the integrated developmental system and for designing research to study the course of human development. That is, Bronfenbrenner believes that, just as each of the four components of the PPCT model must be included in any adequate conceptual specification of the dynamic human development system, so too must research appraise all four components of the model to provide data that are adequate for understanding the course of human development.

Indeed, neither research nor theory could exclude the developmental process, the person, and the context integrated by this process, or the changes over time that occur as a consequence of this process, and still hope to have a full depiction of the dynamics of changes in functioning within the developmental system. Accordingly, in describing the PPCT model, Bronfenbrenner (Bronfenbrenner and Morris, 1998, p. 994) noted that he must explain the

> four principal components and the dynamic, interactive relationships among them . . . . The first of these, which constitutes the core of the model, is Process. More specifically, this construct encompasses particular forms of interaction between organism and environment, called proximal processes, that operate over time and are posited as the primary mechanisms producing human development. However, the power of such processes to influence development is presumed, and shown, to vary substantially as a function of the characteristics of the developing Person, of the immediate and more remote environmental Contexts, and the Time periods, in which the proximal processes take place.

In turn, in regard to the three remaining defining properties of the model—Person, Context, and Time—Bronfenbrenner and Morris (1998, p. 994) noted that they give priority in their scholarship to defining the biopsychosocial characteristics of the "Person," because, as noted by Bronfenbrenner in 1989, his earlier formulations of the model (e.g., Bronfenbrenner, 1979) left a gap in regard to this key feature of the theory. As a consequence, Bronfenbrenner and Morris (1998, p. 995) made several observations in regard to these Person characteristics:

> Three types of Person characteristics are distinguished as most influential in shaping the course of future development through their capacity to affect the direction and power of proximal processes through the life course. The first are dispositions that can set proximal processes in motion in a particular developmental domain and continue to sustain their operation. Next are bioecological resources of ability, experience, knowledge, and skill required for the effective functioning of proximal processes at a given stage of development. Finally, there are demand characteristics that invite or discourage reactions from the social environment of a kind that can foster or disrupt the operation of proximal processes. The differentiation of these three forms leads to their combination in patterns of Person structure that can further account for differences in the direction and power of resultant proximal processes and their developmental effects.

Consistent with the integrative character of development systems theory, Bronfenbrenner and his colleagues point out that, when the characteristics of the Person component of the bioecological model is expanded in this way, the result is a richer understanding for the scholar and, potentially, for parents of the context—the ecological system—with which the developing person is fused. For instance, parents may attain a more differentiated and nuanced appreciation of the resources on which they may call for support. Thus, as explained by Bronfenbrenner and Morris (1998, p. 995),

> These new formulations of qualities of the person that shape her or his future development have had the unanticipated effect of further differentiating, expanding, and integrating the original 1979 conceptualization of the environment in terms of nested systems ranging from micro to macro . . . . For example, the three types of Person characteristics outlined above are also incorporated into the definition of the microsystem as characteristics of parents, relatives, close friends, teachers, mentors, coworkers, spouses, or others who participate in the life of the developing person on a fairly regular basis over extended periods of time.

Indeed, Bronfenbrenner redefined the character of the microsystem to link it centrally to what he regards as the "center of gravity" (Bronfenbrenner and Morris, 1998, p. 1013)—the biopsychosocial person—within his theory as it has now been elaborated. That is, although, as in 1979, he sees the ecology of human development as "the ecological environment . . . conceived as a set of nested structures, each inside the other like a set of Russian dolls" (p. 3), he magnifies his conception of the innermost, microsystem structure within this ecology by incorporating the activities, relationships, and roles of the developing person into this system. That is, he made the following observation

(Bronfenbrenner, 1994, p. 1645):

> A microsystem is a pattern of activities, social roles, and interpersonal relations experienced by the developing person in a given face-to-face setting with particular physical, social, and symbolic features that invite, permit, or inhibit, engagement in sustained, progressively more complex interaction with, and activity in, the immediate environment.

What may be particularly significant to Bronfenbrenner in this expanded definition of the micro-system is that he includes not only the person's interactions with other people in this level of the ecology but, as well, the interactions the person has with the world of symbols and language (with the semiotic system)—a component of ecological relationships that action theorists also believe is especially important in understanding the formulation of intentions, goals, and actions (see, for example, Brandtstädter, 1998, 1999). That is, Bronfenbrenner and Morris (1998, p. 995) noted the following characteristics:

> The bioecological model also introduces an even more consequential domain into the structure of the microsystem that emphasizes the distinctive contribution to development of proximal processes involving interaction not with people but with objects and symbols. Even more broadly, concepts and criteria are introduced that differentiate between those features of the environment that foster versus interfere with the development of proximal processes. Particularly significant in the latter sphere is the growing hecticness, instability, and chaos in the principal settings in which human competence and character are shaped—in the family, child-care arrangements, schools, peer groups, and neighborhoods.

Finally, Bronfenbrenner noted that the emphasis on a redefined and expanded concept of the microsystem leads to the last defining property of the current formulation of his theory of human development. Bronfenbrenner and Morris (1998, p. 995) indicate that

> the fourth and final defining property of the bioecological model and the one that moves it farthest beyond its predecessor [is] the dimension of Time. The 1979 Volume scarcely mentions the term, whereas in the current formulation, it has a prominent place at three successive levels—micro-, meso-, and macro-. Microtime refers to continuity versus discontinuity within ongoing episodes of proximal process. Mesotime is the periodicity of theses episodes across broader time intervals, such as days and weeks. Finally, Macrotime focuses on the changing expectations and events in the larger society, both within and across generations, as they affect and are affected by, processes and outcomes of human development over the life course.

As we have noted, Bronfenbrenner and Morris (1998) indicate that the inclusion of a temporal dimension in the current model draws on the work of Elder (1998), previously discussed, in regard to the multiple dimensions of time that are involved in linking the ecology of human development (or the social system, in the terms of Elder, 1998) to individual development. Thus, as is the case in regard to other instances of developmental systems theory, Bronfenbrenner's theory integrates ideas unique to his model with those associated with other members of the developmental systems theoretical family.

Conclusions Regarding Bronfenbrenner's Model

Bronfenbrenner's bioecological model is, in at least two senses, a living system (Ford and Lerner, 1992). First, the theory depicts the dynamic, developmental relations between an active individual and her or his complex, integrated and changing ecology. In addition, the theory is itself developing (e.g., see Bronfenbrenner, in press), as Bronfenbrenner seeks to make the features of the theory more precise and, as such, a more operational guide for PPCT-relevant research about the dynamic character of the human developmental process.

At this writing, then, the bioecological model has developed to include several propositions (Bronfenbrenner, in press). These ideas promote a dynamic, person–context relational view of the process of human development. As explained by Bronfenbrenner and Morris (1998, p. 996), this is Proposition 1 of the bioecological model:

> Especially in its early phases, but also throughout the life course, human development takes place through processes of progressively more complex reciprocal interaction between an active, evolving biopsychosocial human organism and the persons, objects, and symbols in its immediate external environment. To be effective, the interaction must occur on a fairly regular basis over extended periods of time. Such enduring forms of interaction in the immediate environment are referred to as proximal processes. Examples of enduring patterns of proximal process are found in feeding or comforting a baby, playing with a young child, child–child activities, group or solitary play, reading, learning new skills, athletic activities, problem solving, caring for others in distress, making plans, performing complex tasks, and acquiring new knowledge, and know-how.

Thus, in the first proposition in his theory, Bronfenbrenner emphasizes a theme found in the other instances of developmental systems theory and, as we have noted, developmental contextualism in particular—the role of the active individual as an agent in her or his own development. In fact, the notion that the individual contributes to the developmental process is present as well in the second proposition of bioecological theory (Bronfenbrenner and Morris, 1998, p. 996):

> The form, power, content, and direction of the proximal processes effecting development vary systematically as a joint function of the characteristics of the developing person; of the environment—both immediate and more remote—in which the processes are taking place; the nature of the developmental outcomes under consideration; and the social continuities and changes occurring over time through the life course and the historical period during which the person has lived.

As is evident from these two propositions, Bronfenbrenner regards proximal processes as the primary sources of development and stresses the role of the individual, as an active agent in her or his own development. Indeed, Bronfenbrenner and Morris (1998, p. 996) asked their readers to make the following observations:

> Note that characteristics of the person actually appear twice in the bioecological model—first as one of the four elements influencing the "form, power, content, and direction of the proximal process," and then again as "developmental outcomes"; that is, qualities of the developing person that emerge at a later point in time as the result of the joint, interactive, mutually reinforcing effects of the four principal antecedent components of the model. In sum, in the bioecological model, the characteristics of the person function both as an indirect producer and as a product of development.

In sum, as is the case in regard to developmental contextualism, and indeed all instances of developmental systems theory, the active, developing individual is seen by Bronfenbrenner as a central force of that individual's development. This contribution to the process of development is made by a synthesis, an integration, between the active person and her or his active context. Accordingly, Bronfenbrenner's model converges with developmental contextualism in pointing to the need to adopt a multidimensional approach to conceptualizations of, research about, and applications associated with the character of parenting for child development. It is pertinent to discuss these research and application implications of the two instances of developmental systems theory that we have discussed.

SAMPLE CASES OF A DEVELOPMENTAL SYSTEMS FOCUS ON PARENTING: RESEARCH DIMENSIONS

Several areas of research within the parenting literature reflect ideas associated with developmental systems theory. These areas of scholarship can also be extended through the use of ideas pertinent to developmental systems. In fact, we believe that virtually every area of research on parenting either provides support for the developmental systems framework and/or would benefit from a more concerted and conscious application of that framework in subsequent studies. To illustrate, we briefly discuss five areas of inquiry on parenting, highlighting the relevance of the developmental systems approach in each case.

The Effects of Harsh Discipline

One prominent line of inquiry in the field of parenting concerns the effects of harsh physical discipline on children's externalizing behavior problems (for example, Baumrind, 1971; Glueck and Glueck, 1940; McCord, 1991; Straus, 1994). Confusion about effects of harsh physical discipline (and, relatedly, coercive and authoritarian parenting) persists because of the failure to consider interaction effects. Although most investigators report very negative effects (high externalizing behavior in children), the findings are not consistent and there is strong public sentiment, at least in some quarters, that harshness is sometimes beneficial. The latter belief, reflected in the popular aphorism "spare the rod and spoil the child," is evidenced by findings that the vast majority of young children are physically punished by parents in the United States (Deater-Deckard and Dodge, 1997; Straus and Gelles, 1990). We believe that a developmental systems framework is best suited to account for the complexity of issues in this area.

For instance, racial differences in discipline practices and socialization have been well documented (Coll, Meyer, and Brillon, 1995). Some research has reported that African American parents use high levels of control and physical punishment and high levels of affection and acceptance (e.g., Brody and Flor, 1998). European American families, on the other hand, more often use democratic parenting practices (Hamner and Turner, 1990). Moreover, there is a significant positive correlation between harsh punishment and externalizing behavior for European American, but not for African American, families (for a review, see Deater-Deckard and Dodge, 1997). In seeking to explain these findings, Deater-Deckard and Dodge pointed to the differences between cultural groups in the extent to which harsh punishment is a normative form of discipline that is likely to be viewed as acceptable rather than aberrant.

If parents view physical punishment as aberrant and illegitimate, as opposed to normative and justified, then so too do the children, and they are more likely to react negatively to it. In fact, there is evidence that African American parents view physical punishment (spanking) less negatively than do European American parents (Deater-Deckard and Dodge, 1997). Because the meaning of the parents' behavior is critical in determining its effect on the child and because community standards determine the meaning of parents' behavior, physical punishment is likely to have very different consequences in different communities.

Furthermore, discipline practices differ across socioeconomic groups (e.g., Luster, Rhoades, and Haas, 1989; Steinberg, Lamborn, Dornbusch, and Darling, 1992). McLoyd (1990) has proposed that the stress of poverty takes its toll on parents' resources and ability to parent effectively. Specifically, some evidence suggests that low-income parents use more harsh discipline practices compared with those of middle-socioeconomic parents (Steinberg, Mounts, Lamborn, and Dornbusch, 1991); similarly, low-income parents have been reported to be less involved in their children's schooling (Harris, Kagey, and Ross, 1987).

These findings may have implications for other demographic groups and other parenting practices. Just as there are interactions between ethnic group and physical punishment, there may be interactions of generational group and physical punishment. In America before the 1960s, there was more acceptance of physical punishment (Straus, 1994). As previously suggested, when physical punishment is seen as more acceptable and legitimate, it is likely to have less aversive effects on children. Similarly, there are community differences in many parenting practices, including physical contact (e.g., hugging, kissing, sleeping arrangements) and negotiation (compromising, certain forms of reasoning). In East Asian communities, where these practices are less normative and less valued than they are in the United States (Rothbaum, Pott, Azuma, Miyake, and Weisz, 2000), their effects on children may be less positive. For example, the practice of cosleeping, which is much more widely practiced in Japan, is often seen as problematic in the context of U.S. culture, for example, in regard to having a negative emotional impact on the child, especially if the practice is extended too long into her or his childhood (Lebra, 1994). There is also substantial evidence of cultural differences in parental attitudes regarding the exercise of control and of corresponding cultural differences in the beneficial effects of parental control on children (Chao, 1995; Lau, Lew, Hau, Cheung, and Berndt, 1990; Rohner and Pettengill, 1985). These ideas and findings are consistent with developmental systems theorists' claim that context (culture) and time (generational effects) help shape the effects of parenting practices (see also Chao and Tseng, in Vol. 4 of this *Handbook*).

There is reason to believe that the effects of harsh discipline on externalizing varies as a function of the child's developmental level—the other temporal factor highlighted by developmental systems theory. Findings from a meta-analysis indicate that the effects of rejecting parenting (closely related to harsh discipline) depend on the age of the child—the association between parental rejection and externalizing is greater at older ages than at younger ones (Rothbaum and Weisz, 1994). As noted by Deater-Deckard and Dodge (1997, p. 168), "the meaning that a child applies to a particular parental behavior (such as spanking) is probably based, in part, on past experience and in part on his active construction of the current status of the parent–child relationship." Because "cognition is the filter through which experiences are evaluated" (1997, p. 168) and because children's ability to form abstract conceptualizations about the meaning of parental behavior increases with age, it follows that older children would be more adversely influenced by their parents' negative behaviors. Again, the findings are in line with developmental systems thinking.

Contextual Supports Against Risk

Several reviews of the literature on familial risk highlight the interactive effects of parenting and ecosystemic factors. Rutter (1979) and Sameroff (1983, 1987) reviewed evidence that the adverse effects of negative parenting factors, such as maternal mental illness, paternal criminality, and other disturbances in parental functioning, are much greater when combined with environmental risk factors such as poverty and low socioeconomic status (SES), family size, and inadequate educational and community support services. The combined effect of these multiple risks is much greater than their additive influence, suggesting an interaction of parental and environmental risks. It is possible that the buffering effects of middle to high SES (e.g., educational opportunity) and quality support services (e.g., counseling) is much greater among children with negative parenting than among those with adequate parenting (Sameroff, Seifer, and Bartko, 1997).

Interactive, as contrasted with additive, effects of risk have also been reported by Richters and Martinez (1993). They found that, among inner-city youth, instability at home and lack of safety (i.e., drugs and guns in the home) increased adaptational failure by a factor of 15, but either risk alone increased failure by a factor of only 3. Such findings make us mindful of the dynamical systems model notion that change occurs as a function of a confluence of influences, with decidedly nonlinear effects (Thelen and Smith, 1998). Further investigations of interactions such as these will ultimately enable us to pinpoint the processes that lie at the heart of the developmental systems model.

Family Systems

More than any other literature on parenting, the family systems literature highlights the different factors emphasized by developmental systems theory—process, person, context, and time (McAdoo, in Vol. 4 of this *Handbook*). The theory's consideration of these multiple factors is no doubt responsible for the difficulty in conducting research pertinent to it. Yet, in recent years, there have been valuable empirical efforts to test the theory. For example, Vuchinich, Angelelli, and Gatherum (1996) have shown that parents' agreement with one another can have beneficial effects on children, depending on other family dynamics—particularly whether or not the parents were engaged in a coalition. Vuchinich et al. (1996) have shown that parents and preadolescents' discussion of topics involving autonomy is productive, but only when the adolescents initiate the selection of the topic for discussion.

Other family systems research indicates interactions between children's age and gender in determining children's reaction to marital conflict (Davies, Myers, Cummings, and Heindel, 1999; Grych, in Vol. 4 of this *Handbook*). Research that examines the effects of marital disagreement and conflict through a simpler research lens, failing to consider other familial dynamics, the child's developmental level, and the social context (e.g., the nature of the topic under discussion and who selected it), will yield a much more limited understanding of parent–child relationships.

Attachment

One of the most productive areas of research on children involves attachment (Cummings and Cummings, in Vol. 5 of this *Handbook*). A substantial body of research indicates that infants who receive "sensitive and responsive" caregiving are more likely to develop secure attachment relationships with their caregivers and that secure infants are likely to become more "socially competent" children and adults. Attachment researchers acknowledge cultural influences, but they believe that there are only "specific" differences in "particular situations" and they emphasize "similarities across cultures" (Ainsworth and Marvin, 1995; see also Cassidy and Shaver, 1999, p. 8). The attachment theory position is inconsistent with a developmental systems approach. In support of the latter, research from Japan indicates that the parental antecedents of security (i.e., sensitivity), and the long-term consequences of sensitivity (i.e., social competence) are very different than those in the United States (Rothbaum et al., 2000; Rothbaum, Weisz, Pott, Miyake, and Morelli, 2000). Specifically, parental sensitivity is more likely to be associated with prolonged and skin-to-skin physical contact, anticipation of children's signals, and encouragement of dependence and emotional closeness in Japan than in the United States, and parental sensitivity is less likely to be associated with brief and distal contact, waiting until after children signal their needs, and encouragement of autonomy and exploration. Social competence in Japan compared with that in the United States is more likely to include dependence, emotional restraint, indirect expression of feelings, clear differentiation of behavior with in-group and out-group members and self-effacement, and it is less likely to include autonomy, willingness to discuss strong affect and disagree with partners, sociability with unfamiliar (out-group) members, and a positive view of self (Rothbaum, Pott, Azuma, Miyake, and Weisz, 2000; Rothbaum, Weisz, Pott, Miyake, and Morelli, 2000).

These cultural differences in the kind of parenting that leads to security and in the kind of social competence that security is expected to foster exemplify ways in which parenting and culture interact in determining the antecedents and consequences of children's attachment. Despite their emphasis on the ecology of human adaptation, attachment theorists have not adequately considered the ways in which parental behavior and the social context dynamically interact in determining the import of attachment for development across the lifespan.

Family Type

During the past 50 years, there has been growing awareness of generational differences in family structure and functioning. Research by Hernandez (1993) and others (Hetherington and Stanley-Hagen, in Vol. 3 of this *Handbook*; Lerner, Sparks, and McCubbin, 1999) highlights the increase in divorce and in single-parent, adoptive, dual-wage earner, and lesbian, gay, and blended families, and the decrease in number of children per family. There is also research on the adaptiveness of these different family forms, particularly the effects of divorce on children (Emery, 1998).

However, this research has not adequately explored interactions between generation and family type. Given that different family forms are more or less common in different eras, it is possible that the adaptive consequences of these different families also vary with time. We suspect that any adverse consequences of nonnormative family forms, such as those previously noted, are greatest when they are least common (and thus least likely to be accepted). Thus, for example, divorce is likely to have had more detrimental effects on children in the early and the middle (as contrasted with the late) twentieth century, when it was less common and less accepted and when there were fewer social supports to help children cope with its likely adverse effects (e.g., loss of one parent or financial stress; Demo, Allen, and Fine, 2000).

Interactions between family type and culture are likely for the same reason. In communities where family forms, such as gay, lesbian, or adoptive families, are less common and less accepted or marginalized, children from these families are likely to fare less well (Savin-Williams and Esterberg, 2000). Similarly, in communities where divorce is less common and less accepted, such as Japan, the negative effects of divorce are likely to be accentuated (Hetherington and Stanley-Hagen, 2000).

Conclusions About Research Dimensions

Whether areas of research pertinent to parenting (for example, the literature pertinent to harsh discipline) have a dominant tradition consistent with developmental systems theory or do not have such a history (such as scholarship pertinent to attachment), the substance of all areas can be interpreted and extended by ideas associated with developmental systems. Findings in all areas highlight the need to broaden our thinking about parenting effects. The study of parenting has primarily focused on main effects of parental behavior. Even when social context influences (e.g., culture, poverty) are considered, their effects are seen as mediated through parents. In their review of parenting research, Collins, Maccoby, Steinberg, Hetherington, and Bornstein (2000) extend this focus by explicitly stating that social context factors are in large part "mediated" by parenting (see also McLoyd, 1990; Patterson, 1982). In effect, they maintain that child behavior is a *main effect* of parenting or an additive main effect of parenting and other social context factors.

By contrast, we emphasize the ways in which parenting serves as a moderating factor and stress interaction effects rather than main effects; we point to the ways in which parenting interacts with social context factors. In the analysis of variance, one should not interpret main effects when they are complicated by higher-order interactions; similarly, because any single source of influence in the developmental system is always fused with the other influences in the system, one should not interpret effects of any single source of influence, including parenting, but instead the *relations* among sources.

This is not a novel view, but it has not received the attention it deserves—especially if we are correct that the sorts of dynamic interactions depicted within developmental systems theories, such as the ones we have reviewed in this chapter, account for most of the variance in the parent–child relationship and in child functioning. Indeed, even though they focus on parenting as a mediating variable, Collins et al. (2000, p. 227) endorse Bronfenbrenner's emphasis on the "interactive and synergistic . . . links between the family and other influences." The study of such complex interactions is more consistent with the developmental systems framework than is the study of simple main effects.

Developmental systems ideas also enable the applied import (for child- and family-serving programs and policies) of these research areas to be specified. To illustrate this use of developmental systems theory, consider the previously noted research on the effects of harsh punishment and how the effects are moderated by (interact with) context, generation, and so forth. Investigations of the ways in which culture, developmental level, and other factors influence the effect of harsh punishment will inform policymakers, clinicians, and other change agents of the conditions under which harsh punishment is least likely to have negative effects. To increase the quality of our policies and interventions, it is first necessary to understand why certain parents are likely to adhere to particular practices. Armed with this understanding, change agents should be better able to provide convincing arguments about how the costs of harsh punishment outweigh its benefits, and they should be sensitive to circumstances in which parents will be most receptive to these arguments (Deater-Deckard and Dodge, 1997). Indeed, knowledge about the multiple factors (e.g., such as cultural influences) that interact with harsh punishment may improve program implementation and evaluation of targeted interventions (Deater-Deckard and Dodge, 1997; Last and Perrin, 1993).

In short, an appreciation of developmental systems theory for the extension of research is not discontinuous with the application of such an approach to developmental science to policy and program actions designed to enhance the lives of children and parents. We consider such applications next.

SAMPLE CASES OF A DEVELOPMENTAL SYSTEMS FOCUS ON PARENTING: SOCIAL PROGRAM AND PUBLIC POLICY APPLICATIONS

Given the integrative scholarship associated with developmental systems theory, it would seem logical that social programs and public policies would use this model as a framework for the creation of comprehensive child and family services. At this moment in time, however, this model is rarely, if ever, implemented. Approximately a decade and a half ago at this writing, Brim and Phillips (1988, p. 290) noted that, "Even a cursory examination of federal programs for children reveals that contemporary developments in life-span theory and its associated disciplines have not been incorporated into the assumptions that affect policy. Instead, interventions and benefits characterized by illogical gaps in coverage, contradictory goals, and poor coordination have proliferated." Their observation still holds true. As a result, families often find themselves in the center of a jumble of disconnected, and often overlapping, services, many of which are in competition for the same limited resources. This situation is shown in Figure 11.2.

There are a number of possible reasons for this apparent distance between the *study* of development and the *application* of developmental systems theory in the "real world." First, although in this chapter we highlight research based on such an approach to theory, in reality, many researchers do not use this model in their study of children, families, and communities. Furthermore, it is still the case that the majority of child development research is not focused on the diverse children of America.

Moreover, the manner in which most research is conducted and disseminated by the academic community rarely matches the realities of the political sphere that is actually responsible for the creation and implementation of policies and programs that presumably should be based in this very research (Brim and Phillips, 1988, pp. 293–295):

> ". . . [T]he guidelines for policy-making derived from life-span development theory are mostly incompatible with the familiar political pressures. As a first-instance, the timeframe for problem-solving is set to a large extent by 2-, 4-, and 6-year election cycles. The immediacy of reelection pressures combined with the multitude of issues on the political agenda promotes an episodic rather than a long-range perspective on policy development. There is a fundamental contradiction between a political system that seeks closure on issues and a theory about human development that advances a long-term perspective on intervention." (Phillips, 1988, pp. 293–295).

Nevertheless, even if it is the case that most policy remains uninformed by research and most academic developmental research remains unconcerned with the policy needs of parents and children, there *are* examples of programming on the federal, state, and local levels that seem to represent a convergence of theory and practice. Although no program currently exists that fully encompasses all of the dimensions of the developmental systems model, some recent federal and state family programming initiatives appear consistent with this model. Here we briefly review three of the most comprehensive and promising of these initiatives: Early Head Start (EHS), Healthy Families of Massachusetts (HFM), and full-service schools.

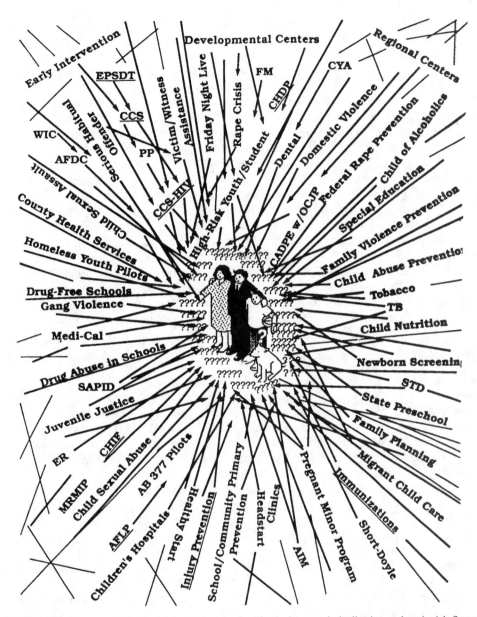

FIGURE 11.2. Programs of the social service system are often unintegrated, duplicative, and territorial. Source: J. G. Dryfoos.

Early Head Start

As explained by the Commissioner's Office of Research and Evaluation and the Head Start Bureau (2001), EHS is a federally funded community-based program for low-income families with infants and toddlers. Established as part of the 1994 Human Services Reauthorization, the EHS initiative is an extension of the Head Start Program, which has been serving older toddlers and preschoolers since 1965. The most recent reports from the Department of Health and Human Services show that in fiscal year 1999 the program was administered locally by 525 agencies across the country, was funded at $349 million, and served approximately 40,000 children. Administered through school systems, Head Start programs, childcare programs, colleges, community centers, medical centers, city and county governments, Native American tribes, and other nonprofit agencies, local EHS programs provide a wide variety of services, including family childcare, center-based care, and home visiting.

The goals of EHS are to promote healthy prenatal outcomes for pregnant women, enhance the development of very young children, and promote healthy family functioning (Commissioner's Office of Research and Evaluation and the Head Start Bureau, 2001). The results of evaluation studies indicate that EHS programs have a significant influence on the development of children and their parents (e.g., Commissioner's Office of Research and Evaluation and the Head Start Bureau, 2001). For instance, compared with children and parents not in EHS programs, participating children show better cognitive, language, and socioemotional development and their parents demonstrate more positive parenting behaviors, less use of physical punishment, and more help to their children to learn at home (Commissioner's Office of Research and Evaluation and the Head Start Bureau, 2001).

Because of the program's two-generational, community-based, comprehensive, and preventive approach, EHS serves as a particularly salient illustration of how developmental systems theory may be translated into practice. That is, with a focus on child development, family development, community development, and staff development, EHS is founded on nine basic principles: (1) high quality; (2) prevention and promotion; (3) positive relationships and continuity; (4) parent involvement; (5) inclusion; (6) culture; (7) comprehensiveness, flexibility, responsiveness, and intensity; (8) transitions; and (9) collaboration. These principles attest to the multilevel integrative approach to the human development system. They focus on the person (child and parent), the process of an individual's relations to others, family, and culture (thus, to context), and on the time and transitions across life.

Healthy Families in Massachusetts

The HFM program is a statewide application of the Healthy Families America home-visiting program (Gomby, Culross, and Behrman, 1999; Gomby, Larson, Lewit, and Behrman, 1993). Administered and monitored by the Massachusetts Department of Public Health and the Massachusetts Children's Trust Fund, HFM provides comprehensive home-visiting services to all first-time mothers under the age of 21 and their families (and thus HFM is a "universal" program). In fact, HFM is unique in that it is the first statewide universal parenting program to be implemented in the United States.

HFM is similar to EHS in its community-based, family-centered, comprehensive, and preventive approach. Although it does target teenagers, believed to be an at-risk parenting population, HFM is available to families across the state, regardless of income, ethnicity, or geographic location.

HFM has four main goals: (1) to reduce state and individual community rates of child abuse and neglect; (2) to promote optimal infant and toddler health, growth, and development; (3) to increase parental levels of education, and of economic self-sufficiency; and (4) to reduce repeat teenage pregnancy rates (Brady, Easterbrooks, Jacobs, and Mistry, 1998, 2000). HFM services for families are provided by paraprofessional home visitors who model and support positive parent–child interactions, teach about child development, support the parent's educational and professional development and goals, provide crisis intervention, and connect the family with other social services as needed. Although home visits are the primary mode of service delivery, each program also has a significant on-site component, in which home visitors provide the same types of services previously described, only with groups of parents and groups of parent–infant dyads.

In several ways, EHS and HFM are similar. Both programs focus on the individual (the teenage mother and her family), the individual's relationships to family, community, and culture, and the evolving processes and needs of individuals and communities over the course of time (Brady et al., 1998, 2000).

Full-Service Schools

The full-service school is a model that attempts to enhance and expand the services provided by public schools to meet the needs of families and communities as well as students. Full-service schools integrate communitywide multiagency collaborations and multiple social service programs into a local public school and involve school administrators and teachers, social service providers and agency administrators, and local citizens (Lerner, 1995). As Dryfoos (1994, p. 12) stated, "The charge to community agencies is to bring into the school: health, mental health, employment services, childcare, parent education, case management, recreation, cultural events, welfare, community policing, and whatever else may fit into the picture. The result is a new kind of 'seamless' institution, a community-oriented school with a joint governance structure that allows maximum responsiveness to the community, as well as accessibility and continuity for those most in need of services." An illustration of applied developmental systems theory, full-service schools are based on (Dryfoos, 1994, p. 12) "the belief that no single component, no magic bullet, can significantly change the lives of disadvantaged children, youth, and families. Rather, it is the cumulative impact of a package of interventions that will result in measurable life scripts."

Recent years have seen the development of many full-service or partial-service schools, including state legislation in Florida to support the establishment of such schools (Dryfoos, 1994; Lerner, 1995). However, the implementation of integrative schools has varied, with a range of services provided and differing levels of community involvement and success. One exemplar of this model, as identified by Dryfoos, is Intermediate School 218 (IS 218), a middle school in Washington Heights, New York. Developed through a partnership between the New York City public school system and the Children's Aid Society (CAS), a nonprofit social agency, IS 218 houses 1,200 students, enrolled in one of four "academies": Math, Science, and Technology; Business; Expressive Arts; and Community Service. In addition to the academic programming, the school provides a range of mentoring, academic enrichment, and sports and arts activities for students and local citizens during the afternoon and evening hours. In addition, the school houses a Family Resource Center staffed by members of the community, a primary health, vision, and dental clinic, and a student-run store. The school remains open during evenings, weekends, and summers to meet the needs of the community (Dryfoos, 1994, 1998). Building on existing institutions already committed to serving the needs of children, full-service schools draw on the principles of developmental systems theory to provide a comprehensive, multigenerational, community-based program for families.

Requirements for Successful Programs

As promising as a program may seem in the abstract, it needs more than a strong intervention theory (that is, a "theory of change" in regard to how the program will influence the developmental process of program participants) and a charismatic leader to ensure long-term success. To progress and reach scale, programs must address issues of political and financial sustainability, community buy-in, and evaluation. One reason the three sample initiatives previously discussed appear to be so promising is that they take into account these factors early in their program development. Recognition of the interrelated importance of these issues for program success is brought to the fore by a developmental systems perspective.

Sustainability. Crucial in the development of a program is the consideration of long-term sustainability; that is, after the initial implementation of an program, what financial, structural, and political supports guarantee its longevity? Issues of sustainability continue to be underemphasized by both private foundations and governmental agencies, and as a result there are few incentives for program developers, evaluators, or both to consider a program's long-term prospects. As a result, many effective programs disappear soon after their inception (Schorr, 1988). As Lerner (1995, p. 67) states, "Accordingly, when the demonstration program parachutes out of the community, just as it was likely to have parachuted into the community when it began, the community will likely feel less hopeful and less empowered than it did before the program was begun." Before a program is implemented, long-term plans for its continued functioning and growth must be firmly in place.

Community buy-in.   Equally crucial to the creation and the implementation of a program is the involvement of the community meant to be served by the program. Too often, well-meaning scholars suggest programs that, if promising on paper, fail to address the needs and desires of the targeted population (Lerner, 1995, p. 55): "Development happens in particular communities, and it involves the attempts of specific children and families to relate to the physical, personal, social, and institutional situations found in their communities." To ensure the targeted population's interest and continued engagement, a successful program must be founded in full collaboration and partnership with the communities and families who will be using the services. The voices of parents, and their values and visions for their families, must be included in such a partnership.

Role of program evaluation.   Finally, programs must be accountable to their various audiences and stakeholders, including the population(s) they serve, the agency responsible for the administration, and various funding streams. Jacobs and Kapuscik (2000, p. 3) define evaluation as "a set of systematically planned and executed activities designed to determine the merit of a program, intervention, or policy, or to describe aspects of its operation." Evaluation is important in identifying the needs of families and communities, helping communities and agencies adopt a programming strategy or model, and demonstrating the effectiveness of particular programs and services (Jacobs and Kapuscik, 2000). Furthermore, evaluation is essential for program sustainability, to ensure continued funding, and for community buy-in to the program, so that communities feel empowered in selecting, implementing, and modifying services.

In sum, as with research pertinent to parenting, there is much to be gained in the application of developmental science by conceptualizing, designing, and evaluating social programs and public policies in a manner that embraces the active relations between developing individuals, their families, and their communities. The importance of this emphasis on the dynamic interactions within the developmental system allows us to frame our concluding observations.

CONCLUSIONS

Together, developmental contextualism and the bioecological model converge in pointing to four dimensions of scholarship that should be involved in research and application pertinent to parenting. The first dimension is *process*. Here what is meant is the need to understand parenting as exerting a role on the child through the basic, relational processes of human development. A dynamic interaction—a fusion among the multiple levels of organization involved in the developmental system—accounts for change. No one level of organization (e.g., biology) is predominant in the system (Collins et al., 2000), and attempts to "split" the system apart by claiming that variables from one level (e.g., genes) have hegemony over others (e.g., as in Rowe, 1994; Rushton, 1999) are egregiously flawed on philosophical, theoretical, and empirical grounds (Collins et al., 2000; Horowitz, 2000; Overton, 1998).

Accordingly, to understand how parenting contributes to the development of a child, one must focus research on relations among levels and not on any one level per se. In turn, research, policies, and programs aimed at understanding and enhancing the positive contributions that parents make to their children's development must be designed in manners sensitive to the diversity of variables from multiple levels of organization that affect the parent–child relation. Policies appropriate for one racial, ethnic, religious, cultural, or geographical group of families may not be assumed to be equally applicable to groups differing in these characteristics or even to the same group at a different point in history (e.g., de Vries, 1984).

To operationally pursue the study of the relational developmental process involved in parenting, one must consider all levels of the developmental system, albeit no one study can appraise all potentially relevant variables or levels (accordingly, limits are placed on the generalizations that may be appropriately derived from any one study; Lerner, 1998b). Key in this appraisal of course are the people involved in the human development system. Accordingly, the second dimension that must be considered in research and application is the *person*. The role of the active individual—the child in affecting the parent as well as the parent in affecting the child—must be of concern and, more specifically, scholars and practitioners must be attentive to the dimensions of individuality (e.g., regarding temperament, attitudes, cognitive styles, values, intentions, goals, and so forth) that enable the individual to influence her or his partner in the parent–child relationship and, as well, the broader ecological systems of human development (the mesosystem, exosystem, and macrosystem).

Of course, to understand how the individual may affect the levels of her or his context, one must appraise variation within and across the tiers of the developmental system. Just as the multiple dimensions of personal diversity must be considered in research and application, a similar consideration of the *context* must occur. In turn, all these assessments are embedded in time and, as envisioned in both developmental contextualism and the bioecological model, *time* has a different meaning at the various levels of organization comprising the ecology of human development.

Policies and programs need to grapple with the different meanings of time at the various levels of the developmental system. Policies or programs instituted to improve the quality of family life (e.g., regarding providing welfare benefits to poor families, enabling nutritious food to be available to women with young children, offering parenting support to new, teenage mothers) may take years, if not decades, to enact or to diffuse in society sufficient to see a general effect on the quality of life of children and parents. The temporal metric for gauging the effectiveness of such macrosystem efforts may therefore mean that a given child or family, or even a cohort of children or families, may progress through their ontogeny before the policy and the program could reasonably be expected to have had a detectable influence.

In sum, whether viewed from the integrated developmental contextual model presented in Figure 11.1, through the comparable lens provided by Bronfenbrenner's PPCT model, or within the frame provided by other comparable models (e.g., Brandtstädter, 1998; Elder, 1998; Thelen and Smith, 1998), developmental systems theory calls for a focus on process, person, context, and time in research and applications pertinent to parenting. At this writing, there are few studies of parenting, and fewer still applications, that have characteristics that reflect all four dimensions of scholarship prescribed by developmental systems theory. As such, one current use of these four dimensions is to organize an evaluation of parenting research and applications, an appraisal that would indicate where research fits into this developmental systems perspective—where it supports, refines, or challenges it—and whether policies and programs sensitive to one or more of the four dimensions seem promising as bases for the promotion of parenting that enhances children's lives.

ACKNOWLEDGMENTS

The writing of this chapter was supported in part by a grant to Richard M. Lerner from the W. T. Grant Foundation.

REFERENCES

Ainsworth, M. D. S., and Marvin, R. (1995). On the shaping of attachment theory and research: An interview with Mary D. S. Ainsworth. In E. Waters, B. Vaughn, G. Posada, and K. Kondo-Ikemura (Eds.), Caregiving, cultural, and cognitive perspectives on secure-base behavior and working models. *Monographs of the Society for Research in Child Development, 60* (2–3, Serial No. 244).

Baltes, P. B. (1987). Theoretical propositions of life-span developmental psychology: On the dynamics between growth and decline. *Developmental Psychology, 23*, 611–626.

Baltes, P. B., Lindenberger, U., and Staudinger, U. M. (1998). Life-span theory in developmental psychology. In R. M. Lerner (Ed.), *Handbook of child psychology: Vol. 1. Theoretical models of human development* (5th ed., pp. 1029–1144). New York: Wiley.

Baumrind, D. (1971). Current patterns of parental authority. *Developmental Psychology Monographs, 4* (Serial No. 1, Pt. 2).

Bijou, S. W. (1976). *Child development: The basic stage of early childhood.* Englewood Cliffs, NJ: Prentice-Hall.

Bijou, S. W., and Baer, D. M. (Eds.). (1961). *Child development: A systematic and empirical theory.* New York: Appleton-Century-Crofts.

Bijou, S. W., and Baer, D. M. (Eds.). (1965). *Child development: Universal stage of infancy* (Vol. 2). Englewood Cliffs, NJ: Prentice-Hall.

Brady, A., Easterbrooks, M. A., Jacobs, F., and Mistry, J. (1998). *Evaluating Healthy Families Massachusetts: Building on the past and charting the future. Report to the Massachusetts Children's Trust Fund.* Medford, MA: Eliot-Pearson Department of Child Development, Tufts University.

Brady, A., Easterbrooks, M. A., Jacobs, F., and Mistry, J. (2000). *Massachusetts Healthy Families: Evaluation plan. Report to the Massachusetts Children's Trust Fund.* Medford MA: Eliot-Pearson Department of Child Development, Tufts University.

Brandtstädter, J. (1998). Action perspectives on human development. In R. M. Lerner (Ed.), *Handbook of child psychology: Vol. 1. Theoretical models of human development* (5th ed., pp. 807–863). New York: Wiley.

Brandtstädter, J. (1999). The self in action and development: Cultural, biosocial, and onotgenetic bases of intentional self-development. In J. Brandtstädter and R. M. Lerner (Eds.), *Action and self-development: Theory and research through the life-span* (pp. 37–65). Thousand Oaks, CA: Sage.

Brandtstädter, J., and Lerner, R. M. (1999). *Action and self-development: Theory and research through the life span.* Thousand Oaks, CA: Sage Publications.

Brazelton, T. B., Koslowski, B., and Main, M. (1974). The origins of reciprocity: The early mother-infant interaction. In M. Lewis and L. A. Rosenblum (Eds.), *The effect of the infant on its caregivers* (pp. 49–76). New York: Wiley.

Brim, O. G., Jr., and Phillips, D. A. (1988). The life-span intervention cube. In E. M. Hetherington, R. M. Lerner, and M. Perlmutter (Eds.), *Child development in life-span perspective* (pp. 277–299). Hillsdale, NJ: Lawrence Erlbaum Associates.

Brody, G., and Flor, D. (1998). Maternal resources, parenting practices, and child competence in rural, single-parent African American families. *Child Development, 69,* 803–816.

Bronfenbrenner, U. (1977). Toward an experimental ecology of human development. *American Psychologist, 32,* 513–531.

Bronfenbrenner, U. (1979). *The ecology of human development.* Cambridge, MA. Harvard University Press.

Bronfenbrenner, U. (1989). Ecological systems theory. In R. Vasta (Ed.), *Six theories of child development: Revised formulations and current issues* (pp. 185–246). Greenwich, CT: JAI.

Bronfenbrenner, U. (1994). Ecological models of human development. In T. Husen and T. N. Postlewaite (Eds.), *International encyclopedia of education* (2nd ed., Vol. 3, pp. 1643–1647). Oxford, England: Pergamon/Elsevier Science.

Bronfenbrenner, U. (in press). The biological theory of human development. In N. J. Smelser and P. B. Baltes (Eds.), *International encyclopedia of the social and behavioral sciences.* Oxford, England: Elsevier.

Bronfenbrenner, U., and Ceci, S. J. (1993). Heredity, environment, and the question "How?" A new theoretical perspective for the 1990s. In R. Plomin and G. E. McClearn (Eds.), *Nature, nurture, and psychology* (pp. 313–324). Washington, DC: American Psychological Association.

Bronfenbrenner, U., and Ceci, S. J. (1994a). Nature–nurture reconceptualized: A bioecological model. *Psychological Review, 101,* 568–586.

Bronfenbrenner, U., and Ceci, S. J. (1994b). *"The Bell Curve:" Are today's "New Interpreters" espousing yesterday's science?* Ithaca, NY: Cornell University, Department of Human Development and Family Studies.

Bronfenbrenner, U., and Morris, P. A. (1998). The ecology of developmental process. In R. M. Lerner (Ed.), *Handbook of child psychology: Vol. 1. Theoretical models of human development* (5th ed., pp. 993–1028). New York: Wiley.

Brooks-Gunn, J. (1987). Pubertal processes and girls' psychological adaptation. In R. M. Lerner and T. T. Foch (Eds.), *Biological–psychosocial interactions in early adolescence* (pp. 123–153). Hillsdale, NJ: Lawrence Erlbaum Associates.

Cairns, R. B. (1998). The making of developmental psychology. In R. M. Lerner (Ed.), *Handbook of child psychology: Vol.1. Theoretical models of human development* (5th ed., pp. 419–448). New York: Wiley.

Cassidy, J., and Shaver, P. R. (Eds.). (1999). *Handbook of attachment: Theory, research, and clinical application.* New York: Guilford.

Chao, R. K. (1995). Chinese and European American cultural models of the self reflected in mothers' childrearing beliefs. *Ethos, 23,* 328–354.

Chess, S., and Thomas, A. (1984). *Origins and evolution of behavior disorders.* New York: Bruner/Mazel.

Chess, S., and Thomas, A. (1996). *Temperament: Theory and practice.* New York: Brunner/Mazel.

Chess, S., and Thomas, A. (1999). *Goodness of fit: Clinical applications from infancy through adult life.* New York: Brunner/Mazel.

Coll, C. T. G., Meyer, E. C., and Brillon, L. (1995). Ethnic and minority parenting. In M. H. Bornstein (Ed.), *Handbook of parenting: Vol. 2. Biology and ecology of parenting* (pp. 189–209). Mahwah, NJ: Lawrence Erlbaum Associates.

Collins, W. A., Maccoby, E. E., Steinberg, L., Hetherington, E. M., and Bornstein, M. H. (2000). Contemporary research on parenting: The case for nature and nurture. *American Psychologist, 55,* 218–232.

Commissioner's Office of Research and Evaluation and the Head Start Bureau. (2001). *Building their futures: How Early Head Start programs are enhancing the lwes of infants and toddlers in low income families.* Washington, DC: Administration for Children & Families, U.S. Department of Health & Human Services.

Damon, W. (Ed.). (1998). *Handbook of child psychology* (5th ed). New York: Wiley.

Davies, P. T., Meyers, R. L., Cummings, E. M., and Heindel, S. (1999). Adult conflict history and children's subsequent responses to conflict: An experimental test. *Journal of Family Psychology, 13,* 610–628.

Deater-Deckard, K., and Dodge, K. A. (1997). Externalizing behavior problems and discipline revisited: Nonlinear effects and variation by culture, context, and gender. *Psychological Inquiry, 8,* 161–175.

Demo, D., Allen, K., and Fine, M. (Eds.). (2000). *Handbook of family diversity.* New York: Oxford University Press.

de Vries, M. W. (1984). Temperament and infant mortality among the Masai of East Africa. *American Journal of Psychiatry, 141,* 1189–1194.

Dixon, R. A., and Lerner, R. M. (1999). History and systems in developmental psychology. In M. Bornstein and M. Lamb (Eds.), *Developmental psychology: An advanced textbook* (4th ed., pp. 3–45).

Dryfoos, J. G. (1994). *Full service schools: A revolution in health and social services for children, youth and families.* San Francisco: Jossey-Bass.

Dryfoos, J. G. (1998). *Safe passage: Making it through adolescence in a risky society.* New York: Oxford University Press.

Elder, G. H., Jr. (1974). *Children of the Great Depression: Social change in life experiences.* Chicago: University of Chicago Press.

Elder, G. H., Jr. (1998). The life course and human development. In R. M. Lerner (Ed.), *Handbook of child psychology: Vol. 1. Theoretical models of human development* (5th ed., pp. 939–991). New York: Wiley.

Elder, G. H., Jr., Modell, J., and Parke, R. D. (Eds.). (1993). *Children in time and place: Developmental and historical insights.* New York: Cambridge University Press.

Emery, R. E. (1998). *Marriage, divorce, and children's adjustment.* Newbury Park, CA: Sage.

Fischer, K. W., and Bidell, T. (1998). Dynamic development of psychological structures in action and thought. In R. M. Lerner (Ed.), *Handbook of child psychology: Vol. 1. Theoretical models of human development* (5th ed., pp. 467–561). New York: Wiley.

Fisher, C. B., and Lerner, R. M. (Eds.). (1994). *Applied developmental psychology.* New York: McGraw-Hill.

Ford, D. L., and Lerner, R. M. (1992). *Developmental systems theory: An integrative approach.* Newbury Park, CA: Sage.

Freud, S. (1949). *Outline of psychoanalysis.* New York: Norton.

Garbarino, J. (1992). *Children and families in the social environment* (2nd ed.). Hawthorne, NY: Aldine de Gruyter.

Glueck, S., and Glueck, E. T. (1940). *Juvenile delinquents grow up.* New York: Commonwealth Fund.

Gomby, D. S., Culross, P. L., and Behrman, R. E. (1999). Home visiting: Recent program evaluations—Analysis and recommendations. *The Future of Children, 9*(1), 4–26.

Gomby, D. S., Larson, C. S., Lewit, E. M., and Behrman, R. E. (1993). Home visiting: Analysis and recommendations. *The Future of Children, 3*(3), 6–22.

Gottlieb, G. (1970). Conceptions of prenatal behavior. In R. Aronson, E. Tobach, D. S. Lehrman, and J. S. Rosenblatt (Eds.), *Development and evolution of behavior: Essays in memory of T. C. Schneirla* (pp. 111–137). San Francisco: Freeman.

Gottlieb, G. (1983). The psychobiological approach to developmental issues. In M. M. Haith and J. Campos (Eds.), *Handbook of child psychology: Vol. 2. Infancy and biological bases* (pp. 1–26). New York: Wiley.

Gottlieb, G. (1991). The experiential canalization of behavioral development: Theory. *Developmental Psychology, 27,* 4–13.

Gottlieb, G. (1992). *Individual development and evolution: The genesis of novel behavior.* New York: Oxford University Press.

Gottlieb, G. (1997). *Synthesizing nature–nurture: Prenatal roots of instinctive behavior.* Mahwah, NJ: Lawrence Erlbaum Associates.

Gould, S. J. (1977). *Ontogeny and phylogeny.* Cambridge, MA: Belknap.

Haeckel, E. (1876). *The history of creation: Or, the development of the earth and its inhabitants by the action of natural causes: A popular exposition of the doctrine of evolution in general, and of that of Darwin, Goethe and Lamarck in particular.* New York: Appleton.

Hall, G. S. (1904). *Adolescence: Its psychology and its relations to physiology. anthropology, sociology, sex. crime. religion. and education* (Vols. 1 and 2). New York: Appleton.

Hamner, T. J., and Turner, P. H. (1990). *Parenting in contemporary society.* Englewood Cliffs, NJ: Prentice-Hall.

Harris, L., Kagey, M., and Ross, J. (1987). A child resource policy: Moving beyond dependence on school and family. *Phi Delta Kappan, 68,* 575–580.

Hebb, D. O. (1949). *The organization of behavior.* New York: Wiley.

Hernandez, D. J. (1993). *America's children: Resources from family, government, and the economy.* New York: Sage.

Hetherington, E. M., and Stanley-Hagen, M. (2000). Diversity among stepfamilies. In D. Demo, K. Allen, and M. Fine (Eds.), *Handbook of family diversity* (pp. 173–196). New York: Oxford University Press.

Horowitz, D. F. (2000). Child development and the PITS: Simple questions, complex answers and developmental theory. *Child Development, 71,* 1–10.

Jacobs, F. H., and Kapuscik, J. L. (2000). *Making it count: Evaluating family preservation services*. Medford, MA: Tufts University.

Katchadourian, H. (1977). *The biology of adolescence*. San Francisco: Freeman.

Korn, S. J. (1978, September). *Temperament, vulnerability, and behavior*. Paper presented at the Louisville Temperament Conference, Louisville, Kentucky.

Last, C. G., and Perrin, S. (1993). Anxiety disorders in African-American and White children. *Journal of Abnormal Child Psychology, 21*, 153–164.

Lau, S., Lew, W. J., Hau, K.-T., Cheung, P. C., and Berndt, T. J. (1990). Relations among perceived parental control, warmth indulgence, and family harmony of Chinese in Mainland China. *Developmental Psychology, 26*, 674–677.

Lebra, T. (1994). Mother and child in Japanese socialization: A Japan–U.S. comparison. In P. Greenfield and R. Cocking (Eds.), *Cross-cultural roots of minority child development* (pp. 259–274). Hillsdale, NJ: Lawrence Erlbaum Associates.

Lerner, J. V., and Lerner, R. M. (1983). Temperament and adaptation across life: Theoretical and empirical issues. In P. B. Baltes and O. G. Brim, Jr. (Eds.), *Life-span development and behavior* (Vol. 5, pp. 197–231). New York: Academic.

Lerner, R. M. (1982). Children and adolescents as producers of their own development. *Developmental Review, 2*, 342–370.

Lerner, R. M. (1984). *On the nature of human plasticity*. New York: Cambridge University Press.

Lerner, R. M. (1986). *Concepts and theories of human development* (2nd ed.) New York: Random House.

Lerner, R. M. (1987). A life-span perspective for early adolescence. In R. M. Lerner and T. T. Foch (Eds.), *Biological–psychosocial interactions in early adolescence* (pp. 9–34). Hillsdale, NJ: Lawrence Erlbaum Associates.

Lerner, R. M. (1991). Changing organism–context relations as the basic process of development: A developmental–contextual perspective. *Developmental Psychology, 27*, 27–32.

Lerner, R. M. (1995). *America's youth in crisis: Challenges and options for programs and policies*. Thousand Oaks, CA: Sage.

Lerner, R. M. (1996). Relative plasticity, integration, temporality, and diversity in human development: A developmental, contextual perspective about theory, process, and method. *Developmental Psychology, 32*, 781–786.

Lerner, R. M. (Ed.). (1998a). *Handbook of Child Psychology: Vol. 1. Theoretical models of human development* (5th ed.). New York: Wiley.

Lerner, R. M. (1998b). Theories of human development: Contemporary perspectives. In R. M. Lerner (Ed.), *Handbook of child psychology: Vol. 1. Theoretical models of human development* (pp. 1–24). New York: Wiley.

Lerner, R. M. (2002-a). *Concepts and theories of human development* (3rd ed.). Mahwah, NJ: Lawrence Erlbaum Associates.

Lerner, R. M. (2002-b). *Adolescence: Development, diversity, context, and application*. Upper Saddle River, NJ: Prentice-Hall.

Lerner, R. M., and Busch-Rossnagel, N. A. (Eds.). (1981). *Individuals as producers of their development: A life-span perspective*. New York: Academic.

Lerner, R. M., Fisher, C. B., and Weinberg, R. A. (1997). Editorial: Applied developmental science: Scholarship for our times. *Applied Developmental Science, 1*, 2–3.

Lerner, R. M., Fisher, C. B., and Weinberg, R. A. (2000a). Toward a science for and of the people: Promoting civil society through the application of developmental science. *Child Development, 71*, 11–20.

Lerner, R. M., Fisher, C. B., and Weinberg, R. A. (2000b). Applying developmental science in the twenty-first century: International scholarship for our times. *International Journal of Behavioral Development, 24*, 24–29.

Lerner, R. M., and Lerner, J. V. (1987). Children in their contexts: A goodness of fit model. In J. B. Lancaster, J. Altman, A. S. Rossi, and L. R. Sherrod (Eds.), *Parenting across the life span: Biosocial dimensions* (pp. 377–404). Chicago: Aldine.

Lerner, R. M., and Lerner, J. V. (1989). Organismic and social contextual bases of development: The sample case of adolescence. In W. Damon (Ed.), *Child development today and tomorrow* (pp. 69–85). San Francisco: Jossey-Bass.

Lerner, R. M., Sparks, E. S., and McCubbin, L. (1999). *Family diversity and family policy: Strengthening families for America's children*. Norwell, MA: Kluwer.

Lerner, R. M., and Walls, T. (1999). Revisiting individuals as producers of their development: From dynamic interactionism to developmental systems. In J. Brandtstädter and R. M. Lerner (Eds.), *Action and development: Origins and functions of intentional self-development* (pp. 3–36). Thousand Oaks, CA: Sage.

Luster, T., Rhoades, K., and Haas, B. (1989). The relation between parental values and parenting behavior: A test of the Kohn hypothesis. *Journal of Marriage and the Family, 51*, 139–147.

Magnusson, D. (1995). Individual development: A holistic integrated model. In P. Moen, G. H. Elder, and K. Lusher (Eds.), *Linking lives and contexts: Perspectives on the ecology of human development* (pp. 19–60). Washington, DC: American Psychological Association.

Magnusson, D. (1999a). On the individual: A person-oriented approach to developmental research. *European Psychologist, 4*, 205–218.

Magnusson, D. (1999b). Holistic interactionism: A perspective for research on personality development. In L. A. Pervin and O. P. John (Eds.), *Handbook of personality: Theory and research* (2nd ed., pp. 219–247). New York: Guilford.

Magnusson, D., and Stattin, H. (1998). Person–context interaction theories. In R. M. Lerner (Ed.), *Handbook of child psychology: Vol. 1. Theoretical models of human development* (5th ed., pp. 685–759). New York: Wiley.

McCandless, B. R. (1967). *Children*. New York: Holt, Rinehart & Winston.

McCandless, B. R. (1970). *Adolescents*. Hinsdale, IL: Dryden.

McCord, J. (1991). Questioning the value of punishment. *Social Problems, 38*, 167–179.

McLoyd, V. C. (1990). The impact of economic hardship on Black families and children: Psychological distress, parenting, and socioemotional development. *Child Development, 61*, 311–346.

Overton, W. (1998). Developmental psychology: Philosophy, concepts, and methodology. In R. M. Lerner (Ed.), *Handbook of child psychology: Vol. 1. Theoretical models of human development* (5th ed., pp. 107–187). New York: Wiley.

Patterson, G. R. (1982). *Coercive family process*. Eugene, OR: Castalia.

Petersen, A. C. (1988). Adolescent development. In M. R. Rosenzweig (Ed.), *Annual review of psychology* (Vol. 39, pp. 583–607). Palo Alto, CA: Annual Reviews, Inc.

Piaget, J. (1970). Piaget's theory. In P. H. Mussen (Ed.), *Carmichael's manual of child psychology* (Vol. 1, pp. 703–732). New York: Wiley.

Richters, J. E., and Martinez, P. E. (1993). Violent communities, family choices, and children's chances: An algorithm for improving the odds. *Development and Psychopathology, 5*, 609–627.

Rohner, R. P., and Pettengill, S. M. (1985). Perceived parental acceptance–rejection and parental control among Korean adolescents. *Child Development, 56*, 524–528.

Roth, J., Brooks-Gunn, J., Murray, L., and Foster, W. (1998). Promoting healthy adolescents: Synthesis of youth development program evaluations. *Journal of Research on Adolescence, 8*, 423–459.

Rothbaum, F., Pott, M., Azuma, H., Miyake, K., and Weisz, J. (2000). The development of close relationships in Japan and the United States: Paths of symbiotic harmony and generative tension. *Child Development, 71*, 1121–1142.

Rothbaum, F., and Weisz, J. R. (1994). Parental caregiving and child externalizing behavior in nonclinical samples: A meta-analysis. *Psychological Bulletin, 116*, 55–74.

Rothbaum, F., Weisz, J., Pott, M., Miyake, K., and Morelli, G. (2000). Attachment and culture: Security in the United States and Japan. *American Psychologist, 55*, 1093–1104.

Rowe, D. C. (1994). *The limits of family influence: Genes, experience, and behavior*. New York: Guilford.

Rushton, J. P. (1999). *Race, evolution, and behavior* (Special abridged edition). New Brunswick, NJ: Transaction.

Rutter, M. (1979). Maternal deprivation, 1972–1978: New findings, new concepts, new approaches. *Child Development, 50*, 283–305.

Sameroff, A. J. (1983). Developmental systems: Contexts and evolution. In W. Kessen (Ed.), *Handbook of child psychology: Vol. 1. History, theory, and methods* (pp. 237–294). New York: Wiley.

Sameroff, A. J. (1987). Transactional risk factors and prevention. In J. A. Steinberg and M. M. Silverman (Eds.), *Preventing mental disorders: A research perspective* (pp. 74–89). Rockville, MD: National Institute of Mental Health.

Sameroff, A. J., Seifer, R., and Bartko, W. T. (1997). Environmental perspectives on adaptation during childhood and adolescence. In L. Suniya and J. A. Burack (Eds.), *Developmental psychopathology: Perspectives on adjustment, risk, and disorder* (pp. 507–526). New York: Cambridge University Press.

Savin-Williams, R. C., and Esterberg, K. G. (2000). Lesbian, gay, and bisexual families. In D. Demo, K. Allen, and M. Fine (Eds.), *Handbook of family diversity* (pp. 197–215). New York: Oxford University Press.

Schneirla, T. C. (1957). The concept of development in comparative psychology. In D. B. Harris (Ed.), *The concept of development* (pp. 78–108). Minneapolis, MN: University of Minnesota Press.

Schorr, L. B. (1988). *Within our reach: Breaking the cycle of disadvantage*. New York: Doubleday.

Steinberg, L., Lamborn, S. D., Dornbusch, S. M., and Darling, N. (1992). Impact of parenting practices on adolescent achievement: Authoritative parenting, school involvement, and encouragement to succeed. *Child Development, 63*, 1266–1281.

Steinberg, L., Mounts, N. S., Lamborn, S. D., and Dornbusch, S. M. (1991). Authoritative parenting and adolescent adjustment across varied ecological niches. *Journal of Research on Adolescence, 1*, 19–36.

Straus, M. A. (1994). *Beating the devil out of them*. San Francisco: Jossey-Bass.

Straus, M. A., and Gelles, R. J. (Eds.). (1990). *Physical violence in American families: Risk factors and adaptations to violence in 8,145 families*. New Brunswick, NJ: Transaction.

Super, C. M., and Harkness, S. (1981). Figure, ground, and gestalt: The cultural context of the active individual. In R. M. Lerner and N. A. Busch-Rossnagel (Eds.), *Individuals as producers of their own development: A life-span perspective* (pp. 69–86). New York: Academic.

Tanner, J. M. (1991). Menarche, secular trend in age of. In R. M. Lerner, A. C. Petersen, and J. Brooks-Gunn (Eds.), *Encyclopedia of adolescence* (Vol. 2, pp. 637–641). New York: Garland.

Thelen, E., and Smith, L. B. (1994). *A dynamic systems approach to the development of cognition and action*. Cambridge, MA: MIT Press.

Thelen, E., and Smith, L. B. (1998). Dynamic systems theories. In R. M. Lerner (Ed.), *Handbook of child psychology: Vol. 1. Theoretical models of human development* (5th ed., pp. 563–633). New York: Wiley.

Thomas, A., and Chess, S. (1977). *Temperament and development*. New York: Brunner/Mazel.

Thomas, A., and Chess, S. (1980). *The dynamics of psychological development*. New York: Brunner/Maul.

Thomas, A., and Chess, S. (1981). The Cole of temperament in the contributions of individuals to their development. In R. M. Lerner and N. A. Busch-Rossnagel (Eds.), *Individuals as producers of their development: A life-span perspective* (pp. 231–255). New York: Academic.

Thomas, A., Chess, S., and Birch, H. G. (1968). *Temperament and behavior disorders in children*. New York: New York University Press.

Thomas, A., Chess, S., Sillen, J., and Mendez, O. (1974). Cross-cultural study of behavior in children with special vulnerabilities to stress. In D. F. Ricks, A. Thomas, and M. Roff (Eds.), *Life history research in psychopathology* (pp. 53–63). Minneapolis, MN: University of Minnesota Press.

Tobach, E. (1981). Evolutionary aspects of the activity of the organism and its development. In R. M. Lerner and N. A. Busch-Rossnagel (Eds.), *Individuals as producers of their development: A life-span perspective* (pp. 37–68). New York: Academic.

Tobach, E., and Greenberg, G. (1984). The significance of T. C. Schneirla's contribution to the concept of levels of integration. In G. Greenberg and E. Tobach (Eds.), *Behavioral evolution and integrative levels* (pp. 1–7). Hillsdale, NJ: Lawrence Erlbaum Associates.

Tobach, E., and Schneirla, T. C. (1968). The biopsychology of social behavior of animals. In R. E. Cooke and S. Levin (Eds.), *Biologic basis of pediatric practice*. New York: McGraw-Hill.

Vuchinich, S., Angelelli, J., and Gatherum, A. (1996). Context and development in family problem solving with preadolescent children. *Child Development, 67*, 1276–1288.

Wapner, S., and Demick, J. (1998). Developmental analysis: A holistic, developmental, systems-oriented perspective. In R. M. Lerner (Ed.), *Handbook of child psychology: Vol. 1. Theoretical models of human development* (5th ed., pp. 761–805). New York: Wiley.

Watson, J. B. (1914). *Behavior: An introduction to comparative psychology*. New York: Holt.

Watson, J. B. (1928). *Psychological care of infant and child*. New York: Norton.

Werner, H. (1957). The concept of development from a comparative and organismic point of view. In D. B. Harris (Ed.), *The concept of development* (pp. 125–148). Minneapolis, MN: University of Minnesota Press.

12

History of Parenting: The Ancient Mediterranean World

Valerie French
The American University

INTRODUCTION

For institutions now believed crucial in any society, parenthood and family received remarkably little attention from historians before the early 1960s. Convinced that the adult-male world of politics, war, diplomacy, and economics should command center stage in historical narrative and analysis, historians gave relatively short shrift to social and cultural history. The 1960s produced many changes in U. S. society as a whole and in historians' approaches to the scope and focus of their work. One result of this revolution within the discipline of history is the now-burgeoning attention given heretofore marginalized peoples—women, ethnic groups, middle- and lower-socioeconomic groups—and institutions—family, childrearing, community groups, and fraternal organizations. Only because of this revolution in historical interest and inquiry is it now possible to reconstruct the often fragmented history of family life and parenting.

Historians who struck out in new directions discovered, however, that the old sources and methods of historical investigation would not work. For modern as well as ancient historians, there is a problem with the evidence. It was produced and transmitted almost exclusively by elite males, and it therefore represents one particular perspective on their world and homes. Only rarely can we hear directly the voices of the women, the children, and the other nonelite members of these male-elite households describing their own experiences from their own points of view.

Moreover, one cannot turn to the masterworks of political history—Thucydides, Tacitus, Machiavelli, von Ranke, Churchill—and find much evidence about family life. The new social historians had to look elsewhere—in letters, diaries, popular literature, manuals of household advice, medical treatises, law codes, and artifacts from everyday life. Before early modern times, we rarely find sustained and well-developed discussions about parenting and childrearing in our historical sources. Ancient and medieval historians thus must root about in all kinds of evidence, gathering nuggets of information wherever they can find them; the picture being reconstructed is not a fully finished painting, but more a jigsaw puzzle with over half its pieces missing and unrecoverable. From bits and pieces of details, they then try to discern the overall puzzle pattern.

Reconstructing the history of parenting and family life is beset not only by difficulties with limited and undoubtedly biased evidence, but also by theoretical problems. Do we work inductively or deductively? If deductively, what general theory or set of questions guides our inquiry? If guided by contemporary theory, will we misinterpret or overlook evidence? If inductively, how shall we give overall shape and meaning to the individual puzzle pieces we do find? The method of "deconstruction" offers a way to mediate and ameliorate these theoretical difficulties. As a method of interpretation and analysis, deconstruction takes as its starting point the axiom that the meanings of texts and images are embedded in the beliefs held by society at large and tend to serve the interests of their creators. Thus the meanings of texts and images are a *social construction*, made from a society's beliefs about what the text or image represents and, often, interpreted to the advantage of the creator. In most cases, regardless of the conscious intent of the creator of the text or image, the meanings come from the social construction of beliefs about the content—both of the society in which the text or image was created and in the society in which the scholar lives and works.

Something that can be constructed can be deconstructed. And scholars in literature, history, art history, and other disciplines are using the method of deconstruction to illumine the underlying and inherent social meanings of their sources, whether literary or visual. Although often mystified by theoreticians, deconstruction requires that scholars ask their evidence, *and themselves*, what fundamental assumptions underlie the categories of analysis and their relations to one another, and how these assumptions give advantage to the user? For example, to end the conflict between Orestes, who has killed his mother, and the furies, who torture him in retribution, the Athenian playwright Aeschylus makes Apollo declare: "The mother is no parent of that which is called/her child, but only the nurse of the new-planted seed/that grows. The parent is he who mounts. A stranger, she preserves a stranger's seed (*Eumenides*, 658–660)." This divine proclamation frees Orestes from the furies, to be sure, and decrees the "natural order" of things. But just what is portrayed here as "natural?" We should not infer that the Athenians believed the womb was simply an empty vessel for gestation (there is plenty of evidence to the contrary). Rather, we must deconstruct the statement and see how it serves male-elite interests as divine sanction of the male-elite domination of the Athenian family and state, confirmation of the dominant ideology of male superiority, and male appropriation of woman's unique contribution to the family—creation of progeny. Aeschylus is here participating in the Athenians' construction of "the natural" and then using this historically specific construction of "nature" to perpetuate the dominant position of elite males (Harkness and Super, in Vol. 2 of this *Handbook*).

The method of deconstruction applies as well to historian as to text or image. This chapter is written from a postmodernist, feminist perspective. That is, in this chapter it is assumed that most truth is historically contingent, that some set of values undergirds *all* forms of inquiry and analysis, and that elite-adult-male is only one of many kinds of valid, authentic human experience deserving of careful, disciplined historical study. The goal of this chapter is to illumine as accurately as the sources and this perspective allow the lives and experiences of *all* the people, particularly parents and young children.

In addition to presenting current scholarly research and interpretation of early childhood, childrearing, parenting, and family life in several ancient Mediterranean civilizations—Egypt, Mesopotamia, Israel, Greece, and Rome—this chapter discusses important theoretical considerations—prehistory, patriarchy, and maternal values—within the context of this historical description and analysis. Of particular significance is an overview of how, over the past 30 years, historians have created a rich, new scholarship on the history of the family and related topics.

HISTORY OF CHILDHOOD, CHILDREARING, FAMILY, AND PARENTING

Four categories of inquiry significantly overlap one another. About which one the historian writes depends mainly on the historian's focus of attention and position in relation to the subject. All draw from basically the same pool of evidence, but they write from different angles. The historian of childhood seeks to reconstruct the experience of childhood, trying to ascertain what it was like to be a child by seeing the adult world from the child's perspective; the historian of childrearing stands back from the child's perspective and looks for common practices, materials, attitudes, and beliefs that guided adult care of the young; the family historian is concerned with the material and emotional relationships within households and may try to stand either inside or outside of the family; the historian of parenting wants to create a picture of children's growth and development from the point of view of the parent, to reconstruct the parents' experiences and perspectives.

A great deal of the work on children and parents in ancient and medieval societies falls mainly into the category of history of childrearing, and this work has produced a considerable range of interpretation. In the nineteenth and the twentieth centuries, the few pieces of scholarship to treat children and families were essays in learned encyclopedias and *Daily Life in XYZ* books, with the obligatory chapters on mothers and the home. Although often providing basic information, these essays offered little critical interpretation of evidence and generally painted a benign picture of home life, rather like *Fun with Dick and Jane*, a first-grade reader popular in the 1940s and 1950s. The English translation of Aries' groundbreaking *Centuries of Childhood* in 1962 challenged the benign picture and prompted a variety of scholars to expand on his work. Although Aries' contention that childhood as a recognized stage of development between infancy and young adulthood did not exist before the early modern era has been overturned (French, 1977), the importance of his positioning of childrearing and childhood as central historical questions can hardly be overestimated.

Hard on the heels of Aries' hypothesis came the ontogenic, psychogenic theory of Western history advanced in the 1970s by deMause, founder of the first journal devoted entirely to the history of childrearing, *The History of Childhood Quarterly*. deMause (1974) argued that, to understand the history of the evolution of civilization in the West, one had to examine changes in childrearing practices over time. In the beginning, deMause contended, childrearing was brutish, cruel, and emotionally distancing because parents were unable to identify psychically with their children's needs. "The further back in history one goes, the lower the level of child care, and the more likely children are to be killed, abandoned, beaten, terrorized, and sexually abused" (deMause, 1974, p. 504). Parenting in antiquity deMause called the "Infanticidal Mode;" in medieval Europe, it was the "Abandoning Mode." Western civilization has progressed, deMause argued, because in each successive era parents have become psychogenically better able to identify with their young and their needs. deMause's monocausal theory explains all adult behavior—political, artistic, social, religious and spiritual, economic—in terms of the dominant childrearing patterns of its historical era. Today, according to deMause, we see the initial stages of the "Helping Mode," in which we recognize that children usually know what is best for themselves, and as parents we follow our children's lead in childcare.

Leaving aside the question of whether one accepts deMause's conclusion that civilization has truly advanced over the past 3,000 years or his belief that children inherently know what they need, deMause seriously distorted the historical record he sought to illumine. deMause's work, along with that of a few other scholars such as Etienne (1973), is a striking example of what happens when an historian presents only one portion of the available evidence. deMause was correct to point out multiple examples of horrendous treatment and abuse of children; but he is silent about all the evidence to the contrary—evidence showing adult knowledge of, attention to, and often delight in children's special characteristics and needs.

The work of the past two decades on the history of childhood, childrearing, family life, and parenting is neither benign portraiture nor a Hieronymous Bosch-like print. Dozens of scholars have extracted most of the available evidence from a plethora of potential sources (Bradley, 1991, 1999; Colon and Colon, 1999; Demand, 1994; Dixon, 1988, 1992; French, 1977, 1987, 1991, 1997, 1999; Golden, 1989; Hallett, 1984; Pomeroy, 1997; Rawson, 1991; Riddle, 1992; Strauss, 1993; Wiedemann, 1989). Their studies have examined such subjects as contraception and birth control, obstetric and neonatal care, pediatrics, wet-nursing, foster parentage, children's legal statuses (freeborn, freed, slave), toys and play, education, efforts at socialization, affective bonds among family members, and images of motherhood. There is no grand overarching scheme or theme that unites these studies save their common subject matter and general recognition of the diversity of both children's and parents' experiences within these complex societies and across time.

Few scholars now working in this field have explicitly considered questions about the vantage point from which they evaluate and interpret their evidence; they rarely attempt distinctions among the histories of childhood, childrearing, the family, or parenting. Yet the perspective from which one writes influences the historical product. This chapter tries to understand and interpret the evidence about families from the vantage points of the parents within the family; it writes a history of parenting of young children from infancy through ages 6 to 8 years.

Taking the position of parents has its own complications, for there are many different parents. In many families in the ancient Mediterranean worlds, the vantage points of mothers differed from those of fathers and from those of foster or adoptive parents. In addition, in many homes, parents were not the primary child caregivers; a variety of forms of surrogate parenthood was common. Moreover, the expectations of parents differed across socioeconomic class and according to subculture. Thus, although working from the basic perspective of parents, the chapter recognizes that parenthood was not a unitary construct, even within a single historical period in a single place such as pharonic Egypt, classical Athens, or imperial Rome.

SOME BACKGROUND: PREHISTORY, PATRIARCHY, AND MATERNAL VALUES

Historians rarely venture into the undocumented domain of prehistoric societies, those that left no written records. However, recent scholarship on the development of the patriarchal state and attempts to show that at least some complex preliterate societies were based on a paradigm of maternal values compel a brief examination of these issues for they bear heavily on our constructs of "father," "mother," and "parent," and our understanding and use of Jungian psychology and all it implies about parenting.

In her provocative and now generally accepted work, *The Creation of Patriarchy*, Lerner (1986) traced the origins of the patriarchal state to the prehistoric transformation of ancient Eastern Mediterranean societies from basically nomadic and gatherer–hunter groups to settled, agricultural communities that had to defend themselves against external enemies. The hallmarks of a patriarchal state are the axioms that males are *naturally* superior to females, that society must have a hierarchical structure, and that production is more valuable than reproduction. According to Lerner, the evolution of the idea of individual property rights alongside the development of male-centered political–military– religious organizations paved the way for the view that all men (not just members of the elite) have rights in all women and that therefore the state must control all women. Elite-male domination of the state and the creation of patriarchy as the dominant ideology gave primacy to paternal authority within the family—the rule not just of fathers, but of the oldest father. It is in the state, not in the family, that we must locate the origin of "naturalized" male domination and androcentrism (male = norm). Lerner's thesis has contemporary significance for parenting as well as for political ideology. She has demonstrated that the patriarchal state and family are products of human society and not natural conditions of humanity; we can therefore create nonpatriarchal states and families.

Lerner and other scholars who have sought to historicize the origins of the patriarchal state have assumed some kind of nonpatriarchal prehistoric period. Serious consideration of the possible prominence of a female or maternal social-organizing principle began in the midnineteenth century with Bachofen's work, a selection of which was published in English as *Myth, Religion, and Mother Right* (1967). On the basis mainly of his analysis of an archaic substratum of Greek and Roman myth that was filled with powerful female divinities and inferences from the famous "Venus" or "Mother Goddess" fertility figurines found throughout late paleolithic and neolithic Europe and in the Eastern Mediterranean, Bachofen hypothesized that the first civilizations were matriarchal.

While rejecting Bachofen's hypothesis of matriarchy as simply the opposite of patriarchy but with women on top, a number of scholars, including Gimbutas (1982), Eisler (1987), Ehrenberg (1989), and Baring and Cashford (1991), concluded that before patriarchy—with its emphasis on militarized hierarchical distribution of power and androcentric axioms—there existed an earlier, widespread prehistoric civilization based on communal or horizontal organizing principles and recognition of men and women as different but nonetheless equal in value. The ethos of these cultures is symbolized in the "Venus" figurines, emphasizing as they do female procreative and nurturing capacities by representing women in the final stage of pregnancy and with engorged breasts. These cultures that prized maternal values of care and nurturing also valued collaborative activity (as opposed to competition) and peaceful conflict resolution (as opposed to the use of force).

In the past 20 years, a burgeoning new field of "goddess studies" has attempted to weave the archaeological evidence from prehistoric Europe and the Eastern Mediterranean together with historical study of the eradication of the female divine from Western monotheisms and contemporary feminist theory and feminist spirituality to argue for a radical transformation of society today. The hypothesis that prehistoric societies were "goddess centered" and therefore based on maternal, life-giving values has been vigorously challenged by Goodison and Morris (1998) and Eller (2000). To date, proponents of the goddess hypothesis have offered the only systematic and comprehensive interpretation of the archaeological evidence; critics have identified problems in the hypothesis but offer no other interpretation. Given the fragmentary nature of the archaeological evidence and the inherent uncertainty of interpreting the meaning of figurines to the prehistoric peoples who made them, the question of the validity of the goddess hypothesis can probably never be settled.

What is of particular importance in this scholarship for historians of parenting is the tendency to assume that there are inherent male principles and female principles and that the form society takes depends on to which principles it accords primacy. Although there are surely other possible organizing principles, the debate over prehistory as currently framed not surprisingly has strong parallels in contemporary philosophical and ideological controversies over women's and men's "proper" or "natural" positions in modern society. These assumed male and female principles splash over into everyone's understanding and interpretation of roles played by mothers and fathers as parents throughout Western history. The tendency to trace the roots of Western father roles back to the beginnings of the patriarchal state and to look for the origins of mother roles in prehistoric times poses the real danger that historians of parenting will impose these gendered parent roles on our sources and either distort or fail to observe parental behavior that runs counter to or is outside of these parental paradigms. These same epistemological problems no doubt beset scholars in other disciplines who study parenting (Barnard and Solchany, in Vol. 3 of this *Handbook*).

The nascent field of evolutionary psychology, combined with primatology and anthropological perspectives on the development of human societies, is offering some new perspectives on these issues. For example, Hrdy (1999) argued that "maternal instinct" is a modern social construction, that in the distant past mothers had to balance conflicting demands and agendas and consequently gave different levels of commitment to each infant depending on the particular circumstances facing the woman at the time the baby was born. This work also compels us to exercise care lest we impose unthinkingly our own conceptions of parenting on the millions of mothers and fathers who came before us (Corter and Fleming, in Vol. 2 of this *Handbook*).

THE ANCIENT EASTERN MEDITERRANEAN

Traditionally, study of Western history has begun with the Greeks. In reality, as the ancient Greeks themselves clearly realized, European Greek civilization was relatively new and rested on foundations laid by truly ancient societies in Asia—Anatolia (modern Turkey), Syria, Israel, Assyria, Babylonia, Akkad, Sumer, and Persia—and in Africa—Egypt, Nubia, and the land of Punt (today's Eritrea, Ethiopia, and Somalia). The ancient eastern Mediterranean world was a product of the confluence of important cultural traditions from three continents. The roots of the European West stretch back firmly into the soils of ancient Mesopotamia and northeastern Africa.

It was in these ancient Eastern Mediterranean cultures that the system of family and social organization now called patriarchy was established. Its basic assumptions underlie not only ancient Eastern Mediterranean but also Greek and Roman civilizations. A brief survey of parenting and family life in Egypt, Mesopotamia, and Israel suggests the variety of ways parents adapted patriarchy to contingent historical conditions.

Ancient Egypt

Of all the ancient Mediterranean civilizations, these people—from pharaohs to peasants—seem to have been, from our contemporary value system, the most devoted parents. Throughout the nearly 2,000 years that pharaohs ruled the Nile River valley (ca. 3000–1000 BCE), the pervasive social expectation was that parents would have large families, enjoy their children, and rear them with love and care. Egyptians also recognized stages of child development and had separate hieroglyphs designating infants, toddlers, youths, and adolescents (Colon and Colon, 1999).

The bulk of the evidence comes from literary and artistic representations of the pharaoh and his family, and of other nobles, giving our picture a decidedly aristocratic cast. However, archaeological evidence from workers' communities, particularly Deir el-Medina of the New Kingdom (ca.1550–1069 BCE), parallels that of elite families. Tomb paintings, from the Old through the New Kingdoms, presumably depicting what the honoree wanted in the afterlife, frequently show father and mother surrounded by their offspring, eating, playing, hunting, and so forth. By the conventions of Egyptian art, the children occupy as important iconographic space as do other relatives and trusted adult servants.

This interpretation of tomb paintings–that parents regarded their children as essential members of the family–is corroborated by the prominence given their children in the official art of the heretic pharaoh Akhenaten and his wife Nefertiti (ca. 1378–1362 BCE). King and queen have their children with them at state ceremonies, hold them on their laps, kiss and embrace them warmly. There is no mistaking the fondness of these royal parents for their children—or at least as part of the public message conveyed by these official representations: Conjugal and parental affection is to be emulated.

Popular stories create the same portrait. In a tale from Middle Kingdom Egypt (ca. 2000–1800 BCE), Sinuhe, a royal courtier, returns home after a long trip. Pharaoh and wife rejoice at the reunion; they are joined in their welcome by their children who swarm over Sinuhe, telling him about their jewelry and toys, as their parents look on fondly. Another Middle Kingdom story, the *Tale of the Shipwrecked Sailor*, recounts the adventures of a nonaristocratic, small merchant stranded on the shores of the land of Punt. Befriended by the Prince of Punt, he finally sets off for Egypt, with the Prince crying after him, "Farewell, farewell . . . to your home! You will see your children . . ." (Simpson, 1972, p. 55). As a piece of popular literature, this tale probably implies that the audience expected the poor sailor to have missed his children especially.

Social expectations encouraged large families, with 8–12 children considered a satisfactory number. Childless marriages were regarded as a disaster; such marriages ended in divorce or with the adoption of children, often those of poorer relatives. Because marriage occurred early for males—in their late teens—men had ample time to sire large families; females married in their early to midteens, common in ancient societies.

Fathers were proud of and honored for their progeny, and bureaucrats kept records of all births. During the eleventh dynasty of the Middle Kingdom, an army captain boasted that he had fathered "seventy children, the issue of one wife" (Tyldesley, 1994, pp. 67–68); hyperbolic claims were not uncommon in ancient Egypt. A book of advice to young men from the New Kingdom counseled "Take a wife while you are young, so that she may give you a son. . . . Happy is the man with a big family. He is honored on account of his children" (Macdonald, 1999, p. 15). This advice shows the habitual ancient preference for males over females, but in Egypt the preference was mild in comparison with that of other societies; in Egypt, there is no evidence of female infanticide and few indications of any kind of deliberate neglect or murder of newborns.

Mothers too took pride in their fertility. In an inscription recording the will of the woman Naunakhte from the workers' village of Deir el-Medina (dated to the twentieth dynasty of the New Kingdom), she proclaims "I am a free woman of Egypt. I have raised eight children, and have provided them with everything suitable to their station in life" (Macdonald, 1999, p. 10). The rest of her will reveals that she disinherited four of her children for not tending to her well enough in her old age, but that she distributed to all eight a portion of the property she had held in trust for them from their late father (Robins, 1997, p. 81). Naunakhte's will is but one of many pieces of evidence showing the unusually high degree of legal and actual independence of Egyptian women. Custom dictated that males headed their households, yet women suffered few legal disabilities; they could own and convey property and could sue in courts in their own right.

Naunakhte's will also shows the expectation of parents that their children would care for them in their old age. An adage from the late period (ca. 664–323 BCE) advises "Do not prefer one of your children above the others; after all, you never know which of them will be kind to you" (Tyldesley, 1994, p. 68). Apparently, not all children lived up to this expectation. However, most children probably did. A New Kingdom scribe's instructions to his son counsels respect and honor for his mother: "Double the food which your mother gave you and support her as she supported you. You were a heavy burden to her but she did not abandon you. When you were born after your months, she was still tied to you as her breast was in your mouth for three years. As you grew and your excrement was disgusting, she was not disgusted" (Tyldesley, 1994, p. 69).

Despite the clear evidence of parental love of and investment in their children, we have relatively little evidence of childrearing practices. Methods of parenting must be inferred from information derived from medical treatments, school texts, and household archaeology. The extensive medical literature reveals an astonishing variety of tests used to try to determine the potential fertility of a woman, whether she was pregnant, and the sex of the fetus; there is little about normal childbirth, except for medicaments and incantations used to induce birth (Nunn, 1996). Birth was handled by midwives and was apparently outside the scope of male physicians. While pregnant, women were protected by the pregnant hippopotamus goddess, Tauret; newborns and young children were protected by a lion-headed dwarf god, Bes.

At birth, the mother conferred the name on the new baby, presumably with the concurrence of the father. Names were thought to carry great power, and children were often named for deceased ancestors who were regarded as continuing members of the family long after their deaths; in some real way, the child bearing an ancestor's name also carried that person's being on into a continuation of life on earth.

Babies and young children spent their time in the household, and their care was entrusted primarily to mothers, elder female relatives living with the family, and older siblings. Babies were laid on cushions when they were not being carried around by their mothers, who used a sling to keep their small children close to the breast until they were weaned. In wealthy families, there were additional child attendants, often slaves purchased especially for this purpose. Elite families had elaborate homes with elegant furnishings. Working-class families had much smaller but well-ventilated houses, usually with a few rooms and a walled-in courtyard, where most of the day-to-day household work took place. Thus children were nearly constantly in the presence of watchful, attentive adults who were interested in and often delighted by their activities; as they became capable, children were expected to help with daily chores. Men and women spent their leisure time together, often in family activities such as picnics or walks through the countryside.

Archaeological remains reveal a wide variety of toys: dolls with real hair and articulated limbs, rattles, balls, tops, animal pull toys with moving parts, puppets, board games like chess, and slingshots;

children apparently also made their own toys out of clay that were then sun dried. Tomb paintings depict children at play in games that appear to range from leapfrog, piggyback riding, to tug-of-war; holding pet cats, monkeys, and birds; and engaging in such activities as acrobatics, swimming, fishing, and wrestling or rough housing. The visual evidence shows small children going naked or with minimal clothing; some wear sandals and jewelry such as necklaces and bracelets. Most boys had their heads shaved save for a long lock, often in a braid, on the left side; girls' hair was cut to neck length, except for the long sidelock they shared with their brothers. Altogether the evidence strongly suggests that parents provided or their young children with toys and activities that helped them develop physically and socially.

Children were breast-fed until approximately the age of 3 years—a comparatively late age for weaning. However, given the contamination of the Nile River water—which the Egyptians understood as a potential source of illness—and the prevalence of barley beer as the main beverage, late weaning makes considerable sense for protecting the well-being of the child. However, given the Egyptians' desire for many children and the likely suppression of ovulation associated with breast-feeding, late weaning is perhaps surprising. Working-class and peasant women nursed their own children; elite families hired wet-nurses, a profession held in high esteem among Egyptians, in contrast to other ancient societies. Otherwise, children probably shared in their parents' diet—bread, vegetables, lentils, beans, fish, some fruit, and honey; for working-class families, bread was the mainstay of the diet, with other foods used sparingly and meat reserved for feast days. Because of the sand that got into the flour, Egyptian bread was very gritty; mummies show that, even in the elite, teeth were chipped and ground down from chewing the bread, and all Egyptians, even children, suffered from cavities and gum disease.

Parents, then, created for their children a safe and pleasurable early childhood. But by the age of 5 or 6 years, children were expected to begin preparation for their adult occupations. In all classes, girls were taught all the domestic skills they would need to manage their households. In working-class and peasant families, the vast bulk of the population, sons learned their fathers' occupations; training began with boys following the men into the fields or apprenticing in crafts. However, here too, parents took great care for their children's training for adult life.

More privileged children—some girls as well as boys—attended school from the age of 4 to 14 years, where they learned reading, writing, math, and singing. A number of school texts from the New Kingdom survive and give us a glimpse of the values and methods of formal education. Children are reminded to "write with your hand and read with your mouth"; they could expect beatings for slacking off; boys are admonished not to pay too much attention to girls (Erman, 1995, p. 189ff).

Sick babies and children caused their parents much anxiety, as did worry about potential illness. Infant and child mortality rates were high. The Egyptians had extensive medical knowledge and advice on treatment ranging from medical to magical, but there was not a specialization in pediatrics. The few references to children in the medical literature usually advise incantations and charms. Maternal milk was used to treat colic, as were poppy pods that may have conveyed some opiates to the baby; milk was also recommended for eye infections, which were nearly epidemic and a major cause of blindness. Diuretics and laxatives were often used to treat sick children; they may well have caused more harm than good.

Examination of the mummies of children shows that they suffered and died from a variety of ailments brought on by worms (round, hook, and flat) as well as other parasites, including schistosoma. Polio is documented as is an eczemalike skin disease. Without modern anasepsis and understanding of infectious disease, parents were in fact helpless in the face of life-threatening illnesses (Colon and Colon, 1999). Children at least had the comfort of loving care and prayers, such as this one, intended to drive away evil spirits (Tyldesley, 1994, p. 79): "Perish, you who come in from the dark. You who creep in with your nose reversed and your face turned back. . . . Did you come to kiss the child? I will not allow you to kiss him." In ancient Egypt, even the demon wanted to kiss the child.

Ancient Mesopotamia

The Tigris–Euphrates River Valley was home to a succession of kingdoms—Sumer, Akkad, Babylonia, and Assyria. Scholars have long noted that in general these Mesopotamian cultures had a darker cast to them than the apparently more easygoing and optimistic Egyptians: Mesopotamian societies were more often engaged in war, were more litigious, struggled with comparatively unpredictable seasonal floods, and had mythologies that depicted a grim life and afterlife. This overall more pessimistic tone seems to have permeated family life as well.

Literary or artistic representations of a happy home life symbolized by parents with their children are nearly nonexistent in Mesopotamia. Children are nearly totally absent from official and funerary art; family life is not celebrated, it is hardly ever even portrayed. Rather we find proverbs, like the following from Sumer, suggesting that, from a father's point of view, having a family was difficult: "Who has not supported a wife or child has not borne a leash!" (Kramer, 1963). Having children, however, was nonetheless important; a barren wife could be divorced, and a wife who refused to have children could be drowned (Eller, 2000).

The famous Babylonian law, the Code of Hammurabi (ca. 1750 BCE) sets forth many provisions about how parents and the community were to care for children, particularly their economic upkeep; that many provisions were needed suggests, perhaps, that the ruler believed that parents had a tendency to shirk these duties. Dowries were returned following divorce so that the mother could support her children. Legally the property of their fathers, children were supposedly protected against physical abuse, against being reclaimed from adoptive parents, and against being disinherited by adoptive parents who then had their own natural-born children. Again, the existence of these protections implies some problem with parental ill treatment of children. However, fathers had the legal right to expose infants and sell their children into slavery. The principle of the *lex talionis* in Hammurabi's Code governed children who were in conflict with their parents. A son who denied that he was the child of either the man or the woman who reared him was to have his tongue cut out; a son who said he hated the man or the woman who reared him and then went back to his father's house was to have his eyes plucked out; a son who struck his father was to have his fingers cut off.

A picture of a desirable home life must be inferred not from literary or artistic representations of happy parents with their youngsters but from descriptions of disasters that could be imposed by the gods or underworld demons, such as these from Sumerian literature (Kramer, 1963):

> The mother will not care for her son, the father will not cry out, O my wife,
> The concubine will not rejoice in the lap, the children will not be fondled on their knees.
>
> Take away the wife from the man's lap, take away the child from the nursemaid's breast.
>
> Sate not with pleasure the wife's lap, kiss not the well-fed children,
> Take away the man's son from his knee.

These images suggest that Sumerians lacked confidence about maintaining a tranquil home life; wife could be ripped away from husband, children from parents by forces beyond their influence, let alone control. This interpretation of such passages finds some support in the etymology of the Sumerian word for freedom, *amargi*, which means literally "return to the mother" (Kramer, 1963). First used ca. 2500, *amargi*'s context indicates that freedom was something valuable. If having freedom was defined as being able to return to one's mother, it is quite likely that having freedom meant being able to be safe, to be protected as a small child would be by her or his mother. Assuming this explanation of *amargi*'s derivation is sound, then we can probably also infer that in Sumerian culture, mothers as opposed to fathers were regarded as the main source of protection and comfort for their children.

The militarism of Mesopotamian cultures shows up especially in Assyria, certainly the most fearsome of these powers. Aristocratic fathers introduced their sons early, possibly when they were

3 years old, to the military life by teaching them to ride horses and to shoot with bow and arrow. The fact that in Assyria the morning greeting involved kisses exchanged among parents and children, however, suggests some expressions of parental affection for the young.

It was generally believed by the Mesopotamians that demons caused illness. One, Labartu, portrayed with a pig nursing at her breast and holding a snake in each hand, was particularly dangerous to newborns (Colon and Colon, 1999). Surviving medical texts, representing both Akkadian and Assyrian medical knowledge, can tell us something about eastern Mediterranean societies' understanding of the health and diseases of young children. The Mesopotamians seemed to have recognized such conditions as scurvy, hydrocephalus, polio, nosebleeds, meningitis, colitis, jaundice, gangrene, epilepsy, ear infections, tuberculosis, abscesses, dysentery, and poisoning from botulism. Recommended treatments included poultices, bathing, and ingestion of a range of herbs and plants such as frankincense, myrrh, and thyme. Only elite families would have been able to engage men learned in medical matters; the poor surely relied on folk remedies and prayer. How efficacious any of these treatments were, we have no way of knowing (Colon and Colon, 1999).

Overall it seems that the rather pessimistic outlook of adult society in ancient Mesopotamia may have served to promote more emotional distance between parents and children than seems to have existed in ancient Egypt. However, no scholar primarily trained in the ancient Mesopotamian languages has yet investigated parenting, family life, or childrearing in these complex cultures; research by specialists may cause a revision of these conclusions.

Ancient Israel

Reconstruction of parenting and childrearing among the ancient Israelites is both important and difficult. Important because the images of and values attached to family life portrayed in the Hebrew Bible provide the foundation for the major religions of the Western tradition; difficult because the Hebrew Bible is organized mainly around a narrative recounting the development of a religion and nation, written from a patriarchal and androcentric perspective that tends to emphasize public as opposed to domestic life and concerns. Despite these problems, when the Biblical literature is supplemented with archaeological evidence, a reasonable although sketchy portrait can be recovered.

The archaeology of ancient Israel in the Biblical period (from the patriarchs through the Babylonian exile, ca. 2000–500 BCE) reveals that the vast bulk of the population lived in an agrarian, subsistence economy based on small family-centered households. These households had at their core a husband and wife, their children, and other kin—often older relatives—and were usually multigenerational; they probably averaged 10–15 people (Meyers, 1992).

The number of people and their differing needs seem to have created families that were characterized both by love and affection and by tension and conflict. These complex family relationships provide the basis for much of the imagery and metaphor of the Bible, particularly that between husband and wife and father and daughter. The authors of the Bible frequently use a metaphor contrasting female infidelity and betrayal with male sorrow, anger, and punishment; the female, representing the Israelite people or Jerusalem, and the male, representing God, experience discord followed by reconciliation and renewal of the marital or parental bond, signifying restoration of the covenant (Ackerman, 1992, on Isaiah; O'Connor, 1992, on Jeremiah). The prevalence of these images and metaphors surely represents a long-enduring use and reuse of a single literary motif but very probably also reflects a real and continuing concern with harmony and conflict within the dominant social and economic unit of the Israelites.

In the Bible, God is often described as a parent, usually as a father; most of these portrayals show "loving ties between fathers and their children" (Gruber, 1999, p. 142). Sometimes God is represented as both mother and father, as in the first creation account (Genesis 1:27) where God creates both man and woman in a divine image, suggesting therefore a deity who embodies both male and female (Gruber, 1999, p. 125). Less frequently, a writer such as Isaiah shows God speaking or acting as a mother: screaming in childbirth (Isaiah 42:13–14); unable to forget her nursing baby (Isaiah 49:15); and comforting her children (Isaiah 66:13).

In a subsistence, agrarian economy, families profited from having many children to help with the intensive labor required for survival. "Biblical injunctions to 'be fruitful and multiply' surely served the interests of Israelite villagers and of society as a whole" (Meyers, 1992, p. 248). Most families probably had three to five offspring who survived into adulthood (Gruber, 1999, p. 142); given infant and early childhood mortality rates, to produce that number of surviving children, women probably had twice as many pregnancies (Meyers, 1992, p. 248). Despite the dangers of death in childbirth, women seem to have wanted large families. Indeed, barrenness—explained as God's closing of the womb—is a theme and dilemma that recurs in the stories of the matriarchs, Sarah, Rachel, and Leah (Exum, 1985). In the eleventh century, Hannah's prayer of petition for a child and her prayer of thanksgiving for her first son provided models repeated in both later Jewish and Christian traditions (Gruber, 1999); she was rewarded with a son, the future king Saul, and then with three more sons and two daughters (1 Samuel 1–2; Hackett, 1992). As in other ancient societies, the Israelites explained barrenness and fertility by divine intervention and regularly prayed for divine favor and protection of the mother and small children.

Despite the clear evidence for a strong desire for many children, there are hints about older traditions of child sacrifice, such as the story of Isaac and the ruminations of Jeremiah (7:31–32; 19:5; and 32:35), which condemn the practice. The date or extent of child sacrifice is unknown (O'Connor, 1992).

Desire for children led some Israelites to adopt orphaned children, as Mordecai adopted his uncle's daughter, Esther, in the late sixth century (Esther 2:7). Several other passages depict an *ōmēn*, a man who provides nursing care to someone else's child (Numbers 11:12; Isaiah 49:23). General community solicitude for parentless children is reflected in Biblical law's demand that orphans and widows be invited to holiday feasts (Gruber, 1999).

The Bible, supplemented with later Talmudic literature (dating from the Israelites' return from exile in Babylonia in the midsixth century BCE, extending into the Hellenistic and Greco–Roman periods, and lasting into the fifth century CE), provides some evidence about the beginning of human life among ancient Israelites. Pregnant women were to avoid alcohol, suggesting an understanding of the possibility of damaging a fetus *in utero* (Colon and Colon, 1999), and pregnant women were excused from fasting. Miscarriages were explained by strife and stress in the home, strong and unpleasant odors, the experience of great pain, or insufficient food. Childbirth was expected to be painful and explained by Genesis's account of God's punishment for Eve's disobedience. The death of a woman in childbirth was attributed to her violation of religious law or breaking a vow; an easy delivery was seen as a reward for righteousness (Ilan, 1996).

Childbirth was superintended by midwives and accomplished by kneeling on bricks or stools. Midwives could exercise considerable authority to judge from the Exodus (1:15–19) account of Shipreh and Puah, who rejected pharaoh's order to kill all newborn boys at birth; their refusal saved Moses and started the Hebrew resistence that culminated in the Hebrews' escape from Egypt.

The twelfth-century story (1 Samuel 4:19–22) of the wife of Phinehas giving birth during a battle against the Philistines shows midwives comforting the new mother with the news, "Do not be afraid, for you have given birth to a son," suggesting a preference for male over female children or perhaps a need for sons to grow up to become soldiers. Preference for male children during the Biblical period, however, may be overstated by the Bible; in a labor-intensive agrarian economy in which many children are desired, females provided not just workers but crucial skilled labor (Meyers, 1992). However, almost certainly a preference for males was clear by the more urban and commercial Talmudic era, when the birth of a daughter became a disappointment. Nonetheless, Jews living in the Greco–Roman world raised all children, and fathers were required to support both sons and daughters while they were minors (Ilan, 1996).

In a metaphor describing God's care of newborn Jerusalem, Ezekiel (16:4–12) provides a good description of the treatment of neonates. The umbilical cord was cut, the infant washed first with water, then oiled and salted with soda ash, which likely served as a bacteriostatic astringent, and finally wrapped in cloth. Evidence from Talmudic sources reveals a variety of remedies for babies who did not breathe readily and for some birth defects, showing "a keen observation of congenital abnormalities and normal newborn behavior" (Colon and Colon, 1999, p. 29). In Ezekiel's account, God provides his infant daughter with the finest embroidered fabrics of linen and silk, sandals made of badger skin, and jewelry—bracelets, a necklace, earrings, and a tiara; this portion of the story of divine care reflects, no doubt, the practices of a few wealthy families; such luxuries were simply unavailable for the bulk of the population. However, these unusually lavish infant accoutrements probably do reflect a general social expectation for basic material investment in the care of newborns.

Infants were named at birth, often for parents or grandparents. The name was usually given by both parents, but could be bestowed by the mother alone, as shown when the wife of Phinehas by herself named her newborn son Ichabod. Circumcision occurred on the eighth day and was carried out by a man, although Exodus 4:24–26 hints that women may have played a role in this ritual in very early times.

Mothers, together with older women and siblings, provided the bulk of the care of young children. In Biblical times, the demands for women's skilled labor in the subsistence, agrarian economy— gardening, transformation of agricultural products into food, weaving and sewing, pot making and basketry—probably consumed an average of 10 hours a day. In such circumstances, mothers likely integrated childcare into their other responsibilities (Meyers, 1989, 1992). Thus we must picture children growing up under the watchful eyes of mothers and adults but also having considerable freedom of movement and action so long as they did not disrupt the extensive and necessary work of adults. We hear nothing about small children's toys or games or play; but some time for maternal play with small children is suggested by Isaiah's description (66:12) of a restored Jerusalem as a happy child "carried on her hip and bounced on her knees."

The most frequent references to early childcare in the Bible concern nursing and weaning, which probably took place around the age of 3 years (Meyers, 1988). The story of Ruth (4:17), from the fourteenth century, shows us an infant left in the care of a grandmother while the mother went to work in the fields. The story of Hannah, however, from the twelfth century, presents a nursing mother who is excused from making the Passover pilgrimage so she can stay home with her infant until he is weaned (1 Samuel 1–2). In Biblical times, mothers very probably nursed their own babies, although a wetnurse is mentioned in 2 Samuel (4:4). In the later Talmudic period, wet-nurses were used in some elite families, as they were in wealthy Greco–Roman ones. Rabbinic opinion was divided on the practice of wet-nursing, as it was on the appropriate time for weaning; there was agreement that the minimum age should be 18 to 24 months, but recommendations for the maximum age ranged from 2 to 5 years. Nursing mothers were encouraged to suckle their children with such incentives as a reduction in other household duties, an exemption from fasts, and the right to have intercourse and use contraceptives while nursing (Ilan, 1996).

Another common reference to young children in the Bible depicts their suffering in war, and the history of the Israelites brought them much strife—both internal struggles and conflict with their aggressive neighbors. Indeed, the suffering must often have been terrible. Writing of events in the sixth century, Jeremiah (15:9) tells how a mother, once honored and blessed for her seven children, is cursed by losing all of them in war. And Jeremiah's prophesy (19:9) that Jerusalem will endure so horrible a famine that parents would eat their children seems fulfilled in Lamentations, in which Jeremiah says the children are desolate (1:16), nursing children and toddlers faint from hunger on the streets (2:11; 2:19), children's tongues stick to roofs of their mouths because of excessive thirst (4:4), and mothers eat their own young (2:20; 4:10).

War and upheaval were regular features of Israelite history, but more peaceful images of daily family life appear as well, if less frequently. A mother's voice in Psalm 131 tells the Lord as she approaches a place of worship that she has quieted her soul; it is calm, "like the contented child I carry" (131:2). Involvement of children in family-centered religious activities, including those the central authorities regarded as acts of apostasy, was probably a regular feature of family life, such as the scene described by Jeremiah (7:18): "the children gather wood, the fathers kindle fire, and the women knead dough, to make cakes for the queen of heaven"; the queen of heaven here may refer to the fertility goddesses so common in the eastern Mediterranean (O'Connor, 1992) or to an earlier Hebraic conceptualization of the divinity as both king and consort (Frymer-Kensky, 1992).

Other evidence suggests sensible, healthy childrearing practices. Parents were advised to keep their youngsters out of the sun during the middle of the day. Children were to eat slowly, chew their food well, and have a good, solid breakfast (Colon and Colon, 1999). Like their parents, children probably lived on a diet in which the mainstays were bread, olives and olive oil, grapes, and dairy products; these principal foods were supplemented seasonally with other fruits, legumes, and vegetables. Meat was probably reserved for feast days. Strict dietary laws and unusual attention to sanitation in food preparation and handling may well have reduced the incidence of foodborn disease among Israelite children (Colon and Colon, 1999).

Primary care of infants and toddlers was the responsibility of the mother and older women, but the Bible clearly reflects an expectation of shared parental authority. Law required respect for and obedience to both mother and father. Besides the commandment to honor both mother and father (Exodus 20:12; Deuteronomy 5:16; Leviticus 19:3), Exodus demanded the death penalty for anyone who cursed or assaulted either parent (21:15–17; Leviticus 20:9). Two injunctions in Deuteronomy (21:18–21 and 22–15) required actions by both mother and father for grown children: turning over a juvenile delinquent to authorities and displaying the bloodstained marital sheet of any bride wrongly accused by her husband of not having been a virgin.

Traditional wisdom expressed in Proverbs (1:8 and 6:20) shows the role both parents played in educating the young: "Hear, my child, your father's instruction, and reject not your mother's teaching." Parents taught children the tasks they would have to carry out as adults: fathers the heavy work of the fields, mothers the more specialized labor of tending the gardens, transforming crops into food, weaving, and sewing. Because both boys and girls spent more time during their formative years with their mothers and elder females, it seems probable that these maternal figures played the greater role in socializing the young into the values and mores of Israelite society and religion (Meyers, 1988). Mothers had a duty to teach their daughters to keen and wail at funerals (Jeremiah 9:19).

The authority and the power of mothers during the Biblical period distinguish the Hebrews from other eastern Mediterranean cultures. Although the Bible mentions women infrequently (only 9% of the named people are female; Meyers, 1992) and mainly as the mothers of important and famous sons, these women often had significant influence in starting and determining the outcome of crucial events (e.g., the matriarchs, Miriam, Bathsheba, Jezebel, Delilah). One of the most powerful women in the Bible, Deborah, was a judge who organized and helped to lead an army that freed the Israelites from Canaanite oppression, probably in the twelfth century. The name of her husband is given, but there is no specific mention of her children. Yet in her victory song, one of the oldest pieces of literature in the Bible, Deborah identified herself first as a "mother in Israel" (Judges 4–5). Inferences from her accomplishments suggest that "a mother in Israel is one who brings liberation from oppression, provides protection, and ensures the well-being and security of her people" (Exum, 1985, p. 85).

There is every reason to believe that within Israelite households of the Biblical period, mothers exercised authority alongside fathers and served as empowering role models for their daughters. However, the legal and cultural authority granted to mothers in the Biblical period was significantly circumscribed by the Talmudic era. In rabbinic literature, mothers have lost their ability to be a guardian of or agent for their minor children, and with respect to "legal responsibility, women were usually bracketed with slaves, minors, deaf-mutes, and persons of double or doubtful sex" (Archer, 1994, p. 63).

Many scholars believe that during much of the Biblical period, ordinary Israelites had rudimentary literacy—in sharp contrast to other eastern Mediterranean cultures. Because there is no evidence of formal schools with paid instructors before the Talmudic period, it seems likely that parents, both mothers and fathers, taught their children the basic elements of reading, writing, and numeracy, as well as the fundamentals of Hebrew cultic and family law (Meyers, 1988). Law required fathers to instruct their children in Hebrew history and tradition (Exodus 10:2; Deuteronomy 32:7).

Eastern Mediterranean Civilizations: Some Conclusions

In these societies, it seems clear that the overall outlook and presuppositions of the general culture permeated to some degree attitudes about children and parenting. Although all of these civilizations recognized infancy and early childhood as distinctive stages of life and took care to safeguard young children, the experience of parenting—and of being a child—seems to have been decidedly different in each. Because of their particular history during the Biblical period, the Israelites seem to have blended into their beliefs about parenting elements of the more harsh and pessimistic Mesopotamian cultures with the more affectionate and optimistic outlook of the Egyptians, combining both with the Israelites' unique conceptualization of their relationship with their God.

THE GREEKS

For the Greeks, there is considerably more historical evidence for investigating parenting, family life, and childrearing practices. As in the ancient Eastern Mediterranean, patriarchy dominated the way Greeks thought about these critical issues. Most of the evidence for ancient Greece was produced in Athens, and an inevitable Athenian elite-male bias colors the sources. What historians reconstruct about Greek parenting pertains primarily to the Athenian upper classes. Inferences about lower classes, slaves, and other Greek communities are difficult and uncertain. However, some important differences between Spartan and Athenian parenting can be seen.

Unlike most of their ancient predecessors in the Eastern Mediterranean, the Greeks thought consciously about thinking and knowing, systemizing their knowledge of the human and natural worlds. Although few Greeks focused their writing on parenting and childrearing, political philosophers saw parenting and childrearing as crucial ingredients in creating and maintaining the ideal state. Greeks were observant and knowledgeable about stages of child development and thoughtful about how parents should respond to the child's changing needs—not so much for the sake of the child, but for the welfare of the community.

Polis and Oikos: The Cultural Context of Greek Family Life

The Greek *polis* or city-state was the fundamental unit of Greek political life. Most were governed by relatively small groups of families who called themselves *aristoi*—the best men; because they held the power, *kratos*, they became known as aristocrats. For our purposes, it is important to note that these aristocrats used the household, *oikos*, as their principal conceptual model for the *polis*. For the Greeks, the aristocratic household embraced a good deal more than the family and its basic dwelling; the *oikos* included family dependents (e.g., servants and slaves; other people, usually kinfolk, who were wards; in-laws of lesser socioeconomic status) and all property (e.g., city house as well as country estates). At the head of each household was the *kurios*, the senior male direct descendant of the former head. Although the *kurios* in theory had primary power, in fact he was expected to consult widely with other senior males; collectively the senior males looked out for the social, economic, and political interests of the family, with the *kurios* serving as their major spokesman. In less affluent families, the *oikos* was, of course, much smaller, corresponding more nearly to a nuclear family that rents its dwelling place. However, regardless of wealth and size, every *oikos* had its *kurios*.

Within the *oikos*, especially the more wealthy ones, there arose a fairly strict division of labor between men and women and a clear demarcation between public and private spheres of action. The world of the *polis* was the world of men; the activities within the *oikos* as a domestic and family unit was a space for both men and women. The women supervised and performed domestic duties—cooking, cleaning, weaving, and childrearing—but were nonetheless accountable for their work and proper behavior to the *kurios*. In practice, daily life saw men of affluence moving freely and frequently back and forth between *oikos* and *polis*; affluent women were mainly confined to the *oikos* because the family could afford to have servants and slaves go out to get water and conduct the family's daily commerce.

Recent work on the domestic architecture of ancient Greece allows us to infer some important ideas about the interaction of adults and children within the Greek house. The focal point of domestic life was a walled-in but open courtyard with a portico for shade in summer and protection from rain in winter. Paved in more affluent houses, packed earth in less, the portico and courtyard complex was where most activities took place. Small, often windowless rooms—including a washroom and kitchen or cooking area—were reached from the portico; only these small rooms were part of the *oikos'* truly private space. Almost always directly adjacent the house's main doorway, the courtyard served as a kind of intermediate ground between the private *oikos* and the public *polis* in that guests, both male and female, were received here. From the courtyard, there were usually clear lines of sight into the rest of the house's rooms. The only interior room that may have been reserved for exclusively male use was the *andron*, a dining area used by the male family members for entertaining other male guests—and sometimes female entertainers—at dinner; although it is certainly possible that during the day, this room could have been used by other members of the family (Levett, 1999). From the architecture of Greek houses, we can infer that children constantly interacted with adults in the household, observed them at work, participated in both daily family religious rituals and other significant events such as weddings and funerals, met most guests, and had ample space to play and exercise. In turn, parents and other adults could keep a constant eye on the young.

For less affluent families, the basic house plan was the same, just smaller. Families that ran artisan businesses—leatherworks, masonry, pottery—generally had their workshops immediately adjacent to the house; it is not unreasonable to infer that children would have gone back and forth between house and workshop, perhaps even helping out with the business. Because by law, Athenian fathers were required either to train their sons in a trade or to provide them with some means of support, we can safely assume that sons of artisans and laborers began some sort of apprenticeship with their fathers at an early age. A large proportion of the male citizens earned a meager living as day laborers—carpenters, agricultural workers, ox drivers. Without domestic servants and with their husbands otherwise fully engaged, women in these families had to go into the public sphere to purchase food and household items; indeed, many women from the lower classes also worked outside their homes for pay as laundresses, midwives, nurses, fishmongers, ribbon sellers, and so forth. Who looked after children while their parents were away running errands or working is unclear; most likely it would have been an older relative living in the household, although it is certainly probable that children from poor families were left unattended for considerable periods of time.

It is into this social, economic, political, and physical context that we put our investigation of Greek parenting and family life. Only the wealthy elite families had the wherewithal to achieve the aristocratic ideal of the *oikos*, but it likely that less affluent families aspired to the same idea. In classical Athens, even among aristocrats, there arose considerable division of opinion about how far into the *oikos* the reach of the *polis* should extend; and when the state tried to reach into the home, it was often about matters of childrearing and sexual activities (particularly relations among men). The more radical democrats drew the line at the front door, claiming a right to privacy in childrearing and sexual conduct much like that contemporary jurists have found in the U.S. Constitution. The conservative aristocratic families, however, alarmed at the demise of the old, highly disciplined approaches to childrearing and the erosion of deference to their position, advocated state-imposed schemes of childrearing that began at birth and continued into early adulthood (Keuls, 1985; Cohen, 1991).

Reckoning with this aristocratic conservative perspective, especially in Athens, is crucial to interpreting parenting, for its major spokesmen—Plato and Aristotle—provide us with the bulk of our information about Greek views of expectations of parents and child development. It is often difficult to separate what parents were actually doing from what Plato and Aristotle say parents should be doing.

The importance these philosophers attached to children and childrearing seems not much different from that found elsewhere in Greek society. A household needed children to be complete; a son was critical for continuing the family line into future generations; at least one daughter was desirable to care for parents in their old age; and children were needed to tend and honor the family graves. Leaving an enemy childless, as Medea does her abandoning husband Jason, was the most devastating revenge possible. These reasons for producing and rearing are fairly devoid of sentimental feelings about small children themselves, and that is an important difference between ancient and contemporary Western attitudes about children. Nonetheless, Greeks seem to have regarded the experience of parenting with interest and felt considerable affection for their offspring *qua* children.

Family Planning

The birth of a child was an important family event, and the child's formal acceptance into the household and naming involved considerable ritual and celebration. A collateral issue here is the extent to which the Greeks practiced infanticide. That infanticide—as we define it, taking away the life of a newborn baby—was a legal option that was exercised by the *kurios* is indubitably true. The vexing historical questions concern how often Greek fathers resorted to infanticide and whether females were more likely to be exposed than males.

In considering infanticide, we must remember that an infant did not become a legal person until it was officially accepted into the family; the act of birth itself did not confer legal status on the baby. The distinction was important to the Greeks. By exposing the child—wrapping it warmly and leaving birth tokens with it—the parents left its fate to the gods; some exposed newborns were rescued and reared by childless families. Thus exposure did not legally constitute murder, and newborns seem to have been conceptualized as being more akin to an unborn fetus than a full person. Given high neonatal mortality rates, it is not difficult to understand why ancient families waited a few days to determine whether the baby would survive; formal acceptance and naming occurred approximately a week after childbirth. However, Pomeroy (1997) suggests that the delay in performing the ritual of acceptance may well have diminished the initial strength of parental bonding with the newborn, creating a more distanced affective tie for both baby and parents.

Many of the crude ancient pots found filled with the bones of newborns—evidence adduced in favor of significant infanticide—are more likely burials of infants who died from natural causes; because they were not yet formal members of the family, the disposal of their bodies did not require the usual funerals and rituals of internment, and they would not have been put in cemeteries. However often fathers resorted to infanticide, it was not a casual decision, and adults felt real unease about the act, as demonstrated by ambivalence expressed in literary texts and the hope that exposed infants would be rescued and reared by another family. There is no consensus among historians about selective exposure of females. Despite recent work (Riddle, 1992) arguing that adult gender ratios favoring men do not demand extensive female infanticide as an explanation, most scholars (e.g., Pomeroy, 1997) maintain that more girls than boys were killed, a reflection of the general social preference for males.

The weight of the evidence and argumentation now suggests that infanticide in antiquity was a relatively uncommon method of controlling family size. Indeed, it appears that ancient families regulated their size through a variety of methods of contraception and abortion. Most of our evidence about contraception and abortion comes from sources later than the classical Greek era, but the information contained therein most likely reflects centuries-old traditional herbal medicine. Riddle (1992), historian of ancient medicine and particularly herbals, conducted an extensive study in which he concluded that ancient people used contraceptives and abortifacients for effective planned parenthood, regulating with considerable success the number and spacing of their children.

The Social Construction of Children and Childhood

In general, Greeks saw their offspring as inheriting both physical and psychological characteristics of their parents and ancestors (Pomeroy, 1997). If there were various views about the relative strengths of male versus female contributions to conception and gestation, there was little doubt that both the mother's and father's families were somehow represented in the children. Adults expected to find both physical resemblances between children and progenitors and personality and character similarities as well. Parental expectations here may have significantly influenced their behavior toward their young.

The Athenians had a well-developed social construct of what children were and how they differed from adults and old people. Above all, Greek parents conceived of their young as plastic, shapable, unformed, impressionable, ignorant, gullible, imaginative—a physical as well as mental–emotional *tabula rasa*. The idea that children were plastic included the child's body as well as the mind. Thus the application of the proper nurture and training was seen as critical in determining what kind of adults children would grow up to be. Collaterally, adults saw children as sometimes unruly, difficult to control, in need of discipline.

Judging from the frequency of remarks in the corpus of Greek literature from the classical period, second to the adult view of the child as plastic comes a recognition of the child as a fearful creature, as easily frightened, given to tears, hiding in mother's skirts, begging to be picked up for comfort. Greeks believed their children would be frightened by strangers, objects of large size, or changes in the family's circumstances. Parents and other adults apparently took advantage of (and perhaps even cultivated) this characteristic by telling stories about ghosts and monsters that would punish children for bad behavior. In addition to these characteristics, the Greek construct of children saw them as loving, happy, playful, and affectionate; as naturally imitative; and as innocent, unworldly, and without sexuality (French, 1991).

Not surprisingly, Greek parents also saw children as helpless, in need of protection, unable to communicate. One adjective frequently associated with small children in Homer is *nepios*, meaning literally "not able to speak." Babies' inability to express their needs clearly was apparently a source of considerable discomfort to Greek parents. In Aeschylus's play, *The Libation Bearers* (753–757), Cilissa, Orestes' aged nurse, recalls caring for her young charge: "A baby is like a beast, it does not think/but you have to nurse it, do you not, the way it wants./For the child still in swaddling clothes can not tell us/if he is hungry or thirsty, if he needs to make/water. Children's young insides are a law to themselves." This recognition of infancy as a distinct phase of life during which a child is in need of special care shows up in medical writings, particularly with respect to the child's greater vulnerability to disease and infection.

Plato and Aristotle on children's development. Writing in the fourth century BCE, Plato and Aristotle undoubtedly drew a good deal of their knowledge about children and parenting from the larger society; neither seems to have devoted himself to empirical studies of the subject. It is important to recognize how much knowledge about children and childrearing was generally available to these wealthy male aristocrats; the scope and depth of that knowledge strongly suggest that Greek fathers were not the absentee, disinterested parents some scholars have posited. Of particular interest is the developmental approach both take to describing the stages of childhood. Table 12.1 sets out their principal observations about the different characteristics or needs children have as they grow up and their prescriptions for the appropriate or proper care for that stage. Plato's prescriptions come from *Laws*, 694D and 789E–795E; Aristotle's come from *Politics*, 1336a-b; the views they set out in these passages are echoed and supplemented in other of their works.

The stages that Plato and Aristotle created correlate reasonably well with many contemporary theories of development, missing only is what today we call toddlerhood. Both Plato and Aristotle included psychosocial as well as physiological growth. Neither philosopher believed that his scheme fit all children uniformly. Both commented on the importance of recognizing differences among individual children and advised tailoring childrearing to suit the particular child. We can find a good deal of evidence in other sources to confirm that these developmental stages were widely accepted and that the generally mild, nurturing parenting practices recommended were also generally agreed on. Indeed these other sources allow us to add a good deal of detail to the stages implicit in Plato's and Aristotle's generic discussions.

TABLE 12.1
Characteristics and/or Proper Care

Age Level	Plato	Aristotle
Birth to weaning (approximately 2 years) 2 to 3 years	Swaddled, much rocking and crooning Carried by nurses Nurses/mothers ascertain wants according to cries Shield from pain, fear, grief, corruption "It is infancy that the whole character is most effectually determined"	Bodily development most important "Training of the body [comes] before training of the mind" Plenty of milk; no wine As free movement of the limbs as possible Accustom to endure cold
2 or 3 to 5 or 6 years	Games played together with other children Mild discipline	Bodily exercise Play in preparation for adult activities Allow to cry Protect from base influences Keep at home
5 or 6 to puberty	Separate the genders Boys go to school; learn gymnastics and music Girls learn gymnastics also	Boys being school Avoid hard diet and severe exercise
Puberty to 21	Rigorous training for boys	Rigorous training for boys

Childbirth and infancy. Demand's (1994) *Birth, Death, and Motherhood in Classical Greece* provides a comprehensive study of this important topic. Demand accepts recent arguments that Athenian citizen women probably underwent six or more pregnancies; the number of pregnancies for women in other city-states may have been lower, in the range of three to five. Ancient Greeks were well aware of the dangers of reproduction for mother and child. We will not be far off the mark if we assume that ancient Greece had maternal and infant mortality rates comparable with those of contemporary cultures lacking modern medical care, particularly anasepsis. There were three major incentives for a woman to undergo so many pregnancies. First was the social belief that childbearing was a woman's primary purpose in life and within the family; a woman with few children had less prestige than a woman with many children. Second was production of many children so that enough of them would survive to adulthood to sustain the family. Third was the belief that frequent pregnancy protected women from the dreaded illness of *hysteria*, the wandering womb; without the weighty fluids produced by pregnancy, a dried-up womb could break free from its moorings and move about the body, causing terrible medical and emotional problems.

Demand's extensive analysis of the Hippocratic writings on obstetrics (some 40 individual cases) and of related sources reveals the social construction of childbirth in ancient Greece, particularly Athens. Care of the pregnant wife, supervision of childbirth, and care of the infant were regarded as the province of women, particularly of midwives. The difficulty of successful obstetrical work was recognized by the Hippocratic doctors (Hippocrates, *Diseases of Women*, I.25): "It requires much care and knowledge to carry and nurture the child in the womb and to bring it to birth." A male physician was called on only for advice on handling complications during pregnancy and delivery—and only when the *kurios* was able and willing to pay the doctor's fees.

Assuming survival of infant and mother, the family celebrated the *amphidromia* (literally "the running around") on the fifth or seventh day after birth, decorating the front door with an olive wreath for a boy and wool for a girl. On this occasion the father carried the newborn around the hearth, signaling his intention to accept it into the family and rear it; the mother and female kin who had attended the birth purified themselves; friends and neighbors sent gifts and congratulations. Families who could afford a second celebration for family and friends officially named the new child on the tenth day.

The day-to-day care of infants was the preserve of the women in the household. An experienced mother would expect and be expected to supervise this care. However, with the notable exception of Sparta, Greek girls became wives and mothers in their early teens and needed the guidance and support of their older female kin, both those of their natal families and those of their in-laws—particularly the women resident in the household. On the whole, we can infer a pattern of babycare that involved cooperative efforts among several women. In wealthy families, there would probably be a wet-nurse and perhaps other nurses hired or purchased for their expertise in tending small babies. And the midwife remained on call for postpartum and pediatric problems.

Swaddling was common among the Greeks, again with the exception of Sparta, whose example probably led Aristotle to recommend that babies have free movement of their arms and legs. Lessons about swaddling in later writers make it clear that adults believed the bands were necessary to ensure the growth of straight limbs, a reflection of their construct of the child as plastic. Along with swaddling went several daily massages, whenever the bands were removed to clean the infant. Greek practice apparently loosed babies from their bands gradually, first leaving the head free, then the arms, and so on down the body; babies were completely out of swaddling probably by the time they were 6 months old.

Breast-feeding was regarded as the best nourishment, but success here seems not to have been universal. We can assume that some very young mothers did not produce enough milk and that some upper-class women preferred to use wet-nurses. At any rate, historical sources attest to wet-nursing as a common phenomenon and a means of livelihood for many lower-class women. Many infant feeding bottles from excavations across Greece indicate that human milk was often supplemented with other foods such as goat's milk, honey water, diluted wine, and strained broth from soups. After a few months, babies were probably introduced to bread soaked in one of these liquids and thin gruel or porridge. Older babies might have mashed vegetables with olive oil and bits of meat that had been masticated by mother or nurse. Full weaning probably took place by a child's second birthday at the latest.

Plato attached special importance to infancy. He argued that it is through its perceptions of pleasure and pain that an infant first begins to gain a conception of good and evil, of right and wrong—a kind of protobehaviorist theory of human motivation. Plato complained that parents were generally not careful enough to make sure that babies found pleasure in people or activities that should be emulated. He criticized, for example, leaving infantcare (Plato surely is thinking here of aristocratic children) to lower-class or slave nurses for two reasons. First, he contended, they probably do not do their work as well as the real (high-born) mother would; second, if they did a good job, the child would associate pleasure with them—people of low status—not with their aristocratic parents.

Mothers and mother surrogates keep nearly constant watch over the infant during the first year of life. Crying was generally interpreted as meaning the baby needed something—as suggested by the nurse Cilissa's observations in *Libation Bearers* about the young Orestes; she implies that babies cry to indicate that they are hungry, thirsty, or need to urinate. We can assume that collectively the infant's "mothers" provided a great deal of stimulation through their attention and ministrations. During a child's first year of life then, a pattern of attentive, gentle female parenting was well established. At what point fathers began to play more than observer roles in their children's life is unclear; but their close observation of infancy is certainly well attested in our predominately elite male literary sources.

Toddlers and preschoolers.   The dominance of females in parenting is clear not only for infants but also for male children before they went to school and for females until they married and left home. However, there is good evidence suggesting that fathers began to interact with their youngsters once they became toddlers (Parke, in Vol. 3 of this *Handbook*). Several passages from Aristophanes' comedy *The Clouds*, portray one middle-class father, married to an upper-class wife, as intimately involved in his young son's daily care. The play's hapless hero, Strepsiades, reminds his now arrogant and rebellious teenage son how well he took care of him as a small child (*The Clouds*, 1380–1384)

    ... You haven't a shred of respect for
    The father who brought you up. Why, before you could speak

I knew if you gurgled 'Bru-Bru,' you wanted your feeding bottle,
And if you went 'Mam-mam-mam' I knew it was bread you wanted–
You hardly had time to say 'Kakka' before I grabbed you
And held you out the door.

The last of the baby-talk words, 'Kakka' (feces), provides one of the very few extant literary references to toilet training; apparently, this aspect of childrearing did not provoke the discussion in the ancient world that it does in our own day. Artifacts and vase paintings, however, allow us to infer something about potty training. Excavated in the marketplace of ancient Athens, the Agora, was a nearly fully intact potty chair. Beautifully painted and crafted, this was undoubtedly intended for sale to a wealthy family. The overall dimensions suggest that the chair was made to hold a child weighing approximately 18 to 22 pounds, probably corresponding to an ancient 2-year-old toddler; from this we can probably safely infer that toilet training took place at approximately this age. Several vase paintings from Athens depict small children in just this sort of chair. More interesting is the fact that the child could not get in or out of the potty chair alone; an adult would have to put the child in, and once in, the child would have to wait until an adult lifted her or him out. Can we infer from this evidence that parents meant toilet training to signal the onset of restrictions on the child's behavior? That such devices were used to make toddlers stay put, at least for a little while? Unfortunately, in the absence of literary evidence, we cannot confidently infer parental intent.

Strepsiades gives us other glimpses of a father's close observations of his preschooler's creative activities (*The Clouds*, 877–881):

When he was just so high he made
His own toy houses, he carved boats,
He knocked up miniature carts from leather,
Cut frogs from pomegranates....

Even allowing for some exaggeration about his son's accomplishments, there is no mistaking the pride father expresses about son. He was a doting parent, as this final passage clearly reveals (*The Clouds*, 860–864):

...When you
Were a little boy I used to spoil you
And do what you asked—with the very first
Obol I earned as a juryman
I bought you a little pushcart
At the Spring feast....

There is additional evidence of male familiarity with the activities of toddlers and preschoolers (French, 1999). Little jugs called *choes* were given to small children or perhaps their families at a spring festival when, probably at 3 years of age, children were officially accepted as members of the father's clan. Hundreds of these jugs have been discovered in excavations, and nearly all use as a decorative theme little children—usually boys—at play. The figures of the children are delightfully plump and happy; the vase painters show children indoors and outside romping, running, throwing balls, playing with hoops and pets—engaged in precisely the kinds of activities we associate with this stage of child development. Other literary and visual evidence confirms the range of toys provided for small children we find on the *choes*.

In his consistent call for close supervision of children in order to maintain a stable, conservative state, Plato (*Laws*, 793E-794B) provides a revealing description of the social life of preschoolers and the importance of play and games:

To form the character of the child over three and up to six years old, there will be need of games....
Children of this age have games which come by natural instinct; and they generally invent them of

themselves whenever they meet together. As soon as they have reached the age of three, all the children from three to six must meet together at the village temples. . . . I assert that in every State a complete ignorance about children's games—how that they are of decisive importance for legislation, as determining whether the laws enacted are to be permanent or not. For when the programme of games is prescribed and secures that the same children always play the same games and delight in the same toys in the same way and under the same conditions, it allows the real and serious laws also to remain undisturbed.

. . . Alterations in children's games are regarded by all lawgivers. . .as being mere matters of play and not as the causes of serious mischief; hence, instead of forbidding them, they give in to them and adopt them. They fail to reflect that those children who innovate in their games grow up to be different from their fathers.

From this remarkable passage we can draw a number of inferences. First, here is clear adult-male recognition of one of the most important characteristics of this age group. Second, Plato sees that play and games can be powerful tools of socialization of the young to the norms of adult society. Third, he notes that children differ from one another; some are more likely to lead and innovate. Perhaps the most interesting inference is Plato's complaint that adults do not make much effort to regulate children's games and seem content to let their preschoolers have control over their own play and games. It is important that Plato does not condemn parents for neglecting their youngsters; rather, he chastises them for letting their children play as the children wish.

A parental tendency to see safeguarding as opposed to carefully controlling preschoolers is confirmed for the wealthy by the institution of the *paidagogue*—literally a person who leads a child around. Probably shortly after full weaning and toilet training, and around the time the child could speak reasonably well, affluent parents turned over the hour-to-hour supervision of their boys to a *paidagogue*, an older male (usually lower class or slave) whose job it was to supervise the child, especially outside the home, and see to it that nothing harmful happened to the boy; we hear of a handful of girls who had a *paidagogue*. The *paidagogue* was also expected to begin to teach the child proper manners and help him improve his speech. In many cases, the *paidagogue* continued in service to the boy and his family throughout his school years and well into adolescence; literate *paidagogues* apparently helped the boy with his school work. Within this relationship, the child probably had a good deal of autonomy so long as the child's behavior did not court danger or seriously violate standards of conduct expected of this age group. Father and son had an intermediary who seems on occasion to have been able to diffuse conflict, especially between an adolescent youth and his father.

Adult interest in and observation of small children is reflected to some degree in the large corpus of Greek medical literature, beginning with that of Hippocrates (ca. 460–370 BCE). Although there is no treatise specifically focused on pediatrics among the Hippocratic works, references to children and the occasions on which special treatment was required are frequent. In the beginning of *Aphorisms* (1:13 and 16), Hippocrates stresses the differences between children and adults, noting that children cannot tolerate fasts and need liquid diets during fevers. One essay, *On Dentition*, discusses not only development of the teeth but also mouth and throat problems. In one section of *Aphorisms* (3:24–26), Hippocrates lists the kinds of diseases most associated with each stage of child development: Infants are said to be vulnerable to aphthae, vomiting, coughing, insomnia, frights, infections around the navel and in the ears; teething babies are subject to gum problems, fevers, convulsions, diarrhea or constipation; toddlers run risks for tonsilitis, spinal disk misalignments, asthma, worms, warts, leprosy, swollen glands in the neck, and tuberculosis. Elsewhere, Hippocrates mentions other childhood diseases such as mumps, convulsions from fever, diphtheria, polio, and meningitis. He also notes that women put medicaments into children's porridge to treat worms and other diseases. The treatise on *Epidemics* shows that in some cases children were treated with surgery. The Hippocratic attention to children's physical health was continued in the biological works of Aristotle, the son of a physician (Colon and Colon, 1999).

What generalizations about parenting in classical Athens can we make with some degree of confidence from this evidence? First, parents—fathers as well as mothers—seem to have had a solid working knowledge of the characteristics and needs of their young children; parents and adult society believed that families should meet these needs. Second, the basic concept of the child as plastic and moldable guided parental efforts to rear and shape the young into the kinds of adults they believed their societies needed. Third, parenting seems to have been attentive to children but not intrusive. Once out of swaddling clothes, small children appear to have been supplied with toys and other objects for play and allowed to follow their own instincts and desires with enough adult supervision to keep them out of harm's way. There is little in the evidence to suggest that Athenian parents became locked in some early struggle for control; the child's efforts to gain autonomy were probably usually successful. Fourth, parenting was often a communal endeavor; society expected that in rearing young children, biological mother and father would share with and receive support from a range of other adults—including men.

The Spartan Anomaly

This discussion has been based mainly on sources for classical Athens, and it is not unreasonable to assume, given the cultural hegemony of Athens during these years, that what we see for Athens can be extended to other Greek city-states as well—with one important exception, Sparta. Sparta was recognized by everyone as having a distinctive, if not totally unique, culture and political life. This difference affected patterns of Spartan parenting significantly.

Classical Sparta lived a state of permanent military preparedness against threats she perceived within her own lands—a huge servile population tied to the soil—and on their borders—members of their own Peloponnesian league as well as Athens and Persia. Until they were in their 40s, Spartan male citizens lived in military camps and rarely spent time in their homes—the places where their wives and small children lived.

As a result of Sparta's thoroughgoing militarism, the rearing of boys up to the age of 7 years and girls until they married was left almost entirely in the hands of Spartan wives. A Spartan women's chief job and basis for judging her worth was to produce more thoroughly Spartan soldiers and wives. A Spartan mother's attention was riveted on training her young children to become good Spartans. Whereas in Athens, children were an important, well-observed, and for the most part welcome part of the household, in early and classical Sparta they were at the center of household attention.

The Spartans apparently practiced eugenics. First, women were not married until their late teens or early 20s on the grounds that they bore more healthy babies and were less likely to die in childbirth than young teenagers. Adolescent Spartan girls participated in rigorous physical fitness programs, and Spartan wives were expected to maintain an extensive program of exercise to maintain their health. Second, Spartan men, apparently older ones, could "breed" their young wives with younger Spartan males whose physical prowess and character they admired; it seems that Spartans believed that, as a man aged, his semen/seed tended to deteriorate also. Third, babies were inspected soon after birth by a team of Spartan men who, probably on advice of the midwife, determined whether the child was healthy enough to rear. How often sickly or deformed neonates were killed by being thrown into a nearby gorge is unknown.

Spartan mothers personally supervised every aspect of her children's growth, assisted by one or more nurses. According to scattered sources (principally Aristotle and Xenophon), Spartan babies were not swaddled at all; they were fully breast-fed, sometimes by both mother and a wet-nurse; they were never fed even diluted wine; they were bathed frequently and in cold water. By the time they were toddlers, mothers and nurses were teaching them not to be afraid of the dark, not to whine, and not to be picky about their food. Lots of vigorous exercise and games under close supervision filled the children's days. Mothers were to imbue their boys especially with the strength and courage needed to withstand the punishing course of military education boys began at approximately the age of 7 years. It appears that the primary mechanism of child discipline was the use of shame; children were encouraged to tease and taunt their peers who stepped out of line.

For well over two centuries, Spartan childrearing produced men and women who were capable of continuing the rigorous, highly disciplined Spartan way of life. During the later stages of the Peloponnesian War in the last decades of the fifth century and into the first decades of the fourth century, when Sparta became the hegemonic power of all Greece, Spartan childrearing practices changed dramatically. The Spartans suffered such heavy losses of men and the remaining citizens became so overextended that Spartan women began to take on additional functions within the state, particularly the management of the huge estates owned by each family and a good deal of the daily commercial and economic activity of the state. The focus of Spartan home life was no longer fixed on the children and on inculcating the values of Spartan society; childrearing was increasingly turned over to the nurses who, because they themselves were not products of the Spartan system, could not transmit successfully Spartan values to their young charges. By the middle of the fourth century and for generations thereafter, when Sparta tried to reclaim power, she tried to reform, to return to the former hard self-discipline of earlier times. She failed, in significant part, because the habits of parenting had so dramatically changed. Here is one excellent example that demonstrates how changes in parenting can be connected clearly with changes in adult society (French, 1997).

The Greeks: Some Conclusions

It is with the Greeks that we find the first systematic observations and thinking, even theorizing, about parenting and childrearing—spurred by their belief that the stability of the society and the state depended on producing new generations capable of and committed to maintaining the community. Greeks created models of child development that closely parallel contemporary theory. Emphasis within the family on parenting practices advocated by the aristocratic elite was probably more prevalent in the upper classes. Because Greek *poleis* were fairly small, it is likely that elite beliefs about proper parenting and childrearing practices permeated the entire community; to what extent parents in the lower classes had the resources and time to emulate aristocratic practices cannot be determined.

THE ROMANS

Historians today, as well as Romans themselves, remarked on the extent to which Rome incorporated many aspects of Greek culture into their own. Many historians posit a Greco–Roman civilization that began soon after Rome added Greece and the Eastern Mediterranean world to its empire in the second century BCE. Indeed, there are many commonalities between Greek and Roman ideas about and practices in parenting and childrearing, and Romans clearly adopted much of what they found in Plato and Aristotle and other Greeks in their own philosophical thinking. However, Roman family relationships were probably more complex and variable than those of the Greeks, and it appears that Romans expressed more interest in and attention to affective bonds between parents and children than did the Greeks.

Familia, Domus, and *Patria Potestas*: The Cultural Context of Roman Family Life

Like the Greeks, the Romans' model of the state grew out of their conceptualization of the household; but unlike the Greeks, the Romans developed two distinct constructs. The first and most commonly used is the Latin *familia*, which is probably closest to the Greek *oikos* in that it encompassed not only the central nuclear grouping of father–mother–children but also coresident kin, retainers and other dependents, slaves and all chattel property, as well as all land and buildings. When Romans meant just the nuclear unit's people and dwelling, they used the word *domus*, which is more like our word home. It was the *familia* that interacted with the state, the public sphere, and it was the *familia* to which Roman law applied; it was the *domus* that connoted the private sphere within which Romans conducted what we would call family life.

Within the home and household, the Roman *pater familias*, like the Greek *kurios*, was in charge. However, the Roman father's power, the *patria potestas*, was absolute; a father had the right to kill anyone—including his grown children; his right to impose less than capital punishment was also absolute; and he could sell his children as slaves. There are a number of examples of fathers who exercised their right to execute their grown children. This absolute power retained legal sanction for nearly a millennium, ending only in the late fourth century CE, after Christianity had significantly changed the core value structures of the Roman imperial world.

In practice, the exercise of *patria potestas* was restrained by a number of factors. First, before killing, exiling, or severely punishing adult children, a father was expected to take counsel with the other adults, including the women, of the *familia*; few fathers risked acting in contravention of this family council. Second, the role of the *mater familias* traditionally expected her to ameliorate the harshness of paternal discipline. Third, a Roman law, allegedly instituted by Rome's founder Romulus, limited a father's right of life or death over his newborn children; Romans were obligated by law to rear all sons and at least their firstborn daughters to adulthood. Finally, surely in the early years of the Republic, fathers were the main teachers of their sons; Romans expected the bonds forged between father–teacher and son–pupil to be strong enough to withstand intergenerational conflicts.

The alleged Romulean law compelling fathers to rear newborns suggests some notion of legitimate state intervention in the private sphere of Roman families. We see later evidence of attempts of the state to address what was apparently a general problem—the failure of Roman families to replenish themselves. The Roman practice of dividing the paternal estate among heirs (daughters as well as sons) seems to have prompted families to adopt a strategy of trying to have but one or two heirs survive their father so as not to divide and redivide the patrimony until each heir's share was so small as to count for very little. The problems of not having a system of primogeniture (i.e., eldest surviving male child inherits the entire estate) extended into the middle classes and small-farm families. Given the nearly incessant and large-scale warfare in which the Romans engaged for many centuries as well as childhood mortality rates, it must have been very difficult to carry out this reproductive strategy successfully. Romans seem to have consistently erred on the side of insufficient reproduction rather than risk excessive division of the estate, probably because the practice of adopting adult male heirs was widely accepted and offered powerful families yet one more way to manipulate kinship ties to their political advantage. The ability of the Romans to err on the side of producing too few children who survived to adulthood suggests not high rates of infanticide—for which there is little evidence and was illegal anyway—but reasonably effective family planning methods of contraception and abortion (Riddle, 1992).

The potentially monstrous powers given to fathers and the centuries-long problem of families failing to reproduce themselves suggest an important element of the social context for investigation and interpretation of the Roman social construction of parenting. At the very least, it seems that there must have been some deep ambivalence about receiving life from the previous generation and handing it over to the next.

One other aspect of the social context of parenting deserves mention—the relatively high rates of divorce and remarriage that seem to have characterized the Roman aristocracy and affluent and aspiring families. Although marriage and divorce surely occurred among the Greeks, the Romans played this game with considerable gusto; many amicable divorces left the ties of friendship that once united the families fairly well intact. Thus the individual Roman *familia* was most often a set of blended and reblended families forming a complex web of blood and current marriage–former marriage relationships (Hetherington and Stanly-Hagan, in Vol. 3 of this *Handbook*). Within the *domus*, the basic unit of husband–wife–children was stable, but the individuals playing those roles could change frequently within one generation. When the death of women in childbirth and the mortality rates in the Roman military are added to the ease and acceptability of divorce, we have to posit nuclear families for Roman parents and children that were fluid at the least. When we examine Roman ideas about and attitudes toward young children, it is important to keep in mind this rather somber background of the *patria potestas*, reproductive failures, and frequent reconfigurations of the people within the *domus*.

The Social Construction of Children and Childhood

There is general agreement among historians of Roman family life that sometime between the beginning of the second century and the end of the first century BCE, the Romans' social construction of the young child changed significantly, and changed in such a way as to emphasize affective bonds between parent and child (Dixon, 1988, 1992). Evidence adduced includes changes in vocabulary used to describe small children, increasing evidence of parental mourning the deaths of small children, and increasing references to the active presence of small children in literature and art (Evans, 1991). However, the emotional investment Romans of the regnal and early and middle republic made in their children should not be underestimated. A number of factors prompt this caution. First, evidence for family life before the second century BCE is extremely meager and cannot be regarded as a random sample of what was once available. Second, the important cult of the *Mater Matuta—the nurturing or nourishing mother*—in early Rome suggests considerable familial and state investment in rearing the young. The cult statues of this goddess show a hefty, mature woman seated on a throne holding from 1 up to 14 swaddled infants. That one of early Rome's major cults centered on this visual representation suggests the crucial importance of the young child in Roman society. Finally, meager though the evidence is, it does contain a number of stories that glorify parents who invest time and effort in rearing their children. For example, Plutarch reports in his life of Cato the Elder that the redoubtable and stern statesman regularly rushed home from the Senate to supervise the bathing of his infant son. Nonetheless, it is probably true that, by the time Rome acquired an overseas empire and came into contact with the Greek East, the Roman social construction of the small child had changed and families paid more attention to affective bonds between parent and child.

Perhaps the most important single source for the current of Greco–Roman thought that put emphasis on loving parents and children is Plutarch, the prolific writer of the second century CE. Throughout his biographies of famous Greeks and Romans, he includes stories of his characters as youngsters, usually to demonstrate that adult characteristics could already be discerned in childhood. In a number of his essays, Plutarch reveals the dynamics of his own family, indicating that he and his wife shared in the parenting of all their children, four sons and a daughter. When his only girl, Timoxena, died at the age 2 years, Plutarch was away from home and composed an elegant letter of consolation to his wife. In it, Plutarch recounts his own fond memories of his little girl (Pomeroy, 1999, pp. 59–60):

> There is a special savor in our affection for children of that age; it likes in the purity of the pleasure they give, the freedom from any crossness or complaint. She herself too had great natural goodness and gentleness of temper: her response to affection and her generosity both gave pleasure and enabled us to perceive the human kindness in her nature. She would ask her nurse to feed not only other babies but the objects and toys that she liked playing with, and would generously invite them, as it were, to her table, offering the good things she had and sharing her greatest pleasures with those who delighted her . . . our daughter was the sweetest thing to fondle, to watch, and to hear; and we ought to let the thought of her also dwell in our minds and lives, for there is much more joy in it than sorrow.

Not surprisingly, given intercultural borrowings, Roman concepts of the child and stages of childhood differed little from those of the Greeks. Like the Greeks, Romans conceived of their

TABLE 12.2
Characteristics and/or Proper Care

Age Level	Quintilian	Augustine
Birth to 3 years	In charge of nurses and then paidagogue Highly impressionable; therefore nurses and paidagogue must speak properly and set fine moral examples Has learned to speak	At first can only suck and cry Then begins' to smile and laugh Frustrated at being unable to communicate and thus cries even more Easily angered; often sullen Jealous of other babies Learning to speak; at first just one word at a time; makes lots of grunting noises; learns without being taught by adults; is aware of nonverbal cues, "body language"
3 to 7 years	Still at home but education and training should being Memory is acute and retentive Not capable of originality Needs studies to be amusing Needs stimulation of praise and sometimes of compeition Suit tasks to child's limited abilities Do not push too hard	Remains at home Learns to speak well At beck and call of others Often disobedient
7 to adolescence	Boys sent out to school Instruction should be tailored to individual student Needs rest and relaxation Play is good for boys Character formation is crucial before boys learn deceit Avoid flogging and abusive punishment	Boys go to school Often unruly and disobedient Does not like to study Loves to play Irrational likes and dislikes Curiosity leads to learning and frightful punishment hampers learning

small children as plastic, unformed, moldable, ignorant, unaware and, thus, susceptible to corrupting influences and potentially fragile. Writing at the end of the first century CE, the rhetorician Quintilian (*Institutio Oratoria,* 1.1.x) illustrates well the Roman belief in the moldability of the young and confidence in children's abilities to learn:

> I would, therefore, have a father conceive the highest hopes of his son from the moment of his birth. . . you will find that most [children] are quick to reason and ready to learn. . . Those who are dull and unteachable are as abnormal as prodigious births and monstrosities and are but few in number. . . . Let us not therefore waste the earliest years; there is all the less excuse for this, since the elements of literary training are solely a question of memory, which not only exists even in small children, but is specially retentive at that age. . . . He will remember such aphorisms even when he is an old man, and the impression made upon his unformed mind will contribute to the formation of his character.

Romans also saw their youngsters as playful, cheerful, affectionate, and gregarious. Romans seem to remark more often on children's unruliness and their natural imitativeness. Probably because of the influence of Stoicism and Christianity, Romans frequently comment on the child's natural innocence. In the Roman construct of the child, there are three traits not recorded among the Greeks: competitiveness, curiosity, and natural facility of memory—all three characteristics put to good use in Roman theories of education (Bonner, 1977).

Just as Plato and Aristotle set out basic theories of child development, so too the Romans Quintilian and Augustine describe similar theories for their own cultures (see Table 12.2). Quintilian and Augustine give more attention to issues of discipline than do their Greek predecessors. There seems to have been more ready use of physical punishment among Romans and more contention—and perhaps feelings of ambivalence—about its successful controlling versus detrimental effects on young children.

Babycare and Childcare in the Roman *Domus*

Pregnancy, childbirth, and childhood for the Romans were just as fraught with the specter of death as for the Greeks. Recent work on Roman demography suggests that about a quarter of Roman babies died before their first birthday and that only half of Roman children lived past the age of 10 years (Bradley, 1999). Parents undoubtedly expected a heavy toll to be paid to neonate and childhood disease; but nonetheless many, like Plutarch, made considerable emotional as well as physical and financial investments in rearing their young.

Quintilian and Augustine describe childrearing practices among the upper classes during Rome's imperial era. In much earlier periods of Roman history, before Rome gained the spoils of an empire that stretched across the Mediterranean basin and well into Western Europe, the care of young children would not have been entrusted to nurses and *paidagogues*; according to the Roman historian Tacitus (*Germania*), mothers and fathers and coresident kin would have done this work. As previously noted, in the centuries before Rome acquired an overseas empire, fathers seems to have taken over the training and education of their male children as early as the age of 3 years.

However, by the second century BCE, both the upper- and the middle-class Roman *domus* would be likely to have several attendants, probably slaves, to nurse and look after babies and preschoolers. The sources describe a considerable range of parental surrogates: other older relatives, such as grandmothers and aunts; wet- and dry-nurses for infants; other people called nurses, some of whom were male, for toddlers and preschoolers; *paidagogues*; and tutors to begin teaching the children the alphabet and simple numbers. It is worthwhile noting that literary references and funeral epitaphs refer to these caregivers with respect and affection (Bradley, 1991). Many children grew up knowing and being able to trust a wide circle of adults and in later years remembered this experience positively. Given the frequent change of the individual people who constituted the Roman *domus* at any one time, it is perhaps not surprising that responsibilities for babycare and childcare would be entrusted to adults who were likely to stay attached to a single child and that, as grown-ups, children would remember these caregivers fondly. The only parental surrogate who seems uniformly despised is the stepmother, who is nearly always portrayed as wicked and mean. We can only speculate that stepmothers were expected to favor their own biological children over those in her new family (Brodzinsky and Pinderhughes, in Vol. 1 of this *Handbook*).

One can hardly mention Roman mothers without immediately thinking of that paragon, Cornelia, daughter of Scipio Africanus, hero of the war against Hannibal, and mother of the Gracchi, her two sons who started the political revolution that eventually led to the demise of the Roman Republic and the imposition of the one-man, imperial rule for the Roman empire. Historical sources uniformly describe Cornelia as the educated and highly cultivated mother of 13 children who, when her husband died, refused to remarry in order to devote her time, energy, and attention to the education of her offspring. Her home was a regular meeting place for discussions among the most notable and intellectually gifted philosophers and politicians in Rome. Cornelia was unaffected by the wealth and status of her family. A story has it that once, while walking along a street, Cornelia was asked by another wealthy matron, "Where are your jewels?" Pushing her two sons in front of her, Cornelia retorted, "Here are my jewels." Cornelia has long been regarded as an incarnation of the ideal Roman wife and mother: married only once, well educated, and intimately and absolutely devoted to the welfare of her children.

In her study of Roman motherhood, Dixon (1988) has compelled a revision of our interpretation of Cornelia, demonstrating that her relationship with her children has been constructed in light of twentieth century ideals of motherhood—making her far closer to her young children than actually was the case. Dixon cogently argued that the conditions within which Romans carried on family life necessarily led to a more distant physical and emotional relationship between mother and child than we, from our late twentieth century perspective, think natural. Dixon has concluded that the ideal or stereotypical Roman mother—including Cornelia—was (1) an important and vocal figure within the household whose position of influence depended heavily on custom and tradition; (2) not connected more intimately with her babies and young children than with them as adolescents and adults; (3) closely associated with the father as a *generic parent* responsible for the children's discipline, education, and development of moral character; and (4) a strong protector of her children's interests and well-being but not a special source of affection and tenderness in comparison with other family members—including fathers. In short, the roles of Roman mother and father do not seem as closely tied to female and male gender constructs as were the Greeks'—or for that matter, those of our own day. Dixon and other scholars believe that Roman mothers generally had stronger bonds of affection and influence with their grown children, particularly their sons, than with their children when they were small.

Of particular interest is Dixon's demonstration of a parallel growth of women's *de facto* ability to bequeath their personal property, usually to their biological children, and social recognition of the importance of the mother–child bond. This aspect of Dixon's work allows us to see a historical change in the Roman's construct of the "natural" relationship between a mother and her children. Dixon's argument, together with some literary and iconographical evidence about early Rome, suggests that, before imperial times and when nuclear units were relatively stable, Romans thought in terms maternal care for children in general. In the main festival for the *Mater Matuta*, the *Matralia*, women carried in their arms to her temples, not their own infants, but those of their brothers and sisters, clearly indicating a collective maternal responsibility for the family's babies. Perhaps as Roman women began to think of themselves, together with their personal property, as unique individuals, they also began to claim a unique relationship with their children, symbolized by their newly acquired right to dispose of their property by testament as men did. Against the backdrop of the *patria potestas*, the growth of a social recognition of the importance of the mother–child bond also appears to coincide with a relaxation in the beliefs about how stern a father should be with his children. Plutarch's essays and biographies indicate that he expected good fathers to be moderate, even compassionate, in their discipline of their children.

Dixon's work on Roman mothers and their bonds with their adult sons was preceded by Hallett's (1984) study of father–daughter relationships among elite Roman families. Relying mainly on Roman legends in which daughters play pivotal and influential roles in motivating their fathers and on the evidence in Cicero's extant correspondence about his doting affection for his daughter, Tullia, Hallett shows that in many families the strongest dyadic bond of affection was likely to be one between a father and his daughter. "Daddy's little girl" was more likely to marry and divorce compliantly; more likely to work hard to further her father's political interests among her in-laws; more likely to bring crucial political and economic intelligence to her father; and less likely to be alienated from her father by the competition that existed between Roman generations. Conversely, daddy's little girl was more likely to receive continued financial support if her in-laws were either stingy or hard up; more likely to be rescued from an unhappy marriage; and more likely to receive a larger share of the inheritance. A good deal of evidence suggests that girls and young women were most likely to receive approval and unconditional acceptance from their fathers than from any other family member. That same evidence also suggests that men were more likely to receive unconditional acceptance from their daughters than from any other family member.

Parents saw to it that their children had ample opportunity to join their peers outside the *domus* for play. The evidence indicates that parents provided a wide range of toys and games for their youngsters. Roman children shared their parents' enthusiasm for gambling and used dice, coins, and nuts in games like heads or tails or odds and evens. Children from wealthy families could expect their parents to give them marbles, balls, spinning tops, spinning hoops, pull toys, push toys, scooters, or even small-scale chariots pulled by a dog, pony, or goat. Archaeological excavations have unearthed a wide variety of dolls from crude figures fashioned from wood or clay to near works of art sculpted from bone or ivory with articulated limbs. Visual and literary evidence depicts children playing a wide variety of games from skipping rocks over waves, building sand castles, tag, leapfrog, and blind-man's bluff. Adults recalled their childhood play with considerable pleasure and apparently enjoyed watching their own youngsters engaging in similar activities (Evans, 1991).

Greek medicine's attention to infants' and children's health continued on into the Roman world, with a good number of treatises that provide significant insight into Roman ideas about pediatrics. The Hippocratic distinction between treatment of children and adults was fully developed by Celsus' (ca. 30 BCE to 45 CE) clear dictum, "Children must be treated entirely differently than adults" (*de Medicina* 3.7). Pliny the Elder (23 to 79 CE) preserves much valuable information about folk medicine in his *Historia Naturalis*; here we catch a glimpse of the kind of treatments—mostly herbal and dietary—most Romans probably used to care for sick children. Some may have been efficacious, such as the use of the plant ephedra for a bloody nose and asthmatic cough, or the liberal use of garlic, oil, and fish sauce. Of particular interest is the extensive treatise on obstetrics and care of neonates written by the physican Soranus in the second century CE; his references to handbooks written by midwives suggest that the corpus of medical literature relating to children was far more extensive in the Roman world than in the Greek. The pediatric sections of late ancient and early Byzantine medical epitomes and encyclopedias by Oribasius, Aetius, and Paul of Aegina confirm this view (Colon and Colon, 1999).

The Romans: Some Conclusions

On the basis of the available historical evidence, it appears that the concept of patriarchal power reached an apogee in the Roman construct of *patria potestas*, the right of the eldest male to execute his children, even as adults. Fathers were undoubtedly powerful figures within their families, but their ability to exercise this power was tempered by informal mechanisms of social control: an expectation of agreement by a family council and an ameliorating influence of the mother.

The Roman mother also played a key role in parenting not only of babies and preschoolers but also of adolescents and young adults. She was seen as a protector of her children's interests. Mother held a position of influence in the home and was closely associated with the father as a *generic parent*, responsible for children's education and training.

Parenting must also be considered in light of two other important characteristics of Roman families: failure of the upper classes to reproduce themselves and fluidity in the composition of aristocratic and affluent nuclear families resulting from relatively high rates of divorce and remarriage. Children of elite families were likely to have a variety of parental surrogates.

Probably from its earliest period, Roman parents regarded their roles as important and devoted considerable time and attention to rearing their young. Fathers were expected to supervise their sons' education personally, and there is good evidence that many did. The bonds tieing parents to children may have become increasingly affectionate beginning in the second century BCE. The most affectionate bond within the family may well have been that between fathers and daughters.

Along with other borrowings, the Romans apparently adopted the Greek social construction of the young child, stages of childhood development, and interest in pediatric medicine. Like the Greeks, Romans saw childrearing primarily in terms of influencing the moral, intellectual, and physical development of the young; education was crucial in this process.

CONCLUSIONS

What conclusions about parenting can be drawn from this ancient historical material? Constructing generalizations about relatively poorly documented societies is fraught with difficulties. The best we can do is to point out that parenting was mainly a private as opposed to public concern, but political philosophers and politicians recognized the critical importance of this activity. A considerable number of people, including males, in ancient societies had an understanding of how children grow and develop that parallels contemporary theory. To what extent such people predicated their parenting behavior on this understanding is unknown. Many parents invested heavily in rearing their children and loved them dearly. Simultaneously, we can be sure that large numbers of children suffered serious physical and psychological deprivation and abuse. Despite detailed knowledge of what parents needed to provide for their offspring, we know of no systematic effort to eradicate child abuse. Perhaps the only safe general conclusion is that the ranges of approaches to parenting we see in contemporary society were paralleled in the ancient Mediterranean world.

Despite these caveats, we can see some differences in approaches to parenting among ancient Mediterranean civilizations. Upper-class Egyptians seem to have delighted in their children, giving them prominent positions in representations of family life. Mothers and slaves probably oversaw the care of babies and preschoolers, but fathers likely personally taught and prepared their sons to follow in their footsteps as adults. In contrast to Egyptians, Mesopotamians did not celebrate family life, and children are nearly absent from official and funerary art. Many Mesopotamians seem to have regarded parenting and family demands as a difficult burden. Legal evidence suggests a perceived need to protect children from ill treatment at the hands of their parents. It appears that Mesopotamian parents were more emotionally distant from their children than were the Egyptians. The ancient Israelites made the family—both its bonds and affection and potential for tension and conflict—a metaphor for writing about the relationship between themselves and their God.

The Greeks were the first to think systematically about parenting and child development, and they laid the theoretical foundations for childrearing and education that dominated the Mediterranean world for nearly a millennium (ca. 600 BCE to 400 CE). Greek and Roman descriptions of childhood and prescriptions for parenting reflect an emphasis on the effects of nurture and the need for parents to invest the time, energy, and resources appropriate for the particular stage of the child's development. Alongside the evidence that demonstrates keen observation of children and their needs comes other evidence pointing to neglect and abuse of the young. Among the Greeks, the picture of parenting and family life derived mainly from evidence for ancient Athens can probably be applied to most other Greek city-states. However, the Spartans developed an anomalous approach to parenting, leaving childrearing of boys until the age of 7 years and girls until they married almost entirely to Spartan mothers. In classical Sparta, children were the central focus of the household; fathers were nearly entirely absent because of their full-time involvement in the Spartan military.

In many respects, the picture of Roman parenting is like that of the Greek. However, fathers had more legal power over their children, and the roles of mothers and fathers may have been more similar, with both responsible for the moral, physical, and educational development of their children. Within the Roman family, the bonds between fathers and daughters may have been the most affectionate.

Can we compare parenting in the ancient Mediterranean world with that of our own era? The most important common elements are the centrality of rearing children in the social construction of the family and the variety of assumptions and practices that underlie childrearing both then and now. Although the Greeks were the first to articulate a prototheory of child development, all these ancient cultures recognized stages of children's growth and sought to use methods of childrearing appropriate for those stages. The most important difference is a tendency in some contemporary Western cultures to romanticize the child and childhood and the appearance of an ideology that seeks to create child-centered societies; in the ancient Mediterranean world, children were an important and integral part of the family—but not its sole focus.

REFERENCES

Ackerman, S. (1992). Isaiah. In C. A. Newsom and S. H. Ringe (Eds.), *The women's Bible commentary* (pp. 161–168). Louisville, KY: Westminster/John Knox Press.

Archer, L. J. (1994). Notions of community and the exclusion of the female in Jewish history and historiography. In L. J. Archer, S. Fischler, and M. Wyke (Eds.), *Women in ancient societies* (pp. 53–69). New York: Routledge.

Aries, P. (1962). *Centuries of childhood: A social history of family life* (R. Baldick, Trans.). New York: Random House.

Bachofen, J. J. (1967). *Myth, religion, and mother right* (R. Manheim, Trans.). Princeton, NJ: Princeton University Press.

Baring, A., and Cashford, J. (1991). *The myth of the goddess: Evolution of an image.* New York: Penguin.

Bonner, S. J. (1977). *Education in ancient Rome.* Berkeley, CA: University of California Press.

Bradley, K. R. (1991). *Discovering the Roman family.* New York: Oxford University Press.

Bradley, K. R. (1999). Images of childhood: The evidence of Plutarch. In S. B. Pomeroy (Ed.), *Plutarch's advice to the bride and groom and a consolation to his wife* (pp. 183–196). New York: Oxford University Press.

Cohen, D. (1991). *Law, sexuality, and society: The enforcement of morals in classical Athens.* New York: Cambridge University Press.

Colon, A. J., and Colon, P. A. (1999). *Nurturing children: A history of pediatrics.* Westport, CT: Greenwood.

Demand, N. (1994). *Birth, death, and motherhood in classical Greece.* Baltimore: Johns Hopkins University Press.

deMause, L. (1974). The evolution of childhood. *The History of Childhood Quarterly, 1,* 503–575.

Dixon, S. (1988). *The Roman mother.* Norman, OK: University of Oklahoma Press.

Dixon, S. (1992). *The Roman family.* Baltimore: Johns Hopkins University Press.

Ehrenberg, M. (1989). *Women in prehistory.* Norman, OK: University of Oklahoma Press.

Eisler, R. (1987). *The chalice and the blade.* New York: Harper & Row.

Eller, C. (2000). *The myth of matriarchal prehistory: Why an invented past won't give women a future.* Boston: Beacon.

Erman, A. (1995). *Ancient Egyptian poetry and prose* (A. M. Blackman, Trans.). New York: Dover.

Etienne, R. (1973). La conscience medicale antique et la vie des enfants [Ancient medical peraption and the life of infants]. *Annales de Demographie Historique, 21, Enfant et sociétés,* 15–61.

Evans, J. A. S. (1991). *War, women and children in ancient Rome.* New York: Routledge.

Exum, C. (1985). 'Mother in Israel': a familiar story reconsidered. In L. Russell (Ed.), *Feminist interpretation of the Bible* (pp. 73–85). Philadelphia: Westminster.

French, V. (1977). History of the child's influence: Ancient Mediterranean civilizations. In R. Q. Bell and L. V. Harper (Eds.), *Child effects on adults* (pp. 3–29). Hillsdale, NJ: Lawrence Erlbaum Associates.

French, V. (1987). Midwives and maternity care and in the Greco–Roman world. *Helios, 13,* 69–84.

French, V. (1991). Children in antiquity. In J. M. Hawes and N. R. Hiner (Eds.), *Children in historical and comparative perspective* (pp. 13–29). Westport, CT: Greenwood.

French, V. (1997). The Spartan family and the Spartan decline: Changes in child-rearing practices and the failure to reform. In C. D. Hamilton and P. Krentz (Eds.), *Polis and polemos* (pp. 241–274). Claremont, CA: Regina.

French, V. (1999). Aristophanes' doting dads: Adult male knowledge of children. In R. Mellor and L. Tritle (Eds.), *Text and tradition: Studies in Greek history and historiography* (pp. 163–181). Claremont, CA: Regina.

Fyrmer-Kensky, T. (1992). *In the wake of the goddesses: Women, culture, and the biblical transformation of pagan myth.* New York: Random House/Ballantine.

Gimbutas, M. (1982). *Goddesses and gods of old Europe.* Berkeley, CA: University of California Press.

Golden, M. (1989). *Children and childhood in classical Athens.* Baltimore: Johns Hopkins University Press.

Goodison, L., and Morris, C. (Eds.). (1998). *Ancient goddesses: The myths and the evidence.* Madison, WI: University of Wisconsin Press.

Gruber, M. I. (1999). Women in the ancient levant. In B. Vivante (Ed.), *Women's roles in ancient civilizations* (pp. 115–152). Westport, CT: Greenwood.

Hackett, J. A. (1992). 1 and 2 Samuel. In C. A. Newsom and S. H. Ringe (Eds.), *The women's Bible commentary* (pp. 85–95). Louisville, KY: Westminster/John Knox Press.

Hallett, J. (1984). *Fathers and daughters in Roman society: Women and the elite family.* Princeton, NJ: Princeton University Press.

Hrdy, S. B. (1999). *Mother nature: A history of mothers, infants, and natural selection.* New York: Random House/Pantheon.

Ilan, T. (1996). *Jewish women in Greco–Roman Palestine.* Peabody, MA: Hendrickson.

Keuls, E. (1985). *The reign of the phallus: Sexual politics in ancient Athens.* Berkeley, CA: University of California Press.

Kramer, S. N. (1963). *The Sumeriáns.* Chicago: University of Chicago Press.

Lerner, G. (1986). *The creation of patriarchy.* New York: Oxford University Press.

Levett, L. C. (1999). *House and society in the ancient Greek world.* Cambridge, England: Cambridge University Press.

Macdonald, F. (1999). *Women in Ancient Egypt.* New York: Peter Bedrick Books.

Meyers, C. (1988). *Discovering Eve: Ancient Israelite women in context.* New York: Oxford University Press.

Meyers, C. (1989). Women and the domestic economy of early Israel. In B. S. Lesko (Ed.), *Women's earliest records from ancient Egypt and western Asia* (Brown Judaic Studies, Vol. 166, pp. 265–281). Atlanta, GA: Scholars Press.

Meyers, C. (1992). Everyday life: Women in the period of the Hebrew Bible. In C.A.

Nunn, J. F. (1996). *Ancient Egyptian medicine.* Norman, OK: University of Oklahoma Press.

O,Connor, K. (1992). Jeremiah. In In C. A. Newsom and S. H. Ringe (Eds.), *The women's Bible commentary* (pp. 169–177). Louisville, KY: Westminster/John Knox Press.

Pomeroy, S. B. (1997). *Families in classical and hellenistic Greece.* New York: Oxford University Press.

Pomeroy, S. B. (Ed.). (1999). *Plutarch's advice to the bride and groom and a consolation to his wife*. New York: Oxford University Press.

Rawson, B. (1991). *Marriage, divorce, and children in ancient Rome*. Oxford, England: Clarendon.

Riddle, J. M. (1992). *Contraception and abortion from the ancient world to the Renaissance*. Cambridge, MA: Harvard University Press.

Robins, G. (1997). Women in Egypt. In D. Silverman (Ed.), *Ancient Egypt* (pp. 80–89). New York: Oxford University Press.

Simpson, W. K. (1972). *The literature of ancient Egypt*. New Haven, CT: Yale University Press.

Strauss, B. (1993). *Fathers and sons in classical Athens*. Princeton, NJ: Princeton University Press.

Tyldesley, J. (1994). *Daughters of Isis: Women in ancient Egypt*. New York: Viking.

Wiedemann, T. (1989). *Adults and children in the Roman empire*. New Haven, CT: Yale University Press.

Author Index

Subject Index